GERMANY AND THE SECOND WORLD WAR

II

Germany's Initial Conquests in Europe

Germany
and the
Second World War

Edited by the
Militärgeschichtliches
Forschungsamt (Research
Institute for Military History),
Freiburg im Breisgau, Germany

VOLUME II
Germany's Initial
Conquests in Europe

KLAUS A. MAIER
HORST ROHDE
BERND STEGEMANN
HANS UMBREIT

Translated by
DEAN S. McMURRY
EWALD OSERS

Translation editor
P. S. FALLA

CLARENDON PRESS · OXFORD
1991

Oxford University Press, Walton Street, Oxford OX2 6DP

Oxford New York Toronto
Delhi Bombay Calcutta Madras Karachi
Petaling Jaya Singapore Hong Kong Tokyo
Nairobi Dar es Salaam Cape Town
Melbourne Auckland
and associated companies in
Berlin Ibadan

Oxford is a trade mark of Oxford University Press

Published in the United States
by Oxford University Press, New York

British Library Cataloguing in Publication Data
Germany and the second world war.
Vol. 2, Germany's initial conquests in Europe.
1. World War 2
I. Maier, Klaus A. II. Militärgeschichtliches
Forschungsamt III. Deutsche Reich und der Zweite
Weltkrieg. English 940.53
ISBN 0-19-822885-6

Library of Congress Cataloging in Publication Data
Errichtung der Hegemonie auf dem europäischen Kontinent. English.
Germany's initial conquests in Europe / Klaus A. Maier . . . [et al.];
translated by Dean S. McMurry, Ewald Osers; translation editor, P. S. Falla.
(Germany and the Second World War; v. 2)
Translation of: Die Errichtung der Hegemonie auf dem europäischen Kontinent.
Includes bibliographical references (p.   ) and index.
1. World War, 1939–1945—Germany. 2. World War, 1939–1945—
Campaigns—Eastern. 3. World War, 1939–1945—Campaigns—Western.
4. Germany—History—1933–1945. I. Maier, Klaus A.
(Klaus Autbert), 1940- II. Falla, P. S. (Paul Stephen), 1913-
III. Title. IV. Series: Deutsche Reich und der Zweite Weltkrieg.
English; v. 2.
DD256.5.D43413 vol. 2 [D90-14262757] 943.086 s—dc20 [940.53'43]
ISBN 0-19-822885-6

Phototypeset by
Dobbie Typesetting Limited, Tavistock, Devon
Printed in Great Britain by
Courier International Ltd,
Tiptree, Essex

Contents

PART VII

The Operational Air War until the Battle of Britain

PART VIII

The Second Phase of the War at Sea (until the Spring of 1941)

PART IX

List of Illustrations

The diagrams and maps are taken from originals by Hans Gaenshirt, Vera Kluge, and Rolf Schindler of the Cartographic Section, Research Institute for Military History.

Notes on the Authors

Dr KLAUS A. MAIER (b. 1940). Publications: *Guernica, 26. 4. 1937: Die deutsche Intervention in Spanien und der 'Fall Guernica'* (Einzelschriften zur militärischen Geschichte des Zweiten Weltkrieges, 17; Freiburg i.Br., 1975; Spanish edn. 1976); 'Die EVG in der Außen- und Sicherheitspolitik der Truman-Administration', in *Die Europäische Verteidigungsgemeinschaft: Stand und Probleme der Forschung*, ed. Hans-Erich Volkmann and Walter Schwengler (Militärgeschichte seit 1945, 7; Boppard, 1985), 31-49; 'Total War and German Air Doctrine before the Second World War', in *The German Military in the Age of Total War*, ed. Wilhelm Deist (Leamington Spa, 1985), 210-19; 'Die Auseinandersetzung um die EVG als europäisches Unterbündnis der NATO 1950-1954', in *Vom Marshallplan zur EWG*, ed. Ludolf Herbst (Munich, 1990), 447-74; 'Die internationalen Auseinandersetzungen um die Westintegration der Bundesrepublik Deutschland und um ihre Bewaffnung im Rahmen der Europäischen Verteidigungsgemeinschaft', in *Die EVG-Phase* (Anfänge westdeutscher Sicherheitspolitik 1945-1956, 2; Munich, 1990), 1-234.

Dr HORST ROHDE (b. 1937). Publications: *Das deutsche Wehrmachttransportwesen im Zweiten Weltkrieg: Entstehung, Organisation, Aufgaben* (Beiträge zur Militär- und Kriegsgeschichte, 12; Stuttgart, 1971); 'Das Eisenbahnverkehrswesen in der deutschen Kriegswirtschaft 1939-1945', in *Kriegswirtschaft und Rüstung 1939-1945*, ed. F. Forstmeier and H.-E. Volkmann (Düsseldorf, 1977), 134-63; 'Kriegsbeginn 1939 in Danzig: Planungen und Wirklichkeit', *WWR* 28 (1979), 154-62; 'Kriegstagebücher als historische Quellen', *Schiff und Zeit*, 12 (1980), 1-8; 'Beispiele für den Einfluß der Logistik auf die Operationsführung des deutschen Heeres im Ersten Weltkrieg', in *Die Bedeutung der Logistik für die militärische Führung von der Antike bis in die neueste Zeit* (Vorträge zur Militärgeschichte, 7; Herford, Bonn, 1986), 135-66.

Dr BERND STEGEMANN (b. 1938). Publications: *Die deutsche Marinepolitik 1916-1918* (Berlin, 1970); 'Hitlers "Stufenplan" und die Marine', in *Festschrift für Richard Dietrich* (Frankfurt am Main, 1975), 301-16; 'Hitlers Ziele im ersten Kriegsjahr 1939/40: Ein Beitrag zur Quellenkritik', *MGM* 27 (1980), 93-105; 'Der Entschluß zum Unternehmen "Barbarossa": Strategie oder Ideologie?', *Geschichte in Wissenschaft und Unterricht*, 33 (1982), 205-13; 'Die italienisch-deutsche Kriegführung im Mittelmeer und in Afrika', in Gerhard Schreiber, Bernd Stegemann, and Detlev Vogel (eds.), *Der Mittelmeerraum und Südosteuropa* (Das Deutsche Reich und der Zweite Weltkrieg, 3; Stuttgart, 1984), 591-682; 'Geschichte und Politik: Zur Diskussion über den deutschen Angriff auf die Sowjetunion 1941', *Beiträge zur Konfliktforschung*, 17/1 (1987), 73-97; articles on naval history and naval warfare.

Dr HANS UMBREIT (b. 1937). Publications: *Der Militärbefehlshaber in Frankreich 1940-1944* (Wehrwissenschaftliche Forschungen, Abteilung Militärgeschichtliche Studien, 7; Boppard, 1968); *Deutsche Militärverwaltungen 1938/39: Die militärische Besetzung der Tschechoslowakei und Polens* (Beiträge zur Militär- und Kriegsgeschichte, 18; Stuttgart, 1977); 'The Development of Official Military Historiography in the German Army from the Crimean War to 1945', in *Official Histories, Essays and Bibliographies from around the World*, ed. Robin Higham (Manhattan, Kan., 1970), 160-208; 'La stratégie défensive de l'Allemagne sur le front de l'Ouest en 1944', *Revue historique des armées*, 4 (1974), 122-38; 'Nationalsozialistische Expansion 1938-1941: Strukturen der deutschen Besatzungsverwaltungen im Zweiten Weltkrieg', in *Dienst für die Geschichte: Gedenkschrift für Walther Hubatsch*, ed. Michael Salewski and Josef Schröder (Göttingen, 1985), 163-86.

Note on the Translation

THE sections by Klaus A. Maier and Bernd Stegemann were translated by Dean S. McMurry; those by Horst Rohde and Hans Umbreit were translated by Ewald Osers. The translation as a whole was revised and edited by P. S. Falla, who also translated the Introduction and Conclusion.

In the Bibliography information has been added concerning English translations of German and other foreign-language works. These translations are cited in the footnotes and have been used whenever possible for quotations occurring in the text.

Abbreviations

AA	Auswärtiges Amt: ministry of foreign affairs
ADAP	*Akten zur deutschen auswärtigen Politik*: Documents on German Foreign Policy
ADC	aide-de-camp
AHA	Allgemeines Heeresamt: general army office
AO	Auslandsorganisation: Party organization for Germans abroad
ASDIC	Anti-Submarine Detection Investigation Committee
BA	Bundesarchiv (Federal German archives), Koblenz
BA-MA	Bundesarchiv-Militärarchiv (Military archives), Freiburg im Breisgau
BEF	British Expeditionary Force
DBFP	*Documents on British Foreign Policy*
DGFP	*Documents on German Foreign Policy* (translation of *ADAP*)
DMO	Director(ate) of Military Operations
DNSAP	Dansk National Socialistisk Arbejderparti: Danish Nazi party
Frhr.	Freiherr (title equivalent to 'baron')
Füst	Führungsstab: operations staff
Gen.d.Fl.a.D.	General der Flieger außer Dienst: retired air force general
Gen.Lt.	Generalleutnant: Lieutenant-General
GenStb.	Generalstab: General Staff
GenStdH	Generalstab des Heeres: Army General Staff
g.Kdos.	geheime Kommandosache: top secret (military)
GL	Generalluftzeugmeister: chief development and production officer of the Luftwaffe
HZ	*Historische Zeitschrift*
i.Br.	im Breisgau
Kdo.	Kommando: headquarters
KFG	Küstenfliegergruppe (q.v. in Glossary)
KG	Kampfgeschwader: bomber Geschwader (q.v. in Glossary)
Kptl.	Kapitänleutnant: naval lieutenant
KTB	Kriegstagebuch: war diary
KTB OKW	*Kriegstagebuch des Oberkommandos der Wehrmacht* (q.v. in Bibliography)
Lfl.Kdo.	Luftflottenkommando: command of a Luftflotte (q.v. in Glossary)
Lw	Luftwaffe: German air force
MGFA	Militärgeschichtliches Forschungsamt: Research Institute for Military History
MGM	*Militärgeschichtliche Mitteilungen*
mot.	motorisiert: motorized
MR	*Marine Rundschau*
NSDAP	Nationalsozialistische Deutsche Arbeiterpartei: National Socialist German Workers' Party (Nazis)
OB	Oberbefehlshaber: commander-in-chief
ObdH	Oberbefehlshaber des Heeres: commander-in-chief of the army
ObdL	Oberbefehlshaber der Luftwaffe: commander-in-chief of the air force
ObdM	Oberbefehlshaber der Kriegsmarine: commander-in-chief of the navy

OKH	Oberkommando des Heeres: army high command
OKL	Oberkommando der Luftwaffe: air force high command
OKM	Oberkommando der Kriegsmarine: navy high command
OKW	Oberkommando der Wehrmacht: high command of the armed forces
PA	Politisches Archiv des Auswärtigen Amtes (political archives of the foreign ministry), Bonn
PRO	Public Record Office, London
R-boot	Räumboot: motor minesweeper
RdL	Reichsminister der Luftfahrt: Reich minister of aviation
RGBl.	*Reichsgesetzblatt*: official journal of laws
RLM	Reichsluftfahrtministerium: Reich ministry of aviation
RUSI	Royal United Services Institute
RVM	Reichsverkehrsministerium: Reich ministry of transport
RWM	Reichswirtschaftsministerium: Reich ministry of economics
S-boot	Schnellboot: motor torpedo-boat
SIS	Secret Intelligence Service
SKl	Seekriegsleitung: naval war staff
SS	Schutzstaffel ('guard detachment'): élite Party troops
VfZG	*Vierteljahrshefte für Zeitgeschichte*
WFSt	Wehrmachtführungsstab: armed forces operations staff
WiRüAmt	Wehrwirtschafts- und Rüstungsamt: war economy and armaments office
WO	War Office
WWR	*Wehrwissenschaftliche Rundschau*
z.b.V.	zu besonderer Verwendung: for special duties
ZfG	*Zeitschrift für Geschichtswissenschaft*
ZMG	*Zeitschrift für Militärgeschichte*

Glossary of German Terms

Ausfuhrstaffel	'Export group', code-name for merchant vessels employed in Weserübung, q.v.
Feldkommandantur	Field headquarters established in occupied countries
Gau (pl. Gaue)	Regional division of Nazi party
Gauleiter	Regional Party leader
Generalquartiermeister	Quartermaster-general
Geschwader (pl. same)	Largest combat unit of Luftwaffe: 3 Gruppen and a staff unit
Gruppe (pl. -n)	Intermediate combat unit of Luftwaffe: 3 Staffeln and a staff unit
Kampfgeschwader	Bomber group
Kreisleiter	District Party leader
Küstenfliegergruppe	Coastal air force unit
Luftflotte	Air fleet (combining fighter, bomber, and dive-bomber aircraft)
Luftwaffe	German air force
Ministerialdirektor	Head of department in a ministry
Oberfeldkommandant	General in charge of military administration in occupied territory
Oberquartiermeister I	Deputy chief of General Staff (Operations)
Regierungspräsident	Senior official of administrative district
SS-Leibstandarte	Crack SS division, originally Hitler's bodyguard
Staffel (pl. -n)	Basic combat unit of Luftwaffe (9 aircraft)
Truppenamt	'Troops office': camouflaged General Staff in Weimar Germany
Wehrmacht	German armed forces
Weserübung	'Weser exercise': code-name for invasion of Denmark and Norway, April 1940
Westwall	Fortifications in Western Germany: the 'Siegfried Line'

Introduction

WITH the second volume of *Germany and the Second World War* we begin an account of the military events of the conflict that was deliberately unleashed by Nazi Germany. The first year of the war, dealt with in this volume, took quite a different course from that which the German dictator had intended, notwithstanding his readiness to take extreme risks; but it led to triumphant successes that hardly anyone had believed possible. At the same time, the establishment of hegemony on the European continent confronted the aggressor with ever new problems; above all it did not bring about the end of war, though this was still essentially confined to Europe. Only to a small extent could Germany's victory on the battlefields be converted into political capital.

The first volume of the present work was divided into four parts describing the build-up of the German war-machine, over a long period of years, from the respective points of view of ideology and propaganda, the economy, rearmament, and foreign policy. Volume II, by contrast, traces the history of the war up to the late autumn of 1940, for the most part as a consecutive account of interconnected political and military events. The account of the successive campaigns—the invasion of Poland, the occupation of Denmark and Norway, and the attack in the west—is complemented by a description of naval and air operations in so far as these were not directly connected with the actions of the land forces. To explain the strategy of the German air force and navy it has sometimes been necessary to go a long way back into pre-war developments. In addition, treatment of the war at sea required a different time-scale. Whereas the volume as a whole ends with the failure of direct strategy against Britain and the decision to invade the Soviet Union, the account of naval operations continues until the spring of 1941, when the second phase of the 'Battle of the Atlantic' was coming to an end.

It is not the purpose of this volume to give a comprehensive picture of the history of Germany during the first stages of the war. The factors affecting strategy—economic, technical, social, and ideological, problems of organization and domestic policy—are only referred to in so far as is necessary for an understanding of war events. Their importance is so great that they require fuller study, to which subsequent 'cross-section' volumes will be devoted. However, Part I of the present volume attempts to survey the politico-strategic scene and, in line with the first volume, to clarify the connection of events that are described more fully in subsequent chapters along with the actual military operations. The latter are treated against the background of Hitler's war policy and in relation to the plans of the German leadership, whether long-term or born of immediate circumstances. This represents a departure from the traditional type of war history; but the general conception of military history nowadays, which the present authors fully share, accords a legitimate place to the analysis of operations. Certainly the conduct of war is not equated with the mere movement of armies on battlefields. Military operations were intended to serve more or less clearly formulated political aims, and the authors' first task was to explain these. But an attempt has also been made to describe the military events of the war with exactitude, albeit concisely, so as to facilitate a critical appraisal of them. Numerous maps, tables, and statistics are also provided for this purpose. The authors hope in this way to have depicted the belligerents' intentions and resources, the execution and outcome of their plans, in such a way as to make clear the reasons for success or failure in each case. It was deliberately decided not to go further and give a complete account of military events in the style of a chronicle.

Like the work as a whole, Volume II is addressed not so much to specialized historians as to a wider circle of readers interested in contemporary events. The former have at their disposal an almost inexhaustible quantity of monographs, and easy access to archives if they wish to investigate military events that have been somewhat neglected by scholars despite the multiplicity of publications. The present authors, on the other hand, have in mind primarily readers who seek information about a period that most of them did not experience directly, but in which the fate of Germany and Europe was decided and the basis created for the present confrontation of the two superpowers. The reader is not deprived of an interpretation of events in the light of present-day research; but the intention is to describe them on a uniform basis, rather than to concentrate on particular 'key issues' with a discussion of existing theories concerning them.

In accordance with this intention, the authors have kept footnotes to a minimum. In order that their account of events may be checked, they give references to the most important publications and sources. But it was not possible, given the method of investigation and presentation chosen by them, to reflect the abundance of scientific literature on the Second World War. Where the account embodies the accepted conclusions of research, footnotes are largely dispensed with for the sake of greater readability.

It would no doubt also have conduced to readability if the authors of this collective volume had always been able to agree on a uniform interpretation of events. This was only possible up to a certain point, as in the present state of knowledge many aspects of the war still admit of different opinions. For example, it is not absolutely certain how far Hitler's war aims continued to be dictated by his programmatic ideas of the 1920s and 1930s. Was his objective still only to win additional 'living-space' for Germany at the expense of the Soviet Union, or did this aim lose its relevance from time to time? Faced with issues of this kind, the authors chose individual liberty rather than a compulsory harmonization that would have been incompatible with their idea of scholarship. Hence, each author is responsible for his own contribution only, though each has endeavoured to achieve a high degree of assimilation to the others' viewpoint and method of presentation. This required not a little self-limitation and avoidance of over-precise formulations. It will nevertheless be clear to the reader where and in what way the authors differ in their viewpoint and understanding of events. Such differences could only be avoided in ideal conditions or by a sacrifice of academic freedom. The authors hope that the reader will not regard them as a defect, but as an encouragement to him to form his own conclusions.

PART I

Politics and Warfare in the First Phase of the German Offensive

BERND STEGEMANN

TODAY historians generally agree that the Second World War did not, in the strict sense, 'break out' in 1939, but was unleashed by the German attack on Poland on 1 September of that year. At most a discussion seems possible about the other powers' share of responsibility.[1] The diplomatic and political mistakes of the Western powers and Poland probably played only a minor role. Undoubtedly, however, the signing of the Soviet–German non-aggression treaty of 23 August 1939 was a decisive factor. In its secret protocol Hitler recognized Finland, Latvia, Estonia, eastern Poland, and Bessarabia as areas of Soviet interest and declared his lack of interest in the south-eastern part of Europe.[2] It cannot be said with certainty whether a successful conclusion of the military negotiations conducted in Moscow between Britain and France and the Soviet Union would have deterred Hitler from attacking Poland; in any case, after signing the pact with Stalin he was convinced that the Western powers would not enter the war merely for Poland's sake. Moreover, on 25 August he announced a 'generous' offer to Britain, which, he hoped, would give him a free hand with regard to Poland.

On the same day, however, after the ratification of the mutual-assistance pact between Poland and Britain had become known, Hitler cancelled the attack order already issued on 23 August for the 26th. Moreover, on that day Mussolini declared definitely that he was not yet in a position to join a war against the Western powers. In view of earlier Italian statements, he could hardly have been expected to do so; but the news was serious, the more so as the German government took it for granted that the Italian attitude was also known in Britain. In considering intervention, the Western powers had no need to worry about Germany's Axis partner. But by 28 August Hitler had recovered his determination and set the attack definitely for 1 September.[3]

The most important factor in his decision was probably his confidence in the deterrent effect of German armaments, which he believed had caused the Western powers to shy away from a military conflict in the Sudeten crisis. Above all, the armaments lead enjoyed and constantly emphasized by the Luftwaffe itself was supposed to induce the British in particular to exercise restraint. Göring, the commander-in-chief of the Luftwaffe, nevertheless considered the risk of a two-front war too great, but his loyalty to Hitler caused him to put aside his doubts.

The Army High Command had prepared for 'Case White', the campaign against Poland, but they feared expanding the conflict to a war with the Western powers, for which in their opinion the army would not be prepared for years; Hitler's assurances that the Western powers would not intervene met with considerable doubts even after the signing of the non-aggression pact with the Soviet Union.

[1] On this problem cf. *Kriegsbeginn*; Hillgruber, *Entstehung des Zweiten Weltkriegs*.
[2] Printed in *DGFP* D vii. 246–7. Soviet historians emphatically deny that the pact between Germany and the Soviet Union played a role in triggering the war. Cf. Yakushevsky, 'Vymysly i pravda'.
[3] Cf. *Weizsäcker-Papiere*, 160–3; Halder, *Diaries*, i. 26–34.

Finally, the navy had been preparing itself for a conflict with the Western powers in the long term, but in 1939 it was the Wehrmacht branch least ready for a war and was hopelessly inferior to the fleets of Germany's probable enemies. For this reason there were numerous voices in the navy warning against a military conflict, but the commander-in-chief, Grand Admiral Raeder, relied on Hitler's assurances that it would be limited to Poland.

Complete certainty about Stalin's motives for concluding the pact with Hitler will not be possible until the Soviet archives are opened, if then. Of course the Soviet need for security played a role, for Stalin feared an understanding between the Western powers and Hitler at the expense of the Soviet Union, in which Poland would either be Germany's junior partner or her first victim. However, the Western powers did not intend to involve the Soviet Union in a war with Germany in which they themselves would stand aside.[4] By the summer of 1939 it had long been clear that Poland would refuse to be drawn into a common front against the Soviet Union by Hitler, while the Western powers, notwithstanding their readiness to make concessions on particular matters, sought to prevent a Polish capitulation to Germany. Hence, a policy of unequivocal support for Poland would probably have met the Soviet desire for security; for even if Stalin doubted that the Western powers would respond militarily to a German attack on Poland, the Wehrmacht would not have been able to attack the Soviet Union from Poland's eastern borders immediately after annihilating the Polish army. Even if the Western powers had remained completely inactive, the Soviet Union would not have been directly threatened; and because of his weak position, Hitler would certainly have had to take Soviet interests into consideration even without a treaty. Khrushchev's statement in 1956 that Stalin wanted to 'push Hitler into a war' by signing the non-aggression pact thus seems much more likely to be correct.[5] The pact with Hitler and the latter's conflict with the Western powers offered Stalin the chance to extend Soviet borders far to the west; this would not have been the case in a different power-constellation. It therefore seemed wise to support Germany as the supposedly weaker side in the conflict. On the other hand, when the Western powers declared war on Germany on 3 September the Soviet Union had no interest in fighting on Hitler's side. Therefore Stalin waited until 17 September, when Poland's fate was already sealed, before ordering the Red Army to march into the areas of eastern Poland to which he was entitled by his pact with Hitler. In the treaty with Germany of 28 September Stalin renounced part of his Polish booty in exchange for Lithuania, which, except for the border area around Mariampol (Mirijampilis), was now included in his area of interest.[6]

According to Hitler's 'step-by-step' plan, which Andreas Hillgruber has explained as the basic guide-line of his decisions, and for whose critical importance in Hitler's policy and strategy Klaus Hildebrand has also sought new evidence,[7] the

---

[4] As is claimed e.g. in *Deutschland im zweiten Weltkrieg*, i. 156.

[5] Rauch, 'Nichtangriffspakt', here 365–6. Cf. also Hillgruber and Hildebrand, *Kalkül*.

[6] Cf. Fabry, *Hitler-Stalin-Pakt*, 82–7. Hillgruber has also pointed out the connection with the ending of the Soviet-Japanese border conflict by the armistice of 15 Sept. Cf. Hillgruber, *Kriegsziele und Strategie*, 24–5.

[7] Hillgruber, *Strategie*; Hildebrand, *Außenpolitik*; id., 'Hitlers "Programm" '.

consolidation of German rule in central Europe was to be followed by the conquest of the European part of the Soviet Union and the establishment of a continental *imperium* together with overseas colonies and bases. As the last phase, originally envisaged for the time after his death, Hitler foresaw a struggle between the United States and Germany as world powers. It is at least very doubtful that, before the Western powers declared war on Germany in 1939, he thought there was bound to be a conflict with them before he had conquered his *Lebensraum* in the east. His earlier plan for an alliance with Poland against the Soviet Union, and also the alliance with the Soviet Union against Poland and the 'pact of steel' with Italy, were alike intended to deter the Western powers from intervening in a territorial reordering of eastern Europe.

In this regard we must mention Hitler's oft-cited statement of 11 August 1939, reported by the high commissioner of the League of Nations in Danzig, Carl J. Burckhardt:

Everything I do is directed against Russia. If the West is too stupid and blind to understand that, I shall be forced to come to an understanding with Russia in order to defeat the West and then, after its defeat, to turn against the Soviet Union with all my forces. I need the Ukraine so that we can't be starved out again as we were in the last war.[8]

Apart from the fact that Germany had to capitulate in 1918 even though it had occupied the Ukraine, Hitler can hardly have wanted to inform the Western powers through a neutral confidant that he envisaged a campaign against them as the next step in his programme. Instead he wanted to point out once again that, in his opinion, his intentions did not affect their interests in any way; he combined this attempt with a threat and an appeal to anti-Soviet feelings in London and Paris. His words should probably not be considered as a statement of his programme in regard to either the Western powers or the Soviet Union.[9]

In any case, the declaration of war by the Western powers on 3 September surprised Hitler. According to his own statements he had taken that risk into consideration, but clearly he believed it to be very small. Moreover, his Axis partner, Italy, refrained from participating in the war. But while Italy described herself as a 'non-belligerent' power and thus announced her position of benevolent neutrality towards Germany, Japan actually declared her strict neutrality. Germany's Far Eastern partner in the Anti-Comintern pact had rejected the idea of an alliance against Britain and was much offended by the German pact with the Soviet Union, the earlier common enemy. Thus, Hitler not only found himself in a war with Britain and France that he had not wanted, and certainly not in 1939; he also did not receive the expected support from his allies. For this reason his partnership with Stalin acquired an even greater importance.

Japan's neutrality and Italy's non-participation in the war made the situation much easier for the Western Allies, even though it also made their strategic planning

---

[8] Burckhardt, *Danziger Mission*, 348.
[9] Cf. the interpretation by Lukacs, *European War*, 42. Hitler's statements of 23 May 1939 are not considered here as they do not reveal any clear plan.

completely redundant, as they had originally planned an offensive against Libya, to be followed by a concentration of their forces against Italy itself, which they considered the weaker Axis partner. On the other hand, the German leaders were also relieved, because the feared enemy offensive in the west did not materialize while the mass of German forces were tied down in the Polish campaign. Because of the inaction of the Western Allies, who at first took measures only to initiate a naval and economic war, Hitler even believed that they had only declared war to save face and that he would be able to detach France, the more passive partner, from her alliance with Britain.[10] After the Soviet–German border and friendship treaty had been concluded on 28 September 1939, which greatly strengthened Germany's position, and after the end of the fighting in Poland, Hitler therefore made the Western powers a 'peace offer', in which he demanded that he be left free to settle conditions within Poland, and again raised Germany's claim to colonies.[11] The French and British leaders, Daladier and Chamberlain, however, were able to win through against opposing tendencies in their governments and countries, and rejected Hitler's peace appeal on 10 and 12 October respectively. For them there could no longer be any question of negotiating with Hitler.

The absence of significant military operations by the Western powers, which Hitler misinterpreted as a readiness to conclude peace, was merely the result of their strategic planning before the start of the war. In the staff conferences which took place in the spring after the guarantee to Poland on 31 March the Allied commanders concluded that the Axis powers should be assumed to be initially superior on land and in the air; the Western powers should therefore conduct a defensive war in the first phase. Basing their plans on the overall superiority of their production potential, and utilizing their strong fleets to control the seas, they intended to create the military means to take the offensive, while the fighting ability of the enemy would decline progressively as a result of the blockade measures to be introduced at the start of the war. This plan was not changed even when the Allies assumed more and more precise obligations towards Poland. In the view of their military leaders, direct support for Poland was impossible in any case. Her fate would be finally determined by the result of the war as a whole. No serious offensive was planned in the west in the event of a German attack on Poland, so that Hitler was able to carry out his first 'blitzkrieg' undisturbed.

Without speculating about the further course and results of the war, it can be stated that as long as the Polish army had not been annihilated a planned offensive by the Western powers with forces available at the beginning of September 1939 would have had far-reaching potential and military consequences, given the relative strength of German and Allied forces in general and especially on the Franco-German

[10] Cf. 'Führer Conferences', 39 (7 Sept. 1939).
[11] The second demand has been interpreted as indicating that Hitler was interested even at this early date in creating the basis for a world-power position to be achieved later, and that the construction of a fleet according to the Z plan was also intended to serve this aim. Cf. Hillgruber, *Strategie*, 146. On Hitler's peace campaign after the conquest of Poland cf. Martin, *Friedensinitiativen*, 57–82; on German colonial planning cf. Hildebrand, *Reich*.

border. And one should not overlook the probable interaction between political and military factors in the event of an Allied breakthrough into the western part of Germany: this would have necessitated the withdrawal of some German troops from Poland, which would have enabled that country to resist longer. It could also have kept the Soviet Union from intervening in Poland, which would have made more difficult the transfer of German forces to the west.[12]

The Allies were certainly correct in their belief that they had not yet intensified their armaments programmes to anything like the same degree as the Germans. But their strategy based on this fact, which took as its point of reference the positional warfare of the First World War and was strongly influenced by propaganda about German strength, was dangerous. By writing off Poland from the very beginning, the Western powers gave Germany the opportunity to overcome her inferiority on the battlefield and then to create the preconditions for a later campaign in the west. It was also a mistake to design Allied strategy around a blockade of Germany. In the First World War, under much more favourable conditions, the effects of the blockade had made themselves felt only after several years. Against a man like Hitler, a strategy which left the initiative to him for years would inevitably have disastrous consequences.

As early as 7 October, the day after his 'peace speech' to the Reichstag, Hitler discussed a possible attack in the west with his commanders-in-chief and the chief of the Army General Staff; preliminary discussions had already begun in September. Within a week the hope that the Western powers would give in had vanished, and the deployment directive of the Army High Command for 'Case Yellow' was drawn up at the same time; it envisaged 15 November as the earliest date for attack. In a memorandum of 9 October Hitler explained the necessity of an early operation. He claimed to fear the possibility of a French attack on the Ruhr through Belgium, which in his opinion might make it impossible for Germany to continue the war. Moreover, he too was of the opinion that time was working for the Allies. He considered the position of the Soviet Union in the long run uncertain, and, like the commander-in-chief of the navy, he firmly believed that the United States would enter the war later, although, unlike Raeder, he wanted to avoid anything that could provoke an early American entry.[13] The Army High Command attempted to change Hitler's mind about an attack because they wanted to prevent an extension of the conflict. Moreover, they had serious reservations because of the late season and with regard to the operational ability of the German units so early after the Polish campaign, as material losses and the consumption of ammunition had been considerable. In these arguments the Army High Command were from time to time supported by Göring, who also considered the Luftwaffe to be unready, and frequently used forecasts of bad weather to persuade Hitler to postpone the attack.[14]

Hitler was well aware of the resistance to his plans, and on 23 November he attempted again in a wide-ranging speech to convince his generals and admirals

---

[12] On the German weakness in the west during the Polish campaign cf. Westphal, *Heer*, 109-15; also Kimche, *The Unfought Battle*.

[13] 'Führer Conferences', 45 (10 Oct. 1939). Hitler's memorandum of 9 Oct. is printed in *Dokumente zur Vorgeschichte*, 4-21.   [14] Cf. Martin, *Friedensinitiativen*, 111.

of the necessity and the prospects of success of an early attack in the west.[15] Nevertheless, for various reasons, the attack had to be postponed repeatedly until 10 May 1940. The delay was certainly useful in working out the final operations plan. It also improved the manning and material readiness of the army[16] and the Luftwaffe, although the constant deployments to operations areas before each new attack-date placed a considerable strain on the Luftwaffe units.

Hitler's judgement of the time factor and the expected shifts in relative strength corresponded to the view of the Allies. On 9 September the British cabinet had decided to prepare for a war lasting three years. The army was to be expanded to fifty-five divisions. Churchill, the First Lord of the Admiralty, was convinced of the correctness of preparing for a long war, because time was working for the Allies, but he also pressed for early operations. On 9 September he had suggested using part of the Royal Navy to gain control of the Baltic in order to interrupt Germany's trade with Scandinavia, especially imports of Swedish iron ore, and to influence the policy of the Soviet Union. But Churchill could not realize his plan (code-name 'Catherine'), if only because modification of the battleships which it required would have taken a year.[17]

In the same month Churchill made a new suggestion: to mine Norwegian territorial waters so that German ore-carriers on the way to and from Narvik would have to leave them and could then be intercepted by units of the Royal Navy. But Lord Halifax, the foreign secretary, rejected this suggestion when it was first made and again at the end of November because he believed that such illegal action would hurt the cause of the Allies more than could be justified by its doubtful effect on the economic war.

Allied planning also concerned itself with the Balkans. If Italy entered the war, which was expected in the event of a conflict with Germany, the sending of a French expeditionary corps from the Levant to Salonika had been planned. In view of Italy's non-participation in the war, however, the basis for this plan was lacking. The Allies did consider whether they could establish a second front against Germany in the Balkans in this way, but, taking into account the weakness of their own forces, the British government thought it advisable to refrain from carrying out this operation in order to avoid provoking Mussolini. While the French expected an increase in Allied strength of up to 110 divisions from the establishment of a Balkan front, the British feared Italian intervention. Although Italy was definitely considered the weaker Axis partner, her strength was still greatly overestimated. British efforts were therefore aimed at creating a neutral bloc in the Balkans and first strengthening British forces in the Middle East.

---

[15] Text in *Lagevorträge*, 49–55.

[16] On the overcoming of the personnel shortages which had become obvious during the Polish campaign cf. Murray, 'German Response'.

[17] On this subject cf. Lorbeer, *Westmächte*, 43–5. Lorbeer judges the chances of success too optimistically. On the strategy of the Allies during the first phase of the war as a whole, up to the German attack in the west, cf. Bédarida, *Stratégie secrète*.

The agreements with Turkey of 12 May and 19 October 1939, in which the Western powers promised to aid Turkey if she became involved in a war or if an attack by a European power should reach the borders of Greece and Bulgaria, were also intended to prevent an Italian entry into the war. For her part, Turkey promised to support the Western powers in the event of a conflict in the eastern Mediterranean. It was stipulated that the agreements were not to involve Turkey in war against the Soviet Union; and the other obligations were made dependent on the delivery of war material to Turkey. But in the autumn of 1939 the Western powers were in a position to deliver only very small quantities of such material. Thus, the most important condition for implementing the treaty could not be fulfilled.[18]

In the end the Allies were unable either to cut Germany off from Scandinavia, and in particular from imports of Swedish iron ore, or to establish a position on the Balkan peninsula and thus make south-eastern Europe part of a blockade directed against Germany. They were therefore unable to prevent the export of Romanian oil to Germany, much less establish a second front in the Balkans.[19]

Germany's continued trade with Scandinavia and the Balkan states was basically dependent on the attitude of the Soviet Union. Direct Soviet economic support for Germany still played no role in the first phase of the war; the volume of deliveries of raw materials became significant only after Germany had occupied Denmark and Norway.[20]

In August 1939 Stalin had accepted Hitler's offer not only in order to involve him in a war with the Western powers and then to help him sustain that war for a long time; Stalin also wanted his share of the booty. Only three days after Soviet troops had marched into Poland, the Soviet Union began to develop its position in the Baltic States, which under the Soviet–German agreements belonged to the Soviet sphere of interest. On 19 September the Soviet foreign minister informed the Estonian minister in Moscow that the Soviet Union would assume the protection of Estonian coastal waters, as Estonian authorities had not been able to prevent the escape of a Polish submarine from internment the day before. In the following negotiations the Soviet Union insisted on the conclusion of a treaty covering mutual assistance and bases, which was signed on 28 September. Similar agreements followed with Latvia and Lithuania on 5 and 10 October.

German reaction to these treaties gave the impression that not all Soviet wishes had been fulfilled by the establishment of bases in the Baltic States. On 15 and 30 October Germany concluded resettlement treaties with Estonia and Latvia which permitted members of the German minorities in those countries to emigrate to Germany. Emigration began immediately. By the end of 1939 about 67,000 ethnic Germans had left the two states. A Soviet–German agreement of 12 November

[18] Cf. Butler, *Strategy*, ii. 63–70; Ackermann, 'Türkei'.

[19] The British were able to persuade Romania to reduce its oil exports only temporarily.

[20] Ambassador Ritter to the embassy in Moscow on 9 Apr. 1940, *DGFP* D x. 110–12; Ambassador von der Schulenburg to State Secretary von Weizsäcker, 11 Apr. 1940, ibid. 134–6; also Birkenfeld, 'Stalin'. In contrast, Hillgruber, *Strategie*, 31–2, and Friedensburg, 'Kriegslieferungen', consider the Soviet deliveries in the first year of the war to have been very important.

provided for the resettlement of about 135,000 Germans from Volhynia and Galicia, areas of eastern Poland which had been occupied by the Soviet Union. In the spring of 1941, after the Baltic States had already become Soviet republics, an additional resettlement operation was carried out in which about 17,000 Germans left Estonia and Latvia and 50,000 Lithuania.[21] For Hitler these resettlement operations were part of a mutual delimitation of interests with the Soviet Union, just as he had renounced South Tyrol in his relations with Italy.[22] Thus, paradoxically, his campaign for 'living-space in the east' began with Germans having to leave their homes there.

However, Soviet aspirations were not limited to eastern Poland and the Baltic. In talks conducted in Helsinki from April 1938 the Soviet Union had already indicated that it was interested in political, economic, and military co-operation with Finland, in joint control of the Åland Islands should they be fortified, and in obtaining a base on the island of Suursaari (Hogland) in the Gulf of Finland. But Finland did not want to endanger her policy of Scandinavian neutrality and primarily sought co-operation with Sweden. On 5 October 1939, when Latvia was forced to sign a treaty with the Soviet Union concerning bases and mutual assistance, the Soviet government also invited Finland to send representatives to Moscow for talks. An answer was required within forty-eight hours. The Finnish delegation, led by the Finnish minister in Stockholm, Paasikivi, who had been Finland's first prime minister in 1918 and had conducted the negotiations with the Soviet government leading to the treaty of Dorpat (Tartu) in 1920, arrived on 11 October. The next day Stalin presented the Soviet demands: conclusion of a treaty of mutual assistance, the leasing to the Soviet Union of the Hangö Peninsula at the entrance to the Gulf of Finland, transfer to the Soviet Union of the western part of the Rybachy Peninsula (near Petsamo) and several islands in the eastern part of the Gulf, and the moving of the border on the Karelian Isthmus thirty-five kilometres to the north in exchange for twice as much territory in northern Karelia.

In the following negotiations Stalin reduced his demands to three islands off the coast instead of the Hangö Peninsula, but the Finnish government were only prepared to make concessions in the eastern part of the Gulf. They feared for the independence of their country, although Stalin's final goals were not clear. After the negotiations had been broken off without results, the Finnish delegation left Moscow on 13 November. On 18–19 October, at a meeting between the three Scandinavian monarchs and Finland's President Kallio in Stockholm, Finland had received only moral support. Prime Minister Hansson of Sweden, the only Scandinavian leader with significant military forces at his disposal, refused to intervene in the event of a Soviet attack as he believed he lacked the necessary political support at home.

While after the start of the negotiations the Finns no longer really believed in the threat of war, the Soviet leaders obviously underestimated Finland's will

---

[21] Figures in Fabry, *Sowjetunion*, 134; id., *Hitler-Stalin-Pakt*, 186; Loeber, *Option*.
[22] Cf. Hitler's letter to Mussolini of 8 Mar. 1940, *DGFP* d viii. 871–80.

to resist. In view of Finland's diplomatic isolation and their erroneous assessment of conditions in the country, which they judged on the basis of the situation during the civil war of 1918, they believed they could quickly subdue the Finnish armed forces. The Soviet attack began on 30 November with troops of the Leningrad military district. It was represented as a response to a call for help from a 'people's government' of Finns in exile headed by the general secretary of the Comintern, Otto Kuusinen—a puppet regime which had been created shortly before for that purpose. On 2 December this group concluded a treaty of mutual assistance with the Soviet Union and fulfilled Soviet territorial demands on paper, in return for which it was to receive parts of Soviet Karelia.[23]

Contrary to all expectations, however, the Red Army did not succeed in overrunning the small country. It suffered serious losses and was not able to advance much further than the border. If the Finno-Soviet war were to last for any length of time it would be bound to affect the war of the Western powers against Germany, and itself be affected by that war. In accordance with the German treaties with the Soviet Union, Hitler refused to give Finland any aid; in this policy he had the especially strong support of Grand Admiral Raeder, who hoped to benefit from co-operation with the Soviet Union in the naval war with Britain. On the other hand, Soviet relations with Italy worsened, and Mussolini even recalled his ambassador from Moscow. He claimed to oppose co-operation between Germany and the Soviet Union for ideological reasons, but his main concern was in fact Soviet activity in the Balkans. The Western powers were faced with the questions of what the Soviet-German pact actually involved, how far they should go in helping Finland, and whether a military confrontation with the Soviet Union could contribute to an early German defeat.

In considering how to help Finland, the Allies soon thought of landing at Narvik and occupying the Swedish iron-ore region from there in order to stop all deliveries of ore to Germany. As an alternative they considered using naval forces to at least stop the shipping of ore from Narvik. At a meeting of the Supreme War Council in Paris on 5 February 1940 the French premier Daladier even suggested a landing at Petsamo,[24] which would probably have meant an open war with the Soviet Union, for it would hardly have been possible to disguise the Allied troops as volunteer units in such an operation. In contrast to the British, the French government even desired to participate in Finland's war with the Soviet Union, for domestic reasons.[25]

The British wanted to avoid a final break with Stalin, but not because they feared him as a possible new enemy; they too considered Soviet military potential to be

---

[23] Jakobson's description in *Diplomatie* is no longer adequate. Cf. now Nevakivi, *Appeal*, and Ueberschär, *Finnland*. The official Finnish account is also available now: *Talvisodan historia*.

[24] Bédarida, *Stratégie secrète*, 254.

[25] On the British and French divergencies of opinion and domestic political influences on French foreign policy and strategy cf. also Dilks, 'Great Britain', and Bédarida, 'France', printed together with other papers presented at the symposium on 'The Great Powers and the Nordic Countries 1939-1940'. On Norwegian and British policies and strategies cf. now Munthe-Kaas, 'Campaign in Norway', and Bayer and Ørvik, *Scandinavian Flank*.

almost insignificant. The British and French chiefs of staff thought it probable that the Soviet Union would quickly collapse in the event of war, but they advised restraint because they did not think such a development would have any decisive effect on Germany.[26] In any case they agreed on 5 February to request permission for Allied troops to pass through Norway and Sweden in response to a call for help from Finland, to land at Trondheim and Narvik, and to occupy the Swedish iron-ore area. Finally, they also wanted to send a smaller part of the expeditionary corps to Finland. Although a formal Finnish request for assistance had not been received, the Allies approached Oslo and Stockholm in this sense on 2 March, but Norway and Sweden refused to abandon their neutrality. They did not want to become theatres of war, and rightly feared that the Allies would not be in a position to protect them from German retaliation.

On 5 February the Finnish foreign minister Tanner met the Soviet ambassador to Sweden, Mme Kollontay, with whom there had been unofficial contacts since 10 January, for a first talk. Finland's fading strength, the inadequate assistance from abroad, and a new Soviet offensive, which had begun on the Karelian Isthmus on 1 February, forced the Finnish government to make a decision. In Stockholm Tanner still attempted to obtain help in the form of regular Swedish troop contingents, but Prime Minister Hansson rejected this request categorically on 13 February, just as he had rejected the request for permission for an Allied expeditionary force to pass through his country. For this reason the Finnish government decided on 29 February to begin peace negotiations on the basis of the Soviet demands. This prompted the Allies to renew their activity: they attempted again to obtain permission to march through Norway and Sweden, and sought to induce Finland to continue the fight by promises of help on the one hand and threats to stop all assistance on the other. For its part Sweden attempted to bring about peace by all possible means, to prevent an invasion of Scandinavia. As it soon became clear that the volume of Allied aid would be modest and that for domestic political reasons the premier of France was making promises he could not keep, the Finns had no choice but to accept the Soviet demands. Finland's appeal of 11 March to the Allies to officially request permission to send troops through Norway and Sweden was intended to improve her negotiating position in Moscow. Beyond that it only amounted to a pretext, as the answer of the Swedish and Norwegian governments could only be negative. Nevertheless, on 12 March the Allies gave the order to prepare their operations, but this was cancelled when it became known that on the same day the Finno-Soviet peace treaty had been signed in Moscow.

In this treaty the Finnish islands near Leningrad were ceded to the Soviet Union and the Finno-Soviet frontier in Karelia was moved to the west of Lake Ladoga. The border in the far north was moved westward, as Finland ceded her part of the Rybachi Peninsula; while the Hangö Peninsula was leased to the Soviet Union for thirty years for the construction of a military base.[27]

---

[26] Cf. Lorbeer, *Westmächte*, 72–5, 102–12.
[27] The texts of the treaty and protocol are in Mazour, *Finland*, 241–6.

The end of the Finno-Soviet war did not mean the end of the danger that the Scandinavian countries would be drawn into the larger war. On the contrary, just three weeks later Hitler and Grand Admiral Raeder agreed on a date for the occupation of Norway and Denmark. Moreover, the possibility remained of a direct confrontation between the Western powers and the Soviet Union. In addition to their plans to establish a front against the Soviet Union in the Caucasus with the help of Turkey and Iran, the Allies developed plans to destroy Soviet oil refineries and storage facilities in the Caucasus region by air attacks, and at times considered using naval forces in the Black Sea. These projects for an attack in the south, initially to support Finland against the Soviet Union, were revived even after the peace treaty between those countries had been signed in Moscow. In this way the Allies sought to restore their prestige, which had suffered considerably because they had not provided any significant help for Finland. However, the British were less and less inclined to yield to the urging of the French premier Reynaud, who had taken office after Daladier resigned on 20 March over the Finland issue. Planning was completed at the beginning of April, but no final decision was taken. As a result of subsequent military developments in northern and western Europe, the projects became irrelevant.[28]

The Finno-Soviet winter war was in Germany's interest in so far as, like the Soviet operations in the Baltic States, it tied down forces of the Red Army; moreover, it could lead to an open war between the Soviet Union and the Western Allies, or at least make the Soviet Union more dependent on Germany. But Allied intervention, the sending of troops to Scandinavia, would have deprived Germany of supplies from the north, especially Swedish iron ore. In addition, with bases in southern Norway Britain would have been able practically to close the sea between the Shetland Islands and Bergen to German surface ships, and it would only have been a matter of time until the British would also have had sufficient mines to block the passage of German submarines.

The first suggestion in the German leadership regarding operations in Scandinavia, which came from Raeder, did not mention these possibilities. In his analysis of the situation for Hitler on 10 October 1939 he argued in the interest of the navy in favour of concentrating the war effort against Britain and of beginning a large-scale U-boat construction programme; the strategy to be followed in the future had not been decided upon at the beginning of October, and the chief of the Army General Staff did not expect a German attack in the west to be a decisive success. Consequently Raeder did not at this time hope to obtain bases in the Atlantic for the war against Britain; as an alternative, he suggested obtaining U-boat bases on the Norwegian coast with the help of Soviet pressure.[29] But Hitler did not accept this suggestion; the day before, he had issued Directive No. 6 for the conduct of the war, which envisaged an offensive in the west in the event of a negative Allied reaction to his 'peace speech' of 6 October. This came on 10 and 12 October, when Daladier and Chamberlain rejected his peace offer once and for all.

[28] Cf. Bédarida, *Stratégie secrète*; Lorbeer, *Westmächte*, 68–85; Kahle, *Kaukasusprojekt*.
[29] 'Führer Conferences', 45–7; cf. also Salewski, *Seekriegsleitung*, i. 121–3; on the development of the operations plan for Weserübung cf. Gemzell, *Raeder*, and Loock, 'Weserübung'. On the trial of this case by the International Military Tribunal in Nuremberg cf. Salmon, 'Crimes against Peace'.

Unlike Raeder, members of the naval war staff regarded the acquisition of bases in Norway with scepticism. They opposed military operations against Norway for that purpose. On 25 November Raeder ordered the problem to be examined with regard to the possibility of a British landing in Norway as a reaction to the intended start of the German offensive in the west. On 8 December he suggested the occupation of Norway to Hitler. This time he defended his suggestion by pointing out the necessity of stopping the larger deliveries of timber and ore to Britain, which the naval war staff had observed in November and which were considered 'vital'. But Hitler still did not act. Only on 14 December, after a visit by Vidkun Quisling, the former Norwegian war minister and leader of the Nasjonal Samling, whom Raeder had recommended, did Hitler order the creation of a staff to examine the possibility of invading Norway. Quisling had described the danger of a British operation in Norway and requested support for his plans for a *coup d'état*.[30]

German plans and preparations for the occupation of Denmark and Norway were speeded up when more and more reports of Allied intentions in Scandinavia were received, and especially after the German supply ship *Altmark* was boarded by British sailors in Norwegian territorial waters. However, when Hitler and Raeder agreed on the latest possible date for 'Operation Weserübung' on 26 March, they both knew that the planned Allied operation had been cancelled on 12 March because of the Finno-Soviet peace treaty. Raeder now argued, and he hardly had to convince Hitler, that it would be better to carry out the operation soon, because Germany would sooner or later be confronted with the problem in any case, and maintaining the state of readiness for the operation forced the navy to remain inactive in other areas.

However, before the German operation began on 9 April, the Western powers had become active again. On 28 March the Supreme War Council had decided to mine the Rhine and Norwegian territorial waters. Moreover, the British put troops on stand-by to land in Narvik, Trondheim, Bergen, and Stavanger at the first sign of German countermeasures. But the French Comité de Guerre rejected the mining of the Rhine, as they feared retaliation in view of the weakness of France's own defences. The British finally decided, instead of the planned joint action on 5 April, to mine Norwegian coastal waters alone on 8 April. But the German countermeasures, which became known the next day, represented considerably more than the sort of minor action which the British desired as a pretext for landing their own troops in Norway. The Wehrmacht was able to occupy the most important ports in the country and all airfields in central and southern Norway, and thus to establish a decisive position for the war on the northern flank of Europe.

The policy and strategy of the Allies, and especially of the French government, were guided by the wish to shift the start of the actual fighting on land to a secondary theatre and thus disrupt the increasingly threatening concentration of German forces on the north-eastern border of France. But while Britain and France sought to divert the war in this way, they hoped at the same time to win new allies among the

---

[30] Cf. 'Führer Conferences', 65 ff; Gemzell, *Raeder*, 268–74. For a full discussion of Quisling's role in the events leading up to the establishment of German rule in Norway cf. Loock, *Quisling*.

previously neutral countries, some of which possessed strong armies (numerically). The spread of the war to Scandinavia gave the Allies the desired secondary theatre, but no significant increase in fighting strength and, above all, no opportunity to thwart Hitler's plans for a campaign in the west. Moreover, the situation in Norway quickly became very unfavourable for the Allies. By 10 May 1940 the southern parts of the country were completely under German control; the Allied troops withdrew to a point north of Mosjöen. Around Narvik the Allies deployed disproportionately strong forces in order finally to advance against the weak and isolated German occupying forces there.

When the German attack in the west began on 10 May strong German forces were indeed tied down in Scandinavia, but this had no effect on the success of the offensive against France. The opposite happened; the rapid German advance there hastened the end of the fighting in Norway. By 8 June the Allies had withdrawn their troops; two days later the Norwegian commander-in-chief in northern Norway had to surrender.

The German operational plan for the western offensive, which had been developed during months of disputes involving Hitler, the Wehrmacht High Command, the Army High Command, and especially the command of Army Group A, envisaged a surprise attack from the Ardennes and a breakthrough on the weak French Meuse front, with the fast units spearheading the drive in order to reach the Channel coast and annihilate the isolated northern part of the Allied armies. Army Group B was given the task of tying down the strong Allied forces on the north-eastern border of France by attacking through Holland and Belgium. The strategic surprise was completely successful.[31] Already on 15 May the Dutch army had to surrender; led by their king, the Belgians followed on 28 May. The British and French withdrew to Dunkirk, but owing to mistakes in the German command nearly 340,000 men were evacuated to Britain before the Germans took the city on 4 June, although most of their weapons and equipment was lost. Next day the actual 'battle of France' began with a German attack on the Somme–Aisne line. On 10 June the French government left Paris; the same day Mussolini declared war on the Western powers, expecting to participate in the peace negotiations as a victor.

Premier Reynaud resigned on 16 June; Marshal Pétain formed a new government and began negotiations with the Germans the next day. In the armistice of 22 June France was forced to agree to the German occupation of 60 per cent of her territory and the almost complete demobilization of her home and colonial armed forces under German and Italian supervision. The armistice went into effect on 25 June, the French negotiators having signed a similar agreement with Italy the day before.

The causes of the rapid and unexpected defeat of France, which had been considered the strongest military power in Europe, have been the subject of numerous studies, especially by the French themselves. A main reason was certainly the inadequacy of the inter-Allied and French command organizations, which were not able to adjust to the pace of the German attack; this had become clear even in Norway.

---

[31] For the extensive literature on the military and political background and history of the campaign in the west cf. Part VI below.

Strategically and tactically the French continued to believe in the superiority of defence; armour was used to support the infantry, and the prerequisites for an operational command of the armoured units as well as the air force were lacking. The slow French pace was simply inadequate to cope with a motorized war of movement.

The domestic situation in France cannot be discussed in detail here, but it must be mentioned that in appointing Marshal Pétain as deputy premier and General Weygand as commander-in-chief after the German breakthrough at Sedan, Reynaud entrusted with decisive positions two 'victors of 1918' who were extreme enemies of the Republic. They wanted to spare the country and the army additional, unnecessary sacrifices and also avoid a total occupation of France; they wished above all to keep the army intact as a means of preserving internal order. They therefore considered the achievement of a cessation of hostilities their most important task. Together with the former premier Laval, Pétain established in Vichy after the armistice a patriarchal, authoritarian regime with himself as head of state and government.

These two men also frustrated Reynaud's intention to move the government and parliament to North Africa after the defeat in France, to transfer as many troops and as much equipment as possible there, and then to use the French fleet and the resources of France's colonial empire as well as aid from the United States to continue the war at Britain's side. This plan was certainly realistic; even though there was not the slightest hope of liberating France itself from German occupation in the near future, a joint Franco-British conduct of the war in North Africa and the Mediterranean in the summer of 1940 would have had even more devastating consequences for Italy than the British were able to achieve alone with much more limited forces at their disposal in the autumn and winter of 1940–1. For Italy a two-front war in North Africa would most probably have meant the loss of Libya, and would thus have decisively changed the situation in the Mediterranean.

The decision to abandon the war, in spite of all British and American entreaties not to do so, severely strained Anglo-French relations. Even before 10 May 1940 there had been serious differences of opinion regarding the proper conduct of the war; then, in defeat, mutual recriminations began; but now Britain felt directly threatened. She overestimated the capabilities of Germany and Italy, and feared that in the hands of the Axis powers the French fleet could endanger her own domination of the seas. French assurances that in no case would the fleet be turned over to the Axis powers did not offer enough security for the British. On 27 June the British government, which had been under the leadership of the new prime minister Winston Churchill since 10 May, decided to act; they did not know that the Germans had made the concession of permitting the French to demobilize their fleet in North Africa and ports in the unoccupied part of southern France, where it would be beyond the immediate reach of German forces.

On the morning of 3 July the British surprised the crews of the French ships that had taken refuge in Portsmouth and Plymouth; in Alexandria negotiations skilfully conducted by both sides made it possible to demobilize the French task-force anchored there on the spot. The British Force H from Gibraltar appeared outside the French naval base near Oran in Algeria and presented the French with an ultimatum in which they were called upon either to continue fighting on the side of the British, or to sail their ships to Britain, or to demobilize them in the West Indies or the United States, or to scuttle them within six hours. As the French refused to accept any of these conditions, the British attacked, and the French suffered heavy losses. On 6 July the operation was repeated with aircraft from carriers, and on 7 July another attack was carried out on a French battleship anchored at Dakar.[32]

The British action was based on an erroneous assessment of the situation, for there was no longer a prospect of the French fleet being turned over to the Axis. Hitler had realized that he could not hope to get it and that attempting to do so would only result in its escaping to join the British. For this reason he ignored the unrealistic ideas of the naval war staff, who had hoped that the addition of the French fleet would greatly increase German naval strength. In any case the French were determined to sink their ships themselves if necessary.

These events clearly showed that Hitler's hope that Britain would accept German domination of the Continent was an illusion. The ruthless elimination of the fleet of their former ally clearly demonstrated that the British were determined to continue the war at all costs; this was definitely the impression their actions made on the American president Roosevelt. In spite of all the indignation aroused in France, the Vichy government did not declare war on Britain; they only broke off diplomatic relations. But the British attacks were a severe blow to all Frenchmen who wanted to keep fighting at Britain's side. General de Gaulle, who had come to Britain for that purpose on 17 June, was for this reason able to find few supporters at first; and the French colonies in North Africa, which had been the strongest advocates of a continuation of the war against Germany, remained on the side of Vichy until the Allied landing in North Africa in November 1942.

Britain's continuation of the war in the hope of receiving political and material support from the United States[33] forced the German leaders to reassess the situation. The problem of an invasion of Britain had been raised in independent studies by the individual Wehrmacht services, but basically Hitler and his political and military advisers had assumed that after a German victory in the west Britain would accept a peace that recognized German domination of the Continent and return the colonies taken from Germany after the First World War. Only the German navy did not completely share this assessment; it considered a phase of intensified sea and air warfare necessary to force Britain to admit defeat. Hitler accepted this view on 21 May 1940 when he decided that after the main operations in France the emphasis in armaments programmes would be shifted to U-boat construction and the production of the Ju 88 aircraft.[34] On this occasion Raeder mentioned for the first time the problem of a landing in Britain. In the following weeks doubts

---

[32] Marder, *Dardanelles*, presents a detailed history of the events.

[33] For the British assessment of the situation cf. Reynolds, 'Churchill and the British "Decision"'.

[34] 'Führer Conferences', 105–6. In contrast to his other statements, Hitler also spoke here of wanting to prepare for a long war.

that Britain would make peace became increasingly strong, so that the question of an invasion moved to the foreground of German planning. As early as 2 July the navy and the army began preparatory operational planning on the basis of an order from the Wehrmacht High Command, and on 16 July Hitler issued his Directive No. 16 for the planning of a landing operation in Britain. This did not mean that a definite decision had been taken concerning the invasion; but, in spite of a vague peace offer in his Reichstag speech of 19 July, Hitler now had hardly any hope of achieving a peaceful settlement with Britain.

During the preparations, however, it became clear that Germany did not have the means and forces at her disposal to carry out such an operation. On the one hand, after the Norway operation only remnants of the German navy, which was hopelessly inferior to the British in any case, were ready for action. On the other hand, the lack of amphibious equipment, which the Allies also developed only in the course of the war, could not be adequately compensated for by improvised measures. Above all, however, in contrast to the Norway campaign, the Luftwaffe was not able to gain control of the air or even achieve adequate air superiority to protect a landing in the projected operations area. On 17 September Hitler postponed 'Operation Sea-Lion' 'until further notice', while the Luftwaffe continued its attacks on Britain, though with fading hopes of being able to force a decision alone.[35]

In the mean time Hitler sought other ways out of the situation in which he had found himself since his attack on Poland. He could not calmly wait, for he clearly saw that sooner or later the United States would enter the war on the side of Britain, and he would inevitably lose a war against these two powers in spite of the forces at his disposal in the summer of 1940. He was also forced to reconsider his relationship with the Soviet Union. Here it should be remembered that his non-aggression pact with Stalin had been intended to deter the Western powers from intervening in favour of Poland when Germany attacked that country. If they had refrained from declaring war on Germany, Hitler would have remained independent of Stalin, while the Western powers would not have been tied down by a war with Germany and would therefore have found themselves in a much stronger position *vis-à-vis* the Soviet Union. It is quite uncertain how much the German–Soviet division of spheres of interest would then have been worth to Stalin. At any rate he would hardly have been able to annex all the areas within his sphere. Especially in the Balkans and over the Turkish Straits question he would have had to expect not only opposition from those states immediately affected and from their neighbours, but also British, French, and Italian intervention. In view of this, Hitler was prepared initially to declare his lack of interest in the Balkans, including the Turkish Straits, and instructed Ribbentrop accordingly before the conclusion of the non-aggression pact.[36] He did

---

[35] The most thorough studies of developments on the German side are still the works by Klee, *Seelöwe* and *Dokumente*.

[36] Ribbentrop was authorized to state Germany's lack of interest in the areas of south-eastern Europe, 'but this topic did not come up': memorandum by the foreign minister, note for the Führer, 24 June 1940, *DGFP* D x. 10–11 (trans. amended).

did not need to worry, because Stalin would, he thought, encounter such strong opposition in that area that he would not be able to achieve his aims, and German economic interests would therefore not be endangered by political or military activities.

However, the declaration of war by the Western powers produced a new, unexpected situation. Moreover, it was directed only against Germany. Several times during the following months a military confrontation between the Western powers and the Soviet Union seemed imminent, but it did not materialize. This produced a basic change in Soviet–German relations. As long as Germany was to a certain extent dependent on Soviet deliveries, which Stalin certainly used to apply political pressure, Hitler could not prevent him from setting about the reordering of the political and military situation in his sphere of interest. In carrying out his plans Stalin had to show much less consideration for the Western powers than would have been the case if they had not already been at war with Germany. The over-hasty measures taken by Hitler, after the signing of the border and friendship treaty, to resettle Baltic Germans in the Reich seem in any case to indicate that no one on the German side had thought of the possibility that the Soviet Union might annex the Baltic States, which she now seemed about to do. For the moment, however, Stalin restricted himself to obtaining military bases and treaties of alliance with Latvia, Lithuania, and Estonia, to the relief of those countries and of neighbouring Scandinavia.

The Finno-Soviet winter war, which started shortly thereafter and in which Hitler was forced to assume a position of benevolent neutrality towards the Soviet Union in order not to endanger the non-aggression pact, created considerable political and strategic problems for Germany. Not only did she lose political credit with neutral states, especially in Scandinavia, but she was also cut off from imports of Finnish wood and nickel. Imports of iron ore from Sweden were endangered. Relations with Mussolini, who watched Stalin's activities with distrust, became even cooler. Undoubtedly only the threat of intervention by the Western powers kept Stalin from realizing his plan to convert Finland into a Soviet republic and incorporate her into the Soviet Union.[37]

However, the British defeat at Dunkirk and the fall of France changed the situation fundamentally. Britain had lost her ally and was isolated, except for the uncertain prospect of help from America. A conflict with the Soviet Union was the last thing she needed. Action to stem Soviet advances, as had been planned in the case of Finland, was now inconceivable, either in Scandinavia or in the Balkans.

Already in May, when the French collapse was becoming evident, Stalin took the next steps within his sphere of interest; for the conclusion of peace would inevitably frustrate his plans, which had been based on the assumption of a long war of attrition between Germany and the Western powers. As Britain continued to fight, however, Stalin hoped that the warring states would court his favour and that he would be able to add other areas to the Soviet Union both inside and outside her sphere of interest as recognized by Germany. Hitler found himself in a situation in which

---

[37] Whether Stalin pursued this aim from the beginning is a matter of dispute among historians. Cf. Ueberschär, *Finnland*, 124-6.

he had not yet won the war but had defeated France and driven Britain from the Continent. These two powers had previously guaranteed the territorial order in east central Europe, and Stalin, overestimating their potential power, had refrained from taking complete advantage of the opportunities offered by his treaty with Hitler. But now Hitler had to show how far he was really prepared to go in his concessions to Stalin, as he could not be indifferent to further developments in the Balkans. If the Soviet Union attempted to make good its claim to Bessarabia and to achieve its further objectives in the Balkans and the Turkish Straits, which were already known even though—by pure chance—they had not been mentioned in the non-aggression pact with Germany,[38] changes affecting the entire area all the way to the Near East could be set in motion without Berlin having any chance to control or influence them. To Hitler it seemed clear that imports of Romanian oil, without which Germany could not continue the war, would then stop and that Britain would take advantage of every opportunity to intervene in the expected developments.[39] On the other hand, Stalin was surely interested in creating a fluid situation in the Balkans, with Hungary and Bulgaria using force to settle their territorial claims against Romania. He would then have an opportunity to intervene and could more easily achieve his goals with dependent allies. For this reason the real danger in German eyes lay not in Stalin's military forces, which in any case were considered inferior, but in the uncertain consequences of his political activity.

The Soviet actions, which had begun in May, led to the occupation of the Baltic States in the following month (15-17 June), when members of the existing governments either fled or were arrested. The area around Mirijampilis was also occupied. At the same time the Soviet Union demanded that Finland grant her a concession for the nickel mines near Petsamo (27 June) and agree to joint control of the Åland Islands. The next day the Soviet Union forced Romania to cede Bessarabia (28 June). The additional demand that all of the Bukovina also be ceded was reduced to the northern part of that area after German protests. Finally, the establishment of diplomatic relations with Yugoslavia on 25 June made it clear that the Soviet Union intended to pursue additional interests in the Balkans, while her agreement at this time (1 July) to receive a new British ambassador for negotiations in Moscow gave the German government cause for speculation, at least, above Soviet intentions.[40]

Hitler seems not to have been especially concerned about Stalin's moves to expand the area under his domination as long as he believed that after the German victory over France a peace with Britain could be expected in the following weeks. On his orders planning was begun in the Army High Command to reduce the size of the army after this had taken place.[41] His attitude towards the Soviet Union began to change in July when he realized that Britain intended to keep on fighting and, he supposed, was basing her hopes on the United States and the Soviet Union.

[38] Cf. n. 36 above.
[39] Cf. Halder, *Diaries*, i. 515.
[40] For details of the Soviet actions cf. Fabry, *Hitler-Stalin-Pakt*; Hillgruber, *Strategie*, 102-15 (see also 86-90).
[41] Halder, *Diaries*, ii. 865, 870-1.

On 22 July, after a conversation with Hitler, the commander-in-chief of the army ordered a preliminary examination of the Soviet problem.[42] On his own initiative the chief of the Army General Staff had already ordered a study of this matter on 3 July. But these steps did not mean that a final decision to pursue a military solution had been taken. Hitler also considered including Spain and the Soviet Union in a political bloc against Britain, a project apparently urged on him energetically by Ribbentrop.[43]

German concern with regard to the United States increased after Roosevelt's hostile speech on the occasion of his receiving the Democratic nomination and as a result of the 'Two-Ocean Navy Expansion Act' of 19 July 1940, which envisaged an enormous expansion of the United States navy. But Hitler lacked the means to undertake any direct action against the United States. For this reason he resolved to annihilate the Soviet Union, which, as a 'British sword on the Continent', could be used against either Germany or Japan. By eliminating the Soviet Union Hitler hoped to make Japan such a threat to the United States that that country would no longer be able to support Britain effectively.[44] In the mean time, however, it had became clear that a campaign against the Soviet Union could no longer be carried out according to plan in 1940. For this reason the date for the attack was postponed until May 1941; by then 180 divisions were to be ready for action.[45]

Hitler did speak of his decision to 'finish off Russia', but there is no evidence that he took an interest in the military planning of the Wehrmacht High Command and the Army High Command for the campaign against the Soviet Union, between 31 July and 5 December 1940; nor was the planning followed by preparations or concrete measures. Some troops were transferred to the east, which had been left almost completely exposed during the campaign in France, but the mass of German units remained in the west.

Hitler was primarily occupied with the political situation. The dispute between Romania and Hungary was settled by the Vienna award pronounced by Germany and Italy on 30 August. Hungary received the northern part of Transylvania and the Székler land from Romania; by the treaty of Craiova of 7 September Bulgaria received the southern Dobrudja. Romania was given a guarantee of her frontiers, which was strengthened in October by the sending of a German military mission to that country. German moves in Finland, which was supposed to belong to the Soviet sphere, were no less clear. After Germany had secured 60 per cent of Finnish nickel production for herself by a treaty in July, in August Hitler approved the resumption of arms deliveries to Finland as a quid pro quo for Finnish permission for German troops and their supplies to be sent to northern Norway through Finnish territory; a formal transit agreement was concluded on 22 September. To avoid a completely unacceptable dependence on the Soviet Union, Hitler was forced to

---

[42] Cf. Raeder's memorandums in 'Führer Conferences', 119-20; Halder, *Diaries*, i. 515-18.

[43] Cf. Michalka, *Ribbentrop*.

[44] Cf. Hillgruber, 'Faktor Amerika'.

[45] Halder, *Diaries*, i. 530-4 (31 July 1940). The genesis of the campaign in the east is presented in detail in *Das Deutsche Reich und der Zweite Weltkrieg*, iv.

assume in new form the protective function previously fulfilled by the Western powers in Scandinavia. But he did not limit himself to creating a glacis against Stalin. He also wanted to determine whether a further balancing of interests was possible and whether the Soviet Union could be drawn into a continental bloc against Britain and the United States.

Already on 30 June the chief of the Wehrmacht operations office, Major-General Jodl, had pointed out in a memorandum the possibility of expanding the circle of powers ranged against Britain to include Italy, Spain, the Soviet Union, and Japan. In particular he thought of closing the Mediterranean to Britain by the capture of Gibraltar and an Italian attack on the Suez Canal.[46] Several German offers to support an attack on the Suez Canal with air and armoured forces were not received with enthusiasm by the Italians, however; their own offensive against Egypt, which began on 13 September, was broken off after only four days and not resumed before the British counter-attack on 9 December. Alarmed by the British attacks on the French fleet at the western end of the Mediterranean (Mers-el-Kébir), Germany had demanded on 15 July that four airfields in Morocco be turned over to her, but this met with the emphatic refusal of Marshal Pétain. On the other hand, on 19 June Franco had offered to bring Spain into the war, but he demanded as a reward not only the recognition of Spain's claim to Gibraltar but also considerable German military aid and the fulfilment of extensive colonial claims at the expense of France. For these reasons Hitler refrained from accepting Franco's offer for the time being. However, he continued to examine the possibility of a Spanish entry into the war and the capture of Gibraltar.

As part of his efforts to create a bloc reaching all the way to Japan, Hitler then negotiated in Berlin with the Spanish foreign minister, Serrano Suñer, in September. But the Spanish government refused to moderate their demands of June, and the only result of the talks was Franco's agreement to meet Hitler.[47]

German negotiations conducted at the same time in Tokyo were more successful. On 27 September the Tripartite pact was signed, which included Italy. It defined the spheres of interest of the signatory powers on the basis of a general expansion to the south, allocating India to the Soviet Union. The automatic mutual assistance that the treaty partners were to afford each other was, however, effectively nullified by secret clauses added at the request of the Japanese. Although these clauses did not become known, the pact did not achieve its goal. The United States refused to be intimidated, intensified its co-operation with Britain, even in Asia, and increased its aid to China, which had been at war with Japan since 1937. Under these circumstances the Japanese intention to obtain concessions from the United States in exchange for Japan's dissociating itself from the Tripartite pact could not be realized.[48]

---

[46] Memorandum in Klee, *Dokumente*, 298–300.

[47] Cf. Hillgruber, *Strategie*, 137–8, 183–7.

[48] On the relations between Germany and Japan in this phase the standard work is still Sommer, *Deutschland und Japan*; cf. now also Krebs, *Japans Deutschlandpolitik*.

In the mean time Hitler had turned his attention to France. His interest was aroused by the energetic local resistance to a British and Gaullist attack on Dakar on 23–5 September, and by the reference of the head of the French delegation in the armistice commission to a possible Franco-German alliance. Moreover, after a long rethinking process within the naval war staff following Mers-el-Kébir, Grand Admiral Raeder presented a plan to Hitler that would shift the main weight of the Italo-German war effort to driving Britain from the Mediterranean and capturing Gibraltar and the Suez Canal, in order to deal Britain a heavy blow and gain a starting-position for additional operations before increasing American help for the British began to affect the course of the war. Raeder specifically referred to the need to secure France's West African colonies. If Spain and Portugal entered the war their islands in the Atlantic would also have to be secured against Anglo-American operations. After the raid on Dakar Raeder pleaded for co-operation with Vichy France. His strategy, which had originally been developed as an alternative to 'Operation Sea-Lion', now seemed to him to offer an alternative to 'Barbarossa', the planning of a campaign in the east.[49]

After informing Mussolini—who was extremely reluctant to renounce his war aims with regard to France, but finally agreed to postpone their realization until a peace settlement was reached—Hitler set about persuading France and Spain to co-operate with Germany. On 22 October he met Laval in Montoire, and on 23 October Franco in Hendaye. The next day he was back in Montoire to meet Pétain and Laval. While Hitler was very disappointed by his talk with Franco, the French seemed prepared to co-operate in ways to be determined from case to case. However, Pétain had a secret agreement negotiated in London at the same time whereby the British government promised to refrain from further actions against French overseas territories as long as France did not co-operate with Germany or allow her the use of bases in the French colonies.[50] Hitler for his part was not in fact interested in a real partnership with France, and continued his ruthless policy towards that country. Planning and preparations for the capture of Gibraltar and the defence of the Canary Islands continued, as did talks with the French, although Hitler had long since realized that a reconciliation of the conflicting French, Italian, and Spanish interests in Africa was 'possible only by a gigantic fraud'.[51]

After Mussolini had completely misjudged the political and military situation and had begun his inadequately prepared campaign against Greece from Albania on 28 October, German planning again concentrated on Spain. The Italian offensive came to a standstill on 9 November, and the British demonstrated their naval superiority in no uncertain manner. For this reason Germany sought to relieve some of the pressure on Italy by obtaining Spanish co-operation in closing the western entrance to the Mediterranean. After new negotiations with Serrano Suñer, Admiral Canaris had talks with Franco in Spain on 7 December. The results were clearly negative;

---

[49] 'Führer Conferences', 132–6 (6 Sept. 1940, incomplete), 141–3 (26 Sept. 1940).
[50] Hillgruber, *Strategie*, 321–2.
[51] Halder, *Diaries*, i. 609 (3 Oct. 1940). Cf. also the detailed account in *Das Deutsche Reich und der Zweite Weltkrieg*, iii.

the Spanish government rejected such plans once and for all. Franco rightly feared that entering the war on the side of Germany would cost Spain her overseas possessions and that the country would not be able to withstand the pressure of an economic blockade.[52]

The Wehrmacht High Command's hope of obtaining French co-operation lasted only a few days longer. As late as 10 December Laval declared at Franco-German talks in Paris that France would begin the reconquest of her lost colonies in Africa at the end of February 1941 and would undertake operations against British possessions in West Africa if, as expected, Britain took countermeasures.[53] But only three days later Laval was dismissed by Pétain, who had reached a second agreement with Britain on 6 December.[54] This meant the end of the Franco-German *rapprochement* and of any chance for Germany to capture Gibraltar and extend her military operations to North-West Africa. Meanwhile, after the Italian defeats in the middle and eastern Mediterranean, German intervention there was not only possible but essential. When Hitler intervened, however, he did so not in pursuit of Raeder's Mediterranean strategy, but only to prevent a total Italian collapse and to secure his southern flank for 'Barbarossa'. A strong German involvement could indeed have led to such important successes as the capture of Malta, the driving of the British out of Egypt and the Middle East, and the establishment of a link to the isolated Italians in East Africa. But all these operations would neither have forced the British to make peace with Germany nor have enabled the Axis powers to cope with America's entry into the war, which they expected to take place in 1942. But the decisive factor in Hitler's strategy was no doubt that he had determined in the mean time to destroy the Soviet Union, believing that only in this way could he secure an adequate base and the necessary rear cover for the struggle against the Anglo-Saxon sea powers. For this reason he rejected the plan of the commander of U-boats, Vice-Admiral Dönitz, to concentrate the entire war effort on a submarine war against British shipping in the Atlantic: the success of this plan was uncertain, and it would require too much time.

Concern about rear cover in the east does not seem to have been a major factor in Hitler's thinking until he learnt of Stalin's further intentions during Molotov's visit to Berlin on 12–13 November. When he planned to extend the war to Africa and the Atlantic islands he must have been aware that after these plans had been carried out Germany's armed forces would be tied down to an extent that would preclude a campaign against the Soviet Union.

The Soviet actions in the summer of 1940 have already been described. In a speech on 1 August Molotov declared that the Soviet Union could not be satisfied with what it had achieved up to that point and that additional successes were essential. Accordingly, Moscow criticized the Vienna award and the explanations for it provided

[52] Report from Canaris in *Kriegstagebuch des Oberkommandos der Wehrmacht*, i. 219–20.
[53] Ibid. 984–94.
[54] Hillgruber, *Strategie*, 333.

by the German government. A Soviet memorandum of 21 September pointed out that the award violated the obligation of the German government to consult with the Soviet Union and that the Soviet Union had by no means renounced its interests in the Balkans, which went beyond Bessarabia and northern Bukovina. At the same time, however, Molotov expressed the readiness of the Soviet Union to negotiate a new delimitation of interest-zones. Molotov voiced Soviet displeasure about the Finno-German transit agreement, which had been answered by increased Soviet pressure on Finland. The Soviet Union also occupied some Romanian islands in the Danube delta to secure control of the mouth of that river.

Hitler's next goal after the conclusion of the Tripartite pact was, in accordance with his plan for a continental bloc, to persuade the Soviet Union to join that pact; for, as long as the Soviet position was uncertain, it would not be possible to achieve the desired effect on Britain or the United States. He therefore had to attempt to reach a global understanding with Stalin in which, as already noted, the regions south of the Soviet Union were to be allocated to her sphere of interest. Hitler thus invited Molotov to come to Berlin on 13 October, before he left for his meetings with Franco and Pétain. Stalin agreed to send Molotov, but not until after the American presidential election. Accordingly, the visit was set for 12–13 November. Stalin was prepared to negotiate, but his ideas of what should be accomplished obviously differed from those of Hitler. Stalin found himself in a situation similar to that of 1939, when he had been free to give his support to the side prepared to pay the most. A British offer of 22 October, to recognize the *de facto* rule of the Soviet Union in the annexed areas pending a peace settlement in which Stalin was to be consulted, was of course in his eyes no basis for negotiations. He expected more from Hitler in exchange for enabling him to continue his war against Britain. For this reason Molotov in Berlin was less interested in the proffered share of the 'British estate in bankruptcy' than in annexing Finland and southern Bukovina, concluding a treaty of alliance with Bulgaria, and acquiring military bases on the Dardanelles. The German government for its part was strongly interested in maintaining peace in the Baltic; there could be no question of violating the guarantee to Romania; Bulgaria was indispensable as a deployment zone for the planned operation against Greece; and in the question of the Turkish Straits only a treaty securing free passage for Soviet ships seemed to be acceptable. Further, Molotov revealed to Ribbentrop on the second day of the negotiations that the Soviet Union was also interested in Romania, Hungary, Yugoslavia, and Greece. The same applied to the future of Poland, and Molotov wanted to know if Germany still considered the maintenance of Swedish neutrality important. Finally, he voiced the opinion that talks would have to be conducted on the Danish entrances to the Baltic as well as on the International Danube Commission, which should be replaced by a joint Soviet-Romanian control of the mouth of the Danube. Evidently Molotov was thinking of a similar Soviet-Danish control of the Sound, the Belts, the Kattegat and Skagerrak.[55]

---

[55] On the talks with Molotov, with an assessment of their importance, cf. Fabry, *Hitler-Stalin-Pakt*, 343–64; Hillgruber, *Strategie*, 300–9.

Molotov's statements showed that Stalin regarded the delimitation of German and Soviet interests in August and September 1939 as by no means final, and in practical terms this was bound to be the case. However, he was evidently not interested in a definitive, precise settlement of interests but rather intended to extract a further high price from Hitler for Soviet support in the various phases of the war. The desire to secure Soviet acquisitions against intervention by the Western powers after a German defeat may also have played a role in his thinking.[56] This was indicated by his desire to control the entrances to the Baltic as well as the Black Sea and to acquire southern Sakhalin and the Kurile Islands from Japan. These efforts were, of course, completely in accord with the tradition of the tsars.

The final Soviet conditions for joining the Tripartite pact, which Stalin communicated to Hitler on 25 November, were more modest: Japanese renunciation of their concessions in northern Sakhalin, recognition of Soviet aspirations in the direction of the Persian Gulf, the withdrawal of German troops from Finland, leasing of a base in the area of the Turkish Straits (a demand which, if necessary, the Axis powers were to support militarily against Turkey), and finally, the conclusion of a pact of mutual assistance with Bulgaria, for which direct negotiations were begun on the same day.

Hitler did not reply to Stalin's suggestions, and concentrated instead on a campaign against the Soviet Union—'Operation Barbarossa'—because he had understood that, in view of the policy Stalin was pursuing, his own strategy of a continental bloc could not be realized. If he wanted to set Japan free for a confrontation with the United States, so as to keep Roosevelt from intervening in the European conflict, then he had to destroy the Soviet Union. Moreover, in and after 1942 he would be able to fight a war against Britain and the United States with some prospect of success only if he had the resources of the Soviet Union at his disposal. His decision was made considerably easier by the fact that his military advisers, who completely underestimated Soviet strength, had no doubts about the feasibility of a campaign against the Soviet Union and were cautious only because they did not see any advantage in it and basically wanted to avoid a war on two fronts. Even Raeder expressed reservations only because such a campaign would mean that the plans and projects of the navy would again be given a low priority for the foreseeable future.

In conclusion, we must consider to what extent Hitler's decision was influenced by the fact that 'the war in the east was for him the real war, the great goal of his policy, which he had been striving to realize since the 1920s'.[57] For those historians who believe this to have been the decisive motive in Hitler's decision to attack the Soviet Union, it is logical to maintain that Soviet foreign policy was not a significant factor in this regard. 'Since for Hitler the war of conquest in the east was the decisive goal itself, whose realization was dependent on several basic political and strategic preconditions, but not on Stalin's more or less limited actions,

[56] Cf. Hillgruber, *Deutschlands Rolle*, 111; Topitsch, *Stalins Krieg*, suggests that the revelation of Soviet ambitions was intended to provoke Hitler into attacking the Soviet Union so that Stalin might achieve his aims all the more easily from the position of a victim of aggression.

[57] Hillgruber, *Strategie*, 362.

a cause-and-effect chain of individual events in the realm of actual politics is not very probable.[58]

In recent years the tendency to explain the decision to attack the Soviet Union as primarily or exclusively the result of Hitler's dogmatically determined programme has become stronger, while strategic considerations, if they are mentioned at all, are considered to have been relatively unimportant. The numerous attempts to show that Hitler was constantly preoccupied with the campaign against the Soviet Union during the first year of the war are examples of this tendency, although they have not as yet been very convincing. Contemporary evidence is lacking of a direct connection between programme and actual policy during this period.[59] Present research seems to indicate that it was Stalin's policy in the summer of 1940, which was not in violation of the pact with Germany but nevertheless endangered German interests, that caused Hitler to view the Soviet Union as a potential ally of Britain. Stalin's refusal to fit into Hitler's strategic plan, and the disclosure of his aims affecting the German spheres of power and interests, led to Hitler's final decision to seek a military solution—always his first choice when policies proved unsuccessful. The question of whether and to what extent Hitler's decision was determined by his ideology, dogma, and programme must remain open as long as there is nothing to go on but conjecture based on his earlier or later statements. Certainly, after 23 August 1939 he did not simply forget what he had been saying and writing about the 'Jewish–Bolshevik enemy' for almost two decades, and this no doubt played a role in his plans for the future destiny of the 'east'. But the connection can be proved only after February 1941, long after Hitler had taken his decision to attack the Soviet Union.[60]

[58] Hillgruber, *Strategie*, 209.
[59] Cf. Stegemann, 'Hitlers Ziele'.
[60] On this still controversial question cf. Stegemann, 'Entschluß'; Hillgruber, 'Hitlers Wendung'; Stegemann, 'Geschichte und Politik'.

PART II

Action Plans and Situation Assessments of the Luftwaffe and Navy before the Outbreak of War

KLAUS A. MAIER
AND
BERND STEGEMANN

I. Total War and Operational[1] Air Warfare

Klaus A. Maier

1. Air War Theory

In his preface to the German edition of Douhet's *Dominio dell'aria*,[2] published in 1935, the then head of the foreign air forces department in the Air Command Office (Luftkommandoamt, later the Luftwaffe General Staff), Lieutenant-Colonel Freiherr von Bülow, wrote that warfare as it had been practised for centuries had been made obsolete by air power, which had transformed the entire living-space of the enemy into a battlefield. In spite of his criticism of the extreme conclusions, the 'air war alone' strategy which the Italian general had derived from this fact, Bülow believed he could see the 'immensely stimulating effect' of Douhet's ideas in the armaments programmes of the European powers, and even perceived an ideological quality in them: 'Douhet's attacks on the bastions of the old principles of warfare were the military equivalent of the Fascist march on Rome. Not their least important aspect was that they were both an expression and a consequence of the Fascist revolution.' This claim, and Bülow's observation that only the Führer had clearly recognized the special threat to Germany posed by air warfare and had put an end to one-sided disarmament by re-establishing Germany's military sovereignty, and especially by creating its air force, suggested to his readers a special relationship between German air armaments and National Socialism.

In Germany, which had been forbidden by the treaty of Versailles to create an air force, military officers concerned with air warfare attempted to compensate for the lack of practical experience by assiduously reading foreign publications on air-war theory.[3] The 'Guide-lines for the Conduct of Operational Air Warfare', compiled in 1926 by the aerial warfare expert of the Truppenamt in the Army Command Staff (Heeresleitung) 'from publications of foreign air powers',[4] described the new strategic possibilities as the specific ability of air forces 'to carry the war immediately to the innermost political, moral, economic, and military sources of a state's strength'. Their attack was directed not only against the enemy's armed

---

[1] In spite of initially different meanings, the term 'operational air warfare' (*operativer Luftkrieg*) gradually came to be used in the Luftwaffe for those actions in an air war which air forces carried out on their own, i.e. independently of the operations of the other armed services, and which are today generally described as 'strategic air warfare'. Cf. Köhler, 'Operativer Luftkrieg'; Förster, *Totaler Krieg*, 156.

[2] Douhet, *Luftherrschaft*, 5; cf. Köhler, 'Douhet und Douhetismus'; Vauthier, *Doctrine*.

[3] On German air-war theory cf. Förster, *Totaler Krieg*, 149 ff.; Völker, 'Entwicklung', 171 ff., 218; id., *Luftwaffe*, 28 ff., 71 ff., 194 ff.; id., *Dokumente*, Nos. 195–200; Rautenberg, *Rüstungspolitik*, 317 ff.; Gehrisch, *Entwicklung*, 227 ff.; Murray, 'British and German Air Doctrine'; id., 'Luftwaffe'; Maier, 'Total War'; Overy, 'Uralbomber'; id., 'Hitler and Air Strategy'; Boog, *Luftwaffenführung*; Feuchter, *Luftkrieg*, 32 ff. Additional literature can be found in Köhler, *Bibliographie*, 80 ff.

[4] BA-MA Lw 106/11.

forces and their installations, but also against the civilian population, industry, and the transport system. The Luftwaffe should try to 'destroy the enemy's moral ability to resist and his will to carry on the war by attacking his large cities, industrial centres, armaments industry, and sources of food for his population'.

The aims of air warfare were also the main subject of a memorandum by Dr Robert Knauss, transport director of Lufthansa, on the 'German air fleet', which was submitted to Göring for approval by State Secretary Milch in the Reich ministry of aviation.[5] Knauss pointed out the vulnerability of the European industrial states, whose complex production and transport systems were such sensitive structures that they could be paralysed by disruption at a single vital point. In addition to these industrial targets, Knauss included the 'concentrations of millions of people in large cities' as targets of air warfare:

It is clear that even the best organization of passive air defence is helpless when confronted with planned attacks by an air fleet against a large city or an industrial area. Terrorizing enemy capitals or industrial areas will lead all the more rapidly to a collapse of morale if the national consciousness of the population is weak and the masses in the big cities have become materialistic and divided by social and party-political conflicts.

Among others, the head of the Army Command Staff (T1, operations department) in the Truppenamt, Colonel von Gossler, raised objections to this plan of air warfare. He agreed that in war there was no longer any separation between the zone of actual combat and the home front, and undoubtedly victory could be achieved more rapidly by attacking the enemy's civilian population than indirectly by defeating his army. But both air fleets in a war would have this advantage. Throughout the course of military history there had been many new weapons which would supposedly consign all others to the scrap-heap. Gossler's objections, which clearly reflected pride in and concern about the future of the more traditional weapons, were also motivated by fear that 'the new weapon could kill war and make it impossible for both sides. Pacifists have been preaching such ideas for a long time.'[6]

The assessments of the threat by the chief of the Air Command Office,[7] Major-General Wever, also reflected concern about internal dangers. In his speech on the occasion of the opening of the Air Warfare Academy on 1 November 1935[8] he described 'Germany's fate' as a constant 'struggle against superior strength', which German armies had had to win since the creation of Prussia and in the world war, 'until a leaderless nation collapsed at home and knocked the weapons out of the hands of its brave army'.

Compared to Knauss, Wever advocated a moderate plan for air warfare which corresponded more closely to the ideas of the other Wehrmacht services.

---

[5] Heimann and Schunke, 'Geheime Denkschrift'. According to the letter of 31 May 1933 the memorandum reflected Milch's views 'as they already formed the basis of my policy in the creation of the Hansa Fleet (Ju 52, He 70)'.

[6] Quoted from Rautenberg, *Rüstungspolitik*, 322 and 466 n. 10.

[7] As of 2 June 1937 officially the 'Chief of the General Staff'. On 3 June 1936 Wever died in an aeroplane crash. Cf. Völker, *Luftwaffe*, 77–8.

[8] Wever, 'Vortrag'.

The fact that at last National Socialism had created a strong Luftwaffe as an independent service did not mean that that service wanted to conduct its own war without taking into consideration the plans of the army and the navy. In Wever's view, the leader principle (*Führerprinzip*) alone forbade such a plan: 'Just as in the national community (*Volksgemeinschaft*) only the united march of all members towards a goal can lead to success, so only the will of one man can direct a war.' Wever gave priority in a future war to attacking the armed forced of the enemy in 'operational co-ordination' with the army and navy. In a war the role of the Luftwaffe could be to subdue the air force, the army, and the naval forces of the enemy, or to destroy his armaments industry—the basis of his armed forces. The situation as a whole would determine where the use of the Luftwaffe should be concentrated. Although he did not want to neglect air defence, Wever was convinced that the 'decisive weapon of air warfare is the bomber'.

Basically Wever's conception of air warfare contained an operational (strategic) component as well as the co-operative (tactical) uses of the Luftwaffe he preferred. With his demand that the Luftwaffe had to paralyse the enemy armaments industry Wever actually crossed the dividing-line, which was in any case not very clear-cut, between the air war against the supply-system of the enemy's forces and one directed against the enemy population itself.[9]

The regulation on air warfare, first issued in 1936, also followed this plan.[10] Air attacks were to be directed against the fighting strength of the enemy as well as against the 'roots of the adversary's will to resist' (point 2). Within this double task the war against the enemy armed forces was given priority, and attacks on the enemy's 'sources of strength' were made to seem less radical by referring to their expected effects on his armed forces:

The task of the Wehrmacht in war is to break the will of the enemy. The Wehrmacht is the strongest embodiment of the will of the nation. The defeat of the enemy armed forces is therefore the most important goal in a war. [Point 9] The task of the Luftwaffe is to serve this aim by its conduct of the air war within the framework of the grand strategy. By attacking the enemy air force, it weakens the enemy armed forces and at the same time protects our own Wehrmacht, our population, and our living-space. By participating in operations and combat on land and at sea it directly supports the army and the navy. By attacking the sources of strength of the enemy armed forces and disrupting the flow of that strength to the front, the Luftwaffe attempts to paralyse the enemy armed forces. [Point 10]

Among the sources of enemy strength the regulation listed in particular production, food supply, imports, the supply of energy, the railway system and other forms of

---

[9] For Ziese-Beringer ('Gefährdungsraum', 77) air attacks on the civilian population also had a military character: 'The typical, unmistakable characteristic is that they contribute to ending the war and thus have a military effect in the true sense of the word.' Cf. also Schmitz and Stauffenberg, 'Angriffsziele'. On the international legal aspects of air war cf. Watt, 'Restraints'; Best, *Humanity in Warfare*, 262 ff.; Messerschmidt, 'Kriegstechnologie'.

[10] L.Dv. 16 *Luftkriegführung* (L.F.), repr. with alterations in Mar. 1940; excerpts printed in Völker, *Dokumente*, 466-86.

transport, military command centres, and government administrative centres (point 143). It warned that actions against them would require much time and large forces. For this reason the 'sources of enemy strength' and the 'flow of that strength to the front' should only be attacked in the following cases (point 22):

1. if targets presented themselves which would be attacked in the expectation that this would have a rapid effect on the course of the war;
2. if the land and sea operations had only paved the way for a conclusion;
3. if the decisive battles had been concluded;
4. if a decision in the war could only be achieved by destroying the enemy's sources of strength.

Attacks on cities 'to terrorize the population' were rejected in principle. However, were the enemy to resort to terror attacks, the regulation described retaliation as the 'only way to persuade the enemy to stop using this brutal form of air warfare'. In any case such attacks had to be clearly retaliatory (points 186 ff.).

In spite of the priority given to the fight against the enemy armed forces in the air warfare regulation, the Luftwaffe did not lose sight of its operational role. In his lecture on the 'principles of operational air warfare'[11] on 29 October 1936 the director of operations in the Air Command Office, Major Deichmann of the General Staff, explained that, although everyone knew that the Luftwaffe had to be in a position to conduct the air war on an operational level, it was all the more astonishing that very few people had any clear idea of how such a war was to be conducted. Deichmann maintained that there could be no question of attacking all enemy armament factories, because consumption of munitions would be too high. It was therefore important to identify targets whose destruction would have a decisive effect. He presented numerous criteria for the selection of targets, which he intended to be used as a basis for training in operational decision-making in war-games. He added that he had confined himself to providing a basis for decisions to attack a nation's defence economy, but likewise a criterion must be found for 'decisions regarding attacks on the moral strength of a nation'.

In a confidential study for Göring at the beginning of 1937, Milch advocated a surprise attack on enemy bases, to be carried out with all available forces either at the same time as or in place of a declaration of war. This would make it possible to use the Luftwaffe early against operational targets, which required the prior defeat of the enemy air force.[12]

The plan of attack of the Luftwaffe, which in principle threatened the civilian population as well as the armed forces of enemy countries, was in complete agreement with a study of 19 April 1938 by the Wehrmacht High Command on 'Warfare as an Organizational Problem'.[13] The study maintained that war served to secure the continued existence of a nation and state or their 'future place in history'. This 'high

---

[11] LA III Nr. 1710/36 g.Kdos. III, 1 B, Berlin, 29 Oct. 1936, printed in Völker, *Dokumente*, No. 198.
[12] 'Gedanken über den Luftkrieg', c.Jan. 1937; Irving, *Rise and Fall*, 53. Milch was familiar with Douhet's ideas. On 22 Oct. 1933 he recorded in his notebook: 'read Douhet': Milch, 'Merkbuch', MGFA.
[13] Cf. esp. the appendix 'Was ist der Krieg der Zukunft?', *IMT* xxxviii. 35 ff.

moral purpose' (*hoher sittlicher Zweck*) gave war its 'total' character. Costs, profit, and losses would reach 'hitherto unheard-of levels', and losing a war would mean the destruction of a state and nation. War was indeed waged primarily against the enemy armed forces, but in addition it was also directed against the enemy's material resources and the 'moral strength' of his population. As the guiding principle in waging war the Wehrmacht High Command recommended: 'necessity knows no law.'

In contemporary German military publications there was no lack of authors who, wedded to the ideology of total war, advocated considerably more radical plans of air warfare. For example, arguing that discussions about air warfare could only produce useful results if the air war were seen as 'part of the total war of tomorrow', Major Gehrts of the supplementary reserve[14] questioned whether the aims described in the air warfare regulation (defeating enemy armed forces within the framework of the grand strategy) were broad enough. He maintained that technology, which had 'shattered the entire structure of all nineteenth-century middle-class ideas of order', had also come to dominate war. Technology had made it possible and even unnecessary to crush the enemy's resistance in a war of movement, however firmly entrenched he might be. And it was essential to do so, for 'where the fronts become rigid, time starts to operate', and in a war on several fronts time would always work against Germany.

A war of long duration would, 'like a landslide, bring subterranean currents to the surface' and revive the 'spectre of a collapse at home'. As the will of a nation at war was embodied not only in its armed forces but also in its industry, the aim of a war had to be more than merely defeating the enemy's armed forces. The will of the enemy nation could also be broken if the will of its workers, its technological and economic arm, were broken, for since the 'collectivization of our existence' brought about by technology the worker as the 'functional exponent' of that technology had become a decisive political factor in war and peace. The result of this collectivization was the 'national community' as the workers' 'common destiny' (*Schiksalsebene*). Anyone who had recognized this historical change would clearly see that the worker could even break the will of the soldier. The world war and the working man's revolution had proved that his revolutionary will could vanquish even the best army and thus deprive the state of an effective instrument of power. The highest priority for German military leaders was therefore to break the will of the enemy in the shortest possible time. On fronts where his armed forces could be defeated quickly, the task of the Luftwaffe was to support this aim within the conduct of the war as a whole. However, on fronts where the decision could not be achieved within a short time it would have to be sought from the very beginning in the conduct of the air war, in which the most important aim was to break the will of the enemy 'home army of workers'. In this regard it was less important to destroy the enemy's 'arsenals of economic technology' than to 'depopulate' them. As Gehrts assumed that Germany's potential enemies also had the same intentions,

[14] Gehrts, 'Gedanken'. This essay was published in the collection of essays on military science *Die Luftwaffe*, ed. by the Luftwaffe General Staff, Department 3 (II); it was for 'official use only'. Although the essays represented the 'completely free ideas of the authors', it can be assumed that the editor considered them especially worthy of discussion.

he called for 'total mobilization' by the 'creation and demonstration of a uniform national consciousness by mobilizing all values, even in peacetime' and by educating the worker to give him a 'soldierly basic attitude'. As in Gehrts's view 'today the worker and the soldier are, in their Prussian-German substance, cast from the same mould', he believed that this aim had been realized to a high degree in the National Socialist state and that in this respect the Third Reich had gained a considerable lead over the Western powers.

The use of air power seemed to indicate that total war was approaching its purest form and to provide the ultimate justification for total mobilization. Gehrts's arguments show, however, that his demand for a completely militarized and authoritarian state was not based solely on perceptions of external, military threats. Behind his militarism, with its mask of revolutionary phraseology, they reveal a desire to put a stop to social changes that had been taking place in Germany since the start of the industrial revolution and were considered no less threatening.[15] In the authoritarian state, in which 'with the socialization of danger as a permanent characteristic of the modern use of force' the nation became 'a uniform technical enterprise',[16] the pursuit of group interests could be punished as sabotage. The most extreme proponents of 'total war' derived their perceptions of the threat from the idea of war as a force of nature rather than from specific traits of an enemy, which might in principle change. In their view a society organized for war was bound to seem only 'natural'.[17]

The mutual affinity of the ideology of total war and total mobilization and the National Socialist world-view is obvious. Supporters of this ideology, regardless of the intensity of their enthusiasm, expected better conditions for success in a future war from the National Socialist 'Führer-state' than from a parliamentary, democratic constitution.[18]

The key position of the Luftwaffe in the National Socialist regime, best expressed in Göring's rank as 'Reich minister of aviation and commander-in-chief of the Luftwaffe', suggests that the spirit of German plans for air warfare, which was 'total' in its basic tendency, exerted an especially strong influence in the Nazi policy of aggression and warfare. But on the other hand it must be pointed out that the German aircraft industry did not and could not create an operational Luftwaffe comparable to the strategic air fleets used by the Allies against Germany in and after 1943. And the Luftwaffe, as is well known, achieved its spectacular initial successes not in operational (strategic) missions, but as a support service for the army. However, this fact should not keep us from describing the mutual dependency between the operational aspects in situation assessments, mission plans, and the conduct of the air war on the one hand, and National Socialist policy and strategy on the other, and, when appropriate, determining the 'total' elements in the former.

---

[15] Cf. Wehler, 'Verfall der deutschen Kriegstheorie', 306–7.
[16] Thus Harold D. Lasswell in 1939 in his 'barracks state' model, quoted in Senghaas, *Rüstung*, 12.
[17] Hillgruber, 'Militarismus', 39.
[18] Cf. Messerschmidt, *Wehrmacht*, 480 ff. (conclusion); Förster, *Totaler Krieg*, 11 ff.; vol. i of the present work, III.iii.

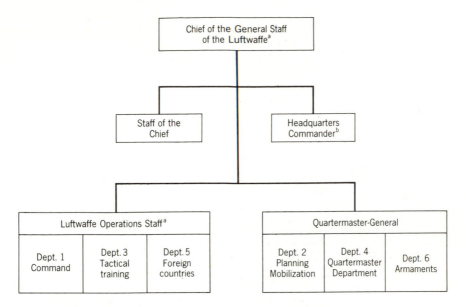

[a] The Chief of the General Staff was at the same time Chief of the Operations Staff.
[b] Only in wartime.

DIAGRAM II.I.1. The Luftwaffe General Staff in 1939 (as of 1 February)

Source: 'Studiengruppe Luftwaffe, Aufbau der Luftwaffe bis 30.8/1939, Gliederung und Befehlsverhältnisse', BA-MA Lw. 101/4, pt. 1.

2. SITUATION ASSESSMENT AND MISSION-PLANNING

Knauss's memorandum of May 1933 on 'The German Air Fleet' was based on the assumption that the foreign-policy goal of the 'national Government' was to re-establish 'Germany's position as a great power in Europe'. Knauss considered that the necessary build-up of the Wehrmacht 'to the minimum strength essential to be able to wage a two-front war against France and Poland with prospects of success' might be endangered by a possible preventive war started by those two powers. To shorten the critical period in which France and Poland would be able to prevent German rearmament, Knauss recommended the construction of a fleet of large, four-engine aircraft with a penetration range of 800 km. and a bomb-load of 2,000 kg. of high-explosive, incendiary, and gas bombs. Even a Luftwaffe with 200 such aircraft, he argued, would dampen the enthusiasm of the enemy for an attack on Germany; overnight it would increase the risk that this air fleet could immediately be used to carry the war to his own country. Moreover, the air fleet would make Germany more attractive as an ally and guarantee the operational mobility necessary for a war on several fronts.

When the secrecy surrounding the German air force was removed in March 1935, the real Luftwaffe bore little similarity to the one Knauss had sketched in his

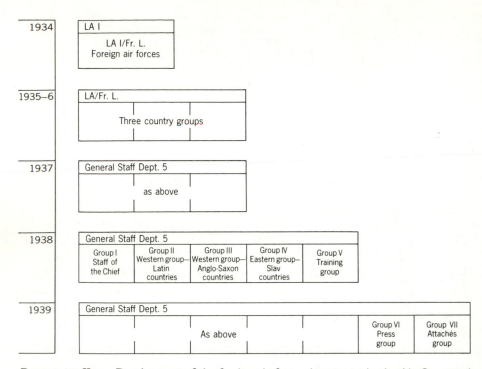

1934	LA I
	LA I/Fr. L. Foreign air forces

1935–6	LA/Fr. L.
	Three country groups

1937	General Staff Dept. 5
	as above

1938	General Staff Dept. 5				
	Group I Staff of the Chief	Group II Western group– Latin countries	Group III Western group– Anglo-Saxon countries	Group IV Eastern group– Slav countries	Group V Training group

1939	General Staff Dept. 5			
	As above		Group VI Press group	Group VII Attachés group

DIAGRAM II.1.2. Development of the foreign air forces department in the Air Command Office (LA: Luftkommandoamt), later the Luftwaffe General Staff, 1934-1939

Source: As Diagram II.1.1.

memorandum. Of its total of 2,500 aeroplanes of all kinds, only 800 were ready for action, and none fulfilled the technical and tactical requirements described in the memorandum. The results of a hectic procurement programme, considerable structural problems of the aircraft industry, and technical difficulties with the engines, as well as a chronic shortage of skilled workers, foreign currency, and precious metals, was a Luftwaffe in which quantity took precedence over quality.[19] When Hitler boasted to the British foreign secretary, Sir John Simon, on 25 March 1935 that the Luftwaffe had already achieved parity with the Royal Air Force and would soon catch up with the French air force,[20] he was using as an instrument of political pressure a Luftwaffe whose inadequacies for much simpler tasks than those envisaged in Knauss's memorandum were soon to become evident in strategic planning.

In the 'Wehrmacht Study 1935/36' of November 1935,[21] prepared on the war

[19] Cf. Homze, *Arming*, 56 ff.; Rautenberg, *Rüstungspolitik*, 323 ff.; Völker, 'Entwicklung', 210 ff.; Overy, 'Production Plans', 792 ff.
[20] Henke, *England*, 38-9; Geyr von Schweppenburg, *Critical Years*, 45 ff.; Hyde, *British Air Policy*, 333 ff.; Gibbs, *Strategy*, i. 174 ff., 543 ff.
[21] Völker, *Dokumente*, No. 195, pp. 445 ff.

minister's instructions, the Luftwaffe was given the task in an assumed war against France, Czechoslovakia, and Lithuania of destroying the French air force and its bases in order to assist the army indirectly in carrying out its mission and to protect Germany as far as possible from air attacks. The plan called for the first attacks to be directed against the French ground-support units and against the French army deployment (railway facilities). As retaliatory strikes for attacks on German cities and to destroy enemy communications centres, operational attacks were to be prepared on Paris (the main storage depots, engine factories, and government buildings) and on industrial targets and radio facilities in Reims, Dijon, and Lyons. The conduct of the air war against Czechoslovakia was based on a 'rapid redeployment of the mass of German combat formations' and on their use here too against the enemy air force and to prevent deployment of the enemy army as well as against 'important armaments and population centres, such as Prague and Pilsen'. According to the report presented on 23 December 1935, the work on the Wehrmacht study had proved that 'German air armaments, at the level of 1 April 1936 assumed in the war-game, are completely inadequate.' Even after the defeat of Czechoslovakia, which was considered essential for a successful war against France, the Luftwaffe, according to the report, would inevitably be defeated in the long term by the far stronger French air force.[22]

If the Luftwaffe's chances of success even in a two-front war against Germany's immediate neighbours were poor, they would be much worse if a new potential enemy appeared against whom an effective air war was impossible for geographical reasons. Since 1935, however, the possibility of such a hostile constellation had been visible on the political horizon. Hitler's hope of conquering living-space in the east under the favourable conditions of an Anglo-German alliance was gradually replaced by doubts about the willingness of Britain to reward German respect for her imperial interests by tolerating a National Socialist policy of aggression in eastern Europe. While on the one hand British attempts to integrate Germany into a European security system reduced more and more the chances of an Anglo-German alliance, on the other the feeble reaction of the British to moves affecting their interests such as the occupation of the Rhineland and the Abyssinian conflict inevitably led Hitler to conclude that if necessary he could pursue his aims without such an alliance.[23] Against this background it is not surprising that in his memorandum on the tasks of the Four-year Plan (approximately August 1936) Hitler energetically pursued his goal of expanding German living-space under the pretence of the need for a defence against Bolshevism, compared to which all other considerations were 'completely insignificant': in four years the German army was to be ready for action and the German economy ready for war.[24]

When Hitler revealed to his closest advisers on 5 November 1937 that in pursuit of his living-space goals in the east he wanted to annex Austria and 'smash'

[22] Ibid., No. 196, pp. 449–50.
[23] On National Socialist foreign policy: *Hitler, Deutschland und die Mächte*; *Kriegsbeginn*; *Nationalsozialistische Außenpolitik*; Messerschmidt, vol. i. of the present work, pt. IV; on the British factor: Henke, *England*.   [24] Treue, 'Hitlers Denkschrift', 210 (trans. 408).

Czechoslovakia, and that in this effort Germany would have to expect resistance from her two 'hate-inspired enemies, England and France',[25] it was clear that in spite of his continued potential interest in an alliance with Britain that country could no longer be ignored in German planning and assessments of the military situation.

In the 'Directive for the Uniform Preparation of the Wehrmacht for War' of 24 June 1937[26] a military confrontation with Britain was treated briefly as a 'special case' ('Extension of Red and Green') with extremely poor prospects of success: 'This would make our military situation unacceptable, even hopeless.' In spite of the promise that the political leadership would do everything to keep Britain neutral, plans were to be made 'even now as additions to deployments "Red" [against France] and "Green" [against Czechoslovakia] in case they are unsuccessful'.

Hitler's ambivalent attitude towards Britain had an adverse effect on the tactical and technical orientation of the Luftwaffe, which had been introducing a new generation of aircraft since the end of 1936. Clear ideas about the military tasks of this new generation would have been necessary for the technical and tactical design of the aircraft. In view of the blitzkrieg plan, the use of 'force involving risks', which Hitler had outlined on 5 November, as well as his determination to take advantage of a civil war in France at any time to crush Czechoslovakia, and considering the personnel and raw-material shortages in the aircraft industry, the Luftwaffe finally chose aeroplanes that could be delivered as rapidly as possible and in large numbers to active units.

After the pre-series production of the four-engine bombers Ju 89[27] and Do 19 had been made uncertain by the aircraft procurement programme of 27 October 1936, on 27 April 1937 Göring ordered development work on these aircraft to be stopped.[28] He calculated that for every four-engine aeroplane two and a half two-engine bombers could be produced; his decision clearly gave priority to quantity over quality (in terms of range and bomb-load). The search for an effective four-engine bomber was not abandoned in principle: Heinkel was commissioned to develop the He 177. But the aircraft industry was told to concentrate in future on the production of medium-range bombers (such as the He 111, the Ju 86, and the Do 17). The development and construction of dive-bombers (such as the Ju 87) and a fast bomber (the Ju 88) were intended to compensate for a lack of effectiveness or inadequate fighter cover and weak defensive armament until a new generation of four-engine aircraft became available.

Göring took advantage of the opportunity provided by the Spanish civil war to test this compromise Luftwaffe.[29] Although the 'Condor Legion' was used primarily as 'flying artillery' to support the nationalist army under the specific conditions of this war and developed an effective tactical command procedure for such

---

[25] Cf. the 'Hoßbach Memorandum', printed in *DGFP* D i, No. 19; *IMT* xxv. 402 ff.
[26] Printed in *DGFP* D i. 433 ff.; *IMT* xxxiv. 732 ff.
[27] For detailed information about the aircraft mentioned here and below: Kens and Nowarra, *Flugzeuge*.
[28] Homze, *Arming*, 119 ff.; id., 'Luftwaffe's Failure'; Irving, *Rise and Fall*, 54.
[29] Cf. Göring's testimony at Nuremberg, *IMT* ix. 281.

missions,[30] its operational use excited the interest and revulsion of world opinion. The destruction of the Basque town Guernica on 26 April 1937 by the Condor Legion and Italian aviators still ranks as a symbol of total air warfare. The fact that this attack was actually intended to serve tactical purposes does not excuse the ruthlessness with which it was carried out against the civilian population.[31] The reports from the Condor Legion clearly show that the operational features of German air doctrines, including war against the civilian population, were being tested in the Spanish civil war. The report of June 1938[32] on the use of the bomber wing K-88 stated that in spite of the unique features of the Spanish war, which could lead to distorted views and conclusions with regard to its implications for a European war, it had been possible to gain valuable knowledge about the moral and physical effects of aerial bombing. Concerning the effect of bombing on morale, it was pointed out that 'the discipline and organization of the working population' were 'in some respects very poor' and that this had produced 'very low powers of moral resistance'. According to the report the K-88 had flown missions against the enemy air force, enemy economic installations (factories), supplies (ports and transportation routes), and troop movements and positions. Concerning the air attacks on the enemy government and population, the report explained that constant attacks by smaller units on particular cities had 'frightened and made a strong impression on' the population, especially where air defences were inadequate.

While the Luftwaffe grew into its role as an instrument of the blitzkrieg with tactical and operational functions in the Spanish civil war, a rethinking of air-warfare strategy had begun in Britain.[33] Whereas previously British air defence had reflected Baldwin's belief that 'the bomber will always get through', which made a successful defence seem impossible and had therefore led to a concentration primarily on creating a powerful instrument of deterrence and retaliation, the new doctrine attempted to achieve a balanced relationship between offence and defence. This change was due to the perception that the attempt since July 1934 to achieve numerical parity with the Luftwaffe would not be successful in time and that it was therefore important to avert defeat in an air war by creating an effective air defence. This would permit the traditional blockade strategy, which was based on the assumption of a long war, to achieve the desired results. The more important role accorded to air defence was also the result of the progress of British radar technology.[34] This development gave reason to hope that attacking aircraft could

[30] Cf. the personal diary of the chief of staff (later commander) of the Condor Legion, Lieut.-Col. Freiherr von Richthofen: excerpts in Maier, *Guernica*, 75 ff.

[31] The purpose of the air attack was to block the Basque lines of retreat, in which Guernica was an important transportation junction. Designated targets were the suburb of Rentería, the bridge between it and Guernica, and the approach roads. On the circumstances which led to the destruction of the entire town cf. Maier, *Guernica*, 55 ff.; Talon, *Arde Guernica*; Southworth, *Guernica!* On the effects on British air-armaments policy cf. Bialer, 'Humanization', 91-2.

[32] Auswertestab R(ügen), Anlagen 1-5 zu LW. Gr. Kdo. 3 No. 7179/38, Heft 3 Kampfflieger (v. Knauer), BA-MA RL 7/57; excerpts printed in Maier, *Guernica*, 150 ff.

[33] On British air strategy cf. Gibbs, *Strategy*, i. 102 ff., 170 ff., 264 ff., 531-604; Hyde, *British Air Policy*; Powers, *Strategy*; Bialer, 'Danger'.

[34] Jones, *Most Secret War*, 135 ff.; Niehaus, *Radarschlacht*, 154 ff.; Mason, *Battle over Britain*, 91 ff.

be located early and as many as possible destroyed before they reached their targets by complete co-ordination of air-space surveillance and interceptor control. Because the British expected to have a qualitative edge in air armaments (the four-engine bomber, the Hurricane and Spitfire fighters), mere numerical comparisons with the Luftwaffe no longer seemed sensible.

The behaviour of the Western powers in the Spanish civil war, in which Britain in particular did not offer military opposition to the German and Italian intervention in spite of the threat it represented to her economic and strategic interests,[35] no doubt seemed to Hitler an invitation to take greater risks in preparing the way for his eventual campaign against the Soviet Union. Providing the necessary military deterrence for this 'risk policy' was primarily the task of the Luftwaffe.

On 18 February 1938, a few weeks before the annexation of Austria, the commander of Luftwaffe Area Command 2 (as of 1 February 1939 Air Fleet Command 2), General Felmy, was ordered by the chief of the Luftwaffe General Staff to make preparations to meet a British intervention in a war in the west. Plans for this mission were to concentrate on the port and the armaments industry in London, on the Channel ports, and on ground-support facilities in Norfolk, Suffolk, and Sussex.[36]

From this point on Britain received special attention in Luftwaffe evaluations of possible enemies. On 23 April 1938[37] in a talk to German air attachés in European countries the head of Department 5 (foreign air forces) of the Luftwaffe General Staff,[38] Lieutenant-Colonel Schmid, mentioned Britain, in addition to Czechoslovakia, France, the Soviet Union, and Poland, as being among those states which, 'given the present political situation, might be of direct significance as hostile air powers in a future war'.

In addition to these main powers, Schmid also regarded Belgium and Holland as 'forward positions' for an Anglo-French air war against Germany. Lithuania and the Baltic States might constitute such positions for the Soviet air force. Schmid considered the Scandinavian countries to be 'economic buffer states' and North America as 'an industrial power whose aircraft production will probably play a role in any European conflict'. He described Britain and her Empire as a 'large economic

---

[35] Deliveries of Spanish iron ore for British industry were particularly at risk. The C.-in-C. of the Condor Legion, Gen. Sperrle, urged Franco to refrain from an offensive against Madrid in the spring of 1937 and, instead, to advance against Bilbao in the north. Among other reasons, he mentioned that the capture of Bilbao would considerably increase ore exports to Germany and reduce the shipping distance while seriously disrupting the British armaments programme: Sonderstab W, Oberst Jaenecke, Dienstreisebericht, 18 May 1937, BA-MA II H 796/1: cf. Schieder, 'Spanischer Bürgerkrieg', 173 ff.
[36] Gundelach, 'Gedanken', 33–4; Klee, *Seelöwe*, 38 ff.; Völker, *Luftwaffe*, 159 ff.; Gemzell, *Raeder*, 178 ff.
[37] Beilage I zu RdL u. ObdL Genst. 5. Abt. No. 360/38 g.Kdos., 12 May 1938, betr. Die Luftlage Europas nach dem Stand vom Frühjahr 1938. According to the accompanying letter (BA-MA PG 32937, Case GE 941), the lecture, given on 23 Apr. 1938 (BA-MA RL 2/534), was distributed to the highest command offices of the Wehrmacht, including the 'Adjutant der Wehrmacht beim Führer und Reichskanzler'. Cf. also 'Englische Luftflotte und ihr Einsatz im Kriege gegen Deutschland', Genst. d. Luftwaffe, 5. Abt., BA-MA PG 32937, Case GE 941, fos. 124 ff.
[38] On Department 5 of the Luftwaffe General Staff cf. Boog, *Luftwaffenführung*; also Diagrams II.1.1–2 above.

unity' with a strategic, defensive military policy. During the previous 140 years
Britain had intervened directly on the Continent only twice, against Napoleon and
the Kaiser's Germany, when they challenged her as a world power. While Britain
had been able to withdraw into 'splendid isolation' after the defeat of Napoleon,
this had not been possible after the First World War because of new weapons, the
submarine and the aeroplane. France was the most dangerous of Britain's possible
enemies: 'Above all France is in such an extremely advantageous position *vis-à-vis*
Britain from the point of view of air strategy that Britain can no longer accept the
risk of a hostile neighbour across the Channel.'[39] Hence Britain could no longer
conduct her foreign policy independently of France and would be forced into any
European conflict. It seemed to Schmid that 'a certain political ruling class' had
already drawn the necessary conclusions from this fact and was determined, 'as in
the last years before the war', to unite again all anti-German forces under British
control. If this view should prove to be correct, Britain must already be considered
'the most dangerous of all Germany's possible enemies in a future war'. It looked
as if Britain, which regarded the growing strength of Germany as a threat to her
world power, was pursuing two solutions to this problem simultaneously. The first
was a peaceful solution designed to confine Germany to the narrow limits of the
Continent by means of a diplomatic understanding which would bind her
economically to Europe. The second situation involved a coalition against Germany,
which Britain would only consider, however, if the first solution should prove to
be impracticable. But Britain would in all probability only intervene directly in the
fighting after Germany had been weakened. The Royal Air Force had about 1,500
front-line aircraft in Britain (800 bombers, 400 fighters, 250–300 reconnaissance
and general-purpose aircraft); the Royal Navy had 200 aircraft, and about 300 were
stationed overseas. There were also about 1,500 aircraft, primarily older types of
bomber, as a reserve. As possible targets of a German air war against Britain, Schmid
mentioned, apart from the Royal Air Force, the area around London, which he
considered a 'target of special importance', and (for attack in co-operation with the
navy) the import harbours with their oil-storage areas, grain silos, and large cold-
storage depots.

With regard to France, Schmid noted that her relations with Germany were indeed
tense, but that at the moment she did not want war. French treaty obligations,
however, might result in France being forced to enter a war almost automatically
at an unfavourable moment. In the spring of 1938 the striking-power of the French
air force, especially the offensive formations, should be considered weak in relation
to its numerical strength, as it was only equipped with 'transitional material'. But
if one took into account delayed orders, due since 1937 (about 400 bombers and
200 fighters as well as 50 reconnaissance aircraft), its striking-power could increase
considerably within a few months. At the moment France had about 1,500 aircraft
at home in front-line formations and 1,700 as a mobilization reserve (among
them 400 short-range reconnaissance aircraft, 500–600 light fighters, 300–50

---

[39] For British ideas on this question cf. Powers, *Strategy*, 183 ff.; Hyde, *British Air Policy*, 110–11.

bomber-reconnaissance aircraft), of which, after an initial period of tension, between 1,200 and 1,300, in addition to the front-line aircraft, could be used in action. Although Schmid considered the French air force qualitatively and quantitatively 'about equal' to the Luftwaffe, he believed it to be inferior in training and 'flying-spirit'. In the event of a war against Germany it was not to be expected that the French air force would concentrate on clearly selected targets. More probably it would attack many different kinds of target at the same time. In this regard it was more inclined to co-operate operationally and tactically with the army than to conduct its own air war. The strength, organization, and use of the French air-defence forces, however, deserved the closest attention in the planning and execution of Germany's own air attacks. Here Schmid explained that a complete paralysis of the extensive French armaments industry could only be achieved by destroying its raw-material base, including imports. This aim, however, required 'a long-term effort and an unusually strong allocation of forces'. The more Germany had to restrict its attacks to 'short-term actions', the more necessary it would be to attack the higher levels of the armaments economy, such as the production of weapons and ammunition. In this connection attacks on French power-stations, especially those of Paris, were especially important. Schmid advised against terror attacks; the fact that France had only a few large cities automatically limited the effectiveness of possible terror attacks from the air.

In conclusion, Schmid observed that France, Britain, and the Soviet Union were still relatively unprepared for war, but were making great efforts to increase their readiness: 'If there are no serious setbacks in aircraft production, we must expect that new equipment will result in a considerable improvement in the combat-readiness of the French and British air forces in and after 1939.' Schmid considered an early improvement in the readiness of the Soviet air force doubtful.

The 'possibility of conducting a war against Britain' as the 'main enemy' was also the subject of a conference between Department 1 of the naval war staff (represented by Commander Heye) and the head of the Luftwaffe operations staff, Jeschonnek, on 4 May 1938.[40] Jeschonnek wanted to know if the army was in a position to occupy Belgium and Holland rapidly and how the naval war staff would view the situation if the Luftwaffe succeeded by a surprise attack in putting important units of the British fleet out of action. Jeschonnek hoped that an entry of Italy into the war and the resulting diversion of British forces would make it considerably easier to conduct a war against Britain.

Despite Germany's own armament problems and warnings about the improving readiness of the Western powers, the General Staff was already making bold plans for a future Luftwaffe. On 23 May 1938 the chief of the organization staff, Major Kammhuber, set as a 'long-term' goal a Luftwaffe which in 1940 and afterwards ('intermediate solution by 1 October 1938, final goal by 1942') was to be prepared to fight the 'main enemies'—Britain, France, and the Soviet Union—with eighteen flying corps (thirty-six air divisions with a total of 144 Geschwade). This Luftwaffe,

---

[40] BA-MA PG 33272, Case GE 1165.

consisting of aircraft with ranges of 6,000–8,000 km. and speeds of 500–600 km. an hour, was to operate from a deployment area already expanded eastward. Its division into the seven command areas Berlin, Brunswick, Munich, Vienna, Budapest, Warsaw, and Königsberg clearly showed the greater importance assigned to the eastern front.[41]

During the crisis of May 1938 Hitler's fears increased that Britain as well as France would try to block an expansion of German power eastward. In a speech on 28 May,[42] however, he calmed the commanders-in-chief of the three Wehrmacht services by assuring them that British rearmament would not play a significant role before 1941–2. Hitler's statement that 'today the aim of a war in the west (against France and Britain) is to expand our coastal base (in Belgium and Holland)'[43] reflected his realization that before he began the conquest of living-space in the east (the Soviet Union) it would be necessary to eliminate France and gain a geographical position from which to deter Britain by military threats from intervening against him on the Continent.

In the partially new version of the directive of 24 June 1937 for the uniform war preparations of the Wehrmacht, ordered on 30 May 1938, Hitler explained that it was his 'unalterable decision to smash Czechoslovakia by military action in the foreseeable future'. For this purpose a minimum number of air units were to be left in the west for defence, while the mass of the Luftwaffe was to be used in a surprise attack on Czechoslovakia.[44] On 18 June 1938 Hitler promised that he would only open hostilities against Czechoslovakia when he had become convinced that 'France will not march and thus Britain will not intervene'. As in his opinion a war begun by the Western powers would also require that Germany 'smash' Czechoslovakia in order to achieve the necessary freedom on her eastern border, the working out of deployment plans for a war with the main effort in the west was no longer given top priority. However, the preparations already made for this 'Case Red' retained their importance and were now supposed to serve as preparations for a rapid shift of the main attack from east to west, which might become necessary, and as 'preliminary work for a possible future war in the west'.[45]

Göring did not believe either that the Western powers would intervene militarily in the foreseeable future,[46] but at a conference with leaders of the aircraft industry on 8 July 1938 he demanded accelerated armament efforts. He claimed that there could be no doubt that Britain did not want war, and neither did France. America's attitude was uncertain, but economic conditions there were 'miserable'. Göring calmed the possible fears of his listeners with regard to the efficiency of the British aircraft industry by urging them to compare their own difficulties with those of a democratic system: 'I am completely convinced, gentlemen, that the new

---

[41] BA-MA Lw 101/4, Teil 3 (Abschrift); cf. *IMT* xxxvii. 443 ff., ix. 488–9.

[42] This speech has come down in Beck's records: Beck Papers, BA-MA N 28/2, 23 ff. For criticism of it as a source cf. Dülffer, *Weimar*, 466–7 n. 55.

[43] Beck's note quoted from Dülffer, *Weimar*, 467.

[44] *DGFP* D ii, No. 221; *IMT* xxv. 455 ff.   [45] Cf. *IMT* xxv. 445 ff.

[46] Cf. Göring's remarks to the Polish ambassador Lipski on 24 Aug. 1938: Lipski, *Diplomat*, 383.

developments we can achieve in one year Britain can achieve, with a maximum effort, in two, perhaps three, years.' Göring urged the industrialists to disregard the interests of their own construction offices and, in spite of the raw-material shortage and lack of skilled workers, to build the aeroplane whose construction was decided upon after a free competition. The important thing was not whether the aircraft were built by Junkers, Dornier, Heinkel, or Messerschmidt, but 'that the best German aircraft is built, that it is built in the greatest possible numbers, and that it is built and delivered quickly'.[47]

While the first and third Luftwaffe command areas concerned themselves with the deployment directives for an attack on Czechoslovakia,[48] on 23 August 1938 the chief of the Luftwaffe General Staff instructed Command 2 to prepare for the addition of three or four bomber Geschwader, should 'Case Green' lead to a war with France and Britain, making it necessary to use the Luftwaffe to attack Britain.[49]

Department 5 of the Luftwaffe General Staff also concerned itself with this possibility in a situation assessment ('Extended Case Green') of 25 August 1938.[50] In the assessment the 'war aim of the Entente' was considered to be the defeat of Germany by attacking her defence economy, 'i.e. accepting a long war'. Attacks by the French air force were expected on economic and Luftwaffe as well as other military targets and the transportation system. These attacks would accordingly fail to achieve any concentrated effect. The offensive strength of the French air force as of 1 October 1938 was given as approximately 640 combat aircraft in front-line formations, of which, however, only 120-50 at most met modern performance standards. There were reserves of 320 combat aircraft in France itself and 120 in North Africa, all of them older models. It was assumed that the British air force would attack the Rhineland-Westphalian industrial area and the German North Sea ports from its home bases, and in doing so would sooner or later violate Belgian and Dutch neutrality. Even in this case only the estimated 300-50 modern bombers out of a total of about 850 combat aircraft in front-line units (with reserves of 200-300) were considered 'serious attack aircraft'. The German plan was based on the assumption that at the start of the war two, and after three or four weeks a total of five, bomber Geschwader would be available; the outcome of the war would be sought in a defeat of the Western powers. The Luftwaffe's task was described as follows: 'As at the moment the Luftwaffe and the navy are not strong enough to seek a resolution by attacking the enemy's war economy, the Luftwaffe has in the present situation the decisive task of helping the army in front of the enemy fortresses to achieve operational freedom.' The question whether it would be advisable in the event of war in the west to wait until spring before making massive use of bomber forces was answered negatively, since because of the further expansion of the French

---

[47] *IMT* xxxviii. 375 ff.
[48] 'Memorandum Green' ('Denkschrift Grün') was worked out in the first half of 1938 and put into force on 11 July 1938 by Luftwaffengruppenkommando 1 in revised form as 'Plan Study Green' ('Planstudie Grün'), effective 15 July 1938: Völker, *Luftwaffe*, 155-6.
[49] Gundelach, 'Gedanken', 35; Völker, *Luftwaffe*, 158.   [50] *IMT* xxv. 381 ff.

and British air-armament industries and supplies from North America, the relative strength of the Western powers' air forces and the Luftwaffe would probably change to the latter's disadvantage by that time.

As Germany's own forces with a total of five Geschwader were considered weak, Department 5 was of the opinion that the Luftwaffe could fulfil its task only by concentrated attacks on the most sensitive enemy targets. For this purpose the Luftwaffe was promised information on targets such as the French air force, its fuel, munition, and electricity supplies, key industries (especially the aircraft-engine industry around Paris), and the 'target area' Paris itself. Target information on air-bases in Britain was about 90 per cent complete, and its printing and the addition of map sections by the Luftwaffe Command Area 2 had been ordered by 15 September. As long as only two Geschwader were available in the west, the war would be fought with delaying tactics in the form of attacks on the French air force and its deployment bases in eastern France, to prevent total domination of the air by the enemy. Attacks on Paris were to be contemplated only as retaliation. Direct co-operation with the army was considered only in the event of the enemy's breaking through or threatening to outflank the German fortifications in the west. Department 5 considered attacks on targets in Britain 'inadvisable' because of the small number of aircraft available for that purpose. Even if more units were used in the west (five Geschwader), with whose help a breakthrough along the French fortifications did seem possible, 'attacks on targets in Britain would by and large not be feasible'. Nevertheless, everything was to be prepared to enable the Luftwaffe to carry out retaliatory attacks on London at any time. As in the opinion of Department 5 an improvement in the chances of successful attacks on Britain could only be expected from a change in the military fronts on the Continent in favour of Germany, the situation assessment concluded, in the chapter 'Proposals for the Wehrmacht High Command, the Army, and the Navy': 'As Belgium and The Netherlands in German hands would constitute an enormous advantage against Britain as well as France, it is considered necessary to ask the army under what conditions and within what time-frame an occupation of this area can be accomplished. In this case a new examination of the use of the Luftwaffe against Britain is considered necessary.'

On 22 September 1938, two days after Göring had demanded that the heavy fighter Me 210 should have a range covering Britain,[51] the commander of Command Area 2, General Felmy, submitted in the form of a memorandum his answer to the order he had been given on 23 August to prepare to receive additional units. His sober judgement that 'a war of annihilation against Britain' seemed 'impossible with the forces available now' caused Göring to note: 'Actually, I didn't ask for a memorandum evaluating the prospects of success and pointing out our weaknesses; I know them best myself. I want to know how you envisage the largest possible operation with the forces planned and what you require as a precondition for this action.'[52]

---

[51] RdL u. ObdL, Chef des Ministeramtes, Min. A. I No. 597/38 g.Kdos., 20 Sept. 1938, BA-MA RL 3/63, 7440.   [52] Quoted from Klee, *Seelöwe*, 39 n. 112. Cf. Gundelach, 'Gedanken', 35 ff.

On the one hand, pessimistic assessments of the prospects of an air war against Britain were probably the main factor that caused Göring to advise Hitler against taking the risk of an armed conflict with the Western powers during the Sudeten crisis.[53] On the other hand, it is known that the fear of German air attacks in particular greatly reduced the freedom of action of the Western powers.[54] Statements by British leaders to the effect that the Munich agreement of 30 September 1938 primarily allowed additional time for British rearmament must have given Hitler the impression that he had missed a favourable opportunity, after which time would increasingly work against him.[55] As the British efforts towards collective security in Europe in the form of a 'general agreement' blocked Hitler's deployment strategy, he had to abandon once and for all his 'without Britain' policy and concentrate on the alternative of eliminating France and forcing Britain to 'keep off the Continent' (Henke) by creating a military threat on the Channel coast.

On 14 October 1938, in connection with the forced pace of rearmament following the Munich agreement, Göring declared that he had been ordered by the Führer to expand the armaments effort enormously, and that this applied first of all to the Luftwaffe, which was to be 'increased fivefold as rapidly as possible'. In view of the 'unimaginable difficulties' (empty foreign-exchange coffers; overloading of production capacity), he would 'turn the economy round by brutal means' if necessary and switch to a 'state economy' to achieve the goal set by the Führer.[56]

The Luftwaffe General Staff attempted to meet this demand with a 'Concentrated Aircraft Programme'[57] which envisaged the creation of a Luftwaffe with a strong offensive component by 1 April 1942. Among other units, it included: 58 bomber Geschwader (Ju 88; 'as many He 177s as possible, at least 4 Geschwader'), 16 heavy-fighter Geschwader (Bf 110, 'at least 7 or 8 Geschwader of Me 210s'), 8 Stuka Geschwader (Ju 87b, later Me 210s), 16 fighter Geschwader (Bf 109 and later models of the same fighter), 500 ships' and carrier aircraft. On 24 November 1938 the Luftwaffe General Staff promised the naval war staff thirteen of the fifty-eight bomber Geschwader under the command of the Luftwaffe for attacks on enemy shipping and the British fleet. Of the remaining bomber Geschwader, thirty were to be deployed for the war against Britain and fifteen for the offensive against France.[58] In spite of objections raised by the technical office and the aircraft industry, Göring insisted on carrying out the 'Concentrated Aircraft Programme'. A short time later even more modest plans (with the same deadline of 1942) proved to be unrealizable.

On 7 February 1939 Göring issued the 'Deployment and Combat Instructions

---

[53] On Göring's role in Munich cf. *Weizsäcker-Papiere*, 144, 169, 171-2, 508 n. 140.

[54] Murray, 'German Air Power'; Gibbs, *Strategy*, i. 583, 642 ff., 598 ff.; Hyde, *British Air Policy*, 414 ff., 448 ff.; Powers, *Strategy*, 206-7; Smith, *Royal Air Force*, 157.

[55] On Hitler's reaction to Munich cf. Henke, *England*, 187 ff.

[56] Conference in Göring's office in the aviation ministry at 10 a.m. on 14 Oct. 1938: *IMT* xxvii. 160 ff.

[57] Generalstab der Luftwaffe No. 3244/38 g.Kdos. 1. Abt. (III), betr. Konzentriertes Flugzeugmuster-Programm, 7 Nov. 1938, printed in Völker, *Dokumente*, No. 89; cf. Irving, *Rise and Fall*, 67; Overy, 'Production Plans', 782; Homze, *Arming*, 221 ff.   [58] Gundelach, 'Gedanken', 37.

for the Luftwaffe'.[59] These 'preparations for action for the mobilization year 1939-40' bore the cover-name 'Plan Study 1939' and were intended to go into effect on 1 March 1939. They envisaged preparing all measures for the worst possible case, 'that a war might start without sufficient time for preparation or a previous mobilization according to plan'.[60]

In the event of a war breaking out in the west—it was assumed that either a war with France ('Case Red') and a war with Britain ('Case Blue') would begin at the same time or that one 'case' would necessarily lead to the other—the Luftwaffe would have the task of attacking the French air force, including its supply-depots and other vital facilities, as long as only a limited number of offensive units were available. If stronger offensive forces were available, in addition to attacks on the French air force preparations should be made for attacks on Paris, on French fuel supplies (refineries and oil-storage depots), and on the unloading of supplies in French ports. Attacks on these targets as well as on air-bases and supply-depots around Paris and on Paris itself required Göring's permission. The French air force, which was expected to be reinforced by British formations, was considered inferior to the Luftwaffe 'in every respect'. A significant change in this situation was not expected in the remainder of 1939, although it was known that the French air force was being equipped with new aircraft. While the war against the French air force was the task of the 'Commander West', the 'Commander North' was to watch the Dutch and Belgian frontiers for violations of neutrality and, if necessary—above all if Belgium entered the war—prevent enemy air formations from using the Belgian ground-support organization. In this case too the initiation of the air war required a special order from the commander-in-chief of the Luftwaffe.

In addition to these combat directives, 'Plan Study 1939' contained statements declared to be 'legal principles' which, in the absence of adequate guide-lines in international law, constituted 'rules adopted by Germany for conducting air warfare', but were intended to restrict the actions of commanders 'only to the extent required by Germany's own military interests'. The clarity and binding force of the guide-lines, which were in themselves very restrictive, were in part considerably weakened by the accompanying 'explanations'.[61]

When German troops marched into Czechoslovakia on 15-16 March 1939, Hitler overstepped the limits of a policy that, in the broadest possible terms, could still be described as revisionist. The ensuing diplomatic activity brought about a new

---

[59] RdL u. ObdL Genst. 1. Abt. No. 5015/39 g.Kdos. Chef-Sache, 7 Feb. 1939, Heft I, 'Allgemeine Anordnungen', with annexes; Heft II, 'Weisungen für den Einsatz gegen Osten', originally dealt with 'Case Green' (action against Czechoslovakia) and was replaced on 1 May 1939 by a revised version for 'Case White' (action against Poland); Heft III, 'Weisungen für den Einsatz gegen Westen', after corresponding changes (the last on 9 Aug. 1939), remained in force after the invasion of Czechoslovakia, as did Heft I; Heft IV, 'Weisungen für Lw. Kdo. Ostpreußen', was cancelled, BA-MA RL 2 II/1-4.

[60] Ibid., 'Heft I', 4.

[61] Anlage 1 zur Planstudie 1939, Heft I, Neufassung Juli 1939, Berlin, 20 July 1939; produced with the collaboration of the Wehrmacht High Command, the Reich aviation ministry, the Navy High Command, the Army High Command, the ministry of justice, the foreign ministry, the Kaiser Wilhelm Institute for the Study of Foreign, Public, and International Law, and the German Society for the Study of Defence Policy and Military Sciences. On the international legal situation cf. Watt, 'Restraints'.

power-constellation in Europe, eventually polarized by the non-aggression pact of 23 August 1939 between Germany and the Soviet Union and the Anglo-Polish alliance of 25 August. The Russo-German pact isolated Poland militarily. On Hitler's orders preparations for an attack on Poland had been in progress since 3 April 1939; the attack was to be possible at any time on or after 1 September 1939.[62]

In this connection, Göring had ordered a map-manoeuvre, 'General Staff Trip of the Luftwaffe', on 24 April 1939,[63] based on the following initial situation: 'Germany (blue) intends to begin the war against Poland (red) with a surprise attack. Preparations are in progress.' It was assumed that the Western powers and the Soviet Union would take up a position of 'benevolent neutrality' towards Poland. Although it was pointed out that this situation did not correspond to reality, the revised version of the 'Instructions for Operations in the East' (Section II of 'Plan Study 1939')[64] issued on 1 May 1939 was based on the same optimistic assumption. In this study 'Case White' was a 'precautionary completion of preparations for the security of the Reich' and was not to be regarded as a precondition for an armed conflict with the Western powers. For this reason it was important to open the war with strong surprise attacks and achieve rapid successes by direct and indirect support of the army.

This calculated optimism also spread to the situation assessments of the Luftwaffe, in which the absence of military reaction by the Western powers to German aggression was attributed primarily to French and British inferiority in the air. The only remainder of the somewhat more cautious assessment before Munich was the reference to the short-term nature of German's relative superiority.

As the technical office had already submitted an extremely favourable report on the level of German aircraft development on 16 March, the quartermaster-general of the Luftwaffe estimated on 12 May that in the period from 1 April 1939 to 1 April 1940 Britain, France, and the United States would build 3,730, 2,450, and 2,700 aircraft respectively, whereas Germany would build 9,192. Thus, in the spring of 1940 the Western powers would have a total of about 6,400 aircraft fully ready for action, including 1,850 fighters and 2,370 bombers. The quartermaster-general also estimated the active strength of the Western powers on 1 March 1939 to be only 790 British and 1,220 French aircraft.[65]

On 2 May 1939 Department 5 of the Luftwaffe General Staff concluded in a long report on the 'Air Situation in Europe in the Spring of 1939'[66] that 'at the present time' the Luftwaffe was superior to any other European air force with regard to the number and quality of its aircraft, its organization, training, and 'especially its tactical and command preparation for an air war'. It was claimed that this would also be true even if in 1939 the British and French air forces should appear as

---

[62] *Hitlers Weisungen*, No. 1a; Trevor-Roper, *Directives*, 3.

[63] RdL u. ObdL Genst. 3. (takt.) Abteilung (I) 230/39 g.Kdos., 24 Apr. 1939, BA-MA RL 2/v. 3404.

[64] For 'Case White', action against Poland, BA-MA RL 2 II/2; cf. Wollstein, 'Politik', 795 ff.

[65] Homze, *Arming*, 244 ff.

[66] Annex to RdL u. ObdL Chef des Generalstabs No. 700/39 g.Kdos. (5. Abt. 1), 2 May 1939; 'Die Luftlage in Europa, Stand: Frühjahr 1939', BA-MA RL 2/535. Cf. n. 70 below.

enemies of Germany at the same time, since, because of the obsolescence of the French and British aircraft, the German offensive forces were considerably stronger than British and French air defences, which could only be used independently. German air defences were so strong that even combined attacks by British and French offensive forces would have little prospect of success. As it was assumed that because of their infrastructure neither Poland nor the Soviet Union was in a position to conduct an effective air war against Germany, the authors of the report were convinced that in a conflict in the east the air war would still be decided in the west if the Western powers intervened. The report warned that Germany's lead in air armaments would be of limited duration, 'in view of the recent accelerated rearmament of the British and French air forces, especially in the area of air defence'. It therefore placed special emphasis on the tactical and command preparations for an air war and observed with satisfaction:

On the basis of all available information, we can say that Germany is the only state to have developed a total plan for the preparation and conduct of an offensive and defensive air war in the areas of equipment, organization, tactics, and command. This means a general advantage in war readiness and thus a strengthening of Germany's overall military position.

In the opinion of Department 5 the thesis of the decisive importance of an air war had not yet been proved, as a war had not yet been fought under the necessary conditions, but in the Abyssinian conflict as well as during the 'Czechoslovak state crisis' the Italian air force and the Luftwaffe respectively had functioned as 'powerful means of applying political pressure', although they had not been able to demonstrate their actual military value. In September 1938 the view of the situation in Paris and London had 'bordered on panic': this had led to repeated attempts at mediation by the British and French governments, driven into a corner, and finally to the Munich agreement. Department 5 believed that an important reason for this development had been the limitations placed upon the Western governments by their democratic constitutions. In the domestic politics of these countries a slow change from a purely parliamentarian to an authoritarian form of government could in fact be observed, above all in France. Although this would undoubtedly increase their ability to act decisively, the British and French governments were still subject to strong restrictions that reduced their freedom and readiness to act in foreign affairs. Viewing the situation from the point of view of this assessment, Department 5 was optimistic about prospects in a war between Germany and Poland:

Although the Western powers seem to have recently assumed serious obligations in eastern Europe, it can be said that, depending on the further development of the total political situation, British and French interests, especially vital interests, do not necessarily have to be affected there. Therefore it seems quite possible that, in spite of the pacts and promises, conflicts arising in eastern Europe will remain local.

The claim that the Luftwaffe was superior in the area of tactical command stood in sharp contrast to the quite different results of air fleet exercises in the conduct of an operational air war. Between 10 and 13 May Air Fleet 2 conducted a map-manoeuvre to determine the command, supply, and communications possibilities in a war against Britain based on the assumed technical data for 1942.[67] According to the record of General Felmy's final conference, commanding large formations in the air still presented problems which the Luftwaffe was tackling for the first time: 'At present the practical ability to command formations in the air does not extend beyond the wings.' In addition to inadequacies in radio technology Felmy blamed the 'extremely rapid build-up' of the Luftwaffe, in which the front-line formations had been 'plundered' in favour of the flying-schools. Following Ludendorff, Felmy argued that, as the Luftwaffe still did not have everything it needed to 'serve its leaders as an instrument', it would 'have to place tactics above operations for the time being'. But in Air Fleet 2 hopes were placed in the deterrent effect of the Luftwaffe. For example, Felmy dealt extensively with the question of a terror war from the air against Britain. While admitting that an attack on London could have political consequences, he would not be afraid to bomb the city as a major industrial centre and because of its significance and psychological importance as the capital of the country: 'If we consider the struggle against Britain as the struggle of the German nation to survive, then the government of the Third Reich will not suffer the attacks of weakness once embodied by the late Bethmann [-Hollweg, chancellor in 1914].' Indeed, in the coming war every bomb flown across the sea would have to be used to terrorize the British population. The attack on the industrial Midlands would have to be carried out 'solely as a terror attack' and possibly even be given priority over attacks on the British ground-support organization. But Felmy warned that if a war with Britain began before the end of 1942 only a small number of forces with sufficient range would be available for terror attacks from the air (the He 111 H and P: 900 km.; the He 111 H with an all-up weight of 11 tons: 1,000 km.). Preparations for such attacks were still completely inadequate: 'Unfortunately, my wish expressed to the field marshal [Göring] in September 1938 to have one division ready for action this summer could not be fulfilled. Here too we shall have to resort to a makeshift arrangement.' For Felmy such an arrangement involved the use of large Lufthansa aeroplanes (the FW 200 Condor), which, simultaneously with direct air attacks on the British west coast, were to 'drop a few incendiary and other light bombs by hand and alarm the British aircraft-warning service'. In judging the effect of such attacks on enemy morale, Felmy referred to the experience of the Sudeten crisis:

We seem to have no real idea in the present situation of the anxiety that has seized broad circles of the enemy population. If during the period of tension last September the British built civilian shelters in their public parks and private gardens, distributed gas masks etc., these events clearly show the pressure to which, unlike Germany, they were subjected by their own overwhelming fear of war. We must increase and exploit this pressure.

The use of special naval units to lay mines in a war against Britain was also rehearsed. As in the matter of terror attacks against Britain, Felmy also seemed prepared to ignore the laws of naval warfare: 'Let us hope that in a conflict between

---

[67] Luftflottenkommando 2, Führungsabteilung No. 7093/39 g.Kdos. Chef-Sache, 13 May 1939, Schlußbetrachtungen des Planspiels 1939, BA-MA RL 7/42; parts printed in Völker, *Dokumente*, No. 199.

Germany and Britain our use of all available weapons will not be restricted even slightly for political reasons.' On 16 May 1939 the office of General for Special Tasks in Air Fleet 2 (after 1 October 1939 called the 'Tenth Flying Corps') was created for the air war at sea, and placed under Lieutenant-General Geisler, whose responsibility it was to study problems related to the preparation and conduct of air attacks across the sea and determine the basic principles necessary for such actions.[68]

The experiences of Air Fleet 2 were reflected in a study by Department 1 (Operations) of the General Staff on 'Operational Targets for the Luftwaffe in the Event of a War with Britain in 1939'.[69] The study concluded that the equipment, level of training, and strength of Air Fleet 2 in 1939 could not force a quick decision in a war with Britain, as the available bombers could not reach the ports of the British west coast, the British fleet could not be effectively attacked because of a lack of proper bombs, and training in bad-weather flying was still inadequate. Moreover, the number of aircraft was not sufficient for the multitude of targets and the larger combat area. No decisive effect was expected from terror attacks on London alone, as Felmy had suggested. Rather it was feared that this would lead to a hardening of the British will to resist. Success was expected in 1939 only in attacks on the British aircraft industry, as they would have a long-term effect and the widely scattered installations could be attacked even by small formations. In addition, if carried out in an uninterrupted but irregular sequence, such attacks could have a 'demoralizing effect on large areas of the island'. Department 1's assessment of the situation was basically shared by the chief of the General Staff, who, after consultation with the head of Department 5, expanded the target group 'aircraft industry' to include all industrial and supply facilities in weakly defended areas. After this list of targets had been approved by Göring on 19 June, a corresponding directive was issued to Air Fleet 2 on 4 July 1939.

On 26 July 1939 the head of Department 5, Schmid, reported to Göring and Jeschonnek in List (Sylt) on the results of the study of Britain's vulnerability to air attack, which had been in progress since January 1939 under the cover-name 'Study Blue'.[70] At that time Schmid apparently advocated an air war against British imports and pointed out that, because of the time this method would require, perhaps air attacks alone would not be sufficient, and that in the final analysis it might be possible to force Britain to surrender only by occupying part of the island. In the study on the 'Targets for the Conduct of an Air War against Britain in the Final Solution', submitted on 7 August 1939 by the chief of staff of the General for Special Tasks in Air Fleet Command 2, among other possibilities the 'threat and carrying

---

[68] Gundelach, 'Gedanken', 44–5.

[69] Generalstab I. Abt. (Chef) No. 5094/39 g.Kdos. Chef-Sache, 22 May 1939 (copy), MGFA Materialsammlung Greffrath.

[70] Milch, 'Merkbuch', entry for 26 July: 'List. Vortrag Schmid über England. Sehr gut' ('List. Schmid's talk on England. Very good'); Klee, *Seelöwe*, 42–3. The complete files 'Studie Blau' no longer exist. According to Homze (*Arming*, 242–3), 'Studie Blau' consisted of several parts, among them 'H', the report on 'Luftlage in Europa, Stand Frühjahr 1939' ('The Air Situation in Europe in the spring of 1939') of 2 May 1939 and Felmy's final conference on the map-manœuvre of Air Fleet 2 of 13 May 1939, erroneously designated by Homze as 'Planstudie 1939'.

out of an invasion within the framework of larger combined operations by the entire Wehrmacht' was considered. Regarding the air war in 1940, this study came to the conclusion that it could only achieve 'partial successes', which could constitute a threat to the total British war effort only in the second year of the war. And even this effect could be achieved only if the British defence forces could be split, surprised, and deceived, Germany's own forces expanded at the same time, and the air war sustained for a long period.[71]

In the mean time Air Fleet 1 had tested the blitzkrieg against Poland. The aim of the map-manœuvre 'General Staff Trip of the Luftwaffe 1939', carried out between 9 and 13 June, was, according to the introductory talk by the chief of the General Staff, Jeschonnek,[72] to determine whether it was possible seriously to damage a hostile air force by surprise attacks and then to eliminate it completely in ensuing battles. The operational mission during the 'General Staff Trip' was the destruction of aircraft in the area of the Polish aeroplane factory at Grodno. But Jeschonnek, like Felmy earlier, was 'seriously worried' that the further development of Luftwaffe tactics was proceeding slowly because of the lack of experienced units. While the map-manœuvres of the air fleets clearly showed the limits of the Luftwaffe's effectiveness, on 3 July at the testing-area near Rechlin Hitler was shown a Luftwaffe whose most recent developments obviously made a great impression on him and apparently caused him to take 'extremely grave decisions'.[73] If the demonstration at Rechlin (a radar early-warning system, a model of the jet fighter Me 262, rocket-assisted take-offs, He 100 and Bf 109 fighters with high-performance motors, a 3-cm. aircraft cannon Mk 101, a pressurized cabin for high-altitude aircraft, etc.) actually encouraged Hitler to attack Poland and to accept the related risk of a war in the west, this was not the intention of its organizers. On 18 April 1939, in agreement with the chief of the General Staff and the quartermaster-general, Milch had put to Göring the idea of organizing such a demonstration to persuade Hitler to give the Luftwaffe preferential treatment in the distribution of scarce raw materials. He argued that the Luftwaffe had to resort to such a demonstration to obtain the critical help it needed in its build-up, as in the coming years it would have to carry the burden of the war against the Western powers practically alone. The fact that Milch considered the new 500-kg. bomb with jet propulsion—'the weapon to destroy enemy naval fleets'—especially well suited for the demonstration shows that this effort by the Luftwaffe was directed primarily against its rival the navy.[74] But Hitler was more interested in the 3-cm. cannon and the high-altitude aircraft; on 12 July Göring ordered that everything be done to accelerate development work on these projects.[75]

[71] General z.b.V. Lfl.Kdo. 2, Der Chef des Stabes B No. 100/39 g.Kdos., 12 Aug. 1939, BA-MA RL 7/29.
[72] Luftflottenkommando 3, Führungsabteilung No. 2778/39 g.Kdos. (no date), 'Verlauf der Generalstabreise der Luftwaffe 1939 und Vorträge bei der Generalstabsreise', photocopy, BA-MA RL 7/159. On 27 Apr. 1939 Jeschonnek had already given a talk on the plan of action against Poland. Cf. Irving, *Tragödie*, 417 n. 30.
[73] On 13 Sept. 1939 Göring recalled this demonstration: 'What bunglers our magicians are! What they showed me, and above all the Führer, hasn't been achieved at all.' Cf. Irving, *Rise and Fall*, 74.
[74] Der Staatssekretär der Luftfahrt und Generalinspekteur der Luftwaffe an Generalfeldmarschall, 18 Apr. 1939, BA-MA RL 3/50, 5667.   [75] BA-MA RL 3/63, 7318-26.

In view of the bottlenecks and the approaching war, the Luftwaffe already had more ambitious development projects than it could afford. For this reason Göring demanded on 5 August 1939 that production of the He 177, the Me 210, the Ju 88, and the Bf 109 be given priority.[76] Production of other types of aircraft was to be stopped or cut back. Göring's order limited the Luftwaffe to basically four aircraft types, of which only the Bf 109 was to prove its worth initially. The He 177 and the Me 210 were, as later became clear, ineffectual; as early as 30 August 1939 Jeschonnek demanded that the He 177 be produced as a substitute for the 'super bomber' Ju 88, whose production delays after numerous changes raised fears of a 'bomber gap' in 1940. It had become obvious that the Ju 88 'will not achieve the promised deep penetration range with performance acceptable for a military aircraft'.[77]

When, on 14 August 1939, Hitler informed the Wehrmacht leaders of his decision to attack Poland,[78] he hoped on the one hand that it would be an isolated campaign, but on the other hand he also accepted the risk of a war with the Western powers.[79] In his talk to the Wehrmacht commanders on 22 August 1939 he reduced the Polish campaign to a question of nerves: ending it quickly would mean less risk of a war in the west.[80] He maintained that political leaders, like military commanders, had to take risks and accept responsibility for them. At present he was once more taking a 'great risk'. Four days later he wrote to Mussolini:

As neither France nor Britain can achieve any decisive successes in the west, while the pact with Russia will free all German forces in the east after the defeat of Poland, and as we clearly have superiority in the air, I shall not hesitate to solve the problem in the east even if this involves the danger of a conflict in the west.[81]

At the start of the war the Luftwaffe had large numbers only of medium-range aircraft capable of carrying average bomb-loads. Because of its shortcomings in equipment and training, it was not able to force a decision in an operational air war, especially against Britain. However, thanks to its superiority in September 1939,[82] its tactical experience in providing direct and indirect support for the army, and its operational mobility, it was the only military instrument with which the risks of a two-front war were, to a limited extent, calculable: it promised quick offensive successes in Poland and could be transferred rapidly to the west in the event of a war there. The front-line strengths of the German, British, and French air forces in September 1939 are shown in Table II.I.1.

On the western front the Luftwaffe was considered capable, in co-operation with the permanent local defence installations (Air Defence Zone West), of preventing decisive offensive successes by the hostile air forces and even of carrying out telling

---

[76] Homze, *Arming*, 229 ff.

[77] Der Chef des Generalstabes No. 2183/39 g.Kdos. 1. Abt. (II), 30 Sept. 1939, betr. Attrappen-besichtigung He. 177 am 10.8.1939; BA-MA Lw 103/65. Cf. also BA-MA RL 3/63, 7318 ff.

[78] Halder, *Diaries*, i.1–12 (14 Aug. 1939).   [79] Cf. Henke, *England*, 276 ff.

[80] Text: *DGFP* D vii, Nos. 192–3; cf. Baumgart, 'Ansprache Hitlers', and Boehm's reply, 'Ansprache Hitlers'; Hillgruber, 'Quellen', 384 ff.

[81] *DGFP* D vii, No. 307; cf. *Weizsäcker-Papiere*.   [82] Cf. Table II.I.1.

TABLE II.1.1. *Bombers and Fighter Aircraft in Front-Line Units of the German, British, and French Air Forces in September* 1939[a]

Aircraft type	Germany	Britain	France
Bombers	1,176	536 (973)	643[b] (485)
	+366 dive-bombers		
Fighters	771	608 (530)	590 (585)
	+408 heavy fighters		

[a] Numbers in brackets indicate the strength assumed by Dept. 5 of the Luftwaffe General Staff.

[b] Only older models.

Sources: Völker, *Luftwaffe*, 184 ff.; Gibbs, *Strategy*, i. 599; Christienne, 'Armée de l'air', 29 ff.; Genstb. 5. Abt. No. 12070/39 g. (1A), Unterlagen über fremde Fliegertruppen, 17 Aug. 1939, BA-MA RL 2/447.

operational strikes against the enemy. Much more important, however, was the fact that the Luftwaffe itself confirmed Hitler's belief that the Western powers would not go to war if Germany attacked Poland. The situation assessments of Department 5 in particular show how much the belief of the Luftwaffe in its own superiority was based on the military structure of the 'Führer'-state, in addition to its temporary lead over other air forces. In the eyes of the Luftwaffe leaders this structure guaranteed that in Germany itself the psychological effects of an air war could be kept under control; in the 'Führer'-state, in contrast to the democracies 'torn by partisan political differences', the danger of an internal collapse had been eliminated, and the creation of the 'national community' ensured a much greater ability to bear the hardships of an air war.[83] The Luftwaffe leaders considered the general advantage in war readiness achieved by this 'total view' (Schmid) to be a great deterrent. This assumption seemed to be confirmed by international political developments since Munich. Göring had weakened the effect of his own warnings against a war with Britain:[84] his eagerness to carry out Hitler's orders and his sabre-rattling towards other countries had been an important factor in making Hitler's Luftwaffe feared abroad, and so reducing the risk of such a war.

In 1938 Hermann Rauschning had commented on the abnormal readiness to take risks which Hitler later demonstrated in his decision to attack Poland, and the high

[83] Cf. Macht, 'Wehrwirtschaftliche Grundlagen', 165: 'The ideological position of the Western democracies, the emphasis on individual freedom, prevents them from understanding the nature of total war; for if war is the continuation of politics by other means, only a people with a totalitarian leadership can adequately prepare and carry out a total war; only then will it be possible to fight the war to the finish with the strength of the entire nation'; Herhudt von Rohden, 'Betrachtungen', 213: 'The idea of a national community, which finds its fullest expression in our state, is a guarantee of the successful air defence of our country ... The unity of the nation has toughened our spiritual powers enormously.'

[84] According to Weizsäcker, Göring remarked to Hitler on 29 Aug.: 'Let's call off this dangerous game (*Vabanquespiel*).' Hitler answered: 'I have played dangerously all my life': *Weizsäcker-Papiere*, 162. Cf. also Speer, *Inside*, 162. As late as 2 Sept. Milch still hoped that Göring's attitude towards Britain would make mediation possible: 'My suggestion to Göring: he should go to London' (Irving, *Tragödie*, 421 n. 1).

value placed on ideological factors in German military situation assessments. He described them as typical features of a degenerate 'broadened strategy' under National Socialism, displaying the 'resolute and ruthless character that marks all operations of the Party, with everything staked on a single card'.[85]

The declaration of war by the Western powers on 3 September 1939 meant that the deterrent strategy of the Luftwaffe had failed. Hitler became involved in a war he did not want at that time and for which his Luftwaffe was still unprepared.

[85] Rauschning, *Germany's Revolution*, 151.

II. Germany's Second Attempt to Become a Naval Power

BERND STEGEMANN

As long as the size and composition of the German navy were determined by the treaty of Versailles, the operational planning of the Navy Command was mainly concerned with Poland and France. The navy estimated the chances of success in a war at sea against those countries far more optimistically than could be justified by the strength of German land forces. After the National Socialists came to power, the Soviet Union was also considered a potential enemy. The relative strength of German and British naval forces was ostensibly settled by the agreement of 18 June 1935, which limited the size of the German fleet to 35 per cent of the Royal Navy. However, Erich Raeder, the head of the Navy Command, considered the restrictions imposed by the agreement acceptable only for a limited time, and already in 1934 he and Hitler had evidently agreed that the later expansion of the German fleet might have to be carried out against British opposition. At first this idea was not reflected in German operational thinking. The expert in the fleet department, Commander (Fregattenkapitän) Heye, pointed out the hopelessness of a naval war against Britain in an official study on 1 October 1936.[1] A study by the Navy High Command of 4 May 1937 came to the same conclusion and expressed the view that military success was possible only in a war with France and the Soviet Union, and that this hypothesis was also the more probable—a view which did not remain unchallenged.[2] In May 1938 Hitler informed Raeder that in a war France and Britain could be expected to be Germany's enemies, but the question of when such a war might start remained open. Nevertheless, Heye was ordered to examine the possibilities of conducting a naval war against Britain. His memorandum served as a basis for the discussions of the planning committee Raeder formed on 19 September 1938. In a revised version of 25 October 1938 it also formed the basis for construction planning which led to the Z plan in 1939, and for operational thinking regarding a naval war against Britain.[3]

The main suggestion of the memorandum was the idea of building a special fleet for a cruiser war against Britain, as it was not possible to create a battle fleet superior to the British. To build such a cruiser fleet the traditional types of ships had to be replaced by new, faster models able to stay at sea longer, and superior to the British fleet on a ship-for-ship basis. Supported by a fleet of supply-ships, these new models were if possible to be on station in the Atlantic at the start of a war so as to force the enemy to divide his forces and loosen his blockade. This would make it possible for Germany to send further ships into the Atlantic. The following

---

[1] Salewski, *Seekriegsleitung*, i. 30–1.   [2] Ibid. 32–6.   [3] Ibid. iii. 27–63.

figures were mentioned as a provisional final goal of fleet construction by 1948 (figures for the end of the first construction period scheduled for 1942-3 in brackets): 10 (6) battleships, 12 (4) new, 3 (3) old pocket battleships, 5 (5) heavy cruisers, 24 (4) new light cruisers, 36 (?) new small cruisers, 8 (2) aircraft-carriers, 249 (133) U-boats, 70 (48) destroyers, and 78 (36) torpedo-boats. Evidently at the urging of Hitler, who gave naval armaments the highest priority on 27 January 1939, completion dates for the 6 battleships (construction designations 'H' to 'N') were moved up to the period before 1945. Construction of the new pocket battleships and the small cruisers was temporarily postponed, and it was decided not to order additional aircraft-carriers. On the other hand, 3 additional battle cruisers were included in the programme (construction designations 'P' to 'R'), and 6 light cruisers were ordered. Before the start of the war a total of 42 destroyers, 36 torpedo-boats, and 131 U-boats was also ordered.[4]

However, German shipyards were unable to meet the demands of this ambitious programme before the start of the war. Warship construction had suffered from delays since the beginning of rearmament, with the result that in 1939 the only ships ready for action were those whose construction had begun by 1935. The main causes of this situation were the shortage of capacity in the shipyards and of the necessary materials, and the increasingly frequent shortages of skilled workers. The slow growth of the fleet worried Hitler and Raeder, both of whom attempted with different methods to accelerate the pace of construction.[5] Nevertheless, at the start of the war only 2 battleships, 3 pocket battleships, 1 heavy and 6 light cruisers, 21 destroyers, 12 torpedo-boats, and 57 U-boats were in service.

But not only the small number of ships ready for action was disquieting. To carry on a naval war in the Atlantic, the navy needed fast ships which if necessary could escape from a superior enemy and which had a great cruising-range, as Germany could not expect to have bases near the operations area. It was planned to meet these requirements by using diesel engines, which had proved their worth in pocket battleships but were not yet available with the necessary performance for battleships, heavy cruisers, and destroyers. For this reason high-pressure, superheated-steam engines were chosen, but they quite failed to measure up to expectations. Cruising-range was reduced, mechanical and technical problems were frequent, and repairs were extremely complicated. This meant that in a war heavy cruisers could hardly be used successfully in the Atlantic. The effective range of the destroyers was limited to 1,000 nautical miles—a journey as far as Narvik, for example.[6]

In 1938-9 Reader repeatedly pointed out to Hitler that the planned expansion of the navy in the coming years would still not give Germany a fleet able to conduct an effective naval war against Britain. For this reason he suggested the creation of a

---

[4] Cf. Dülffer, *Weimar*, 496-505; Salewski, *Seekriegsleitung*, i. 57-61.

[5] Cf. Dülffer, *Weimar*, 503-12; Salewski, *Seekriegsleitung*, i. 61-2.

[6] These problems are described in a memorandum of the naval war staff of 4 Feb. 1941 on requirements for future warship construction on the basis of experience gained in the first year of the war with regard to the military effectiveness of the new German ships: Salewski, *Seekriegsleitung*, iii. 168-88.

special fleet with the emphasis on U-boats, which could be built faster. But as late as 22 August 1939 Hitler still expressly denied that an early military conflict with Britain was possible; and he continued to give priority to battleship construction.[7] An alternative was urged energetically by the leader of U-boats, later grand admiral, Karl Dönitz.[8] Basing his planning on personal experience in the First World War,[9] he had developed the tactic of nocturnal surface attacks on convoys by large groups of U-boats; he assumed that in the event of war the London agreement, which made a submarine war against enemy trade practically impossible, would be disregarded by its signatories, including Germany. Moreover, he did not believe that the British device for locating submerged submarines (ASDIC) was effective.[10] ASDIC, however, had led the British to believe that U-boats no longer represented a serious threat.[11] After a war-game in the winter of 1938-9, Dönitz concluded that a decisive success would be possible in a war against enemy trade with a fleet of at least 300 operational U-boats. Since then he had been demanding a corresponding expansion of the U-boat fleet. In his opinion an expansion of the navy according to the Z plan would only lead to an arms race which Germany would lose; U-boats would be able to reach the operations area in the Atlantic, without being discovered and attacked, more easily than could surface ships. As a result of the growing threat from the air it had become necessary to build protective bunkers for ships at bases; this was possible for U-boats but not for large surface ships.[12] Dönitz was correct in his belief that, in view of the superiority of the enemy, moving German naval forces into the Atlantic represented a problem for which it had not been possible to find a satisfactory solution in the memorandums that preceded the Z plan. Even ships equipped with diesel engines were not capable of unlimited action, and moreover they were dependent on supplies that also had to pass the British blockade.

But this problem applied also to U-boats; in the First World War the British had succeeded in completely closing the Channel with mines, though the 'Northern barrage' laid between the Shetland Islands and Bergen had not been satisfactory from a technical point of view. It had not been possible to clear these obstacles with minesweepers operating from Germany itself, and the mine war in the North Sea had also presented increasing difficulties in proportion to the growing distance of the areas mined by the British from the Heligoland Bight, as German minesweepers had had to operate under greater danger of attack by British forces.[13]

The question of acquiring Atlantic bases also arose in this connection; but here

[7] As one of many pieces of evidence, Raeder's memorandum of 3 Sept. 1939, printed in 'Führer Conferences', 37-8.

[8] Dönitz, Memoirs. Dönitz's ideas are summarized in his memorandum 'Gedanken über den Aufbau der U-Bootwaffe' of 1 Sept. 1939, printed in Salewski, Seekriegsleitung, iii. 64-9.

[9] Dönitz professed ignorance of the work done in the navy on submarine warfare in the First World War; cf. Dönitz, Memoirs, 4-5, 18-20.

[10] The name is derived from the 'Allied Submarine Detection Investigation Committee' of the First World War.

[11] On the development of the Royal Navy between the wars cf. Marder, Dardanelles, 33-63.

[12] Dönitz, Memoirs, 38-40. 　　　　　　　　　　　　　[13] Gladisch, Nordsee, vol. vii.

co-operation could be expected at most from Spain, which, however, was so weak militarily that she could not be considered as an ally for the foreseeable future.[14] The occupation of the northern coast of France, including Brest, was regarded as the ideal solution because it would outflank the British blockade and at the same time give Germany bases on the Atlantic. But such an operation required at first a concentration on the armaments programmes of the army and the Luftwaffe and could not therefore be in the interest of the navy.

The air threat, which Dönitz had seen clearly, was a danger not only to German naval bases. At a time when Lufthansa was establishing routes across the Atlantic, it could be foreseen that an increasing use of land-based aircraft had to be expected in any naval war there, which, however, would not be possible from German territory. Therefore Dönitz could assume that his U-boats would not receive any support from the Luftwaffe in their intended operations area. On the other hand, the Z plan envisaged the construction of, at first, two aircraft-carriers, but typically these ships were given lower priority than the small cruisers in the construction plan of the memorandum of 25 October 1938. For the German navy, aircraft-carriers and carrier warfare were a new dimension; with the expected commissioning of the first carrier at the end of 1941 a training- and test-ship would have been available, but not a strong carrier air force to support operations in the Atlantic.[15] As the construction of a second carrier was stopped even before the start of the war and there were no other concrete construction plans, the ships of the Z plan fleet would have had to fight a war in the Atlantic without air support. It must also be noted that Germany's probable enemies in such a war, Britain and France, were not only able to make increasing use of land-based aircraft but also had 8 aircraft-carriers in service and another 8 under construction, although they too still accorded primacy to the battleship. Even from the perspective of 1939-40 the belief that Germany would nevertheless be able to conduct a successful naval war against a vastly superior enemy must be considered completely unrealistic.

However, Dönitz's favoured alternative, the submarine war against enemy shipping, involved additional problems. His plan for attacks on convoys assumed not only that the U-boat would continue to be able to escape by submerging, but also that it would remain almost invisible at night on the surface because of its small silhouette. In reality its safety under water was threatened by ASDIC, which was quite effective if sufficient escort vessels were used, and darkness would soon offer U-boats no protection on the surface. Already in 1938 Dönitz was aware of the development of devices using radio waves which, like the radar developed by the British, could locate ships at night beyond the range of optical instruments. In 1939 such equipment was even tested on U-boats, where, however, it did not prove to be very useful. From surface ships, however, the 'Sea Tact' (*Seetakt*) device was able to locate targets at a distance of 14 km.[16] Of course these devices were still far from being fully developed, but it was already clear that they represented the start

---

[14] On the question of bases on Italian territory cf. Schreiber, *Revisionismus*, 139-43.
[15] Hadeler, *Flugzeugträger*, esp. 110-14.
[16] Gießler, 'Funkmeß', 182; id., *Marine-Nachrichtendienst*, 64-6.

of a technical development which endangered the tactical plan of the German U-boat command, and thus also cast doubt on the effectiveness of a strategy which regarded a submarine war against enemy shipping as the decisive instrument of naval warfare.

The feasibility of a naval-war strategy like the one on which the Z plan was based, and to a certain extent of a submarine war like the one Dönitz advocated, was doubtful for another reason. In 1938 Germany produced 145,000 tons of diesel and 372,000 tons of fuel oil; however, at the same time she consumed 1,650,000 and 1,025,000 tons respectively. The navy calculated that after the completion of its construction programme mobilization requirements would be 2m. tons of diesel and 6m. tons of fuel oil, which would enable it to carry on a war for twelve months. On the one hand, the navy wanted to take these quantities from current production, which would reach 1.34m. tons of diesel and 2m. of fuel oil annually by 1948; on the other hand, it wished to have available storage facilities with a capacity of 10m. m.³, which, however, still had to be built.[17] If the envisaged efforts to increase fuel production were not successful, or not as successful as planned, the effectiveness of the navy would be very limited, for in the event of war supplies could not be expected from overseas. Nor could oil imports from other European countries, in particular Romania, close this gap. Even the very modest German fleet began to suffer noticeably from oil shortages in 1941.

In conclusion, we must ask what aims Hitler and the navy were pursuing in the expansion of the fleet according to the Z plan. It is fairly certain that Hitler considered an early military conflict with Britain improbable. Otherwise he would have accepted the navy's suggestions and ordered an accelerated construction of U-boats. As he had not been able to reach his expansionist goals in an alliance with Britain, he decided to achieve them against her. This was announced openly with the denunciation of the Anglo-German naval agreement on 28 April 1939, for the German government had assured Britain that the agreement represented a final and permanent fixing of the relative strength of the British and German navies. However, the question remains whether threatening Britain by constructing a fleet was a suitable means to ensure that she would not intervene when Germany plunged into military campaigns on the Continent. The view is not convincing that Hitler was already thinking of the time after the conquest of 'living-space in the east' and the acquisition of a colonial empire overseas, and wanted to build in good time the fleet he would need for the defence of his 'world power' position against the United States and possibly also against Britain.[18] It was already uncertain whether the Z plan could be carried out in the time demanded, and the expansion of the navy would certainly have to be interrupted if the army and the Luftwaffe were supposed to carry out large-scale military operations. Apart from the question whether Hitler considered these factors, German naval armaments must be seen in comparison with those of the Western powers. Already in 1938 Germany had calculated the strength

---

[17] Figures according to Birkenfeld, *Treibstoff*, 218–19, and Meier-Dörnberg, *Ölversorgung*, 29–31. Cf. also Zetzsche, *Logistik*.   [18] e.g. Hillgruber, *Strategie*, 36–7.

of the Royal Navy by 1942 at between 22 and 25 battleships, 12 aircraft-carriers, over 80 cruisers, and 200 destroyers; while the French fleet had 11 battleships, 3 aircraft-carriers, 22 cruisers, and 79 destroyers.[19] In the same year the United States decided to increase its fleet by 20 per cent; by 1942 it would consist of 21 battleships, 7 aircraft-carriers, 40 cruisers, and 252 destroyers.[20]

The figures for the first period of the German construction plan make it clear that the German navy would inevitably remain hopelessly inferior to the fleets of her potential enemies, even if the construction of battleships and battle cruisers were accelerated. For this reason too the idea of conducting a successful naval war with battleships in the Atlantic was unrealistic. It must also be considered that the British and French naval construction programmes were based on the assumption that Germany would continue to abide by her naval agreement with Britain; the effect which Germany's denunciation of that agreement would have on British and French planning remained to be seen. Even after reaching his 'provisional final goal', however, Hitler certainly would not have had a 'world-power fleet' that would have enabled him to form an alliance with Britain and embark on a conflict with the United States.[21]

An additional factor in the expansion of the navy's demands beyond the ship-construction programme based on the 35 per cent agreement was the international arms race which started after Japan announced at the end of 1936 that she would no longer abide by the London agreement. The change in the operational planning of the German navy against Britain can be adequately explained as the result of a sober assessment of the international political situation, which made it increasingly improbable that Britain would stay neutral, let alone support Germany in a war with her neighbours. However, the developments which took place primarily in 1938 involved not only a strengthening of naval armaments and consideration of Britain as a potential enemy in operational planning, but also the conscious adapting of the navy to, at first, peaceful rivalry with Britain.[22] Hitler's foreign-policy successes, the annexation of Austria and the Munich agreement, apparently caused the Navy High Command to believe that now the time had come to realize their boldest ambitions, which had been more or less repressed since the Tirpitz era.[23] These plans were not based on present realities but took as their point of orientation a distant future. It seemed necessary to prepare for a war with half or even two-thirds of the world in order to achieve access to the oceans if, 'according to the will of the Führer, Germany is to achieve a secure world-power position'.[24] One naval commander, however, was of the opinion (which the Navy High Command did not share) that the aim of

---

[19] Figures in *Nauticus*, 22 (1939), 21-4, already compiled in 1938.   [20] Cf. *Weyer* (1939).

[21] Cf. Dülffer, *Weimar*, 546.

[22] Cf. the memorandum of 25 Oct. 1938: Salewski, *Seekriegsleitung*, iii. 27-63.

[23] This was very clearly expressed in the conclusions of the Navy High Command regarding the war-game of Feb.-Mar. 1939; quoted in Gemzell, *Raeder*, 135.

[24] Comment of the C.-in-C. of the fleet, Adm. Carls, on Heye's memorandum of Sept. 1938, quoted in Gemzell, *Raeder*, 87-9; Salewski, *Seekriegsleitung*, i. 55, and Dülffer, *Weimar*, 486-7.

German policy was to 'unite' Europe from Germany's western frontier to the Urals in order to be independent of imports of raw materials and food.[25]

Evidently the Navy High Command did not believe that expansion in the east represented an indispensable prerequisite for the next step, expansion overseas. But even in 1939 there were still those who pointed to the First World War and doubted that Germany could rise to the level of a naval world power against British opposition.[26] The naval war staff fell back on the assumption that Italy and Japan would co-operate with Germany in the event of a war with Britain and France, thus tying down a considerable part of the Royal Navy. The naval strength of the United States as a possible ally of Britain was not even considered.[27]

Hitler and the Navy High Command generally agreed that Germany must become a world power again, but the navy had no clear idea of the steps it would have to take on the way to realizing this aim. In view of the uncoordinated armaments programmes of the three Wehrmacht services, it cannot be argued convincingly that Hitler's intention in pursuing the Z plan was to prepare for a precisely definable phase of his expansion programme, namely a conflict with the United States in the second half of the 1940s.[28] In 1941 the naval war staff did plan an offensive fleet of 25 battleships, 8 aircraft-carriers, 50 cruisers, and 400 U-boats for this purpose, but they 'realistically' allowed twelve to fifteen years for its construction.[29]

The idea of a naval war against the enemy's sea links remained the decisive factor in German naval planning before the start of the Second World War. Considerably better chances of success were expected with the increase in the size of the navy after 1943. As mentioned above, a Wehrmacht operation to occupy the northern coast of France, including Brest, was considered to be the solution to the problem of getting German naval forces into the Atlantic.[30] However, even in the military and geographical situation of 1939 the Navy Command believed they could wound Britain at her most vulnerable point by carrying on a war against British trade; they also hoped that by concentrating their forces in the northern part of the North Sea they would be able to breach the British blockade there and thus make it easier for German naval forces to enter and leave the Atlantic.[31]

---

[25] The Navy Group Commander East, Adm. Albrecht, in a study of spring 1939; Gemzell, *Raeder*, 68-9; Salewski, *Seekriegsleitung*, i. 68-9; Dülffer, *Weimar*, 524-6.

[26] Adm. Saalwächter, commanding admiral of the North Sea station, in a war-game in Jan. 1939, quoted in Dülffer, *Weimar*, 538.

[27] Cf. Salewski, *Seekriegsleitung*, i. 74-6; 'Führer Conferences', 37, and Schreiber, *Revisionismus*, on the role of Italy in German planning.   [28] Cf. e.g. Hildebrand, *Foreign Policy*, 80.

[29] Cf. Salewski, *Seekriegsleitung*, iii. 135-6. On the ideas of the naval war staff in July and Aug. 1941, which went even further, and on the relationship between naval visions of the future and Hitler's goals, cf. Schreiber, 'Kontinuität'; Salewski, 'Das maritime Dritte Reich'.

[30] At the final conference of the Navy High Command war-game in Feb.-Mar. 1939: Gemzell, *Raeder*, 143.

[31] Cf. combat instructions for the navy (May 1939), BA-MA II M40, ii, and the Navy High Command to the Wehrmacht High Command, No. A I Op. 113/39 g.Kdos. Chefs., 29 July 1939 (Verfügung), betr. Weisungen für den Kampf gegen die feindliche Wirtschaft . . ., BA-MA, Case 1169.

PART III

Hitler's First Blitzkrieg and its Consequences for North-eastern Europe

HORST ROHDE

I. Germany and Poland in the Prelude
to the Second World War

In the early hours of 1 September 1939 German air force and naval units opened the attack on Poland. Shortly afterwards five armies of the German land forces crossed the frontiers of East Prussia, Pomerania, Silesia, and Slovakia. The plans for this offensive were based on the 'Directive for the Uniform Preparation of the Armed Forces for the War for 1939–40' issued by the OKW between 3 April and 10 May 1939.[1] It can be fully understood only by an examination of the development of German–Polish relations since Hitler's seizure of power and of his earlier statements.

Before 1933 Poland had not been the subject of any special mention in the programmatic utterances of the future 'Führer'.[2] His constant demands for an extension of German 'living-space' in the east had referred mainly to the Soviet Union, suggesting that the lesser countries of east central Europe were of no particular importance to him. This applied also to Poland, although Hitler seemed to regard it, at least for a limited period, as a useful potential bulwark against Bolshevism and later as a potential 'ally' in a joint 'crusade' against the east. Such considerations were a factor in determining his policy as chancellor. This did not mean that he had renounced the territorial demands made of Poland which enjoyed such popularity in Germany. But he believed he might be able, at a later date, to achieve a solution by negotiation with a Polish 'junior partner', if need be by offering compensations in Lithuania or the Ukraine.

The National Socialists' assumption of governmental responsibility in Germany, however, at first resulted in a deterioration of relations with Poland: the latter's military demonstrations, designed above all to secure her western frontier, made Hitler aware of Germany's political isolation. He therefore initiated a new era of relations between the two countries in his very first conversation with the Polish minister Wysocki, on 2 May 1933. The German–Polish non-aggression treaty concluded in January 1934 met with reservations in both countries. Nevertheless, it reflected an improvement in

---

[1] OKW/WFA No. 37/39 g.Kdos. Chefs. L Ia (2. Ausf.), 3.4.39, BA-MA PG 33276; Der Oberste Befehlshaber der Wehrmacht/OKW No. 37/39 g.Kdos. Chefs. WFA/L 1 (2. Ausf.), 11.4.39, BA-MA PG 33276; OKW/WFA No. 37/39 g.Kdos. Chefs./WFA/L I 2. Angel. (2. Ausf.), 13.4.39; Der Oberste Befehlshaber der Wehrmacht No. 48/39 g.Kdos. WFA/L (1) (2. Ausf.), 10.5.39, BA-MA PG 33276. The different dates are due to the consecutive publication of the directive's six parts. The central section, 'Case White', must have been completed before 1 Apr. as Hitler was on a holiday cruise from 1 to 4 Apr. aboard the Kraft durch Freude ship *Robert Ley*, with the result that Keitel signed the document of 3 Apr. with the note that Hitler's signature would be supplied later; this was done on 11 Apr. Cf. Domarus, ii. 1119.

[2] This is not the place for a discussion of Hitler's war aims. For this cf., in addition to Zipfel, 'Hitlers Konzept', *passim*, mainly the most recently published collections: *Kriegsbeginn* and *Hitler, Deutschland und die Mächte*. These provide a comprehensive survey of the present state of research and of existing controversies.

mutual relations, which not only persisted but was further developed over the next few years. This was still true at the turn of 1937/8, when the Polish foreign minister, Józef Beck, began to pursue his plan for the creation of a 'Third Europe'. What he had in mind was the foundation of an independent east central European bloc of states. An essential element of this concept was the establishment of a common frontier between Poland and Hungary at the expense of Czechoslovakia. Budapest was to make the greater territorial gains, by absorbing the Carpatho–Ukraine (also known as Sub-Carpathian Ruthenia) and Slovakia, while Warsaw on the other hand was to play the dominant role in this neutral zone, forming a barrier between the Soviet Union and Germany.

In accordance with this plan the Polish government not only acquiesced in the German annexations of 1938, but played into German hands by occupying the Těšín (Teschen) region of Czechoslovakia and certain frontier districts in the Carpathians, since these actions gravely compromised it *vis-à-vis* the Soviet Union and, above all, *vis-à-vis* France and Britain.

Following these developments Hitler believed the time had come to test Poland's readiness for further-reaching agreements. The German proposals between October 1938 and January 1939, both at first very cautiously formulated and relatively restrained, presented Warsaw with a difficult decision. If the Polish government were to accept Danzig's return to the Reich as well as an extraterritorial communication link across the 'Corridor', in return for a twenty-five-year extension of the non-aggression treaty, a guarantee of common frontiers, and concessions on the Polish–Hungarian issue, it was bound to forfeit even further the goodwill of the other powers and drift into even greater dependence on Germany. Realization of this dilemma, combined with an exaggerated confidence in its own military strength, was the reason for Warsaw's dilatory replies to Hitler's offers. These unresolved German–Polish problems became factors in the situation leading up to the Second World War from about the beginning of 1939.

Hitler's foreign-political procedure had until then consisted not only of premeditated actions but also of more or less skilful improvisations by which he swiftly reacted to any weaknesses of other governments, exploiting them for his purposes. 'To that extent the prelude to the Second World War was not determined rectilinearly by Hitler's will but was the history of changing situations which included the failure of the forces opposing him.'[3] These tactics did not, of course, mean that Hitler ever lost sight of his long-range objectives. The growth of real power and the success of German propaganda were alike intended to prepare a basis for the conquest of living-space in the east.

In the case of Poland too Hitler was primarily interested in clarifying that country's attitude to his plans. To that end he focused on the Danzig and 'Corridor' issue, allegedly the last remaining foreign-policy problem created by the treaty of Versailles and one which, camouflaged as a justified and, above all, limited demand for revision, might be expected to meet with understanding abroad. In this respect, however, the liquidation of Czechoslovakia in March 1939 proved to be a mistake: by sending

---

[3] Broszat, *Polenpolitik*, 253–4; on the entire period of 1930–9 here described see ibid. 234 ff., as well as Roos, *History*, 125 ff.; latest synopsis in Piekalkiewicz, *Zweiter Weltkrieg*, 34 ff.

the Wehrmacht into that territory Hitler had forfeited all foreign-policy credibility. Strategic and economic advantages did not make up for the deterioration of the political climate. Chamberlain's speech in Birmingham on 17 March and Daladier's statement to the French Assembly shortly afterwards signalled the turning-point. What was decisive from the point of view of the Western democracies was not only Hitler's first departure from his proclaimed 'policy of revision' (ostensibly confined to populations of German race) but also his unscrupulous treatment of international agreements and the alarming increase of German power. Poland, on the other hand, was released from its quandary with regard to Germany. With the inclusion of former Czechoslovakia into the German sphere of power, Germany's seizure of the Memel region on 25 March, and the conclusion of the German–Romanian trade agreement of 23 March, Poland's encirclement had become virtually complete, so that it could now credibly speak of being threatened and hence count on help from London and Paris.

Poland's foreign minister, on the other hand, was bound to realize, by that time if not before, that his policy of a 'Third Europe' had failed. Hungary, prior to and following the Munich agreement, had displayed cautious reserve *vis-à-vis* Germany and had only partially achieved the territorial claims it had formulated in concert with Poland. Thus, the greater part of the Carpatho–Ukraine came to it only after the German occupation of Bohemia and Moravia, while Slovakia, whose secession from Prague had originally been welcomed by Poland, was kept by Berlin—which realized its strategic importance—within its own sphere of power.

In consequence of these developments Poland's attitude stiffened. When on 21 March the German foreign minister von Ribbentrop requested J. Lipski, the Polish ambassador, to call on him so that he could explain the German entry into Czechoslovakia and the establishment of the Protectorate of Bohemia and Moravia as well as that of an independent Slovak state, he repeated the German proposal for a final solution of common problems, now for the first time in the tone of an ultimatum. In reply the ambassador left him in no doubt that Poland regarded Germany's assumption of the guardianship of Slovakia as an unfriendly act. Not even Ribbentrop's hints that, in the event of Poland adopting a benevolent attitude, the Slovak and even the Ukrainian issue might well be resolved to mutual advantage produced any change of reaction from his Polish interlocutor.[4] Poland's partial mobilization on 23 March, principally in the region around Danzig, was a further symptom of increased self-assurance in Warsaw. At the same time Warsaw agreed to a British proposal for a consultative agreement, to embrace several nations, which was immediately followed by Beck's request for the speedy conclusion of a bilateral British–Polish alliance.[5]

Hitler was increasingly convinced that the limit of expansion without warlike entanglements had now been reached. He therefore, for the first time, revealed in an instruction to the commander-in-chief of the army, dated 25 March 1939, that he was considering the idea, given favourable political conditions, of solving the Danzig or indeed the whole 'Polish question' by military means. He ordered a start

---

[4] *DGFP* D vi, No. 61; *Weizsäcker-Papiere*, 174 ff.
[5] Denne, *Danzig-Problem*, 178-9; Roos, *History*, 158-9.

to be made on preparing a plan of operations against the eastern neighbour.[6] When the Polish note presented on 26 March in response to the German demands turned out to be a clear rejection, Hitler no longer showed any interest in embarking on talks unless a positive outcome was visible in advance. Moreover, just as on the German side the issue of German minorities—temporarily neglected for the sake of other political objectives—was once more being played up, so the war psychosis and hatred of Germans was growing in Poland on the same scale. A further escalation occurred when on 31 March the British government issued its guarantee of Polish independence, in which the French joined. On 2 April the Polish foreign minister went to London and four days later signed a provisional two-page treaty of mutual assistance.

From what is known today of Polish policy during those months the British and French promise of support merely corroborated Poland's already firm intention to resist German demands. Hence, even a failure to obtain Western support would scarcely have resulted in a fundamental change in Warsaw's attitude. On the other hand, the expectation of help from Britain and France naturally had a massive effect on the morale of the Polish armed forces and population. For Hitler, however, who had misjudged the mood in Poland, the London agreement was a painful setback. He had now brought about the very thing he had tried to avoid at all costs, i.e. inducing Poland to lean more heavily on Britain on account of Danzig. The British government, admittedly, had no intention of giving its ally *carte blanche*: this was evident from the fact that the guarantee was framed so as to apply to Poland's independence and not to her frontiers. In practice, however, the decision on the *casus foederis* had largely been handed to Warsaw.[7]

Hitler reacted to this changed situation with the already mentioned directive for the Wehrmacht's uniform preparation for war; this represented the Third Reich's first complete plan of aggression against another state.[8] In memorandums presented in Warsaw and London on 27 April, as well as in a speech to the Reichstag the following day, he denounced both the 'German–Polish Declaration', i.e. the non-aggression treaty of 26 January 1934, and the Anglo-German naval agreement of 18 June 1935. He added that any new contractual arrangement between Germany and Poland would have to be based on 'a clear obligation binding on both parties'.[9] A similar sentence concluded the reply to this invitation, presented by the Polish chargé d'affaires in Berlin to the secretary of state in the foreign office, von Weizsäcker, on 5 May.[10]

The next few weeks and months were marked by more or less open diplomatic activity, triggered off mainly by conditions in Danzig and by the treatment of the

---

[6] *DGFP* D vi, No. 99; Hillgruber, *Germany*, 65 ff. For details of Poland's partial mobilization cf. III.II.3 below.

[7] Broszat, *Polenpolitik*, 258 ff.; Roos, *History*, 160 ff. For details of Anglo-German relations at the time cf. esp. Henke, *England*, *passim*.

[8] Cf. n. 1 above; Broszat, *Polenpolitik*, 259 ff.; Roos, *History*, 161-2.

[9] *DGFP* D vi, Nos. 276 (quotation), 277; Reichstag speech: Domarus, ii. 1148 ff., here esp. 1161 ff.

[10] *DGFP* D vi, *passim*, e.g. Nos. 334, 335, 350, 355, 367, 387, 418.

German and Polish minorities. At the same time hatred grew, systematically whipped up by propaganda on both sides.[11]

In spite of these developments there were a number of indications, especially on the Polish but also on the German side, suggesting that, in the spring of 1939, fatalistic ideas about the inevitability of war had not yet prevailed.[12] Thus, among other things, the economic agreement of 1 September 1938 remained essentially in force, even though this was predominantly owing to pragmatic considerations. On the one hand, the Reich was anxious to avoid major obstacles to its own industry and, on the other, the chances of weakening its neighbour by economic means were regarded as relatively slight after the experiences of the nine-year 'economic war' with Poland between 1925 and 1934.

For Hitler himself, however, the decision in favour of war had meanwhile become virtually immutable. The fact that, as he saw it, German policy on the Danzig and 'Corridor' problem had driven Poland into the arms of Britain and that the last revisions of the treaty of Versailles, regarded as absolutely indispensable, could apparently no longer be achieved by peaceful or *coup de main* methods now led him to regard the solution of the entire 'Polish question' as the first step in his 'living-space' programme. His conference with leading military figures on 23 March 1939 reveals this quite clearly, as it does also his fear that, in the event of a conflict with the Western powers, now assumed to be almost inevitable, Germany might be faced with a war on two fronts.[13] In his opinion Britain had become the main obstacle to eastward expansion. As for relations with Poland, it appears that Hitler wanted to safeguard his rear prior to an attack on the West. If, as a result of a German-Polish conflict, a war with the West was no longer avoidable, then the struggle was to be primarily against Britain and France. If these two powers intervened after the launching of a German campaign against Poland, then, according to Hitler's intention, they had to be attacked as well, with Poland at the same time being 'finished off'. The wish to separate the timing of the wars continued, as is clearly demonstrated by subsequent events. Finally, it is interesting in this context that the Soviet Union was at that time still considered by Hitler as a potential adversary in a German operation against Poland.

Although German-Polish relations continued to deteriorate over the next few months, mainly because of Danzig, it was clear that Berlin was endeavouring to keep events under control in order not to be forced into action. Hitler, moreover, speculated on the possibility that Poland might take a rash step or that some other favourable opportunity might offer itself for a swift seizure of the Free City.

---

[11] On developments in Danzig from Mar. onwards, see Denne, *Danzig-Problem*, 176 ff. On the role of German propaganda against Poland during the period leading up to the Second World War cf. the detailed account in Sywottek, *Mobilmachung*, 209 ff. On Polish propaganda regarding Germany, see Golczewski, *Deutschlandbild*, esp. 262 ff.

[12] e.g. *DGFP* D vi, Nos. 261, 387/annex 2 (economic reprisals), 394, 429; *Weizsäcker-Papiere*, 153 ff.

[13] *DGFP* D vi, No. 433; Domarus, ii. 1195 ff.; Hillgruber, 'Quellen', 110 ff. The gradual switch towards Poland's inclusion in the living-space programme likewise began to be reflected in German propaganda after the end of 1938 and was intensified from the spring of 1939: Sywottek, *Mobilmachung*, 180 ff., 227.

Such a step immediately before the beginning of operations against Poland would have enabled the Wehrmacht to improve its operational starting-position. On the other hand, Germany's ever increasing war preparations on Reich territory and especially along its entire frontier strengthened the impression in Poland and abroad that Germany had opted for a military solution.[14]

In view of the emerging escalation, Western diplomatic wooing of the Soviet Union had been intensified. This was of particular importance as the guarantee to Poland of 31 March 1939 was doomed to ineffectiveness without Soviet military support. The negotiations, begun about mid-April 1939, appeared to be nearing completion—at least when viewed from Germany.[15] But appearances were deceptive: Stalin from the outset regarded an alliance with the Reich as offering a stronger guarantee than a treaty with the Western powers, which would not be able to offer him sufficient protection against a potential German attack, since Japan, as a member of the Anti-Comintern pact, might arise as a second adversary in his rear. In view of the hastily given British guarantee to Poland he was moreover entitled to assume that, in the event of a German attack on his Polish neighbour, war between the 'capitalist' great powers was inevitable.

Hitler, on the other hand, for some time during the summer of 1939 showed no great interest in an arrangement with the Soviet Union. However, events suddenly came to a head in the second half of July: Hitler was bound to assume, from British and French negotiations in Moscow as well as from their follow-up by military missions, that a positive outcome was on the cards. A campaign against Poland with the Soviet Union and the Western powers as additional adversaries was too great a risk even for his gambler's nature. Moreover, he had to bear in mind not only Germany's exposed position in a future war but also that he was increasingly finding himself under pressure of time with regard to his plans against Poland. And when Japan refused to enter into an anti-British coalition the road was now clear for an alliance that was to cause a good deal of surprise, mainly in view of the many years of anti-Communist propaganda by the National Socialists.

At the end of May Hitler had instructed the state secretary in the foreign office to inform the Soviet chargé d'affaires, Astakhov, that the development of relations between Warsaw and Berlin had brought about greater latitude in the east. From this it was clear that territorial issues—at least with regard to Poland—would no longer represent a decisive obstacle. The only remaining problem from the Soviet point of view was the Baltic States and Finland, but that was solved relatively easily when Hitler was forced into precipitate negotiations in Moscow. Compared with what the Germans were prepared to concede, the offers of the Western powers did not stand a chance. Having until then discussed no more than procedural questions, the Western military missions were informed on 25 August by the defence minister, Voroshilov, that their task in Moscow was at an end.

---

[14] *DGFP* D vi, 189 (n. 6), and e.g. Nos. 470, 471, 515, 622, 702. On detailed developments in Danzig after the end of May see Denne, *Danzig-Problem*, 210 ff.

[15] *DGFP* D vi, e.g. No. 441; on this and the following also Broszat, *Polenpolitik*, 262 ff.; Hofer, *War Premeditated*, 17 ff.; Roos, *History*, 154 ff., 164 ff.; detailed and reliable synoptic account of German-Soviet relations in Allard, *Stalin*, passim.

The pact between Poland's two great neighbours gave rise to alarm, even though its published text seemed inoffensive: in the event of one of the partners being attacked by a third party, the treaty did not oblige the other to give assistance, but merely to preserve benevolent neutrality. The decisive point, however, was the secret supplementary protocol which delimited the parties' 'spheres of interest' in the event of 'territorial-political restructuring' in eastern Europe. Finland, Estonia, Latvia, Poland east of the rivers Pisa, Narew, Vistula, and San, as well as Romanian Bessarabia, were to be part of the Soviet sphere of influence, while Lithuania and Poland west of the above-mentioned line were to be part of that of Germany. It was further decided that 'the question whether the interests of both parties make the maintenance of an independent Polish state appear desirable and how the frontiers of this state should be drawn can be definitely determined only in the course of further political development'.[16]

The importance Hitler attached to the German–Soviet pact emerges from his addresses to military leaders at the Obersalzberg on 22 August 1939: the agreement, he explained, not only prevented the Soviet Union from being used as the spearhead of an anti-German coalition but, as a result of the 'credit agreement' concluded on 19 August, would also render ineffective any blockade of Germany by the Western powers, as the Soviet Union had promised extensive deliveries.

The road to military conflict with Poland was thus clear for the German dictator. Without ruling out the possibility of a simultaneous or immediately consecutive war with the Western powers as a result, he was now, on the strength of the power-situation he had brought about, determined to act. 'Now Poland is in the position in which I wanted her . . . I am only afraid that at the last moment some swine or other will yet submit to me a plan for mediation.' He also said: 'The way will be open for the soldiers, after I have made the political preparations . . . Act brutally . . . The wholesale destruction of Poland is the military objective.'[17]

On 23 August the NSDAP organization in Poland received instructions to destroy all party documents immediately. Simultaneously the warship *Schleswig-Holstein* was ordered to Danzig, where she arrived on 25 August without, as was normal custom, notifying the Polish government. This training-ship was taking the place of the cruiser *Königsberg*—which had been scheduled to pay an official visit to the Free City since the middle of May—because her guns were of sufficient range to bombard the installations at Gdynia and to protect Danzig itself. As possession of the Westerplatte, the Polish-fortified peninsula off the Vistula estuary, was a prerequisite of secure and successful operation from the intended firing-position near Neufahrwasser in Danzig harbour, the first task of the *Schleswig-Holstein* was to assist in the elimination of the fortress, which also served as an ammunition depot.[18]

---

[16] Non-Aggression Treaty between Germany and the Union of Socialist Soviet Republics, text in *DGFP* D vii, Nos. 228, 229 (secret supplementary protocol).

[17] *DGFP* D vii, Nos. 192, 193; cf. also the detailed examination by Baumgart, 'Ansprache Hitlers', and Boehm and Baumgart, 'Miszelle'.

[18] *DGFP* D vii, Nos. 204, 225; MDv No. 601/11: 'Die deutsche Kriegsmarine im Feldzug gegen Polen, September 1939', 7, BA-MA RM D4 601/11. Cf. also Stjernfelt and Böhme, *Westerplatte*, 7 ff. and the German trans.

On 24 August Gauleiter Forster was elected by the Danzig senate to be head of state of the Free City, and Burckhardt, the League of Nations high commissioner, was privately advised by Senate President Greiser to leave Danzig as soon as possible. The clashes there, as well as excesses against German nationals in Poland, were on the increase and presented German propaganda with welcome material for reports of hostile 'provocations'. The Wehrmacht's move into the assembly areas and Polish reactions to the German deployment led to frequent frontier violations, exchanges of fire, and attacks on civil aircraft. On 25 August the German embassies and consulates in Poland, Britain, and France received instructions to send all Reich Germans to Germany or to neutral foreign countries immediately.[19]

In view of these developments the question arises as to why Hitler on the evening of 25 August again called off the attack on Poland he had ordered for the following morning.[20] His action is generally ascribed to either or both of two events that occurred just before: Mussolini's warning that Italy was not yet ready either militarily or economically for participation in a war, and the conclusion of the final Anglo-Polish treaty of alliance. In point of fact the events came as no surprise and changed nothing as regards the immediate strategic position. Hitler, however, under Ribbentrop's influence, was evidently a victim of wishful thinking and suddenly found himself faced with a reality which did not match his expectations. When he gave orders for the offensive to start on 1 September nothing had in fact changed in the situation as against 26 August; but his readiness to take risks had increased, as had his determination to conduct the campaign against Poland under any circumstances.

These motives behind Hitler's attitude undoubtedly provide a partial explanation of events on the eve of the Second World War. Yet the order of 25 August may have been additionally motivated by the fact that, faced with increasing opposition from world public opinion to his intended military operation, Hitler thought it opportune to dissuade the Western powers from supporting Poland by a last-minute diplomatic ruse. If this failed he hoped that, together with the staging of alleged Polish 'provocations'—of which only the attack on the Gleiwitz radio transmitter was in fact carried out[21]—he would at least furnish himself with some more alibis for domestic and foreign consumption.

But there was yet another reason for wanting to gain time: on 26 August the attack would have begun on the first day of mobilization. By postponing the launching of the attack to the seventh day of mobilization a speedier and more effective

---

[19] *DGFP* D vii, e.g. Nos. 5, 197, 218, 224, 231, 259, 286, 330, 355; Groscurth, *Tagebücher*, 152. For the situation in Danzig during the last few weeks before the war see Denne, *Danzig-Problem*, 165 ff. On the intensification of German anti-Polish propaganda cf. Sywottek, *Mobilmachung*, 209 ff.

[20] On the decisions of 25 Aug. see *Weizsäcker-Papiere*, 156 ff., esp. 161 ff. and above all 177-8. Along very similar lines also Vormann, *Feldzug*, 43 ff., Groscurth, *Tagebücher*, 183 ff.; *Heeresadjutant bei Hitler*, 58 ff.; Hofer, *War Premeditated*, 94 ff. For a graphic account of the situation see Speer, *Inside*, 236 ff.; *IMT* ix. 596 ff. (Göring's evidence), x. 269 ff. (Ribbentrop's evidence).

[21] Groscurth, *Tagebücher*, 180, 258; Runzheimer, 'Überfall', 408-26. There is a list of numerous, evidently genuine, frontier incidents from the German and Polish point of view 25-31 Aug. 1939 in Hofer, *Entfesselung*, 95 ff. (passage not included in English edn.).

execution of military operations was achieved. This was of particular importance for a war on two fronts—traditionally the greatest problem of German deployment planning. In such a war there was only one really practicable solution for a planned German attack—massed concentration on the offensive front, even at the risk of having, for the moment, only inadequate cover in the rear. Thus, given the situation in the summer of 1939, there could logically be no other objective than to conclude operations, or at least bring about a decision, in Poland as quickly as possible. Only thus might a timely transfer of major units to the west be accomplished and a possible Franco-British penetration deep into German territory prevented. But the concentration of troops necessary for such a plan did not yet exist on the Polish front on 25 August.[22]

An exact calculation of the difference in strength between 26 August and 1 September is of course difficult, since in the case of lesser units only fragmentary information is available on whether they were mobilized in the normal manner or whether they too were subject to the special regulations which (as will be seen) made a speedy move possible. Yet these units were often of particular importance, especially for certain tasks in the initial phase of operations, such as the securing or repair of bridges and the restoration of communications.

Even so, a comparison of divisions provides an approximate picture: whereas the number of armoured formations available for the offensive on the second date was the same as a week earlier, there were 21 more infantry divisions and 2 more motorized divisions. In addition, it was possible to improve the personnel staffing and the material equipment of available units, which would be bound to have an effect on operational and tactical planning.[23] The importance which attached to these military considerations—alongside the political ones, generally mentioned in isolation—emerges also from the fact that on 25 August the army commander-in-chief warned emphatically that the army required another week to be brought to the peak of mobilization.[24] On the other hand, the loss of the element of surprise on 26 August—though by then already somewhat questionable—must be set against the greater strength on 1 September.

Regardless of how Hitler's motives for his decision on 26 August are assessed, it should be pointed out once more that none of the listed reasons was capable of making him give up his plans for war; they merely induced him to postpone the date of attack by a few days. This delay was designed to gain further strategic advantages as well as to convince the world of the alleged justification of a German attack on Poland and thereby to achieve that country's isolation.

Although mobilization was steadily progressing in Germany, Poland, Britain, and France, diplomatic activity once more revived, giving rise to hopes that peace might after all be saved. During the final days of August nearly all the responsible figures in the states directly or indirectly affected were feverishly working to save the world from another blood-bath. Their hopes seemed to receive new nourishment from

[22] Cf. also Hofer, *Entfesselung*, 277–8 (passage not in English edn.).

[23] Mueller-Hillebrand, *Heer*, ii. 17 (table 7).

[24] Hofer, *Entfesselung*, 277–8 (passage not in English edn.); Groscurth, *Tagebücher*, 184.

some results of Hitler's decision of 25 August inside Germany; it also had a lasting effect on certain military leaders. To begin with, no one knew any longer what was bluff and what real intent, and there was even the comforting conviction in various quarters that the present crisis would end peacefully just as earlier ones had. A few senior officers, moreover, believed that their supreme commander had, by his wavering, suffered a political defeat and could therefore no longer afford to provoke a war. For a short time there was even a revival and intensification of plans for his overthrow and a simultaneous *coup d'état*.[25] Hitler himself, however, precisely because of this supposed defeat, was all the more determined to launch the attack against Poland.[26] His talks with the British ambassador, Henderson, and the latter's French colleague Coulondre on 25 August clearly represented a renewed attempt to prise the Western powers away from Poland and to drive a wedge between Britain and France. The reply of the French premier, Daladier, on the following day, left no room for such hopes. London took a little more time to react to Hitler's 'generous' offer. An essential part in this was played by Göring's attempt, with the help of his friend Birger Dahlerus, to influence the course of events. While there is scarcely any doubt about the sincerity of the Swedish industrialist's efforts, the motives of the German politician are still not entirely clear. But regardless of whether Göring's purpose was the preservation of peace or support of Hitler's aims, it is certain that the British government was fortified in its desire to seek a solution to the conflict. Its hope was based on the fact that on 27 August Dahlerus presented in London a new version of Hitler's demands. Whereas Henderson had earlier reported Hitler's firm resolution not to resume negotiations with Britain until the 'German–Polish question' had been solved, Hitler now seemed once more to desire Britain's co-operation. His object was mainly to gain German possession of the Free City and the 'Corridor' (i.e. the Polish province of Pomorze), while Poland was to enjoy free-port facilities in Danzig and a corridor to Gdynia. Even though realization of this new proposal was scarcely within the realm of the possible, it at least offered London a new starting-point for encouraging direct German–Polish negotiations. In a message of 28 August the British government urged such negotiations and expressed willingness to join in an international guarantee of any agreed settlement.

Hitler, according to Henderson's impression on 29 August, seemed to like the British offer, except that he raised his territorial claims against Poland by demanding additional frontier rectifications in Silesia. However, he gave an evasive reply to the straight question of whether he was now willing to have direct negotiations with Poland. He would have to study the British note carefully and would transmit a written reply to the ambassador the following day. British optimism was reflected in messages sent from London to Rome. Mussolini thereupon sent a telegram to Hitler, urging his ally to choose not the road to war but that of negotiation. Hitler replied that he had already declared himself prepared to receive a Polish negotiator. He had in fact done so at a further conversation with Henderson on the evening

---

[25] Hofer, *War Premeditated*, 96; cf. also Ueberschar, 'Halder', 24–5.; for a graphic description of the effects of the 'halt order' among the troops see Heusinger, *Befehl*, 57 ff.

[26] On the following see esp. Hofer, *War Premeditated*, 100 ff.

of 29 August, when he assured the latter that he had no intention of 'attacking Poland's vital interests or questioning the existence of an independent Polish state'—a statement obviously in conflict with his secret remarks to the military leaders on 22 August and with the supplementary protocol to the German–Soviet non-aggression treaty of 23 August. Hitler then declared himself ready to accept 'the despatch to Berlin of a Polish emissary with full powers' in Berlin not later than the following day (30 August).[27] Henderson rightly pointed out that this short deadline gave the German offer the character of an ultimatum. This observation was borne out by Hitler's answer that the urgency stemmed from the danger caused by the confrontation of two fully mobilized armies. He thereby confirmed publicly for the first time that the Wehrmacht was standing ready to attack Poland.

In view of the excessively short time allowed, the realization of German–Polish talks on 30 August became increasingly doubtful. The hopelessness of the situation emerges even more clearly if one directs one's attention to Warsaw. There the Polish government informed the diplomats of the Western powers on the afternoon of the 29th that general mobilization would start the following day. Even though this was no more than a completion of defence preparations in progress for some time, the British and French ambassadors were anxious to avoid upsetting the political negotiations at all costs. In their difficult situation the Poles could only undertake to postpone mobilization by one day.[28] In the mean time the Western powers tried to persuade the Poles to at least enter into negotiations. They could not, however, advise the Polish politicians to conduct these negotiations in Berlin, whereas the Germans for their part insisted on negotiating at the place 'where Reich Chancellor Hitler happens to be'.[29]

Apart from the issue of the venue of negotiations, the details of the territorial changes desired by Germany increasingly became the focus of interest. On 29 August Hitler announced to the British ambassador that he would have proposals for a solution worked out immediately, and that these were to form the basis of talks with the Polish plenipotentiary. A first version of these was given by Göring to his Swedish friend on the following day, to take to London with him; Hitler now wanted the cession of Danzig as well as a plebiscite in the 'Corridor'. Whoever lost the plebiscite would receive extraterritorial right of passage to Gdynia or Danzig respectively. Any impression of German readiness for a compromise, however, was wiped out on the same day by Ribbentrop's behaviour. In the course of his conversation with Henderson during the night of 30–1 August the German foreign minister acted so provocatively that even the normally restrained Englishman lost his composure. Henderson received the impression that the Reich government had deliberately and forcibly slammed the last door on peace. Nevertheless, he and Coulondre continued to endeavour to get the Poles to the negotiating-table. The Polish foreign minister promised a reply by noon on 31 August, and this in fact he sent to Lipski. In it he stated that the British proposals (for direct discussion and an international

[27] *DGFP* D vii, No. 421.
[28] For details cf. III.II.3 below.
[29] Hofer, *War Premeditated*, 126.

guarantee) were being thoroughly examined and would be answered within a few hours. The Polish ambassador was to maintain contact with the Reich government, without, however, receiving official full powers to negotiate. At 1 p.m. Lipski therefore requested an interview with the German foreign minister, which was not granted to him until 6.30 p.m. As he made it clear that he possessed no special powers to negotiate, Ribbentrop very quickly brought the conversation to an end with the remark that he would inform the Führer accordingly. This meant the final rupture of official German–Polish contacts.

The German attitude makes it clear that Hitler was concerned only with gaining time for the final opening of the attack and with creating an alibi for himself. That the road ahead had been unambiguously chosen emerges from the fact that since 28 August, at the latest, the date of 1 September had been firmly set for the opening of the attack. On 31 August at 12.40 p.m. Hitler issued to the Wehrmacht his 'Directive No. 1 for the Conduct of the War',[30] which stated that as 'all political possibilities of peaceful settlement' of a situation 'intolerable' to Germany on its eastern frontier were now 'exhausted', he had decided on a 'solution by force'. The offensive was to be conducted in accordance with the preparations for 'Case White', with certain changes arising for the land forces from the fact that deployment had meanwhile been almost completed. The rest of the directive was chiefly concerned with behaviour *vis-à-vis* the Western powers. On the German side the greatest possible restraint was to be observed. If Britain and France opened hostilities on their part, then the Wehrmacht formations operating on the Western frontier were to practise a 'maximum preservation of their strength to ensure the prerequisites of a victorious conclusion of operations against Poland'. Towards 4 p.m. on 31 August the High Command of the Armed Forces ordered the three services to 'get ready to move'. Hence, the conversations between Henderson and Göring and between Lipski and Ribbentrop that afternoon were virtually pointless from the start, as Hitler's decision was already taken.

There exist numerous accounts[31] which deal with the tense and dramatic sequence of events of those final days of August 1939 in far greater detail than is possible here. Even though their often minute descriptions of the supposedly knife-edge decisions on war and peace invariably make fascinating reading, it should not be forgotten that the die had long been cast. Thus, the Second World War—though perhaps not at first seen as such—had its momentous beginning, after only a few days' delay, in the early dawn of 1 September 1939.

---

[30] *Hitler's War Directives*, 3 ff.; for military events 28–31 Aug. 1939 see Halder, *Diaries*, i. 40 ff.

[31] e.g. Halder, *Diaries*, i. 34 ff.; Hofer, *War Premeditated*, 269 ff.; Benoist-Méchin, *Wollte Adolf Hitler*, 383 ff.; the most recent synopsis is Piekalkiewicz, *Zweiter Weltkrieg*, 61 ff.

II. Military Preparations for a German–Polish War

1. THE GERMAN PLAN OF OPERATIONS

THE first part of the OKW directive 'for the Uniform Preparation of the Armed Forces for War for 1939-40' of April and May 1939 dealt with 'securing the frontiers of the Reich and protection against surprise air attack'. As between 'frontier security east' and 'frontier security west', greater importance was now attached to the latter. By means of strategic defence in the west the Wehrmacht was hoping to keep its rear covered for a war with Poland.

Completion of plans for an attack on Poland was ordered in part II, the central feature, of the OKW's directive. Preparations for the enterprise, covered by the code-name 'Case White', were to be completed by 1 September. To Hitler the employment of military means for the overthrow of Germany's eastern neighbour was the next phase in the realization of his programme of expansion. A more modest solution, the surprise entry of German forces into Danzig and West Prussia alone, was no longer regarded by Hitler as a possibility after the adverse international reaction produced by the dismemberment of Czechoslovakia. In consequence, parts III and IV of the directive, the 'Seizure of Danzig' independently of 'Case White' and the 'Regulation of Authority of Command in East Prussia in the Event of Warlike Developments' (i.e. in the event of having to defend it), were no more than relics of earlier instructions.[1] Their purpose now consisted purely in allowing for all eventualities and, moreover, in maintaining the pretence that a peaceful solution of the 'Polish question' was still possible. The final two parts of the OKW order, on the other hand, were again tailored to the event of a conflict. They regulated the rearward delimitation of the theatre of operations in the east and west of Germany and contained instructions on the conduct of economic warfare.

The directive for 'Case White' was essentially confined to an exposition of probable or possible political situations at the time of a German attack and of the consequences arising for mobilization and deployment. The 'Instructions to Wehrmacht Services' were still couched in general terms, offering little guidance for the further strategic planning of the individual High Commands.[2] In the case of the army this was evidently done deliberately by the chief of the Wehrmachtführungsamt (the armed

---

[1] Der Oberbefehlshaber des Heeres, 1. Abt. (I) GenStdH No. 3634/38 g.Kdos. (3. Ausf.), 8 Dec. 1938 = 'Weisung für das Oberkommando der 3. Armee im Kriegsfall', BA-MA PG 33276; in connection with the deployment instructions for 'Operation West' and 'Operation East'. The latter were dated 18 Jan. 1939, effective from 1 Mar. 1939, and represented purely defensive measures. A useful survey of events leading up to German operational planning against Poland is to be found in Berberich, 'Militärische Planungen', 3 ff., 62 ff.

[2] On the OKW instruction for 'Case White' dated Apr. and May 1939 cf. III.1 n. 1.

forces operations office) in agreement with OKH (the Army High Command), in order to allow the principal branch of the Wehrmacht and the army commander-in-chief the greatest possible freedom of action.[3] Much the same applied to the navy and the air force. The formulation of their tasks was modelled on those for the army.

The army operations branch was initially instructed only to establish a link between Pomerania and East Prussia as quickly as possible; permission was also given to include Slovak territory in the south for deployment. OKH did not have much time to prepare detailed plans. Although it could proceed from existing mobilization and operation orders, it was nevertheless compelled to improvise to some extent in planning a large-scale offensive. On 26 or 27 April Brauchitsch, the commander-in-chief, submitted his first plans to Hitler. These having been approved in principle, and—unlike those for subsequent campaigns—without any substantial changes being requested, the two staffs earmarked as army group headquarters received on 1 May the 'Draft Deployment Directive for Case White' for comment.[4]

The 'Rundstedt working staff', earmarked for the role of 'Army Group Command South', and the 'Army Group Command 1', earmarked for that of 'Army Group North', submitted their drafts on 20 and 27 May respectively.[5] Following further discussions, mainly concerning Army Group North, the definitive operations order of OKH was finished on 15 June.[6] The army command was anxious to eliminate Poland as quickly as possible, to enable the bulk of the German formations to be switched to the west; in spite of Hitler's optimistic assurances they feared an intervention by the Western powers and hence a war on two fronts. The unfinished Westwall and the forces initially available for deployment in the west seemed scarcely able to stand up to an Allied attack for long.

There were no fundamental differences of opinion within the military leadership concerning the objectives of the operation against Poland. OKH intended to smash the Polish formations even before they were fully mobilized and before they could assemble west of the Vistula–Narew line. To this end it was intended to overrun the Polish frontier positions with infantry forces held in readiness near the frontier and, more particularly, with motorized units brought up at speed. By moving the bulk of the German forces forward the initial superiority over the deploying Polish army was to be maintained. The overriding purpose was: 'By swift action and ruthless attack to maintain an advantage over the opponent.'

---

[3] Warlimont, *Headquarters*, 19–20.

[4] Arbeitsstab Rundstedt Ia No. 1/39 g.Kdos., 20 May 39 = draft deployment instruction 'White', BA-MA RH 19 I/9. This directive makes it possible to reconstruct almost entirely the (so far undiscovered) OKH instruction of 1 May. Cf. also Kennedy, *German Campaign*, 59.

[5] Cf. previous n.; also Heeresgruppenkommando i/Ia No. 40/39 g.Kdos. Chefs. (3. Ausf.) = deployment directive for 'Case White', 27 May 1939, BA-MA II H 821.

[6] Der ObdH (1. Abt./I) GenStdH No. 4200/39 g.Kdos. (Prüf.-Nr. 16), 15 June 1939, BA-MA RH 15/v. 159. The following account and Map III.II.1 are essentially based on this directive; the quotations are likewise taken from it. For the further course of strategic planning at Army Group North cf. Heeresgruppenkommando i/Ia No. 57/39 g.Kdos. Chefs. (5 Ausf.), 1 July 1939 = deployment instruction for Fourth Army in the event of 'Case White', BA-MA RH 19 II/8 (also contains all important information for Third Army). Admittedly, Fourth Army had already issued its own 'directives' for deployment and initial conduct of operations on 20 June (BA-MA P 218 g, k). Much the same is likely to have been the case with the other armies.

Since the development of the political situation had resulted in heightened readiness for defence on the part of the Polish army, ruling out the element of surprise, OKH now planned not to give the order for the opening of hostilities until adequate forces had been assembled. The organization and disposition of the Wehrmacht had to make the transition from surprise attack to full-scale offensive possible at any time. This was ensured by a complicated and painstakingly calculated timing of the mobilization and deployment of the German formations.

Generally speaking, OKH intended to aim the attack concentrically at the bulk of the Polish army, with Army Group North striking from Pomerania and East Prussia, and Army Group South from Silesia. Eliminating the Polish forces advancing from Galicia, Army Group South was to thrust with powerful units towards the Vistula on both sides of Warsaw, while Army Group North was to establish a link between Pomerania and East Prussia and simultaneously attack from East Prussia across the Narew in the direction of Warsaw.

Although the main effort was to have been in the south, most of the problems in fact arose in connection with the planning and execution of the initial moves in the north. This was because the army group there had to move off from two separate zones and had two tasks to accomplish simultaneously. Fourth Army, on the day of the attack ('Y Day') had to thrust across the frontier with formations held in readiness in Pomerania, reaching the opposite bank of the Vistula between Chełmno and Grudziądz, in order to continue the offensive across the Drwęca in a south-easterly direction. It was important for it to secure road and rail communications to East Prussia and not to allow itself to be diverted from the proper direction of the attack by scattered Polish forces in the 'Corridor'. In the arc between the Oder and Warta there were only weak forces available for the diversion and pinning down of the enemy.

Third Army was to assign some of its forces to help Fourth Army in the crossing of the Vistula and in its further advance. With the bulk of its forces it was to move off from the Neidenburg area across the frontier with the aim of smashing enemy forces on the near side of the Narew and subsequently thrusting towards Warsaw and the area east of the city. Along the rest of the East Prussian frontiers with Lithuania and Poland the Germans intended to confine themselves to safeguarding their own territory. At first there were no Third or Fourth Army formations available for Danzig. The city was to be secured by local units which, at the start of the war, were to come under the command of Army Group North. Elimination of Polish formations to be expected in the area around Gdynia had to be postponed until later.

The disposition of Army Group North had been preceded by differences of opinion between OKH and the commander-in-chief of the army group, Colonel-General von Bock, differences which had not been entirely ironed out even by the operations order of 15 June. On the whole, however, Bock had prevailed, with the support of Hitler, who at that time was not yet greatly interfering with OKH planning.[7]

---

[7] Heeresgruppenkommando i/Ia No. 40/39 g.Kdos. (3. Ausf.)=deployment instruction 'Case White', 27 May 1939, BA-MA II H 821. Diary notes on the Polish campaign May/June 1939–3 Oct. 1939 by Field Marshal von Bock, BA-MA III H 53/1; also 'Bemerkungen zu dem Manuskript "The German Campaign in Poland", here Antworten zum Questionnaire für General Halder v. 1. 4. 55 und Anmerkungen von Gen.d.Art. a.D. Warlimont v. 27. 1. 55', MGFA MS D-399.

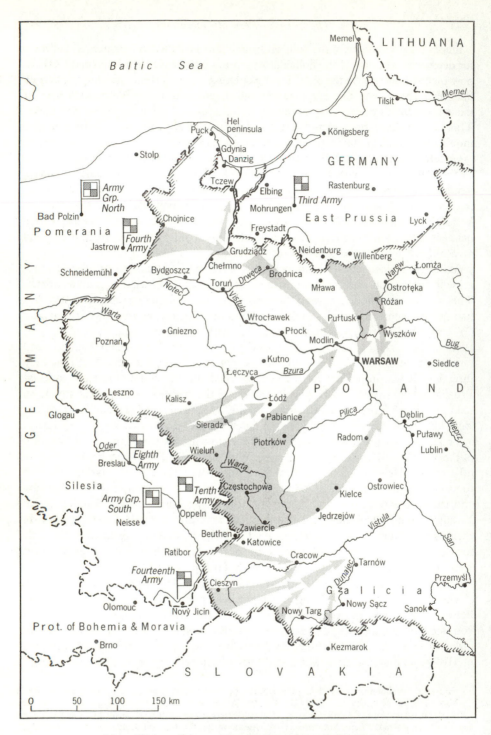

MAP III.II.1. German Plan of Operations against Poland

The issue had been whether the strength of the Army Group would permit the simultaneous establishment of a link between Pomerania and East Prussia across the Corridor and an attack from East Prussia southwards towards Warsaw. Both operations were of approximately equal urgency from the strategic point of view: the prompt link-up of the two armies was an indispensable condition of a successful pincer movement towards the Polish capital; in order not to over-extend Army Group South, which in any case would have to bear the main brunt, it was absolutely necessary for Army Group North to mount its southward offensive at an early stage.

In his first proposal to OKH Bock had come out in favour of pushing as far as the Grudziądz area with a reinforced army corps from Third Army and of keeping the Vistula crossings there open for the forces advancing from Pomerania. He consciously accepted the risk that this operation might prove to be 'beating the air' if the Corridor was not seriously defended and the Polish forces speedily withdrew across the Vistula. In that event Bock intended to switch the Third Army formations intended for the attack on Grudziądz immediately to its left wing and thus to lend greater weight to the attack of the other two corps in a southerly direction towards Różan and Pułtusk. He was well aware that, if the enemy offered serious resistance, the employment of these two corps would not bring about any decisive success. Hence, the real objective of this attack was initially seen as pinning down Polish formations and relieving the parts of Army Group North which were thrusting towards the Vistula, until such time as the capture of the Corridor permitted a switching of major forces to the left wing of the offensive.

This operational intention too had been the subject of lively discussion between OKH and Army Group Command North. The Army General Staff attached great importance to the bulk of Fourth Army continuing its offensive in the same direction after reaching the Vistula. Bock, on the other hand, took the view that an offensive with its main thrust from southern East Prussia across the Narew and then bypassing Warsaw in the east would be the most effective. OKH in the end yielded and amended its deployment orders accordingly. The army group was not to be restricted in its freedom of action. Army command had proceeded from the view that the encirclement of the opponent would succeed in the Warsaw region, whereas the army group wished to cover itself more strongly towards the east, hoping to surround east of the Polish capital those enemy forces which might escape encirclement there.

Lesser problems arose from the deployment instruction for Army Group South,[8] where the size of the forces to be committed by Tenth Army, the protection of the southern flank, as well as the question of how far toward the east the pincer movement was to reach out, still awaited clarification. The army group was eventually ordered, by advancing from Silesia and 'by concentrating strong forces (Tenth Army)' between Wieluń and Zawiercie, to attack in the direction of Warsaw and to seize the Vistula above and below the Polish capital. The bulk of the Polish army was to be encircled and destroyed while still west of the Vistula.

[8] As III.II n. 4; the documents there quoted cover virtually the whole process of strategic planning at what became Army Group South from 20 May to 28 June 1939, as well as amendments up to 15 July 1939; for supplements to it cf. BA-MA RH 19 I/159.

The main part in this operation was to be played by Tenth Army, half of which consisted of motorized corps. Taking full advantage of its mobility, and by concentrating its armoured formations, it was to make a rapid advance across the Kielce–Pabjanice line to reach the Vistula between the debouchments of the Wieprz and the Bzura. The final elimination of scattered enemy units could be left to the infantry divisions which were following up. Provident and meticulous organization of supplies served to keep the risk of the armoured thrusts being impeded as low as possible.

The relatively weak Eighth Army had the task of securing the northern flank of Tenth Army against Polish thrusts from the Poznań–Kutno area and was, initially, to advance towards Łódź as rapidly as possible.

Even greater importance attached to the protection of the southern flank, as hitherto unidentified Polish forces were discovered to be present there. At the request of the commander-in-chief of Army Group South, Colonel-General von Rundstedt, the Fourteenth Army, earmarked for flank cover, was therefore reinforced. The army group also had additional reserves assigned to it. It was planned to transfer several German divisions into northern Slovakia, to ensure that the enemy could also be enveloped from the south. The main body of Fourteenth Army was to capture Upper Silesia, push through to Cracow, and cross the Dunajec as soon as possible. The next task was to screen the Tenth Army's advance against Polish attacks from western Galicia.

Together with the Army High Command, those of the air force and the navy had likewise been requested to comment on the general outline of their tasks as set out in the OKW directive for 'Case White' and to report their views to OKW. The task of the Luftwaffe, apart from protecting Reich territory, was to eliminate the Polish air force as speedily as possible and to disrupt the enemy's mobilization, deployment, and supplies. Also envisaged was a raid by all available units on the Warsaw area in order to eliminate military installations and armament factories there. Göring had reserved authorization of this operation for himself. He similarly made the destruction of economic establishments, to whose possession Germany attached importance, subject to his authorization, as well as attacks on the centre of Warsaw. Puck and Hel, on the other hand, had been authorized targets from the start; in the case of Gdynia the departure of the ships of neutral countries was to be awaited.

The army attached great importance to massive air support, right from the crossing of the frontiers. In addition, the air force, with Air Fleet 1 in the area of Army Group North and Air Fleet 4 in that of Army Group South, was to prevent the enemy from establishing himself along the river-courses and preparing for defence.

Luftwaffe operations were based on 'Planning Study 1939', the 'Deployment and Operations Directives'.[9] Part II, dated 1 May 1939, in its 'Directives for Operations

---

[9] Der Reichsminister der Luftfahrt und Oberbefehlshaber der Luftwaffe, Generalstab 1. Abt. No. 5085/39 g.Kdos. Chef-Sache (19. Ausf.), 15 May 1939 = covering letter of revised edn. of 1 May: structure of 'Planning Study 1939' = pt. I: General Instructions, dated 7 Feb. 1939; pt. II: Directives for Operations against the East, dated 1 May 1939; pt. III: Directives for Operations against the West, dated 7 Feb. 1939, BA-MA II L 10; cf. also 'Die Luftwaffe im Polenfeldzug 1939', vols. i, iv, MGFA MS Lw 2/1, 2/4.

against the East', already contained the operations plan against Poland. It had only to be adapted to the development of the situation and to the results of the 'General Staff exercises' in which the co-operation between land and air forces had been 'played through'. There were a few problems concerning the method of dividing the available air force formations between the eastern and western fronts. For the sake of a rapid conclusion of the war in Poland it was eventually decided to assign two-thirds to the eastern front.

OKL (the Air Force High Command) expected the enemy air force to be employed mainly in conjunction with land forces, with individual squadrons and wings being subordinated to army formations. Sporadic attacks were also expected against the deployment of the German land forces and against towns and military installations near the frontier. Enemy fighter and anti-aircraft opposition above the army's front line was thought to be likely, as was also some, though incomplete, aerial protection of Warsaw, Gdynia, and the Upper Silesian industrial region. Other centres, however—and this applied to the central Polish industrial area and the oil region—could scarcely be adequately defended. Only in the Dęblin–Radom–Lublin area did OKL expect some slight anti-aircraft defences.

The navy had been ordered to eliminate the weak Polish naval forces, to bar the sea routes to enemy bases, and to strangle Polish merchant shipping. German shipping-routes in the Baltic were to be kept free from interference as far as possible.

OKM (the Navy High Command) informed OKW of its plans on 25 April 1939,[10] and on 16 May Raeder, the commander-in-chief, issued his first operations order for 'Case White'.[11] On its basis the commander-in-chief of Naval Group East, responsible for the Baltic, was to carry out all further planning.[12] On 2 June OKM in addition reissued the so-called 'Operations Directives for the Navy' of earlier years, which set out the 'tasks to be expected in view of the present situation'.[13] In this document the Soviet Union was still envisaged as the principal adversary in a war in the east.

On 26 June Naval Group Command East issued 'Directive No. 1 for Case White'. It contained only a few changes compared with the OKM order of 16 May, chiefly to ensure better co-ordination with the other two services. In the foreground of its considerations was the operation against the Polish naval base of Gdynia.

[10] Der Oberbefehlshaber der Kriegsmarine B. No. 1/Skl Ia 45/39 g.Kdos. Chefs. (Vfg.), 25 Apr. 1939, BA-MA III M 155/1; cf. also Salewski, *Seekriegsleitung*, i. 80 ff., 92.

[11] Der Oberbefehlshaber der Kriegsmarine B. No. 1 Skl. Ia Op 48/39 g.Kdos. Chefs. (Vfg.), 16 May 1939, BA-MA III M 155/1.

[12] Supplementary orders: OKM AI op 55/39 g.Kdos. Chefs. (Vfg.), 23 May 1939 (with reference to discussion on 12 May), BA-MA III M 155/1; OKM AI op 53/39 g.Kdos. Chefs. (Vfg.), 19 May 1939, and 56/39, 25 May 1939, BA-MA III M 155/2; B. No. AI op 57/39 g.Kdos. Chefs. (Vfg.), 25 May 1939, BA-MA III M 155/2; cf. also BA-MA III M 155/1–5, *passim*; Salewski, *Seekriegsleitung*, i. 92 ff.

[13] Kampfanweisungen für die Kriegsmarine (Ausgabe Mai 1939), BA-MA II M 40, i–iii; cf. also Salewski, *Seekriegsleitung*, i. 76 ff. He is mistaken (p. 76) in dating the latest rules of engagement from 20 Apr. 1938. Although a new edn. had been completed by that date, this was not issued, according to a prefixed decision (AI op 222/38) of 22 June (?), because the instructions had meanwhile been overtaken by the political situation (BA-MA PG 33306 B). This is corroborated by the new rules of engagement of 1939, which quote only the 1936 edn. and supplements.

General-Admiral Albrecht, the commander-in-chief of the naval group, did not believe a direct attack with surface units to be possible in view of the strong shore defences. All that was possible in his view was a blockade of the Gulf of Danzig. The Polish navy was to be destroyed during its expected break-out into the open Baltic.[14]

The final operations plan of Naval Group Command East, dated 15 August, based as it was on the controversial division of naval forces between the eastern and western theatres of war, as decided by the naval war staff,[15] summed up its latest thinking as follows: while the Luftwaffe was ready to conduct air raids also on Gdynia from the very first day, the navy nevertheless regarded the intended treatment of neutral ships as highly unsatisfactory. Admittedly, mines without delayed detonators were to be laid off Gdynia on the day of the offensive, and neutral ships in the harbour would not be given time to leave port. An attack on the merchant port of Gdynia, however, was prohibited and an attack on the naval base was permitted only in the event that no neutral warships were lying at anchor there. Neither closure of the sea area around Hel nor a warning to neutral ships lying there was to be effected, out of consideration for the army, until the start of the war.[16] A special group, consisting of a cruiser, a destroyer, and the torpedo-training flotilla, was to patrol the sea area south of the sound. The warship *Schleswig-Holstein* was earmarked for Danzig.

2. MOBILIZATION AND DEPLOYMENT OF THE WEHRMACHT

In considering German mobilization and deployment measures in 1939[17] a fundamental distinction must be made between general measures—serving the transformation of the Wehrmacht, the economy, and the administration from a peacetime to a war footing—and those which were tailored to specific offensive plans. Any directives for the raising of wartime armed forces and all other arrangements to be made in the event of war were essentially covered in the mobilization plans of the three services as well as in the mobilization manual issued by the High

---

[14] Marine-Gruppenkommando Ost B. g.Kdos. 160/39 Chefs. (1. Ausf.), 26 June 1939, BA-MA III M 155/4; cf. also Marine-Gruppenkommando Ost B, No. g.Kdos. 154 Chefs., 13 June 1939, and Der Oberbefehlshaber der Kriegsmarine B. No. A I Op 66/39 g.Kdos. Chefs. (Vfg.), 16 June 1939, both in BA-MA III M 155/3, and other correspondence filed there, esp. on the discussion on the booms to be laid.

[15] Cf. the memorandum by the C.-in-C. of the fleet, Adm. Boehm (Flottenkommando B, No. 107 g.Kdos. (Vfg.), 21 Aug. 39, BA-MA III M 155.3), who called for a greater concentration of effort in the west, esp. in view of British intervention (which he considered probable) in the German–Polish conflict: Salewski, *Seekriegsleitung*, i. 82, 92 ff.

[16] Marine-Gruppenkommando Ost, g.Kdos. B. No. 230/39 and 250/39 Chefs. AI, 15 and 21 Aug. 1939: operations order No. 1 for the 'Königsberg' group in the event of 'Case White' (Prüf.-Nr. 1) and for the warship *Schleswig-Holstein* (Prüf.-Nr. 2), BA-MA III M 155/4; Der Reichsminister der Luftfahrt und Oberbefehlshaber der Luftwaffe/GenStb 1. Abt. No. 5234/39 g.Kdos. (op 1) Chef-Sache, 17 Aug. 1939, BA-MA III M 155/2; Salewski, *Seekriegsleitung*, i. 93 ff.

[17] Mobilmachungsbuch für die Zivilverwaltungen, new edn. 1939, 18 Feb. 1939, BA-MA H 1/332; Reichsverteidigungsgesetz of 21 May 1935 (*IMT* xxx. 59 ff.) and 4 Sept. 1938 (*IMT* xxix. 319 ff.); quotations in the text derive from these documents. Partial accounts of German mobilization and deployment preparations, which can only be referred to briefly here, in Mueller-Hillebrand, *Heer*, i. 47 ff.; Rohde, *Wehrmachttransportwesen* 71 ff.; Elble, 'Mobilmachung', 365 ff.

Command of the Armed Forces for the civilian authorities. They contained, in great detail, full instructions for the necessary organizational changes, for reinforcements of personnel and material, as well as all other measures—especially in the economy—which might be introduced either separately or as a package.

Mobilization was potentially preceded by a 'state of tension'. This, of course, did not have to be proclaimed but merely represented 'the technical term for a period of especial international tension, during which preparatory measures . . . might be ordered'. These were to ensure that, 'while avoiding as far as possible any political strain or provocation, the foundations were laid for a reliable progress of mobilization proper and that individual mobilization measures were anticipated'. The 'period of tension' therefore served to facilitate and accelerate the subsequent mobilization. In this way a lead could be gained over the potential enemy. Concealment, or at least camouflage, of all these measures was made the easier as peacetime legislation was sufficient for their implementation.

Under the second 'Reich defence law' of 1938 the Führer was entitled to declare a 'state of war' or a 'state of defence'. With the declaration of a state of war the wartime laws and war ordinances automatically came into force with appropriate legal consequences. As the political and military leaders of the Third Reich did not, for 'political reasons (the question of war-guilt etc.)', intend to combine aggression with a simultaneous proclamation of a state of war, a number of ordinances anticipated those legislative regulations which would be indispensable in the event of war. This had the advantage that 'war' within the meaning of Reich law did not yet exist. In this way the government, while mobilizing, avoided some of the legal consequences provided for in war legislation.

Declaration of a state of defence normally preceded the proclamation of a state of war. If this was not the case, then the regulations of the state of defence automatically entered into effect with the beginning of the state of war. These provided, in essence, that executive power within a zone of operations was transferred to the army commander-in-chief and, within certain limits, to the commanders-in-chief of the armies concerned.

Mobilization itself could take place also without official announcement ('Case X'). This provision, 'using the greatest possible measure of concealment of its purpose, served the systematic mobilization of the Wehrmacht, as well as, if necessary, the camouflaged mobilization of state, economy, and nation'. There existed also the possibility of proclaiming 'Case X' for just the Wehrmacht, or for one of the services; this could be done on the basis of peacetime regulations such as the Wehrleistungsgesetz (military service law) or the Notstandsverordnung (state-of-emergency decree), without the need for an earlier 'period of tension' or any other 'preliminary measures'.

The final stage was 'General Mobilization with Public Proclamation (Case Mob.)'. This implied the comprehensive systematic switch-over of the entire country to a state of war, likewise initially on the basis of peacetime legislation.

The highly complicated mobilization machinery of the Wehrmacht was designed primarily to apply all the necessary laws and decrees while avoiding any undesirable escalation, especially as concealment of aggressive intentions ruled out the declaration of a state of war or a state of defence in any case. This made it possible to step up political and military pressure to the utmost and, in the event of a peaceful settlement, to call off military preparations without any great damage or loss of face. On the other hand it was possible, if the method was applied repeatedly and the adversary's watchfulness was flagging, to launch an attack with a 'flying start', as in fact happened in the case of Poland.

In addition to the possibilities arising from graduated mobilization, measures were taken to ensure rapid readiness for action. These included, in particular, the establishment of 'accelerated marching-out capability'. The troops earmarked for this achieved their 'readiness to move' (army and navy) or their 'readiness for action' (air force) within twelve hours by drawing on instantly available replacements of personnel and material. Those sections which were still lacking, mainly rear services, were mobilized according to plan and brought up in due course.

On an overall view the German mobilization system prior to the Second World War enabled the National Socialist leadership to keep its freedom of decision-making during a period of political tension. At the same time it was able, in consequence, to secure an important lead in mobilization and deployment. These two advantages, however, were offset by the drawback that not all the necessary legislative regulations had as yet come into force, e.g. (in September 1939) in the economic sphere. Hitler had ordered mobilization without public announcement ('Case X') for the 'bulk of the Wehrmacht' with effect from 26 August. Orders went out at the same time that 'Case X' was not to be extended to the whole civilian area. The civilian authorities were merely to make the necessary provisions for safeguarding the mobilization of the Wehrmacht and for the maintenance of their own capacity to function, unless these had already come into effect in the form of preliminary measures. All actions and demands were to be based on peacetime legislation, as neither a state of defence nor a state of war had been proclaimed within the meaning of the Reich defence law of 4 September 1938.[18]

It was within the framework of this mobilization that the German deployment took place in the east and the west. The army alone was enlarged for this purpose by just short of three million men, 400,000 horses, and 200,000 vehicles. In addition there were extensive replacements of weapons, ammunition, and other material.[19] For the concealment of Germany's aggressive intentions against Poland two distinct kinds of measures were adopted; the first of these could unroll independently of the second, though both of them were an indispensable prerequisite of complete deployment.[20] The first phase comprised numerous manœuvres and exercises, due to be held mainly in the east from the end of June onwards and consisting of three parts:

1. 'Entrenchment moves of the first and second instalment.' These consisted essentially of the transfer of nine infantry divisions in peacetime formation to the eastern frontier districts between 26 June and 4 August. There, according to the official version, the operational consolidation of existing fortifications was to be continued

---

[18] *DGFP* D vii, No. 293.
[19] Mueller-Hillebrand, *Heer*, i. 55–6.
[20] On the following see mainly Rohde, *Wehrmachttransportwesen*, 74 ff., 90–1.

'within the framework of the measures ordered by the Führer for the security of the eastern frontier'. Moreover, deceptive measures and exercises were intended in rail transport and overland marching. These troops returned to their peacetime stations.

2. Manœuvres by formations in order of battle by way of camouflaging the start of deployment. These exercises were carried out only in part because the participating formations went over directly to the attack at the beginning of the war. The most important part of this second wave of deployment was the 'entrenchment move of the third instalment', due to have been executed between 3 and 14 August. It comprised thirteen divisions and, for the first time, also envisaged the transportation of units to East Prussia. The pretext used, among others, was a manœuvre of the I (East Prussian) Army Corps as well as the annual 'Tannenberg celebration'. This, in particular, enabled many 'former veterans' to be brought up more or less unnoticed, especially as 1939 was the twenty-fifth anniversary of the great battle of the First World War.

3. Manœuvres designed predominantly to serve as camouflage for organizational and material preparations and cancelled when the deployment took place in earnest. In this context mention should be made of the 'Reich Party Rally of Peace', which, though cancelled on 15 August, made it possible for rolling-stock to be unobtrusively assembled by the Reich railways.

The second phase, the actual deployment against Poland, was composed of a so-called 'A' movement and a 'Y' movement. The Wehrmacht leaders were well aware that, with an increase in troop transports, effective camouflage would become increasingly difficult. The 'A' movement began on 19 August. It comprised all those troops which had to be transported, or had to be on the march, at least six days before 'Y Day', the first day of the attack. These movements were complete by 23 August. The formations intended for the first action were now in two 'zones of readiness', staggered towards the rear and within one to two days' march of the Polish frontier. Thus, an excessive and hence conspicuous concentration was avoided, the more so as the motorized forces were located even further to the rear.

The subsequent 'Y' movement consisted of transports and marches to be executed following the fixing of 'Y Day'. It began on the evening of 24 August and continued into September. It involved formations and units which had been moved forward towards the frontier either from their regular stations or from assembly areas further to the rear. By far the greatest part was provided by all those troops whose mobilization proceeded according to plan.

On the evening of 25 August the troops moved off from their assembly areas towards the Polish frontier. Hitler's 'halt order', as is well known, affected mainly operational control and communications. They achieved the incredible by halting the offensive formations already on the move. The deployment movement proper continued according to plan, as did mobilization. Altogether more than 5,000 trains were used for troop transports within the framework of 'Case White' (see Diagram III.II.1).

The nature and scope of German mobilization and deployment planning prior to the Second World War was thus all-embracing, extending to every conceivable area.

The trigger-period could thus be kept very short: depending on the intensity of other concomitant measures, an offensive—at least a limited one—was possible

ARMY	Army Group North Army Group reserves: 73rd Inf. Div. 206th Inf. Div. 208th Inf. Div. 10th Armd. Div.	Third Army Army reserves: 217th Inf. Div.	I Army Corps	11th Inf. Div., 61st Inf. Div., Armoured Formation Kempf
			XXI Army Corps	21st Inf. Div., 228th Inf. Div., Frontier Rgt. 11
			Special operational staff (Wodrig)	1st Inf. Div., 12th Inf. Div., Frontier Rgt. 31
			Group Brand	Fortification Section Lötzen, Brigade Goldap, Fortification Section Königsberg, Frontier Rgt. 41
			Frontier Sector Detachment 15	Frontier Rgt. 21
			Mixed formation Danzig	
			Frontier Rgt. 1	
			Group Col. Medem	
		Fourth Army Army reserves: 23rd Inf. Div. 218th Inf. Div.	II Army Corps	3rd Inf. Div., 32nd Inf. Div.
			III Army Corps	50th Inf. Div., Brigade Netze
			XIX Army Corps	2nd Inf. Div. (mot.), 20th Inf. Div. (mot.), 3rd Armd. Div.
			Frontier Sector Detachment 1	207th Inf. Div.
			Frontier Sector Detachment 2	
			Frontier Sector Detachment 12	
	Army Group South Army Group reserves: VII Army Corps {27th Inf. Div., 68th Inf. Div.} 62nd Inf. Div. 213th Inf. Div. 221st Inf. Div.	Eighth Army Army reserves: 30th Inf. Div.	X Army Corps	24th Inf. Div.
			XIII Army Corps	17th Inf. Div., 10th Inf. Div., SS-Leibstandarte 'Adolf Hitler'
			Frontier Sector Detachment 13	
			Frontier Sector Detachment 14	
		Tenth Army Army reserves: 1st Mobile Div. (part mot.)	IV Army Corps	4th Inf. Div., 46th Inf. Div.
			XI Army Corps	18th Inf. Div., 19th Inf. Div.
			XIV Army Corps	13th Inf. Div. (mot.), 29th Inf. Div. (mot.)
			XV Army Corps	2nd Mobile Div. (part mot.), 3rd Mobile Div. (part mot.)
			XVI Army Corps	14th Inf. Div., 31st Inf. Div., 1st Armd. Div., 4th Armd Div.
		Fourteenth Army Army reserves: 239th Inf. Div.	VIII Army Corps	8th Inf. Div., 28th Inf. Div., 5th Armd. Div., SS-Stand. 'Germania' Frontier Sector Detachment 3
			XVII Army Corps	7th Inf. Div., 44th Inf. Div., 45th Inf. Div.
			XVIII Army Corps	3rd Mountain Div., 4th Mobile Div. (part mot.), 2nd Armd. Div.
			Slovak Army	1st Slovak Div., 2nd Slovak Div., 3rd Slovak Div., mobile detachment
AIR FORCE	Air Fleet 1	Luftwaffen-Kommando East Prussia	Luftwaffe Training Div.	Training Geschwader 1, Bomber Geschwader 2
			directly subordinate: Bomber Geschwader 3, I/Stuka Geschwader 1, I/Fighter Geschwader 1	
		1st Air Division		Bomber Geschwader 1, Bomber Geschwader 26, Bomber Geschwader 27, II+III/Stuka Geschwader 2, IV/Training Geschwader 1, I/(Fighter) LG 2, I+II/Pursuit Geschwader 1
	Air Fleet 4	2nd Air Division		Bomber Geschwader 4, Bomber Geschwader 76, Bomber Geschwader 77, I/Pursuit Geschwader 76
		Air Commander, special duty		Stuka Geschwader 77, Stuka Training Geschwader 2, I/Pursuit Geschwader 2
NAVY	Naval Group Command East	Directly subordinate: 1st Destroyer Division, TS Flotilla, battleship *Schleswig-Holstein*		
		Naval Commander Baltic		Commander of Torpedo-Boats, 3rd Destroyer Division, 6th Destroyer Division, 1st MTB Flotilla, Escort Flotilla, Commander of Minesweepers East, 1st Mine-Locating Flotilla, Boom Defence Command (formation), 3rd Sweeper Flotilla
		Leader of U-Boats		U14, U18, U22, U56, U57, U5, U6, U7
		Leader of Naval Aviation East		Küstenfliegergruppe 306, 506, 706, Carrier Wing II/86

DIAGRAM III.II.I. Order of battle in the east, 1 September 1939

Sources: Organization of the army: BA-MA RH 60/v. 1, H 1/533b, and H 10-3/48; air force combat formations: MGFA MS Lw 2/4; navy: BA-MA RM D 4 601/11 = MDV No. 601/11: Die deutsche Kriegsmarine im Feldzug gegen Polen, Sept. 1939.

approximately from the second half of the second day after receipt of an appropriate order. Knowledge of the intention could remain restricted to a relatively small circle of persons directly concerned.

3. THE POLISH PLAN OF OPERATIONS AND DEPLOYMENT[21]

Plans for simultaneous deployment and operations against both an eastern and a western adversary never existed in Poland, as waging a war on two fronts was considered impossible. When the German annexation of Austria in March 1938 prompted the Polish General Staff to intensify its planning against Germany—which had been resumed a few years earlier—preparations for the event of war were now concentrated almost exclusively on the western enemy.

However, planning against Germany enjoyed little continuity during the ensuing period, as the Polish General Staff repeatedly found itself faced with new strategic situations as a result of German territorial expansion. Detailed work on 'Operations Plan West', ordered by Rydz-Śmigły, the Polish inspector-general, in February 1939, was fairly well advanced when the break-up of Czechoslovakia once more changed the terms of the problem and simultaneously called for accelerated preparations. Many subsequent improvisations can only be understood against this background. For that reason also the Polish plan of operations was never completely set down in writing. Only at the top level did planning during the next few months—owing to new German measures and to Polish requirements of secrecy—progress with any measure of continuity. This planning was intended, at least, to update the principal directives on the assembly, first deployment, distribution of forces, and the tasks of the several armies as a basis for the work of subordinate commands. Shortage of time, however, resulted in inadequate harmonization with the commanders in the field. Commanders-in-chief of armies frequently found themselves compelled to change their instructions, either wholly or in part, which led to considerable complications and unfavourable effects on morale. Only the first phase of the deployment plan was in fact completed; concerning the ensuing phase, all that existed at the onset of the war were a few top-level observations.

In its assessment of the German attacking formations the Polish plan of operations proceeded from more or less correct evaluations. Likewise, there were no illusions about the danger of a German surprise operation (however limited) before Polish deployment, or even full mobilization, was completed. There was scarcely any doubt either about the strategic feasibility or intentions of a full-scale German offensive; only the depth of the outflanking movements, which proved fatal to the Polish army, could not be foreseen. This was true in particular of the south, where—until Slovakia was included in the German sphere of interest—the weakness of her forces compelled Poland to rely, more or less, on the protection of the mountain ranges there and to hope that the Germans, if only because of transport difficulties, would not extend

---

[21] Unless otherwise stated, for the whole section see *PSZ* i/1. 109 ff., 114–15, 257 ff.; Roos, 'Militär-politische Lage', 189 ff. (applies also to Map III.II.2). A few further details in Berberich, 'Militärische Planungen', 57 ff., 76.

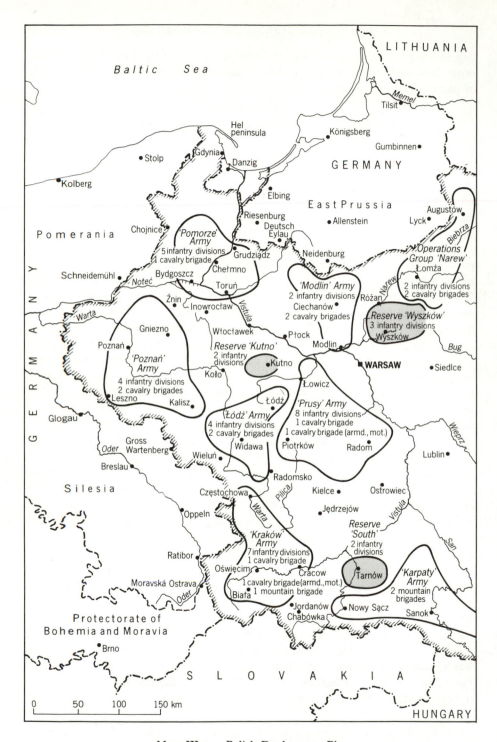

MAP III.II.2. Polish Deployment Plan

their envelopment too far towards the east. In the north, on the other hand, the German intentions were forecast with great accuracy: it was assumed that an excessively powerful and deep outflanking thrust from East Prussia need not be feared at the outset.

As the region west of the Vistula was their main mobilization and war-economy base, the Poles had to accept engagement as close to their frontier as possible. Pulling their main line of defence back behind the Vistula would have drastically reduced the depth of their own hinterland and would therefore have required close political and military reliance on the Soviet Union; this option had to be eliminated from the start in view of poor Polish–Soviet relations. The Poles were hardly able to comply with the strategic precept of never locating important mobilization or economic centres in the most threatened parts of the country. Even a mitigation of this unfavourable state of affairs, for instance by the establishment of supply-bases in the area east of the Vistula, was, for reasons of time, only beginning to be implemented by the summer of 1939.

In view of the superiority of the Wehrmacht and the fact that its own forces were inevitably exposed to the German outflanking thrusts, Poland could do no more than yield as little of its territory as possible until the confidently expected British and French offensive in the west, in order to gain time, to conserve forces, and inflict maximum losses on the enemy. A German surprise attack was on the cards, and the Polish army was, with its alert and mobilization system, well designed to meet just such an attack, being able to deploy a large proportion of its fighting forces, as well as its entire air force and anti-aircraft defences, while still in the 'period of tension'; in this way the threatened areas were to be made safe and strengthened at an early date, so as to ensure that the first German attack was contained and the mobilization and full deployment of the remaining forces covered.

The inspector-general therefore intended to employ the armies of the 'first echelon'—which consisted almost entirely of so-called 'stand-by units'—with their main effort in the area south of Bydgoszcz as well as west of Łódź and in the Upper Silesian industrial area, in order to repulse with every means possible the enemy forces expected to thrust forward from central Silesia towards Warsaw. Nevertheless, relatively strong flanks—especially in the north—based on the Vistula, the Narew, and the Biebrza, and in the south on the Carpathians, would have to protect the main forces against local surprises.

The course of the defensive battle was visualized on the Polish side as follows:

1. In the forefield of the main positions a 'delaying action' was to slow down the German advance, to allow for the main defences to be better prepared and to gain time for the completion of full mobilization. That action was to be based essentially on existing frontier fortifications—to be further strengthened—and on others to be newly constructed.

2. The principal defence was envisaged along the following line: Augustów forest—Biebrza—Narew—Vistula with bridgeheads at Modlin and Toruń—Bydgoszcz—the Żnin lakes—the Gopło lakes—the Gopło-Warta canal—the Warta

with a bridgehead at Koło—Widawa—Częstochowa—the Silesian fortifications—Oświęcim—Bielsko-Biała—Żywiec—Jordanów—Chabówka—Nowy Sącz.

3. The reserves were to block the German formations advancing from Silesia towards Warsaw and go over to the counter-attack.

As for the distribution of forces, the Polish command decided to commit all formations, with the exception of insignificant units protecting the less threatened frontiers, against Germany—i.e. initially five armies and an independent group as the first echelon in the front line, as well as one army and two lesser groups as a second echelon in reserve. The main concentration in the south was with the 'Kraków' Army and the 'Łódź' Army, which were to oppose the expected main body of the attacking Germans. It depended on them whether the front line could be held or whether a retreat towards the south-east would be necessary so that, after regrouping, the defence could be resumed. The employment of the reserve army and its counter-attacks, planned in a south-westerly direction towards Radom-Piotrków, would depend on the resistance offered by the front-line armies. Provided it was possible systematically to absorb any retreating troops in a new front, there would still be forces available to slow down the main German thrust, prevent envelopment from the south, and provide an opportunity for the rest of the Polish units to withdraw in good order to new positions.

Adjoining these southern groups were two armies well advanced towards the west and the north—'Poznań' and 'Pomorze'. Rear cover for them was to be provided by a group 'Kutno'. The exposed position of these formations would have particularly adverse consequences if a rapid German penetration in the direction of Łódź and Warsaw succeeded in cutting them off from the main body. In spite of this risk there was scarcely any other solution available in view of mobilization in this region, the richest in reservists, and of the need to prevent the seizure of these territories, which until 1919 had belonged to Germany.

To its north the 'Pomorze' Army was to be flanked by the 'Modlin' Army, mainly in order to block the way to Warsaw against the German forces attacking from East Prussia. This army was supported on its eastern flank by the independent operational group 'Narew', which was to hold a line along the Biebrza and the Narew, and by the reserve group 'Wyszków', intended either for a counter-offensive from the Narew elbow against the wing of the Germans attacking in the Ciechanów-Modlin direction or as support for the 'Narew' group.

The overall objective of the Polish operations was thus to hang on for as long as possible to the regions necessary for military operations, in the expectation that a Franco-British offensive in the west would bring timely relief to the Polish forces. The first attack had to be endured to an extent that made it possible to continue fighting, especially as supplies of material from the west were shortly expected via Romania.

Military preparations were therefore paralleled by Polish efforts to conclude a new military convention with France; this was accomplished on 19 May. In it the French command undertook to open an offensive against Germany 'with the bulk of its forces' not later than on the fifteenth day following French mobilization. Subsequently a fierce controversy arose between representatives of the two countries about the binding nature of that promise. Warsaw at any rate relied on such Allied support.[22]

Further negotiations with Paris and London on immediate financial, material, and military assistance, however, produced only slight results, as the two Allies, owing to shortages at home and to Poland's unfavourable strategic and geographical situation, to a great extent avoided firm commitments.

Polish mobilization had started on 23 March. Altogether five formations, predominantly in the western districts, were brought up to war strength, and two divisions as well as a cavalry brigade were transferred from the interior of the country to the western frontier. These measures represented a reply to increasingly threatening German demands; at the same time they served the purpose of putting the highly complicated Polish mobilization and deployment system—in many respects similar to the German—to a first test. It was also important to set in motion the measures necessitated by the new plan of operations, e.g. in the field of transport and communications, anti-aircraft defence, supplies, and fortifications. In view of rapidly deteriorating German–Polish relations these measures were taken very hurriedly; they remained incomplete and were not always sufficiently thought through. Additional problems arose from the changes to which the plan of operations itself was subject up to the last moment.

The main difficulty lay in protecting the Polish flanks. A threat to the Carpathian frontier was taking ever clearer shape, and the situation in Danzig likewise called for a re-examination of existing plans. Thus, the left wing in the south was extended all the way to the Hungarian frontier by the creation of a new 'Karpaty' (Carpathians) Army. As a result the Polish main front was extended by nearly 300 km. The assembly area of the reserve army was shifted to the south to relieve the 'Łódź' Army and, if necessary, also the 'Kraków' Army. The latter was reinforced by the 10th Cavalry Brigade, which, being the only armoured and motorized formation of its size, had originally been earmarked for the reserve army. Moreover, the Polish command created an additional reserve of two infantry divisions in the Tarnów area. In the north, the situation in Danzig led to the establishment of an intervention corps, which was to prevent the seizure of the Free City by a *coup de main* prior to the outbreak of war. Two of its three divisions were taken from the 'Pomorze' Army and the 'Prusy' (Prussia) Army, as the reserve army was subsequently named. It was intended to pull this corps back from the Corridor at the outbreak of war and to dissolve it again. For the time being, however, it meant a further lengthening of the front and a further frittering away of Polish strength.

Difficulties in Poland's mobilization arose also from political and economic causes. In spite of the now patent German war preparations the Western powers were urging their Polish allies to show restraint in their countermeasures. In their opinion any

---

[22] Roos, *History*, 162 ff.; id., 'Militärpolitische Lage', 198–9, with listing of further sources on the Polish-French controversy on this issue.

attempt to forestall a German deployment might serve Hitler as a welcome pretext for accusing Poland of aggressive intentions. Such an accusation might gain wide credence and lead to Poland's isolation. Economic factors, moreover, were playing a major part: even partial mobilization in March had been a heavy burden on the national budget. With the possibility of the international crisis persisting for several months, and with only little support to be expected from her allies, an intensified mobilization could bring Poland's economy to the verge of collapse. Such makeshift solutions as a heightened state of alert in the frontier districts, the reinforcement of frontier guards, the temporary call-up of reservists and territorial volunteers for exercises, as well as partial mobilization, diminished neither the political risks nor the economic burdens. Also, the call-up at any one time of only part of the reservists was leading to considerable unrest among those concerned, especially since their dependants were as a rule inadequately taken care of. There were numerous desertions and even some instances of collective disobedience. In the frontier regions, especially in Upper Silesia, this mood of dissatisfaction was further fanned by Germany. More and more deserters, predominantly ethnic Germans, crossed the frontier in uniform and with their weapons.

From the beginning of August the Polish government was increasingly convinced that the German government were not just concerned with the training of troops, the construction of fortifications in the frontier districts, or the unleashing of a war of nerves, but that they were getting ready for deployment, presumably to be followed by an early attack. From mid-August onward, therefore, Polish mobilization was accelerated. When Ribbentrop's trip to Moscow became known on 22 August Warsaw decided on further measures, including an immediate 'alarm mobilization', initially in six corps areas bordering on Germany. These measures, which became effective on 23 August, were almost tantamount to general mobilization in Pomerelia (the 'Corridor'), Wielkopolska (Great Poland), and Upper Silesia. They concerned all as yet unmobilized major formations in those areas—twenty-eight in number— as well as the air force throughout Poland, the anti-aircraft defences, all senior staffs, and the principal signal units. The railways were, for the time being, still exempt, even though a great many transports had to be handled by then. The mobilized units still remained in or near their garrisons. Only in exceptional cases were they already being moved to their final positions. On 27 August the mobilization of the remaining 'stand-by units' was ordered. This concerned mainly nine major formations in two corps areas as well as railway transport units. On 28 August followed measures for 'frontier clearance west' and for the evacuation of reservists.

In view of further frontier incidents the inspector-general issued an order urging the Polish troops not to allow themselves to be provoked. Only unambiguous frontier crossings were to be repulsed. On the same day the commander-in-chief of the 'Pomorze' Army, General Bortnowski, proposed to carry out a limited offensive in the direction of Riesenburg–Deutsch Eylau for the purpose of establishing a more favourable line of defence and simultaneously forestalling the danger of encirclement of his main forces. Permission was not granted. In the south new problems were arising as the Bratislava government declared its solidarity with Germany and news was received of the entry of German troops into northern Slovakia. The Polish General Staff transferred a division of the 'Łódź' Army into the area south of Tarnów as an additional reserve.

Between 22 and 28 August there may still have been some occasional doubt among the Polish leadership concerning whether war with Germany was imminent. This was certainly supported by the view, held to the very end by the foreign minister, Beck, that a peaceful solution was possible, as well as by the circumstance that only limited German actions—especially against Danzig—were expected in some quarters. Not until the evening of 28 August did the military leadership consider the situation so serious that the inspector-general, after hearing a report from the chief of the General Staff, decided to request the president to order general mobilization for 30 August. On the morning of 29 August the army commanders received orders to move their troops into their jumping-off positions. Simultaneously the 'national guard (militia) battalions' were called up.

On the afternoon of 29 August general mobilization was cancelled again. The French and British ambassadors had pointed out that such war preparations would wreck the last chance of a peaceful settlement of the conflict, especially as the British government was just then awaiting a decisive reply to its latest proposals to the Reich government. The countermanding order resulted in considerable confusion, especially on the railways, which were already over-extended by deployment transports.

On 30 August mobilization was once more ordered with effect from the following day. With considerable delay the battle formations so far mobilized now moved into their assigned jumping-off positions. Additional delays and confusion were created by orders from the General Staff authorizing army commanders-in-chief to decide for themselves on their definitive lines of defence. In consequence, many formations were moved even further to the west. When the German offensive started, only about one-third of the troops in all the armies of the first echelon were ready for action.[23] The intervention corps set up for the protection of Danzig could no longer be disbanded in time. Mobilization of the 'stand-by units', at least, had been completed, as had the transportation to the front of the formations mobilized on 23 August. Movement of the formations on stand-by since 27 August was in full swing, while those made ready for combat by 'general mobilization' became available only on 3 September. The major part of the air force had been transferred to advanced airfields by the morning of 1 September.

The reasons for Poland's subsequent defeat have to be sought in her unfavourable geographical situation as regards defence and in Germany's numerical, technological, and organizational superiority. Besides, the Polish operations and mobilization plan was marked by many shortcomings. Apart from clinging to the 'strategic central territory' and to exposed lines of defence near the frontiers, there was an underestimation of the striking-power of the modernized German army and of its strategic potential, especially in the south. The dissipation of Polish strength, inadequate communication links, delays in mobilization and deployment, as well as

---

[23] Roos, 'Militärpolitische Lage', 200; id., *History*, 165.

inadequate support by the Western powers, which in no way matched up to the obligations undertaken by them—all this weakened the resistance of the bravely fighting Polish armed forces. The sudden Soviet invasion of eastern Poland on 17 September finally shattered all hopes that Poland might be able to hold out for three months or so. Not even guerrilla warfare in the east of the country, until such time as Allied help could become effective, was possible any longer.[24]

[24] Roos, 'Militärpolitische Lage', 200, 202.

III. The Course of the Polish Campaign from 1 September to 6 October 1939[1]

1. THE SMASHING OF THE POLISH DEFENCE SYSTEM

THE German deployment continued according to plan even after 25 August; on the morning of 1 September Army Groups North and South launched their offensive. Although the Poles were aware of the German troop concentrations, they were nevertheless taken by surprise by the actual start of operations. The Germans were thus able to seize the initiative.

The German public, generally speaking, entered the new war calmly and with little enthusiasm. Only a small proportion were fooled by the propaganda of their National Socialist leaders, according to which the Poles and the Western powers were solely responsible for the aggravation of the situation. The majority of Germans simply obeyed. Even so, the authorities were evidently not too sure of the public mood and during the first weeks of the Polish campaign still occasionally referred to 'police operations' or 'retaliatory measures'.[2]

TABLE III.III.1. *German and Polish Strength on 1 September 1939*

	Men	Incl. frontier guards	Armd. and mot. divs.	Inf. divs.	Mtn. divs.	Cav. brigs.	Total form-ations	Armd. vehicles	Guns	Planes	Ships
Wehrmacht Eastern front	1.5m.	90,000	15	37	1	1	54	3,600	6,000	1,929	40
Poland	1.3m.	60,000	1 brig.	37	—	11	49	750	4,000	900	50

[1] III.III (including maps) is generally based—except where otherwise stated—on the following sources: Kriegsgeschichtliche Forschungsanstalt des Heeres, 'Der Feldzug in Polen 1939', BA-MA III H 165; Gen.d.Fl. a.D. Wilhelm Speidel, 'Die Luftwaffe im Polenfeldzug 1939: Karlsruher Studie in wesentlicher Anlehnung an die "Kriegsgeschichtliche Studie über den Polenfeldzug 1939"' (1956), MGFA MS Lw 2/1-6; *Operationen und Taktik: Auswertung wichtiger Ereignisse des Seekrieges*, No. 11 = *Die deutsche Kriegsmarine im Feldzug gegen Polen, September 1939* (publ. by OKM; Berlin, 1943), BA-MA RM D 4 601/11; *PSZ*, vol. i, pts. 2, 3, 5. Additional data from FM von Bock, 'Tagebuch-Notizen zum Polen-Feldzug, Mai/Juni 1939-3. Oktober 1939', BA-MA III 53/1; Kriegswissenschaftliche Abteilung des Generalstabes des Heeres, 'Die operativen Nachrichtenverbindungen des deutschen Heeres im Polenfeldzug 1939' (completed 1942), BA-MA RH 60/v. 1; Garliński, *Poland*, 12-13; Mueller-Hillebrand, *Heer*, i. 71 ff., 132 ff., ii. 13 ff. See also Kennedy, *German Campaign*, 78 ff.; Roos, 'Feldzug', 504 ff.; Piekalkiewicz, *Polenfeldzug*, 72 ff., 83, 95; id., *Zweiter Weltkrieg*, 66-7, 72, 77 ff.; Tippelskirch, 'Operativer Überblick', 252 ff.; Vormann, *Feldzug*, 73 ff. Generally speaking, all figures should be viewed with reserve as only few official records exist, which are, moreover, often open to a variety of interpretations. Statements of strength or losses published beyond these records are not as a rule verifiable. They also often suffer from being based on different criteria.

[2] Mann, *Deutsche Geschichte*, 186-7, 196, 202-3.

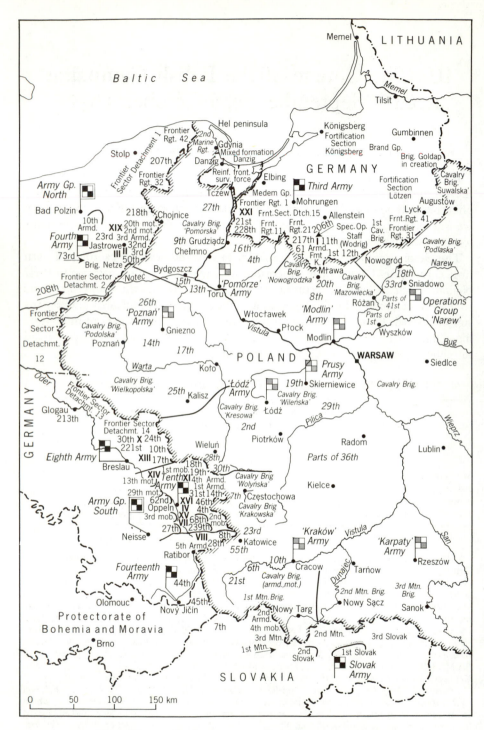

MAP III.III.1. Deployment on 1 September 1939, 04.45 hrs.

Danzig immediately proclaimed its 'accession' to the Reich. The League of Nations high commissioner, Carl-Jakob Burckhardt of Switzerland, left the former 'Free City'. On the same day Hitler addressed the Reichstag to justify the German attack.[3] On that same evening of 1 September, in spite of Hitler's protestations of peaceful intentions towards France and Britain, the ambassadors of those countries presented their governments' demands for an immediate cessation of operations and for the Wehrmacht's withdrawal from Poland. The same day also saw a mediation proposal from Mussolini, which failed chiefly because Hitler refused to accept the restoration of the status quo ante, without which Britain in particular was not prepared to negotiate. On 3 September, following the expiry of their ultimatums, Britain and France declared war on the German Reich. Hitler left Berlin and went to the army training-area of Gross-Born in Pomerania to demonstrate his 'proximity' to the front.

In Danzig the operations of minor units were concentrated mainly on the Westerplatte. Inadequately prepared assaults by a naval shock-troop company, which had been secretly transferred to Danzig on board the *Schleswig-Holstein*, failed at first in spite of the employment of the training-ship's heavy guns.[4] Another failure was the coup against the important bridges at Tczew, which the Poles had managed to blow up in good time. Rail communications between East Prussia and the rest of the Reich territory thus remained disrupted for some time.[5]

The navy, supported by the air force, had been blockading the Gulf of Danzig since 1 September, operating mainly against the port installations of Gdynia and Hel, clearing mines and hunting submarines. It scored its greatest success on 3 September with the sinking of the modern minelaying vessel *Gryf* and the destroyer *Wicher*. The other three Polish vessels of that category had left port bound for Britain on 30 August. The German naval command had therefore transferred numerous units to the North Sea as early as 31 August.[6]

The western wing of Third Army, which was to support the attack of Fourth Army, ran into considerable opposition soon after crossing the East Prussian frontier. Not until 4 September did it succeed in taking Grudziądz and linking up further to the south with the forces which had come up from Pomerania.[7]

The left wing of Fourth Army forced a crossing of the Brda north-east of Chojnice on the very first day of the war. Parts of its right wing advanced along the Noteć, and by the evening of 2 September they were 10 km. north-east of Nakło. The centre of the army burst through the strongly held Brda position to both sides of Koronowo, crossed the Bydgoszcz–Tczew railway line, and reached the Vistula at Chełmno. On 3 September the first overland link was established between Pomerania and East Prussia north of the Bory Tucholskie forest. Moreover, a crossing of the Vistula

---

[3] Domarus, ii. 1312 ff.

[4] Latest detailed account of the fighting in Stjernfelt and Böhme, *Westerplatte*.

[5] Details in Schindler, *Mosty und Dirschau*, 101 ff.

[6] Among the numerous detailed studies of naval warfare during the Polish campaign only the following need mention: Bachmann, 'Hela', 275 ff.; id., 'Polnische U-Boot-Division', 17 ff.; id., 'Seekriegführung', 197 ff., 273 ff., 352 ff., 407 ff.

[7] See also Schindler, *Mosty und Dirschau*, 136 ff., 152–3 (Grudziądz bridge).

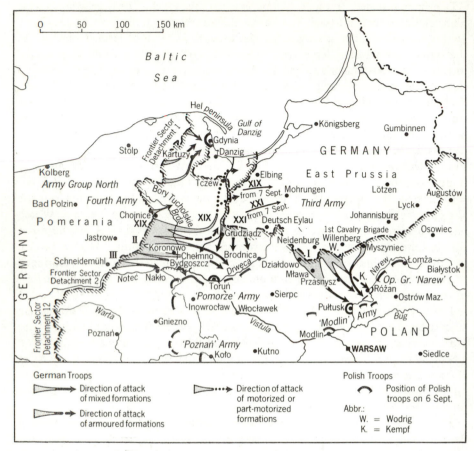

MAP III.III.2. Northern Front Sector, 1–6 September 1939

near Chełmno was achieved without major Polish opposition. At its centre Fourth Army rapidly advanced further east as far as the Drwęca.

The Polish forces encircled in the Bory Tucholskie forest desperately tried to break through towards the south. Their fighting-power, however, soon flagged. By 5 September it was possible to make a start on 'mopping up' operations, in the course of which losses were incurred through attacks by irregulars. On the right wing III Corps reached Bydgoszcz without major fighting and from there wheeled south towards Inowrocław. There, from 6 September onward, the resistance of Polish rearguards began to stiffen once more.

In the northern part of the Corridor, where Polish forces were earmarked for the defence of Gdynia, Fourth Army during its advance to the Vistula had merely protected its flank. Not until 6 September was a start made on the encirclement of these Polish forces by a 'Northern Group' formed under General Kaupisch from the Frontier Guard Sector Command No. 1; this group advanced against the Polish port from Danzig, Kartuzy, and Wejherowo.

As soon as operations had been successfully concluded in the Corridor the XIX Corps, composed of armoured and motorized infantry divisions, was detached and moved towards the left wing of Third Army. The XXI Corps was likewise pulled out once it had accomplished a link-up with Fourth Army south-east of Grudziądz. It was transferred—together with some further divisions, mainly from the reserve of Army Group North and of Fourth Army—to the Pisz–Łyck area. In addition, all units not absolutely needed were detached from the forces present in the Giżycko area in order to support the emerging point of main effort on the eastern wing of Third Army.

The main strength of Third Army, concentrated in the Nidzica–Wielbark area, had at first made rapid progress but had then come up against strong concentrations of the Polish Northern Army, who benefited from well-established bunker positions flanked on both sides by swampy terrain north of Mława and Przasnysz for conducting a vigorous defence and counter-attacks. However, by 6 September the Narew had been reached and at Różan crossed.

With the transfer to East Prussia of all formations that could be spared from the Corridor, conditions were now ready for a vigorous pincer movement from the north. As a result, however, the intended thrust of Third and Fourth Army forces—which, after linking up on the Vistula, were to strike directly towards Warsaw—proved correspondingly weaker. On the other hand, the reinforcement of the eastern wing was entirely in line with the ideas of Colonel-General von Bock, who had from the outset called for a far-reaching encirclement all the way to Brześć nad Bugiem (Brest-Litovsk) and Lublin. Meanwhile he had begun to doubt, as had Rundstedt, whether the concentration of Polish forces in the Łódź–Piotrków and Radom–Kielce–Sandomierz area was still intended to establish a new line of defence west of the Vistula and the San. In that case it would have been possible to entrap them in central Poland. However, the army groups thought it more likely that the Poles were preparing to withdraw to the east.

The Army High Command did not yet fully endorse that view. In its estimate of the situation it proceeded from the argument that it might suddenly become necessary to pull divisions out of Poland in order to employ them in the west. Thus, no excessive time was to be lost in the east, as might happen with far-reaching movements. A signal from the army commander-in-chief, Colonel-General von Brauchitsch, therefore ruled on 5 September:

It is the intention of the army C.-in-C. for Fourth Army to advance towards Warsaw on both sides of the Vistula, for Third Army to advance with its right wing to Warsaw, with its left wing towards Ostrów-Mazowiecki. Army Group's intention to reinforce Third Army with forces—especially mobile ones—from Fourth Army is in line with the thinking of the army C.-in-C. Avoidance of far-sweeping movement of eastern wing and limitation of disposition to the Warsaw–Ostrów-Mazowiecki line is considered advisable. This does not affect bringing the Giżycko group forward to Łomża and Osowiec in order to tie down enemy forces.[8]

---

[8] Cited from Vormann, *Feldzug*, 90.

Apart from the pressure of time under which the German army command believed itself to be operating, this order was evidently also inspired by the hope that the Polish enemy was already sufficiently mauled for him to be encircled while still west of the Vistula.

In OKH's opinion the Poles had lost their freedom of action after a few days. Their only choice now was to stand and fight the decisive battle west of the Vistula, seeing that the main German offensive had made surprisingly rapid progress in the south as well. After two days of war Eighth Army had reached the Prosna. Tenth Army was east of the Warta and had occupied Częstochowa. Its tanks were already rolling towards Radomsko. Fourteenth Army had crossed the upper Vistula and was fighting its way forward, with rather more difficulty, in the Western Beskidy mountains into the plain of Nowy Targ. The Upper Silesian industrial region was occupied by members of the *K(ampf)-Organisation* of the military security service before the Poles found much time to carry out their planned demolitions.[9] 'Mopping up' of the industrial region took some considerable time.

On the Polish side the 'Kraków' and 'Łódź' Armies were already badly mauled and engaged in evasive movements towards the east. The 'Pomorze' Army was in a similar situation, while the 'Modlin' Army was in danger of being outflanked from both sides by the German Fourth and Third Armies. Retreat, on the other hand, would have prematurely opened the way to Warsaw. Less critical was the situation of the 'Poznań' Army, although it was withdrawn too late to a common line of defence with its neighbouring formations and in consequence was unable to give them any appreciable support. There were no further reserves available, as the 'Narew' operational group was tied down in defensive fighting against the extreme left wing of the Third Army, and as the main Polish reserve, the 'Prusy' Army, had been caught by German aircraft and armour while still assembling and now had virtually no freedom of movement left. It was understandable, therefore, that the head of the Polish armed forces, Marshal Rydz-Śmigły, became convinced that the war was already lost for Poland. In that connection it was of no particular importance that the German air force, which had achieved virtually unchallenged command of the air after a mere couple of days, missed the disengagement of the 'Poznań' Army, which was yet to play a part in the battle on the Bzura.

Within a few days the main task of the German air force no longer consisted of strategic operations but of direct or indirect support for the army.[10] The Polish airmen—those that had not already been eliminated—seldom engaged in combat and withdrew to remote airfields. The Luftwaffe flew missions against Polish armament factories and communications, attacked the retreating enemy, and supported the advance of Eighth and Tenth Armies by bombing the cities of Łódź, Warsaw, Dęblin, and Sandomierz.

---

[9] See also Groscurth, *Tagebücher*, 196, 199; de Jong, *Fünfte Kolonne*, 42 ff. A well-founded study of the strike and sabotage organization of German counter-intelligence in the Polish campaign is still unfortunately lacking, in spite of sufficient documentary material.

[10] On the situation of the Luftwaffe in Sept. 1939 see also the graphic account in Bekker, *Angriffshöhe 4000*, 11 ff.; the situation of the Polish air force at that time is described by e.g. Cynk, *Polish Air Force, passim.*

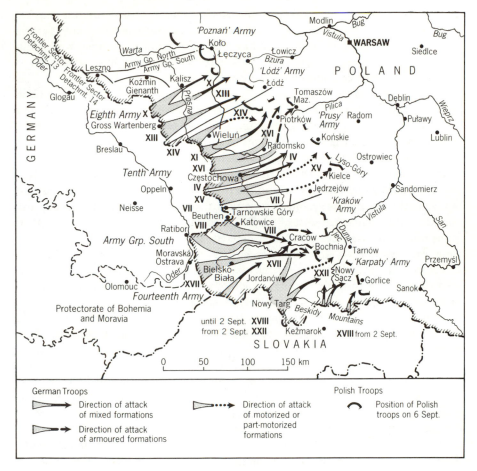

MAP III.III.3. Southern Front Sector, 1–6 September 1939

In the area of Army Group South the enemy was already engaged in an often disorderly retreat before the Eighth and Tenth Armies. While the occupation of the former German province of Posen (Poznań) was assigned to a 'Group Gienanth', composed of frontier guard units, Eighth Army was rapidly advancing towards Łódź. On the right wing of Tenth Army the mobile troops of XV Corps reached the northern part of the Łysa Góra range on the evening of 6 September, roughly between Kielce and Końskie. There was a gap of over 90 km. between it and the left wing of Fourteenth Army, but that was speedily closed. Further north the armoured forces of XVI Corps, following their breakthrough at Piotrków and the repulsion of Polish counter-attacks, were pursuing the enemy towards Tomaszów.

On 6 September Fourteenth Army had taken Cracow virtually unchallenged. Though initially hanging back in the south-west, XXII Corps, having penetrated into the plain, was thrusting vigorously towards Bochnia and Tarnów. In the extreme south XVIII Corps, consisting mainly of mountain divisions, had to overcome very heavy opposition in the Beskid mountains. Only later did the general weakening of the Polish enemy begin to show also in these parts, so that the Dunajec was crossed at Nowy Sącz and the region west of Gorlice reached.

Army Group South was still hoping, by means of a rapid advance of its mobile troops, to engage the main Polish forces in a decisive battle west of the Vistula and the San. To be on the safe side, however, it wanted to cross the Vistula at Dęblin and Puławy with the right wing of Tenth Army as well as to reinforce the eastern wing of Fourteenth Army, enabling it to reach out even further. Although the Army High Command essentially shared the opinion of the army group, it nevertheless found it necessary to intervene when the centre of Fourteenth Army was pushing too far to the north. One reason for this was the latter's intention to envelop the 'Kraków' Army while still west of the Dunajec, and another was the inferior state of the roads in the Beskidy mountains, where the few existing lines of communication were nearly all north–south. On 5 September, therefore, the commander-in-chief of Fourteenth Army, Colonel-General List, received orders, first from OKH and then also from his own army group, to wheel towards the north-east and to thrust as rapidly as possible across the San towards Lublin.

On 6 September the High Command feared that it would scarcely be possible to encircle the bulk of the Polish army west of the Vistula and the Narew. In an estimate of the situation, demanded by Hitler, OKH pointed further to the creation of appreciable Polish groupings on the Narew and mainly around Łódź; these might conceivably be moved closer to Warsaw in order to increase protection for the capital and at the same time absorb the retreating forces. In the south a major concentration in the Kielce area no longer looked probable, though a new one in the Lublin area did. About 5 Polish divisions were regarded as routed, another 24 as probably only capable of limited operations, with only the remaining 10 being left intact. OKH did not consider new decisions to be immediately necessary as its instructions of 5 September had largely allowed for the existing situation.

Not until 9 September was the German plan of operations adjusted to a new estimate of the situation after the Polish evasive movements had become a certainty. OKH instructed both army groups to perform a second pincer movement east of the Vistula. To accomplish this, Army Group North was now after all to reach out towards the east with mobile troops—if necessary even beyond the Bug—and to link up with Army Group South. The latter had the task, above all, of thrusting with its right wing east of the San towards Chełm, if necessary crossing the upper waters of the Bug.

A few days later the enemy's position appeared hopeless. In the opinion of the army commander-in-chief the remnants of the Polish army now only had the alternative of withdrawing either eastwards towards the Soviet frontier or towards the south-east in the direction of Romania. In consequence Bock's army group was ordered to advance its left wing towards the south-east and then south into the Słonim–Kowel area. Army Group South was instructed to continue its advance

MAP III.III.4. Northern Front Sector, 7–11 September 1939

towards Kraśnik with elements of Tenth Army and beyond Lwów with Fourteenth Army. In doing so the German command underestimated the fighting capacity of the Polish forces still west of Warsaw. In the area of Army Group North the newly established eastern wing of Third Army broke through the Polish defences on the Narew to both sides of Łomża. The Białystok–Warsaw railway line was reached on 11 September. Mobile troops were already advancing towards Brześć nad Bugiem. In the centre and on the right wing of the army the penetration of the Polish lines of defence on the Narew and the establishment of bridgeheads south of the Bug likewise succeeded.

On 15 September Guderian's XIX Corps captured Brześć nad Bugiem and two days later it took Włodawa. Reconnaissance forces probed as far as the Lublin–Kowel railway at Chełm, while other units took the town of Kobryń east of Brześć.

The XXI Corps had advanced from Łomża towards the south and on 12 and 13 September had enveloped and wiped out major enemy forces near Ostrów-Mazowiecki. It next turned east towards the Bielsk–Białystok railway. Białystok fell on 15 September.

On the right wing of the army west of the Bug the Wodrig Corps had pushed forward through Węgrów to Siedlce. On 16 September, instead of maintaining its south-easterly line of attack, it was turned west against the Mińsk-Mazowiecki-Karczew line, where major remnants of dispersed and disintegrating enemy forces had been identified east of the Vistula. The I Corps on the extreme right wing of the army likewise wheeled towards the northern and eastern front of Warsaw. The German ring was progressively closing around Modlin and the Polish capital. The Poles' determination to resist, however, was not yet broken. A demand for the surrender of Warsaw, brought under a flag of truce, was

MAP III.III.5. Southern Front Sector, 7–11 September 1939

rejected. On Hitler's orders an attack on Praga, the eastern part of the city, had to be suspended.

Fourth Army meanwhile was fighting its way forward towards the south-east along both sides of the Vistula. North of the river the II Corps encountered a weak enemy and advanced through Płock to Modlin. In front of III Corps south of the Vistula,

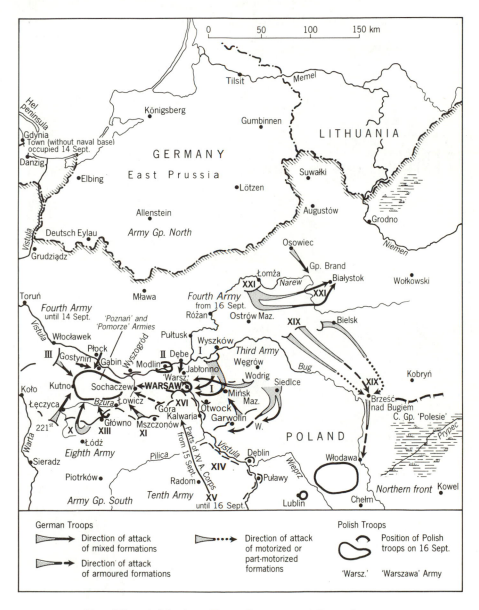

MAP III.III.6. Northern Front Sector, 12–16 September 1939

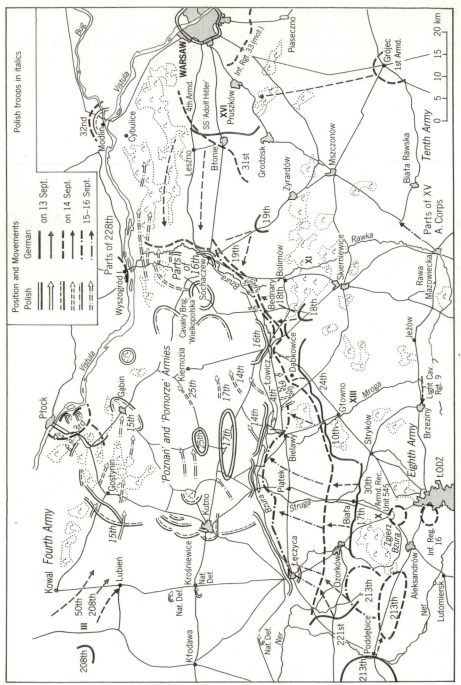

MAP III.III.7. Situation on the Bzura, 13–16 September 1939

however, enemy opposition stiffened considerably. It was evident that this German group had been furnished with insufficient forces. It was unable to keep step with the left wing of Eighth Army, whose task, in addition to protecting Tenth Army's flank, now also included the pursuit and overtaking of the Polish 'Poznań' Army. The gap which resulted was the main cause of the subsequent battle on the Bzura.

In the rearward zone Poznań had been occupied by German troops on 11 September. That same day General von Vollard-Bockelberg assumed command of the forces in his sphere as 'Military Commander, Posen'.

The failure of the attack against the Westerplatte had been assessed by the Germans as a loss of face and resulted in the strength of the Polish defence being overrated. While the air force and naval High Commands were reconsidering the situation and while Hitler, for propaganda reasons, demanded a repetition of the attack of 2 September, OKW on the same day put Army Group North in charge of operations. Bock convinced OKH and Hitler of the need for more careful planning in order to avoid a renewed setback. Thus, 4 September was fixed as a new date for the German thrust; but this had to be postponed several times. Meanwhile there was repeated bombardment as well as a raid by 60 dive-bombers. The Germans moreover transferred a sapper company to Danzig and reinforced their infantry units. After a heavy bombardment by the *Schleswig-Holstein* the garrison of the Westerplatte surrendered on 7 September.[11] During the next few days the Kaupisch Group advanced ever more closely to Gdynia. After heavy fighting German troops penetrated into the city on 13 September. The naval base and the Oksywska Kępa succeeded in holding out for some time. The last resistance was broken only on 19 September with the aid of the navy and the air force.

In the sector of Army Group South advanced armoured formations of Tenth Army had reached the outskirts of Warsaw by the beginning of the second week of the war. On 10 September units of 4th Armoured Division penetrated into the capital but, to avoid major losses, were pulled back again to the western outskirts, especially as the Poles themselves were directing heavy artillery fire on the city from the eastern bank of the Vistula.[12] At the same time the division had to resist fierce attempts at a breakthrough by other Polish troops from the west, so that its position suddenly seemed to be getting precarious.

Further south armoured forces established a bridgehead on the eastern bank of the Vistula at Góra Kalwaria. The right wing of the army attacked further towards the south-east, took Opatów, Ostrowiec, and Sandomierz, and then wheeled north along the Vistula. East of Radom it blocked the crossing of the river to six Polish divisions. Thus, the encirclement of the troops fighting in the Łysa Góra mountains and near Radom was completed, and after devastating attacks by the Luftwaffe from 11 September onward they laid down their arms. The Germans took approximately 60,000 prisoners. On the right wing of the army the attack continued eastward across the Vistula, while the other corps were still mopping up the Radom pocket or taking part in the fighting on the Bzura.

[11] Stjernfelt and Böhme, *Westerplatte*, 100 ff.   [12] Reinhardt, '4. Panzer-Division', 237 ff.

The Eighth Army had captured Łódź on 9 September and next moved against an enemy group located south-west of Warsaw; with its road to the east being blocked by the XVI Corps of Tenth Army there was stubborn resistance and from time to time the mounting of counter-attacks.[13] Suddenly the Germans found themselves threatened from the north-west south of the Bzura: the hitherto inadequately considered 'Poznań' Army was falling back towards the east and was attempting to fight its way south out of the Kutno area. It was joined by formations from other Polish armies in the north which had already withdrawn to the Modlin–Warsaw–Bzura area. These Polish forces were threatening Eighth Army not only from the flank but, above all, from the rear. In consequence the army commander-in-chief, General Blaskowitz, found himself compelled to perform not only a left turn but in part even an about-turn. Only thus could the Poles, who in some places had already advanced across the Bzura, be contained and their encirclement be initiated.

The increasingly encircled enemy was offering desperate resistance with his powerful rearguards and continued in every possible way to try to achieve a breakthrough in the south. However, the XIII and X Corps were standing firm in the Głowno–Łęczyca area. The XVI and XI Corps were pushing, from Warsaw and from the Mszczonów area, against the eastern flank of the Poles who had managed to get across the Bzura. On 16 September XV Corps arrived to reinforce them. Eventually Fourth Army, coming from the west and the north, also struck at the Polish forces concentrated in the Kutno area. While Polish rearguards dug in south of Włocławek were offering stubborn resistance to III Corps, preventing it temporarily from making further progress, II Corps had reached Modlin on 11 September, where it left some forces facing the western and northern fronts of the fortress. The bulk of its forces meanwhile thrust against Dębe, situated further east on the Bug, penetrated into the Polish bridgehead position there, crossed the Bug, and reached Jabłonna. One division had previously wheeled south towards Kutno, where all encircling forces were placed under the command of Eighth Army on 13 September. Command on the former left wing of Third Army was assumed by Fourth Army headquarters.

On 16 September the concentric attack of all German forces began on the Bzura. The main effort was on the eastern wing of Army Group South, where the XV, XVI, and XI Corps remained under the command of General von Reichenau, who for this purpose came under Eighth Army but otherwise retained command of his army's formations engaged near Radom.

Coming from the west and north-west, III Corps pushed east across the line Gąbin–south-east of Gostynin–east of Kutno. At Wyszogród meanwhile parts of Third Army had blocked the Vistula crossings. On the right wing the XIII and X Corps succeeded on 17 September in crossing the Łowicz–Kutno road by a northerly attack and in capturing Kutno.

---

[13] A comprehensive view of operations in the Kutno area may be found in the study by Elble, *Schlacht an der Bzura*; Map III.III.7 closely follows the one found there on pp. 170–1.

Of the three corps of Tenth Army, XV Corps crossed the Warsaw–Sochaczew road on 17 September, maintained the capital's southerly encirclement from the west by repulsing various breakthrough attempts, and on 19 September reached the Vistula. On 17 September XI Corps finally crossed the Bzura between Sochaczew and Łowicz and advanced further in a north-westerly direction.

On 13 September all bomber formations of the German air force had been employed against the area north-east of Łódź, where they operated against crowded enemy marching columns. As no operations were possible on the two succeeding days because of bad weather, the next attacks did not take place until 16 September,

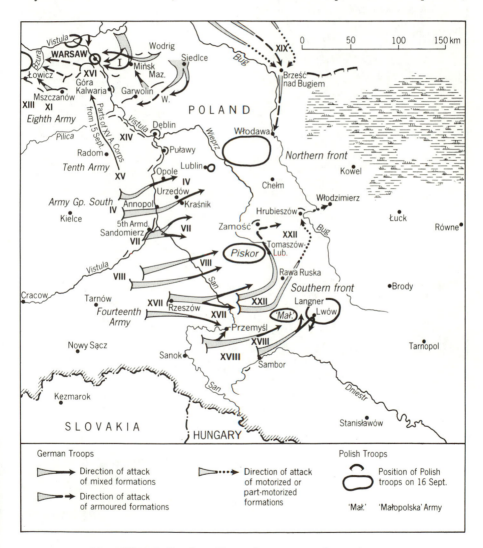

MAP III.III.8. Southern Front Sector, 12–16 September 1939

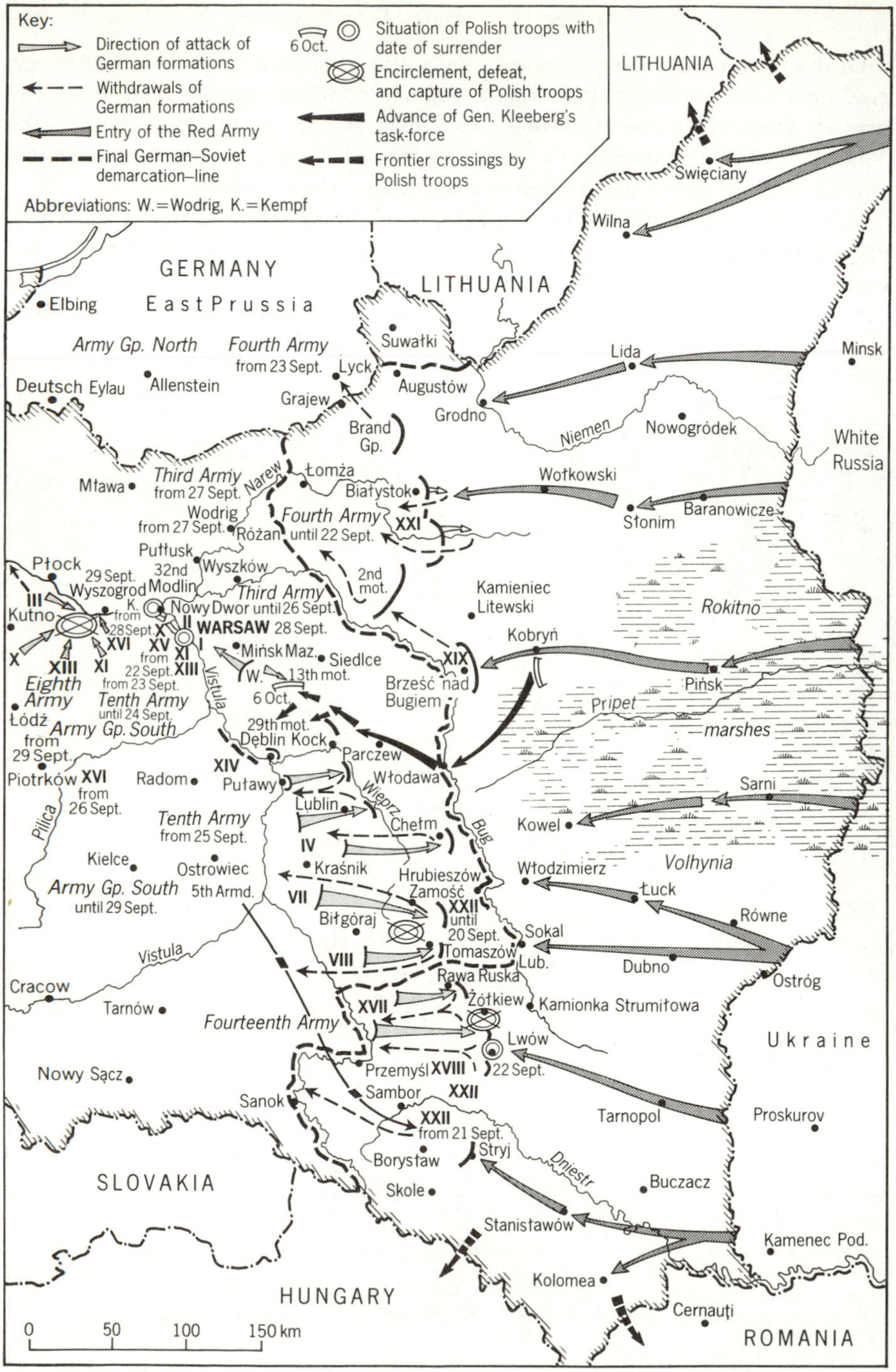

Key:
Direction of attack of German formations
Withdrawals of German formations
Entry of the Red Army
Final German–Soviet demarcation–line
Abbreviations: W.=Wodrig, K.=Kempf
6 Oct.
Situation of Polish troops with date of surrender
Encirclement, defeat, and capture of Polish troops
Advance of Gen. Kleeberg's task-force
Frontier crossings by Polish troops
LITHUANIA
Święciany
Wilna
GERMANY
East Prussia
LITHUANIA
Elbing
Army Gp. North
Fourth Army
from 23 Sept.
Suwałki
Minsk
Lida
Deutsch Eylau
Allenstein
Lyck
Augustów
Grajew
Grodno
Brand Gp.
Niemen
Nowogródek
White Russia
Mława
Third Army
from 27 Sept.
Narew
Łomża
Białystok
Wołkowski
Wodrig
from 27 Sept.
Fourth Army
until 22 Sept.
XXI
Różan
Słonim
Baranowicze
Pułtusk
Płock
32nd
Wyszków
2nd mot.
29 Sept.
Wyszogrod
Modlin
Third Army
Kamieniec Litewski
III
Kutno
K. from 28 Sept.
Nowy Dwor until 26 Sept.
WARSAW 28 Sept.
Rokitno
X
XV
II
I
XVI
XI
Kobryń
X
XIII
XI
from 22 Sept.
XIII
Mińsk Maz.
Siedlce
XIX
Eighth Army
from 23 Sept.
Vistula
W.
13th mot.
Brześć nad Bugiem
Pińsk
Pripet
Łódż
Tenth Army
until 24 Sept.
6 Oct.
marshes
from 29 Sept.
Army Gp. South
29th mot.
Dęblin
Kock
Parczew
XIV
Piotrków
XVI
from 26 Sept.
Radom
Puławy
Włodawa
Sarni
Pilica
Lublin
Wieprz
Tenth Army
from 25 Sept.
Chełm
Kowel
Bug
IV
Kielce
Ostrowiec
Kraśnik
Hrubieszów
Włodzimierz
Volhynia
Army Gp. South
until 29 Sept.
5th Armd.
Zamość
Łuck
VII
XXII
until 20 Sept.
Równe
Biłgóraj
Sokal
Tomaszów
Lub.
Vistula
VIII
Dubno
Ostróg
Cracow
Rawa Ruska
Żółkiew
Kamionka Strumiłowa
Tarnów
XVII
Fourteenth Army
Ukraine
Lwów
Nowy Sącz
Przemyśl
XVIII
22 Sept.
XXII
Sambor
Sanok
Tarnopol
Proskurov
XXII
from 21 Sept.
Stryj
Borysław
Dniestr
SLOVAKIA
Buczacz
Skole
Stanisławów
Kamenec Pod.
Kolomea
HUNGARY
Cernauţi
0
50
100
150 km
ROMANIA

MAP III.III.9. Situation from 17 September to the End of Hostilities in Poland

when they were directed against extensive Polish columns north of Łowicz and Sochaczew. As Eighth Army had still not succeeded in making any lasting penetrations into the enemy's troop concentrations, and as the three corps of Tenth Army had been forced to defend themselves since early morning against powerful Polish attacks from the west, an extensive Luftwaffe offensive was mounted with massive formations and repeated strikes against major troop concentrations and assembly positions. The result was so effective that all Polish attacks petered out. Frequently the effect was so demoralizing that the Poles threw away their weapons and German commanders in the field requested a discontinuation of air attacks on a totally helpless opponent. On 16 September 820 aircraft were engaged in operations, with 328,000 kg. of bombs being dropped.

After 18 September the battle of encirclement gradually came to an end. OKH reported over 120,000 prisoners from 19 divisions and 3 cavalry brigades.

In the south Fourteenth Army was trying to cut off the enemy's retreat across the San. On its right wing mountain troops, in spite of difficult terrain, had crossed the river on 11 September and were advancing towards Przemyśl. Not until 15 September was the fortress taken by troops of XVIII Corps, which had been weakened by transfers to the western front—although some of its advance units had been outside Lwów several days earlier. Capture of this city failed on 16 September. The German units which had penetrated into it were unable to hold out and had to be pulled back again.

While the left wing was trying to block the road over the San to the retreating enemy, the motorized XXII Corps at the centre of the army thrust across the San in a north-easterly direction and on 15 September reached the Tomaszów–Lubelski area with its main forces, some advanced units actually reaching Włodzimierz and Hrubieszów and establishing bridgeheads over the Bug. Reconnaissance units linked up with XIX Corps of Army Group North, coming from a northerly direction. On 16 September eventually XXII Corps again wheeled south-west in the direction of Rawa Ruska–Lwów.

The Luftwaffe, whose formations were being increasingly pulled back into the Reich for replenishment, simultaneously kept up its support for army operations. It disrupted road and rail transport, prevented break-outs by encircled Polish troops, and undertook supply-flights for the army's offensive spearheads, which had outrun their supply-bases. A new task emerged for the Luftwaffe as a result of Polish efforts once more to gain the operational initiative east of the Vistula.

Facing Fourteenth Army, the bulk of the Polish formations fell back via Lwów towards Tarnopol and tried to turn north-east, where massive troop concentrations were observed in the Równe–Kowel area. Simultaneously German air reconnaissance identified railway transports and marching columns from the area between Bug and Vistula in a south-easterly direction: these were Polish forces retreating in the face of the Third and the reorganized Fourth Armies. Other enemy movements aimed from Brześć towards the north-east, so that—considering that eastern Poland was divided into two halves by the Pripet marshes—the German command considered it possible that a southern group of forces was being established in the

Równe-Kowel-Brody area and a northern group in the Baranowicze-Lida-Wołkowski area. Since, following the loss of the communication centre of Brześć, the two areas were linked only by a railway line following the Soviet frontier from Równe to Baranowicze, the Luftwaffe aimed its strikes against Polish columns and railway transport so as to prevent the systematic conduct of any new Polish operation from the outset. All railway lines in the south-east and north-east, as well as the linking line between the two areas, were therefore systematically wrecked. Soon there were rail transports piling up at stations. Moreover, columns of trucks and marching columns were scattered, and Polish headquarters as well as the government, fleeing from Warsaw via Lublin to the Romanian frontier, were bombed every day at their identified locations, so that it became impossible for them to control whatever fighting forces remained. In consequence, the enemy's remaining forces east of the Vistula were already badly mauled by the German air force when on 17 September the Soviet army crossed the frontier and marshalled for operations against these Polish troops in the east of their country.

2. The Invasion by the Red Army and the Collapse of Poland

The Red Army's intervention in the German–Polish war was of decisive importance to further developments in eastern Europe. To the German leaders it came—at least in its timing—as a surprise, even though they had for some time been trying to induce the Soviet Union to move into eastern Poland. The hope was that the Western powers would in that case refrain from intervening or else would declare war on Moscow as well. Stalin, however, saw through Hitler's calculations and deliberately awaited the optimal moment. He extended the period of conscripted service and on 7 September ordered a partial mobilization under the cover of 'reserve exercises'.[14] However, another ten days were to pass before the situation seemed sufficiently opportune for him to claim, after alleged frontier violations and provocations by the Poles, that the entry of Soviet troops was aimed solely at 'the protection of the Ukrainians and Belorussians, with full preservation of neutrality in the present conflict; with no Polish government in existence, the Soviet government is therefore no longer bound by the Soviet-Polish non-aggression treaty'.[15]

The German military command, which was evidently completely unprepared for the new situation, was now concerned to avoid clashes between the two armies as well as unnecessary losses, especially as German formations had meanwhile reached positions up to 200 km. east of the line defined in the treaty of 23 August as the boundary between the two countries' 'spheres of interest'. On 17 September OKW first of all laid down an extreme limit to the advance of German troops. Units which had moved beyond that line had to be pulled back. The subsequent lines, laid down anew each day from 18 to 21 September, no doubt reflected German hopes of

---

[14] Soviet preparations for and justification of the invasion of Poland are summed up in Mäkelä, *Im Rücken des Feindes*, 25. Details of fighting between the Polish and the Soviet army in Piekalkiewicz, *Zweiter Weltkrieg*, 116 ff.   [15] Cited from Vormann, *Feldzug*, 154.

renewing negotiations with the Soviet government about certain territories conquered by the Wehrmacht east of the demarcation of interests.[16] The principal purpose, however, was to enable the German forces to conduct a reasonably orderly withdrawal, taking with them as many wounded as possible, as well as their own and captured material. For that reason time-intervals of several days each were laid down for reaching the successive lines. The Red Army then followed up in stages. In this way it was possible to keep the German and Soviet formations apart and generally to avoid clashes. A further reason for the staggered pull-back was the fact that in the not yet occupied or no longer occupied areas there were still remnants of Polish armies which might otherwise have been given too much elbow-room and might have threatened the retreating German units. This argument also met with understanding from the Soviet leadership. While there had been a good deal of initial mistrust of German intentions, and indeed fears of a German breach of the agreement, the Soviets were subsequently prepared even to postpone the deadline, laid down as 1 October, for the definitive evacuation of Poland east of the four main rivers.

A new situation arose following the conclusion of the German–Soviet 'boundary and friendship treaty' of 28 September.[17] Since Lithuania was now also recognized as being part of the Soviet sphere of interest, Germany was additionally given the Suwałki corner, as well as parts of the Voivodship of Warsaw and the entire Voivod-ship of Lublin, i.e. the central Polish region between Vistula and Bug. In consequence some of the German troops had to about-turn once more and occupy regions which they had only just, precipitately and with the greatest difficulties, evacuated. There were units which had to traverse that area for the third time within a few weeks.

After the Red Army had crossed the frontier along its entire length in Belorussia and Volhynia on the morning of 17 September, OKW defined the line Grajewo-Białystok-Kamieniec Litewski-Brześć nad Bugiem-Włodawa-Włodzimierz-the eastern edge of Lwów-Stryj-Skole as the extreme limit for the advance of German troops.[18] On 18 September OKH of its own accord defined the demarcation-line in greater detail, with small amendments in favour of the Red Army and instructions for the German troops near the line. These were ordered to move right up to the limit of advance, search the territory for any remnants of Polish troops, and marshal their own units. The two army groups were also instructed to report which of their formations were ready for transportation to the west. German units which had penetrated too far east were to start withdrawing not later than the following day and by 21 September to have completed their withdrawal everywhere. OKH pointed out that a further withdrawal to a 'definitive' demarcation-line was to be expected shortly.

---

[16] Ibid. 153 ff.; see also n. 18 below.

[17] Vormann, *Feldzug*, 199 ff. Text of German–Soviet treaty of 28 Sept. 1939, with confidential and secret supplementary protocols, and declaration on the continuation of the war, in *Nazi-Soviet Relations*, 105-8.

[18] For the demarcation-line see Map III.IV.1; sources: orders of Army Group North of 18, 19, and 20 Sept. 1939, BA-MA P 214c; war-diary entries by Army Group North of 17 and 19 Sept. 1939, BA-MA E 80/1; OKW No. 1866/39 of 17 Sept. 1939 with additional note No. 0360/39 geh. Aus. III L/b of 18 Sept. 1939, BA-MA RW 4/v. 144; see also Vormann, *Feldzug*, 153 ff. For details of Red Army operations against Polish forces see Piekalkiewicz, *Polenfeldzug*, 168 ff.

On 19 September OKH announced a new boundary-line which—except for the area around Lwów—essentially followed the rivers San, Vistula, and Narew. Withdrawal to the territory assigned to Germany was scheduled to start on 22 September.

On 20 September a further change occurred: in the south too the demarcation-line was shifted westward, to the line Przemyśl–Užok Pass. On Hitler's explicit order all fighting east of the line was to cease. Withdrawal to the west was to start at once. On the following day there was once more a rectification in the south, to the effect that the San was to be the demarcation-line there as well. The demarcation agreed on 23 August was now in force everywhere.

The order instructing German formations not to risk any losses after 20 September in the areas ceded to the Red Army could not, in view of still existing groups of Polish forces, be observed everywhere. Thus, the formations of Fourth Army on the left wing of Army Group North—as also the independent XIX Corps—had for the most part been advancing until the evening of 18 September and could not even consider rallying and then gradually turning until the following day. These movements did not pass without clashes with the enemy. It was in this area between Białystok and Brześć that German forces first made contact with the Red Army. Arrangements were made with their advance guards about procedure on both sides, including the provision that the Soviet troops during their advance would follow the withdrawing Germans at a distance of 25 km. On 22 September the fortress of Brześć was ceremoniously handed over to the Red Army.

In addition to the elimination of the last major centres of opposition, a large number of scattered forces had to be liquidated behind the German lines. The terrain with its extensive forest and swamp areas offered superb opportunities for concealment over considerable periods, and indeed for recovering and resuming military action, especially as the rapid German advance had largely been confined to the major roads and had therefore favoured such a situation.

On 22 September Fourth Army began its systematic withdrawal towards the west and north-west; this was completed on 26 September. Thereupon the army was dissolved. Third Army had linked up with Tenth Army at Góra Kalwaria and had thereby firmly closed the ring around Modlin and Warsaw. Praga was bombarded. Polish attempts to break out from Modlin near Nowy Dwór on 19 September and from Praga on 20 September were repulsed. The problem of pulling Third Army back behind the demarcation-line while maintaining the encirclement of Warsaw was solved by Hitler's order for I Corps to be kept facing Praga even beyond the agreed date of evacuation. If the capital did not surrender in time it would be necessary, there and at Modlin, for Soviet troops to take over the German positions. Some 11,000 prisoners whom the Germans were no longer able to transport back were handed over to the Red Army. On the morning of 22 September, on the front facing Praga, the former army commander-in-chief, Colonel-General von Fritsch, was killed in action. He had accompanied the 12th Artillery Regiment, whose chief he was, to Poland.[19]

---

[19] On the controversy about the circumstances of von Fritsch's death see Brausch, 'Tod', 95 ff.

On the right wing of Tenth Army IV Corps had meanwhile pushed through Lublin, which it took on 18 September, to Chełm and on to Hrubieszów. Two bridgeheads were established on the eastern bank of the Wieprz and a link was established with the spearheads of Fourteenth Army at Kock and Zamość. The advance came to an end on 19 September. To avoid exposing the northern flank of Fourteenth Army the withdrawal was delayed. This delay subsequently saved numerous formations from having to advance once more over the whole distance after 28 September. Massive streams of refugees from east to west, as well as Polish troops withdrawing in the face of the Red Army, created particular difficulties in the Lublin area. Thus, IV Corps alone took 12,000 prisoners within a few days. Even after 25 September German soldiers were left in Lublin to prevent the outbreak of disturbances prior to the town's surrender to the Red Army on 30 September.

In the area of operations of Fourteenth Army heavy fighting was still going on near Tomaszów–Zamość. After a battle lasting three days four Polish divisions and a cavalry brigade were forced to surrender on 20 September. Further south a major enemy group was encircled in the forests north of Lwów, between Żółkiew and Kamionka, and on 19 September forced to lay down its arms. Lwów itself was surrounded in the south, west, and north by parts of XVIII and XVII Corps, but continued to offer fierce resistance and on 19 September still rejected an appeal to surrender. Break-out attempts were repulsed. On the evening of the same day there was the first inadvertent clash with Soviet armoured scouting cars on the eastern edge of the city. On 20 September troops of XVII Corps penetrated as far as the upper Bug. On the following day the relief of the German forces by the Red Army was set in motion. The start of the pull-out of the German formations was scheduled for 22 September and the moving-off of the Soviet troops for 23 September.

Following the conclusion of the Bzura battle Eighth Army prepared to attack Warsaw. For this purpose parts of Tenth Army were ordered to annihilate the enemy—of a strength of approximately three divisions—between Warsaw and Modlin.

Hitler wanted a quick capture of the Polish capital, if only for political reasons. From the Wehrmacht's point of view, however, Warsaw was not only the enemy's capital but also an important traffic junction and the centre of the Polish armament industry. The Luftwaffe, having postponed the originally considered mass raid because of the weather and because of urgent tasks elsewhere, now sent parts of its formations into action against predominantly military targets in Warsaw: railways, bridges, artillery positions, and armament works. There were losses among the civilian population, especially as the Germans used incendiary bombs to eliminate small and difficult targets by area conflagrations. On the afternoon of 20 September the Luftwaffe employed 620 aircraft in order to add to the disruption of the connection between the fortresses of Modlin and Warsaw by aerial attack. On the following day Göring ordered Air Fleets 1 and 4 to concentrate their remaining forces on Warsaw and its environs.

The army formations—Eighth Army reinforced by two corps of Tenth Army—at first encountered considerable resistance. On 22 September the breakthrough to the Vistula was accomplished, and hence the final separation of Modlin and Warsaw.

Blaskowitz decided to attack the capital with XIII and XI Corps on the left bank of the Vistula. Modlin was sealed off in the south by XV and X Corps.

The assault on the Polish capital began on 25 September. The Luftwaffe employed approximately 1,200 planes, including transport aircraft unsuitable for aerial attack; these dropped about 13 per cent of all incendiary bombs. The result was a wide scatter of bombs and such an intense formation of smoke that both the Luftwaffe's and the artillery's accuracy of aim was greatly impaired. There were heavy casualties among the civilian population, and even the German troops on the north-western edge of the city suffered casualties. This led to conflicts between army and air force commands, making it necessary for Hitler to intervene. Although he ruled that the Luftwaffe should 'carry on' as before, both services endeavoured to achieve greater accuracy in bombing and shelling. On 26 September 450 German aircraft made an attack on Modlin, while there was only reconnaissance activity over Warsaw. Leaflets called on the Poles to surrender.

Meanwhile the army offensive had made some progress. On 25 September XIII Corps broke into the first and the following day into the second line of fortifications, while XI Corps for its part occupied the first line of fortifications. Simultaneously, I Corps, with Hitler's approval, thrust east of the Vistula to the southern edge of Praga in order to eliminate Polish attacks on the German flank. Here two representatives of the commandant of Warsaw, General Rómmel, appeared on the evening of 26 September, requesting a twenty-four-hour cease-fire and negotiations about the surrender of the city. They were informed that nothing short of unconditional capitulation would be considered. Following renewed artillery bombardment during the night of 26–7 September and the continuation of the infantry assault along the entire front, General Rómmel offered unconditional surrender on the morning of 27 September. Negotiations between Blaskowitz and Rómmel produced as a first outcome a temporary cease-fire which came into effect in the early afternoon. By noon on 28 September the fighting for Warsaw was at an end: the fortress garrison of more than 120,000 surrendered, having received German assurances that officers would be allowed to keep their swords and that non-commissioned officers and other ranks would be released to their homes after brief captivity. The exit of Polish troops from Warsaw began on the evening of 29 September. On 1 October at 17.00 h. General Rómmel formally handed over the defeated forces to the commander-in-chief of Eighth Army at the Raków command-post. Warsaw was occupied by the 10th Infantry Division and Praga by I Corps. On 2 October, in Hitler's presence, the troops principally concerned in the capture of the Polish metropolis entered the city.

Since Luftwaffe operations against Warsaw were no longer needed by 27 September the bomber formations were directed that same day against Modlin. The raids by 550 aircraft were aimed in particular against the suburb of Nowy Dwór. As the entire city was simultaneously under heavy artillery fire and as reconnaissance units of II Corps were thrusting against the inner line of fortifications, the commandant of the fortress, General Thommé, offered to surrender that evening. Following negotiations conducted by Third Army the surrender was scheduled for 29 September. Here more than 30,000 Polish troops were taken prisoner.

The last Polish centre of resistance eventually fell on 1 October—the Hel peninsula, where the defenders, approximately 4,500 men under the command of Rear-Admiral Unrug, had to surrender unconditionally.[20]

For Tenth Army the pull-back of the corps already beyond the Vistula passed without appreciable fighting. In agreement with the Soviet Union a temporary boundary was established here pending the final definition of the demarcation-line; this temporary line ran roughly from Parczew, 25 km. to the east, beyond Lublin and Kraśnik. The pull-back of Fourteenth Army behind the San began on 22 September and was completed by the morning of 29 September. In the course of it some heavy fighting still occurred for VII and especially for VIII Corps against Polish forces which were for the most part trying to fight their way through to Hungary between the retreating German and advancing Soviet forces. Thus, the two corps were again attacked at Tomaszów–Zamość on 21 and 22 September by a strong enemy pressing forward from the Hrubieszów area. They about-turned, partially encircled the Poles, and thwarted their breakthrough attempt for the time being. When on 23 September the corps once more turned westwards, the Poles exploited the gaps which resulted. Thus, on 25 September parts of VIII Corps once more found themselves in a tricky situation when they were attacked from the flank, about half-way between Tomaszów and the Tarnogród–Biłgoraj line, by superior forces of a strength of approximately one and a half divisions and three cavalry brigades. However, they managed to shake off the enemy and take a considerable number of prisoners.[21]

On 3 October a reorganization of command came into effect in the east.[22] The hitherto commander-in-chief of Army Group South now assumed overall command as 'Commander-in-Chief East', i.e. also over the 'military commander, Posen' and the previously appointed 'military commander, Danzig–West Prussia'. The staff of Army Group North was pulled out when, on 2 October, Third Army headquarters assumed command over the remaining troops. Eighth Army assumed the tasks of Tenth Army, which was likewise pulled out. As a result, there remained under the command of the Commander-in-Chief East, Colonel-General von Rundstedt, the Third, the Eighth, and the Fourteenth Armies, now renamed Frontier Sector North, Centre, and South respectively, as well as the two military commanders. At the same time the exchange of first-wave divisions for third-wave divisions was set in motion.

The German advance which, in some parts, had been made necessary again by the definitive delineation of the boundary between German-occupied and Soviet-occupied territory began on 5 October and was completed by 13 October. In the course of it there were still occasional clashes with Polish forces which had been left behind between the major roads, a situation favoured by the precipitate first German withdrawal in mid-September and the Red Army's suspended advance in late September. On 6 October Polish troops of the strength of about two divisions, commanded by General Kleeberg, surrendered at Kock east of Dęblin.

[20] Detailed account of the fighting for Hel in Bachmann, 'Hela', 275 ff.
[21] Detailed account of the final operations in south-east Poland in Piekalkiewicz, *Zweiter Weltkrieg*, 106 ff. [22] Details in Umbreit, *Militärverwaltungen*, 98 ff.

TABLE III.III.2. *German, Polish, and Soviet Losses in the Polish Campaign, 1939*

	Poland against Germany	Poland against the Soviet Union	Germany	Soviet Union
Killed in action	70,000	50,000	11,000	700
Wounded	133,000	?	30,000	1,900
Missing	?	?	3,400	?
Prisoners	700,000	300,000	—	—
Escaped abroad	150,000		—	—
Armoured vehicles	700	?	300	?
Guns	?	?	370	?
Other vehicles	?	?	5,000	?
Aircraft	330	?	560	?

Sources: see n. 23.

With the last engagements between Vistula and Bug the Polish campaign was definitely at an end. The superiority and mobility of the Wehrmacht had surprised both friend and foe. However, the losses suffered—especially in terms of personnel—proved very serious, as was to emerge during the subsequent years of war. Lost or damaged material was only more or less quantitatively offset by captured Polish weapons, equipment, and stores (see Table III.III.2).[23]

For Poland, however, the consequences were disastrous. The country suffered painful losses in men and in material assets, it lost its political existence, and it became the object of an unscrupulous policy of exploitation and racial and cultural extermination.

If one seeks the reasons which led to the rapid conclusion of the campaign in September and October 1939, the first to be listed must be the marked inferiority in armaments of the Polish compared to the German forces. Moreover, the military and geographical situation was so unfavourable to the Poles that any defence based solely on their own efforts was possible only for a limited period against either, let alone both, of their great neighbours. This dilemma was made much worse by Poland's well-nigh complete encirclement by Germany during the last few months prior to the war, an encirclement which culminated in the German-Soviet alliance of 23 August, as well as by the surprise strike with which the Wehrmacht started

[23] On this and the following see esp. Roos, 'Militärpolitische Lage', 200, 202. The tabulation of losses etc. in Table III.III.2 comes from numerous, widely dispersed data; the most important are contained in OKW/WFSt/Abt. L, No. 3340/40 g. (I M²), of 9 Sept. 1940 (German losses in the first year of the war, 1 Sept. 1939–31 Aug. 1940), BA-MA RW 4/v. 170; figures for use of ammunition from various reports, BA-MA III H 49 and W 01-8/22 (also contains further data on material losses). Overall report on the Polish campaign by the Luftwaffe to OKW for the period 1–30 Sept. 1939 in MGFA MS Lw 107/20; Molotov's speech of 31 Oct. 1939 is reproduced in Molotov, *Soviet Peace Policy*, 25–46; see also Carl, *Geschichte Polens*, 134; Garliński, *Poland*, 25; Vormann, *Feldzug*, 184, 191–2; Piekalkiewicz, *Zweiter Weltkrieg*, 115; Zentner, *Kriegsausbruch*, 220. See also the general observation on the problem of numerical data at the end of n. 1 above.

the campaign. This latter fact was in many respects decisive for Poland's inadequate defence. The failure of French or British help to materialize accelerated the Polish defeat.

The German armed forces showed a great skill, in their first blitzkrieg, in exploiting the advantages of motorization and thereby, in effective interplay between armour and aircraft, in waging an unrestricted war of movement. Shortcomings in training, equipment, and communications were of slight significance in view of the rapid and bold thrusts of the German forces. Generally speaking, therefore, the German victory represented the first successful application of a new strategic concept. It set new standards of warfare and, with the 'blitz' campaigns of 1940 and 1941, largely determined the further course of the Second World War.

A second reason for the swift German victory was clearly the high standard of General Staff training in the Wehrmacht. Operational intentions were formulated and implemented within a very short period of time. The advantages of strength, military geography, and concept were skilfully exploited and Germany's strategic situation in the east and west was decisively improved by swift actions resulting in the seizure of territory.

The Polish army, on the other hand, was insufficiently prepared for modern warfare. Pilsudski had earlier repeatedly pointed to shortcomings in the command of the armed forces, and the Polish commander-in-chief Marshal Rydz-Śmigły subsequently confirmed the correctness of that judgement by numerous wrong decisions. These began with the fundamental planning of Poland's defence, characterized by the refusal to yield any ground voluntarily. This meant that existing forces were hopelessly frittered away, strips of territory were chosen which were totally unsuitable for defence, and necessary flank cover was frequently disregarded. The inadequacy of Polish political judgement was reflected in the belief in effective support from Britain and France and in the neutrality of the Soviet Union. After the beginning of the war the mistakes were continued: large formations, until then scarcely under attack, were kept in their forward positions even though neighbouring formations had already suffered deep penetrations. This rigid conduct of operations not only virtually preprogrammed the battles of encirclement but also wasted what opportunities there were of reabsorbing retreating formations. Much the same was true as regards a timely retreat beyond the Vistula and the San, or a systematic defence of Warsaw.

Similar shortcomings in flexibility and striking-power were also reflected in the plans of subordinate staffs. Yet the decisive factor was the political and military starting-position, which, it has to be admitted, could not have been greatly improved. The gallantry in action shown by the overwhelming mass of Polish troops and acknowledged by the Wehrmacht could do no more than mitigate the weaknesses just listed.

Politically the success of the German campaign against Poland was less impressive than in the military field. Although in his 'peace speech' to the Reichstag on 6 October Hitler tried to give the impression that the continuation of the war depended solely on Britain and France, he was not prepared to make any major concessions, let alone comply with the demanded restoration of the status quo ante in Poland. The victory in the east did not undo the isolation in which the Reich was largely finding itself and from which Hitler, in view of the continuing war in the west, was trying to free himself by a new campaign. Nevertheless, the fact that the Wehrmacht was able to keep the initiative from the start was a vital prerequisite of its subsequent successes. And that was made possible only by the rapid victory over Poland and the subsequent concentration of all German forces in the west.

An equally important consequence of the Polish campaign was that National Socialist Germany now had the opportunity for an almost unrestrained exploitational and racist policy which, in its inhumanity, surpassed the imagination of even most Germans. The Wehrmacht, which had gone to war willingly if not enthusiastically, relying on the political leadership and its seemingly justified demands against Poland, had created the prerequisites of an occupation policy that ran counter to international law, an occupation policy which it often watched helplessly and which attracted to it the odium of shared responsibility. Its general passiveness, soon to find a consistent continuation in its unprotesting surrender of the administration of occupied Poland, could not therefore—in spite of the need to differentiate—acquit it of shared guilt for the conditions which now came into being.[24]

---

[24] Even the attested championing of law and justice by many individual soldiers can but little brighten the gloomy general picture of that period.

IV. Consequences of the Military Events in the Autumn of 1939

1. THE ESTABLISHMENT OF GERMAN ADMINISTRATION IN OCCUPIED POLAND

BY the final definition of the German–Soviet demarcation-line just under half of the Polish state came under National Socialist domination.[1] The German-occupied territory had a population of roughly 20 million—approximately 65 per cent of the country's population—of whom 15 million were Poles, 2 million Jews, and over 1 million ethnic Germans. Hitler did not yet have any definite plans for the treatment of the conquered country. He wanted to await further political developments before making up his mind about Poland's future destiny.[2]

The German-occupied area of Poland was, for the time being, under military administration. As neither a 'state of defence' nor a 'state of war' within the meaning of the Second Law on the Defence of the Reich had been proclaimed, Hitler, by ordering 'Case X' on 25 August, had expressly assigned to the army commander-in-chief the authority to exercise executive power in the east and west operational areas of the army. Brauchitsch in turn decreed that in the occupied areas of Poland sole responsibility was to lie with the commanders-in-chief of the individual armies.[3] However, their staffs were not adequately prepared for this task, either in terms of personnel or in terms of organization. Added to this was the fact that their authority—in line with the National Socialist style of leadership—was not clearly delimited from that of other institutions of the state or the party. Initial uncertainty about further political and military developments was probably a reason for the Army High Command to avoid major clashes with persons or administrative bodies if these were unwilling to submit to the military administration. Divergent intentions and objectives, each supported by a particular 'power-group', resulted in considerable confusion of competences and in conflicting measures which were hardly in line with German interests.[4]

The German–Soviet treaty of 23 August expressly stated that a decision on the continued existence of an independent Polish state would only be taken in the course of further developments. In Berlin, however, the intention from the outset was to

---

[1] Umbreit, *Militärverwaltungen*, 223.

[2] Broszat, *Nationalsozialistische Polenpolitik*, 14 ff.; Roos, *History*, 171-2.

[3] *DGFP* D vii. 302; cf. above, III.II.2, 'Mobilization and Deployment of the Wehrmacht', fourth paragraph.

[4] Umbreit, *Militärverwaltungen*, 65 ff., contains the first detailed report on the origin, circumstances, and consequences of German military administration in Poland 1939. Now and again, though, the role—and hence the responsibility—of the Wehrmacht in the National Socialist state is overrated. Cf. therefore also Broszat, *Nationalsozialistische Polenpolitik*, 19 ff., 29 ff., 44 ff.; id. *Polenpolitik*, 280 ff.; Roos, *History*, 177 ff.

Baltic Sea

Memel

Memel (R)

Königsberg

Stolp

Gdynia
Danzig

East Prussia

Tczew   Elbing

Lötzen

Neustettin

Chojnice

Deutsch Eylau

Allenstein

Stettin

Pomerania

Grudiądz

Schneidemühl

Chełmno

Bydgoszcz

Mława

Łomża

Oder

Noteć

Toruń

Ostrów Maz.

Berlin

Warta

Włocławek

Płock

Vistula

Frankfurt a.d. O.

Poznań

Kutno

Wyszków

Kościan

Warta

WARSAW

Mińsk
Maz.

Glogau

Kalisz

Łódź

Skierniewice

P

O

L

Dresden   Görlitz

Oder

Wieluń

Piotrków

Radom

Breslau

Silesia

Oppeln

Częstochowa

Government-

Kielce

San

Gleiwitz

Vistula

PRAGUE

Katowice   Cracow

Protectorate of

Mor. Ostrava

Tarnów

Bohemia and Moravia

Nowy Targ   Nowy Sącz

Brno

Zilina

returned to Slovakia
on 21 Nov. 1939

Keźmarok

S   L   O   V   A   K   I   A

Danube

Košice

VIENNA

Bratislava

H   U   N   G   A   R   Y

| 0 | 50 | 100 | 150 | 200 km |

Map III.iv.i. Poland, 1939–1940

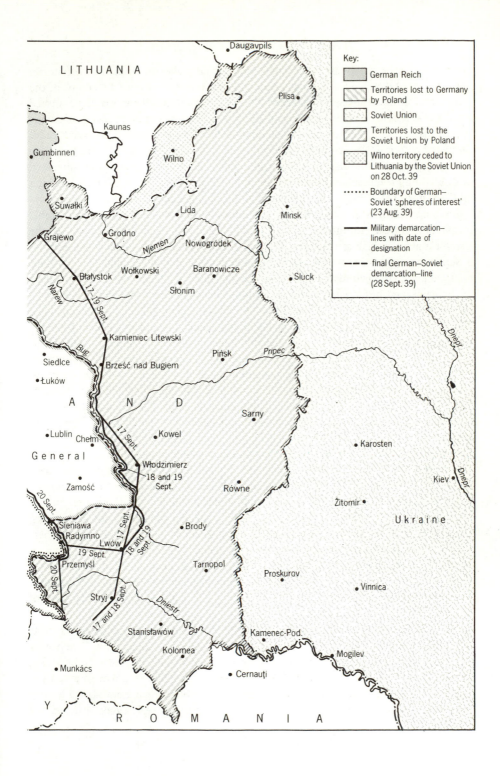

Key:

German Reich

Territories lost to Germany by Poland

Soviet Union

Territories lost to the Soviet Union by Poland

Wilno territory ceded to Lithuania by the Soviet Union on 28 Oct. 39

········ Boundary of German–Soviet 'spheres of interest' (23 Aug. 39)

——— Military demarcation-lines with date of designation

– – – final German–Soviet demarcation-line (28 Sept. 39)

LITHUANIA

Daugavpils

Plisa

Kaunas

Gumbinnen

Wilno

Suwałki

Lida

Minsk

Grodno

Grajewo

Njemen

Nowogródek

Białystok

Wołkowski

Baranowicze

Słonim

Sluck

Narew

17–19 Sept.

Kamieniec Litewski

Pińsk

Pripec

Bug

Siedlce

Brześć nad Bugiem

Łuków

A N D

Sarny

Karosten

Lublin

17 Sept.

Kowel

Chełm

General

Włodzimierz

Zamość

18 and 19 Sept.

Równe

Žitomir

Kiev

Dniepr

Ukraine

20 Sept.

Sieniawa

Radymno

17 Sept.

Brody

Lwów

18 and 19 Sept.

19 Sept.

Przemyśl

20 Sept.

Tarnopol

Proskurov

Vinnica

Stryj

17 and 18 Sept.

Dniestr

Stanisławów

Kamenec-Pod.

Kolomea

Mogilev

Munkács

Cernauți

Y

R O M A N I A

Dniepr

incorporate in the Reich not only Danzig but certainly also the remaining territories that had once belonged to Prussia. These therefore were soon bracketed out of the competence of the army commands. On 8 September a military commander assumed office in Poznań and two days later a military commander assumed office in Danzig-West Prussia. On 13 September the eastern part of Upper Silesia was placed under the Frontier Sector Detachment Headquarters established there. At the same time heads of the civil administration assumed their functions. Their duties consisted of discharging the actual administrative tasks in the occupied territories, working on the staff of the military commanders.[5] However, the rapid German advance and numerous unclarified personal and organizational problems resulted in considerable initial difficulties. Admittedly, Hitler had issued the first 'Directives for the Establishment of Military Administration in the Occupied Eastern Territory' on 8 September.[6] But this merely regulated the subdivision of Poland into military districts under the command of a 'Commander-in-Chief East', the filling of posts in the envisaged headquarters and administration staffs, and the first measures to be taken. On 25 September Hitler issued a second decree, on the 'Organization of Military Administration in the Occupied Former Polish Territories', which the Army High Command—who had drafted the decree—hoped would remain in effect for some time. The new structure, which a few days later was adjusted to allow for the extension of German-occupied territory under the German-Soviet treaty of 28 September, provided for four military districts (Danzig-West Prussia, Poznań, Łódź, and Cracow) under the control of Commander-in-Chief East. Special regulations were announced for eastern Upper Silesia and south-eastern Prussia. The entire military administration was to be headed by Colonel-General von Rundstedt; Reich Minister Hans Frank was appointed his head of administration.[7]

In spite of his irritation at Poland's earlier 'intransigence' and his bitterness about the treatment of ethnic Germans in Poland, Hitler at the outset did not rule out the continued existence of a truncated Polish state. In this he was motivated mainly by pragmatic considerations: for one thing, he expected Soviet wishes to be along these lines, and, for another, he was hoping, well into the second half of October, that the Western powers might yield if he proposed a reduced Polish state as an object of negotiation. Nevertheless, on the German side there were also some early reflections about an annexation of all conquered territories or about the maintenance of a residual area for economic exploitation by Germany and for the settlement of Jews.[8]

After the occupation of eastern Poland by the Red Army it gradually became clear that Stalin had no interest in the continued existence of a Polish state. The Soviet dictator had included a passage in the new German-Soviet treaty on joint action against any Polish national 'agitation'. Moreover, the Soviet government, by a rigorous occupation policy aimed at the annexation of eastern Poland, made sure of a *fait accompli* and thus induced Hitler, for his part, to seek a regulation in the

---

[5] Umbreit, *Militärverwaltungen*, 13-14, 85-6.
[6] Ibid. 91 ff.   [7] Ibid. 98 ff.
[8] Broszat, *Nationalsozialistische Polenpolitik*, 14 ff.; Roos, *History*, 171 ff.

German-occupied territory.[9] Following Chamberlain's negative response to his 'peace speech' of 6 October, Hitler finally abandoned the idea of a Polish rump state in favour of an unscrupulous 'policy of suppression and exploitation'.[10]

On 3 October Rundstedt assumed command of the occupied territory, which was now divided into the military districts Danzig–West Prussia and Poznań, the military area Upper Silesia, and the frontier sectors North (including the Suwałki corner), Centre, and South. However, the continuing uncertainty about the ultimate fate of the occupied territory and increasing clashes between political and military interests prevented an orderly discharge of his duties as Commander-in-Chief East. By mid-October Hitler decided that the time had come for a final settlement.

The first stage was his decree of 8 October 'on the Structure and Administration of the Eastern Territories', which reflected the wishes of some Gauleiters, now working as administration heads, to have the territories which were earmarked for annexation—their future sphere of activity—withdrawn from military administration as quickly as possible. Frank, too, was intent on sole responsibility for the rest of the occupied territory. On 12 October Hitler signed an order for the establishment of a 'Government-General' composed of all areas not earmarked for annexation. The new arrangement, combined with the replacement of the military administration, was originally to come into effect on 1 November, but on 20 October Hitler ordered it to be implemented as early as 26 October. The annexations—the new Reich Gaue West Prussia–Danzig and Poznań (Wartheland), as well as the Polish areas now joined to East Prussia and Silesia[11]—far exceeded the territories lost by Germany after the First World War. Germany's new eastern frontier, to be kept secret for the time being, thus included extensive areas populated purely by Poles. A police boundary was therefore designed to prevent the uncontrolled influx of Poles into original German territory. The old Reich frontier was initially also kept as a customs border.

The constitutional position of the territory not incorporated into the Reich and its position under international law remained unclarified right to the end of the German occupation. On the one hand, the intended policy of exploitation would obviously most easily be practised if the status of the 'Government-General' remained vague. On the other hand, the experience of the occupation authorities soon showed that any administration, of whatever kind, needed at least certain legal principles unless total chaos was to make the intended exploitation of human and material resources needlessly difficult.

Although the definition of the central Polish territory as an indispensable 'subsidiary country' (*Nebenland*) of the Reich gained ground in the course of 1940, its situation continued to be marked by an antagonism which had existed from the start. Its main representatives were Hans Frank and Heinrich Himmler. Admittedly, the flashy figure of the governor-general residing at the royal castle in Cracow was not predestined for the role of champion of a more or less orderly administration of the German-occupied zone. The striking contrast between the abstract demands

---

[9] Broszat, *Nationalsozialistische Polenpolitik*, 17–18.
[10] Ibid. 18.
[11] Umbreit, *Militärverwaltungen*, 98 ff., 109 ff.; Broszat, *Nationalsozialistische Polenpolitik*, 29 ff.

of leading National Socialists, especially Hitler himself, and the purely material prospect of long-term exploitation of the human and economic resources of the occupied territory soon brought the governor-general into conflict with the representatives of both trends. Initially he had fully and unreservedly embraced the National Socialist programme, but later he became open to pragmatic considerations. Moreover, he soon began to enjoy his post, and believed that an improvement in conditions within his realm would simultaneously mean a strengthening of his position in the power-structure of the Third Reich. This emerged with particular clarity from the administration of the Government-General.[12]

With the main exceptions of budget approval by the Reich ministry of finance, the legislative rights of the ministerial council for Reich defence, and the right of the Four-year Plan plenipotentiary to issue direct instructions, all the authorities of the Government-General were independent of Berlin and had to develop their own style. To Hitler the principal difference between the Reich administration and that of the Government-General was that the latter should not aim at perfection but should exploit and suppress the country by a kind of colonial administration. In actual fact, the small number and often the low quality of the German administrative officers never ensured the establishment of orderly conditions. But this was something the regime of the Government-General soon refused to accept. It tried to avoid chaotic conditions and endeavoured to have additional, and adequately qualified, administrative officials sent out. However, these efforts were not too successful.

2. German Occupation Policy[13]

The chaotic conditions in occupied Poland soon provided an opportunity for numerous party and SS authorities to adopt all kinds of arbitrary measures. Special-task units of the security police, while implementing their instructions to eliminate all 'anti-Reich and anti-German elements', simultaneously pursued their secret objective, at Hitler's behest, of taking action against all those inhabitants who could be potential figures in any future Polish resistance. Members of the Wehrmacht too were guilty of infringements of international law, often out of panic or indignation

---

[12] Among the many publications on the Government-General only the following need to be mentioned: Broszat, *Nationalsozialistische Polenpolitik*, 70 ff.; Eisenblätter, *Grundlinien, passim; Diensttagebuch*, esp. 7 ff. (introduction); Klessmann, *Selbstbehauptung, passim*; Kuby, *Polen*, 71 ff. (with reservations).

[13] Broszat, *Nationalsozialistische Polenpolitik*, 19 ff.; Umbreit, *Militärverwaltungen*, 137 ff. Cf. Figs. III.IV.1–2 (Allied propaganda leaflets).

Translation of Figure III.IV.1

Do you want to snuff it for the sake of annexation mania?

They tell you you're fighting for freedom and socialism against the plutocracies

What has the annexation of Poland to do with freedom and socialism?

Man erzählt Euch, dass Ihr für Freiheit und Sozialismus gegen die Plutokratien kämpft

Was hat die Annektion Polens mit Freiheit und Sozialismus zu tun?

FIG. III.IV.I. Allied leaflet against annexation of Poland

GESTAPOLEN

„Denn ihr pflüget Böses und erntet Übeltat und esset Lügenfrüchte. Weil du dich verläſſeſt auf dein Weſen und auf die Menge deiner Helden, ſo ſoll ſich ein Getümmel erheben in deinem Volk, daß alle deine Feſten zerſtört werden."

Hoſea, 10. Kapitel, Verſ 13/14.

"Das Schicksal der Polen wird hart aber gerecht sein."

GAULEITER GREISER

Das Schicksal des polnischen Volkes ist ein Terror der Gestapo und SS-Verfügungstruppe von unvorstellbarer Brutalität, die die ganze Welt mit Entsetzen erfüllt.

Authentische Berichte wurden zum ersten Mal durch den Rundfunk des Vatikans bekanntgegeben. Nach den Berichten, die dem diplomatischen Korps des Vatikans zugingen, wurden bisher nicht weniger als fünfzehntausend Polen aller Schichten hingemordet.

Ganz Polen liegt verwüstet. Warschau, das vor dem Kriege eine Bevölkerung von 1 200 000 hatte, und während der Belagerung 170 000 Menschen verlor, hat jetzt durch den Zustrom obdachloser Flüchtlinge eine Bevölkerung von 1 500 000. Und in Warschau—wie in anderen Städten Polens—herrscht Hungersnot.

Nazi-Gerechtigkeit . . . . . .

Radio Vatikan über Polen

" Zahllose polnische Familien sind in dem von den Deutschen besetzten Westpolen auseinander gerissen worden. Die Väter sind im Gefängnis, die Kinder zur Zwangsarbeit nach Deutschland verschickt und die Mütter nach Zentralpolen deportiert worden . . . . . ."

" Innerhalb von Minuten wurden polnische Bürger gezwungen, ihre Häuser und alles Hab und Gut im Stiche zu lassen und in Viehwagen nach unbekannten Bestimmungsorten abtransportiert . . . . . ."

" Diejenigen, die aus den Massen-Konzentrationslagern befreit' wurden, sind zu völlig mittellosen Bettlern geworden—dem Hungertod und Elend preisgegeben . . . . . ."

All das im Namen des

ANNEKTIONSWAHN.

FIG. III.IV.2. Allied leaflet against annexation of Poland

over Polish excesses against ethnic Germans or German troops. On the whole, however, the behaviour of the Wehrmacht contrasted favourably with that of other German organizations. There were numerous squabbles and conflicts between them which soon kept their superior authorities in the Reich busy. There were two opposing main trends: Hitler's destructive ethnic programme, aimed at the violent oppression and the spiritual and physical weakening of the Poles, and the predominantly pragmatic approach of the Wehrmacht, which soon met with the backing of some sensible authorities. The military leaders, however, did not do enough to get their views accepted. The result was that, if only for this reason, military administration in Poland was not of long duration. The Wehrmacht readily withdrew from any kind of responsibility and confined itself to more or less half-hearted protests. This merely gave fuller rein to arbitrariness. The Wehrmacht restricted itself to recording the countless excesses, murders,

---

TRANSLATION OF FIGURE III.IV.2

GESTAPOLAND

'Ye have plowed wickedness, ye have reaped iniquity; ye have eaten the fruit of lies: because thou didst trust in thy way, in the multitude of thy mighty men. Therefore shall a tumult arise among the people, and all thy fortresses shall be spoiled.'

Hosea 10: 13–14

'Poland's fate will be hard but just.'

Gauleiter Greiser

The fate of the Polish people is terror of unimaginable brutality by the Gestapo and the SS special squads, brutality which fills the whole world with horror.

Authentic reports have for the first time been made public by Vatican radio. According to reports received by the Vatican's diplomatic corps, no fewer than fifteen thousand Poles of all classes have been murdered so far.

All Poland lies waste. Warsaw, which before the war had a population of 1,200,000 and which during the siege lost 170,000 dead, now, through the influx of homeless refugees, has a population of 1,500,000. And in Warsaw—as in other cities of Poland—there is famine. Nazi justice . . .

VATICAN RADIO CONCERNING POLAND

'Numerous Polish families have been torn apart in German-occupied western Poland. Fathers are in prison, children have been sent to Germany into compulsory labour, and mothers deported to central Poland . . .'

'Within minutes Polish citizens have been forced to abandon their homes and all their belongings and have been transported in cattle-trucks to unknown destinations . . .'

'Those discharged from the mass concentration camps have become penniless beggars—left to die of famine and destitution . . .'

All this for the sake of

ANNEXATION MANIA

lootings, and expulsions by SS, police, or Party bodies and reporting them to Berlin.

An improvement of conditions was not to be achieved in this way. Even Party members posted to Poland, and many ethnic Germans who, believing in the Party's 'self-cleansing power', had so far accepted such incidents as probably inevitable initial difficulties, soon found themselves at the limit of what they could take. But even their queries and representations to leading figures produced virtually no results. In the winter of 1939–40 the large-scale de-Polonization measures in the annexed territories, as well as their consequences for the Government-General, were meeting with growing opposition from various supreme Reich authorities, such as the chancellery and the ministry of the interior, as well as from prominent National Socialists such as Göring and Frank. The reasons for this were not so much humanitarian as pragmatic. The principal result was that the racial-policy measures of Himmler and Heydrich, in particular, were henceforward pursued with less emphasis. For the Poles, however, this hardly meant an improvement.

Relations between the Wehrmacht and the SS and Party authorities continued to be tense, both in the incorporated territories and—to an even greater extent—in the Government-General.[14] The main task of the troops left in Poland was to secure the new territory as well as the frontier with the Soviet Union. In addition, with a view to improving the deployment basis in the east, they were responsible for developing lines of communication. The Commander-in-Chief East was responsible for internal security, for the functioning of transport and telecommunications, and for production in armament enterprises. During the first winter of the war his influence went even further in that he controlled the only functioning network of territorial authorities. They alone were really capable of gradually restarting industry and general supplies, as well as initiating the systematic listing and removal of booty and confiscated goods. On the other hand, the commander-in-chief was scarcely able to check the activities of other German authorities in the occupied country, which sometimes undid his own endeavours. Major personal clashes between Frank, who—regardless of his difficult position—was answerable for the situation, and Colonel-General Blaskowitz, Rundstedt's successor, were therefore unavoidable.[15] Although in May 1940 the governor-general succeeded in having his opponent relieved of his post, this controversy was by then paling against his ever more pronounced difficulties with the SS and the police. These two institutions—with their close personal and organizational links back in the Reich—refused to consider themselves as mere executive aides even in such tasks as they were given (for lack of sufficient personnel) by the Government-General's administration, e.g. the forcible collection of prescribed farm deliveries or the struggle against the black market, but instead preserved their own scope of activity. Frank tried to remedy this state of affairs by setting up an auxiliary police force recruited mainly from ethnic Germans, but failed to achieve any substantial changes.

---

[14] Broszat, *Nationalsozialistische Polenpolitik*, 44 ff., 75 ff.
[15] The C.-in-C. East thereby also became a personal symbol of the fact that the Wehrmacht, or at least a minority of it, actively opposed the inhuman outrages of the other occupation authorities.

Even greater differences of opinion existed with regard to criminal prosecution between the government of the Government-General on the one side and the SS and the police on the other. During the first few months, given the exceptional war situation and its immediate consequences, there may have been more or less plausible reasons for setting up special courts, which functioned alongside the Wehrmacht jurisdiction, but these reasons ceased to exist by the spring of 1940, when general German jurisdiction was introduced. Nevertheless, Himmler's henchmen continued their terror methods, as reflected, for instance, in the establishment of the notorious Auschwitz (Oświęcim) concentration camp. In this camp, situated immediately west of the frontier of the Government-General, the arrested Poles, unaffected by the intervention of other authorities, were detained under the most brutal conditions, used as labour slaves, and exterminated almost at will. This development, which was continued in other fields, was made possible by the fact that Frank in reality had but little influence.[16]

In the administration of the German occupation a programme was being implemented which aimed at 'total disorganization'. This was true both of the Government-General and of the western Polish territories annexed to Germany. The arbitrary terrorist measures, directed mainly against the Polish upper class and the Jews, were—if possible—even more far-reaching and barbaric in the western parts of the country than in the Government-General, as Himmler and the Gauleiters were trying to implement 'National Socialist self-realization' in the annexed area as rapidly and as radically as possible.[17]

Disregarding measures taken by the German occupying power arbitrarily, for special reasons, or for the securing of economic interests, there were three programmes which became characteristic of occupation policy in Poland: resettlement, transportation of Polish workers to Germany, and the struggle against the Catholic Church.

Expulsion of large portions of the Jewish and Polish population from the annexed territories into the Government-General began soon after the conclusion of military operations. It was part of the population-policy programme of National Socialist Germany; the manner of its execution, however, was also a reaction against the treatment of the German ethnic minority prior to and during the war.[18]

The situation of the ethnic Germans, already difficult, had worsened as Hitler's pressure on Poland increased. The consequences were a comprehensive ban on cultural activities, obstruction in professional practice, expulsions, and other forms of oppression. A mass flight to Germany began. On 21 August 1939 there were approximately 70,000 ethnic Germans in hurriedly established reception camps in the east of the Reich. The Polish government justified its procedure, which met

---

[16] On Frank's attitude and personality cf. esp. Broszat, *Nationalsozialistische Polenpolitik*, 79 ff.; *Diensttagebuch*, 23 ff.

[17] Broszat, *Nationalsozialistische Polenpolitik*, 15 ff., 41 ff., 128 ff., 158 ff.; Umbreit, *Militärverwaltungen*, 190 ff.

[18] Broszat, *Nationalsozialistische Polenpolitik*, 50-1, 62 ff., 112 ff.; id., *Polenpolitik*, 280 ff.; Roos, *History*, 165 ff., 178 ff.; Umbreit, *Militärverwaltungen*, 200 ff.; Kuhn, 'Deutschtum', 138 ff.

with understanding in other countries also, by claiming that those concerned had been active on Germany's behalf as agents and saboteurs. This is contradicted by the fact that the Polish measures had actually begun even before the German-controlled subversion and were directed not only against the presumed culprits but against entire families. Moreover, the strike and sabotage organizations set up for the event of war by German intelligence were composed for the most part of infiltrated agents. Anti-Polish activities by ethnic Germans as a rule began only with the invasion of the German armies, often indeed out of a need for self-defence. Very much greater was the number of ethnic Germans who served in the Polish army.

The real sufferings of the German ethnic group in Poland began in the early days of September, when the Polish administration collapsed. Mass arrests on the basis of prepared lists, aimless marches on which the elderly and children in particular fell victim to fatigue and hunger, executions, murders, and arson were regular features. The climax was the notorious 'Bloody Sunday' of 3 September, when about 1,000 Germans were murdered at Bydgoszcz (Bromberg) on the pretext of having fired at Polish troops. Altogether some 13,000 ethnic Germans lost their lives. Subsequent exaggerations by National Socialist propaganda caused the reports of what really happened to meet with disbelief outside Germany.

After the end of the Polish campaign the ethnic Germans found themselves on the side of the victors. Some of them yielded to the temptation to take revenge for injustices suffered. Yet the majority saw their task as helping to re-establish peace and order. Their gratitude to their liberators and their faith in National Socialism were frequently abused. Those who saw through the new injustices were hardly in a position to dissociate themselves from the practices of those in power. These in turn used the sufferings of the ethnic Germans as a welcome justification both for the German attack and for the terror in the occupied country. The ethnic Germans in the new eastern territories of the Reich found themselves declared the 'ruling stratum' and seized some of the posts and property of their Polish fellow citizens. But the real masters in the land, as was soon to emerge, were the SS, police, and Party officials sent out from the Reich, and they attached scant importance to the knowledge and experience acquired by the ethnic Germans in living together with other nationalities. The ethnic Germans had to submit to prolonged screening, as did the newly arrived resettlers, and only some of them were recognized as full German citizens.

Linked to this partial upward revaluation of the ethnic Germans was the expulsion of the Polish inhabitants from the annexed territories. What was initially seen as arbitrary action by local authorities and as part of anti-Polish terror was soon, following Himmler's appointment as 'Reich Commissioner for the Consolidation of German Nationhood', practised systematically and on a far larger scale.[19]

The Poles destined for deportation were allowed to take only the barest necessities with them. Those needed as labourers remained, often separated from their families,

---

[19] On the following in detail: Broszat, *Nationalsozialistische Polenpolitik*, 64 ff., 84 ff.; Roos, *History*, 178 ff.

in the new Reich Gaue or else were taken to Germany. The bulk of the deportees
were transported to the Government-General, where a particularly grim fate awaited
them. For the most part no preparations had been made for their accommodation.
Destitute and without appreciable help from the few existing authorities, throughout
a severe winter they drifted about the Polish 'settlement area', which was overcrowded
with refugees and in part devastated by the war. The Commander-in-Chief East
and the government of the Government-General soon protested against this kind
of ethnic 'consolidation', which rendered impossible the establishment of more or
less orderly conditions in their territory and moreover involved the risk of mass
epidemics. They achieved an almost complete temporary cessation of deportations at
the beginning of 1940 and a subsequent more systematic operation on a reduced scale.

The property of the expelled Poles was mostly shared out among the ethnic German
inhabitants. However, it was also to provide a livelihood for the ethnic Germans
to be newly settled there; already 70,000 from Estonia and 135,000 from Volhynia,
Polesie, eastern Galicia, and the Narew area had opted for Germany.[20] This option
had been given them by Germany's treaties with Estonia (15 October), Latvia (20
October), and the Soviet Union (16 November). The German government's intention
behind this resettlement programme was to settle the newly conquered eastern
territories with persons of German stock and not to allow these ethnic groups to
remain in the Soviet sphere of interests. For those concerned fear of Bolshevism
was the main motivation for abandoning their possessions and making a new start.

Hitler intended Poland to meet Germany's great demand—even greater since the
beginning of the war—for labour, especially in agriculture. However, the transport of
workers to the Reich was slow to get going.[21] Although the military administration
had already set up labour exchanges and made a start on registering and hiring
unemployed workers, in October 1939 Frank introduced general labour conscription.
Nevertheless, the voluntary principle was maintained for engagement in the Reich.
Even though the idea of paid work in Germany, so far untouched by the war, was
attractive to many Poles, actual volunteer figures fell far short of expectations. The
principal reasons were inadequate remuneration and insufficient support for
dependants remaining behind. When the Reich authorities called more urgently for
an at least approximate fulfilment of the target figure of one million workers—
75 per cent of them for agriculture—the competent authorities in the Government-
General increased their pressure. But even intensified measures proved unable to
satisfy more than a third of the demand by the end of the first year of occupation.

A further typical example of arbitrary procedure and of failure to harmonize such
steps with the other objectives of German occupation policy was the treatment of
the Catholic Church in the new Reich Gaue.[22] The SS and Party authorities

[20] Broszat, *Nationalsozialistische Polenpolitik*, 95; Kuhn, 'Deutschtum', 154-5.
[21] Broszat, *Nationalsozialistische Polenpolitik*, 99 ff.; Umbreit, *Militärverwaltungen*, 265 ff.
[22] On the following see Broszat, *Nationalsozialistische Polenpolitik*, 143 ff.; also the separate studies
in *Osteuropa-Handbuch Polen*: Stasiewski, 'Die Römisch-Katholische Kirche' (103-8), Koch, 'Die Unierte
Kirche' (109-13), Spuler, 'Die Orthodoxe Kirche' (114-18), Beranek, 'Das Judentum' (119-27), Wagner,
'Die Evangelischen Kirchen' (128-37).

regarded themselves as responsible for ideological matters and hence also for church policy. In the Polish Catholic Church they saw perhaps the most important champion of Polish nationalism, and a potential nucleus of resistance to German rule. They used every opportunity, under the pretext of indispensable security measures, to implement the fundamentally anti-clerical programme of National Socialism in those areas where practically no account needed to be taken of popular feeling or international consequences. Diocesan administrations and cathedral chapters soon lost their most important representatives through arrest or liquidation. Monasteries and institutions of religious orders were for the most part shut down, and members of religious orders as a rule imprisoned. The same happened to all priests who had been outspoken in any way.

Upper Silesia still had the most favourable conditions for church activities, and those in West Prussia were gradually improving a little. Here the clergy were given a chance to undergo a more or less formal Germanization procedure, and in this way managed to remain in the country. On the other hand, in the winter of 1939–40 Gauleiter Greiser in Poznań proceeded radically by initiating the expulsion of numerous still practising priests to the Government-General. In the Warthegau ecclesiastical life was suppressed to an extent that could no longer be accepted by the Vatican or the German foreign ministry. Their objections, however, remained largely ineffective.

In the Government-General the population had to endure less interference; in spite of the effects of the lost war their living conditions had not changed dramatically or radically.[23] But they too were not spared arbitrariness or terror. Nevertheless, owing to Germany's uncoordinated occupation policy, the Poles had more latitude there than in the territories dominated by an all-powerful Germanizing bureaucracy. The administration in the Government-General was not in a position to pervade the country organizationally to the extent that it could manage without the co-operation of the local population. It was here that the first beginnings of self-help and self-assertion by Poles were seen, as well as the beginnings of organized resistance to the oppressors.[24]

3. THE POLISH GOVERNMENT-IN-EXILE AND RESISTANCE IN POLAND

The head of state and the government of the Polish republic, having withdrawn in stages from Warsaw to eastern Galicia, fled the country on 17 September and, following German pressure, were interned in Romania.[25] As they no longer had any freedom of action and could not count on any decisive help from Britain or France, both President Mościcki and Premier Sławoj-Składkowski resigned on 30 September and designated W. Raczkiewicz, the former president of the senate and voivod of

[23] Broszat, *Nationalsozialistische Polenpolitik*, 158 ff.
[24] Ibid. 159; Klessmann, *Selbstbehauptung*, 99.
[25] On the following see esp. Roos, *History*, 168–9, 175 ff.; Rhode, 'Politische Entwicklung', 194 ff.; Broszat, *Nationalsozialistische Polenpolitik*, 162 ff.

Pomorze, as the new head of state. On the same day in Paris Raczkiewicz took the oath under the Pilsudski constitution of 1935. Although he regarded himself as a follower of the late marshal, he appointed the leading representative of the opposition, General Sikorski, to be the new head of government. In order to place the exile government on the broadest possible basis, Raczkiewicz instructed Sikorski to form a cabinet of members of the four major Polish opposition parties who had either escaped from Poland or were living abroad. Recognition by Britain, France, and the United States followed swiftly. In November Sikorski, who was also commander-in-chief of Polish forces, transferred the seat of his government to Angers, where he concerned himself mainly with the creation of armed forces in order to present himself as an equal member of the Western alliance and to lend greater weight to his demands.

The Polish exile army was composed of various elements. First, during or immediately after the fighting against Germany and the Soviet Union, a large number of men had escaped to Lithuania, Latvia, Romania, or Hungary. Thence, often with the connivance of the local authorities or after brief internment, they made their way via Scandinavia or the Middle East to France or Britain, where many reported for active service. Next there were called-up workers in France who still held Polish citizenship, as well as the crews of the few warships which had managed to escape from the Baltic. Altogether the Polish armed forces at the beginning of 1940 numbered approximately 84,000 men. From these three divisions were recruited and set up in France in the spring of 1940, as well as a mountain division which participated in the fighting in Norway. Subsequently Sikorski refused to have his troops included in the French surrender, and roughly 17,000 men, as well as the Polish air force in process of reconstruction, succeeded in escaping to England.[26]

From December 1939 Poland had a parliament-in-exile, the National Council, consisting of 19 members headed by the former premier Paderewski, who was living in Switzerland. In June 1940 this body, together with the government, withdrew from Bordeaux to London, so that Sikorski now possessed a number of institutions which lent him some weight *vis-à-vis* the Allies. However, the government and parliament were almost exclusively composed of opponents of Pilsudski, had not been popularly elected, and scarcely had any contact with Poland. From the winter of 1939–40 Sikorski tried to establish closer ties with his compatriots in Poland, especially with the nascent underground organizations. In order to gain their support he appointed his deputy, General Sosnkowski, as their commander-in-chief.

The beginnings of Polish resistance date from the siege of Warsaw. An organization under the leadership of General Karaszewicz-Tokarzewski, which called itself 'Service to Polish Victory', and which soon subordinated itself to Sikorski, began to grow rapidly, especially after organized opposition ceased with the destruction of the last regular troops near Kock on 6 October. Numerous smaller groups continued the struggle, especially where Poland's huge forest and swamp regions favoured guerrilla warfare. After the withdrawal of the bulk of the German forces the security bodies, at least in the Government-General, were hardly capable of effective counter-measures.

---

[26] Roos, *History*, 176–7; Rhode, 'Politische Entwicklung', 195–6; Garliński, *Poland*, 54 ff.

They confined themselves to overall reprisals and occasional punitive actions, but these merely stiffened Polish resistance. Even though partisan warfare abated in the spring of 1940 and the first resistance cells, especially in the new Reich Gaue and in the Soviet-occupied territory, were time and again broken up, the Polish underground movement experienced a vigorous growth. Its centre was in the Government-General, where it numbered some 100,000 members by mid-1940. The movement regarded itself as following an ancient Polish tradition and, after its amalgamation into a 'Union for Armed Struggle' (Związek walki zbrojnej: ZWZ), as part of Poland's armed forces. Tokarzewski, who had been earmarked as head of the organization in eastern Poland, was arrested by Soviet security officials towards the end of 1939 while crossing the demarcation-line. His successor, with headquarters in Warsaw, was the subsequent General Rowecki, better known by his cover-names 'Rakon' and 'Grot'. Southern Poland came under Colonel Count Komorowski ('Bór') in Cracow. From 1940 onward the underground army confined itself mainly to preparations for a general uprising, to military intelligence, and to propaganda. Armed operations and sabotage were exceptions. Alongside it there were a few clandestine groups, mostly associated with the major political parties. Establishment of an underground civil administration, on the other hand, was only partially successful.[27]

Poland remained one of the few German-occupied countries in the Second World War where there was no collaboration with the occupying power. Such attempts as there were got bogged down in their beginnings or were quickly frustrated by the German terror against the population. Indeed, the German reign of terror induced most Poles, who had at first not been too sorry to see the former government depart and had been indifferent to the new conditions, to practise increasingly a passive or active resistance. Even the seeming hopelessness of their situation and the reprisals of German and Soviet security forces were unable to halt this development.

4. EASTERN POLAND UNDER SOVIET RULE

The Soviet government, by limiting its claims to eastern Poland and giving up the area between the Vistula and the Bug in return for a free hand in Lithuania, had succeeded in acquiring a territory in which Ukrainians and Belorussians together formed the strongest ethnic group. This enabled it to maintain its assertion concerning the 'liberation of sister nations' and, before the world public—though at first only implicitly—to put the whole blame for the break-up of ethnic Poland, and the country's further fate, on the shoulders of the German government.

The Soviet Union proceeded far more skilfully than the Germans not only with the annexation but also with the administration of its occupied territory. It operated with the slogan of every nation's right to self-determination. Thus, it handed Wilno and the surrounding area over to Lithuania, which now belonged to its 'sphere of

---

[27] On the Polish resistance to Germany cf. mainly the detailed study of Jacobmeyer, *Heimat und Exil*, 11 ff.; id., 'Widerstandsbewegung', 658 ff. Further Garliński, *Poland*, 40 ff., which also deals extensively with Polish resistance to the Soviet Union.

interest' and was to be annexed in the following year. In October 1939 sham elections were held in eastern Poland, producing a West Ukrainian and a Belorussian body which promptly 'requested' the incorporation into the Soviet Union of the regions they presented. Simultaneously the entire area was subjected to increasing Sovietization through the expropriation of peasants, especially the big landowners, and through the nationalization of industry and the banks; these measures were a painful blow to the former Polish upper class. At the beginning of November eastern Poland was thus shared out between the Ukrainian and the Belorussian Soviet republics.[28]

With eastern Poland the Soviet Union gained a population increase of a little over 5 million Poles, 4.5 million Ukrainians, 1 million Belorussians, and 1 million Jews.[29] Their fate seemed, but was not, less hard than that of their compatriots in the German-occupied territory. Hand in hand with the 'Ukrainization' and 'Belorussianization' of the new territories there was also a political restructuring of the new population. This was achieved by means of extensive deportations, which fundamentally altered the entire ethnic and social structure. Forcible population transfers to the Soviet Union proceeded in several waves; they began at the end of 1939 and by the summer of 1941 embraced some 1.5 million inhabitants, of whom more than 700,000 perished. Those affected were mainly civil servants, landowners, entrepreneurs, and other leading figures, as well as priests and officers. Many professional soldiers and landowners were liquidated on the spot. Of the approximately 15,000 Polish officers taken prisoner by the Soviets, the murdered bodies of roughly 5,000 were later discovered in the Katyń forest near Smolensk.[30] 'Soviet government practice was in theory based not on a nationalities policy but on a social-political class-war "liberation programme".'[31]

The German–Soviet attack on Poland resulted in that country's renewed disappearance from the map as a state. On the German side, at least, this had not been the intention from the outset. Poland had not been earmarked from the start as a natural German 'living-space'—at least not the entire territory of the state. Hitler's decision to dispense with a Polish rump state was more recent, and based mainly on international developments up to mid-October 1939. The destruction of Poland, admittedly, then opened the door to an unrestrained policy of extermination and exploitation, which—with all its consequences—must, in spite of appearances, be charged to the account of both victorious powers.

---

[28] Garliński, *Poland*, 32 ff.; Roos, 'Polen in der Besatzungszeit', 173.

[29] Ibid. 178; according to Molotov's speech of 31 Oct. 1939 there were over 7m. Ukrainians and over 3m. Belorussians living in the territory concerned (ibid.).

[30] Principal studies of Katyń include Zawodny, *Death in the Forest*; Mackiewicz, *Crime*; Bergh, *Wahrheit*.

[31] Roos, 'Polen in der Besatzungszeit', 178–9.

V. Development of the Situation in North-eastern Europe: Effects of the Hitler–Stalin Pact[1]

B Y the German–Soviet treaties of 23 August and 28 September 1939 Hitler had acknowledged that north-eastern Europe belonged to the Soviet sphere of interest. Very soon the German leaders tried to divert attention from the consequences of this arrangement:

Whereas the press still continues in many ways to represent the German–Russian agreement as having been reached at the expense of the Baltic States and Finland, this is quite untrue. On the contrary, it is to be expected that, as a result of the conclusion of the German–Russian Pact, the whole area of the Baltic States, which felt itself to be seriously endangered in consequence of Anglo-Russian negotiations, will in future experience peaceful conditions, and the individual Baltic States will now more easily be able to reach a satisfactory settlement in their relations with Soviet Russia, such as is known to have already been reached in Germany's relations with the Baltic States.[2]

In point of fact Berlin had not given much thought to the fate of the so-called border states during the preliminary phase of the German–Soviet treaties, and had therefore, under the constraints of the late summer of 1939, pursued a policy which was not compatible with its earlier objectives in the Baltic region. Even if the Baltic States and Finland did not discover what secret supplementary agreements had been concluded on 23 August, there were bound to be presumptions along such lines. The period of uncertainty, however, was of short duration, for soon after 23 August the problems which had been brushed aside emerged anew. The Soviet Union proceeded to claim the 'sphere of interest' conceded to it. Following the Red Army's invasion of eastern Poland on 17 September, Stalin began to apply heavy pressure with a view to including these states in the Soviet power-sphere. Except for Finland this policy was put into effect without difficulties. Estonia, faced with an ultimatum on 28 September 1939, had to sign a 'treaty of mutual assistance' with the Soviet Union. Soviet troops were stationed in the country and naval bases were set up on Saaremaa (Ösel), Hiiumaa (Dagö), and at Paldiski.

Latvia, having concluded its 'treaty of assistance' on 5 October, had to cede bases to the Soviet Union at Liepāja and Ventspils. On 10 October Lithuania too was incorporated into the Soviet 'security zone' by an analogous treaty.[3]

---

[1] The following account is essentially based—except where otherwise stated—on the latest study of German–Finnish relations during the first phase of the Second World War: Ueberschär, *Finnland*, 61 ff. Cf. now also Myllyniemi, *Krise*, *passim*; a detailed if incomplete bibliography, though not free from ideological 'inhibitions', is found in Oberdörfer, 'Militärische Pläne', 430 ff.

[2] *DGFP* D vii, No. 297 (telegraphic circular from the head of the political department of the foreign ministry, Woermann, 25 Aug. 1939), here p. 306.

[3] Jakobson, *Diplomatie*, 127 ff.; details of the coercion of the Baltic States, illustrated by the example of Estonia, in Mäkelä, *Im Rücken des Feindes*, 25 ff.

Although Germany had made it clear that it was interested in undisturbed trade relations with Scandinavia and the north-eastern European states, no help was to be expected from it against Soviet expansionist tendencies. With the German-Soviet 'frontier and friendship treaty' of 28 September Hitler had secured his rear in the east and deliberately accepted a threat to the *dominium maris Baltici* as the price for it.

This political and strategic constellation left Finland little freedom of action *vis-à-vis* Moscow. Its hopes of German mediation were bound to be disappointed. The Scandinavian countries, in spite of public declarations, were not prepared to offer joint support as Helsinki found itself under increasing Soviet pressure. On 5 October Molotov summoned his Finnish opposite number Erkko, or his representative, to Moscow at two days' notice for discussion on an 'improvement' of mutual relations. In spite of the earlier rather discouraging German attitude, Finland thereupon once more tried to win German support, but Berlin left the Finns in no doubt of its lack of interest. Simultaneously, on 6 October, Hitler announced the resettlement of ethnic Germans from the Baltic area. This move, which ran directly counter to earlier policy and to the demand for 'living-space in the east' for the German nation, further revealed the extent of German concessions to Stalin.

In this situation, and with the news of the Soviet-Lithuanian 'treaty of assistance', just concluded, the Soviet-Finnish talks began in Moscow on 12 October. The Helsinki government was prepared to cede a few islands in the Gulf of Finland. But there were points in the Soviet demands which stood in the way of agreement—especially the leasing of Hanko (Hangö) as a naval base in the south-western skerries area directly at the entrance to the Gulf of Finland, the cession of the western half of the Rybachy peninsula in the Arctic Ocean, and the cession of a major strip of land in the Karelian isthmus. Although the Soviet negotiators, by way of compensation, offered to cede a territory twice the size in eastern Karelia, and although they were pressing for a speedy conclusion of a treaty, the Finnish government was not prepared to accede to these terms. Nor did the delegations find a compromise solution later. Although the Finns offered concessions in the eastern part of the Gulf of Finland, they mistrusted Stalin's motives and feared that a Soviet military presence would jeopardize their independence. Negotiations continued unsuccessfully in Moscow in October and November.

Following the failure of the talks there was clearly surprise in the Kremlin that it had not been possible to reach agreement with Finland in the same way as with the Baltic States. This is borne out by the fact that, after the diplomatic breakdown, the Red Army was not immediately in a position to start military operations.

The second half of November 1939 was primarily characterized by Finnish efforts to gain time in order to find support somewhere after all; they also speculated on a deterioration of German-Soviet relations. Help from Berlin seems to have remained the last hope of many Finns, even though official German quarters kept reiterating their loyalty to the treaty with the Soviet Union. When Berlin pointed out to the Finns that surely there was no danger of an armed clash and that the Soviet demands were modest indeed compared with those made on the Baltic States, this was no doubt merely a case of delaying tactics. Such views, which Hitler personally expressed to the Swedish explorer Sven Hedin in mid-October, were supplemented by the assurance that Germany would not attack Sweden from the rear if it should decide to come to Finland's aid. Stockholm assumed that in a possible conflict between Sweden and Finland on one side and the Soviet Union on the other there could be no question of German aid to the former. As the Soviet–Finnish conflict became more acute, so German reserve became more marked, as did the Finnish feeling of being let down by Germany, which in some quarters led to hatred of all things German. The German navy, on the other hand, earned itself Moscow's displeasure when on 13 October it extended its operational area against merchant shipping all the way to the Åland islands and Tallinn. Following a protest by Molotov, the measure was rescinded and the boundary-line of mutual interests on land was applied—at least temporarily—to the Baltic Sea as well, extending due north from the German–Lithuanian frontier (longitude 20° 30′ E.).

A special problem concerned German–Finnish trade relations. The Wehrmacht was interested in Finnish copper and nickel, and Finland in war material, especially from the stocks captured in Poland. After agreement had been reached on certain aspects the talks got bogged down as the Soviet–Finnish negotiations began.

Roughly from the moment of the final breakdown of the Finnish–Soviet negotiations an increasing concentration of Red Army forces was observed on the common frontier, entailing a growing risk of local incidents. The first major conflict occurred on 26 October near the Karelian frontier town of Mainila.[4] To all appearances it was—in the style of the faked German attack on the Gleiwitz transmitter before the start of the Polish campaign—deliberately provoked by the Soviet side; it allegedly cost the Russians four men killed and nine wounded from shelling by Finnish artillery. Molotov demanded the withdrawal of Finnish troops from the frontier. Finland rejected Moscow's demand but declared itself ready to negotiate about the appointment of a mixed commission to investigate the incident and to discuss a withdrawal of both countries' armies from the frontier region. The Soviet Union thereupon gave notice of termination of the non-aggression pact which had been in existence since 1932 and—despite Finland trying to prove its readiness for peaceful negotiations by offering a unilateral withdrawal of its troops in the Karelian isthmus—broke off diplomatic relations on 29 November. On the same day the first frontier violations by the Red Army began in the Petsamo area, and on the following day the Red Army opened military operations on a broad front, on land and in the air, without a declaration of war.

Although Helsinki immediately proclaimed a state of war and appointed Marshal Mannerheim commander-in-chief, the government continued to seek a diplomatic solution of the conflict. On 3 December a request was addressed to Germany to support a mediation attempt made by Sweden in Moscow. However, the request soon became irrelevant as Molotov had already rejected Stockholm's representations.

---

[4] For details of the Mainila incidents see Mäkelä, *Im Rücken des Feindes*, 35 ff.

During those months there was an unexpectedly fast and favourable growth in Soviet–German trade relations—so much so that towards the end of 1939 and in the first few months of 1940 they reached a substantial volume. That too was a reason why Hitler had no wish to impair German–Soviet relations over the Finnish question, especially as the outbreak of the 'Winter War' had led to reductions in Finnish raw-material deliveries in any case.[5]

Nevertheless, Berlin felt it necessary to justify its attitude with regard to Finland. It was pointed out that Finland, ever since 1933, had been extremely reserved towards National Socialism. Besides, as recently as at the beginning of 1939 Helsinki had not been prepared to accede to the proposal for a non-aggression and neutrality treaty. What was not mentioned in this context was that, in spite of just such an agreement with the Reich government, the Baltic States had been unhesitatingly 'sold out' to the Soviet Union. On 9 November Molotov nevertheless accused Germany of supporting Italian aircraft supplies to Finland, and the Soviet press followed suit by reproducing Swedish reports of alleged German war-material deliveries to the Finnish army. Investigation showed that, with a few insignificant exceptions, the ban on armament deliveries to Finland, imposed by Hitler after the outbreak of hostilities, had been observed. Admittedly, there had been some discussion in Berlin of whether the imposed restrictions might not be somewhat relaxed to enable Germany to receive larger supplies of Finnish raw materials, especially copper and nickel; after the protest from Moscow, however, this idea was quickly dropped again.

Strict observance of the German–Soviet non-aggression treaty led to intensified anti-German sentiment throughout Scandinavia and Finland. Among the German public there was lively interest in the state of a traditionally friendly nation, as well as considerable unease at Soviet penetration of the Baltic area; this sentiment persisted to the end of the 'Winter War', despite the ceaseless efforts of Goebbels and his propaganda ministry to counteract it.

Its accommodating attitude to the Soviet Union cost the German government not only annoyance among its own people and in the Scandinavian region, together with irritation from its Axis partner, Italy, at Germany's ban on the transit of arms supplies to Finland, but also some solid economic losses, which were deliberately accepted. These arose mainly from the Baltic trade, more particularly from the obstruction of shipping from and to Finland by a Soviet naval blockade. Now and again German steamships were sunk or damaged without protests being voiced in Berlin.

The fact that the Soviet Union was tied down in the north was, all in all, of advantage to German and Italian policy in the Balkans. However, Soviet expansion, which grew to be strategically significant at a small cost to the Soviet Union, began to worry Hitler as time went on. The Winter War might provoke Allied intervention and thus threaten ore deliveries from Sweden—which were vital to the German war effort—and other important raw-material supplies from the Scandinavian area. Orders

[5] For details of German-Soviet economic relations at the time see Fabry, *Hitler-Stalin-Pakt*, 168 ff.; Friedensburg, 'Kriegslieferungen', 331 ff.

were therefore issued for preliminary work by the Wehrmacht on a 'Study North', in order to be in a position to forestall an Allied landing in Scandinavia.[6] On the other hand, Berlin could not make up its mind to press Moscow to bring about an early conclusion to the war.

On 30 November 1939 Molotov indicated to the German ambassador von der Schulenburg that Soviet troops had started the war in order to bring about the formation of a new Finnish government with which a settlement of the controversial issues might at last be reached. At the same time he suggested that Germany should recognize the 'people's government' of Otto Kuusinen, the secretary of the Comintern, who was living in exile in Moscow; this government was proclaimed on the following day. The matter was carefully watched in Berlin, and with some concern, but that soon became immaterial as neither the Soviet Union nor Kuusinen himself officially requested recognition. The German government was therefore able, right to the end of the Winter War, to avoid committing itself in any way and to maintain contact with Ryti's constitutional government in Helsinki.

Altogether the role of the Kuusinen government in Soviet plans for Finland during the winter of 1939–40 has not yet been fully clarified by historians, and it is bound to remain in doubt so long as access to the relevant documents in Moscow remains barred. It is possible that during the talks with the Finnish delegation Stalin was really mainly interested in strategically securing the approaches to Leningrad, as well as in a few additional security requirements, rather than in taking possession of the whole country. After the rupture of diplomatic relations, on the other hand, the principal endeavour was probably the subjection of the entire Finnish state by means of the Red Army. In this context it is largely irrelevant whether the objective was a total military defeat, or subjection by a combination of external attack and internal subversion, or merely acceptance by the Finns of a puppet government and military control. Kuusinen and his associates, moreover, had the task, during the initial phase of the war, of presenting the invasion by the Soviet army as an act of assistance to the fraternal Finnish communist party. As the war dragged on, Moscow evidently lowered its sights in Finland. Kuusinen's 'people's government' was scarcely heard of and finally vanished imperceptibly from the stage.[7]

Military operations lasted longer than had been expected by either the European powers or the Soviet Union.[8] The Red Army had employed only limited forces. Its reorganization following the purges of the thirties was not yet complete. Thus, the Finnish army at first managed to offer successful resistance, even though the approximately 30 Soviet divisions were opposed by only 8 inadequately equipped and not yet full-strength Finnish divisions. In terms of numbers the ratio was roughly 500,000 to 200,000. Nearly 2,000 Soviet tanks were opposed by 60, and about

---

[6] Cf. Hubatsch, *Weserübung*, 31 ff.

[7] On Otto Kuusinen's personality and career cf. Aino Kuusinen, *Before and after Stalin*, and Hodgson, *Communism*.

[8] Recent detailed studies of military operations in the Winter War include Chew, *White Death*; Mikola, *Finland's War*; Nyman, *Finland's War Years*; interesting details, mainly from the field of Finnish intelligence, are also found in Mäkelä, *Im Rücken des Feindes*, 24 ff.

2,000 aircraft by a little under 300. The forces of Field Marshal Mannerheim, appointed commander-in-chief by the Finnish president Kallio immediately after the declaration of a state of war, nevertheless succeeded during the first weeks of the war—on terrain familiar to the Finns and exceedingly favourable to defence, and often helped by extreme winter cold—in halting the enemy, who suffered heavy losses, or even in repulsing him, so that the fronts became static about the turn of 1939–40.

The Red Army command therefore increased the number of its divisions to about 45, with now more than 3,000 tanks. With reinforcements brought up also in other sectors, as well as with a reorganization resulting in clearer command-relations in the staffs of the troops engaged against Finland, and with better co-operation between the different services, the Soviet army in mid-February 1940 achieved the decisive breakthrough in the Karelian isthmus, penetrating the 'Mannerheim Line'. Although they were once more halted, the Finnish formations by then were exhausted and lacked significant reserves, so that an encirclement and hence the loss of Viipuri and the whole of southern Finland was to be feared, especially as the rearward positions, now manned by the Finns, were only provisionally consolidated.

Various members of the Finnish government had sent out feelers as early as the turn of 1939–40 about the possibility of an early termination of the war. On 4 January 1940 Foreign Minister Tanner confidentially informed the German minister, von Blücher, of his own ideas concerning a mediation attempt, and in this connection skilfully referred to the obstacles encountered by German Baltic trade as a result of the Winter War. The German foreign ministry was not averse to the suggestion, especially as Ambassador von der Schulenburg had learnt in his first talk on the subject with Molotov that the Soviet government was no longer insisting on the Kuusinen government as the sole partner in negotiations. On the other hand, Moscow linked any possible concession to its wish that Germany should bring influence to bear against Italy's anti-Soviet attitude. However, as Mussolini proved intransigent on this point Hitler decided that no further mediation effort was to be made by Germany. Meanwhile the Finnish government made contact with the Soviet leaders via Stockholm.

At the same time the unexpectedly prolonged and until then successful resistance of the Finnish army had made various British and French plans of military intervention once more topical. Apart from the fact that any assistance could only be via Norway and Sweden, the principal objective was less to help Finland than to cut off Germany's ore supplies. Although the government in Helsinki was not of course unaware of these intentions, it was faced with the alternative of either accepting the Soviet peace terms or officially requesting help from the Western powers. The scope of possible Allied help, however, was highly doubtful, and Norway and Sweden steadfastly refused to allow an expeditionary corps to pass through their territory. The Swedes also refused to support Finland with regular troops—not so much because they feared a German reaction, but because they would be making themselves dependent on aid from the Western powers and would then be unable to prevent their intervention in the conflict. Faced with the threatening situation at the front, the Finns had no alternative but the journey to Moscow. On 13 March 1940 the peace treaty was signed there.[9] Stalin broke off the war so as not to risk intervention by the Western powers, which would have jeopardized his long-term strategy. The gains of the Soviet Union were kept within limits: Finland ceded the Karelian isthmus, parts of eastern Karelia, and a few islands in the Gulf of Finland; it had to grant transit rights in the Petsamo area and lease the Hanko (Hangö) peninsula for thirty years for the establishment of a military base. The Soviet Union's strategic position in the north was thereby greatly improved.

Germany, in view of its strategic situation and economic interests, was unable to thwart Stalin's skilful policy. For his impending about-face to the west Hitler depended on Soviet economic aid. Imports of grain, oil, cotton, and other raw materials, and of iron and precious metals, which had lately been increasing on the basis of the economic agreement of February 1940, would make Germany blockade-proof and eliminate any worries prior to the opening of what might prove to be a protracted campaign. Thus, Hitler's agreements with Moscow now enabled him to transfer the bulk of his divisions to the west.

With regard to the more distant future, it should be noted that the initial weaknesses of the Red Army in the war with Finland had resulted in an apparently ineradicable underestimation of its real quality by the German leaders. It is true that military experts observed, and subsequently emphatically pointed out, that the Soviet forces had very quickly adapted to new requirements and, after a certain regeneration phase, presented themselves in superb condition in terms of structure, equipment, and training. However, first impressions evidently proved hard to dispel, as was later to be seen, to Germany's great disadvantage, over the preparations for Operation Barbarossa against the Soviet Union.[10]

[9] Text of the peace treaty with attached protocol in Mazour, *Finland*, 241-6. Cf. also Map V.I.1.
[10] Cf. also Mäkelä, *Im Rücken des Feindes*, 74, 99-100.

PART IV

The First Phase of the War at Sea
up to the Spring of 1940
BERND STEGEMANN

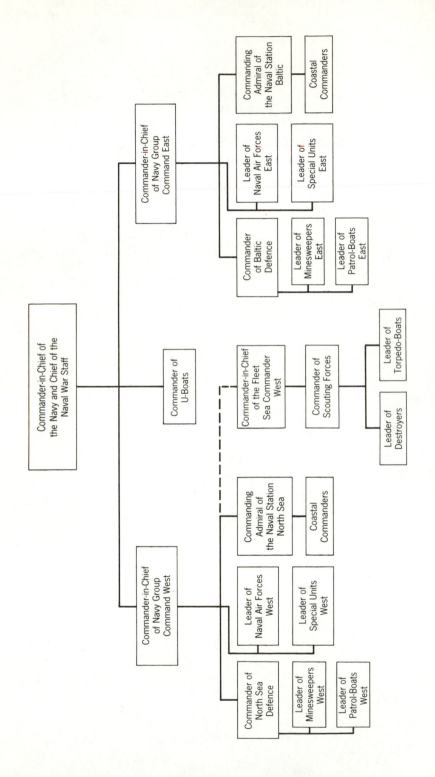

DIAGRAM IV.I.I Command organization of the navy at the beginning of 1940

I. The War in the Baltic

THE combat instructions issued for the German navy in May 1939 stated that 'the clear alignment of the European great powers' made it 'improbable that a war will be confined to a limited area. It is therefore necessary to prepare for the possibility of a two-front war: against Britain and France in the west and at least one enemy—Russia or Poland—in the east.'[1] Hitler's orders for 'Case White' assumed that it would be possible to isolate Poland. The tasks assigned to the navy in the Baltic were based on this assumption. In the North Sea measures against an unexpected intervention by the Western powers were to be limited to the necessary minimum.[2]

Raeder accepted Hitler's assurances that there would be no war with the Western powers; he was only too happy to concentrate on his own special area and relied on the judgement of the political leadership. Most German ships ready for action were placed under the Navy Group Commander East, Admiral Albrecht. On 19 August, as a precautionary measure, a total of 16 U-boats and the pocket battleships *Graf Spee* and *Deutschland* put to sea to take up waiting-positions in the Atlantic. The commander-in-chief of the fleet, Admiral Boehm, criticized this distribution of forces as indecisive: the forces left in the west were insufficient if a British intervention was expected, and the strong concentration of ships in the east was not necessary against the small Polish navy, which consisted of only 4 destroyers, 2 torpedo-boats, 5 submarines, 1 minelayer, 6 minesweepers, and 2 gunboats. On 31 August, however, after three Polish destroyers had been observed sailing for Britain, the commander of scouting forces was ordered to transfer some of his units to the west. By 7 September all cruisers, destroyers, torpedo-boats, U-boats, and patrol-boats had been placed under the Navy Group Commander West in Wilhelmshaven, Admiral Saalwächter.[3]

The task of the German navy in the war against Poland was to close the Gulf of Danzig, to eliminate Polish naval forces, and to support the army, especially in the conquest of the Westerplatte, Gdynia, and the Hel peninsula. For this last action the old battleships *Schleswig-Holstein* and, after 21 September, the *Schlesien* were used.[4]

On 3 September dive-bombers of the leader of Naval Air Forces East sank the remaining Polish destroyer, the minelayer, and a gunboat in the harbour of Hel. Thereafter there were no more Polish surface ships capable of action in the Baltic. However, German minesweeping units were prevented from completely clearing the Gulf of Danzig by Polish coastal batteries, which could not be silenced before the surrender of Hel on 1 October.[5]

---

[1] BA-MA II M 40, vol. ii, p. 5.
[2] Trevor-Roper, *Directives*, 4-5.
[3] Cf. Salewski, *Seekriegsleitung*, i. 92–5.
[4] For more details of the land war and the support provided by the navy cf. III.III above.
[5] For this and the following passage cf. Ruge, *Küstenvorfeld*, 27–35.

German forces were not able to sink the five Polish submarines, which, however, were unable to achieve any successes against German ships. For this reason they were ordered to try to break through to Britain on 11 September. On 14 September one submarine succeeded in breaking out of the Baltic. Between 17 and 24 September three others reached Sweden and were interned. The fifth Polish submarine had put into Tallinn to disembark her captain, who was ill. However, the Estonian authorities were not able to take this opportunity to intern the submarine. She operated in the Baltic until 6 October and was subsequently able to reach Britain. The German navy attributed the sinking of a German minesweeper on 1 October by a submarine-laid mine to a torpedo attack. As it also seemed possible that British and French submarines could penetrate the Baltic, the hunt for enemy submarines was continued until the middle of October.[6]

On 12 October the position of commander of German forces in the Gulf of Danzig, which had been created on 19 September and filled by the chief of staff of the Navy Group Command East, Rear-Admiral Schmundt, was eliminated.

Already on 4 September the German navy laid the first mine barrage in international waters south of the Great Belt and the Sound, which was intended to improve the control of shipping and to make it more difficult for enemy submarines to slip into the Baltic. However, the Sound barrages respected the Swedish claim to territorial waters with a limit of 4 nautical miles; ships passing through the Sound were thus able to avoid German surveillance. The German commander of Baltic Defence, Rear-Admiral Mootz, had little more than auxiliary and training-ships at his disposal. For this reason the war against enemy shipping begun on 10 September hardly produced any results in the Baltic. An operation on 1–2 October carried out east of Bornholm and supported by aircraft of the leader of Naval Air Forces East, which performed reconnaissance and ordered suspicious ships to steam towards the participating German naval units, was more successful. A similar operation between 8 and 10 October extended to the waters near the Åland Islands. As a consequence of these actions, more ships stayed in neutral territorial waters and passed through the Sound using a new shipping channel marked off by Sweden near Falsterbo.[7]

For this reason the naval war staff started an operation between 25 and 27 October to watch those points where ships had to leave neutral waters. The necessity of respecting Soviet interests in the Baltic States, however, placed certain restraints on a war against enemy shipping. In contrast, Sweden's claim that her territorial waters extended 4 nautical miles from her coast was no longer respected. After several incidents involving Swedish units and German naval forces looking for and seizing enemy ships, the naval war staff issued an order to respect only the 3-nautical-mile limit of Swedish waters in future. German–Swedish talks in which the suggestion was considered to close the Kogrund Channel to foreign ships, as had been done in the First World War,[8]

---

[6] Bachmann, 'Polnische U-Boot-Division'.
[7] For this section cf. Bachmann, 'Seekriegführung'; also Kutzleben, Schroeder, and Brennecke, *Minenschiffe*, 34–8.
[8] Cf. Grohmann, *Öresund*.

and for Germany to continue to respect the 4-mile limit, did not produce any results. The Swedish government also rejected a German suggestion that they should prevent submarines from entering the Baltic through Swedish territorial waters. Already at the beginning of September Denmark had laid a mine barrage off Copenhagen and, in compliance with German wishes, she now began to mine the Belts on 20 November.

The war against enemy shipping, conducted primarily by German minelayers off the Swedish east coast and extending to the Gulf of Bothnia, led to further incidents as Sweden did not comply with German wishes. Finally, on 25 November the German mine barrage in the Sound was extended to 3 nautical miles off the Swedish coast. This disrupted shipping for only a few days, however, as the shipping channel had been moved to within the 3-mile limit shortly before.

After the outbreak of hostilities between the Soviet Union and Finland, the German naval war in the Baltic was restricted even more. The blockade zone of 20 nautical miles declared by the Soviet Union on 8 December along the Finnish west coast and the entrance to the Gulf of Finland was outside the German operations area, which Hitler had limited to longitude 20° E. on 1 November. The mine-barrages laid by Sweden and Finland between the Swedish east coast and the Åland Islands precluded the possibility of future surprise operations by German naval forces in the Gulf of Bothnia. The naval war staff also considered Sweden's extinguishing of beacons and the removal of buoys at the southern entrance to the Sound to be clearly directed against Germany. Another such measure was the construction of a canal cutting the Falsterbo peninsula off from the Swedish mainland, to permit an undisturbed passage completely within Swedish waters. At any rate, in December the naval war staff was working on a study to determine what forces would be necessary to occupy the province of Scania and thus place all exits from the Baltic under German control.

The use of minelayers in the war against enemy shipping was continued until February 1940. In order to seize steamers transporting Polish refugees from the Baltic States to Sweden, even the light cruiser *Karlsruhe* was used for a time.

II. The War in the North Sea and the Arctic in 1939

THE strength of the fleets of the main sea powers in 1939 is given in Table IV.II.I. Raeder's assessment of the situation, written on 3 September, the day Britain and France entered the war, was correspondingly pessimistic.[1] In the Atlantic neither the weak German submarine fleet nor the two pocket battleships could achieve a 'decisive effect'. The few German surface ships could only show that 'they know how to die gallantly and thus are willing to create the foundations for later reconstruction'. On the other hand, the picture sketched by Raeder of operational opportunities had the war begun around the end of 1944 or the beginning of 1945 was excessively optimistic, for he counted on having ships which could not be ready for action by that time, and he assumed that Italy and Japan would co-operate with Germany against Britain, which was by no means taken for granted in other naval studies and plans.

TABLE IV.II.I. *Fleets of the Main Sea Powers in 1939*[a]

	Britain	USA	Japan	France	Italy	Germany
Battleships	15	15	9	7	4	2
Pocket battleships	—	—	—	—	—	3
Aircraft-carriers	7	6	6	1	—	—
Heavy cruisers	15	18	12	7	7	1
Light cruisers	49	19	25	11	14	6
Destroyers	192	236	112	61	61	21
Torpedo-boats	—	—	12	12	70	12
Submarines	62	96	60	79	106	57

[a] As of 1 Sept. 1939 (Germany); other countries around that date.

Sources: Gröner, *Schiffe*; *Weyer* (1940).

The construction-planning of the navy, which took as its point of orientation the distant future, could certainly not be realized under war conditions. Construction of battleships already begun as part of the Z plan was stopped and the main emphasis of naval armaments shifted to U-boats, minesweepers, torpedo-boats, and destroyers. Of the large ships only the completion of the two battleships *Bismarck* and *Tirpitz* and the heavy cruiser *Prinz Eugen* was given top priority. But even these relatively modest plans could only be realized to a very limited extent, as soon became evident.[2]

---

[1] Printed in 'Führer Conferences', 37–8.
[2] Cf. Salewski, *Seekriegsleitung*, i. 132; Rössler, *Ubootbau*, 186–8, and IV.VII below.

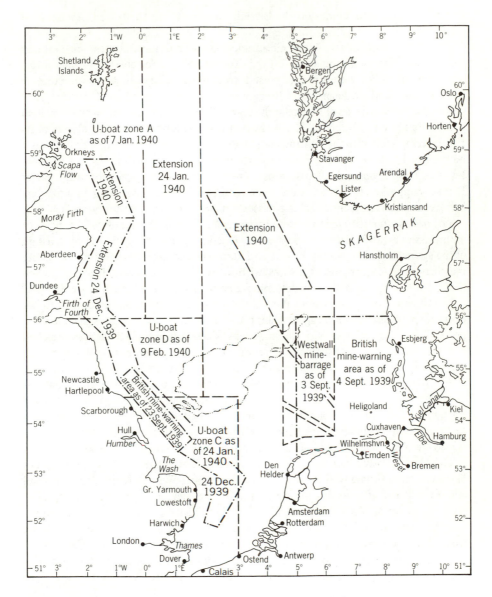

MAP IV.II.1. War Areas of the North Sea

At first the navy was mainly concerned about keeping enemy ships out of the Heligoland Bight. The commander of scouting forces, Vice-Admiral Densch, used the cruisers, destroyers, torpedo-boats, and minelayers under his command to start laying the 'Westwall' mine-barrage. This extended from Dutch territorial waters to west of Norway, and was completed by 24 September. At the same time U-boats began to lay magnetic mines off the British east coast, but the feared repetition of 28 August 1914 did not take place.[3]

The British immediately began air attacks on German naval forces, without any success, and stationed submarines off the German North Sea coasts. Surface ships, on the other hand, were primarily used to intercept German blockade runners between the Shetland Islands and Bergen and between Iceland and The Faeroes.[4]

Because of the attitude of France at the start of the war and the still hesitant British conduct of the war, Hitler and Raeder hoped that Britain would not be able to draw France completely into the fighting and, after the collapse of Poland, perhaps would be prepared to accept to a certain extent the situation created in eastern Europe. For this reason the pocket battleships were ordered not to begin the war against British shipping yet; U-boats were to conduct such a war according to prize law but were to refrain from attacking passenger ships or any French vessels.[5]

The navy soon attempted to remove these restrictions on the use of its few ships. In a conversation with Hitler on 23 September, Raeder was able to obtain the cancellation of the special orders regarding France and also received permission to attack enemy merchant ships (except passenger ships) without warning. However, Hitler still hoped that he would be successful in detaching France from her alliance with Britain.[6]

In a directive of 17 September the naval war staff stressed the importance of an operation with surface forces against shipping between Norway and northern British ports. Raeder and the Group Commander West, Admiral Saalwächter, reached complete agreement that such an operation should be carried out with at least ten destroyers in the Skagerrak and Kattegat on 26-7 September. If this caused the enemy to switch to a convoy system, the battleship group and destroyer formations could be used against them.[7] The planned operation was carried out on 26-8 September, but with only 4 destroyers and a torpedo-boat flotilla, which stopped and searched 45 merchant ships. However, this action is primarily of interest because it also involved the first use of the Luftwaffe against enemy naval forces.

The German navy had no air arm of its own. The leader of Naval Air Forces West was subordinate to the naval Group Command West only on a tactical level and in matters of mission assignments. At the start of the war, he together with the leader of Naval Air Forces East, commanded 14 coastal Staffeln, 1 ship's seaplane Staffel, and 2 aircraft-carrier Staffeln in the process of basing. Apart from the aeroplanes for the carriers, which were assigned to Air Fleet 2 on 25 September, these units consisted of flying boats and seaplanes suitable primarily for reconnaissance and patrol missions. The Luftwaffe wanted to carry out

---

[3] At that time British naval forces succeeded in sinking three light cruisers and a torpedo-boat of the German coastal defence forces near Heligoland.

[4] On the attempts of German merchant ships in foreign ports to break through and return to Germany after the start of the war cf. Dinklage and Witthöft, *Deutsche Handelsflotte*.

[5] 'Führer Conferences', 39 (7 Sept. 1939).

[6] 'Führer Conferences', 41. On 27 Sept. 1939 Hitler declared his intention to attack in the west between 20 and 25 Oct. if peace could not be concluded after the end of the Polish campaign: Halder, *KTB* i. 89 ff. (the trans. in *Diaries*, i. 91-2, is incomplete).

[7] Cf. Salewski, *Seekriegsleitung*, i. 114-15.

attacks at and across the sea and along the coasts itself. For this reason a special staff was formed in Air Fleet 2 and expanded into the Tenth Flying Division on 3 September, from which the Tenth Flying Corps finally emerged; this corps was directly subordinate to Göring. It was equipped with He 111 and Ju 88 aircraft, and reached a total strength of 150 aeroplanes in 1939.[8]

On 26 September aircraft of the Naval Air Forces West on reconnaissance missions in the operation against enemy shipping reported two British formations with large ships in the North Sea north of the Great Fisher Bank. These ships were involved in an operation to salvage the submarine *Spearfish*, which had been badly damaged off Horns Reef and was unable to dive. The Germans, however, assumed that this operation was a test of their reaction to a British sweep through the Heligoland Bight. Following the shadowing reports of the flying boats, four Ju 88s and nine He 111s of the Tenth Flying Division attacked the British ships. The Ju 88s scored a near miss on the carrier *Ark Royal* and a hit on the battle cruiser *Hood*, but the bomb did not explode. The He 111s did not achieve any hits.

The Luftwaffe was convinced it had sunk the *Ark Royal* and concluded as a result of this experience that even small air units were able to inflict serious damage on large ships. The naval war staff were sceptical about the claims of sinking, but they too believed that the enemy must now consider any attempts to penetrate the Heligoland Bight or the Baltic hopeless, although the British had not even made such an attempt. The apparent successes led to a considerable overestimation of the Luftwaffe's possibilities and concealed the shortcomings in the organization and chain of command in the conduct of the air war at sea.[9]

On 26 September restrictions on the use of the two pocket battleships in the Atlantic had been removed. Raeder now intended to keep the heavy British ships, especially battle cruisers, near home by increasing the activity of German naval forces in the North Sea. He also wanted to give the Luftwaffe and the U-boats new opportunities to attack British forces. For this purpose the commander-in-chief of the fleet, Admiral Boehm, carried out a sally on 7–9 October in the direction of the Shetland–Bergen line, with the *Gneisenau*, the *Köln* and 9 destroyers. Although the British sent strong forces to intercept this group, there was no contact. The use of air units by both sides also produced no results. This was especially disappointing for the Tenth Flying Corps, which had sent out 127 He 111s and Ju 88s to attack the British ships reported by the aircraft of Naval Air Forces West. The operation made the adversary uneasy, but no ships were withdrawn from the eight groups the British and French had formed on 5 October to hunt the German pocket battleships.[10] German naval forces were not sufficient to achieve a strategic reciprocal effect in which they could tie down significant numbers of enemy ships by their activity in one theatre of the war and thus take pressure off German units elsewhere.

[8] More details in Bidlingmaier, 'Grundlagen'; Hümmelchen, 'Luftstreitkräfte'.
[9] Additional criticism in Salewski, *Seekriegsleitung*, i. 117.
[10] Bidlingmaier, *Einsatz*, 43–4, 68; Roskill, *War at Sea*, i. 70–2.

Already on 17 September the operations department of the naval war staff had suggested, in addition to sallies by smaller ships, seizing the initiative in the North Sea by using surface forces to carry out mining operations. As the commander-in-chief of the fleet had not encountered any merchant ships during his operations in the North Sea, he suspected that they sailed between Norway and Britain further north. He therefore suggested gradually sealing off the British east coast with mine-barrages. For this purpose between 17 October 1939 and 10 February 1940 eleven operations were carried out and about 1,800 mines were laid off the British east coast near ports and estuaries; 66 merchant ships totalling 238,467 gross registered tons were sunk, also 3 destroyers and 1 trawler.[11]

There were differences of opinion between on the one hand Raeder and the Group Commander West, Saalwächter, and on the other the commander-in-chief of the fleet, Boehm, about the execution of the mining operations; this finally ended in Boehm's resignation. According to Boehm, initially the first operation was to be carried out with destroyers alone. The leader of destroyers, Rear-Admiral Lütjens, expressed his reservations because of their frequent engine problems. Thereupon Boehm promised him an escort by the *Scharnhorst* and the *Gneisenau* the morning after the minelaying operation about thirty miles from the British coast. But Saalwächter considered the danger of an air attack too great and rejected the use of the two battleships. Asked to decide the matter, Raeder agreed with Saalwächter; Boehm's first staff officer, Captain Weichold, then wrote in the instructions for Lütjens that the group command had ordered the mining operation to be carried out 'using destroyers, without cover and escort by stronger forces at daybreak'. Raeder considered this formulation a serious breach of discipline in the fleet and demanded that Weichold be relieved. Boehm was not prepared to accept this demand and immediately requested to be relieved of his duties as commander-in-chief of the fleet when the order for the removal of Weichold arrived. On 18 October his request was granted.[12]

In judging the decisions of the persons involved, it is necessary to accept the fact that Boehm's concern about the problems with the destroyer engines was justified, although no ship was lost during the mining operations. On the other hand, the intention to send battleships to within thirty miles of the British coast to provide protection for destroyers at daybreak hardly reflected an awareness of naval realities in 1939, even though none of the air forces of the warring states had previously demonstrated its ability to attack naval targets. Very soon it was proved that large ships could no longer provide adequate protection for destroyer operations near the enemy's coast.

Boehm's arguments must have made a certain impression on Raeder and Saalwächter, for in subsequent mining operations units of the commander of scouting forces were regularly sent to protect the destroyers. In the sixth operation

[11] Cf. Hümmelchen, 'Minenerfolge'; Rohwer and Hümmelchen, *Chronik*, 20–31. On the operations in the English Channel cf. Smith, *Narrow Sea*.
[12] Cf. Salewski, *Seekriegsleitung*, i. 136–8; Boehm, 'Seekriegsleitung'; id., 'Richtigstellung'; id., 'Stellungnahme'; Salewski, 'Erwiderung'.

off the English coast near Newcastle, on 12–13 December, Vice-Admiral Densch used the light cruisers *Nürnberg, Köln,* and *Leipzig* for this purpose. The *Nürnberg* and the *Leipzig* were torpedoed by the British submarine *Salmon*. When the two damaged ships were being brought back to Germany the next day an escort vessel was lost, again to submarine attack. The subsequent mining operations were carried out by the destroyers without cruiser escort. This dispute within the navy is noteworthy because it clearly shows their lack of unity and certainty with regard to operational questions.

In addition to these questions other problems emerged in the conflict involving Raeder, Saalwächter, and Boehm. The navy group commands, as links between the naval war staff and the sea commander east or west (i.e. the commander-in-chief of the fleet), had existed only since November 1938 and August 1939 respectively. Boehm and his successor, Vice-Admiral Marschall, commander of the pocket battleships, considered these commands an example of excessive organization that led to unnecessary friction, restricted the freedom of action of the commander-in-chief of the fleet, and did not provide him with adequate information. For this reason Marschall's command of the fleet soon led to new disputes. This situation was aggravated by the fact that Raeder did not abide by the regulation he had issued on 21 September governing co-operation between the group commanders and the commander-in-chief of the fleet. This clearly stated that 'Operations of the naval forces are conducted on the basis of orders from the group commanders. These orders should be limited to a general description of the tasks involved. The planning and execution of the operations are the task of the sea commanders, who obtain approval of the group commanders for operations they wish to undertake on their own.'[13] In practice the group commanders were responsible for operations and the commander-in-chief of the fleet had only the task of carrying out their orders as exactly as possible.

On the basis of previous experience, the naval war staff were extremely optimistic about the possibilities of using the two German battleships. Raeder was even of the opinion that 'the *Gneisenau* and the *Scharnhorst,* operating together, have nothing to fear from the three British battle cruisers, especially as they can withdraw from them if necessary'.[14] The commander-in-chief of the fleet and the naval war staff were, however, agreed that there were no real tasks for the battleships in the North Sea: 'The actual operations area for our battleships and heavy cruisers lies outside of this area.'[15] On 12 November, at a discussion of the situation at the naval war staff, it was decided to carry out an operation with the battleships to outflank the enemy blockade forces between The Faeroes and Iceland, and possibly those between the Shetland Islands and Bergen, and to threaten British sea routes in the North Atlantic by an apparent breakthrough. With this operation the naval war staff wanted

---

[13] Marschall, 'Stellungnahme', 60.
[14] 'Führer Conferences', 46. On the following section cf. Bidlingmaier, *Einsatz*, 79–88; Salewski, *Seekriegsleitung*, i. 158–63; Marschall, 'Vorstoß'; id., 'Stellungnahme'; Fechter and Schomaekers, *Seekrieg*, 16–19.
[15] Marschall, 'Vorstoß', 22.

to achieve a diversionary effect and take enemy pressure off the *Graf Spee* to prevent the enemy from taking advantage of the return of the pocket battleship *Deutschland* to Germany. (The *Deutschland* entered the Baltic on 14 November.)

On 21 November Marschall put to sea with the *Gneisenau* and the *Scharnhorst*, accompanied by forces from the commander of the scouting forces, which were to attack enemy shipping in the Skagerrak as a diversion. Because of bad weather this last operation had to be abandoned the following day; for the same reason and because of the lack of air reconnaissance the commander-in-chief of the fleet decided to forgo an operation against shipping between Norway and Britain. On 23 November the two battleships reached the area between The Faeroes and Iceland, where the *Scharnhorst* sighted a third ship at 4.07 p.m., which later turned out to be the British armed merchant cruiser *Rawalpindi*. At 5.04 p.m. the *Scharnhorst* opened fire. Twelve minutes later she ceased firing; the uneven battle was finished. The battleships were occupied with saving survivors for two hours; then the commander-in-chief gave the order to depart on an easterly course, immediately before the *Scharnhorst* reported sighting a darkened ship, the light cruiser *Newcastle*, which tried unsuccessfully to maintain contact with the German ships. At 7.40 p.m. Marschall received a radio message that the *Rawalpindi* had reported his battleships as the *Deutschland* on a south-easterly course. Two hours later he was informed that the British Home Fleet had been at sea since 6.00 p.m. and that other measures were being taken.

Marschall believed that the British ships would in any case reach the narrow part of the North Sea between the Shetland Islands and Bergen before he did, although the Home Fleet had left from the Clyde. Since the sinking of the battleship *Royal Oak* by the German submarine *U 47* in Scapa Flow on 14 October, that naval base could not be used until its defences had been strengthened considerably. Marschall no longer believed that it would be useful to pretend to break through to the west and decided to withdraw to the north-east, beyond the range of British air reconnaissance, to await reports from German air reconnaissance. He also hoped that bad weather would make it easier for him to escape enemy surveillance. On 25 November German air reconnaissance was able to confirm the reports of the very efficient signals intelligence service for the first time: the two battleships of the Home Fleet were north of the Shetland Islands, and cruisers and destroyers were watching the sea between that area and the Norwegian skerries. Marshall waited for the predicted storm front and passed by the patrolling British ships without being seen on 26 November, while the British continued to search until 30 November.

Immediately after Marschall's return, the naval war staff declared the operation a complete success; it had shown Britain how little she was in a position to maintain her domination of the sea in her home waters. Above all, the pressure seemed to be taken off the pocket battleship *Graf Spee*; enemy naval forces were now assumed to be concentrated in the North Atlantic. In fact, however, the British did not withdraw any ships from the hunt for the *Graf Spee* in the South Atlantic. On 13 December she was intercepted by a British cruiser group in the River Plate estuary. But there were other reasons for the criticism of the planning and execution of the operation which was soon heard. The naval war staff criticized Marschall for not having attacked the *Newcastle* or made any attempt to pretend a breakthrough into the Atlantic. Moreover, they were of the opinion that passage of the Shetland–Bergen line on 25 November would have offered good chances to attack the light enemy surveillance forces on station there. They also rejected Marschall's argument that enemy forces in the operations area had enjoyed an overwhelming superiority. But he was convincing in his objection that it would not have been possible to sink the *Newcastle* without serious mistakes by her captain; moreover, an attempt to sink her would have contradicted the basic principle that heavy ships should seek to break off contact with light enemy forces and ships armed with torpedoes attempting to keep in touch with them, and should not attack them at night. In 'Operation Juno' on 4–10 June 1940 it became clear that as few as two ably commanded destroyers could create considerable difficulties for the two battleships operating alone, even during the day.[16]

It is not clear how the commander-in-chief of the fleet could have pretended to break through into the Atlantic after the *Rawalpindi* had incorrectly reported him to be on a south-easterly course. Regarding the concentration of enemy forces, it should be mentioned that only two battleships of the Home Fleet were in the operations area. The two German ships were superior in speed but completely inferior in their armour and guns. For this reason a hit received during a battle with light enemy forces which reduced their speed would have exposed them to mortal danger as soon as they were beyond their own coastal waters.

The British history of the naval war is illogical in its criticism of Marschall: he is accused of having broken off the operation after sinking the *Rawalpindi* and of reducing his already limited operations plan, even though there were no British ships within a radius of several hundred miles that would have been able to oppose his ships on anything like equal terms. On the other hand, the *Newcastle*'s failure to perform the traditional cruiser task of keeping in touch with the German ships until larger British ships could arrive is put down as an unfortunate accident. (A rain-cloud is mentioned as the cause of this failure, but according to Marschall it was due to a successfully laid smoke-screen.) Unfortunately it is also not explained why many of the British ships took up positions south-west of the Shetland–Faeroes–Iceland–Greenland line, although the British believed at the time that the operation in question involved a breakthrough of the pocket battleship *Deutschland* returning to Germany.[17]

In conclusion, we must observe that the destruction of a British armed merchant cruiser or an old light cruiser was in reality all that could be expected from the plan of the operation. Beyond that it was perhaps possible to gain valuable knowledge about British reaction to a breakthrough attempt. However, it is doubtful that these results justified the risks involved in using Germany's only two battleships. The operations would have had a purpose if it had been possible to exploit the withdrawal of enemy forces from other theatres, but, as already mentioned, Germany lacked the naval forces for that purpose.

---

[16] Cf. V.III below.   [17] Roskill, *War at Sea*, i. 82–7.

III. The Use of Pocket Battleships against Enemy Shipping

SWEEPS by the German fleet were unable to force the British to keep heavy ships in home waters, and Raeder's hope that such sweeps would facilitate the operations of the pocket battleships in the North and South Atlantic (and in turn be facilitated by them) also proved unrealizable. At the start of the war he noted: 'The pocket battleships cannot be decisive for the outcome of the war either.'[1] This formulation, in itself a truism, was probably intended to indicate that Raeder did not expect much from the use of those ships. The initial German hopes concerning France required restraint in their use and led to a change in the assessment of their chances of success. After the restrictions were lifted on 26 September, the naval war staff hoped to 'achieve the greatest possible effect' by 'pushing into enemy trade routes, seizing and sinking numerous merchant ships, and destroying enemy convoys . . . and by paralysing enemy and neutral trade over a long period . . . achieving a maximum effect . . . upon the enemy'. They sought quick and impressive successes by using the pocket battleships, but did not want to achieve such successes at the price of losing one of them.[2]

The desired effects were hardly to be expected from the activities of only two ships, especially if the risk of losing them was to be avoided. At first the excessive optimism persisted. The naval war staff prepared to resupply the pocket battleships all over the world and informed them: 'If necessary, it is possible to visit Murmansk or Vladivostok for several days. Fitting-out possibilities and the question of overhauling engines will be settled. We hope for similar assurances from Japan.'[3] But the pocket battleships had no chance to make use of Soviet or Japanese bases. In view of the British and French counter-measures and the modest successes compared with the initial, unrealistically high, expectations (both pocket battleships had seized or sunk only 7 enemy merchant ships by the end of October), the naval war staff's assessment of the situation on 28 October was considerably more sober: attacks on shipping 'under the restraints imposed on the use of the ships' were only possible to a limited degree.[4] 'On the other hand, the other purposes of the use of pocket battleships—achieving a direct effect on the total volume of trade of the hostile countries, as well as tying down strong enemy naval forces and subjecting their ships to increased wear and tear—have been completely realized.' In spite of these successes, such as they were, it was decided to prepare for the return of the pocket battleships to Germany, for the naval war staff wanted at all costs to avoid losing one of

---

[1] 'Führer Conferences', 38.
[2] Cf. Bidlingmaier, *Einsatz*, 67; Salewski, *Seekriegsleitung*, i. 125.
[3] Bidlingmaier, *Einsatz*, 69.
[4] Ibid. 70.

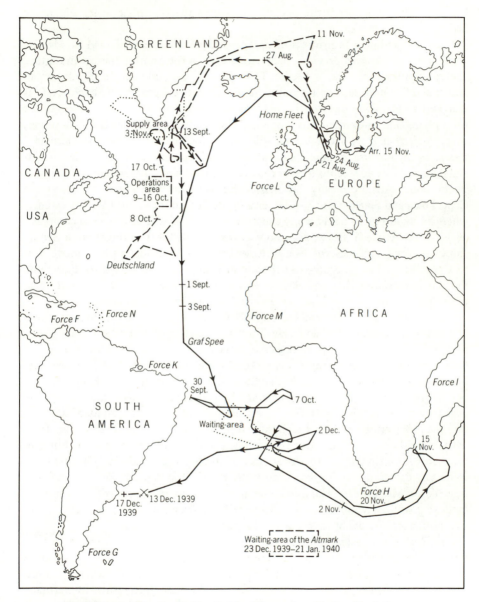

MAP IV.III.1.The Pocket Battleship War against Enemy Trade in 1939

them, and also hoped to be able to use them more effectively after Italy's entry into the war in the spring of 1940, which would tie down large British and French naval forces in the Mediterranean. In the case of the *Deutschland*, Hitler's desire to avoid the loss of a ship bearing that name also played a role. This was the reason why the *Deutschland* was rechristened the *Lützow* after her successful return from the operations area in the North Atlantic, which she had begun on 3 November.[5]

The commanding officer of the *Graf Spee*, Captain Langsdorff, had decided on 28 October to leave his previous operations area in the South Atlantic and attack enemy shipping in the Indian Ocean. On 15 November, after he had sunk a small tanker and had been seen by several neutral ships, he believed he had achieved his aim and returned to the South Atlantic to his supply-ship, the *Altmark*, for resupplying and to overhaul his engines. The condition of the engines, however, soon required an early overhaul in a shipyard, which meant a return to Germany. Before setting a course for home, Langsdorff wanted to attain an even greater success and thought he could accept a greater risk, as he would have to terminate his activities in the South Atlantic in any case. After he had sunk two more ships between Cape Town and Freetown on 2–3 December, he headed for the River Plate estuary, where he could expect to find many enemy merchant ships. The officer in command of the British Force G, Harwood, who was responsible for the protection of British shipping along the coast of South America, also expected such a move. On 12 December he had concentrated a force consisting of the heavy cruiser *Exeter* and the two light cruisers *Ajax* and *Achilles* 150 miles off the River Plate. An additional heavy cruiser, the *Cumberland*, lay at Port Stanley in the Falklands.

On the morning of 13 December Langsdorff approached the River Plate in search of a convoy about which he had received information from the naval war staff. When he sighted ships' masts at 5.30 a.m., he believed he had found the convoy and held his course towards the enemy ships. After he had recognized their true identity, he assumed—wrongly—that they had sighted him and decided to attack immediately before the enemy cruisers could reach their maximum speed and escape an engagement. At 6.17 a.m. the *Graf Spee* opened fire. Harwood divided his ships into the heavy cruiser and the two light cruisers, in order to attack the enemy from both sides. Langsdorff succeeded in putting the *Exeter* out of action, but was prevented from sinking her by the attacks of the two light cruisers. The *Ajax* was so heavily damaged that Harwood broke off the fight at 7.40, while the *Graf Spee* headed for Montevideo. Harwood managed to keep in touch with the pocket battleship while staying beyond the range of her guns until 11.17 p.m., when there was no longer any doubt that she would put into Montevideo.

The *Graf Spee* had also received several hits, which had put out of action two-thirds of her anti-aircraft as well as one of her medium-calibre guns. She had 36 dead and 59 wounded, and had suffered damage to electrical and mechanical equipment. Above all, she was no longer seaworthy enough to return to Germany through the wintry North Atlantic. Langsdorff had to consider too that the speed of his ship had been reduced by the growth of barnacles on her hull, and her engines could not operate without problems at a speed greater than 17 knots. His hope of being able to make his ship seaworthy again in Montevideo was, however, in vain.

[5] For details of the operations cf. (in addition to Bidlingmaier, *Einsatz*) Hümmelchen, 'Handelskriegsoperationen'; on the British countermeasures cf. Roskill, *War at Sea*, i. 111–21.

In the ensuing negotiations the Uruguayan government granted him permission to remain in Uruguayan waters for only seventy-two hours.

After the first reports of the battle, the British commander-in-chief in the South Atlantic had immediately ordered reinforcements to the area. But by the evening of 14 December only the *Cumberland* had arrived from Port Stanley. Two other heavy cruisers from South Africa and a light cruiser, an aircraft-carrier, and a destroyer division from Brazilian waters would not be able to reach Harwood before noon on 19 December. But in part as a result of deceptive British reports and in part because the first artillery officer of the *Graf Spee* believed he had seen the fighting-top of the battle cruiser *Renown* through his ship's range-finder (although the *Renown* no longer had a fighting-top), Langsdorff assumed that these ships had already arrived off Montevideo on 15 December. Having concluded that a breakthrough was impossible, as only 42.5 per cent of the normal supply of ammunition for his heavy guns remained, and fearing that in the relatively shallow water of the River Plate important parts of his ship would fall into enemy hands after an attempted breakthrough and the exhaustion of his ammunition, Langsdorff finally decided to destroy the vessel himself. On the evening of 17 December he blew the *Graf Spee* up in the River Plate. The crew were interned in Argentina; Langsdorff took his own life.

In retrospect it is difficult to understand what Langsdorff hoped to achieve by heading for Montevideo. If the government of Uruguay had granted him more time to make his ship seaworthy again, the enemy would have been able to concentrate overwhelming forces off the River Plate. And Langsdorff could not assume that the Uruguayan government would give him several months, during which he could tie down strong British forces until the enemy in a moment of weakness or carelessness gave him the opportunity to break through. From this point of view it would have been better, after Harwood had broken off the fight, to force him to resume the battle by pursuing the heavily damaged *Exeter*. On the other hand, it is certainly understandable that Langsdorff considered the chances of such an attempt to be very unpromising in view of the condition of his ship and the superior speed and manœuvrability of the two light cruisers.

In the naval war staff the question was raised afterwards as to whether it would not have been better to give Langsdorff a clear order to attempt a breakthrough.[6] In addition, the staff pointed out that putting into Montevideo underlined the problem of the lack of overseas bases, without realizing that this addressed questions which cast doubt on the whole programme on which the expansion of the fleet, according to the Z plan, was based. If even a pocket battleship, which was considered a well-designed and well-built vessel, was no longer seaworthy and was not able to break through and return to Germany after three and a half months at sea and a successful battle with weaker enemy ships, doubts were probably justified about the possibility of conducting an uninterrupted naval war with strong surface forces

---

[6] On the assessment of the situation on 15 Dec. cf. Bidlingmaier, *Einsatz*, 102–3, *Lagevorträge*, 64–5. On the following passage cf. also Salewski, *Seekriegsleitung*, i. 164–5.

in the Atlantic. However, the naval war staff believed that the operations of the two pocket battleships had had a very positive effect, although they had sunk only 11 ships, totalling 57,048 gross registered tons. In contrast to the intention, expressed in September, to achieve impressive successes by sinking numerous enemy merchant ships and destroying enemy convoys, the naval war staff now claimed that the purpose of a war against enemy shipping was 'not so much to sink merchant ships on a large scale as to disturb British merchant shipping continuously over a long period of time and to divert strong defence forces to the high seas, thereby relieving the home theatre'.[7] No longer was the fleet supposed to undertake operations, as in November, in order to make a war against enemy trade easier by forcing the withdrawal of significant hostile naval forces from the Atlantic; the war against enemy trade was now intended to facilitate operations by the fleet. The commerce raiders were, however, to avoid encounters with enemy warships. In cases in which this was impossible, the guide-line for the future was: 'The German warship and her crew are to fight with all their strength to the last shell, until they win or go down with their flag flying.' Raeder could hardly have expressed his criticism of Langsdorff more clearly, although he officially defended him.

A resumption of the war against enemy shipping could not be expected in the coming weeks. At the end of January Raeder expected to be able to send out the *Lützow* at the end of March and 5 armed merchant raiders between the beginning of February and the middle of April; in fact only 2 raiders put to sea during this period.

[7] 'Führer Conferences', 76-7 (26 Jan. 1940).

IV. The War in the North Sea and the Arctic in 1940

ALTHOUGH after the self-destruction of the *Graf Spee* a considerable number of British ships were able to return to duty in home waters, the naval war staff now believed that conditions were more favourable for fleet operations. A directive of 21 December informed the Group Commander West that for this reason he should bring the two battleships and the heavy cruiser *Hipper* into action frequently so as to achieve successes beyond the North Sea. The main aim was the destruction of enemy naval forces. The directive contained clear criticism of Marschall's decisions after the sinking of the *Rawalpindi*: 'The first battleship operation was broken off at the point at which tactical and strategic successes became possible . . . Unlike that action, in future operations every possibility of achieving successes must be sought and exploited.'[1] It is unclear, however, and was not explained in the new directive, exactly what strategic successes the naval war staff believed to have been possible in November. The directive envisaged an 'effective attack on the vital flow of contraband goods from Norway to the enemy' and 'disruption of the convoy system used up to now by the enemy' by means of attacks on the convoys from Canada, which were accompanied by only light escort forces. 'This is to force Britain to assign heavy escort forces, which would then have to pass through the operations area of our U-boats.' This intention seems rather strange, as the North Atlantic convoys had been escorted by battleships since 5 October; moreover, the British ships operating in waters around the British Isles were already in the operations area of German submarines, but not those in the mid- or western Atlantic. But even the first point of the directive, which called for the 'destruction of weaker hostile forces by surprise attacks', did not exactly provide a clear mission.

Group Command West was, for its part, of the opinion that the condition of the engines of the two battleships still did not permit operations in the Atlantic, and therefore wanted to carry out attacks only on convoys between Bergen and the Shetland Islands. There were also disputes between the naval war staff and the group command because the latter wanted to combine the operation with an action by U-boats against parts of the Royal Navy, and postponed it several times when the commander of U-boats could not provide enough U-boats in time because of icy conditions. In addition, no intelligence reports had been received about the sailing of a convoy, and finally, the *Gneisenau* suffered ice damage which had to be repaired. As a result, a further postponement of the operation could not be avoided.[2]

---

[1] Bidlingmaier, *Einsatz*, 115.
[2] Ibid. 116–18; Salewski, *Seekriegsleitung*, i. 168–71; Roskill, *War at Sea*, i. 153–4; Marschall, 'Stellungnahme', 68–9.

On 17 February a convoy was made out off the British east coast heading north; a second convoy was believed to be in the same area. The operation was ordered for the following day. Marschall was determined to reverse his course as soon as it became dark if he was seen and reported by the enemy on the day he left port. Because of weather conditions he moved his ships to the Wangerooge Channel the evening before he was to leave; on the morning of 18 February he was sighted and reported by a British bomber. Thereupon the commander-in-chief of the Home Fleet, Admiral Forbes, sent the one real convoy, which was bound for Norway, to Scapa Flow and put to sea with heavy ships of the Home Fleet from the Clyde. Marschall sailed about 11 a.m., accompanied by the second destroyer flotilla, which he left in the Skagerrak to carry out a separate operation. With two destroyers attached to his ships, he then proceeded to 61°N. and sent his ships' seaplanes as far north as the area off Stadlandet, without, however, sighting the enemy. Reconnaissance aircraft from Germany also reported no contact with the enemy. German signal intelligence did realize on 19 February that there was only one convoy, which had been waiting near the Orkneys, but signal intelligence was not aware that the Home Fleet had put to sea. Therefore the naval war staff wanted the commander-in-chief of the fleet to remain for an additional day in the area between the Shetland Islands and Bergen. The chiefs of staff of the naval war staff and Group Command West even agreed on an operation against the cargo ships and light escort vessels assembled off Kirkwall. But Raeder refused to interfere with an operation already in progress. Group Command West hoped that Marschall could be persuaded to stay in the operations area longer, even without a direct order, by constantly sending him information on the enemy's activities. They reported: 'Wireless traffic remains normal. No recognizable effect of operation. Heavy enemy forces expected near Clyde and in North Channel. Further stay in operations area on 20 February probably not dangerous and with prospects of success.'[3] The naval war staff did not agree with this wireless message, but they did not intervene.

As Marschall still had not sighted any ships of the convoy by 3 p.m. on 19 February, he concluded that the enemy was aware of his operation and had stopped all convoy traffic, so that remaining in the operations area would serve no purpose. He set a course for home and anchored off Wilhemshaven on 20 February. On the same day Admiral Forbes reached the operations area, and the convoy continued on to Norway. The naval war staff were very disappointed by the lack of results from the operation, as they had considered the operational situation very favourable. They decided that the group commander should not restrict himself to sending the sea commander intelligence about the position of the enemy but should in future intervene with clear instructions if the sea commander were uncertain about what to do. The staff did not perceive the mistake in their assessment of the situation and were not certain about what measures had been taken by the enemy. Raeder therefore explained the lack of results to Hitler on 23 February as a consequence of the fact that 'the convoy reported to be proceeding northward

---

[3] Quoted in Salewski, *Seekriegsleitung*, i. 171.

(towards Kirkwall) from the Scottish coast had evidently continued on a course further north'.[4] He wanted to repeat the operation soon and believed that the good work of signal intelligence would reduce the risk involved. This was a much too optimistic estimation of his own possibilities, as the ships of the Home Fleet had in fact been able to reach the operations area without being detected.

Before the two battleships could be made ready for action again on 25 February, the first destroyer flotilla with 6 ships was sent to the Dogger Bank on 22 February to attack British fishing-vessels reported there. Although on that day the Tenth Flying Corps had repeatedly informed the navy Group Command West of its planned actions off the British east coast, it was not told of the destroyer operation. Only the request of the group command late in the afternoon to provide air cover for the returning destroyers on the following day caused the Tenth Flying Corps to ask whether German destroyers were at sea; the answer came too late. At about 8.00 p.m. the destroyers were attacked by He 111s of the Second Gruppe of Kampfgeschwader 26, which scored three hits on one ship. In taking evasive action that vessel and a second destroyer struck mines and sank; the action was then broken off.[5] Now, owing to the loss of the two destroyers, the operation had to be postponed. Since the group commander was ill, it had been planned by his deputy, Admiral Carls, and in accordance with the wishes of the naval war staff it had been fixed for 25 February. Carls himself considered such an operation beyond the Shetland–Bergen line too risky, and wanted instead to carry out another mining operation with destroyers. Moreover, the repairs to the *Scharnhorst* were finished only on 4 March. On 1 March Hitler issued his directive for Weserübung, the occupation of Denmark and Norway, for which the navy had to use all available ships. This meant, however, that after the naval war against enemy shipping, the battle for the 'gates to the Atlantic' also had to be stopped for the time being.

---

[4] *Lagevorträge,* 81.
[5] Cf. Hümmelchen, 'Untergang'; Rohwer and Hümmelchen, *Chronik,* 32.

V. Preparations for the Campaign in the West

PREPARATIONS for 'Case Yellow', the campaign in the west, influenced the current operations of the navy considerably less than did those for Weserübung.[1] Hitler's Directive No. 6 of 9 October 1939 on the conduct of the war laid down that 'The main task of the naval war during this attack is to support directly or indirectly the operations of the army and the Luftwaffe'. In their discussions following receipt of the directive the naval war staff came to the following conclusion: 'The tasks of the navy are limited to the indirect support of the army and the Luftwaffe in the form of individual special operations, for example, the conquest of the West Frisian Islands or the support of Luftwaffe attacks over the North Sea.' If Holland, Belgium, and Luxemburg should become involved in the war, the navy would of course have the task of protecting the flank of the army right wing along the coast. Here the naval war staff were thinking of destroyers laying mine barrages off the Scheldt estuary and in the area of Texel and Den Helder, and of torpedo and mine missions by U-boats in the Hoofden. On 30 October the Group Commander West was entrusted with the preparation of these operations. For the planned start of the attack on 12 November 4 destroyers and 5 U-boats were kept ready; after the attack had been postponed they carried out mining and torpedo operations off the British east coast. In their further planning the naval war staff concentrated on the occupation of the Dutch island of Texel. In response to the wishes of the Army High Command, the islands of Schiermonikoog, Ameland, Terschelling, and Vlieland were included in the planning, which envisaged the transfer of the army troops to the islands by requisitioned Dutch boats with crews provided by the navy.

On 4 January 1940 the Tenth Army Corps of Army Group B also asked that the Navy High Command be requested to occupy the Dutch port of Delfzijl from Emden and to send light forces to protect the operations against the West Frisian Islands. The naval war staff, however, had to refuse the request to occupy Delfzijl since the navy did not have suitable troops at its disposal. Nor was it possible to send light naval forces against the West Frisian Islands. Some of them were defended by Dutch marines and mine-barrages whose positions were not known. Support of the operation by air units, suggested by the naval war staff, was refused by Air Fleet 2. In the end Army Group B decided not to carry out the operation, which was insignificant within the framework of the operations planned by the army as a whole.

After the date of the attack in the west had been repeatedly postponed and Hitler had not set a new date by 16 January, the naval war staff directed the Group

---

[1] On the following section cf. Jacobsen and Rohwer, 'Planungen und Operationen'.

Command West to prepare the laying of mine-barrages with surface forces in such a way that it could be carried out within the available time when the attack date was finally set. U-boats were not to be kept on station for this operation; rather, several of them operating in the North Sea would be sent to the area of the Hoofden. The occupation of the island of Texel was still planned. Should Anglo-French forces enter Belgium and Holland, preparations were to be made for at least three destroyers to lay the most important mine-barrages within twenty-four hours. In May and June 1940, because of other tasks, the navy was able to deploy only a total of five U-boats in the planned area, where they were able to achieve very little and one was lost.[2]

[2] Cf. Rohwer, 'U-Bootoperationen'.

VI. The Mine War

AFTER the introduction of magnetic mines by the British off the coast of Flanders in 1918, the navy of imperial Germany had also turned its attention to this type of mine. Development work was continued in the German navy during the Weimar republic by the Mine Barrage Test Command (Sperrversuchskommando), and in 1929 the first ground-mines with magnetic detonators were procured. Special types of mines were also developed by the navy to be laid by U-boats through their torpedo-tubes or by being dropped from the air.[1] Before the start of the war only a small number of ground-mines were produced; plans based on a mass use of the new weapon could therefore not be realized in the foreseeable future. In spite of the danger that too early use of such mines could provide the enemy with knowledge of their detonator mechanism and give him an opportunity to develop defences, the naval war staff did not believe that they could wait until a large number of mines were available. Ground-mines were laid along the coasts of Britain, first by U-boats and later by destroyers. Because of the small supply available, however, conventional anchored mines were also used.

As early as 10 October Raeder reported to Hitler on the successes of the mine war and the Royal Navy's obvious lack of mine-sweeping gear.[2] For this reason the naval war staff were eager to increase production of magnetic mines; the dropping of mines by aircraft of the Naval Air Forces West was begun. Between 20 November and 7 December 68 mines were dropped in a total of five operations before icing over forced the seaplanes used to stop their activity. Already in the first operation a mine fell on the mud-flat off Shoeburyness, where it was discovered and rendered harmless by the British, who were then in a position to take specific countermeasures.[3]

Meanwhile, Raeder attempted to persuade Hitler of the effectiveness of the mine war. Group Command West and the commander of U-boats were even informed that the mine war had priority over the war in the Atlantic and that U-boats must be used primarily to lay mines. After news had been received on 20 December that the British now knew how German magnetic mines functioned, the continuation and even expansion of mining operations off the British coasts seemed even more urgent. But the naval war staff still wanted to wait until a sufficient number of mines and aeroplanes were available before using air-dropped mines off the British west coast. They expected that, together with other measures in the war at sea, a large-scale mining offensive would possibly have a decisive effect.

[1] Cf. Bauermeister, 'Magnetminen', and the comment by W. Hagen. On the British side cf. Elliott, *Minesweeping*.
[2] 'Führer Conferences', 46. On the problem of the mine war in the winter of 1939-40 cf. Salewski, *Seekriegsleitung*, i. 141-7; Hümmelchen, 'Luftstreitkräfte'.
[3] Cf. Roskill, *War at Sea*, i. 98-102.

Raeder was unable to persuade the Luftwaffe to continue the dropping of mines from land-based aircraft in place of seaplanes of the Naval Air Forces West, which could not be used because of ice conditions. The Luftwaffe wanted to start dropping mines only when it had a supply of 5,000, which it could not reach alone before the middle of October 1940, or August if its output were combined with the production of the navy. The immediate result of Raeder's efforts was that a resumption of mining with aircraft of the Naval Air Forces West was impossible even after ice conditions improved. Three days after Raeder presented his views on 23 February, Hitler decided that the navy should wait until the Luftwaffe too was prepared to start dropping mines. Only after a second talk by Raeder on 26 March[4] did Hitler approve the resumption of mining operations from the air to 'effect a diversion of the British from the North', although only 1,274 air-drop mines were available by the middle of April and the Ninth Flying Division, planned specifically for the mine war, was still being based. From 2 April until the beginning of the attack in the west on 10 May aircraft of this division, together with those from the leader of Naval Air Forces West, dropped 188 mines in six operations off the south-west coast of Britain and the French Channel coast, which sank 7 merchant ships totalling 14,564 gross registered tons.

[4] 'Führer Conferences', 80-2, 87-8.

VII. The Submarine War

GERMANY began the Second World War with 57 U-boats, of which, however, 32 were too small to be used in the Atlantic. An additional 79 were under construction, or at least had been ordered from the shipyards. The planned commissioning dates extended until 1943. The mobilization programme applicable since 1 April 1939 envisaged a delivery rate of 9 U-boats per month: 2 of the large type IX, 4 of the medium-size VIIc, and 3 small submarines of type II. It was planned, however, to reach these delivery figures only after a period of eighteen months.[1] In his memorandum of 1 September 1939 Dönitz had, on the other hand, called for 300 U-boats for use in the North Atlantic as a precondition for 'forcing Britain to her knees with the weapons of the navy'.[2] A quarter of these U-boats were to be of type IX and three-quarters of type VII. In addition, Dönitz wanted 48 large U-boats for use in distant oceans. His arguments, which were supported by the commander-in-chief of the fleet, Admiral Boehm, convinced Raeder, who explained to Hitler on 23 September that the construction programme originally drawn up within the framework of the mobilization plan was inadequate and that a delivery rate of at least 20–30 U-boats must be achieved. Hitler accepted the arguments for carrying out such a programme and ordered that labour and material requirements be determined.[3] The expanded construction programme then worked out, about which Raeder informed Hitler on 10 October, envisaged an additional 658 U-boats by the end of 1942. But this programme was not begun; already on 1 November Raeder noted that Hitler had declared the U-boat construction programme to be not urgent and had given priority to re-equipping the army after the Polish campaign. In negotiations with the Wehrmacht High Command it was possible by December only to reach an agreement to determine whether the early allocation of the tin quota envisaged for the navy in the period from 1942 would make it possible to deliver the planned 316 new U-boats by the end of 1941. But an actual decision was postponed until May or June 1940. The navy had to continue to assume that its allocation of raw materials would be inadequate.[4] Because of the raw-material situation no construction of new ships was expected after 1 January 1942.

Moreover, U-boat construction was slowed by the unusually cold winter of 1939–40, which made work in the shipyards more difficult. In the remaining months of 1939 7 U-boats were delivered, and 13 in the first half of 1940. But in these two periods 9 and 18 U-boats were lost respectively; the total was thus reduced by 7.[5]

German submarines began the war against enemy shipping under prize instructions which respected the London submarine agreement of 1930. Moreover, acts of war

---

[1] Cf. Rössler, *Ubootbau*, 180-1.
[2] Printed in Salewski, *Seekriegsleitung*, iii. 64-9. Cf. II.II above.
[3] 'Führer Conferences', 41. Cf. also Salewski, *Seekriegsleitung*, i. 129-32; Rössler, *Ubootbau*, 196-9.
[4] Cf. 'Führer Conferences', 45-7, 55, 58, 62, 72. Rössler, *Ubootbau*, 198-201.
[5] Herzog, *Uboote*, 209.

against French ships were at first forbidden for political reasons. However, the mistaken sinking of the British passenger steamer *Athenia* on 3 September led to an acceleration of the use of convoys on 6 September. Additional British measures such as the arming of merchant ships and the issuing of instructions for them if they encountered enemy submarines made it possible gradually to relax restrictions on U-boat warfare. On 17 October 1939 limitatations on the use of weapons against enemy merchant ships in the seas around Britain (except passenger ships) were removed, and in the same month this was extended to ships which showed their hostile intent by travelling without lights. Between January and May 1940 all restrictions on attacks against enemy shipping in the waters around the British Isles and in the Bay of Biscay were gradually removed.[6] In contrast to developments in the First World War, this action did not lead to any conflict with the United States; after that country had proclaimed her neutrality on 5 September 1939, parts of the seas around Europe were declared to be a war-zone which American ships were not allowed to enter. They were also forbidden to put into ports of the warring states in Europe and Africa north of 30° latitude.

In the first phase of the submarine war, from the outset until the war against enemy shipping was suspended owing to the preparations for Weserübung in March 1940, U-boats were at first deployed singly in the eastern Atlantic between the Hebrides and Gibraltar. After the British had gone over to the use of convoys, Dönitz concluded in October 1939 that he could introduce for the first time the tactic he had developed in peacetime of co-ordinated attacks by groups of U-boats. The first attempt failed, however, as did two more in the same month and in November, because the number of U-boats available at any given time was still too small. It also became clear that it was neither possible nor necessary for a senior officer of a flotilla to exercise tactical command over U-boats attacking a convoy. Dönitz therefore decided to go back to sending individual U-boats into the operations area as soon as they were ready to put to sea, until he had a larger number at his disposal in the summer of 1940. By May 1940 the few U-boats in the Atlantic had sunk 148 ships totalling 678,130 gross registered tons; in addition, there were further losses due to mines and torpedo attacks by smaller U-boats off the British coasts.[7] Such losses, however, did not constitute a serious threat to Britain, as the British merchant fleet reached a total of 17,984,000 gross registered tons in 1939, and British shipyards had delivered 1,030,000 gross registered tons of shipping capacity the previous year.[8]

The use of U-boats in the Atlantic was made more difficult by the long distance they had to travel north around the British Isles, for, unlike the situation in the First World War, the British succeeded in blocking the Straits of Dover shortly after the start of the war in 1939: on 13 October the third and last attempt of a U-boat to break through the Channel ended when it was sunk by a mine. An additional serious problem for the U-boats and their commander was the frequent

---

[6] Cf. Sohler, *U-Bootkrieg.*
[7] Cf. Rohwer, 'U-Bootkrieg', 329-31; Dönitz, *Memoirs*, 51-74. Figures on losses to U-boats in Rohwer, *Submarine Successes.*
[8] Figures in *Nauticus*, 23 (1940), 344, 355.

malfunctioning of their torpedoes, which had originally been designed to be launched from surface vessels. The torpedoes available at the start of the war could be used with contact detonators or magnetic ones, which were supposed to detonate the torpedo under the keel of the ship being attacked and thus produce the greatest explosive effect. The first U-boat operations in September demonstrated that the magnetic detonators did not function reliably. The torpedoes usually exploded too early and targets were not sunk. This represented an extremely serious danger for the U-boats, as the alerted defence forces were able to destroy them in several cases. Various changes and adjustments of the proximity detonation device in the torpedoes did not lead to any improvement; in June 1940 Dönitz decided to stop using magnetic detonators. Only in December 1942 could a usable proximity detonation device be delivered. After Dönitz had ordered on 2 October 1939 that only torpedoes with contact detonators were to be used, numerous problems were discovered in them as well. The torpedoes ran too deep and did not detonate if they struck the side of a ship at an angle of less than 50°, although the minimum angle of impact was supposedly 21°. The cause of the depth problems, viz. leaks in the depth-apparatus container, was discovered in 1940 but not completely eliminated until 1942.

As the exact cause of the torpedo malfunctions could not be determined at first, a flood of directives was issued on torpedo attacks using various complicated procedures, which created many problems for U-boat captains without improving the situation. The crisis reached its high point during 'Operation Weserübung'. According to the calculations of the commander of U-boats, because of torpedo malfunctions only one attack in four on battleships, in fourteen on cruisers, and in twenty on destroyers and transport ships was successful. The repercussions in the navy were so strong that Raeder was forced to give an official explanation and form an investigating commission, which court-martialled four officers and naval officials. The causes of the problems were probably the inadequate testing of the contact detonator and the fact that, because of the magnetic detonator and the development of new types of torpedoes, the testing-station had not considered the faulty depth-control devices to be very important. The magnetic detonator, however, had not been tested under war conditions.[9] Yet in spite of its numerous weaknesses and the shortcomings of the torpedoes, it became clear that on the whole, as in the First World War, the U-boat was still the most effective weapon in the battle against the flow of supplies to Britain. Its successes against enemy shipping were far greater than those of the pocket battleships (which accounted for 57,048 gross registered tons) and the Luftwaffe (32,332 gross registered tons). The naval staff also complained constantly that the development and expansion of the U-boat fleet were not supported to the extent justified by its role in the war against Britain. In general, however it can be said that the naval staff were uncertain about what their real possibilities were. Following the initially pessimistic and realistic assessments of the situation, far-reaching or even decisive results were expected from the use of magnetic mines, pocket battleships, or the two battleships—results which these modest forces could not achieve together, much less individually.

---

[9] Cf. Dönitz, *Memoirs*, 80–97, 473–8; Rössler, *Ubootbau*, 215; Salewski, *Seekriegsleitung*, i. 188–90.

PART V

Securing the Northern Flank of Europe

Klaus A. Maier

AND

Bernd Stegemann

I. German Strategy

Klaus A. Maier

THE collapse of the political and military power of Germany and Russia after the end of the First World War gave the states of northern Europe a period of freedom from foreign pressure and threats. With the recovery of these two powers, they were affected more and more by the interests and policies of their Continental neighbours. The relationship between Germany and the Soviet Union was of decisive significance for the fate of the northern European states, as they formed the common flank of these two countries. Therefore the Hitler–Stalin pact gave rise to the unfounded hope that northern Europe would not become a battlefield. At the start of the war the relations of Denmark and Finland with their Continental neighbours were regulated by treaties. Denmark and the Third Reich had signed a ten-year non-aggression pact on 13 May 1939. The non-aggression pact between Finland and the Soviet Union had been renewed in 1932 and was originally intended to remain in effect until 1945. This condition of the states on the northern edge of Europe was not only a consequence of their exposed geographical position; it was at the same time an indication of their lack of political, military, and economic solidarity. The different economic ties of the northern European states with the countries involved in the war after 3 September 1939 made it more difficult for them to preserve their traditional neutrality and their own socio-economic systems when confronted with the demands of their warring trade partners, primarily Germany and Britain.[1]

In analysing the foreign-policy, economic, and military-strategic interests of Germany in northern Europe after 1933, it is necessary to consider, in addition to the interdependence of these factors, above all the National Socialist system of power and its racist ideology. However, as long as historians are not able to answer adequately the question of ambivalent factors and contradictions in the relationship between monolithic, dualistic, and polycratic aspects of this system (Bracher),[2] a distinction between traditional and specifically National Socialist elements in German policy towards northern Europe will remain of doubtful value. According to previous studies of the Third Reich's policy in Scandinavia,[3] the first ideological efforts to create a 'German–Scandinavian block' were undertaken by the head of the Aussenpolitisches Amt (Foreign Policy Office) of the NSDAP, Alfred Rosenberg, and the director of its department responsible for the northern countries, Thilo von Trotha.

---

[1] For comprehensive information on Scandinavia in the first year of the war cf. the collection of papers delivered in Oslo 15-19 Aug. 1976, 'Great Powers'; Martin, *Friedensinitiativen*, 176 ff.; Ludlow, 'Scandinavia'.
[2] On this problem cf. *Hitler, Deutschland und die Mächte*; *Nationalsozialistische Außenpolitik*; Messerschmidt, in vol. i of the present work, pt. IV.
[3] Loock ('Nordeuropa', 684 n. 1) offers a survey.

The Foreign Policy Office, whose staff considered their task to be to 'prepare the forces and instruments which, on the basis of the foreign-policy programme of its director, would be necessary in future to carry out a National Socialist foreign policy',[4] made use of the Nordic Society, which had existed in Lübeck since 1921, and attempted to establish it all over Germany by recruiting members for its offices in the NSDAP Gaue. Convinced that Scandinavia would sooner or later experience the same political development as Germany in the form of a 'common ideology within Germandom', the Foreign Policy Office sought to prepare the way by means of cultural propaganda and subversive activities there. But Rosenberg, whom Hitler himself did not value highly as a foreign-policy expert and ideological teacher of the Party,[5] was unable to achieve any great success in Scandinavia.

Internal conflicts within the Nordic Society after Trotha's death in 1936, and the lack of interest shown by the Scandinavian countries themselves, led to Rosenberg being pushed into the background by the competing Auslands-Organisation (Organization for Germans Abroad) of the NSDAP and Goebbels's propaganda ministry, both active in 'Nordic work'. While the attempts of the Auslands-Organisation to infiltrate Scandinavia politically and ideologically through groups of Germans living in the Scandinavian countries were unsuccessful (four NSDAP functionaries were expelled from Sweden), little is known even today about the details of the activities of the Nordische Verbindungsstelle (Nordic Liaison Office) of the Reich propaganda minister.[6] This is also true of the activities of Himmler's SS in Scandinavia. In 1938 Himmler did mention his intention to obtain 'Germanic blood' from northern Europe for the SS: 'I have set myself the task of replacing all Germans in the Germania regiment with Teutonic non-Germans within two years at the most.'[7]

Compared with these programmes based on Nazi racism and myths, the policy of the German foreign ministry was relatively traditional. In July 1938 German embassies and consulates were instructed to attempt to induce the governments of the small states to base their foreign policies on the general principles of neutrality, and reject any obligation to participate in sanctions under Article 16 of the League of Nations covenant.[8] Within the framework of this revisionist policy, for example, the foreign ministry exerted a moderating influence on the activities of the German minority in North Schleswig so as to encourage a friendly Danish neutrality towards Germany.

Although the German navy was much interested in Scandinavia, specifically in widening its base of operations to escape from the 'wet triangle' into the Atlantic and in dominating the Baltic to secure iron-ore imports from Sweden, before the war it had virtually no operational plan directed against this region. In his numerous attempts to achieve clarity about the operational possibilities and necessities of

---

[4] Quoted in Loock ('Nordeuropa', 689).
[5] Bollmus, *Amt Rosenberg*, 9: Ueberschär, *Hitler und Finnland*, 36 ff.
[6] Loock, *Quisling*, 182; Jacobsen, *Außenpolitik*, 488.
[7] Himmler, *Geheimreden*, 38; quoted in Loock, 'Nordeuropa', 692.
[8] *DGFP* D v, No. 436.

conducting a naval war, given the possible hostile combinations and Germany's own naval armaments, Raeder was guided by the following principle: 'The soldier must demand that the political leaders be concerned about creating favourable conditions for a conflict, which, however, does not relieve him of his duty to adjust to changes in the political situation and the possible conflicts that result from it.'[9]

We shall attempt to show how ideological and political ideas and aims influenced the strategic thinking of the navy command, and how, conversely, these strategic ideas influenced the decision-making process of the National Socialist leaders, especially Hitler. Raeder's role as commander-in-chief of the navy deserves special attention.

The combat instructions for the navy issued on 27 May 1936 still rejected the idea of a conflict with Britain, as 'such a war would have to be fought under special conditions and accordingly no combat instructions with the aim of ending the war successfully could be issued in advance'.[10]

In a report of 2 February 1937 on 'Basic Thoughts about Conducting a Naval War'[11] Raeder attempted to gain Hitler's support for a Wehrmacht strategy based on the concerns and aims of the navy. Basing his arguments on the experiences of the First World War, and clearly following Wegener's ideas on naval strategy,[12] Raeder considered the main task of the navy to be the protection of German sea routes and attacks on those of the enemy.[13] In his opinion it was for the political leaders to prepare such a strategy in peacetime by pursuing a far-sighted naval armaments programme: 'A strong and long-term policy of ship construction in peace is therefore an essential part of strategy in war.' The improvement of the operational basis was also the task of the political leaders: 'The operational use of the fleet is . . . determined by ships and bases. These two factors together, in comparison with the naval forces of the enemy, determine a navy's actual fighting ability.' For a foreign-policy strategy in peacetime Raeder advocated forming coalitions, favourable neutrality treaties, and the 'acquisition of bases or at least the creation of a friendly attitude towards Germany in neutral countries'. In war, however, operational possibilities should be sought, allowing the navy to seize the initiative by offensive actions and avoid assuming a rigid defensive posture. Raeder based his views on an 'assumed war in the near future' with France and the Soviet Union. But he added as a warning: 'Under certain circumstances political constellations can change more rapidly than ships can be built.'

With Hitler's 'change to a course against Britain'[14]—the acceptance of the risk of a war with that country, given the continuation of the National Socialist policy of aggression—the navy was forced to begin making plans for this increasingly probable conflict. In the 'Study of the Tasks of Conducting a Naval War 1937–8' of 4 May 1937 by Captain Heye,[15] which was intended to serve as preparation for the

---

[9] Quoted in Dülffer, *Weimar*, 441.   [10] Quoted ibid. 440.
[11] 'Grundsätzliche Gedanken der Seekriegführung', Vortrag ObdM, gehalten am 3.2.37, BA-MA RM 6/53.   [12] Wegener, *Seestrategie*.
[13] Details in Gemzell, *Raeder*.   [14] Details in Henke, *England*.
[15] BA-MA III M 151/2. Cf. Salewski, *Seekriegsleitung*, i. 33 ff.; Dülffer, *Weimar*, 440 ff.

combat instructions for 1938, the possibility of a war with Britain in which the navy was assigned a decisive role was mentioned for the first time. There was, however, one cautious note: 'As long as British strength in relation to that of Germany remains unchanged and the military advantages of the British geographical position cannot be overcome, we must not expect to achieve lasting and decisive success.'[16]

The reactions of the navy leaders[17] to Heye's study ranged from the warning in principle against 'even mentioning such a possibility [i.e. a war with Britain] in an internal service memorandum'[18] to reflections on the political consequences of such a war. The fleet commander-in-chief, Admiral Carls, observed: 'If Britain is against us, political inhibitions about attacking Denmark will probably be overcome.' Raeder noted that he was of the same opinion.[19] The war-game of the Navy High Command in February and March 1939 clearly showed the 'new strategic aims' against Britain. In the concluding conference[20] it was stated, without any attempt to determine Germany's responsibility, that the 'crisis of 1938' had shown that Britain and France must be considered as a single power-bloc.

While in May 1937 the navy leaders still did not believe that Germany had any chance of victory in a naval war against Britain, the final conference represented an attempt to adjust naval strategy to German foreign policy in spite of the navy's inadequacies and lack of sufficient operational possibilities. Assuming a war in 1943, it was recognized that of course in the foreseeable future it would not be possible to achieve a purely quantitative equality with the British fleet. However, as Britain was forced to divide her naval forces to protect a large number of objectives and interests, a war against her sea routes by highly mobile forces would give the numerically weaker side the possibility of 'tackling certain military tasks with good prospects of success'.

The lack of suitable bases was mentioned as the main obstacle to such a German naval war in more distant waters. For this reason the question was discussed of 'what Wehrmacht operations could improve the starting-position for a decisive naval war in the oceans of the world, in view of the fact that political successes in peacetime do not give us the chance to acquire and develop bases beyond the North Sea and the Baltic'. An expansion of German control of coastal areas within the limits of a Franco-British blockade would produce a 'tactical improvement' but no change in the 'overall strategic situation'. In this regard it was noted at the final conference that: 'The occupation of the French Atlantic coast or of central and northern Norway would solve this problem.' However, as German bases in central and northern Norway would not enable Germany to prevent the British blocking the northern route into the Atlantic, it was decided 'to give the aim of establishing bases on the French Atlantic coast absolute priority'. The navy leaders entertained no illusions

---

[16] Quoted in Dülffer, *Weimar*, 441.   [17] BA-MA III M 151/2.
[18] e.g. the commanding admiral of the North Sea station, Schultze; quoted in Dülffer, *Weimar*, 442.
[19] Ibid.
[20] The final conference of the war-game at the beginning of Mar. 1939 was probably given by Raeder: BA-MA M 29/34 148/1; cf. Dülffer, *Weimar*, 527 ff.; Gemzell, *Raeder*, 131–46. Quotations in the following passage are from Gemzell, *Raeder*, unless otherwise stated.

about the difficulty of carrying out a Wehrmacht operation to realize this aim, but they hoped that the 'top leadership' would be inclined to 'consider such an operation, as control of the French Channel coast would probably also yield important advantages for the Luftwaffe in a war with Britain'. This analysis of the problem of bases was intended to convey the ideas of the navy leaders as to desirable objectives for the Wehrmacht, without going into their feasibility at this point.[21]

In a report of 8 March 1939 the head of the office of warship construction in the Navy High Command, Admiral Fuchs, doubted that it would be possible to break through the Maginot Line and considered 'given the geography of Europe . . . [the capture of] Polyarny [near Murmansk]' as the only task for the army capable of fulfilment—apart from taking Brest—which would help the navy. In reply to the critical objections of his superior Schniewind, who did not want to drop Brest as an objective, Fuchs observed that in a war 'the army will be grateful if it is given a task essential to deciding the war in the form of an ambitious and realizable operational aim'.[22] The operational ideas of the navy were based on the level of armaments envisaged for 1943 at the earliest. The combat instructions of May 1939 for a naval war[23] contained no plans for the acquisition of bases, although these would be all the more important if the navy had to fight a war against Britain before reaching the level of armaments planned for 1943.[24]

In a war with Britain Germany's supply of Swedish iron ore through the Norwegian port of Narvik would be endangered because of the threat to the sea route.[25] On 2 November 1934 Raeder noted down Hitler's thoughts as expressed in a talk with him and Göring: Hitler considered 'an expansion of the navy . . . absolutely vital, as the war could not be carried on at all if the navy did not protect the ore shipments from Scandinavia'.[26] The navy reminded the foreign ministry of this fact in a letter of 12 October 1938: 'The ore shipments are so absolutely important that in our opinion every effort should be made and no expense spared to make sure that deliveries in wartime remain as close as possible to the peacetime level.'[27] Germany remained dependent on large deliveries of Swedish ore, because of its high iron content, for her industry in spite of the expanded mining of German ore, which had a much lower metal content, under the 'Four-year Plan' in and after 1936. Sweden thus acquired increasing significance as an important part of a future 'large economic area' in Europe with co-ordinated production and demand structures.[28]

---

[21] Quoted in Dülffer, *Weimar*, 529.

[22] Quoted ibid. 523.

[23] BA-MA II M 40/1-3.

[24] Cf. Dülffer, *Weimar*, 530 n. 67.

[25] On the controversy about the importance of Swedish iron ore to the German war economy cf. the studies by Karlborn, 'Sweden's Iron Ore'; Milward, 'Sweden'; and Jäger, 'Sweden's Iron Ore'; also Fritz, *German Steel*; Lutzhöft, *Deutsche Militärpolitik*.

[26] BA-MA, Sammlung Raeder, iii. 41-2.

[27] Quoted in Dülffer, *Weimar*, 521.

[28] Wittmann, *Schweden*, 432.

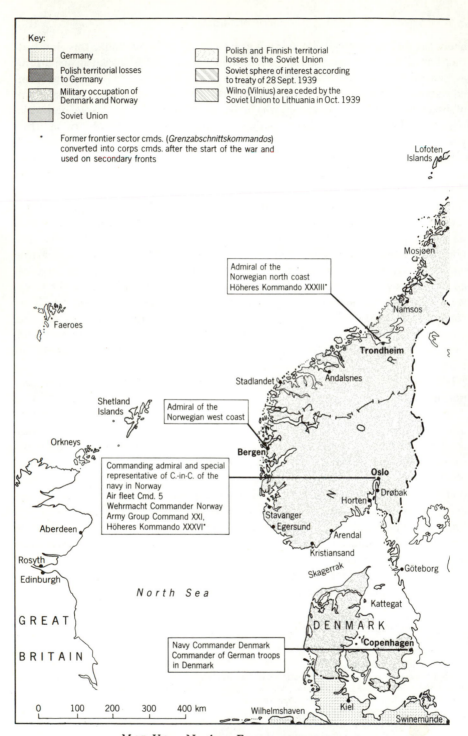

Key:

Germany

Polish territorial losses to Germany

Military occupation of Denmark and Norway

Soviet Union

Polish and Finnish territorial losses to the Soviet Union

Soviet sphere of interest according to treaty of 28 Sept. 1939

Wilno (Vilnius) area ceded by the Soviet Union to Lithuania in Oct. 1939

* Former frontier sector cmds. (*Grenzabschnittskommandos*) converted into corps cmds. after the start of the war and used on secondary fronts

Lofoten Islands

Mo

Mosjøen

Admiral of the Norwegian north coast Höheres Kommando XXXIII*

Namsos

Faeroes

Trondheim

Stadlandet

Andalsnes

Shetland Islands

Admiral of the Norwegian west coast

Orkneys

Bergen

Commanding admiral and special representative of C.-in-C. of the navy in Norway
Air fleet Cmd. 5
Wehrmacht Commander Norway
Army Group Command XXI,
Höheres Kommando XXXVI*

Oslo

Drøbak

Horten

Aberdeen

Stavanger

Egersund

Arendal

Rosyth

Kristiansand

Edinburgh

Skagerrak

Göteborg

North Sea

Kattegat

G R E A T

D E N M A R K

B R I T A I N

Copenhagen

Navy Commander Denmark
Commander of German troops in Denmark

| 0 | 100 | 200 | 300 | 400 km |

Wilhelmshaven

Kiel

Swinemünde

MAP V.I.I. Northern Europe, 1939–1940

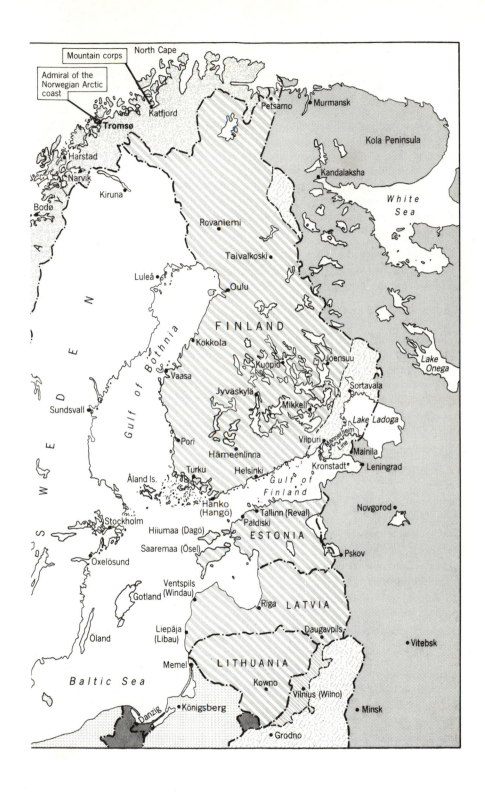

Mountain corps

North Cape

Admiral of the
Norwegian Arctic
coast

Petsamo

Murmansk

Katfjord

Kola Peninsula

Tromsø

Kandalaksha

Harstad

*White
Sea*

Narvik

Bodø

Kiruna

Rovaniemi

Taivalkoski

Luleå

Oulu

F I N L A N D

Joensuu

*Lake
Onega*

Kokkola

Kuopio

Sortavala

Vaasa

Jyväskylä

Mikkeli

Sundsvall

Lake Ladoga

Pori

Viipuri

Mannerheim Line

Mainila

Hämeenlinna

W

Åland Is.

Turku

Helsinki

Kronstadt

Leningrad

*Gulf of
Finland*

E

Stockholm

Hanko
(Hangö)

Tallinn (Reval)

Novgorod

Gulf of Bothnia

D

Hiiumaa (Dagö)

Paldiski

E

Saaremaa (Ösel)

E S T O N I A

Oxelösund

Pskov

N

Ventspils
(Windau)

Gotland

Riga

L A T V I A

Liepāja
(Libau)

Daugavpils

Vitebsk

Öland

Memel

L I T H U A N I A

Kowno

Baltic Sea

Vilnius (Wilno)

Minsk

Danzig

Königsberg

Grodno

That such imperialistic economic views were held within the navy is clearly shown by the statements of the operations officer of Group East, Lieutenant-Commander Assmann, in May 1939:[29]

Close observation and following of economic conditions in northern Europe increasingly confirm the impression of a stabilization and constant improvement of the German position. It must be the aim of German economic policy, especially in the northern states, to turn this improvement into a dominating factor in the policies and attitudes of the northern countries. Under German economic influence northern Europe will then come to realize more and more that it is linked with Germany in a common destiny from which there is no escape and that with the closest possible political and cultural ties it is dependent for better or worse on a dominant Germany.

Clearly following the ideas of Hitler's 'living-space' programme, the Group Commander East (Marinegruppenbefehlshaber Ost), Admiral Albrecht, formulated his ideas in a study 'Conducting a War in the Baltic' in the spring of 1939:

The great aim of German policy is considered to be to bring the whole of Europe, from the western frontier of Germany to the eastern limits of European Russia, under the military and political leadership of the Axis powers. Such a central and eastern Europe would be strong enough to feed itself in war and to defend itself even without raw materials from other continents . . . This involves moving away from a policy with aims overseas in the West and turning towards the east, a development in which we presently find ourselves.[30]

In the Navy High Command Albrecht's ideas were dismissed with the remark that it was not the business of a group command to think up such plans; only the political leaders could tell the Wehrmacht what to do in this way.[31]

According to a report of 6 March 1939 on figures for iron-ore imports from Sweden in 1937 and on 'probable conditions of a mobilization', compiled by the plenipotentiary for the economy,[32] Germany's total imports of iron ore in 1937 amounted to 20.62m. tons (1938: 21.92m. tons). Of this figure, 9.1m. tons (1938: 8.99m. tons) came from Sweden. After conversations with the German legation in Stockholm, the Swedish government had declared their readiness to continue deliveries from northern Sweden.[33] But the plenipotentiary for the economy expected an interruption of ore shipments from northern Sweden 'if, as expected, Britain and Russia are our enemies', as the sea routes from Narvik and Luleå could be attacked by Britain and the Soviet Union. Because of the lack of adequate transportation, shipping the ore by land to central and southern Sweden (1,350 km.)

---

[29] Marine-Gruppenkommando Ost, Studie Ostsee-Eingänge, ihre Bedeutung und Sicherung, Heft III, BA-MA M/32/PG 34161.

[30] Quoted in Dülffer, *Weimar*, 525; cf. Salewski, *Seekriegsleitung*, i. 68–9; Gemzell, *Raeder*, 68–9.

[31] Dülffer, *Weimar*, 526; cf. Gemzell, *Raeder*, 69.

[32] BA-MA Wi/I 3, 12, addressed to OKW, OKM, AA, RWM, and RVM.

[33] On 26 Jan. 1939 Thomas was informed by the Swedish military attaché that Sweden could not be adequately supplied by Britain in a war and therefore wanted to supply iron ore to Germany in exchange for raw materials she had previously received from Britain. Cf. Dülffer, *Weimar*, 520 n. 37, citing BA-MA Wi I E 3, 22.

TABLE V.I.1. *Swedish Exports of Iron Ore, 1937* (1,000 t.)

Port	Total		To Germany		To Britain	
	No.	%	No.	%	No.	%
Narvik	7,580	54	4,889	54	1,611	74
Luleå[a]	3,102	22	1,877	20	217	10
Other Swedish ports	3,086	24	2,310	26	343	15
(incl. Oxelösund)	—	—	(1,560)	(17)	—	—
TOTAL	13,768	100	9,076	100	2,171	100

[a] In 1937 the harbour at Luleå was frozen from the beginning of the year until 1 May: it was expected to be closed by ice for four months every year.

was prohibitively expensive and was not even considered. Table V.I.1 shows the exports of Swedish iron ore through the various ports.

As Germany was only in a position to protect the sea links with Stockholm and ports in south and south-west Sweden, only ore from central Sweden would be available in the event of war. The plenipotentiary for the economy came to the conclusion that 'In a war Germany is dependent on the production of central Sweden, at the present time 3 million tons a year. It is the task of the German authorities to establish contact with the responsible Swedish officials and to use their influence to help resolve the problems mentioned (increasing ore production and the efficiency of the transport system).'[34]

The economic staff of the Wehrmacht High Command came to a similar conclusion in a study of 29 April 1939,[35] in which they argued that maintaining Swedish ore deliveries during a war was a 'basic demand of the Wehrmacht'. Using figures for German ore production and their probable rise in 1939–40, the Wehrmacht High Command calculated the following import requirements for iron ore (m. tons, Swedish quality = 60 per cent):

(Official estimate at start of 1939:	8.4 iron p.a. = 14.0 ore p.a.)
1939	7.0 iron p.a. = 11.7 ore p.a.
1940	5.5 iron p.a. = 9.2 ore p.a.

In a war the Wehrmacht High Command expected only 3m. tons of ore from central and southern Sweden, with an iron content of 5–10 per cent less than ore from northern Sweden, as well as 2.5m.–3.0m. tons of ore that could be brought from northern Sweden by rail; total expected shipments were therefore 5.5m.–6.0m. tons. A comparison with mobilization requirements revealed the shortfalls shown in Table V.I.2. The Wehrmacht High Command argued that in spite of a reduction of imports by 1940 from 8.5m. to 3.2m. tons through increased German production,

[34] On the efforts of the German steel industry in this regard cf. Dülffer, *Weimar*, 521.
[35] Wstb W Wi VI 340/39 g.Kdos., 29 Apr. 1939: 'Die Eisenerzversorgung Deutschlands im Kriege unter besonderer Berücksichtigung der schwedischen Einfuhr, abgestellt auf die Versorgungslage in den Jahren 1939 und 1940'. Cf. also the letter OKM i. Abt. Skl. (same date), BA-MA Wi/I E 3, 22.

TABLE V.I.2. *German Estimate of Shortfalls in Iron Ore, 1939–1940* (m. t.)

	Mobilization requirement	Swedish deliveries	Shortfall
(Official estimate at start of 1939	14.0	5.5	8.5)
1939	11.7	6.0	5.7
1940	9.2	6.0	3.2

Source: Wstb W Wi VI 340/39 g.Kdos., 29 Apr. 1939; 'Die Eisenerversorgung Deutschlands im Kriege unter besonderer Berücksichtigung der schwedischen Einfuhr, abgestellt auf die Versorgungslage in den Jahren 1939 und 1940'.

'even a shortfall of 3.2 m. tons of ore is not acceptable for the German war economy in a war lasting significantly longer than six months'. The question of whether sufficient workers were available to achieve the increase in production expected in 1940 was not considered. On the basis of their observations, the Wehrmacht High Command then listed the following requirements: maintaining shipments through Luleå, maintaining Sweden's readiness to deliver, protecting the mining areas and the transportation system, protecting German domestic production, combating anti-German propaganda in Sweden, expanding the German 'ore base' in Sweden, stockpiling ore in Germany, and solving transport problems.

The Hitler–Stalin pact of 23 August 1939 eliminated the possibility of any Soviet threat to German sea links in the Baltic, which, as recently as 18 August 1939, had caused the Navy High Command to plan a mine-barrage in the Gulf of Finland in the event of a war with the Soviet Union.[36] After the start of the war the Wehrmacht High Command considered a neutral Scandinavia the most favourable possibility for Germany. In a memorandum of 9 October 1939[37] the High Command observed with regard to the northern states: 'Barring completely unforeseen developments, they will probably remain neutral in future. The continuation of German trade with these countries seems possible even in a long war.' The economy and armaments office of the Wehrmacht High Command was not satisfied with mere Scandinavian neutrality. In a study of 26 November 1939 on the effects of trade 'losses for the Western powers after the conquest of the Netherlands', the office explained: 'The effects would be all the more serious for the Western powers if at the same time supplies from other countries (the eastern Baltic area, Denmark, Norway, and Sweden) could be stopped.'[38]

The ultimate argument for the German occupation of Denmark and Norway did not come, however, from the Wehrmacht High Command, but from the navy, presented by its commander-in-chief. Encouraged by the offer of the Soviet Union to give the German navy a base east of Murmansk, Raeder pointed out to Hitler the value of bases on the Norwegian coast, which he wanted to acquire with the help

---

[36] Cf. Dülffer, *Weimar*, 523 n. 48.

[37] 'Denkschrift und Richtlinien über die Führung des Krieges im Westen', Berlin, 9 Oct. 1939; printed in *Dokumente zur Vorgeschichte*, 4 ff.

[38] Quoted in Volkmann, 'Autarkie', 61.

of Soviet pressure, for the U-boat war.[39] When the Soviet Union began to develop the spheres of interest agreed upon in the Hitler–Stalin pact and attacked Finland on 30 November, Scandinavia became directly involved in the conflicting strategic calculations of the warring states. Again it was Raeder who pointed out to Hitler the significance of Scandinavia for the German war economy:[40] 'It is important to occupy Norway. The northern countries should route their exports to Germany, among others.' Four days later, on 12 December, Raeder introduced Vidkun Quisling, the former war minister and the leader of the Norwegian nationalistic splinter party, the Nasjonal Samling, to Hitler and was able to persuade the latter to order the Wehrmacht High Command to study the problem of occupying Norway.[41]

Fearing an occupation of Norway by British Finland volunteers, Raeder again stressed to Hitler on 30 December that Norway must not fall into British hands: 'Therefore it is necessary to be prepared and ready. Serious resistance in Norway, and probably also in Sweden, is not to be expected.'[42] On 13 January the naval war staff discussed critically the study of the Wehrmacht High Command, which generally reflected Raeder's views. Raeder supported (probably only outwardly) the opinion within the naval war staff that the neutrality of Norway was the best solution for Germany, but he pointed out that because of the uncertain situation it was necessary to be prepared for the worst possible case; he therefore ordered the naval war staff to work out an operational study.[43] On 13 January 1940 a special staff N (North) was formed in the Wehrmacht High Command; on 5 February 1940 they were informed of their tasks as the 'special staff Weserübung' by the head of the Wehrmacht High Command. On 21 February Hitler named General von Falkenhorst, who had acquired experience of Finland in the First World War, to head the special staff (later 'Group XXI').[44]

After the attack on the *Altmark*, a supply-ship of the *Graf Spee* which was transporting British prisoners of war, by the British destroyer *Cossack* in Norwegian waters on 16 February, Hitler demanded an acceleration of preparations for Weserübung.[45] On 1 March he issued the directive bearing that name.[46] After receipt of an alarming report from the German legation in Stockholm on 29 February that a 'major operation' in Scandinavia by the Western powers was imminent, the naval war staff were determined to prevent a British intervention in the north with 'all available forces', although they still considered the 'continuation of the present situation with the safe use of Norwegian waters for ore shipments as the best

[39] 'Führer Conferences', 45 (10 Oct. 1939). On the literature on preparations for the German attack on Denmark and Norway cf. the extensive survey in Loock, *Quisling*, 207 n. 1.

[40] 'Führer Conferences', 62 (8 Dec. 1939).

[41] Jodl, *Tagebuch 1939-40*, entry for 12–13 Dec. 1939. On Quisling and his contacts with German representatives cf. Loock, *Quisling*, 207 ff.; id., 'Weserübung', 80 ff.

[42] 'Führer Conferences', 70 (30 Dec. 1939).

[43] Skl, KTB, 13 Jan. 1940, printed in Hubatsch, *Weserübung*, 391 ff.; cf. also ibid. 31-2.

[44] Jodl, Tagebuch, 1940, entry for 5-24 Feb. On 23 Jan. Hitler had cancelled the originally planned creation of a special staff under the commander-in-chief of the Luftwaffe.

[45] Jodl, 'Tagebuch 1940', entry for 19 Feb.   [46] Trevor-Roper, *Directives*, No. 10a.

solution'.[47] In a discussion of the situation on 2 March it was pointed out that the 'problem has ceased to be purely military and has become a political and war-economy issue of the greatest importance'. Putting aside their military reservations, the naval war staff now took the view that 'The demands of the political leaders that the Wehrmacht solve this problem using all available forces must be fulfilled'.[48] It was overlooked that the navy leaders, and primarily Raeder himself, had suggested those demands to Hitler. By professing readiness blindly to carry out orders resulting from their own wishes, the navy leaders attempted to escape the political responsibility for their actions. The operational preparation of the action as a whole in the Wehrmacht High Command, and not in the staffs of the Navy High Command, made it easier to assume such an attitude.

On 3 March Hitler 'spoke very strongly on the need to intervene in Norway quickly and with force'. He demanded the maximum acceleration of preparations and refused to accept objections put forward by the Wehrmacht services, primarily the Luftwaffe and the army, chiefly with regard to the command organization of the forces involved. While Göring, out of jealousy for his own service, 'flew into a rage' (Jodl) in front of Keitel, the head of the Wehrmacht High Command, he was like the army leaders basically concerned that the deployment for the offensive in the west ('Case Yellow'), whose chances of success they considered poor in any case, should not be further endangered by a significant withdrawal of forces for Weserübung. For on 3 March Hitler also demanded that 'Operation Weserübung' be carried out several days before the offensive in the west.[50] Halder noted in his diary: 'Führer demands that movements for "Operation Weserübung" start immediately. Timetable: movement to training centres completed by 7 March. Assembly of units there by 10 March. Ready for jump-off as of 13 March, so that landing in the northernmost parts would be possible about 17 March.'[51]

On 5 March, in a conference between Hitler and the three commanders-in-chief of the Wehrmacht services, Göring, who showed anger at not having been sufficiently consulted in the previous planning, demanded that the navy should keep its ships in the ports to support the invasion troops after the landing. Hitler supported this demand, but in the end, on 2 April, 'did not want to intervene too much in purely naval matters'.[52] The naval war staff pointed out that the importance and size of the Norway operation required 'the complete concentration of the whole navy on this task'; it was therefore necessary to stop the Lützow, the supply-ships, and the auxiliary cruisers from putting to sea, to halt the minelaying operations by destroyers off the east coast of Britain, and to make all U-boats not at sea available for Weserübung. Naval operations planned for the offensive in the west would have to be cancelled or greatly reduced. This complete stop of other naval activity could, however, in the words of the naval war staff, be justified only

[47] Skl, KTB, 29 Feb. 1940, quoted in Salewski, Seekriegsleitung, i. 180.
[48] Quoted ibid. 181.
[49] Jodl, 'Tagebuch 1940', entry for 3 Mar. 1940.   [50] Ibid., 1–3 Mar. 1940.
[51] Halder, Diaries, i. 260 (3 Mar. 1940).
[52] Jodl, 'Tagebuch 1940', entry for 5 Mar.–2 Apr. 1940.

if the decision to carry out Weserübung was irrevocable and if it took place soon.[53]

On 7 March Hitler signed the directive for Weserübung, which had been amended after the conference on 5 March. The next day the naval war staff expressed their concern that because of a concentration of British naval forces observed off Scotland, 'the transfer of heavy ships to Scapa must be closely connected with a support action of the Western powers for Finland and an imminent landing in Norway'.[54] This fear was strengthened by the suspicion that, because of the start of peace negotiations between Finland and the Soviet Union, Britain had to act promptly if she wished to justify her intervention as aid for Finland.[55] Therefore on 11 March the preparation of 'measures to be taken in the event of British operations against Norway' was ordered.[56] On the day peace was concluded between Finland and the Soviet Union the fears of the naval war staff were calmed: 'The naval war staff do not believe that the Western powers will undertake a military action in Norway at the present time. Instead, it is probable that Britain, in so far as she continues to pursue her strategic aims in the north, which must be expected, has been forced to wait for a more favourable moment to carry out the operation.'[57]

In the Wehrmacht High Command the reaction to the Finno-Soviet negotiations was mixed. Jodl wrote: 'The news of the negotiations is very good from a political point of view. The French press is in a rage, as it considers it necessary to cut Germany off from Swedish ore. For us the situation interferes with our military plans, as the early conclusion of peace would make it difficult to justify the already prepared operation of the Falkenhorst Group.' On 12 March Jodl wrote: 'The conclusion of peace between Finland and Russia deprives us, but also Britain, of the political justification for landing in Norway.' The preparations for such an operation had progressed so far that '20 March could be W[eser] Day'; but the ice forced a postponement of one or two days.[58]

While Hitler was 'still searching for a justification', Raeder doubted whether 'it is still important to take preventive action [*praevenire*] in Norway'.[59] When on 23 March Hitler asked him about the possibilities of maintaining the iron-ore shipments from Narvik after a German occupation of Norway, Raeder replied that the most favourable situation for the ore shipments, 'as generally', was one of Norwegian neutrality. But he added: 'As explained earlier, the occupation of Norway by Britain is unacceptable, as it could not be reversed. It would mean increased pressure on Sweden and perhaps the spread of the war to the Baltic, the loss of all ore shipments from Sweden.' On the other hand, after a German occupation of Norway only 2.5m.–3.5m. tons of ore a year would be lost, 'at least temporarily', as ore shipments on the 800-nautical-mile route along the Norwegian coast could not be adequately

[53] Skl, KTB, 5 Mar. 1940, quoted in Hubatsch, *Weserübung*, appendix B1, pp. 361–2.
[54] Skl, KTB, 8 Mar. 1940, quoted in Salewski, *Seekriegsleitung*, i. 182.
[55] Cf. Salewski, *Seekriegsleitung*, i. 182.
[56] Skl. 1/Skl I op 300/40 g.Kdos. Chefs., 11 Mar. 1940, KTB B V, BA-MA III M 1005/2.
[57] Skl, KTB, 12 Mar. 1940, quoted in Salewski, *Seekriegsleitung*, i. 183.
[58] Jodl, 'Tagebuch 1940', entry for 10–12 Mar. 1940.
[59] Ibid., 13–14 Mar. 1940.

protected. Raeder did not omit to mention that a German occupation of Norway would make it possible to exert strong pressure on Sweden to fulfil all German demands.[60]

The naval air staff pressed for an early decision, as they felt condemned to inactivity by the deployment of forces for Weserübung.[61] Raeder informed Hitler of this concern on 26 March and urged that the attack be carried out early, although he no longer believed that the danger of an Allied landing in Norway was imminent. His answer to the question of British intentions in the north in the near future was: 'They will make further attempts to disrupt German trade in neutral waters and to cause incidents, in order perhaps to create a pretext for action against Norway. Their main aim is and remains to stop the ore shipments via Narvik.' With the remark that a German occupation of Norway would also lead to a temporary interruption of shipments via Narvik, Raeder came to his main argument:

Sooner or later Germany will be faced with the necessity of carrying out operation Weserübung. Therefore it is advisable to do so as soon as possible, by 15 April at the latest, since after that date the nights are too short; there will be a new moon on 7 April. The operational possibilities of the Navy will be restricted too much if Weserübung is postponed any longer. The submarines can remain in position only for two to three weeks more. Weather of the type favourable for operation Yellow [attack on the West] is not to be waited for in the case of operation Weserübung; overcast, foggy weather is more satisfactory for the latter. The general state of preparedness of the naval forces and ships is at present good.

Raeder achieved his aim; at the end he noted: 'the Führer agrees to operation Weserübung on D-day about the time of the new moon.'[62]

In a conference with commanders on 1 April Hitler justified the Scandinavian operation by pointing out the necessity of countering British attempts to disrupt German sea links along the Norwegian coast, and, after occupying Norway, to put pressure on Sweden to cut Germany off from raw-material deliveries from Scandinavia. Moreover, he emphasized that Germany must finally acquire access to the open sea: it was intolerable that every successive German generation should be confronted with the problem of British pressure. The conflict with Britain was inevitable sooner or later; it must be fought to a finish. Weserübung was only part of a larger operation.[63]

The similarity between Hitler's statements and Raeder's arguments is striking. It shows that the planned occupation of Denmark and Norway was intended to be permanent and not limited to the duration of the war.

The question of how important race-ideological factors were in Hitler's decision to conquer Norway and Denmark cannot be answered from available sources. It is certain, however, that he completely accepted the strategic and defence-economy arguments of the navy leaders, which had been relevant for a long time and which,

---

[60] Quoted in Hubatsch, *Weserübung*, appendix B1, p. 365.
[61] Cf. Salewski, *Seekriegsleitung*, i. 183.
[62] 'Führer Conferences', 87–8 (26 Mar. 1940).
[63] Jodl, 'Tagebuch 1940', entry for 1 Apr. 1940; Notiz für das KTB der Skl, 1 Apr. 1940, quoted in Loock, *Quisling*, 258.

after the 'change of course against Britain', apparently had such a high priority for the navy, in spite of its obvious weaknesses compared with the British fleet, that it was prepared to undertake an operation which in itself 'violated all the rules of naval warfare'.[64] That Raeder was the chief proponent of this plan is shown by a note of the naval war staff of 11 July 1940 in connection with the planned landing in Britain ('Operation Sea-Lion'): 'The Commander in Chief, Navy, cannot for his part, therefore, advocate an invasion of Britain as he did in the case of Norway.'[65] On 2 April Hitler ordered Weserübung to be carried out on 9 April, after the commanders-in-chief of the Luftwaffe and the navy as well as General von Falkenhorst had confirmed that preparations had been completed. At 2 a.m. the next day the first ships of the transport fleet left port.[66]

The German operations plan[67] was divided into 'Weserübung Nord' (Norway) and 'Weserübung Süd' (Denmark). The army deployed the following forces:

1. *against Norway*: (first wave) the third mountain division; the 69th infantry division; the 163rd infantry division; (second wave) the 181st infantry division; the 196th infantry division; (third wave) the 214th infantry division;

2. *against Denmark*: the 170th infantry division; the 198th infantry division; the 11th rifle brigade (motorized).

These units were to land by sea and air at seven places in Norway and seven in Denmark: Narvik, Trondheim, Bergen, Egersund, Kristiansand, Arendal, Oslo, Copenhagen, Middlefart, Esbjerg, Tyborøn, Korsør, Gjedser, and Nyborg. They had orders, in the event of encountering resistance, to hold the landing areas and establish contact with each other as rapidly as possible, at first in south and central Norway, and then with the German forces in Narvik.

The navy was responsible for the sea transport of the landing forces in 11 warship groups and 8 transport squadrons. Reconnaissance and long-range security to protect these transports were the main tasks of the submarine forces. They were also supposed to frustrate landing attempts by the Allies and secure the supplying of German units by sea. On and after 4 March the navy kept its submarines ready for this task, and on 11 March the submarines intended for Narvik and Trondheim were ordered to go on station. The remaining submarines left port on 31 March and 6 April.

With the reinforced Tenth Flying Corps the Luftwaffe took over the transport of paratroops and airborne units to Oslo, Bergen, Stavanger, Kristiansand, and Ålborg. The importance attached to Weserübung can be seen in the fact that the new tactic of landing troops from the air was used, although it was planned as a key element in the surprise operations which were to start the offensive in the west ('Case Yellow'). The main task of the Tenth Flying Corps was to protect the landing forces against British attacks from the air and sea and to prevent enemy landing attempts.

---

[64] Skl KTB, 5 Mar. 1940, quoted in Loock, *Quisling*, 252.
[65] 'Führer Conferences', 113 ff. (11 July 1940).
[66] Jodl, 'Tagebuch 1940', entry for 2-3 Apr. 1940.   [67] Cf. Hubatsch, *Weserübung*, 39 ff.

Winston Churchill wrote in his memoirs that the German and British naval staffs had come to the same conclusions (in December 1939) on the basis of strategic considerations, but only the German naval staff had received the necessary authority to act from their government.[68] On 4 April 1940, on the basis of reports concerning British landing preparations, the German naval war staff realized that the Royal Navy had also been given the necessary authority. After that a 'race between Britain and Germany for Scandinavia began to develop'.[69] Jodl noted in his diary on 7 April: 'no disturbing news.' But 8 April was a 'very tense day'.[70] On that day the British mined the Norwegian waters off Narvik ('Operation Wilfred').

[68] Churchill, *The Second World War* (US edn.), i. 538; Loock, *Quisling*, 259 n. 94. Churchill's observation, quoted above, does not appear in the British edn. of his work.

[69] Skl, KTB, 4 Apr. 1940, quoted in Salewski, *Seekriegsleitung*, i. 185.

[70] Jodl 'Tagebuch 1940', entry for 7–8 Apr. 1940.

II. Allied Strategy

Klaus A. Maier

THE strategy of the Allies was based on the assumption of a long war.[1] On the one hand, their inadequate armaments forced the Western powers to assume initially a defensive position; on the other hand, confident in their reserves and their more favourable geographical position, they could hope to win the war, especially as they were convinced that they were fighting for a just cause and that in the course of time other states would join the coalition against Hitler. Nor had they lost all hope that the German people would see the light and themselves put an end to Nazi aggression.

The Hitler–Stalin pact endangered the success of this strategy: it created an important breach in the Allied blockade of Germany and made it possible for Hitler to conquer Poland and then turn west with rear cover in the east. If Hitler could maintain the initiative over a longer period of time, the possibility existed that smaller countries, if they had not already been occupied, would come to terms with the 'bigger battalions'. Their will to resist was more dependent on their confidence in the effectiveness of early Allied help than on their belief in a final Allied victory at some point in the future.

In their relations with the neutral states of Europe, the Allies found themselves in the dilemma that, in so far as they were fighting to re-establish the international rule of law, they could not afford to appear in the eyes of the world as being the first to violate the rights of neutral states for the sake of strategic advantage, even if this were also in the interest of the states concerned.

After the defeat of Poland the Allies were mainly concerned with offsetting the Soviet gap in the blockade against Germany and gaining the initiative. Strategic operations on Germany's flanks in the north and south offered the chance to deliver telling blows to the German war economy: in the north against Swedish iron ore, and in the south against Romanian or Soviet oil. In both cases a conflict with the Soviet Union had to be expected and accepted.[2] An analysis of Allied plans gives one the impression that the French government had fewer reservations than the British with regard to the possibility of a conflict with the Soviet Union. Britain's areas of influence had more sensitive points of contact with the Soviet Union than did those of France.[3] However, neither side had a very high opinion of the fighting ability of the Red Army.[4]

The different geographical conditions and the different degrees of threat which each country faced as a result, as well as the different emphasis in their armaments

---

[1] Butler, *Strategy*, ii. 9 ff.; Gibbs, *Strategy*, i. 657 ff.; Bédarida, *Stratégie secrète*, 79 ff.
[2] Lorbeer, *Westmächte*.
[3] On Anglo-Soviet relations after the start of the war cf. Woodward, *British Foreign Policy*, i. 33 ff.
[4] Lorbeer, *Westmächte*, 36 ff.

programmes (Britain concentrated on the navy, France on the army), led to difficulties in co-ordinating plans, although the Allies had created an effective instrument for that purpose in the Supreme War Council. The French were more interested in diverting German forces and taking pressure off their own front, while the British wanted to concentrate on the creation of a blockade. The British, who preferred to respect the Italian position of being a 'non-belligerent' state by supporting the development of a neutral Balkan bloc,[5] did not support the French desire for a second front in the south, which had led to the creation of the Levant Army under General Weygand in the summer of 1939.[6] The British plan for the Balkans failed in the final analysis because of unfulfillable demands for economic and military assistance. The attempt, prepared from 28 September 1939 onwards, to sabotage Romanian oil shipments to Germany by blocking the Danube was also unsuccessful.[7] The Allies expected better results from attacks on the Transcaucasian refineries in Batum, Baku, and Grozny, for which planning was in progress from December 1939 at the latest,[8] while reconnaissance missions to gather information about possible targets were still being flown as late as mid-April 1940.[9]

In contrast to the plans for south-eastern Europe or against Soviet oil centres, which envisaged primarily the use of army and air force units, Allied operations in northern Europe could use the only superior military instrument at the disposal of the Western powers at that time, the British fleet. The fact that Allied operations in this area were dependent on the use of the Royal Navy gave the British more influence in the alliance. The first suggestion to use British domination of the sea to stop German ore supplies from Narvik came from Churchill, then First Lord of the Admiralty. On 19 September 1939 he suggested to the War Cabinet that if the Norwegian government could not be persuaded to intervene against German ore transports, Norwegian waters should be mined to force the German ships to come out into international waters.[10] Two months later, on 19 November, Churchill suggested laying a mine-barrage between the Orkneys and the Norwegian coast, as had been done in the First World War. Although his earlier suggestion was not accepted by the cabinet, preparations for a new northern barrage were ordered on 30 November; it was assumed that they would require six months.

The Soviet attack on Finland on the same day, which led to the expulsion of the Soviet Union from the League of Nations, created a new situation.[11] Under the impression of the initial Finnish defensive successes and the pressure of public opinion, the Allied governments considered ways of helping Finland and at the same time stopping ore shipments to Germany from Sweden. As the use of Allied troops

---

[5] Woodward, *British Foreign Policy*, i. 22 ff.; Butler, *Strategy*, ii. 65–6.
[6] *Weißbuch*, No. 6, docs. 2, 5.   [7] Ibid., doc. 11.
[8] Kahle, *Kaukasusprojekt*; Chassin, 'Plan grandiose'.   [9] Chassin, 'Plan grandiose', 848.
[10] On Allied plans for Scandinavia see War Office, Mar. 1940, Historical, PRO WO 106/1650; Dilks, 'Great Britain'; Woodward, *British Foreign Policy*, i. 31 ff.; Butler, *Strategy*, ii. 91 ff.; Derry, *Campaign in Norway*; Lorbeer, *Westmächte*, 43 ff.; Bédarida, 'France'; Häikiö, 'Race for Northern Europe'; Munthe-Kaas, 'Campaign in Norway'.
[11] On Allied plans for northern Europe in connection with the Finnish 'Winter War' cf. Nevakivi, *Appeal*; Bédarida, *Stratégie secrète*, 235 ff., 279 ff.

was dependent on the only efficient transportation link in Scandinavia, the ore railway from Narvik to Sweden, it required the agreement of the Scandinavian governments, which, however, showed little inclination to become involved in the war. They believed that military support for Finland and co-operation with an Allied landing force would inevitably lead to a German or Soviet attack on the model of the campaigns in Poland. They were sceptical about the volume and prospects of success of Allied aid in the event of such a development. The British were not interested in the French plan for a landing near Petsamo (Pechenga), which would not have been dependent on the consent of the Scandinavian countries. It would have meant a war with the Soviet Union and would not have enabled the Allies to occupy the Swedish ore-fields or provide effective help for Sweden. British plans to stop the supply of Swedish ore to Germany by persuading the Scandinavians to impose an embargo on ore shipments to all belligerents became untenable when it turned out that Britain herself had ore reserves for only one week.[12]

At a meeting of the Supreme War Council in Paris on 5 February 1940 the British prime minister said that his government realized that help for Finland was important because of the negative effect a Finnish defeat would have, above all on morale in the Dominions and the United States, but the main purpose of a Scandinavian operation must be to defeat Germany. Aid for the Finns must be combined with the stopping of ore deliveries to Germany. He proposed landing regular troops in Narvik as a 'volunteer force' and occupying the Swedish ore-fields on the way to Finland. He wanted to obtain the agreement of the Scandinavian governments to this operation by pointing out to them the consequences of a Finnish defeat for Scandinavia and getting the Finns to appeal to them to permit the Allies to send troops through their territory. Daladier accepted this plan, which would place the moral responsibility for a possible Finnish defeat on the Scandinavians, but he also reminded the meeting of the Petsamo plan, in case the Scandinavians refused to permit Allied troops to march through on their way to Finland.[13]

In a memorandum[14] for the British War Cabinet on 16 February the chiefs of staff mentioned 20 March as the earliest possible landing date. The order for the transport fleet to sail would have to be given on 11 March; because of probable German countermeasures, 11 March was the earliest date the Scandinavian governments could be requested to permit the transit of Allied troops. The latest possible date for the order to put to sea would be the end of March, as the expeditionary force would have to land in Scandinavia in the first week of April if it was to help the Finns in time and occupy the ore-mines before the melting of the ice in the Gulf of Bothnia permitted a German landing near Luleå.

The chiefs of staff considered the political implications of this timetable to be (1) that the Finns must delay their official request for help until the Allied landing

---

[12] Dilks, 'Great Britain', 37. Between Sept. 1939 and Mar. 1940 Britain received ore deliveries of 797,612 t. via Narvik; Germany received 762,612 t. (Skodvin, 'Norwegian Neutrality', 142).

[13] Woodward, *British Foreign Policy*, i. 78 ff.; Dilks, 'Great Britain', 40-1.

[14] Notes for War Cabinet meeting 16 Feb. 1940, Annex to C.O.S. (40) 30th Meeting, 15 Feb. 1940, PRO Cab. 79/85.

fleet was ready to sail, and (2) that the expeditionary force could land in Norway only if the Finns agreed to an Allied intervention with regular troops and if the governments of Norway and Sweden permitted an Allied march-through to Finland. But all attempts to obtain such permission failed, and with the *Altmark* incident on 16 February Anglo-Norwegian relations reached their lowest point.[15]

At the end of February, as the military position of the Finns deteriorated and domestic pressure on the French government increased, Daladier pressed the British to take energetic measures. On 21 February he had his ambassador in London inform the British government that 'only the certainty that the Allies are in a position to give Sweden immediate and effective help against German countermeasures' would persuade Sweden to support the Allied plans. He suggested that, even if the Finns did not appeal for help, the Allies should occupy the parts of Scandinavia from which it would be possible to block German ore supplies.[16] However, Chamberlain opposed the plan, which Churchill had submitted once more, to mine Norwegian waters. He did not want to do anything which would jeopardize the chance, however small, of receiving permission from the Scandinavian countries to send troops through their territories. He pointed to the possible negative effect on neutrals, above all the United States, and to the British dependence on Swedish ore, the export of which to Britain would probably be stopped by Norway. The Anglo-Norwegian negotiations for a trade agreement, on which British use of Norwegian shipping depended, required caution and self-restraint.[17]

On 1 March the Finnish ambassador to London enquired whether Britain was in a position to send 100 bombers with crews to Finland immediately and 50,000 soldiers in the course of March. The military situation was so serious that the Finns had to decide within twenty-four hours if they should enter into negotiations with the Soviet Union.[18] While the French showed greater willingness to co-operate, the British raised technical objections and in any case suspected that Finland had made such an impossible request in order to use its rejection as a pretext to start peace negotiations with the Soviet Union.[19]

When the Allied discussion about how to proceed produced further differences of opinion, the Finnish position became almost hopeless. Having little hope that the Scandinavians believed in the success of an Allied operation and would permit Allied troops to pass through their territory, the Finns hesitated to endanger the peace negotiations with the Soviet Union by making an official request for Allied help. From the British point of view, however, such a request was a precondition for moral pressure on the Scandinavian governments to give the required permission. In order to at least win time, the Finns needed Allied military equipment, which,

---

[15] Dilks, 'Great Britain', 41.
[16] *Weißbuch*, No. 6, doc. 21.
[17] Dilks, 'Great Britain', 44.
[18] Nevakivi, *Appeal*, 128 ff.; Woodward, *British Foreign Policy*, i. 92.
[19] Dilks, 'Great Britain', 45.

however, the British did not want to deliver in case it should be lost as a result of a Finno-Soviet peace.[20]

On 5 March the Finns drew the logical conclusion from their increasing losses and entered into peace negotiations with the Soviet Union. On 11–12 March Norway and Sweden again refused categorically to permit the passage of Allied troops. At the same time Britain demanded that the Finns say clearly by 12 March whether they still wanted an expeditionary force. Under the pressure of Daladier's threat to resign, the War Cabinet planned to land an expeditionary force in Narvik and demand permission to march through; but the Finno-Soviet peace treaty was signed before the order to go into action could be given. Although Churchill suggested occupying Narvik nevertheless, the order was given, against the advice of the chief of the imperial general staff, to disband the troop contingents of the expeditionary force. This would probably not have been done if the Allies had then possessed any information about German plans to occupy Denmark and Norway.

Chamberlain tried to see the positive side of developments in northern Europe and confessed that he was rather relieved that he would not have to send an expeditionary force to Scandinavia. Such an operation would have involved many risks and would have tied down valuable forces which could now be used elsewhere. He would not be surprised if the Soviet Union, having achieved all her aims in the Baltic, would now try to move away from Germany rather than develop closer relations.[21]

On the other hand, the Directorate of Military Operations (DMO) was very critical: after the end of the Finno-Soviet war relations with the most important neutral states would have to be reconsidered and the necessary conclusions drawn.[22] The directorate believed that Italy was now confronted with the unavoidable decision between entering the war on the side of Germany or continuing her policy as a 'non-belligerent' nation. They expressed indignation at the position of the United States: the lack of a clear American reaction to the Russian attack on Finland had discouraged the neutrals and played into Hitler's hands. Apparently it would take a long time before the United States understood the German threat and their own responsibility. The small neutral states had been intimidated militarily and politically by the German successes and Allied inactivity. Previously Allied strategy had been based on the assumption that time was working for the Western powers. The Allies had also believed after the German and Russian attacks on Poland that they were in a good moral position and that gradually the world would come to support the Allied cause. In the first three months of the war this had indeed been the case, as everyone had thought that the Allies were preparing to take the initiative in the Spring. But (the DMO continued) the conduct of the Allies during the Russo-Finnish

---

[20] On 5 Mar. the Finnish minister remarked to Lord Chatfield, minister for the co-ordination of defence, that things would now move in a circle. The Allies did not want to send Finland any military equipment if she did not keep on fighting, but in order to keep on fighting Finland needed military equipment: Nevakivi, *Appeal*, 133.

[21] Neville Chamberlain to Ida Chamberlain, 16 Mar. 1940, quoted in Dilks, 'Great Britain', 47.

[22] Notes on the Situation, 17 Mar. 1940 (No. 3), 14 Mar. 1940, PRO WO 106/1650.

war had given rise to doubts. People now believed that Germany and her new ally were possibly so strong that Britain and France could not undertake any operations against them and would have to use all their forces for their own defence; therefore it would be wiser to come to terms with the dictators while there was still time. This situation meant that the Allies must abandon their policy of gradually closing the blockade around Germany in order to defeat her on land and in the air in 1941 or even as late as 1942. The alternative was to seize the initiative from Germany, extend the war, and make the blockade even tighter, without respecting excessively the rights of other states. But the Allies must decide whether they were prepared to abandon their 'high moral tone' in order to counter adequately the unscrupulous German conduct of the war. In terms of fighting-strength the Allies were superior to Germany, but they lacked the firmness of purpose to stop trying to fight the war on League of Nations principles.

The DMO suggested two measures that might provoke Germany to over-react: (1) disrupting the sea links in Norwegian waters, and (2) mining the Rhine and other waterways ('Royal Marine').[23] Both measures would have positive effects on all states waiting for a demonstration of Allied ability to take the initiative. This suggestion was based on the assumption that German strategy had to choose between two alternatives: the decisive battle in the west in 1940 or negotiations. In the mistaken belief, strengthened by the *Sitzkrieg* or 'phoney war', that Hitler would shrink from the risk of an offensive in the west, for which he would have to take precautions with regard to the Balkans and keep the Soviet Union content, the DMO believed he would probably opt for negotiations.

Continuing his efforts to achieve a strategic diversion, on 14 March Daladier sent Corbin, his ambassador in London, a war plan which Corbin communicated to the Foreign Office on the following day.[24] The plan contained the suggestion of a quick initiative without respect for Norwegian neutrality: the Allies should immediately take control of Norwegian waters and occupy bases along the Norwegian coast. In this way they could consolidate their domination of the North Sea and stop Swedish ore deliveries to Germany. The broader French aims were indicated by Daladier's expressed hope that German countermeasures would justify a considerable expansion of the war to Norwegian and Swedish territory.

In the meeting of the War Cabinet on 19 March,[25] at which Daladier's plan was discussed, Halifax cautioned against overestimating the psychological damage that had been caused by events in Norway, not least because they had coincided with the meeting between Hitler and Mussolini at the Brenner Pass and the visit of Sumner Welles to Europe. After considering other possibilities (blocking ore shipments from Narvik, bombing the Russian oil-fields in the Caucasus, opening a Balkan front), Halifax supported operation 'Royal Marine', arguing that French objections were not convincing. Instead of the operation against Narvik suggested by Daladier, Halifax recommended informing the Scandinavian governments that the Allies

[23] For 'Royal Marine' see Woodward, *British Foreign Policy*, i. 101 n. 2.
[24] Text in *Les Événements survenus en France*, ii. 349 ff.; Bédarida, 'France', 22.
[25] PRO Cab, 65/6, pp. 97 ff.; printed in Lorbeer, *Westmächte*, 116 ff.

reserved the right to do whatever they thought proper if their vital interests were threatened in any of the following ways:

1. if the Scandinavian governments placed their countries under the protection of Germany or the Soviet Union;
2. if they joined a defensive alliance from which Britain was excluded;
3. if they increased ore exports to Germany to an unacceptable extent;
4. possibly even if the negotiations with Norway on merchant-ship tonnage broke down.

Even Churchill advocated postponing the Narvik operation, and Chamberlain was prepared to try to obtain Daladier's immediate agreement to 'Royal Marine' (the mining of the Rhine) by means of a personal letter. While Halifax feared German retaliatory attacks on British industry and warned against pressing the French too hard on this question, the chancellor of the exchequer, Simon, suggested putting the same pressure on the French to agree to 'Royal Marine' which they had put on the British to agree to the Scandinavian operation. 'Royal Marine' would be extremely effective and could be carried out immediately, if only the French would agree. Halifax wanted to inform Corbin about the British ideas and leave no doubt that the British government considered 'Royal Marine' a matter of urgency. The French should also be requested to provide more details about Daladier's plan.

While the British did not seem to be in a hurry to make a decision, the domestic political crisis forced Daladier to resign on 20 March. Political and personal rivalry between the new premier, Reynaud, who had to distinguish himself by energetic steps in public, and Daladier as defence minister made it even more difficult for the Allies to develop a common strategy for Scandinavia, especially as the different options for a total strategy were still available. Today, as the relevant sources are open to historians, it is clear that much of the contemporary criticism of Daladier was unjustified.[26] On the day on which he resigned a new war plan he had authorized was completed, and it was this plan which Reynaud presented to the British on 25 March.[27]

The new plan included the northern and southern components of the French diversion strategy. Germany was to be cut off from imports vital to her war effort by a disruption of the ore shipments from Narvik[28] and in the south by submarine attacks in the Black Sea and air attacks on the Caucasus oil-fields. The French programme of paralysing the entire Soviet economy before Germany could mobilize it to her own advantage shows how ready the French government were to accept a military conflict with the Soviet Union. From their previous experience with the Scandinavian governments, the French, like the British, came to the conclusion that before adopting this new strategy it was necessary to review 'a certain legal conception of neutrality'.[29]

---

[26] Cf. Bédarida, 'France', 23, 26.

[27] French text in *Les Événements survenus en France*, ii. 351 ff.; English text: PRO Cab 66/6 WP (40) 109

[28] This part of the plan repeated Daladier's suggestion of 14 Mar.

[29] In a note of the Sous-Direction Europe of the French foreign ministry of 24 Mar.: 'We should not let ourselves be bound . . . by some juridical scruples which our enemies have since thrown to the winds'; quoted from Bédarida, 'France', 23.

In contrast to the French conviction that it was a mistake to believe that time was working for the Allies, the British chiefs of staff maintained in a study of 'Certain Aspects of the Present Position',[30] also submitted on 25 March, that the Allies had been able to make up much lost time as a result of the absence of a German offensive on land and in the air. The chiefs recommended continuing the waiting strategy: the Allies had not yet reached the level—and would probably not reach it in the current year—at which, apart from naval and economic warfare, they would be able to shift to a generally offensive strategy. The chiefs of staff were assisted by Lord Hankey (minister without portfolio), who, in a memorandum on 'The Grand Strategy of the Allies',[31] advised continuing the previous British policy as an 'offensive-defensive strategy', but approved of the 'Royal Marine' operation and a more active policy in the Near East and towards the Soviet Union.

On 27 March the French plan of 25 March was discussed by the War Cabinet, together with the assessment by the chiefs of staff and Hankey's memorandum.[32] Chamberlain found 'little of value' in the French proposal but admitted that something must be done for psychological reasons, and mentioned two criteria an Allied operation had to fulfil: it must be directed against Germany, and in the eyes of the world it must be a legitimate measure that did not violate the rights of innocent parties. In his opinion the French plan did not meet either of these conditions, whereas 'Royal Marine' would. He could not understand why the French hesitated to agree to this operation. With regard to the Narvik plan proposed by the French, he observed that a minelaying operation off Narvik could be carried out at any time; the important thing was to choose the right moment. This clearly shows that Chamberlain did not expect an unprovoked German attack on Scandinavia, any more than did Reynaud's cabinet. The latter took the view on 27 March that an Allied operation in Norwegian waters could force Germany to extend her front, whereas at present she was primarily interested in keeping it as short as possible.[33]

At a meeting of the Supreme War Council on 28 March the British prime minister succeeded in persuading Reynaud to abandon all plans which would have led to a war with the Soviet Union. Reynaud also agreed that, provided the Comité de Guerre approved, 'Royal Marine' should be carried out at the beginning of April, whereupon Chamberlain agreed to the mining operation off Narvik on 5 April, without, however, the occupation of Norwegian coastal bases.[34]

The result of these negotiations was approved by the War Cabinet the following day.[35] On the British as well as the French side there were influential people who hoped secretly that the German reaction to the Allied Narvik operation would lead to a greater military involvement in Scandinavia. Churchill argued for putting a landing force on stand-by, as he expected the Norwegian operation to be followed by German intervention in that country, which would give the Allies the opportunity

[30] PRO C.O.S. (40) 270, Cab 80/9; Dilks, 'Great Britain', 48.
[31] PRO Cab 66/6 WP (40) 103.
[32] PRO Cab 65/6 WM (40) 76; quoted in Lorbeer, *Westmächte*, 121 ff.
[33] Bédarida, 'France', 24.
[34] PRO Cab 99/3; Bédarida, *Stratégie secrète*, 311 ff.   [35] PRO Cab 65/6.

to carry out a landing with Norwegian consent.[36] On 30 March Churchill's French counterpart, Admiral Darlan, wrote to Daladier expressing the view that the Germans would probably react to the Allied operation by attempting to seize control of the ore-mines. In that case it would be the task of the Allies to forestall such German action. Darlan considered that putting an Allied expeditionary corps and the necessary transport ships on stand-by was essential to the implementation of the decisions of 28 March.[37]

These decisions were wrecked, however, when the Comité de Guerre under Daladier's influence postponed approval of 'Royal Marine'. Reynaud had to ask the British for a postponement of three months, which Chamberlain rejected, as he did the request that he and Halifax should come to Paris to persuade Daladier to change his mind. He insisted: 'No mines—no Narvik.' On 1 April Cadogan observed with resignation that the French constantly called for a more resolute conduct of the war, but that this demand was exclusively addressed to the British. He added: 'We really must try to bring them to heel.'[38]

The attempts of the two Allies to bridge the gap between their different points of view had cost valuable time. While Churchill in Paris tried without success to win Daladier's support for 'Royal Marine', on the evening of 5 April the British government decided to waive the agreement, reached on 28 March, that it be tied to the Narvik operation. This was done on Churchill's advice that the question should not be allowed to jeopardize the alliance. The order to carry out the operation was issued without any knowledge of the impending German invasion of Norway.[39] On the morning of 8 April mines were laid off Narvik.

---

[36] PRO Cab 65/12 WM (40) H, quoted in Bédarida, 'France', 24 n. 63.
[37] Bédarida, 'France'.
[38] Quoted in Dilks, 'Great Britain', 50.
[39] Ibid. 50-1.

III. Operation Weserübung

BERND STEGEMANN

ON 26 March Hitler and Raeder agreed on the latest possible date for Weserübung, and one week later Hitler fixed the actual date for 9 April. Of the 31 U-boats envisaged for use in conjunction with the operation, those assigned to Trondheim and Narvik had already received orders to put to sea on 11 March. The first of 7 merchant ships of the 'export group' (Ausfuhrstaffel—a code designation), which were to transport equipment and supplies to Norway, put to sea on 3 April, as did the first 8 tankers. On and after 6 April the ships of the sea transport groups (Seetransportstaffeln) followed, of which 26 were available for the transport of troops, equipment, and supplies. Vice-Admiral Lütjens, who had taken over the duties of the commander-in-chief of the fleet, Marschall, owing to the latter's illness, set sail from Schillig Reede in the Jade estuary at 5.10 a.m. on 7 April with the warships assigned to Narvik and Trondheim: the heavy cruiser *Admiral Hipper*, 14 destroyers, and the battleships *Scharnhorst* and *Gneisenau*. The warships carried 2,000 troops for Narvik and 1,700 for Trondheim. In spite of the bad weather the force was sighted by British air reconnaissance and attacked by 35 aircraft of Bomber Command, which, however, did not score any hits. The commander-in-chief of the British Home Fleet, Admiral of the Fleet Sir Charles Forbes, received exact information about the composition of the German force only during the afternoon and was thus not able to put to sea with all his ships before 9.15 p.m. When they reached the waters off the Norwegian coast, the German ships had already passed. Because of the heavy sea the German destroyers were widely scattered when, at 9.00 a.m. on the morning of 8 April, the *Bernd von Arnim* sighted the British destroyer *Glowworm* on an opposite course. The *Glowworm* belonged to the escort group of the battle cruiser *Renown*, which was stationed off the Vest Fiord to cover the mining of Norwegian waters as part of 'Operation Wilfred', and had become separated from the other ships of her group while searching for a sailor who had fallen overboard. She turned to pursue the German ship, and *Bernd von Arnim* being less able to cope with the heavy seas, could not shake her off. The commander-in-chief of the fleet thereupon detached the *Hipper* to intervene, with the result that the British destroyer was sunk after she and the cruiser had rammed each other.[1]

After this fight the *Hipper* and her four destroyers left the main group and, as it was still too early to put into Trondheim, at first set a westerly course. At 3.30 p.m. they were discovered by a British flying boat, which, however, reported a battle cruiser, two cruisers, and two destroyers. To intercept these ships Admiral Forbes

---

[1] This account is based on Roskill, *War at Sea*, vol. i; Ziemke, *Northern Theater*; and Hubatsch, *Weserübung*. These works should be consulted for sources and further literature.

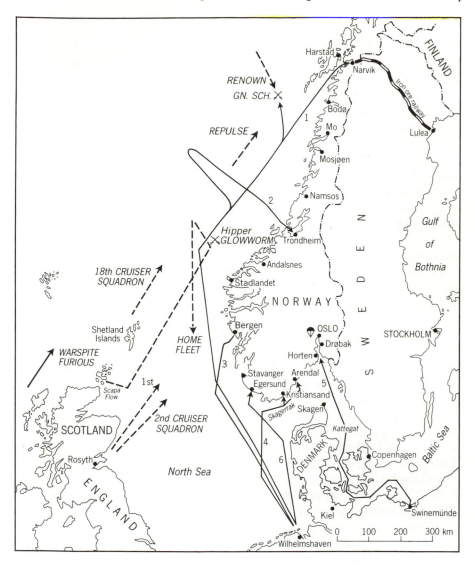

MAP V.III.1. Operation 'Weserübung N', 8-9 April 1940

changed his course to north and then north-west, and thus moved further away from
the Norwegian coast. The *Renown* was assigned to intercept any German force trying
to enter the Vest Fiord. For this purpose the Admiralty placed all destroyers involved
in mining operations under her command. On the morning of 9 April the battle
cruiser and her destroyers were, however, about 50 nautical miles west of the Lofoten
Islands; the Vest Fiord was unprotected. Moreover, the first cruiser squadron, which
lay ready in Rosyth with troops on board for a landing in Stavanger, was ordered by

the Admiralty to put them ashore and join the Home Fleet. The covering force of the group assembled on the Clyde, which was supposed to bring troops to Trondheim and Narvik—a light cruiser and six destroyers—was also withdrawn and sent to the Home Fleet. This meant that a landing operation could not be carried out in Norway in the foreseeable future.

Admiral Forbes had decided on the evening of 8 April to break off the search in the north-west and try to intercept the strong German forces reported on a northerly course in the Skagerrak. After he had detached a battle cruiser and a light cruiser with destroyers to support the *Renown*, he took a southerly course at 9.00 p.m. and continued on it until the next morning. Early on 9 April he was 80 nautical miles south-west of Bergen. At 9.00 p.m. the night before the commander-in-chief of the German fleet had reached the entrance to the Vest Fiord, where he sent the destroyers on to Narvik while setting a north-westerly course with the two battleships. On the morning of 9 April he encountered the *Renown*, which opened fire on the German ships at 5.07 a.m. and after 18 minutes scored a hit on the *Gneisenau* which knocked out the fire control in her topmast. A further hit caused a leak in turret A which led to the failure of all electrical equipment. A leak without a hit also caused the failure of turret A on the *Scharnhorst*.

Vice-Admiral Lütjens then decided to break off the fight as he believed he was facing two battleships, a mistake probably due to the flashes from the guns of the British destroyers. At 5.28 a.m. he therefore set a north-easterly course, but was able to shake off his enemy only at 7.30 a.m. He took a northerly and then a westerly course to gain time to put his two battleships back in fighting condition.

On the morning of 9 April, under the leader of destroyers, Captain and Commodore Bonte, the German destroyers entered the Ofot Fiord. At 4.40 a.m. two destroyers landed troops near Ramnes and Hamnes intending to occupy Norwegian coastal batteries there, only to find that they did not exist. Three destroyers were detached to land troops in the Herjangs Fiord while Bonte sailed for Narvik with three other ships. Shortly after 6 a.m. the leading destroyer was stopped by the Norwegian coastal-defence ship *Eidsvold*. Negotiations with the Norwegian captain were fruitless, and the *Eidsvold* attacked the German destroyer, which responded by firing several torpedoes at her. The *Eidsvold* suffered a number of hits, broke up, and sank. Her sister ship, the *Norge*, which fired on a German destroyer trying to tie up at the pier, was also sunk by torpedoes. Thereafter the operation was carried out without difficulty. The Norwegians, taken by surprise, surrendered Narvik and Elvegaardsmoen to Major-General Dietl, the commander of the German troops; only a small group of 250 troops withdrew to the east.

The *Hipper* spent 8 April steaming back and forth off the Norwegian coast with her four destroyers. At 12.30 a.m. on 9 April the group set a course for Trondheim and entered the inner fiord shortly after 4 a.m. It had already passed the searchlight stations at 25 knots when the battery in Hynes opened fire. The *Hipper* returned the fire with both rear turrets; her shells threw up such clouds of dust and smoke that the Norwegians had no clear field of view and ceased fire. Three destroyers landed troops to occupy the batteries while the *Hipper* and a destroyer anchored in the harbour at 5.25 a.m. The Norwegians in the city did not resist, but only part of the batteries could be captured by evening, and the airfield in Værnes remained in Norwegian hands.

The force assigned to Bergen was composed of the light cruisers *Köln* and *Königsberg*, the gunnery training-ship *Bremse*, 2 torpedo-boats, 5 motor torpedo-boats and a depot-ship. Under the commander-in-chief of scouting forces, Rear-Admiral Schmundt, it had 1,900 troops on board. On 9 April the ships entered the Kors Fiord at 2 a.m. They were seen by a number of Norwegian coastal-patrol vessels but were not attacked. Off the By Fiord troops were landed to occupy the Kvaven battery at 4.30 a.m. But as time was short the ships then entered the fiord immediately and came under fire from the coastal batteries at 5.15 a.m. The *Königsberg* took three and the *Bremse* two hits. The *Köln* was still fired upon by the battery Sandviken after she had anchored in Bergen. German aircraft intervened, and by 9.35 both batteries were occupied; Bergen itself did not offer any serious resistance.

Following attacks by air, Stavanger was occupied from the air by a paratroop company and two infantry battalions. The German steamer of the Ausfuhrstaffel assigned to Stavanger was sunk by a Norwegian torpedo-boat, but the three ships of the Seetransportstaffel (sea transport group) with the troop reinforcements arrived on time, and the airfield Sola was occupied. The telegraph station Egersund was taken without resistance by 150 men who had landed from four minesweepers.

The landing in the Kristiansand was carried out by the light cruiser *Karlsruhe*, 3 torpedo-boats, and 7 motor torpedo-boats with their depot-ship carrying 1,100 troops. It succeeded only on the third try. When the force reached the entrance to Kristiansand at 3.45 a.m., the fog was so thick that it could not enter the harbour. After 6 a.m., when the visibility was better, the Norwegians had already sounded the alarm, and the coastal batteries opened fire on the ships, which withdrew under cover of a smoke-screen. A second attempt after an attack by five German aircraft was also repelled by the coastal batteries. After a stronger air attack resistance ceased, but the ships were able to enter the fiord only at 11 a.m., as visibility had again become poor. During the afternoon three ships of the sea transport group reached the harbour. A torpedo-boat had been detached and, although hindered by fog, had landed a cycle squadron in Arendal at 9 a.m.

For Oslo a numerically strong force had been assembled: the heavy cruiser *Blücher*, the pocket battleship *Lützow*, the light cruiser *Emden*, 3 torpedo-boats, 8 R-boats (motor minesweepers), and 2 armed whaling-ships with 2,000 troops. The *Blücher*, however, had finished her sea trials only on 30 March and it had not originally been planned that she should take part in the operation. In spite of serious reservations, Raeder decided to use the heavy cruiser in order to have the pocket battleship *Lützow* free for a strategic diversion. The naval war staff planned to use her and the first two armed merchant raiders—simultaneously with action in Scandinavia—to start a new phase of the war against supply shipments for Britain across the Atlantic, but the Wehrmacht High Command ordered her to be used in Weserübung. The intention to assign the ship to the Trondheim group and then have her sail into the Atlantic after landing troops there could not, however, be realized, as damage was discovered in her engines which made shipyard repairs necessary before any long operation. For this reason the *Lützow* was assigned to Oslo.[2]

The force left Kiel on the morning of 8 April, passed Skagen around 7.00 p.m., and reached the entrance to Oslo Fiord shortly before midnight, when the Norwegian beacons had been extinguished. A Norwegian patrol-ship that opposed the Germans was sunk. Another patrol-vessel and the batteries on the islands Bolärne and Rauøy were passed, as the worsening visibility prevented them from firing more than a few shots. Troops to occupy these batteries and the navy base of Horten were then taken over by torpedo-boats and R-boats.

However, the assumption of the officer in command of the force, Rear-Admiral Kummetz, that it would be possible to pass the Drøbak narrows and the Oskarsborg fortress more or less without encountering any resistance proved to be a mistake. At 5.20 a.m. the fortress batteries opened fire on the leading German ship, the *Blücher*, with 150- and 280-mm. guns. The *Blücher* immediately suffered serious hits and was struck by two torpedoes a few minutes later, which knocked out her engines. She could not be saved and sank at 7.23 a.m.[3] The *Lützow* was also hit and then withdrew with the other ships, put troops ashore to take the narrows by land, and called for air support. On the morning of 10 April the fortifications at the Drøbak narrows were in German hands, and the German ships were able to reach Oslo at 11.45 a.m.

The air landings in Oslo also failed to go according to plan, because of ground fog. At 8.38 a.m., in spite of the Norwegian defence, the transports began to land at Fornebu airfield. By evening a total of eight companies had been flown in to occupy Oslo.

A much more serious problem than the carrying out of a surprise landing across waters controlled by the Royal Navy was the return of the ships involved after the enemy had already been alarmed. Originally it was planned to have the commander-in-chief of the fleet return together with the forces detached to Narvik and Trondheim. But only the *Hipper* was able to reach the two battleships and enter the Jade with them on 13 April at 8 p.m. The ten destroyers in Narvik found only one instead of the expected two tankers, which greatly slowed refuelling and made it impossible for them to put to sea on the evening of 9 April. On the morning of 10 April five German destroyers were in the harbour at Narvik, two of them being refuelled by the tanker. The remaining five were anchored in two side-fiords. For protection the leader of destroyers relied heavily on the four U-boats stationed at the entrance to the fiord, which, however, did not notice the entry of a group of five British destroyers.[4] Aided by heavy snow, the British ships were able to surprise the Germans in Narvik at 5.30 a.m. and sank two German destroyers. When they attempted to withdraw, however, they were attacked by five destroyers from the side-fiords and lost two of their own ships; a third was heavily damaged. While

---

[2] On criticism of the assignment of the two heavy ships to the Oslo group cf. Salewski, *Seekriegsleitung*, i. 186–7.
[3] A detailed account in Birnbaum, 'Untergang'.
[4] On criticism of the British measures cf. Marder, *Dardanelles*, 174.

withdrawing they still succeeded in sinking the only freighter of the Ausfuhrstaffel
that had been able to reach Narvik.

The senior officer of the fourth destroyer flotilla, who had taken over after the leader
of destroyers had been killed, attempted to break out with the two seaworthy destroyers
during the night of 10-11 April, according to the order of the navy group command,
but he abandoned the attempt after discovering enemy ships. Even though four
destroyers were ready to sail the next day, he considered another attempt to break out
useless. At noon on 13 April the British battleship *Warspite* and nine destroyers
entered the fiord, proceeded to Narvik, and annihilated the German destroyers, or at
any rate those which did not sink themselves after using up their ammunition.

The *Hipper* had already left Trondheim on the evening of 10 April; by 10 June
the four destroyers had also returned to Germany. The commander of scouting forces
left the *Königsberg* and the *Bremse*, which were both damaged, and put to sea on
the evening of 9 April with the *Köln* and four torpedo-boats. To avoid air attacks
he spent the next day in a narrow fiord and reached Wilhelmshaven at 5 p.m. on
11 April. The *Königsberg*, however, took two bomb hits on the morning of 10 April
and sank before noon. The *Karlsruhe* had also left Kristiansand with three torpedo-
boats on the evening of 9 April. At 8 p.m. she was attacked by a British submarine.
Although she suffered only one torpedo hit, she could not be saved and was finally
sunk by a torpedo-boat. The *Lützow* was also hit by a torpedo from a submarine
on 11 April off Skagen while returning to Kiel. She lost her rudder and both
propellers and had to be towed; there could therefore be no question of her being
sent into the Atlantic in the foreseeable future.

Of the 7 ships of the Ausfuhrstaffel, 6 were lost; of the 8 tankers, 3—those assigned
to Trondheim and one of the two sent to Narvik. Of the 26 ships of the
Seetransportstaffeln (sea transport groups), 6 were sunk. On account of these losses
the troop transports from north Jutland to southern Norway were carried out by
fast, shallow-draught ships of the navy. For transports of material about 100 luggers
were used on this route as well. By 15 June 270 German merchant ships had
transported 107,581 men, 16,102 horses, 20,339 vehicles, and 101,400 tons of
supplies to Norway. A total of 21 ships and about 2,000 men were lost. By 30 April
the Luftwaffe had flown 29,280 men and 2,376 tons of supplies to Norway. In
addition, U-boats carried out eight transport missions, mainly carrying aviation fuel,
bombs, anti-aircraft guns, and ammunition to Trondheim.[5]

The occupation of Denmark was carried out without great difficulty. The army
troops intended for the Jutland peninsula moved towards the border at 5.25 a.m.
on 9 April; the airfields of Ålborg were captured by paratroops and an infantry
battalion brought in by air at 7.30 a.m. The landings of troops in Nyborg, Korsør,
Copenhagen, Gedser and Middelfart were also successful, although the old battleship
Schleswig-Holstein ran aground in the Great Belt. On 10 April Bornholm was
occupied by a battalion. The important bridge between the islands of Falster and
Zealand was captured unopposed. An essential factor in the complete success of

---

[5] Figures from Hubatsch, *Weserübung*, 120.

'Weserübung Süd' was that, in contrast to the attack on Oslo, German troops were landed in Copenhagen in good time from the minelayer *Danzig* and were able to take the citadel by surprise. The Danish government decided to accept the German ultimatum, and the king ordered all resistance to cease at 7.20 a.m.[6]

Developments in Norway were different. When the German minister Bräuer informed the Norwegian foreign minister of the terms of the German ultimatum shortly after 5 a.m. on 9 April, no German troops were in or near Oslo. The Norwegian government had already ordered mobilization and were determined to resist. At 8.30 a.m. the royal family, the government, the parliament, and a large part of the ministerial bureaucracy left the city and proceeded by special train at first to Hamar and then to Elverum. Vidkun Quisling, supported by the German naval attaché and a representative of the Foreign Policy Office of the NSDAP, took advantage of this to attempt to form a government of his own the same day. As Hitler applauded this effort, Bräuer's negotiations with the king and the legal government could not lead to any positive results; the king was not prepared to appoint Quisling prime minister. Finally Bräuer and the president of the supreme court agreed that the latter would convene an administrative council consisting of seven persons from public life to take over the civil administration of the occupied areas. Quisling was persuaded to resign and given the position of special commissioner for demobilization. Hitler, however, had clearly expected that the administrative council would replace the legal government and end military resistance, which they were neither able nor willing to do. For this reason Bräuer fell into disfavour and Hitler, by a decree of 24 April, appointed Gauleiter Josef Terboven to be Reich commissioner, i.e. supreme civil authority, of the occupied areas in Norway.[7] This made it impossible to achieve an understanding with the Norwegian government. The attempt to carry out the landings as a 'peaceful occupation' had largely failed because of Norwegian resistance. However, Norwegian mobilization was made extremely difficult by the fact that many depots and communications centres were already in German hands. But the mobilization was carried out fast enough to deny the Germans the use of interior transportation links; the groups of troops that could be landed were largely isolated and dependent on supplies and reinforcements from the air.

On 9 April the British admiralty had decided to attack Bergen and Trondheim with parts of the Home Fleet but had cancelled this decision in the course of the day, probably in the mistaken belief that the coastal batteries were already in German hands. The War Cabinet for their part were convinced of the importance of taking Narvik, and on 11 April the first convoy with troops on board put to sea. On 13 April, however, the War Cabinet considered using part of the troops against Trondheim. Churchill, the First Lord of the Admiralty, expanded this idea into 'Operation Hammer', an amphibious assault on Trondheim supported by flanking landings at Namsos and Andalsnes. While these last two landings were carried out

---

[6] Captains' report in Kutzleben, Schroeder, and Brennecke, *Minenschiffe*, 41–8.
[7] For an extensive account cf. Loock, *Quisling*, 277–340.

on 14 and 17 April, Admiral Pound was able to obtain the cancellation of the direct attack on Trondheim.[8]

Meanwhile the events in Norway had caused a serious top-level crisis in Berlin on 13 April. Raeder complained that the landings had taken place two days late. Hitler wanted to order the troops in Narvik to fight their way through to the south and believed that they had simply had bad luck, while other persons present reported extreme agitation and scenes of 'panicky excitement'.[9] Hitler even gave the Dietl group permission to allow itself to be interned in Sweden, probably the only time he was ever prepared to sign such an order. After a temporary calm the situation again became critical when reports were received of landings of large numbers of British troops at Namsos and Andalsnes. Hitler now wanted to send reinforcements to Trondheim with the two fast steamers *Bremen* and *Europa*. When Raeder declared that this operation was impossible, Hitler wanted to use two large ships of the East Asia service and four banana-carriers to transport troops and equipment at least as far as Bergen, as he thought the units in Norway were extending their control northward too slowly. Only on 26 April was Raeder able to persuade him to abandon the idea of a sea transport to Bergen. On 30 April a land link between the German forces in Oslo and those in Trondheim was established. In the mean time it had become clear that the 12,000 British and French troops who had landed could not hold their positions against the superior German forces without adequate supply-harbours and air support. By 2 May they had to abandon Adalsnes and by 3 May Namsos. Subsequent fighting was concentrated around Narvik and involved mainly attempts by the Allies to stop the German advance on that port.

British advance troops arrived off Narvik on 15 April, but the commander of the army forces, Major-General Mackesy, refused to undertake an improvised landing and insisted that the operation against Narvik be carried out systematically and methodically. Therefore at first, on 24 April, the Allied naval forces only bombarded the port, without results. In the mean time the British established a base at Harstad. The fighting on land began with a Norwegian attack from the north on 24 April. On 28–9 April British and French troops landed north and south of Narvik. After two battalions of the French foreign legion and a Polish brigade had arrived, additional French troops landed in the Herjans Fiord on 13 May. Dietl, who only had 2,500 crew members of the lost destroyers in addition to his 2,000 mountain troops, came under increasing pressure and had to withdraw some of his forces from forward positions.

In view of the adverse situation in France[10] the Allies decided on 24 May to break off the battle around Narvik, but not before they had captured the town and completely destroyed the harbour. The Allied attack began during the night of 27–8 May; the Germans were forced to withdraw from the town. The attacks in the north and south also forced Dietl to shorten his lines and pull back along the ore railway towards the Swedish frontier. His position became extremely difficult.

[8] On 'Operation Hammer' cf. Marder, *Dardanelles*, 154–62.
[9] Evidence in Hubatsch, *Weserübung*, 373–80; Warlimont, *Hauptquartier*, 93–7.
[10] Cf. VI.1 below.

Sweden allowed only very limited transport of personnel, medical material, equipment, and food through her territory to Narvik.[11] Supplies of weapons and ammunition, as well as reinforcements, could only be brought in by air. Only the Luftwaffe was available to attack enemy naval forces in the area around Narvik, but it could often not be used because of the bad weather. A total of 1,050 men were sent to Narvik as reinforcements.

The 'Combat Group Feurstein', composed of parts of the second and third mountain divisions, had begun a march north from Grong in order to establish a land link with the German forces in Narvik on 5 May. Their advances were made difficult by the bad condition of the only road, which did not go all the way to Narvik; very often ferries had to be used to cross the fiords. In spite of Allied naval superiority, the German units reached Bodø on 1 June and Sørfold the next day, where the road ended. The remaining distance, 150 km., was to be covered by three reinforced battalions in a ten-day mountain march, with supplies delivered only by air. The first group reached Dietl on 13 June.

There were plans to give Dietl stronger support: the navy began 'Operation Juno' on 4 June.[12] In the next several days 2,800 mountain troops and paratroops were to be flown in. 'Operation Naumburg' was planned for the second half of the month. It involved sending troops on the *Bremen* and the *Europa*, this time to Lyngen Fiord, about 145 km. north of Narvik, and also the capture of Bardufoss airfield by the Luftwaffe. The navy ships used in 'Juno' were then to cover the two fast steamers, which, however, would not return to Germany but proceed on to Base North on the Soviet Arctic coast.[13] But these operations were never carried out, with the exception of 'Juno'. On 4 June the first of the 24,500 Allied soldiers boarded transport ships, and on the morning of 8 June the rearguard left Harstad. The Germans realized this only later during the day, as the Norwegians continued to attack with undiminished force.

An attempt to neutralize northern Norway under Swedish protection failed. When the British and Norwegian governments declared their readiness to accept such a measure, it was too late. Unlike the German General Staff, who were evidently still occupied with the relief operation for Narvik on 7 June, State Secretary von Weizsäcker in the foreign ministry suspected correctly that an Allied evacuation of Narvik must be imminent when the Swedish minister submitted this project to him on 4 June. On the evening of 7 June the king of Norway and his government left Trømso and went into exile aboard the cruiser *Devonshire*. On the king's orders the Norwegian troops in northern Norway stopped fighting, and the high command signed the act of surrender. However, the king, his government, and Major-General Ruge made it clear that the state of war between Germany and Norway continued and that the struggle would be carried on beyond the borders of his country.

Before the fighting in Norway stopped, however, the German navy was used once more, with far-reaching consequences. Already on 18 April the naval war staff had

---

[11] On the problems mentioned here cf. Lutzhöft, 'Deutschland und Schweden'.
[12] Cf. the following pages.   [13] On this base cf. Salewski, 'Basis Nord'.

informed Group Command West that in their opinion the two battleships *Scharnhorst* and *Gneisenau* should be deployed as soon as possible for continuous operations. Saalwächter agreed at first to postpone the planned shipyard period, but after energetic protests from Marschall he realized the necessity of at least a two-week training-period in the Baltic; reluctantly the naval war staff agreed. The training-period was even extended until 24 May, but Raeder now considered it necessary to make known his ideas about naval warfare in a directive of 18 May.[14] He regarded the areas between the Vest Fiord and Harstad, around the Shetland Islands and The Faeroes, the convoy route to Narvik, the blockade line Hebrides–Iceland, and finally the sea off Bodø as possible operations areas. He mainly wanted to achieve 'a frequent, active, and many-sided use' of the battleships. He was less concerned about particular targets than, 'with an eye on one of the operations areas, to be present so frequently that direct or indirect successes will be achieved because of this frequency alone'. As he evidently did not receive the desired support for his views, he expressed them even more clearly in a second directive.[15] After sketching an extremely optimistic picture of the possibility of actually improbable operations, which were to be carried out by ignoring the basic rules of naval warfare and accepting great risk, he demanded especially the use of the battleships. He considered them to be 'the strongest and toughest ships beyond the coastal zone; they combine the essential combat characteristics of all types of ships'. The loss of one of the two ships would change little in the situation at sea or in the final result of the war, but 'a navy which is led in bold attacks against the enemy, and as a result suffers heavy losses, will rise again after victory even larger and more powerful. If, however, it does not carry out such attacks, its existence will be threatened even after the war has been won'. These ideas repeated almost verbatim those of the naval war staff in October 1918, but, whereas then defeat was imminent, Raeder now believed victory to be near. Therefore the ships must be used more often even if this had no real military purpose. In spite of all the losses the navy had suffered in Norway, the two battleships had hardly made contact with the enemy, but battleships were to be the core of the future fleet. After the successes of the army in France it seemed necessary to justify their existence as rapidly as possible.

On the basis of the directive of the naval war staff, the group commander wrote in an order to the commander-in-chief of the fleet that his main task was to destroy hostile forces and installations in the And-Vags Fiord or the Ofot Fiord. At the same time or later he was to escort supply-ships from Trondheim to Bodø. In a private talk with Marschall on 31 May Raeder expanded the order to include attacks on enemy ships between the Vest Fiord and the area of Tromsø. Moreover, Marschall understood Raeder's instructions as giving the same top priority to protecting supply shipments for the Feurstein Group. Marschall did not understand that it was Raeder's intention to let the battleships be based in Trondheim for a long time to operate

---

[14] Repr. in Salewski, *Seekriegsleitung*, i. 519–22; cf. also the account on pp. 194–212. Marschall ('Juno' and 'Stellungnahme') and Schuur ('Auftragserteilung') were also consulted.

[15] 23 May 1940; Salewski, *Seekriegsleitung*, i. 522–4.

against British supply-routes and the blockade-line and to protect the sea route between Trondheim and Bodø.[16]

When Marschall put to sea from Kiel at 8 a.m. on 4 June with the two battleships, the cruiser *Hipper,* and four destroyers, he had no photo-reconnaissance results from Harstad. In particular he lacked information about possible mine-barrages and nets, torpedo batteries, and artillery emplacements. Nor did he receive any current reports from the commanding admiral Norway about the situation on land. On the evening of 6 June the fleet met its supply-ship south-east of Jan Mayen and took on fuel for the next twenty-two hours on a north-easterly course. On the following evening Marschall called a captains' conference to discuss details of the attack on Harstad. During the conference, however, reports were received that several groups of enemy ships were off the coast of northern Norway, while a German aeroplane over Harstad had only been fired upon by a gunboat. Marschall decided to abandon the attack on Harstad for the time being and to proceed against the nearest group of enemy ships, which was reported to be operating south of his position. He did not change his decision in spite of reminders from Group Command West in three radio messages that his main objective was still Harstad or Narvik. By noon on 8 June the German fleet had sunk a tanker, a trawler, and an armed troop transport; larger enemy ships could not be found. After this Marschall was finally convinced that the intended raid on Harstad would be futile. Therefore at 1 p.m. he decided to send the commander of scouting forces to Trondheim with the *Hipper* and four destroyers to take over the protection of supply shipments for the army as planned. He himself wanted to proceed with the two battleships to the area near Harstad and Tromsø. While he was looking for his own supply-ship, which seemed to be in danger, he sighted smoke at 4.45 p.m. It turned out to be the British aircraft-carrier *Glorious,* which, accompanied by two destroyers, was transporting fighter aircraft back from Norway. Strangely enough, however, neither had the *Glorious* launched any aircraft for her own safety, nor were any ready to take off. As a result the British ships were completely surprised when the Germans opened fire at 5.28 p.m. and by 8 p.m. they had been sunk. But the two destroyers defended the *Glorious* so skilfully that the two battleships had to expend half their medium-calibre ammunition; one destroyer even scored a torpedo hit on the *Scharnhorst,* whose captain broke off an evasive manœuvre too soon. The ship took in 2,500 tons of water; her rear turret was put out of action and her speed reduced.

---

[16] On Raeder's intentions cf. his report on the situation dated 4 June 1940 ('Führer Conferences', 105):

   (d) It will therefore be possible to relieve Narvik as follows:
     (1) By operating against the British naval forces and transports *en route* to Narvik.
     (2) By attacks to be made on bases by suitable forces if no contacts are made at sea and if air reconnaissance indicates a favourable situation in the fiords.

   (e) The following plans have been made for later execution with Trondheim serving as a base. Light enemy forces in the coastal waters near Trondheim and Bodø are to be eliminated; the supply lines for the Feurstein group are to be secured; the coastal artillery defences are to be extended as far as Bodø.

As he could find no more targets within reach,[17] Marschall decided to return the damaged *Scharnhorst* to Germany, but first he set a course for Trondheim. On orders from the group command he arrived there on 9 June at 4 p.m. to undertake operations against transports carrying troops and equipment back to Britain. After taking on supplies, he put to sea again on 10 June at 9 a.m. with the *Gneisenau*, the *Hipper*, and the destroyers so as to reach a more westerly position by the time he received reconnaissance reports. But the two convoys sighted by German reconnaissance during the day were already 400 nautical miles west of Trondheim. Marschall decided to break off the operation at 10 p.m. and returned to Trondheim at noon on 11 June.

When Marschall heard the harsh criticism of the naval war staff regarding his command of the fleet, he reported sick on 13 June. Thereupon Vice-Admiral Lütjens was appointed his successor. On 20 June Lütjens put to sea with the *Gneisenau* and the *Hipper* for an attack on the Northern Patrol, which was also intended to make easier the return of the *Scharnhorst* to Germany. Upon leaving the skerries, however, the *Gneisenau* suffered a torpedo hit in the bow from a British submarine; the operation had to be broken off. Unlike the group command, who now saw no possibility of continuing the operation in northern waters, the naval war staff wanted the *Hipper*, the *Nürnberg*, and four destroyers to continue operating from Norway. Only on 25 June did the *Nürnberg* and four destroyers return to Kiel as an escort for the *Gneisenau*, while the *Hipper* put to sea on the same day to carry out attacks on shipping between Petsamo and Britain. However, as no British merchant ships were at sea in that area, she was only able to capture a small Finnish steamer as a prize before returning to Wilhelmshaven on 9 August.

The naval war staff criticized Marschall's conduct of the operation because he had not fulfilled his main task, an attack on Harstad; but, given the development of the situation as he understood it, this could not seriously have been expected. At most it must be conceded that if he had continued his course towards Harstad he would presumably have encountered evacuation convoys. The criticism of his sending the *Hipper* and the destroyers to Trondheim was obviously the result of a misunderstanding on his part, or of Raeder's misleading words with regard to the importance of protecting supplies for the army. The demand that Marschall should have immediately resumed operations after returning the damaged *Scharnhorst* to Trondheim, i.e. without replenishing his ammunition, ignored all basic principles of naval warfare. More important than these and other detailed points, however, was the fact that the naval staff wanted 'Juno' to be regarded as the beginning of continuous, extensive operations. As already mentioned, the war could not in their view be permitted to end without the navy, and especially the battleships, having proved their value and justified their existence. Marschall, on the other hand, as the responsible commander, saw no purpose in an operation without any clearly recognizable aim, in which the risks were out of all proportion to the possible successes. Nor did he share the naval staff's optimistic assessment of the qualities

---

[17] Roskill on the other hand points out that a slow and only lightly protected convoy was approaching the area in which Marschall was operating; moreover, the heavy cruiser *Devonshire* with the king and government of Norway was only 100 naut. m. west of his position: Roskill, *War at Sea*, i. 196-7.

of the two battleships, i.e. evidently the belief that good luck was one of their construction features.

The new commander-in-chief was also criticized because he had not ordered the *Scharnhorst* and the *Gneisenau* to put to sea separately, so as to be able to concentrate all anti-submarine forces to protect each ship and her escorts. This immediate criticism by the naval war staff of his first operation as commander-in-chief decisively influenced Lütjen's later command of the fleet.[18] The fact remains that the naval war staff ordered Lütjens to carry out an operation in northern waters although France had sued for an armistice three days earlier. They did not recognize that a war at sea with operations based on the French Atlantic coast offered far more possibilities than Norway, although this had been clearly understood before the war.[19] As a consequence of the damage they had suffered, the two battleships were able to sail for their first operation in the Atlantic only on 28 December.

German losses during the operations in Denmark and Norway were 1,317 dead, 1,604 wounded, and 2,375 missing, according to official figures issued during the war. The Luftwaffe lost 242 aircraft, and the navy 1 heavy and 2 light cruisers, 10 destroyers, 1 torpedo-boat, 4 U-boats, 1 gunnery training-ship, and 1 R-boat; excluding auxiliary vessels, 18 ships with a total weight of 88,604 gross registered tons had been lost by 22 May. On the Allied side, in the fighting on land the British lost 1,896 men, the Norwegians 1,335, and the French and Poles together 530. At sea the British lost more than 2,500 men; the Royal Air Force and the Fleet Air Arm are said to have lost only 112 aircraft. Allied naval losses were 1 aircraft-carrier, 2 light cruisers, 9 destroyers, 6 submarines, and numerous auxiliary vessels. Although the naval losses were more or less equal on both sides, the German navy's losses were nevertheless much more serious. After the conclusion of the operation it had only 1 heavy cruiser, 2 light cruisers, and 4 destroyers ready for action. Especially disappointing was the fact that, in spite of numerous opportunities, German U-boats had not been able to play an important role because of torpedo malfunctions. They had been able to sink only one British submarine.[20]

In the campaign in Norway the Royal Navy had been the first navy to learn that even a vastly superior fleet could not operate successfully in waters dominated by the enemy air force. Nor did the superior British transport capacity play a significant role. Already on the second day of the campaign the Germans achieved a decisive advantage: they were able to occupy all important ports and airfields in southern and central Norway. At this point in the war neither was it possible to supply large numbers of troops by using open beaches to land supplies, nor had the aircraft-carrier been developed to the point that its aeroplanes represented an effective instrument against land-based air forces.

On the German side it became clear that Hitler was not up to a military crisis, and his inclination to meddle and give orders regarding the details of military

---

[18] For Raeder's criticism of the use of the battleships and the cruiser *Hipper* in the first year of the war see his order of 16 July 1940, repr. in Salewski, *Seekriegsleitung*, i. 527–33.
[19] Cf. II.II above and VIII.IV below.   [20] Cf. IV.VII above.

operations became evident for the first time. The success of the operation strengthened his tendency to place too much faith in surprise and readiness to take high risks as a prescription for victory. With this faith he could win individual campaigns, but not the war.

The first combined action of all three Wehrmacht services remained an isolated episode, while in the further course of the war and under different conditions the Allies gradually perfected the execution of such operations. The successful conclusion of Weserübung did not encourage critical analysis; rather, it tended to divert attention from the shortcomings of the German command organization and the weaknesses of the Wehrmacht.

Generally historians consider the operation to occupy Denmark and Norway as such to have been a clear German success. On the whole, however, it led to more problems than advantages for Germany. It is idle to speculate whether, if Germany had held back, an Allied operation in Norway and especially Allied occupation of the Swedish iron-ore fields would have led to a confrontation with the Soviet Union. It is also impossible to be certain whether Britain could have defended her position in Norway alone after the German victory in France, or whether an easy German occupation would have been possible if the German leaders had still considered it necessary at that time.

IV. Securing Germany's Political and Military Hold on the Occupied Territory

BERND STEGEMANN

As the Reich Commissioner for the occupied areas of Norway,[1] Terboven exercised the highest authority in civilian affairs, while the 'commander of German troops in Norway' (later 'Wehrmacht Commander Norway') represented the military forces. Terboven also had the German police forces at his disposal; he could enact laws by decree, and received his guide-lines only from Hitler, to whom he was directly responsible. Moreover, he succeeded in creating a position for his office that corresponded to that of the highest Reich authorities without being bound by their routine and procedures. The senior SS and police chief was formally not under Terboven's control, but in fact the latter was able to influence the filling of SS positions and thus to pre-empt any threat to his position from that quarter.

After a build-up phase, the Reich Commission was organized into sections for administration, economy, and propaganda, comprising a total of twelve departments. In addition to the main sections there was the senior SS and police chief. Not including the police, the personnel strength of the Commission was 239 in October 1940.[2]

In its memorandum of April 1940 the German government had stated that 'Germany has no intention of interfering with the territorial integrity and political independence of Norway, now or in the future'.[3] Hitler of course did not abide by this promise once the country had been occupied. Already at the end of April he spoke of building a motorway to Trondheim and of a military enlargement of the town compared to which that of Singapore would be 'child's play'.[4] In addition to the naval base, where the biggest ships were to be built and which was to be defended by a division from each of the Wehrmacht services, it was planned in July to build separately from Trondheim a 'beautiful German city, the most northerly cultural centre of the Great German Reich'.[5] Accordingly, Terboven's task was to strengthen German rule in Norway and to work to form a National Socialist government. In the opinion of Raeder and the head of the Foreign Policy Office of the NSDAP, Rosenberg, the man best suited for that task was Quisling with his Nasjonal Samling. That party, however, had not won a single seat in the elections of 1936 and had shrunk to fewer than 1,500 members by 1940. Moreover, most Norwegians considered Quisling a traitor because he had declared himself prime

---

[1] Cf. V.III above.　　　　　　　　　　　　　　　　[2] Figures in Loock, *Quisling*, 365-6.

[3] Printed in full in Hubatsch *Weserübung*, 509-12.

[4] Rosenberg's diary, quoted ibid. 488. Between 1923 and 1939 the British had turned Singapore into a modern fortress at a cost of £15m.

[5] Cf. 'Führer Conferences', 113; Loock, *Quisling*, 457.

minister after the king and the government had left Oslo on 9 April, and had ordered Norwegian troops to cease firing at the Germans and to arrest the king and the legal government. For these reasons, and because he personally considered Quisling unsuitable, Terboven rejected the idea of forming a government with him and his party alone. Through negotiations with the Norwegians he wanted to convene the Storting, the Norwegian parliament, eliminate the monarchy, depose the exile government in London, and form a new government to preserve the appearance of legality. The Storting would then be made superfluous by an enabling act in favour of the new government, the Riksrådet (National Council). The council's composition would at first have to be a compromise in order to be accepted by the Norwegians, but Terboven's ultimate aim was to fill it with men of his own choosing.

Leading figures of Norwegian public life participated in the ensuing talks and negotiations: members of the administrative council, the supreme court, and the presidium of the Storting, representatives of the four main parties, and the head of the Norwegian state Church. They gradually accepted the German demands because they feared either a new Quisling government or direct German rule, and because resistance hardly seemed possible after the French sued for an armistice on 17 June. On the other hand, in order to have a National Council with a membership reflecting his own wishes, Terboven was even prepared (as he told the Norwegians) to deport Quisling to Germany. This made it possible to reach an agreement on 29 June; the Storting was to meet on 15 July.

Quisling received an invitation to come to Germany, and left on 5 July. But Terboven could not push his plan through: Hitler decided that Quisling should return to Norway and retain the leadership of the Nasjonal Samling. His decision seems to have been influenced by Rosenberg and Raeder, who sharply criticized Terboven, supported Quisling, and above all saw to it that the relevant reports, some of them written by Quisling and his assistant Hagelin, reached Hitler. Terboven now wanted to replace the National Council with a German administration and postpone the formation of a government under Quisling, who of course did not agree to this plan. Asked to make a decision, on 5 September Hitler ordered that a government should be formed which included supporters of Quisling, but it should also be approved by the Storting.[6] Terboven resumed negotiations with the Norwegians and confronted them with new demands. The presidium of the Storting accepted a fifteen-member National Council in which four representatives of the Nasjonal Samling were to sit. The Storting convened on 10 September and, as a test, voted on the arrangement demanded by the German side. When Terboven again raised his demands in response to pressure from Quisling, the Norwegians realized that co-operation would not give them any protection from further pressure and broke off the negotiations. Thereupon Terboven dissolved the National Council

---

[6] Loock (*Quisling*, 510-13, 517) assumes that Hitler abandoned Terboven's original plan because he no longer expected an early peace with Britain and instead assumed that the war would spread. He therefore wanted a stronger guarantee of German influence on the Norwegian government. The method used was also, he suggests, determined by the arrangement in the Netherlands.

on 25 September and appointed thirteen state councillors to conduct the business of government; nine of these belonged to the Nasjonal Samling.

However, the attempt to achieve a 'certain political development in Norway' with this government apparatus failed. A decree that abolished the election of lay judges was declared illegal by the supreme court. When Terboven then denied that the court had the authority to rule on the legality of decrees by the state councillors, all the judges resigned and in this way clearly demonstrated that the methods of the occupiers had nothing to do with legality, the appearance of which they were trying to preserve. Terboven also wanted to start the Nazification of all societies, clubs, and unions; he began by ordering all sports clubs to join a new umbrella organization. The result of this attempt foreshadowed similar reactions to subsequent measures: the athletes and spectators stayed at home; no athletic events could take place.

Terboven was more successful in exploiting the potential of the Norwegian economy, and was able to secure the aluminium production for Göring's benefit. He began the process of penetrating the Norwegian economy with German capital and saw to it that industrial production was increased or decreased solely in accordance with German interests. He also tried to limit Norwegian trade with third countries to goods Germany did not need.[7]

The Wehrmacht commander in Norway, General von Falkenhorst, who was at the same time commander-in-chief of Army Group XXI, headed the German military organization in Norway. He was still in charge of all army units used in Weserübung: five infantry and two mountain divisions. An additional infantry division was deployed in Norway in the course of 1940. On 13 August Hitler ordered a great expansion of the German military presence and installations in Norway, to deter possible Soviet attacks there and to create a base for the occupation of Petsamo. The next day he ordered the two mountain divisions to be transferred to the north. By November an 810-km. road had been built from Narvik to Kirkenes. As the navy did not have sufficient forces available, army artillery units were used for coastal defence for the first time in Norway. On 1 March 1941 thirteen batteries were in position; it was planned to increase their number to 160 by 1 August.[8]

The importance of Norway in Raeder's thinking can be seen in his appointment of the former commander-in-chief of the fleet, Admiral Boehm, as 'commanding admiral and special representative of the commander-in-chief of the navy in Norway'. Unlike the coastal commanders in Germany, Boehm commanded not only the naval units on land and the port-defence flotillas, but also the coastal-zone defence forces. Under his command were three admirals—of the Norwegian west, north, and Arctic coasts—each of whom in their respective areas had three subordinate commanding officers: for sea defence with port-defence flotillas, for naval artillery, and for naval anti-aircraft units. There were also minesweeper, patrol-boat, and anti-submarine flotillas, most of which, like the other units, were quite new and had been created

---

[7] For a detailed account of the use of the Norwegian economy for the German war effort cf. *Das Deutsche Reich und der Zweite Weltkrieg*, vol. v.

[8] Mueller-Hillebrand, *Heer*, vol. i.; Harnier, *Artillerie*, 29–33.

for duty in Norway. All this placed a great strain on the resources of the navy. But Raeder was prepared to concentrate all the navy's efforts on Norway to defend the German positions and the transport routes there.

On 13 October British destroyers carried out a raid on the Lofoten Islands, which, however, did not cause any vigorous reaction on the German side. Nevertheless, concern about the threat to Norway continued, especially in relation to 'Barbarossa', the planned campaign against the Soviet Union. It was increased by a new action of the Royal Navy on 3 March, which succeeded in destroying fish-processing plants in four places and in sinking seven merchant ships totalling 14,929 gross registered tons. As a result of these events Hitler ordered the strengthening of the army coastal artillery mentioned above, and on 26 March he issued a 'combat directive for the defence of Norway'.[9]

For Denmark and Norway the Luftwaffe created Air Fleet Command 5 under General Stumpff with headquarters at first in Stavanger and later in Oslo. Stumpff was in charge of the Tenth Flying Corps, which had the following forces at its disposal: two bomber Geschwader of two Gruppen each, one heavy fighter and one fighter Geschwader of one Gruppe each, a coastal air wing (Küstenfliegergruppe), two reconnaissance Gruppen, and two reconnaissance Staffeln. Its main base was in Stavanger, with units also stationed in Ålborg and Trondheim.[10] After 3 March it became clear that the available units were not sufficient to deter the enemy from attacking the coast, and Göring, as Hitler informed Raeder on 18 March, therefore made available 'air units composed of various types of planes' for southern, central, and northern Norway.[11] Bardufoss in particular was to receive air units.

In Denmark developments took a different course. On 9 April the Danish government under Thorvald Stauning had protested at the violation of Danish neutrality, but they also accepted the German demands. King Christian X and the government remained in the country. Already on 10 April, however, a coalition government was formed in which the four major parties were represented in order to have a better chance of influencing the actions and policies of the occupiers. On the German side only the foreign ministry and the German minister in Copenhagen, Renthe-Fink, remained responsible for dealings with the Danish government. Renthe-Fink now received an addition to his title: 'and special representative of the German Reich'. The responsibility of the German commander in Denmark, General Kaupisch, was limited to purely military matters. He was permitted to have direct contact only with the Danish armed forces, while, however, working closely with Renthe-Fink. The latter was assisted by an expert on economic matters and a specialist in internal administration as well as by an official of the German foreign ministry, whose duty was to superintend Denmark's foreign policy. As the Danish government

    [9] Repr. in *KTB OKW* i. 1007–10; cf. also the 'Weisung an den Wehrmachtbefehlshaber Norwegen über seine Aufgaben im Fall "Barbarossa"', dated 7 Apr. 1941, pp. 1011–13. On this section cf. also Lohmann and Hildebrand, *Kriegsmarine*; Salewski, *Seekriegsleitung*, i. 191–4, 457–9; Boehm, 'Stellungnahme'.   [10] Figures in Mason, *Battle over Britain*, 594 (for 13 Aug. 1940).
    [11] 'Führer Conferences', 182–3.

and administration continued to function, German authorities limited themselves to supervisory tasks. This made it possible to keep the bureaucratic apparatus under Renthe-Fink small: at the beginning of 1942 it consisted of only 89 persons.[12]

At first Renthe-Fink co-operated with the coalition government, but his aim was to create a government friendly to Germany in which the democratic parties would no longer be represented. However, he was not able to influence the reshuffle of the government on 8 July as his efforts were not supported by the German foreign ministry. After negotiations in July and August on a customs and currency union had not produced any results, Renthe-Fink tried in vain to form a government using members of the Dansk National Socialistisk Arbejderparti (DNSAP: the National Socialist Party of Denmark), which, however, was even more insignificant and had an even worse reputation than Quisling's Nasjonal Samling in Norway. On the other hand, Renthe-Fink did obtain the resignation of an undesirable minister. Around the end of 1940 he attempted once again without success to persuade Stauning to resign the premiership so that he could form a government of independent ministers. Thereafter he limited his efforts to persuading individual ministers and party politicians to renounce their offices; here the Danes complied.

Under German pressure the Danish government closed the British and French legations in Copenhagen after the German invasion of Denmark. The Germans also monitored the communications of the Danish foreign ministry with Danish legations and consulates abroad. The latter were instructed to present their country's relations with Germany in a favourable light, and the local German missions kept a close watch on their behaviour. Germany also insisted that the Danish Government protest against the landing of British troops in Iceland on 10 May, after The Faeroes had already been occupied.[13]

The Danish government again made a formal protest when the United States and Canada opened consulates in Greenland, while the Danish minister in Washington concluded an agreement with the United States on 11 April 1941 by which he placed the island under American protection and permitted the United States to construct air-bases there. He was recalled by the government in Copenhagen, but he declared them to be lacking in competence to act for the country and remained in Washington as the representative of Denmark recognized by the American government. Other Danish diplomats abroad followed his example by ceasing to accept instructions from their home government.

While the German economics expert in Copenhagen saw to it that the Danish government introduced measures to guarantee the economical use of stocks so that the economy could continue to function, a Danish–German government committee had been responsible for supervising the exchange of goods between the two countries since 1937. This trade was based on a clearing agreement in accordance with which

---

[12] Figures in Thomsen, *Besatzungspolitik*.

[13] In June Hitler ordered the navy to plan and prepare a landing in Iceland. The naval war staff disliked this project (known as 'Ikarus') because they expected it would involve heavy losses, the island could not be supplied regularly, and there could be no question of using it as a base for German naval forces. Cf. Salewski, *Seekriegsleitung*, i. 272; 'Führer Conferences', 110; Ziemke, *Northern Theater*, 108.

it was evenly balanced and payments were made through state credit institutions. Danish deliveries of agricultural products were greatly increased and German contracts awarded to Danish enterprises. In addition, German troops in Denmark purchased directly from the economy and employed Danish workers, which resulted in a growing German trade deficit. Germany had to increase coal deliveries, but as a set-off Danish labourers were recruited to work in Germany. At the end of 1940 they already numbered 28,000; in the course of the war this figure increased many times.

Höheres Kommando XXXI,[14] which was in charge of German troops in Denmark and had been placed under the command of Army Group XXI during Operation Weserübung, was put directly under the Army High Command on 12 April, but Reich authorities had to communicate with the commander of German troops in Denmark through the Wehrmacht High Command. Because of the relatively secure geographical position of Denmark, only one army division was stationed there. In the negotiations on 9 April German military representatives had secured control of the country's defence installations and a reduction of the Danish army to 2,200 men. The Danes were assured that they would be permitted to keep their weapons, but already on 15 April the German commander demanded that they should turn over 24 light anti-aircraft guns; on 25 April they also had to turn over 36 heavy and 50–60 light anti-aircraft guns. After the Army High Command had demanded 2 batteries of 105-mm. howitzers, which it also received, the German foreign ministry was able to persuade Hitler to order on 20 May that no further demands for weapons were to be made on the Danes.[15]

The navy appointed a 'Navy Commander Denmark' based in Copenhagen. He was responsible to the Baltic naval station, and consequently only the commanding officers of the ports, the naval artillery, and the anti-aircraft units in the area of the Baltic were directly and completely under his command. He was the superior of the commanding officers of sections on the Danish west coast and northern Jutland only in matters related to stationing. In other respects they were under the North Sea naval station. Apart from port-defence flotillas, the commander did not have any naval forces at his disposal. The Danish navy had to lay up part of its ships; with the others it took over defence, patrol, and minesweeping tasks, keeping the east–west channels open while the German navy was responsible for the north–south channels. Raeder was anxious for friendly relations with the Danish navy based on mutual trust, but the Danish naval commander, Admiral Rechnitzer, resigned on 10 April because the officer corps condemned the passivity of the Danish navy on 9 April as well as the new agreements with Germany. When the Germans demanded that the Danes sell them 12 torpedo-boats in January 1941, of which they finally took over 6 as torpedo recovery-vessels, the basis for co-operation was completely destroyed.

---

[14] For Höhere Kommandos cf. note to Map V.I.1.
[15] Cf. Hubatsch, *Weserübung*, 130-1; Thomsen, *Besatzungspolitik*, 48-50. On the following paragraph cf. Thomsen, 51-3; Wesche, 'Dänische Marine'.

PART VI

The Battle for Hegemony in Western Europe

Hans Umbreit

I. Strategic Defence in the West

'GERMANY has no interests in the west,' Hitler declared in the Reichstag on 1 September 1939.[1] The fact was that for the time being he could well do without complications on Germany's western frontier. His programme of expansion was based on the expectation of an arrangement with Britain; this would, first of all, give him a free hand on the European continent. France, on the other hand, which—according to Hitler's original estimate—could not accept any substantial increase in German strength, would have to be eliminated as a power-factor at some future time. Hitler, morever, had some territorial demands to be pressed when the opportune moment presented itself: the return of Alsace and Lorraine[2] as well as the cession of parts of north-eastern France,[3] which had been part of the Empire in early modern times. Hitler believed that by concluding his alliance with the Soviet Union he had effected a lasting improvement of his position. It might not have gone very well with his anti-Communist policy over the years, but it brought him inestimable strategic and economic advantages. However, it also established an increasingly irksome dependence on a power which, in the long run, Hitler believed he must mistrust. Yet he does not appear to have ruled out the possibility of a satisfactory delimitation of the German from the Soviet sphere of interest, at least for a time.

Britain and France certainly recognized Hitler's programme for what it was—not perhaps in all its details but in its overall objective: the step-by-step rise to world power. They believed the time had arrived to oppose Hitler's unquenchable expansionist desires by military means and thus to discharge their obligations vis-à-vis their Polish ally.[4] Hitler probably did not expect such determination. He had tended for a long time to underestimate British interest in a balance of power on the continent of Europe.[5]

The Allied declaration of war on 3 September 1939, followed at once or within a few days by the Commonwealth countries, also came as a surprise to the German military leaders. They had not prepared any offensive plans for a war in the west. All that was ready was a deployment instruction of the Army High Command of January 1939, according to which the western fortifications were to be held in the event of a French attack.[6] Further orders specified the measures to be taken for the contingencies expected—'Frontier Security West' or, in case of a major enemy offensive, 'Defence in the West'. In his 'Directive No. 1 for the Conduct of the War'[7] Hitler had ruled that the opening of hostilities in the west was to be left to

---

[1] Domarus, ii. 1314. [2] *Heeresadjutant bei Hitler*, 58 (22 Aug. 1939).
[3] The intended redrawing of Germany's western frontier was based on the 'north-east line' which Germany imposed on occupied France at the end of June 1940. Cf. Map VI.v.6.
[4] Butler, *Strategy*, ii. 1. [5] Hillgruber, *Strategie*, 29.
[6] Deployment directive 'Operation West', ObdH/GenStdH/1. Abt. (I) No. 4010/39 g.Kdos., 18 Jan. 1939, in *Dokumente zur Vorgeschichte*, 31 ff.
[7] Supreme commander of the armed forces/OKW/WFA No. 170/39 g.Kdos. Chefs. L I, 31 Aug. 1939: Directive No. 1 for the conduct of the war, ibid. 1–2; Trevor-Roper, *Directives*, 3 ff.

the enemy. All preparations were to be made merely to ensure that French thrusts across the common frontier were repulsed and that an encirclement of the German northern wing was prevented in case the enemy—against all expectation—seized the initiative by violating Belgian and Dutch neutrality. The German forces had been ordered to 'observe meticulously' the neutrality of Switzerland, Luxemburg, Belgium, and Holland. The frontier of the Reich was to be crossed only with Hitler's express approval. Similar restraints had been imposed on the navy and air force. Naval forces, for the time being, were to conduct only a limited 'merchantmen war' against Britain. The air force—Air Fleet 2 for the protection of the Ruhr and Air Fleet 3 in support of the ground forces deployed in the west—was to prevent enemy penetrations of Reich territory and merely prepare for offensive operations, likewise against Britain. Intensive aerial warfare was to be avoided in view of the exposed situation of the Ruhr. Generally speaking, Hitler was anxious to keep the western theatre of war quiescent for as long as the bulk of the German forces was tied up in Poland, and to avoid provoking the British and French into major operations. He believed that the enemy countries had no real war aims, and he was initially hoping that a clash in the west might be avoided or that France might be prised away from her alliance with Britain.[8]

The ratio of forces along Germany's western frontier was at first very favourable to the Allies. At the beginning of the war Germany could not deploy even half as many divisions as France—a mere 32, whose state of training and equipment, moreover, was anything but first-rate. This army group, under Colonel-General Ritter von Leeb, consisted, from north to south, of the Fifth, First, and Seventh Armies. These forces would have scarcely been sufficient to halt a vigorous attack, especially as construction of the Westwall had been completed only in a number of places.

Construction of the western fortifications had begun in 1936. The time required for the completion of this counterpart to the Maginot Line was originally estimated at twelve years. In May 1938, in connection with his plans of aggression against eastern Europe, Hitler gave orders for the construction of the Westwall to be accelerated and for it to be extended to the Aachen area. This was possible only by using a less expensive method of construction, by means of a system developed from field fortifications. This was also to ensure operational flexibility and prevent the offensive spirit of the troops from flagging. Massive concrete roofing, in consequence, was the exception. The line—600 km. from Basle to Geilenkirchen—did not necessarily follow the frontier but frequently took account of the nature of the terrain and of tactical requirements. Building work was intensified, especially at the presumed points of the enemy's main thrusts: the sectors of Saarbrücken, Homburg, the Pfälzer Wald, Trier, and Aachen. During the twelve months up to the beginning of the war over 160,000 men were employed on the Westwall, without being able to complete the project. The programme was carried out predominantly by the Todt Organization (OT), which was able to continue the work (with reduced manpower) even after September 1939.

---

[8] Conversation of the chief of naval staff with Hitler at Zoppot, 23 Sept. 1939, in *Lagevorträge*, 41.

The German fortifications in the west were supplemented by an 'Air Defence Zone West'.[9] This consisted of a strip of territory from 20 to 100 km. deep, running along the Reich frontier from north to south. The concentration of anti-aircraft artillery for the protection of industrial centres was intended to inflict maximum losses on enemy aircraft.

According to German estimates, the French would need roughly three weeks to mobilize and deploy the (calculated) 91 divisions of their wartime army. Added to these were a few British formations which might by then have arrived on the Continent. By that time, however, considerable German forces should have become available from Poland. The critical period would be about the tenth day of mobilization, when France would be able to mount an offensive with approximately 50 formations. This assessment of the ratio of strength led the German authorities to carry out the evacuation of the population from the German–French frontier areas, an operation long prepared for in the event of war. Shortly after the Allied declaration of war a start was made on a precipitate 'thinning out' or evacuation of limited areas.[10] Executive power had partly been transferred to the commanders-in-chief of the armies as early as 26 August, a decision which, especially in view of the politically delicate evacuation, led to some friction with the Gauleiters. On the other side of the frontier the population endured the same fate. More than 250,000 inhabitants were evacuated from the eastern parts of Alsace-Lorraine to inland France. As early as the second week of the war further divisions were moved into the German western defences, which rendered possible the establishment of a short-lived Army Detachment A (from 11 September to 10 October 1939, under Colonel-General Freiherr von Hammerstein) at the northern sector of the front. But a major transfer of forces was possible only after the conclusion of the Polish campaign. On 10 October Colonel-General von Bock assumed command of the newly formed Army Group B, on the northern wing, and on 25 October Colonel-General von Rundstedt that of Army Group A, which adjoined it in the south.

Operations in the west still had to remain defensive. Reconnaissance patrols were still not allowed to cross the frontier, and reaction to attacks was to be only local. Until 13 September not even the artillery was permitted to fire across the frontier. Not until 10 September was the Luftwaffe authorized to fly reconnaissance missions over French territory. Military operations during this 'phoney war', the *drôle de guerre*, were thus confined to skirmishes in the forefield of the Westwall, in particular in the area of the Palatinate and the Saar. On Hitler's order the British troops alone, whose presence had been established in December facing the front of First Army, were to be vigorously attacked: the purpose was to weaken their morale and to lower their standing with the French.

---

[9] Speidel, 'Westfeldzug', MGFA Lw 3/4, fos. 35 ff.
[10] H.Gr.C/Ia No. 102/39 g.Kdos. Chefs., 31 Aug. 1939, in *Dokumente zur Vorgeschichte*, 72–3.

II. Hitler's Decision to Attack the Western Powers

1. MILITARY DECISION IN THE WEST?

HITLER was not clear at first whether the Western powers intended to fight or merely to preserve appearances. In any case he attached importance to Soviet participation in the occupation of Poland, so that the Western powers should be faced with the question of whether to declare war on the Soviet Union as well. And as, in his opinion, they would shrink from that step, there might perhaps be a chance to end the conflict. He was therefore anxious to have a *fait accompli* established in Poland in order to avoid a real war on the western front.

By about the middle of September, however, his rapid success in the east induced Hitler to contemplate offensive action also in the west, in order to defeat France militarily and to compel Britain, with her numerically weak ground forces, to come to terms. An arrangement by purely political means—an 'understanding' of the kind he had originally imagined—he increasingly came to regard as unlikely, even though, in view of differences of opinion in the enemy camp and for propaganda purposes, he encouraged various feelers for peace or, to the extent that he was aware of them, at least tolerated them. On 27 September, at the Reich chancellery, Hitler officially informed the commanders-in-chief of the three services of his offensive intentions. He justified his plan by the argument that Germany could not stand idly by while the enemy was getting stronger all the time. She should make use of her superiority while it lasted to avert a serious threat to the Ruhr, Germany's 'Achilles' heel'. Hitler was well aware that Germany was 'unable to see the war through in the long run'. He wanted to stake everything on one card, to deliver the 'big blow' even before Christmas 1939, ideally by the end of October, and bring the war that was 'forced upon him' to an end in this manner: 'smash' France, which he regarded as militarily weak, and 'force Britain to her knees'[1] by securing for Germany favourable bases in Holland, Belgium, and northern France for the war in the air and at sea. He rejected any compromise solution which would have demanded the renunciation of his Polish spoils. He regarded a major action as necessary, if only to preserve German influence on the neutral countries,[2] whose supplies were indispensable to the German war economy. Hitler mistrusted Belgium's willingness to preserve its neutrality. He pointed to its one-sidedly eastward-looking defence measures. He also claimed to have knowledge of secret consultations of the Belgian general staff with the British and the French. As for Holland, he believed he might reach a temporary arrangement, even though the involvement of at least the Maastricht corner in the German area of operations was unavoidable.

---

[1] Halder, *KTB* i. 89 ff.; the trans. in *Diaries*, i. 91-2, is incomplete.
[2] KTB OKW/WiRüAmt/Stab/, entries for 4 and 6 Dec. 1939, BA-MA W 01-8/16.

The Army High Command was instructed to prepare appropriate plans. Hitler had probably not finally made up his mind: he intended first to appeal to the Allies and persuade them to accept the results of the war so far, or else hold them responsible, in his propaganda, for the continuation of the conflict. He was greatly displeased by Army High Command's disinclination to wage a war in the west, and he was determined to override this resistance if necessary. He himself would decide the framework within which all planning was to be done. The military leaders, in consequence, exercised influence only on decisions of detail.

Even before Chamberlain had rejected his vague peace offer of 6 October 1939, Hitler set out his ideas in a memorandum dated 9 October,[3] which he brought to Brauchitsch's and Halder's notice the following day. The two-part structure of this lengthy document made it clear that it served a double purpose: on the one hand it was a disavowal of those military leaders who advised against an extension of the war, and on the other it gave a rough outline of various possible strategic starting-points. Hitler did not, of course, ignore the advantages of concluding peace on the basis of his forcibly achieved territorial accretion in the east, provided this was feasible. In the long term, however, he aimed at the final military elimination of his enemies, to an extent when they could no longer oppose a possible German 'further development' towards the east—which only the British, in Hitler's view, would be capable of doing anyway. He did not have a high opinion of the vigour of the French nation, and regarded Holland and Belgium as of even slighter political weight; he did not believe they would be able to preserve their neutrality against the demands of the Western powers. This put the Ruhr at the kind of risk that Germany could not afford. Occupation of Belgium and Holland by the Wehrmacht, on the other hand, would improve Germany's initial situation to such an extent that the Western powers would have to do all they could to prevent just that situation. Hitler therefore believed that swift action was called for—also in view of the hostility of the United States and the basically uncertain attitude of the Soviet Union—to exploit Germany's momentary advantage. Time, he felt sure, was working for the enemy, who was only temporarily inferior in military strength, i.e. in terms of personnel and armaments.

Hitler did not trouble to support his thesis. He did not even have reliable data on the state of his own forces. It was, in fact, the Wehrmacht which benefited considerably from the the breathing-space granted it, involuntarily, by Hitler. Not only were the losses incurred during the Polish campaign (up to 50 per cent) by armoured and motorized formations made good, but the situation with motor vehicles was generally improved by the spring of 1940, stocks of ammunition were built up, and the training of newly established formations and command personnel was carried out more thoroughly. The last of these measures greatly contributed to the success of the campaign in the west.

As for its actual schedule, Hitler in the second part of his memorandum confined himself to a few general directives. The aim was to annihilate the Franco-British

---

[3] Memorandum and guide-lines for the conduct of the war in the west, dated 9 Oct. 1939, in *Dokumente zur Vorgeschichte*, 5 ff.

forces and to conquer at least enough space to allow the war at sea and in the air to be conducted with greater prospects of future success. Strategically, his idea was to drive rapidly across the Luxemburg-Belgian-Dutch area in two offensive wedges, engage the enemy, and defeat him. The armoured formations would have the role of preventing a congealing of the fronts. The ultimate aim, however, was victory over the French, making full use of the German air force, which would eliminate the enemy's air forces and make operations as difficult as possible for the enemy command. And all this 'as strongly and as early as possible', as demanded by OKW 'Directive No. 6 for the Conduct of the War',[4] dated 9 October, which already summed up the maxims of Hitler's memorandum. This therefore was now a written instruction to the Army High Command to start planning an attack on the northern wing of the deployment front. The objective was 'to defeat as much as possible of the French army and of the forces of the Allies fighting on their side, and at the same time to win as much territory as possible in Holland, Belgium, and northern France, to serve as a base for the successful prosecution of the air and sea war against England and as a wide protective area for the economically vital Ruhr'. The timing of the attack was to depend on the operational readiness of the mobile formations and on the weather.

2. ASSESSMENT OF THE WESTERN OPPONENT BY THE GERMAN ARMY COMMAND

Hitler's low opinion of the French enemy was only partly shared by the German generals. Their way of thinking was largely moulded by the First World War, and they still had 'great respect'[5] for the military capabilities of the neighbour nation. Important circles within the Army High Command were therefore inclined to advise against German initiatives to continue the war. A German offensive would place the enemy in the favourable position of having to defend himself, and this would enhance his fighting spirit. Behind this positive assessment of the French was no doubt the intention to prevent, or at least to delay, the western offensive called for by Hitler. But this proved unsuccessful. Hitler subsequently described these assessments as an 'unparalleled disgrace' of the general staff.

The German army had thoroughly studied the French strategic and tactical principles. It was thought that the enemy would proceed very methodically, cautiously, and according to a definite pattern. In the German view, however, the enemy lacked the ability to react to changing situations by rapid decisions. As for the fighting-strength of the French forces, the German view was that the active German divisions were superior to the French, whereas the French were credited with superiority with regard to their artillery.

The British army in the field was assessed by the German military command as of 'very high quality'. Nor was the strength of the Royal Navy or the efficacy of the Royal Air Force underrated. True, the Germans also criticized the British system

---

[4] Supreme commander of the armed forces OKW/WFA/L No. 172/39 g.Kdos. Chefs., 9 Oct. 1939: Directive No. 6 for the conduct of the war, ibid. 21-2; Trevor-Roper, *Directives*, 13-14.
[5] Liss, *Westfront*, 24.

for undue inflexibility, while acknowledging the courage and tenacity of the British soldiers—to be subsequently confirmed in Norway. Moreover, there were vast reserves of personnel and material available to Britain in her empire.

The Belgian armed forces, on the other hand, were considered mediocre with the exception of the Ardennes chasseurs. The Belgians were expected, even if incapable of offensive operations, to offer vigorous resistance to a German attack.

The fighting performance of the Dutch army was assessed even lower. In view of the weakness of the Netherlands army, both in personnel and material, and because of its lack of war experience (it was also in the course of being reorganized), the Germans believed that only brief resistance need be expected from the Dutch, unless the Allies came to their help promptly.

Deployment and disposition of the Allies had been quite well identified. Useful indications were gleaned from French radio communications, which had successfully been deciphered to a large extent.[6] The great unknown quantity for a long time was the enemy's operational intentions. There was uncertainty, above all, over the question of whether the French would stop at the Meuse south of Namur.[7] An advance to the Dyle in the event of a German attack was, however, considered to be highly probable. That an attack would be launched against the left flank from the south and south-west was regarded as certain. However, this danger was not given excessive weight, so that the German plan of operations seemed secure also from the point of view of enemy reconnaissance.

Although in the judgement of the senior German commands the German forces were superior to all the enemies, these same quarters were well aware of the weakness which attached to the Wehrmacht—its lack of regular officers.[8] There was also a shortage of junior leaders for the newly activated divisions, whose fighting value therefore had to be judged as being correspondingly low. Confidence in the Luftwaffe and the armoured forces, on the other hand, was limitless, so long as conditions existed for their full deployment.

3. MILITARY OPPOSITION TO AN EXTENSION OF THE WAR

The hesitant attitude of the Allies at the beginning of the war had nurtured hopes in the Army High Command that the conflict in the west might somehow be settled by political means. On 17 September it issued a 'Directive for Reorganization of the Army for Defensive War in the West'.[9] Although this was intended to provide for rapid re-equipment of two-thirds of the army for mobile warfare, it generally laid emphasis on the creation of locally based command organizations in the west,

---

[6] Tippelskirch, 'Vorgeschichte Westfeldzug', i. 76; Liss, *Westfront*, 96; Irving, *Hitler's War*, 69. The French, for their part, had succeeded in doing the same. Cf. Bertrand, *Enigma*.

[7] Chef GenSt H.Gr.A/Ia No. 597/39 g.Kdos., 18 Dec. 1939: Proposals for the conduct of the offensive in the west, in *Dokumente zur Vorgeschichte*, 131 ff.

[8] Communication from Rundstedt to the army C.-in-C., 31 Oct. 1939, ibid. 119-20; cf. vol. i of the present work, III.II.2(*d*).

[9] ObdH/GenStdH/Org. Abt. (1. Staffel) No. 86/39, g.Kdos., 17 Sept. 1939, in *Dokumente zur Vorgeschichte*, 35 ff.; Müller, *Heer*, 471 ff.

on restructuring and new structures, and on intensive training. On 25 September the Army High Command was informed of Hitler's offensive intentions against the enemy in the west.[10]

The Army High Command at first reacted disapprovingly to the planned extension of the war and to the violation of Belgian, Dutch, and Luxemburg neutrality. But in accordance with orders it embarked on offensive planning and also revoked the recently decreed reorganization of the army. This was done against the basic convictions of several of the military leaders and caused some conflicts of conscience, especially to those who still had a part in the then lively activity of the intra-German opposition to Hitler.

It is against the background of these tensions that the Army High Command's plans for the western campaign have to be viewed. Their misgivings were further strengthened by warnings from the chief of the war economy staff, Major-General Thomas, in whose opinion Germany was in no position, either militarily or economically, to fight a prolonged war.[11] Towards the end of September, for instance, Brauchitsch expressed a rather critical view of the prospects of an offensive to Keitel, which led to considerable ill feeling between the Army High Command and the High Command of the Armed Forces. The commander-in-chief of the army was in agreement on this issue with the Oberquartiermeister I of his general staff (the deputy chief of the Army General Staff, operations), Major-General von Stülpnagel, who on 24 September set out his view in a memorandum[12] to the effect that no means for an attack on the French or even the Belgian fortification line were available for the next two years. Armoured and motorized formations had suffered too much in the Polish campaign to be employed again so soon. Supplies of weapons and ammunition, he argued, were also still inadequate.

The Army High Command would have preferred simply to react to a British–French attack on the Ruhr. Brauchitsch and Halder were hoping to persuade Hitler at least to postpone the German offensive so as to create the necessary conditions for a political arrangement with the enemy. Göring too seemed to take a sceptical view of the prospects of success if the blow was struck too soon. The commander-in-chief of the navy was alone in not voicing any misgivings.

Uncertainty continued throughout the first weeks of October. While the Army High Command had to concern itself, against its own convictions, with plans for an offensive, Hitler's 'peace speech' to the Reichstag on 6 October seemed to suggest that no decision had as yet been taken. But what he offered to the Western powers could scarcely be acceptable to them: conclusion of peace on the basis of their acceptance of German conquests to date. It seems hardly credible that Hitler seriously expected the Allies to accept his offer. He was probably only making allowance for the public's longing for peace, of which he could not be unaware, by shifting responsibility for the continuation of the war on to the shoulders of the Allies and thereby buttressing his lie concerning the conflict 'forced upon him'.[13] For

---

[10] Halder, *Diaries*, i. 90 (25 Sept. 1939).   [11] Ibid. i. 92 (29 Sept. 1939).
[12] Cf. *KTB OKW* i. 950.   [13] Messerschmidt, *Wehrmacht*, 248; Steinert, *Hitlers Krieg*, 108.

simultaneously he was discussing with the Army High Command his idea of a pre-emptive strike. 'Hitler's speech in the Reichstag was therefore just a case of lying to the German people,' Leeb noted in his diary on 9 October.[14] He too decisively rejected an offensive in the west and tried to persuade the commanders-in-chief of the other two army groups to resign their commands simultaneously. Just as unconvinced of the prospects of success as Rundstedt was the commander-in-chief of Army Group B, although this army group had not so far received any offensive instructions from the Army High Command. Bock was to inform the Army General Staff of his ideas on possible offensive operations. He had also been requested to consider a potential invasion of Holland and Belgium in case the political situation rendered this necessary.

The Army High Command could hardly avoid obeying the unambiguous order in OKW Directive No. 6 of 9 October 1939, instructing it to submit a plan of operations as quickly as possible. The alternative presumably would have been a *coup d'état*, but neither Brauchitsch nor Halder—although the latter had seriously considered this possibility and had even made some preparations—was the right figure for that. Even though the plans of resistance groups within the Army High Command were crystallizing about that time, Halder did not believe that he could count on the majority of senior commanders, let alone on the troops, to take part in actions against Hitler. Hence the commander-in-chief of the army and the chief of his general staff, demoralized and nervously exhausted, found themselves in the moral dilemma of having to apply their entire professional skill to a project which, on military as well as on moral grounds, they opposed. Their traditional concepts of orders and obedience helped them in this situation.[15] They salved their consciences by their intention of presenting the prospects of the enterprise soberly and of 'promoting . . . every possibility of making peace'.[16] Their scepticism was shared by many an army group or army commander-in-chief who, remembering the experience of the last war, expected an early bogging-down in the area of Belgium and northern France.

The first deployment directives from Army High Command were hardly designed to overcome the widespread military, political, and at times also moral disapproval of an early offensive in the west. The army group commands issued memorandums advising against the attack. Leeb implored the commander-in-chief of the army to urge Hitler to go for a political conclusion to the war.[17] Even before Hitler's decision concerning the date of the attack was made on 5 November 1939, the Army High Command, on an inspection tour of the front, got the commanders-in-chief to supply it with arguments about the weaknesses of the forces in personnel and material. Brauchitsch, still in Hitler's bad books for issuing his order of the day on the death of Colonel-General von Fritsch, drew up a memorandum the presentation of which on 5 November aroused Hitler's anger. In particular, the argument that the infantry had been lacking in offensive spirit in Poland[18] and that

---

[14] Leeb, *Tagebuchaufzeichnungen*, 53, 188, 199.   [15] Cf. ibid. 201.
[16] Halder, *Diaries*, i. 105 (14 Oct. 1939).
[17] Letter from Leeb to Brauchitsch of 31 Oct. 1939, in Leeb, *Tagebuchaufzeichnungen*, 472.
[18] Such at least was the impression of Col.-Gen. von Bock: Bock, 'Tagebuch-Notizen', i. 43-4 (22 Sept. 1939).

there had been serious instances of indiscipline enraged Hitler, who sensed the intention of Army High Command to make him abandon the western offensive. The army commander-in-chief was brushed off with the instruction to supply evidence of his assertions. His dismissal was a matter of touch and go.[19]

The Army High Command was unable to obtain the evidence that it sought. Neither Brauchitsch nor the chief of the general staff, Halder, who continued to be allied to the military opposition against the regime, was therefore able to prevent Hitler, on 5 November, from ordering the opening of the attack for 12 November. It was mainly the weather that saved the Army High Command from launching the attack they regarded as a nightmare. Attempts by various military figures to organize concerted opposition to the extension of the war planned by Hitler remained without appreciable results. One man who was not prepared to compromise was the chief of Abwehr-Zentralabteilung (Counter-Intelligence Central Department), Colonel Oster, who repeatedly betrayed the dates of attack to the Dutch military attaché, a friend of his.

Peace-feelers by individuals from civilian resistance groups proved unsatisfactory. Their attempts to receive firm assurances from British government circles in the event of a change in Germany produced only vague results. The significance of the German resistance was soon assessed soberly and realistically by the Allies. The expectations of men like Carl Goerdeler, Ludwig Beck, and the Kordt brothers that Britain might concede to a new German government some of the results of Hitler's policy of expansion and thereby strengthen its domestic standing were based on a mistaken assessment of both their own chances and of Allied interests.

Equally ineffective were oppositional stirrings among the German working class, partly controlled by remnants of Communist and Social Democrat groupings and nurtured by dissatisfaction over socially disadvantageous consequences of the war.

4. PREPARATIONS FOR AN OFFENSIVE IN THE WEST

(a) *The Plans of Attack*[20]

The military leadership's disinclination to mount an offensive in the west was clearly expressed in the comment which Army Group B had been invited to make by the High Command of the Armed Forces. It recommended that attack and violations of neutrality be left to the enemy.[21] The commander-in-chief of Army Group C opposed a German initiative even more resolutely.[22] The Army High Command meanwhile had prepared a plan of operations. On 15 October Halder presented it not to Hitler but, demonstratively, only to the chief of the Wehrmacht operations staff, Major-General Jodl.[23] He proposed to employ 75 divisions, attack north of Liège with the bulk of armoured and motorized formations, and, without avoiding

---

[19] Jacobsen, *Fall Gelb*, 47; *Heeresadjutant bei Hitler*, 67 (7 Nov. 1939).

[20] Jacobsen, *Fall Gelb*; Koeltz, *Destin*.

[21] Bock, 'Tagebuch-Notizen', ii. 2 (11 Oct. 1939); H.Gr.Kdo.B/Ia No. 24/39 g.Kdos., 12 Oct. 1939, BA-MA RH 19 II/32.   [22] Leeb, *Tagebuchaufzeichnungen*, 466 ff.

[23] Jodl, *Tagebuch 1939-40*, 277 (15 Oct. 1939); Müller, *Heer*, 483.

The Netherlands, engage the enemy in fighting at as many points as possible. The decisive order would have to be given seven days in advance, to enable the formations to move into their area of attack in good time. Although the chief of the Army General Staff did not expect the enemy to invade Belgium, Army Group B was nevertheless ordered to oppose the enemy, if necessary, on Dutch or Belgian territory.[24]

The Army High Command issued this first instruction for 'Case Yellow' on 19 October,[25] after Hitler had once more reiterated his determination to defeat the Western powers and only then to negotiate with them. The Army High Command order therefore complied with Hitler's ideas with regard to the objective of the campaign: annihilation of major portions of the enemy forces and extension of the basis for the war at sea and in the air. Army General Staff assumed that the Dutch forces would offer no more than delaying resistance to the German invasion. The bulk of the Dutch forces would not take up battle positions in front of the more strongly fortified Grebbe Line (between the IJssel and the lower Meuse), so as, if necessary, to be able to withdraw into 'Fortress Holland', the triangle formed by the cities of Rotterdam, Utrecht, and Amsterdam. It was therefore important for the German forces to cross the IJssel and burst through the Grebbe Line, to seize the big cities of Amsterdam and Rotterdam, and to pre-empt any establishment of the British in south Holland—i.e. to eliminate the Dutch armed forces and occupy the largest possible tracts of the country. This was to be the task of the short-lived Army Detachment N on the northern wing.

The Army High Command expected Army Group B to encounter greater difficulties in smashing the Belgian forces, who would likewise withdraw behind the more easily defended lines of the Albert Canal and subsequently the Dyle. The Ardennes region was not, it was thought, being strongly held, and the Ardennes chasseurs would withdraw to the line of the Meuse: Givet-Namur-Liège. The main effort of the Belgian deployment was assumed to be north of Liège because it might there be possible, on the Albert Canal–Meuse line, to halt the Germans until the Western powers came to Belgium's aid. If the worst came to the worst the Belgian army would also be able to withdraw into the *réduit national* north of the Ghent-Termonde-Antwerp triangle, or else all the way to the French frontier. The Army High Command did not expect intervention by the British and French until after the piercing of the Belgian frontier defences. It hoped that numerous troops would be eliminated by these operations and that, in a second phase, the powerful northern wing would push through to the Belgian coast. The point of main effort on the German side, therefore, was also with Army Group B—two of whose armies were to engage and tie down the enemy, with a third army on the left wing of the army group front encircling him—while Army Group A, with two armies, had the task of crossing the Meuse south of Namur and covering the entire operation against the south. Army Group C (two armies) was merely to hold its positions and feign offensive intentions.

[24] OKH/GenStdH/Op.Abt. No. 44414/39 g.Kdos., 15 Oct. 1939, BA-MA RH 19 II/20.
[25] ObdH/GenStdH/Op.Abt. No. 44440/39 g.Kdos., 19 Oct. 1939: Deployment directive 'Yellow', in *Dokumente zur Vorgeschichte*, 41 ff.

This deployment directive was not just a reissue of the Schlieffen Plan, as was instantly claimed by critics. Schlieffen's intention in his day had been a rapid annihilation of the French enemy, whereas Hitler had in mind the limited aim of eliminating major portions of the enemy forces and gaining possession of the Belgian-French coast in order to fight Britain to her knees. How this was to be achieved was, for the moment, unclear. In contrast to the well-thought-out Schlieffen Plan, the Army High Command had converted Hitler's vague ideas into a provisional plan of operations, a plan which was little more than the 'expression of an imposed, ill-thought-out improvisation'.[26] Unlike the concentration of the German main effort on the right wing, as under the Schlieffen Plan, the intention in 1939 was a westward attack by a merely reinforced northern wing, while the southern wing was to cover this operation. A major strategic concept of how, following a breakthrough to the coast, the war was to be decided in Germany's favour did not at that time exist.

The Army High Command's plan therefore became the subject of lively discussion in the senior staffs and quickly ran into criticism. Colonel-General Keitel, in agreement with Hitler, disapproved of the move against the Grebbe Line, a move he did not consider very promising, as well as of the concentration of the main effort on Sixth Army and the north-westerly direction of the thrust of Fourth Army, which, in his opinion, must advance further to the west after crossing the Meuse.[27] Altogether he thought the envisaged employment of forces too weak. On 22 October there was a first conference between Army High Command and the High Command of the Armed Forces, at which the idea was once more aired of dispensing with the occupation of Holland. Keitel for the first time presented Hitler's ideas of *coup de main* strikes against Belgian bridges and fortifications.

Hitler at that time intended to order the attack for 12 November. By then the armoured and motorized formations were to be ready for action again. First, however, he wanted to consult with some military leaders. At noon on 25 October he had Brauchitsch and Halder report to him, and in the afternoon he received Bock, Reichenau (Sixth Army), and Kluge (Fourth Army) together with the Army High Command, for discussions. This circle also advised Hitler to postpone the date in view of the uncertain weather conditions. Hitler, however, believed that he should lose no time. As for the conduct of operations, he now posed the question whether the main attack had not better be launched south of Liège, in order, by a subsequent wheeling to the north-west, to cut off the enemy forces assembled in Belgium. He immediately demonstrated his idea on a map: the German forces west of Namur were to turn towards the coast.

The Army High Command was—such, at least, was Bock's impression[28] —'completely surprised' by this idea. After the war Halder claimed that he himself had suggested a kind of sickle movement as early as September 1939.[29] On 25 October, however, he did not comment on such a far-reaching move.

[26] Jacobsen, *Fall Gelb*, 32.   [27] Jodl, *Tagebuch 1939-40*, 279 (21 Oct. 1939).
[28] Bock, 'Tagebuch-Notizen', ii. 9 (25 Oct. 1939).
[29] Jacobsen, *Fall Gelb*, 273; Schall-Riaucour, *Aufstand*, 145 ff.

Hitler instructed the Army High Command 'to examine the new idea', which was by no means fully worked out. On the following day he remarked that he was not thinking about any major changes in the plans prepared. However, the main effort was to be south of Liège, with a simultaneous attack on the Belgian fortifications.[30] Halder recorded the impression at the time that the 'attempt' was to be made 'everywhere'.

Further talks between Hitler and the Army High Command took place during the next few days. Hitler decided in favour of a double main effort north and south of Liège. The principal objective of the attack must be the destruction of major portions of the enemy forces. The breakthrough to the coast would merely be the consequence. One armoured group was to be employed at each of the points of main effort, whereas employment of armoured formations at Sixth Army was to wait until it seemed likely that a crossing of the Meuse would succeed. The main uncertain factor was the possible reaction of the Western powers, on whose intentions reconnaissance had so far been unable to provide sufficient information. The Army High Command still had to take account of the possibility that the enemy would not move into Belgium, so that a German main thrust south of the Meuse–Sambre line would strike straight into the enemy's deployment.[31]

Army High Command made allowance for this estimate of the situation by a second deployment instruction, dated 29 October.[32] This stated that the German offensive depended on the 'attitude of the Western powers'. The objective of the enterprise must be to defeat 'major parts of the French army and its allies on northern French and Belgian soil' and to improve conditions for a continuation of the war by a thrust to the Channel coast. An occupation of Holland would be dispensed with. The main effort would again lie with Army Group B, which would have to pierce the Belgian belt of fortifications in order to advance, on both sides of Liège, in two offensive wedges on a broad front against Antwerp, Brussels, and Charleroi. Any subsequent wheeling to the north-west or south-west would depend on the situation at the time, which would also govern the employment of massed mobile troops and the bringing up of the reserves which were still echeloned in depth. Army Group A still had the task of using two armies to cover the attack against the south. With its right wing Rundstedt's army group was at the same time to cross the Meuse quickly and advance on Laon. The final assembly of the troops should be possible by 11 November. Luftwaffe reconnaissance was to establish the enemy's concentration in good time.

This did not mean that the Army High Command had given up its opposition to a western offensive yet. But this had no effect on the decisions of Hitler, who believed that attack alone was as an effective protection of the Ruhr. On 5 November

---

[30] Jodl, *Tagebuch 1939–40*, 281 (26 Oct. 1939); Halder, *Diaries*, i. 38–9 (26 Oct. 1939).

[31] Only the observation of Allied troop movements in response to identified German offensive intentions—particularly in Jan. 1940—revealed the plans of the Western powers. Cf. the study by Gen. (Inf.) (retd.) Edgar Röhricht, 'Aufmarsch an der Westfront', BA-MA N 204/2.

[32] ObdH/GenStdH/Op.Abt. No. 44440/39 g.Kdos. II. Ang., 29 Oct. 1939: Deployment directive 'Yellow', in *Dokumente zur Vorgeschichte*, 46 ff.

he gave the first order for the attack. But there was a string of postponements and new dates—nearly thirty in all until May 1940. These were due not to objections by the Army High Command but to Hitler's misgivings about weather conditions and the transport situation. In addition, presumably Hitler was not yet absolutely certain of his own judgement. None the less, right into January he adhered to his intention of ordering the attack at short notice. But his hesitation and the continual postponements provided time to rethink the order of assembly once again.

In fact the Army High Command's directives were far from convincing—either to the formation commanders or to Hitler. Hitler, simultaneously with but independently of the chief of staff of Army Group A, Lieutenant-General von Manstein, was considering moving a mobile formation via Arlon towards Sedan, since motorized forces might encounter greater difficulties in the unfavourable Belgian terrain. The army commander-in-chief only reluctantly accepted this suggestion. On 11 November the Army High Command gave orders for the establishment of a third mobile group, concentrated in General Guderian's XIX Army Corps within Army Group A,[33] and thereby, though unwillingly, met Hitler's wishes. To Hitler the creation of an additional point of main effort on the southern wing of the offensive front was merely a first step in his plans. He doubted that it would be possible to gain control of the Belgian bridges over the Meuse and the Albert Canal undamaged, so that a massed attack by armoured forces would not pay off there. He calculated that the chances on the southern wing were better, even though he did not wish to stake everything on one card.

The delay caused by the weather, however, also provided an opportunity, quite apart from the location of the main effort, for rethinking the usefulness of involving Holland. The army intended to content itself with a tactically necessary passage through the Maastricht corner and to await the attitude of the Netherlands government before deciding whether to exercise the rights of an occupying power.

But the Luftwaffe raised objections to this plan. It feared that in the event of a German invasion of Belgium the British might transfer air forces to Holland, which would present a direct threat to the Ruhr. At the end of October Hitler felt obliged to override these objections. At the beginning of November he merely authorized the extension of German strategic aerial reconnaissance to include Holland. Following the postponement of the first date of attack, however, the Luftwaffe's point was accepted by him, and on 15 November the High Command of the Armed Forces issued a so-called Holland Directive,[34] which attached considerable importance to the furthest possible 'forward move of the aircraft-warning organization and of anti-aircraft defence' into Holland.

The army was to prepare for the occupation of Dutch territory, initially as far as the Grebbe Line, and, jointly with the navy, plan the seizure of the West Frisian Islands. Army Group B received a relevant order from Army High Command for the occupation of the country with the exception of 'Fortress Holland'—a 'half-way

---

[33] OKH/GenStdH/Op.Abt. (Ia) No. 44485/39 g.Kdos., 11 Nov. 1939, ibid. 53 ff.
[34] Cf. order ObdH/GenStdH/Op.Abt.(II) No. 44493/39 g.Kdos., 15 Nov. 1939, to Army Gp. B HQ, ibid. 55–6.

house' which neither satisfied the Luftwaffe nor was much to the liking of Army Group B. In Bock's view he had been charged with a 'water pantomime'.

On 20 November the High Command of the Armed Forces issued 'Directive No. 8 for the Conduct of the War',[35] which summed up all operations plans according to the latest ideas. Contingency measures were to be taken in case a rapid switch of the main effort from Army Group B to Army Group A should prove necessary.

What was by no means settled was the crisis of confidence dividing the top generals from the supreme commander of the armed forces. Hitler seized the initiative and called a conference at the Reich chancellery for 23 November. With the commanders-in-chief of the three Wehrmacht branches, the commanders-in-chief of army groups and armies, the chiefs of the Luftflotten, the commanding generals, the chiefs of staff down to army corps, and their opposite numbers from the Luftwaffe and the navy, there were just under two hundred persons present. Hitler told them he had always considered settling accounts with the West because it had always opposed a consolidation of the Reich. Now the favourable situation had arisen, for the first time for a long period, when Germany would have to fight on one front only. This circumstance had to be exploited, especially as the Soviet Union could be regarded as a reliable partner only for a limited period of time. For Hitler there was but one way of bringing the war to a conclusion and of establishing German hegemony in Europe: by annihilating the enemy while he was still militarily inferior to the German forces. To achieve this objective he was prepared to extend the war to northern Europe, to the Balkans, and even to the Middle East. What had been achieved to date 'I am ready to stake. I have to choose between victory and destruction.'[26] He rejected all references to weaknesses in the structure of the Wehrmacht. Britain could be defeated once Germany possessed better operational bases for her U-boats and mines. Violation of Belgian and Dutch neutrality was of no consequence by comparison.

Addressing a smaller circle of commanding officers, Hitler subsequently dealt with some questions of the planned offensive in the west. The objective, he explained, was the defeat of Britain by the German air force and navy, once Germany possessed suitable operational bases. He was firmly counting on the British and French advancing into Belgium. It was important for the German armoured formations to gain territory quickly and to hinder the enemy from an orderly deployment.

The meeting of 23 November did not, however, clear up the strained relations between Hitler and the Army High Command. On that same evening Brauchitsch and Halder had to listen once again to grave accusations. However, the army commander-in-chief's letter of resignation was not accepted. Tensions between Hitler and the army generals were to continue until the military successes of the following spring eclipsed the conflicts.

[35] Supreme commander of the armed forces/OKW/WFA No. 213/39 g.Kdos. Chefs. Abt. L (I), ibid. 23-4.
[36] Minute of the address on 23 Nov. 1939 in the naval staff documents, *Lagevorträge*, 49-55; Halder, *Diaries*, i. 133 (25 Nov. 1939): 'drafts on operations in all corners of the world'.

While the deliberations of Hitler and the Army High Command about shortening the period between the issuing of the order and the opening of the attack, as well as about the most favourable location of the main effort, were continuing, Lieutenant-General von Manstein had intensively studied the deployment directive of the Army High Command. In his opinion it would not guarantee the intended annihilation of the enemy. Towards the end of October Army Group A therefore submitted to Army High Command a memorandum,[37] which was followed by others dealing with the same subject and was designed to convince Army High Command of the advantages of Manstein's plan of operations. His aim was to bring the war to a decisive conclusion on land; to this end the main effort of the overall operation should be shifted to the southern wing of the front. The objective was a breakthrough to the Somme. Manstein envisaged a campaign in two stages: first, the enemy in Belgium and northern France was to be cut off from the south and eliminated, which would mean, at the same time, gaining possession of the Channel coast all the way to the Somme estuary. In the second phase a wheeling to the south would confront the French counter-attack and attempt an encirclement from the west.

As the point of main effort of an attack on the southern wing Manstein envisaged the area south of the Namur–Arras–Boulogne line, and thereby, without realizing it, took up the operations plan suggested by Hitler. For the moment he envisaged a second concentration of effort only if the demand was maintained that the right wing of Army Group A had to cross the Meuse. The attack was to be mounted as vigorously as possible both north and south of the Liège fortress. Manstein, however, expected the decisive action to fall on the southern wing. As for the forces required, he envisaged three armies: Second Army headquarters in the north (12 infantry divisions) pushing across the Meuse, between Dinant and Fumay, in the direction of the lower Somme; at the centre Twelfth Army headquarters with altogether 12 divisions (combined armoured, motorized, and infantry) in the direction of the Aisne to provide offensive flank cover; and in the south Sixteenth Army headquarters with 12 infantry divisions to provide cover for the offensive front. This, compared with the subsequent plan of campaign, envisaged something more like a sickle move,[38] i.e. the encirclement of the enemy by the army on the right wing of Army Group A. However, Manstein saw the main task of his army group as the containment of the French counter-attack from the south-west. He therefore thought it advantageous, after the first breakthrough, roughly at the latitude of Namur, to have the forces there brought together under a new army headquarters of Army Group B, which would be charged with the continuation of the operation in the direction of the coast or the lower Somme. He further envisaged a strong northern wing for Army Group B, which would have to force a breakthrough with armoured forces north of the Meuse and the Sambre. These forces might then advance across the lower Somme as soon as the counter-attack was broken in the area between Aisne and Oise.

---

[37] Communication by OB H.Gr. A to ObdH, 31 Oct. 1939, in *Dokumente zur Vorgeschichte*, 119. Cf. now also Deighton, *Blitzkrieg*, 207 ff.; Uhle-Wettler, *Höhe- und Wendepunkte*, 280 ff.
[38] Jacobsen, *Fall Gelb*, 75.

Manstein, who had consulted with Guderian about a possible armoured attack through the Ardennes towards Sedan, had at first no success with Army High Command. The army commander-in-chief initially opposed any change in the deployment plans, especially as the postponements of the date of attack at short notice left no time for any changes. He refused to allow Army Group A an additional army headquarters and merely promised a few mobile formations. Halder for his part did not believe either in a French counter-attack into the area between Aisne and Oise. The assignment of a further mobile formation to Army Group A on 11 November was therefore due only to Hitler's suggestion, and was hardly the result of Manstein's representations. The Army High Command, which was still trying to persuade Hitler to abandon the idea of an offensive in the west, was not even prepared to discuss Manstein's proposals. The military opposition's plans for a political overthrow were taking on the form of personal conflicts between the generals. Not until early December was Army High Command prepared to comment:[39] Halder wished to reserve for himself the creation of a point of main effort at a later time, once the operation had got going. This would not rule out consideration of the proposals submitted by Army Group A. Manstein reacted to this vague assurance with a new memorandum. Halder instructed his operations department to examine the various plans of attack in a paper exercise. Manstein's draft of an operations plan, available complete on 18 December, was therefore at least seriously discussed in the Army High Command in the second half of December. The High Command of the Armed Forces had earlier made it known that Hitler reserved the choice of the point of main effort to himself.

The new laying down of the date of attack for 17 January 1940 thwarted all hope of a change in the allocation of forces. Nevertheless, Manstein, supported by the commander-in-chief and staff of Army Group A, was not prepared to yield, even though the Army High Command had refused to submit his proposal to Hitler. At the end of January he was appointed general commanding XXXVIII Army Corps in Stettin (Szczecin). Before he assumed his new post he lived to see Halder, at a paper exercise of his army group, moving closer to his ideas and accepting the concentration of mobile troops in Army Group A—XIX Army Corps (General Guderian) and XIV Army Corps (General von Wietersheim) being ranged alongside each other.[40]

Brauchitsch and Halder had meanwhile given up hope of getting Hitler to abandon the attack in the west. This made them more open again to other strategic considerations. Time was working for Manstein's operational concept, the basic idea of which had been known since the second half of December to the Wehrmacht operations staff and also to Hitler. What caused the offensive to be postponed until the spring was not so much the forced landing of a German aircraft at Mechelen on 10 January with important documents on board, some of which fell into Belgian hands, but rather the mobilization measures in Holland and Belgium and a further

[39] Communication by Chef GenStdH No. 660/39 g.Kdos., 5 Dec. 1939, to Manstein, in *Dokumente zur Vorgeschichte*, 57. [40] Halder, *Diaries*, i. 213 ff. (7 Feb. 1940).

deterioration of weather conditions. Hitler at the same time voiced his intention of giving the enterprise a new basis and, more particularly, ensuring secrecy and surprise.

During the ensuing period the deployment of the forces was changed to enable them to be assembled for attack at short notice, and this contributed to the subsequent success of the German campaign in the west. Hitler also issued an order tightening up instructions on secrecy: no authority was to be informed of secret matters in future beyond the extent, and before the time, that it needed to know them. No decision was taken for the time being on the still controversial issue of the location of the main effort—each army group headquarters believed that the bulk of the enemy's forces must be expected at its own front. Army Group B warned against any shifting of the point of main effort. Hitler and the Army High Command, on the other hand, were now inclined to do just that, since, following the Mechelen incident, they thought the chances of taking the enemy by surprise would be better for Army Group A. To prevent the preparations for the main effort on the southern wing from being discovered too soon, the assignment of a further army headquarters and of additional formations to Rundstedt's army group was not to be effected until after the start of the operation. Army Group B meanwhile, on Hitler's orders, was to prepare for the occupation of Holland. All instructions for 'Case Yellow' and for 'Case Immediate' (Sofortfall)—assembly within twenty-four hours in the event of the enemy moving into the neutral countries—were summed up by Army High Command in a third deployment directive dated 30 January.[41] As the objective of the campaign the Army High Command now also envisaged the annihilation of the French and British forces.

The creation of a point of main effort for the German attack, and hence a possible strategic (as against a merely tactical) surprise of the enemy, now became the subject of detailed examination in connection with the above-mentioned paper exercise staged by Army Group A during the first half of February. Halder, present at the exercise, allowed himself to be persuaded of the usefulness of an increased employment of mobile forces. What remained controversial was the timing of the continuation of the attack following the crossing of the Meuse. Halder was unwilling to see the southern flank of the army group stretched excessively, and favoured a pause until the infantry divisions had closed up. He did not regard continuation of the attacks possible before Day 10, in contrast to the commanders of the armoured formations, Guderian and Wietersheim, who wanted the advantages of their equipment—speed and mobility—used to the full.

Also under renewed scrutiny was the conduct of operations by Army Group B. The point at issue was whether Fourth Army should be employed to the north or to the south of Namur. Following a paper exercise in mid-February, the commander-in-chief of that army declared himself in favour of the northern area of attack, whereas Halder preferred its employment solely south of Namur to prevent a gap from opening between the two army groups.

---

[41] ObdH/GenStdH/Op.Abt. (Ia) No. 074/40 g.Kdos. Chefs., 30 Jan. 1940: new version of deployment directive 'Yellow', in *Dokumente zur Vorgeschichte* 59 ff.

Thus, the crucial question remained unresolved. It was owing to an initiative by Lieutenant-Colonel Schmundt, Hitler's Chief ADC, that the supreme commander of the armed forces—who was not greatly satisfied with Army High Command's planning to date ('Thoughts of a Student of War')[42]—was once more reminded of Manstein's ideas. Schmundt arranged a conference with Hitler. Before that, on 13 February, Hitler had again discussed the question of the main effort with Jodl and had favoured employment of the bulk of motorized forces in the direction of Sedan,[43] where the enemy would certainly not expect the main German thrust. Jodl informed Army High Command and invited it to submit appropriate proposals.

On 17 February Hitler consulted with Manstein. The general had an opportunity to outline his plan, and Hitler was impressed. A day later, when he received the Army High Command officers for another conference, the latter, working on Hitler's ideas as communicated by Jodl and utilizing the lessons of the paper exercises, had already arrived at new conclusions: Fourth Army was to be placed under Army Group A and very powerful armoured forces were to be concentrated in front of Twelfth Army and Sixteenth Army. Hitler concurred. He attached importance to Sixteenth Army, on the southern flank, being prepared to repel a French attack from the hinterland of the Maginot Line, and to Twelfth Army, adjoining to the north, being used for the 'offensive extension of the defensive front'. A further army was soon to be brought forward on the army group's sector. For German divisions on the western front on A (Attack) Day see Table VI.II.1.

Thus the long-disputed decision was made. By 24 February the Army High Command worked out the new deployment instruction according to the 'sickle-cut plan', which must be viewed as a fortunate 'convergence of Manstein's inspired concept and Hitler's ideas',[44] further developed by Army High Command, which proposed a different distribution of forces and dispensed with excessive flank cover. The High Command realized the risk involved in this plan, and the army groups for their part voiced serious misgivings. Army Group A, for instance, did not want to send the armoured formations into action until the infantry divisions had succeeded in forcing a breakthrough on the Meuse.[45]

One of the objectives of the campaign, as seen by Army High Command, was the early occupation of Holland in order to eliminate the country as a potential base for Britain. The thrust across the Belgian-Luxemburg frontier, however, was designed chiefly to defeat the greatest possible number of enemy forces and thereby to prepare for the annihilation of them all. The German main effort was south of the Meuse–Sambre line. While the formations of Army Group B, attacking north of this line, had the task of piercing the Belgian frontier fortifications and then of advancing further west in order to engage major portions of the French and British armies, Army Group A, employed south of the Liège–Charleroi line, was to force a crossing of the Meuse and then penetrate to the lower Somme.

---

[42] Cf. *Heeresadjutant bei Hitler*, 75 (19 Feb. 1940). [43] Jodl, 'Tagebuch 1940', 402 (13 Feb. 1940). [44] Jacobsen, *Fall Gelb*, 153; the revised version of the deployment directive 'Yellow', ObdH/GenStdH/Op.Abt. (Ia) No. 130/40 g.Kdos., 24 Feb. 1940, is reproduced in *Dokumente zur Vorgeschichte*, 64 ff. [45] KTB No. 2 H.Gr. A (draft), 22 Feb. 1940, BA-MA RH 19 I/37.

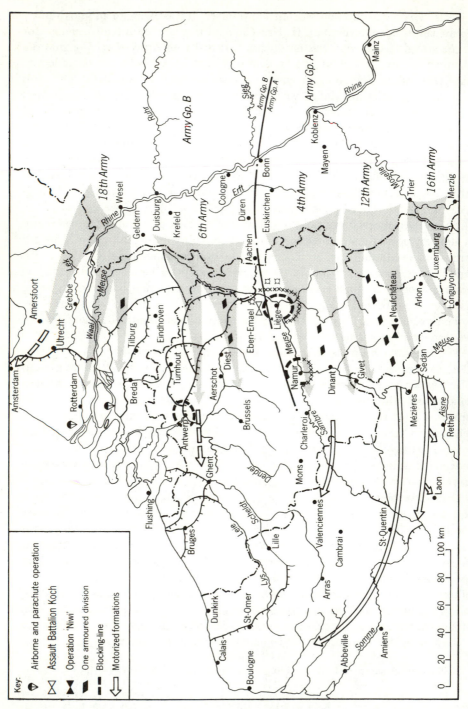

MAP VI.II.1. The 'Sickle-Cut Plan' According to the OKH Directive of 24 February 1940

Key:

- Airborne and parachute operation
- Assault Battalion Koch
- Operation 'Niwi'
- One armoured division
- Blocking-line
- Motorized formations

TABLE VI.II.1. *German Divisions on the Western Front on A (Attack) Day*

Grouping	No.	
Army Gp. B (Col.-Gen. von Bock)		
Eighteenth Army (Gen. von Küchler)	10⅓	(1 armd. div.)
Sixth Army (Col.-Gen. von Reichenau)	19	(2 armd. div.)
TOTAL	**29⅓**	
Army Gp. A (Col.-Gen. von Rundstedt)		
Fourth Army (Col.-Gen. von Kluge)	13	(2 armd. div.)
Twelfth Army (Col.-Gen. List)	10	
Armoured Group von Kleist	8⅓	(5 armd. div.)
Sixteenth Army (Gen. Busch)	13	
TOTAL	**44⅓**	
Army Gp. C (Col.-Gen. Ritter von Leeb)		
First Army (Col.-Gen. von Witzleben)	13	
Seventh Army (Gen. Dollmann)	4	
TOTAL	**17**	
Available to Army High Command (incl. 7th Air Div.)	28	(3 brigades)
Total	**118⅔**	(3 brigades)
Reserves employed by the end of June	**23**	
TOTAL NUMBER OF DIVISIONS PARTICIPATING IN THE CAMPAIGN IN THE WEST	**141⅔**	(3 brigades)

Source: Situation-maps and data in Tessin, *Verbände und Truppen*.

More particularly, Army Group B was instructed to occupy Holland in the shortest possible time in order to prevent any joint action of Dutch forces with those of the Belgians, French, and British. To this end Eighteenth Army was to advance swiftly, to prevent the enemy gaining a foothold on the Dutch coast and, by forcing a breakthrough on both sides of the Waal, disrupt the rearward communications of the Dutch army and prevent its reinforcement by the British and French. The Scheldt estuary was to be blocked with a front against Antwerp. Another important task was the rapid occupation of the West Frisian Islands, in which the Luftwaffe was interested.

Further to the south, Sixth Army had to cross the Meuse between Venlo and Aachen, pierce the Belgian frontier fortifications, and advance to the west. The encirclements of Liège and Antwerp were to be ordered separately.

Army Group A was ordered, while continually covering its left flank, to cross the Meuse and, with the strongest possible forces, to push through, behind the French fortification zone, in the direction of the Somme estuary. Second Army command was additionally available for this operation. Mobile forces, concentrated in the Kleist armoured group ready in deep echelon ahead of the Army group front, were to clear the road. Fourth Army was committed in the Liège–Houffalize area; it was to cut Liège off from the south and, covering itself against Namur, to cross the Meuse between Yvoir and Fumay in order to continue its westward advance. Twelfth Army, adjoining in the south, was rapidly to follow the motorized forces between Fumay and Sedan, across the Meuse, and then attack in a westerly direction parallel to Fourth Army. Sixteenth Army was charged with covering the overall attack against the south, and was to maintain contact with the German fortifications in the west. Later it would be placed under Army Group C.

In the south of the front there was to be a kind of position warfare. It had been the task of Army Group C from the outset to tie down the largest possible number of enemy forces in front of its sector. A multitude of diversions helped to serve this aim. At the beginning of 1940 Army High Command instructed Leeb's army group to give thought to a penetration of the Maginot Line once the bulk of French and British troops had been defeated or pinned down in the north. The army group thereupon submitted several plans under the code-name 'Green'. During the second half of March, after Mussolini had declared his readiness in principle to enter the war, though as yet without a fixed date, a new operation code-named 'Brown' was examined, envisaging the slotting of Italian forces into the offensive front on the Upper Rhine. Army Group C worked out a number of detailed plans: 'Bear' (breakthrough between Breisach and the Swiss frontier in the direction of both sides of Belfort), 'Lynx' (thrust through the Vosges from the Breisach–Strasburg area), 'Panther' (attack in the area north of Strasburg in the direction of Sarrebourg–Blamont), and 'Tiger' (breakthrough between Saint-Avold and the Saar), all of which became largely irrelevant because Mussolini and the Italian army command were not very keen on having their troops employed on the Upper Rhine. The joint general staff talks did not materialize. In consequence, the preparations of Army Group C were soon restricted to two operations without Italian participation—'Tiger' and 'Bear'—which were begun in mid-June.

Luftwaffe operations were conducted mostly in line with the principles set out in a 'Plan Study 1939' in February of that year.[46] Two Air Fleets with about a third of available German forces had to ensure the safety of the western Reich territory: Air Fleet 2 'North' and Air Fleet 3 'West'. In terms of strength, at least numerically, these were at first inferior to the enemy. Air Fleet 3 was soon authorized to counterattack in the event of a French thrust, whereas Air Fleet 2 was meanwhile merely to prepare for operations against Britain while awaiting a specific order from the supreme command. Reflections on aerial warfare against Britain had been continuing since 1938.

Following the Western powers' declarations of war, therefore, the German air force had to hold back for political as well as military reasons. It was not at first permitted to cross the frontiers. On no account was an air war in the west to be provoked. This attitude was the easier for Germany as the British for their part confined themselves mainly to dropping leaflets over Reich territory—although of

---

[46] Speidel, 'Westfeldzug', and II.1.2 above.

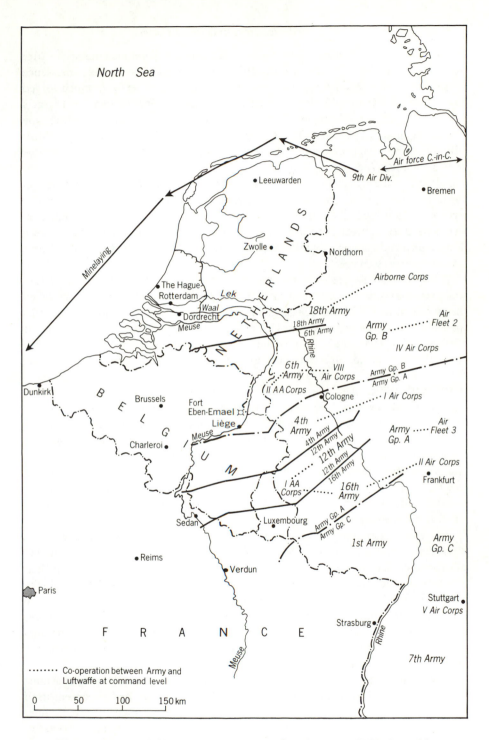

North Sea

Leeuwarden

Air force C.-in-C.

9th Air Div.

Bremen

Minelaying

Zwolle

Nordhorn

NETHERLANDS

Airborne Corps

The Hague
Rotterdam

Lek

18th Army

Air
Fleet 2

Waal

Dordrecht

18th Army

Army
Gp. B

Meuse

6th Army

IV Air Corps

Rhine

Dunkirk

Brussels

6th
Army

VIII
Air Corps

Army Gp. B

Army Gp. A

BELGIUM

Fort
Eben-Emael

II AA Corps

Cologne

I Air Corps

Liège

4th
Army

Army
Gp. A

Air
Fleet 3

Meuse

4th Army

Charleroi

12th Army

12th Army

II Air Corps

12th Army

Frankfurt

Sedan

I AA
Corps

16th Army

16th
Army

Luxembourg

Army Gp. A

Army Gp. C

Reims

1st Army

Army
Gp. C

Verdun

Paris

Stuttgart

V Air Corps

Strasburg

FRANCE

Rhine

Meuse

7th Army

········ Co-operation between Army and
Luftwaffe at command level

0   50   100   150 km

MAP VI.II.2. Army and Air Force Deployment for 'Operation Yellow', 10 May 1940

course in doing so they gained experience for subsequent operational missions. After the second week of the war the Luftwaffe was authorized to fly reconnaissance missions over enemy territory, and soon afterwards to drop leaflets, which served also as a training in night flying. Gradually operations against British naval targets were taken up. Neither Germany nor the Western powers were anxious at that time to unleash an air war of the kind the French had originally promised their Polish allies—both because they realized the inadequacy of their own forces at the time and for political and tactical reasons.

Even before the conclusion of the Polish campaign the Air Force High Command began to transfer formations no longer needed in the east to Germany's western territory. These forces, admittedly, were not immediately usable. Although they were shared out between Air Fleet 2 and Air Fleet 3, they still needed replenishing in personnel and material. By mid-October the deployment of the German air force was more or less complete.

With a certain delay, as compared with the planning of the army, consideration was given to the offensive employment of the Luftwaffe in what the code-name called the 'defensive battle' (*Abwehrschlacht*). Time and again during the next few months these plans had to be adapted to the changing plans of campaign. The requirements of the different services had to be harmonized, great importance being attached to the Luftwaffe demands for advanced bases in north-western Europe and for awaiting favourable weather conditions.

The method successfully applied in Poland was valid also in the west: following a surprise strike against the enemy's ground organization on the day of attack, the Luftwaffe, above all, was to support the operations of the land forces by attacking enemy reinforcements at an early phase of their being brought up and by helping the ground troops to overcome lines of fortifications and river-courses. Moreover, two anti-aircraft corps, made available by the Luftwaffe to the two army groups leading the attack, served as 'assault artillery' and for anti-tank defence. The enemy was expected to use his air forces in much the same way. For the Luftwaffe command structure in the west on 10 May 1940 see Table VI.II.2.

Even after the assembly of all its forces, the Luftwaffe was not interested in an intensive war in the air. It was preparing for the decisive offensive, to be mounted in close co-operation with the army, and it wanted to conserve its strength for that. The tactics to be used were further refined in joint paper exercises. Meanwhile the Luftwaffe flew intensive short-range and long-range reconnaissance missions, also over the neutral countries, utilizing its findings in order to complete its target-maps (airfields, industrial establishments, road bottlenecks, railway lines). Attacks on non-military and non-war-industry targets, as well as on major cities, were permitted only on specific orders.

Only the army could bring about the military decision in the west, at least against France and the British Expeditionary Force (BEF). The navy had to content itself with a more modest role, and with regard to nearly all its rearmament programmes it had to take second place to the other services. Its task, as formulated in 'Directive No. 6 for the Conduct of the War' of 9 October 1939, was to consist of the 'siege

TABLE VI.II.2. *Command Structure of the German Air Force in the West, 10 May 1940*

Air Fleet 2 (north): Gen. (Air Force) Kesselring
   IV Air Corps
   VIII Air Corps
   II AA Corps
   General (spec. employment):
      7th Air Division
      22nd Airborne Division
   Fighter Commander 2
   Long-Range Reconnaissance Gp. 122

Air Fleet 3 (west): Gen. (Air Force) Sperrle
   I Air Corps
   II Air Corps
   V Air Corps
   I AA Corps
   Fighter Commander 3
   Long-Range Reconnaissance Gp. 123

of Britain' and the covering of army operations in the west from the sea. Generally it was to support the army and the air force in their operations. This soon included the task of interfering with Allied naval transports of troops and material in the Channel, predominantly by the laying of mines and by U-boat attacks. Hitler progressively lifted the restrictions which had originally been imposed on naval warfare. For a more effective war at sea the navy, in addition to submarines still to be built, needed operational bases on the French Atlantic coast or in Norway. Although a swift capture of the Dutch and Belgian ports would have been of some tactical significance, plans to this effect had to be abandoned in favour of the Scandinavian operation.[47] And after the losses of vessels in the north the navy was not for the time being capable of major operations in the west. The French campaign essentially took place without naval participation. After June 1940 U-boats were increasingly used in the war against British merchantmen.[48] As Dutch, Belgian, and French ports fell into German hands, the navy embarked on a transfer of light naval units as well as of coastal artillery to the west. From the second week of May onward motor torpedo-boats (*S-Boote*) operated in the Channel, at times successfully. However, when asked by the High Command of the Armed Forces to mount a massive operation against the transports used towards the end of the month for the evacuation of Dunkirk—an operation whose chances of success the navy had underrated—the naval operational command was in no position to do so.[49] Moreover, it proved impossible to clear all mines from coastal approaches in sufficient time for part of the army and air force supplies to be brought up by sea.

---

[47] Cf. V.1 above.   [48] Jacobsen and Rohwer, 'Planungen und Operationen', 76–7.
[49] Naval warfare command war diary No. 1, pt. A, 28 May 1940, BA-MA RM 7/12.

(b) *Special Operations*

German planners examined at an early stage the possibility of improving the initial situation for the offensive by means of special operations. On 21 October Hitler suggested employing a special commando force in troop-carrying gliders against the much-feared Belgian fort of Eben-Emael south of Maastricht. He was anxious to gain swift possession of the vital bridges over the Meuse and the Albert Canal before the Dutch and the Belgians could carry out their expected destruction. Only the swift pouring of a whole German army through this bottleneck would guarantee a rapid push to the west, preventing the Allies from full deployment and, at the least, forestalling their link-up with the Dutch troops. Hitler was not put out by the initial scepticism of the Army General Staff. He was in any case considering employing the newly formed airborne force for the first time in the west. On 27 October Hitler summoned its commander, Lieutenant-General Student, to the Reich chancellery and informed him of his intention to have air-landed troops seize the bridges concerned as well as the fort and the Belgian *réduit national* in the Ghent area, where the Germans had had bad experiences in the First World War, and hold them until the ground forces had pushed through to them. Student expressed some doubts. Nevertheless, 7th Air Division embarked on appropriate preparations in the greatest secrecy. As the plans were being worked out, doubts of success with an air landing in the *réduit* grew. Elimination of the Eben-Emael fort in the gateway to Belgium, on the other hand, was considered easier, and Hitler insisted on it being captured by a *coup*. From the beginning of November onwards a special commando of 7th Air Division, the 'Koch Assault Detachment', was to prepare for the execution of this task as well as for the seizure of several bridges across the Albert Canal. Whether the problem of the bridges could satisfactorily be solved in this manner remained a controversial issue in the German staffs. Still in November a special formation of the Counter-Intelligence Station Breslau, the 'Special Operations Battalion 100', was instructed to prepare for the capture of the bridges in the Dutch town of Maastricht. A decision on the *réduit* was put off, and other potential operations were examined for the airborne force: in the north of Holland, in Belgium between Namur and Dinant, or in France near Sedan. In mid-January a provisional decision was made about 'Fortress Holland'.

Simultaneously a number of lesser actions were planned. Thus, advance parties of the 3rd Battalion, 'Großdeutschland' Infantry Regiment, were to be set down by Fieseler Storch aircraft in the forefield of Army Group A south-west of Bastogne, near Nives and Witry (Operation 'NiWi') to prevent demolitions and facilitate the German advance.[50] Commandos of 34th Infantry Division were to be flown to vital crossroads near the French–Luxemburg frontier (Operation 'Stork'), and parts of the 'Construction Training Battalion for Special Operations 800' (Brandenburger) were to seize a number of Dutch bridges and also go into action in Luxemburg. Principal attention, however, was focused on three major special operations, some

---

[50] *Geschichte des Panzerkorps Großdeutschland*, i. 75–108; Buchheit, *Geheimdienst*, 314 ff.; Brockdorff, *Geheimkommandos*, 105 ff.

of them meticulously planned up to 10 May: the air landing of a 'Group North' under Major-General Count von Sponeck of members of 7th Air Division and especially of 22nd Airborne Division at three airfields in the area of The Hague, to eliminate the military command and the government and take the queen prisoner; this would compel The Netherlands to surrender. A 'Group South', provided mainly by the parachute force and commanded by Student, who was simultaneously in charge of the entire operation against 'Fortress Holland', would operate against bridges in and near Rotterdam. The Koch Assault Detachment, taken from 7th Air Division, was to be landed in four groups by troop-carrying gliders, here used in war for the first time, within the fortress area of Eben-Emael and at three bridges of the Albert Canal, while the bridges in Maastricht would be seized by a *coup* by the Counter-Intelligence Battalion for Special Operations 100. Disguise by Dutch gendarmerie uniforms was to facilitate their drive through enemy territory. Men of the Counter-Intelligence Battalion not needed for this operation, along with the reinforced 151st Infantry Regiment and an anti-aircraft detachment, had the task, within the formation of 4th Armoured Division, of pushing through as quickly as possible to the advance parties which had penetrated into enemy territory.

(c) *Propaganda*

Hand in hand with the planning of the campaign went an intensive and sophisticated propaganda drive. Although Army Group C as recently as September 1939 had warned against provoking the French, and although Halder had wanted to avoid anything that might offend the enemy's sense of honour,[51] the propaganda ministry, the ministry of foreign affairs, and the department for Wehrmacht propaganda in the High Command of the Armed Forces very soon set out to weaken the morale of the French by the use of loudspeakers, leaflets in print-runs of millions, and postcards. Secret transmitters of the Goebbels ministry (Office 'Concordia'),[52] camouflaged as French stations, supported by the regular Reich radio stations, unsettled the French population and spread rumours. In this way panic was to be caused, the conflict between public and government deepened, and the government finally forced to halt the war. The French were persistently told that they were to be sacrificed for Poland and for some armament interests, seeing that Germany had no territorial demands on France whatever, any more than on Belgium or Holland. The central theme of German propaganda was the latent Anglo-French antagonism:[53] France was being used by Britain to do her dirty work, while Britain herself participated in the war with only slight forces.

This propaganda offensive, for which even Hitler and his deputy Hess supplied texts for leaflets, was a great deal more effective than the Allied, especially

---

[51] Record of a long-distance telephone conversation of the chief of the Army General Staff, 5 Sept. 1939, BA-MA RH 19 III/87.

[52] Drechsler, 'Zersetzungsarbeit'; *Secret Conferences of Dr Goebbels*, 68–9. On this see now the basic work by Buchbender and Hauschild, *Geheimsender*, 34 ff.

[53] Memorandum H.Gr.Kdo. A/Ia No. 20/40 g.Kdos., 12 Jan. 1940, concerning offensive in the west, in *Dokumente zur Vorgeschichte*, 137 ff.; *Heil Beil!*, 49.

LE JOURNAL DE CAMBRONNE

1ère année   N° 2

MAIS OUI, NOUS REVOILÀ

Nous tombons juste pour vous exprimer tous nos vœux pour 1940.

Ces vœux, vous les devinez. Mais n'en dites rien aux Anglais si vous ne voulez pas avoir d'histoires.

Avouez que 1939 a fini d'une manière assez médiocre. On est dans les tranchées et on ne sait pas quand on en sortira.

On ne sait même pas si l'on en sortira.

La guerre traîne. C'est comme un enlisement dans lequel disparaît tout espoir d'une vie meilleure, d'un avenir mieux assuré et du vrai progrès social. Votre Gouvernement s'acharne à démolir tout ce que vous avez gagné, comme amélioration de votre sort depuis la der des der. Nous, les Allemands, ne sommes que de pauvres ouvriers qui travaillons pour réaliser un modeste socialisme bien compris. Nous ne pouvons rien faire pour vous, sauf de vous raconter comment les choses vont chez nous. La comparaison fera toujours plaisir à tout le monde.

Et maintenant cachez cette feuille. Parce que voilà un Anglais qui s'approche.

Il est vrai que ce n'est qu'un aumônier.

Le contre-bobardier.

COURRIER DE LA SEMAINE

Récemment a été publié un Livre jaune français. Le Gouvernement français y prétend avoir victorieusement réfuté l'assertion mensongère qu'au début de la guerre il se serait employé à maintenir la paix.

On mande de Londres: La perte totale en sous-marins allemands s'élevait le 1er octobre à 60 unités. Le 1er novembre elle était déjà montée à 40 unités. Le 1er décembre elle avait atteint vingt unités. Vers la fin de janvier elle atteindra très probablement le chiffre véridique.

Les mutineries dans l'armée allemande prennent de plus en plus d'ampleur. Après les anciens Autrichiens c'est maintenant le tour des soldats de l'ancien grand-duché

FIG. VI.II.I. German leaflet

the British, leaflets dropped over Germany since 4 September—18 million were said to have been dropped by the Royal Air Force during the first month of the war alone.[54] France's rapid military and moral collapse is partly explained by the demoralization systematically spread among her forces by Germany.[55] The employment of agents and commando units in France, Belgium, Holland, and Luxemburg, as well as the exploitation of dissatisfied minorities, further contributed to confusion and to the fanning of a hysterical fear of a 'Fifth Column'.

In the German hate propaganda against Britain the figure of Churchill played an ever increasing part. He was accused of being responsible for the continuation of the war. Another standard theme was London's 'plutocracy'.

Little was done, on the other hand, to arouse hostile feelings against the French in the armed forces. Nor did the strictly disciplined Wehrmacht need any special

[54] Barker, *Dunkirk*, 18.   [55] Horne, *To Lose a Battle*, 98.

TRANSLATION OF FIGURE VI.II.1

LE JOURNAL DE CAMBRONNE

1st year   No. 2

For the City which piles up gold the French are sent to their death

YES, WE'RE HERE AGAIN!

Just in time to convey to you our best wishes for 1940.

You'll guess what those wishes are. But don't tell the English about them unless you want trouble.

Admit that 1939 has ended rather shabbily. Men are in the trenches and there's no telling when they'll be out of them.

There's no telling even *if* they'll be out of them.

The war is dragging on. It's like a quagmire into which all hope of a better life disappears, hope of a more secure future and of real social progress. Your government is bent on destroying all you have achieved, such as an improvement in your lot since the 'war to end all wars'. We Germans are just poor workers striving to carry out a modest amount of socialism properly understood. All we can do for you is to tell you how things are going in our country. Comparisons always please everybody.

And now hide this leaflet. Because there's an Englishman coming.

Of course, he's only an army chaplain.

The anti-claptrap man

NEWS OF THE WEEK

A French Yellow Book was published recently. In it the French government claims to have victoriously refuted the false allegation that at the beginning of the war it did its best to preserve the peace.

It is reported from London that losses of German submarines reached a total of 60 units by 1 October. By 1 November the total was already 40 units. By 1st December it had reached 20 units. By the end of January it will probably reach the true figure.

Mutinies in the German army are growing in scale all the time. After the former Austrians it is now the turn of the soldiers of the former Grand Duchy [. . .]

motivation for the western campaign. Among the older generation, especially the officers, there was an occasional revival of resentment based on the outcome of the First World War. This culminated in formulae such as 'reparation of the injustice of Versailles' or 'expunging the disgrace of 1918', phrases frequently found also in official proclamations. Sporadically there was also a thirst for revenge based on

---

TRANSLATION OF FIGURE VI.II.2

1st year, No. 5   Airmail edition

OBSERVER IN THE CLOUDS[a]

'The best government is that which teaches us to govern ourselves.'—Goethe.

That is the whole difference. [between Hitler and Stalin]

'That big stupid flock of sheep.'

'Hitler and Stalin are not the creators of despotism; it is the other way round: the readiness of the masses to tolerate despotism made a Hitler and a Stalin possible.' *New York Times*.

'That big stupid flock of sheep'—this is how Hitler described the German people in *Mein Kampf*.

For seven years the German people have tolerated the most despicable dictatorship of all times. Must the world therefore believe that Hitler was right?

THE THREEPENNY REVOLUTION

Seven years ago a clique of so-called revolutionaries came to power in Germany; they succeeded in fooling their followers and nearly all the German nation with a hullabaloo of slogans. But all that this clique achieved with its threepenny revolution was destruction.

Everything that had made Germany great in her history was wiped out. Statesmen, scholars, and artists who had achieved great things in post-war Germany were driven into exile.

What still remained in Germany was condemned to an insignificant shadow existence. Even their own followers were fobbed off with phrases and—on the pretext that these were revolutionary deeds—misused for street violence and battles at political meetings.

OSTRACIZED

That clique of so-called revolutionaries banned the world from Germany, and banned Germany from the world. They are to blame if being German is synonymous today with barbarism, and if Germany's name has been dragged through the mud. The German people allowed it to happen—unable or unwilling to call a halt to the wreckers.

The world is still asking: Is the German people really 'a big stupid flock of sheep'?

The German people itself must provide the answer.

NEWS IN BRIEF

On 12 January British leaflets were dropped on Prague and Vienna.

On 11 January British aircraft bombed three German destroyers at Horns Reef.

The Italian Ambassador in Berlin protested against the detaining in Sassnitz of war material destined for Finland.

Sweden is negotiating with America for a major loan.

[a] Pun on *Völkischer Beobachter*.

1. Jahrgang Nr. 5 — Luftpost-Ausgabe

WOLKIGER BEOBACHTER

"Diejenige Regierung ist die beste, die uns lehrt, uns selbst zu regieren."—Goethe.

Das ist der ganze Unterschied.

„Die große stupide Hammelherde."

"Hitler und Stalin sind nicht etwa Schöpfer des Despotismus, sondern umgekehrt, die Bereitschaft der Massen, den Despotismus zu ertragen, machte einen Hitler und einen Stalin möglich."

New York Times.

„Die große stupide Hammelherde." So bezeichnete Hitler in „Mein Kampf" das deutsche Volk.

Sieben Jahre lang ertrug das deutsche Volk die verabscheuungswürdigste Diktatur aller Zeiten. Soll die Welt deshalb glauben, daß Hitler recht hatte?

Die Drei-Groschen-Revolution.

Vor sieben Jahren gelangte in Deutschland eine Klique sogenannter Revolutionäre an die Macht, die es verstand, ihre Gefolgschaft und fast die ganze Nation mit einem Wust von Schlagworten zu betören. Aber alles was diese Klique mit ihrer Drei-Groschen-Revolution erreichte, war — Zerstörung.

Alles, was Deutschland in der Geschichte groß machte, wurde ausgemerzt. Staatsmänner, Gelehrte und Künstler, die im Nachkriegsdeutschland Großes leisteten, wurden ins Exil getrieben.

Was noch an Wertvollem in Deutschland verblieb, wurde zu einer bedeutungslosen Schattenexistenz verdammt. Selbst die eigene Gefolgschaft wurde mit Phrasen abgetan und — unter dem Vorwand, daß es sich um revolutionäre Taten handle — zu Straßenkrawallen und Saalschlachten mißbraucht.

In Acht und Bann.

Diese Klique sogenannter Revolutionäre war es, die die Welt aus Deutschland verbannte, und Deutschland aus der Welt. Sie ist schuld, wenn Deutschtum heute gleichbedeutend ist mit Barbarei, und wenn Deutschlands Name in den Schmutz gezerrt wurde. Das deutsche Volk ließ es gewähren, — unfähig oder ungewillt, den Zerstörern Einhalt zu gebieten.

Die Welt fragt immer noch: Ist das deutsche Volk wirklich eine „große stupide Hammelherde"?

• Das deutsche Volk muß selbst die Antwort geben.

Kurze Nachrichten.

Am 12. Januar warfen englische Flugzeuge über Prag und Wien Flugblätter ab.

Am 11. Januar bombardierten englische Flugzeuge bei Horns Riff drei deutsche Zerstörer.

Der italienische Botschafter in Berlin protestiert gegen das Anhalten des für Finnland bestimmten Kriegsmaterials in Sassnitz.

Schweden verhandelt mit Amerika wegen einer grossen Anleihe.

FIG. VI.II.2. Allied leaflet

experiences during the Allied occupation of the Rhineland and the Ruhr. As a rule, however, the German troops harboured no special hostility towards the enemy, even less so towards the civilian population. Hostility was, admittedly, aroused by irregulars and by colonial troops.[56] Reich citizens who fought on the side of the Allies—these included Czechs and Poles from the new German eastern provinces— were not recognized as combatants.

(d) Military Administration

In line with the stipulations of the Second Reich Defence Law, on 26 August 1939, the day of camouflaged mobilization, Hitler transferred executive power within the intra-German operational zone to the army commander-in-chief. This operational zone, defined in advance, embraced a number of urban and rural districts forming wide strips along Germany's eastern and western frontiers. Brauchitsch delegated some of his authority to the commanders-in-chief of the separate armies. Their staffs were joined by Chefs der Zivilverwaltung (CdZ: Chiefs of Civil Administration), appointed long in advance, whose task was the co-ordination of all administrative activities within the army area and the orientation of these activities in line with military requirements. Further Chiefs of Civil Administration, known as 'CdZ Enemy Country', followed the armies into Poland and ensured the establishment of an occupation administration.

This CdZ organization did not prove successful anywhere. Whenever the Chiefs of Civil Administration or other administrative chiefs also held a senior party post they found it easy to escape Wehrmacht supervision. They enjoyed greater support from Hitler, who found his generals lacking in the understanding he believed he was entitled to for his racial policy. The military administration in the east was replaced after two months by a genuine civil administration. Even before that time special police and SS units had exploited the non-uniform structure of the military executive for embarking on a programme of extermination directed primarily against Poland's upper classes and Jewish population. Army High Command was content to be 'exempted' from responsibility for the crimes.[57] Nevertheless, senior officers opposing the regime, or critical of it, tried to prevent a similar situation from arising in the west. This was the easier for them as Hitler was not yet pursuing a similar racial programme there.

The Generalquartiermeister, the officer responsible in the Army General Staff for questions of executive power, designed a 'pure' military administration for the territories to be occupied. Army Groups A and B were assigned Oberquartiermeister— officers responsible for occupation administration until the appointment of special military commanders—and these soon had available to them military administration staffs under Ministerialdirektor Turner and Regierungspräsident Reeder. The Oberfeldkommandanturen (chief field commandants' offices) were joined by

---

[56] Cf. Report AOK 16/Ic/A.O.—06 No. 362/40 g., 28 May 1940, to OKW/Abw. II, BA-MA RW 4/v. 247.   [57] Umbreit, *Militärverwaltungen*, 116–17.

military-administration departments, and the Feldkommandanturen (field commandants' offices) by appropriate groups. Some administrative personnel were found also at local Kommandantur level.

These experts wore uniform, held the novel and not fully clarified status of war administrative officials, and were much more strongly linked to the military hierarchy than were, a few months earlier, the purely civilian Landräte (regional councillors) who represented the military administration at the lowest level in Poland. Army High Command believed this would ensure uniform direction and greater homogeneity of its rather unpolitical executive. It also hoped that in this way it might prevent undesirable measures by Himmler's authorities, especially as it had been possible to block a participation in the western campaign by the meanwhile notorious Einsatzgruppen (special-duty squads) of the Sicherheitspolizei (security police). Only a few small commandos managed to push forward into the western capitals in the train of the Wehrmacht, but they were not allowed to operate there freely.

In contrast to the Polish campaign, representatives of the war-economy organizations were slotted into the military administration staffs. Groups for war-economy matters were set up in these staffs and at the Oberfeldkommandanturen, and staffed with personnel from the war economy and armaments office of the High Command of the Armed Forces. Liaison officers represented the latter's interests also at the office of the Generalquartiermeister and his economic deputy, State Secretary Posse, who was in charge of economic preparations for the military administration. Colonel Nagel, previously responsible for the war economy in the Government-General (rump Poland), was put in charge of the economic department in the military administration staff of Army Group B.

Map exercises and first administrative directives eventually crystallized into detailed regulations such as had never existed for Poland.[58] They essentially followed the lines of the Hague Land War Convention and were communicated in good time to the military administration authorities. Posters with the first appeals and ordinances had been prepared. Hitler had not interfered with these preparations, made mainly by the Oberquartiermeister of Army Group B and State Secretary Posse, even though the NSDAP was already training Kreisleiter to head the administration in any potential new Reich Gaue.[59] On 9 May, as expected, he authorized the army commander-in-chief to wield executive power in the occupied territories of Luxemburg, Belgium, Holland, and France.[60]

But even this did not prevent various Reich authorities from wishing to have their own interests safeguarded by their own representatives on the spot, and these only occasionally liaised with the military authorities. Thus, the ministry of foreign affairs employed its own personnel to search for French official documents, and Heydrich dispatched a special team of Gestapo officials and SD (SS security service) specialists to Paris.

---

[58] Id., *Militärbefehlshaber*, 4 ff.   [59] Halder, *Diaries*, i, 347–8 (9 May 1940).
[60] Wagner, *Belgien*, 110; see also Kwiet, 'Vorbereitung'.

(e) War Economy

The success of the German forces in the early summer of 1940 was due to their acquired skill in combining modern technology with efficient organization[61] and adapting the conduct of operations to Germany's limited potential. The Reich's resources, though not fully exhausted in all spheres during the first years of the war, permitted only short wars—the so-called blitzkrieg, in which the opponent is knocked out by sharp well-aimed blows through the massive employment of all means, above all of armour and the air force.

The Reich did not have any 'armament in depth'. What mattered to Hitler was the armament industry's output at the moment.[62] It was Britain that had the longer breath, the greater production capacities. By the end of 1939 its production figures began to outstrip the German ones. However, Germany for the time being managed, by means of rapid concentration on time-limited programmes, to adapt itself for the next phase of the war—albeit with much friction and many conflicts. More than that was impossible, both because of Germany's natural shortage of raw materials and because of Hitler's opposition to long-term economic planning and to a cut in the production of consumer goods, both of which were demanded repeatedly by the war-economy organization.

Even before the beginning of the campaign in the west stocks of German raw materials had in some areas been drawn upon to the limit. Hitler, inadequately informed of the seriousness of the situation,[63] accepted the risk in the hope of an early end to the war and of a breathing-space. His economic experts were trying meanwhile to improve the distribution of what was available. Subsequently the booty taken in the western theatre of war brought temporary relief to the gloomy raw-material situation.

The main efforts in the armaments sector were characterized by priorities attaching, usually in accordance with Hitler's orders, to the different programmes. A certain measure of chaos in this field too was inevitable under the National Socialist system. There was invariably some project which was even more urgent than earlier plans. The navy, for instance, was not too successful in getting its U-boat construction programme implemented, in spite of the priority officially assigned to it—unlike the Luftwaffe with the construction of Ju 88 machines and anti-aircraft equipment. For the army the priorities were ammunition and weapon production as well as the equipment of the mobile troops.

The ammunition situation, still critical at the outbreak of the war and after the high expenditure in Poland, was improved on a lasting basis by the spring of 1940, simultaneously with an increase in naval mine production. During the western campaign, admittedly, expenditure of ammunition fell short of calculations. Weapons manufacture, on the other hand, was unable to keep pace with the newly established formations. The gaps had to be filled by captured arms. The appointment of a Reich

---

[61] Jacobsen, *Fall Gelb*, 180 ff.   [62] Milward, *German Economy*, 6.
[63] Report of OKW/WiRüAmt, Mar. 1940, concerning centralized war-economy control, BA-MA Wi/IF 5.2151.

TABLE VI.II.3. *Armoured Fighting Vehicles in the German Army, 1939–1940*

	1 Sept. 1939	10 May 1940	31 May 1940
Panzer I	1,445	1,276	1,132
Panzer II	1,224	1,113	927
Panzer III	103	429	358
Panzer IV	211	296	236
Panzer 35/38 (t)[a]	274	391	338
TOTAL	3,257	3,505	2,991

[a] (t)=manufactured in Czechoslovakia.

Source: OKW/WiRüAmt: Dekaden-Übersichten 1939–41, BA-MA Wi/IF 5-366.

minister for armament and munitions generally proved a sound move. On 17 March 1940 Hitler appointed his inspector-general of construction, Fritz Todt, to this post, much to the chagrin of the war economy and armaments office of the High Command of the Armed Forces, whose influence on the war economy, and especially on the output of armaments, was dwindling all the time.[64]

Absolute priority was eventually given to the motorization of the Wehrmacht. In Poland some formations had lost up to 50 per cent of their vehicle stock. Repairs often proved rather time-consuming, so that the motorized formations were scarcely in a position to mount a further, let alone a geographically extended, offensive. Hitler forced the Army General Staff to ensure, emphatically, the re-employability of the mobile formations. The army gave 11 November as the earliest possible date, which Hitler reluctantly accepted. Each subsequent postponement of the day of attack thus favoured the motorization of the Wehrmacht. However, the shortfall of motor vehicles, especially for the newly established formations—7 corps HQs, 8 HQs below corps level, and 32 divisions from the fifth to the eighth wave[65]—was not made good, especially as the army could not expect more than 1,000 newly manufactured vehicles per month. This was not even enough to make up continuing losses in the event of war, so that the forthcoming operation appeared in jeopardy.[66] It was possible, however, to make commercial vehicles available for army purposes; moreover, by various expedients, such as the demotorization of certain formations, the situation was improved by the spring. And even though, at the beginning of the western campaign, the less well equipped formations were up to 10 per cent short of their vehicles establishment, the necessary conditions existed for the calculated blitzkrieg. Conditions were soon further improved by large numbers of captured vehicles. Another successful move was the transfer of various competences to Major-General von Schell, who, as 'general plenipotentiary for motor vehicles'

---

[64] Cf. Thomas, *Wehr- und Rüstungswirtschaft*, 199 ff.   [65] Mueller-Hillebrand, *Heer*, ii. 35-6.
[66] Halder, *Diaries*, i. 207 ff. (4 Feb. 1940).

TABLE VI.II.4. *Fuel supplies 1939/1940* (1,000 t.)

	Stocks 1 Sept. 1939	Stocks 1 Apr. 1940	Booty (west)	Reserves 1 Sept. 1940	Estimated monthly consumption end 1939	Actual monthly consumption 1 Jan.–1 Sept. 1940
Motor petrol	300	110	350	540	170	134
Diesel fuel	220	73	50	470	160	128
Fuel oil for the navy	350	255	180	430		
Aviation fuel	442	480	210	620	100	61

Source: OKW/WiRüAmt: Inspectors' conference on 13 Sept. 1940, BA-MA Wi/IF 5. 378.

under the Four-year Plan and, from March 1940 onward, as under-secretary of state in the ministry of transport, was able to promote the motorization of the Wehrmacht. This aim was served by a unification of models, practised since 1938, which made for cheaper mass production and facilitated the problem of spares. Motor-vehicle production controlled in this manner was therefore swiftly adjusted to war production. For the number of armoured fighting vehicles in the German army in 1939–40 cf. Table VI.II.3.

The long pause in operations had made it possible to speed up the equipment of armoured divisions with modern types, the Panzer III and Panzer IV. Motorization of the Wehrmacht was, admittedly, limited by the bottlenecks which beset German motor-fuel and rubber supplies. The Polish booty made little change. Motor-fuel stocks available on 10 May 1940 were just about sufficient for four months' unrestricted warfare; rubber supplies, according to initial calculations, were enough for six months. For supplies of fuel in 1939–40 cf. Table VI.II.4.

In accordance with mobilization plans the war-economy organization was represented also in the senior commands in the west. Officers of the war economy and armaments office were initially concerned, as army economic officers, with the economic evacuation of the frontier zone, and maintained contact with the armament authorities in the military districts. The number of these liaison officers increased in line with preparations for the campaign. The war economy and armaments office assigned to them technical squads and economic units to be used in the occupied areas for repair work and for the collection of booty. As earlier in Poland, the war-economy organization was again able to supply the functionaries of the future occupation administration with detailed documentation on their area of employment. A new feature was the fact that, in contrast to the Polish campaign, the representatives of the war-economy and armament organization were more closely integrated into the military administration.

III. Deployment and Strategy of the Western Powers until 10 May 1940

WHEN Britain and France declared war on the German Reich on 3 September, having allowed it two days for reflection, they were acting in line with the joint programme laid down after the German entry into Prague, as well as meeting the political obligations they had assumed *vis-à-vis* Poland—London most recently in the Anglo-Polish treaty of assistance of 25 August 1939. Neither the British nor the French could or would suffer any further loss of face. Initially, however, they were neither willing nor in a position to launch appropriate military operations. In France, in particular, broad circles were anxious to avoid a war that was neither seen to be vital nor received with any enthusiasm by a predominantly pacifist public, who were content provided the concessions demanded from the Western powers concerning a reorganization of conditions in eastern Europe made allowance for certain essential requirements. A prerequisite of any further concessions, however, would have been some sign of German respect for treaty obligations. As it was, the various peace contacts which still existed between the belligerents, either directly or through mediation by willing neutrals, failed above all in the face of Hitler's policy and personality,[1] rather than through the intransigence of some British politicians. The latter, indeed, could rely on a greater readiness for war among their population than their opposite numbers in Paris[2] who would, of course, be more immediately exposed in the event of war. The elimination of Hitler soon became the declared war aim of the Allies,[3] along with the intention of limiting Germany's rise to an extent where it did not essentially disturb the balance of power in Europe. Right-wing politicians and the right-wing press, however, soon also discussed plans which amounted to a partitioning of the over-mighty German state. Such circles were playing into the hands of Goebbels's propaganda ministry.

Although France had concluded a treaty of mutual assistance with Poland in 1921, this was followed up by few specific promises. Not until the spring of 1939, when the Polish war minister visited France, did the French hold out the prospect of taking action against Germany in the event of a conflict, once certain mobilization periods had elapsed.[4] By 31 May the chief of the French general staff, Gamelin, had an operations order prepared which envisaged a limited attack in the area between the Rhine and the Moselle. This provided the basis for the tentative French thrusts following the outbreak of the war.

Gamelin had counted on more protracted Polish resistance, allowing France time for deployment behind her secure fortifications and for adapting herself to the new situation; time also for the moving up of sufficient British formations, for a stepping up

---

[1] Cf. Martin, *Friedensinitiativen*, 54–5. [2] Michel, *Drôle de guerre*, 60–1.
[3] Butler, *Strategy*, ii. 2. [4] Gamelin, *Servir*, ii. 420–1.

of French armament production, and for increased arms purchases in the United States. Gamelin had no intention of bringing about an early military decision. Premier Daladier shared this view. After three weeks of war, when French mobilization (begun on 21 August) and deployment were more or less concluded, Gamelin had at his disposal, in metropolitan France, 51 regular divisions and 37 reserve divisions. Ten formations secured the Alpine frontier against Italy, a dozen at least were manning fortifications, so that approximately 65 divisions would have been available for an attack on Germany. But, from the very outset, no such attack was planned. Gamelin did not believe he would be strong enough for an offensive before the autumn of 1941. He shrank from taking risks. He regarded the Westwall and the Rhine valley as insuperable obstacles. He had entertained some hopes of an overthrow of the regime in Germany, such as the British were seeking to promote by contacts with the internal German opposition. In line with the generally defensive military doctrine among the French forces, Gamelin further believed that, unlike Germany, France was not only vulnerable because of her geographical position, but was inevitably bound to disperse her forces to defend her extensive frontiers and her overseas possessions.[5] He regarded London too as being within dangerous reach of the German air force, which he judged to be very powerful.

As a kind of interim solution, designed to force Germany to dissipate her resources and therefore to postpone her offensive in the west, Gamelin had considered an attack against the enemy's sphere of power and economic resources in east and south-east Europe.[6] The necessary conditions for such a project, which followed certain ideas from the First World War, seemed to exist in view of France's traditional system of alliances in that area, as well as Britain's recent diplomatic agreements with Romania, Greece, and Turkey. The situation was complicated, however, by the German–Soviet friendship treaty, the elimination of Poland, and the equivocal attitude of Italy. Greece and Turkey, like most of the countries still neutral, were anxious to keep out of the conflict. Britain too counselled caution as the slight Allied forces in the Middle East were not, in her opinion, strong enough to meet a reaction from the Axis or to comply with the obligations undertaken. Gamelin's plan was supported only by the local commanders-in-chief, Weygand and Wavell, and thus remained controversial within the Allied Supreme War Council. Military means available were totally inadequate to this project, which anyway became irrelevant in April 1940 with the Allied intervention in Scandinavia. The same was true of another new plan, one not fully thought out in terms of its political consequences, envisaging, as a supplement to the economic blockade of Germany, the bombing of Soviet or Romanian oil-fields, or the severing of the Danube shipping route. Germany did not rule out the possibility of such diversionary operations by the Allies.[7] Hitler instructed Army High Command to prepare a deployment plan against Romania, but this pre-emptive operation seemed, for the time being, to have become unnecessary following the German successes on the western front.

---

[5] Michel, *Drôle de guerre*, 13–14.   [6] Hoop, 'Projects d'intervention'.
[7] Halder, *Diaries*, i. 248 ff. (26 Feb. 1940); OKW No. 494/40 g.Kdos. WFA/Abt. L—Ausl/Abw, 21 Mar. 1940: The military-political situation in the Middle East (copy), BA-MA RW 4/v. 35.

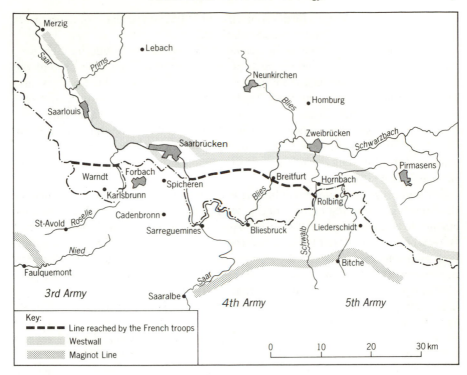

MAP VI.III.1. French Thrusts across the German Frontier in the First Half of September 1939

Generally speaking, Germany's military strength, in particular that of the Luftwaffe, was certainly overrated in London as elsewhere. Churchill was the only exception from the very start. But his proposal for the Rhine to be mined failed in the face of objections by the French, who feared retaliatory measures by the Luftwaffe. The principal British strategic ideas were of a defensive nature: the Atlantic sea routes must be safeguarded and the position in the Mediterranean maintained as long as possible. Britain believed in a lasting effect of her economic blockade and hoped that, after a period of time, she would be able to weaken Germany from the periphery and then finally defeat her.

The Allied initiative was thus at first limited to skirmishes along the German-French frontier. French patrols first thrust across the frontier on 6 September, between the Moselle and the Pfälzer Wald. The attack was followed up by troops in battalion strength, so that the German Army Group C at first feared that the enemy was preparing a full-scale offensive. Operations, however, did not go beyond insignificant thrusts between the Saar and Hornbach, and in the direction of Saarlouis. The Poles called for vigorous intervention by France, but the German success in the east made Gamelin doubt the usefulness of a further advance. Protection of his own territory seemed to him more important for the time being, especially within the French fortification-line or at least on the basis of appropriate natural or artificial obstacles favouring defence.

Gamelin decided in favour of a 'strategically defensive attitude'[8] which was, initially, in line with the German concept too. From mid-September onward the French went over to defence, limiting themselves to individual local actions, and by mid-October they withdrew again. They thereby relieved their German adversary of some anxiety. While following the advances of his armies in Poland, Hitler had been watching Germany's western frontier with great disquiet.[9] But as there were no signs of the indispensable preparations for a major Allied offensive, he soon calculated that he would be able to transfer the bulk of his forces from the east to the west in good time.

Gamelin subsequently justified his passivity by the late operational readiness of the French air force and heavy artillery, without which he did not think he could attempt to break through the Westwall.[10] Added to this was the fact that the Second Bureau of his general staff generally overestimated the German forces facing him; it also failed to identify clearly the creation of a point of main effort in the German deployment.[11] What Gamelin realized from the outset was the unsatisfactory state of training and equipment, and hence the limited fighting capacity, of his troops. The fighting spirit of the French army was not very high in any case, and a traditional excessive reliance on the Maginot Line and the flagging of morale during the long months of the *drôle de guerre* also had their effect. This was matched by the general political state of the country. On the very eve of the German attack France experienced a government crisis which very nearly led to a change of regime and to the dismissal of Gamelin, whose prestige had certainly not gained by the failures in Norway in mid-April.

Intervention in Scandinavia had been considered by the Allies for a long time. A landing at Petsamo, and perhaps an occupation of west Norwegian ports and airfields, as well as a move into Sweden, would cut off German ore supplies. The British, to whom Norway seemed the safer objective, were responsible for further planning and would, if the operation materialized, exercise supreme command. The Soviet–Finnish treaty of 13 March 1940, which was seen in France as a reverse for the Daladier government and brought about its fall, came just in time to restrict the laboriously prepared Allied intervention plans to those parts of Scandinavia where a confrontation with the USSR need not be feared—a risk more acceptable to Paris than to London. The course of the Allied operation against Norway convinced the new French premier Reynaud that the replacement of the 'nerveless philosopher'[12] Gamelin was a matter of increasing urgency.[13] By the middle of April the French commander-in-chief was ready to resign on his own initiative, but

---

[8] 'Instruction personnelle' No. 6, 29 Sept. 1939, in Gamelin, *Servir*, iii. 82–3. A detailed exposition and documentation of Allied strategy in 1939–40 is now available in Bédarida, *Stratégie secrète*.

[9] Irving, *Hitler's War*, 4.   [10] Gamelin, *Servir*, iii. 36.

[11] Brausch, 'Sedan', 64 ff. On the effects on French morale of inactivity, drunkenness, and German propaganda cf. Deighton, *Blitzkrieg*, 112.

[12] Reynaud's description of him. Cf. Horne, *To Lose a Battle*, 155.

[13] Le Goyet, *Gamelin*, 258.

allowed himself to be swayed by Daladier, who had retained the defence ministry, and by President Lebrun. His position remained precarious, and the conflict with Reynaud, who had only slight support in parliament and was himself considering resigning, continued. The German attack left them no time to settle their differences.

There was far more unanimity in the attitude of the British leadership and public. This was reflected also in the change of government effected on 10 May. Winston Churchill, a Conservative, assumed the post of prime minister and minister of defence; Clement Attlee, the leader of the Labour Party, became deputy prime minister; and Anthony Eden, champion of an intransigent policy towards Germany, took over the War Office.

The all too obvious organizational weaknesses and the low fighting spirit in the French army, the inappropriate cumulation of offices in the hands of a few politicians, and the passive attitude of Gamelin, charged with numerous but ill-defined responsibilities, also caused anxiety to the British.[14] Yet they too, as the Germans were aware, took the view that a protracted conflict was of advantage to the Allies, who were not yet ready for war, whereas Germany, weakened by the blockade, would soon find herself in economic difficulties. London's hopes were therefore based on the greater war-economy potential of the western democracies. The British, moreover, set aside their misgivings by trusting to the military qualities their Allies had displayed in the First World War, in order not to complicate even further their relations with Paris, strained as they were by political and psychological problems and divergent interests. The French, on the other hand, wanted to see a larger number of British formations on the Continent and relied on Britain, if necessary, to engage her entire air force. Gamelin was not interested in a joint general staff, as proposed by Chamberlain in July 1939. There was merely the Allied 'Supreme War Council', set up at the end of August, for the occasional discussion of political and general military issues.

British troops—initially two army corps of two divisions each—had arrived in France by the beginning of October and had taken over a defensive sector along the Franco-Belgian frontier. They represented the BEF, which by mid-May 1940 was reinforced to 14 variously trained and equipped infantry divisions and 1 armoured division. Only one of these formations was not posted on the Belgian frontier but was employed along the Saar river within the framework of the French Third Army. The British commander-in-chief, Lord Gort, had instructions to follow the orders of the French commands placed above him so long as the British forces— altogether half a million men—were not endangered. In the latter event, as arranged between London and Paris, he was to consult his government.

As for British air force units, approximately 261 fighters, 135 bombers, and 60 reconnaissance aircraft had been moved to the Continent.[15] The BEF could, moreover, count on air support from Britain itself.

---

[14] Müller, *Entente Cordiale*, 3. A detailed study of the organizational problems which impaired France's conduct of the war from the top downwards may be found in Réau, 'Haut commandement'.

[15] Hillgruber and Hümmelchen, *Chronik*, 10.

Franco-British defence strategy was based on the assumption of a German attack which, bypassing the Maginot fortifications, would be aimed at the less well protected region of northern France, and which, having failed, would provide an opportunity for an Allied counter-offensive. It was in line with this concept that the most efficient formations had been deployed. The value of that strategy depended largely on whether negotiations at the political level would make it possible to include Belgian territory in the Allied deployment area. As the advantages of such a move were obvious, Hitler had made allowance for such plans. In this he underrated the Belgians' firm intention of clinging to their neutrality as long as possible. Allied overtures along those lines yielded no satisfactory results. They had to reconcile themselves to the idea that only after a German attack would the Belgians and the Dutch invite them into their countries. In order to be able to meet the guarantees given to these countries, Gamelin equipped his armies with the necessary operations orders and, with some effort, achieved a few indispensable arrangements with the governments in Brussels and The Hague.

The Allies' 'Scheldt Plan' of October 1939[16] for supporting the Belgian army was designed to bar the Germans from access to the country's great ports, secure bases for the British air force, and facilitate the protection of the economically important region of northern France. To this end Allied Army Group 1 was expected to advance to the Scheldt and make contact with the Belgian defenders of the *réduit national*. Simultaneously, however, Allied Army Group 1 had to be ready, if there was time, to advance further into Belgium, to a line Namur-Gembloux-Wawre-Dyle-Antwerp. The Allied supreme command was convinced that the Belgians would be able to halt the German advance long enough for the execution of these further-reaching intentions to be made possible. This 'D[yle] Plan' had the merit of not letting the north-east French industrial region become a battlefield, and of facilitating Allied intervention, from more easily defended positions, against an enemy advancing through Holland. As soon as detailed information was available concerning the Belgian plan of defence, new deployment instructions were issued in mid-November.[17] Light mechanized divisions would, from a line along the Albert Canal and the Meuse, support the Belgian forces roughly between Liège and Namur, but, in the event of a German breakthrough, they would withdraw behind the Louvain–Namur line. The French Seventh Army, still being held back at that time as a reserve in the area west of Antwerp, soon received special orders to safeguard the Scheldt estuary north of Antwerp and to maintain the link of the French–British–Belgian front with the retreating Dutch by advancing into the area around Breda, Turnhout, or even Tilburg.[18]

---

[16] GQG/E.-M.G./3ᵉ Bureau No. 0559 3/N.E., 17 Nov. 1939: 'Instruction personnelle et secrète pour le Général Commandant le Groupe d'Armées No 1 et le Général Commandant en Chef la "B.E.F."', in *Dokumente zur Vorgeschichte*, 208 ff.

[17] GQE/E.-M.G./3ᵉ Bureau No. 0773 3/N.E., 17 Nov. 1939: 'Instruction personnelle et secrète pour le Général Commandant le Groupe d'Armées No 1 et le Général Commandant en Chef la "B.E.F."', ibid. 212–13.

[18] Order by Gamelin, 12 Mar. 1940, ibid. 214.

The entire plan, which tied down nearly all the revenues of the army command,[19] was based on the assumption that a German attack could only be expected through Belgium and Holland, or possibly also—and here German deception manœuvres paid off—across Swiss territory, bypassing France's south-eastern fortifications. The Maginot Line itself was regarded by the French as impregnable, and the Ardennes and the Meuse valley as scarcely negotiable natural obstacles. Allied troops were deployed accordingly. The best formations were concentrated in the north, while further south on the Meuse two less effective armies went into position. This error, and more especially a multitude of omissions—including the failure to learn the necessary lessons from the accurate analyses of German operations to date made by subordinate commands[20]—resulted in one of the greatest military defeats suffered by France in her entire history.[21]

[19] Horne, *To Lose a Battle*, 113.

[20] Michel, *Drôle de guerre*, 123; Dutailly, 'Faiblesses et potentialités', 28. The possibility that German forces might, in certain circumstances, attempt a crossing of the Meuse at Sedan was considered in a map-exercise of the Supreme War Council as early as 1936-7. It was time and again dismissed by Gamelin. Cf. Delmas, 'Exercices', and Paillat, *Répétition générale*. According to Gunsburg, *Divided and Conquered*, 92-3, however, the French, including Gamelin, correctly understood the basic tactics applied by the Wehrmacht in the Polish campaign, before the German campaign in the west.

[21] Le Goyet, *Gamelin*, 77.

IV. Policies and Defence Efforts of the Neutral Countries: Belgium, Holland, and Luxemburg

FOR the Germans it was an axiom that neither belligerent party could deny itself the advantages to be gained from involving the neutral countries in its theatre of operations. With equal certainty it was assumed that Belgium and Holland would resist an Allied invasion far less vigorously than a German attack.[1] If, against expectation, they nevertheless reacted passively to the Germans, arrangements made on the spot were to ensure an undisturbed advance.

Belgium from the outset missed no opportunity to declare its firm resolution to adhere to its neutrality, which Germany, Britain, and France shortly before the outbreak of the war had promised to respect. King Leopold III and his government of national unity regarded this policy, pursued since 1936, as offering at least a small chance of keeping the country, despite its exposed position between the fronts, out of a war. The German deployment in the west, however, was bound very soon to cause even that feeble hope to fade. As a countermove the Belgian forces were more strongly concentrated on the country's eastern frontier. Reports coming in on an increasing scale gradually left no doubt that the country had to prepare for a German invasion or—what was seen as an almost equal threat—for a German attack against Holland.

The Allied military command saw Belgium's strict neutrality as a complication in its own operational planning.[2] If it proved impossible to induce the Belgians to request assistance beforehand, thereby rendering possible a pre-emptive Allied advance, it was important, at the least, to have talks between the general staffs to prepare for swift and smooth co-operation between the forces in the event of resistance becoming necessary. The British took the initiative by putting out feelers in Brussels as early as September 1939. They referred to Britain's and France's contractual obligations of coming to Belgium's assistance if necessary. That, however, could be accomplished only if a series of indispensable preparations were made for such a move. The Belgian government, however, believed it could not run such a risk, lest it should provide Germany with a pretext for aggression. The British offer was declined, as was a French offer made some time later.[3] Brussels merely evinced non-committal interest in the military plans of the Allies, who, in the view of the Belgian minister of the interior, were sufficiently well informed of the Belgian defence system anyway. On 7 November Leopold III and Queen Wilhelmina of The Netherlands once more offered to mediate between the warring parties. Then, however, further

---

[1] OKH/GenStdH/Op.Abt. (Ia) No. 072/40 g.Kdos., 30 Jan. 1940: Directive for 'Operation Immediate', in *Dokumente zur Vorgeschichte*, 63-4. [2] *Relations militaires*, 80. [3] Ibid. 139 ff.

reports of German aggressive intentions triggered off a first state of alert and readiness in Belgium. Britain and France redoubled their efforts for prompt talks with the Brussels government, which in turn wished to know from the Allies what forces, in the event of a Belgian request for assistance, they could move to the Albert Canal within 48 hours. Belgium, however, was not prepared to have regular negotiations, and Gamelin for his part was not in a position to give firm assurances. The decision to advance over the Dyle, i.e. across the Antwerp–Namur line, could, in his opinion, be taken only on the basis of the immediate situation. This non-committal reply was a disappointment to the Belgian general staff, implying as it did that a large part of the country would have to be surrendered to the attacker. The general staff did not therefore content itself with this position but succeeded, during continuous secret exchanges of ideas through the Belgian military attaché in Paris, in extracting further undertakings from the French high command: arrival at the Albert Canal possibly within six days—a manœuvre not seriously considered possible on the Allied side. The tricky question of a joint high command was not even broached.

No sooner had the November crisis abated than, at the beginning of January 1940, new discouraging information was received. The 'Mechelen incident'[4] confirmed suspicions and—together with a date of attack passed on by Colonel Oster of the foreign counter-intelligence department of the High Command of the German Armed Forces via the Dutch military attaché in Berlin, Colonel Sas, as well as increasing incursions by German reconnaissance aircraft—triggered off additional measures. Leopold III had the British and French military attachés informed and ordered further mobilization measures. Paris and London were notified that, in the event of a German attack, Belgium would request both countries to implement the guarantees given by them. During the night of 13–14 January—and this was subsequently used as a German justification—the Belgian chief of the general staff Van den Bergen ordered the removal of the barriers on the French frontier, where a number of formations were standing ready to move into the country. Following this unauthorized decision he had to request a transfer to another post. And when Britain and France once more proposed that Belgium should request pre-emptive assistance, they again met with refusal. The same happened following the German attack on Denmark and Norway. Until 10 May there was, between Belgium and the Allies, especially in connection with reports of German aggressive intentions, no more than an exchange of ideas through the military attachés, though this at least allowed for a rough harmonization of intended operations. Detailed arrangements, however, did not come about. Co-operation among intelligence services was closer, and included also Dutch and Swiss agencies. A Belgian warning that the Germans might also launch a thrust from the Ardennes did not, however, worry Gamelin.

Nothing had changed in the official Belgian attitude, and this was appreciated, at least by the German embassy. The only suspicious feature, in the interpretation

---

[4] On 10 Jan. 1940 a German courier aircraft en route for Cologne lost its way in fog and landed at Mechelen-aan-de-Maas. On board was a Luftwaffe General Staff officer with secret deployment orders, which he only partially succeeded in destroying. Cf. their reproduction in *IMT* xxxix, doc. No. TC-58 (a).

used in subsequent German propaganda, was that the Belgian troop deployment was directed predominantly against the eastern neighbour. This had no bearing whatever on Hitler's determination to conduct the offensive in the west without regard to the neutral countries' rights. The Allies, for their part, intended to march into Belgium even if the Germans attacked solely across Holland. However, they were going to give the Brussels government three hours' grace, during which it might request the Western powers to take this step.[5]

Belgium had an army field force of 600,000 men, mobilized progressively since 25 August 1939 and consisting in the main of 22 divisions. Of these, 15 were stationed in the east and north-east. Their state of equipment and training varied. There was a shortage of tanks and anti-aircraft artillery. The principles of employment likewise were not up to the level of modern warfare. The air force possessed just under 250 aircraft—fighters, reconnaissance planes, and bombers.[6] A large proportion of these machines were outmoded. There were no naval forces worth mentioning.

The Belgian general staff intended to meet the first assault of the Germans with their own forces and then to withdraw their troops to prepared defensive positions. This necessity arose from the unsatisfactory promises of the Allies, who envisaged a considerable lapse of time before the arrival of their advancing force and who would not promise the air support asked for.

The continual postponement of the German attack gave Belgium an opportunity to improve its defence system. This was divided into three sectors. The attacker was first to be resisted in a frontier zone from Arlon via Maaseik to Antwerp. The bulk of the Belgian troops were stationed on its northern sector on 10 May. Further back ran a second line of fortifications along the Albert Canal between the fortress areas of Liège and Antwerp. The third zone of defence, begun in August 1939 and hence still in varying stages of completion, was based on the fortress area of Namur and on the 'K.-W. position'[7] (partly running along the Dyle), which linked up with the fortifications around Antwerp, behind which was the *réduit national*. This was additionally protected, further to the west, by the fortifications around Ghent. The Belgian defence strategy, which was impaired by the inadequate number of Belgian troops and which initially had probably overestimated the significance of such natural obstacles as the Ardennes and the Meuse, assumed that the forces in the K.-W. position would have to integrate with the advancing Allied armies in order to oppose the German attack with any prospect of success. Any fighting in the approaches could, at best, delay the German advance. The Franco-British Dyle Plan was founded on these considerations. No Belgian–Dutch arrangements existed. The northern flank was to be covered, if necessary, by the French Seventh Army.

The Netherlands government had calculated that there was a chance, as in the First World War, once more to keep out of military events. Hence it was not prepared to enter into any joint defence planning with the Belgians or with the Allies. In the

---

[5] Allied Military Committee: Record of the 101st Meeting of the Military Representatives, 30 Apr. 1940, PRO FO 371, vol. 24901.
[6] Charles, *Forces armées belges*, 24. [7] Koningshooikt–Wavre.

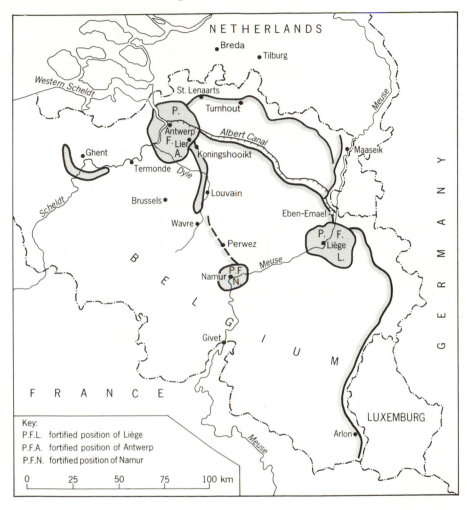

MAP VI.IV.1. The Belgian Fortifications

event of the country nevertheless being attacked, a defence was envisaged along three successive, not particularly well fortified, lines: Meuse-IJssel, the Peel-Raam position in the south and the Grebbe Line in the north, and finally on the boundaries of 'Fortress Holland', which comprised the cities of Rotterdam, Amsterdam, and The Hague. It was hoped that the putative enemy might be held up long enough at the middle position for Allied assistance to arrive. It was expected that the Belgians would continue the Peel-Raam position to the south, i.e. that they would still in part be defending a line east of the Albert Canal.

The weak spot of this plan was that Gamelin did not intend to move as far into Holland as the Dutch government, with a view to holding its middle defensive line, was hoping for. The Allied commander-in-chief did not propose to let his troops

MAP VI.IV.2. The Dutch Fortifications

advance beyond Breda, and the Belgians, in particular, did not think it possible, without Allied help, to start the defence of their country so close to the German frontier. Gamelin was unable to harmonize the different operations plans with each other. The Dutch commander-in-chief, General Winkelman, thereupon decided in early April 1940 to pull the bulk of his forces back, if necessary, to 'Fortress Holland'.[8] Brussels and Paris were notified of the Dutch intention of not embarking on all-out defence against the south until they were behind the Grebbe Line and north of the rivers Waal and Meuse. North Brabant therefore remained essentially unprotected. Yet this had no effect on Gamelin's intention to engage his Seventh Army against Breda.

[8] *Relations militaires*, 129.

The Dutch army consisted of 4 army corps of 2 divisions each, 4 brigades, and a multitude of lesser units.[9] The state of its training and equipment was even below the Belgian level. The air force was able to employ 125 aircraft, most of which, however, were outdated and insufficiently equipped.[10] Its personnel amounted to approximately 3,000 men. Equally outdated were the roughly 50 naval aircraft not required for training purposes. They were intended to be used, carrying bombs and torpedoes (not then capable of being delivered), against landing operations. The Dutch navy was for the most part in south-east Asia. In the mother country there were, among major though largely outdated units, 1 cruiser, 1 destroyer, 10 minelaying vessels, 11 gunboats, 3 torpedo-boats, 6 submarines, and a few mine-sweepers. Some of the numerous ships still under construction were subsequently saved from German seizure and transferred to Britain.

Mobilized deployment of the Dutch army had been in force since 3 September 1939. Having again been informed through Oster of the final date of attack, the Dutch were able to prepare for the mining of bridges and to close the frontier barriers. From 03.00 hours on 10 May the highest stage of alert was in operation, though only for the frontier troops and the anti-aircraft artillery. At any rate, troops were already moving into the foremost defensive positions.

The feeble hope of being able to avoid involvement in the conflict through unarmed neutrality was indulged in also by the government and population of Luxemburg. Some anxiety, however, was caused by statements about a historically and 'ethnically' justified attachment of the small country to the Greater German Reich—arguments used frequently, in contrast to official German policy, by representatives of the NSDAP. Further disquiet was caused by intensified German propaganda and underground activity within the country.[11] The vast majority of the population sympathized with the cause of the democracies. Voluntary enrolment in the French army was not unusual, and French intelligence found operation in Luxemburg easy.

During the 'phoney war' Luxemburg customs personnel as well as gendarmerie, reinforced by police and volunteers, protected the country's frontiers against both east and west. These lightly armed law-and-order forces totalled approximately 1,300 men.[12] Ten radio centres were to ensure a rapid alarm system, independently of the vulnerable telephone network. Some 60 road-blocks were established and, during the night of 9–10 May, also closed—at least on the Luxemburg-German frontier. These were unable to delay the invasion to any marked extent. The security forces had orders not to resist the German invaders and merely to point out to them their violation of neutrality. Approximately 40,000 inhabitants of the country fled across the frontier into France.

[9] Melzer, *Albert-Kanal*, 29–30; 'Comment le Corps aéroporté', 3.
[10] De Jong, *Het Koninkrijk*, ii. 374 ff.
[11] Weber, *Geschichte Luxemburgs*, 11 ff.; Koch-Kent, *10 mai*.
[12] Information kindly supplied by Henri Koch-Kent, 9 Aug. 1977.

V. German Victory in Western Europe

1. THE MILITARY RATIO OF STRENGTH

FOR the strength of the respective forces on A (Attack) Day see Table VI.v.1.

The military potential confronting the Wehrmacht in its attack in the west was approximately equal to the strength of the German forces. In some respects the west was stronger numerically. France, together with her British ally and the overseas possessions of both, held virtually unlimited reserves of raw materials. Like Britain, France had started too late and not rationally enough on the equipping and modernizing of her land and air forces. However, the relative quiet until the spring of 1940 enabled the French to raise some new formations and restructure others. Mechanization was vigorously promoted, less so battle training. Further mobile formations and the first few armoured divisions were established, in addition to the numerous tank battalions which served the reinforcement of infantry divisions.[1] Employment of these tanks (technically often superior) was thought by the Germans to have been 'not very skilful'.[2] The Allied forces were poorly equipped with anti-tank and anti-aircraft weapons, and their system of communications was totally inadequate. With a shortage of fighters and, even more so, of bombers there was marked inferiority in the air. The French air force was in the process of undergoing major changes in equipment and, as a result of being partly assigned to the armies, was inefficiently organized. War with Germany broke out at an unfavourable moment for it. The French aircraft industry, moreover, had not been able to replace the often outmoded machines by modern mass-produced types. Efforts towards an extension of capacity and towards securing deliveries of American material began too late.

Britain's capability in the air, on the other hand, was superior to Germany's in the long run. Its strength lay in the fact that Britain had realized the importance of strategic aerial warfare at an early date, and had created both the technical and the organizational preconditions for it. What the British underestimated, however—and this was to put them, as well as the French, at a great disadvantage in the course of the campaign in the west—was the need for tactical ground support. Neither the British nor the French then possessed an aircraft type that was as suited to this task as the German Ju 87. The lessons of Poland should have made the Western powers realize that it was part of German strategy to destroy the enemy's air force on the ground by a surprise strike at the opening of the attack. There was altogether a failure to learn appropriate lessons from the Polish campaign.[3] A technological

---

[1] Owens, 'Anatomy', 34.

[2] Fourth Army war diary No. 4, 16 May 1940, BA-MA W 6965a. On the relationship of French equipment and conduct of operations cf. also Lee, 'Strategy'.

[3] Le Goyet, Gamelin, 238-9.

TABLE VI.V.1. *Comparison of Strength on A (Attack) Day*

1. ARMY

	Divisions	Guns	Tanks
France	104[a]	10,700	3,063[a]
Britain[b]	10	1,280	310
Belgium	22	1,338	10
Netherlands	8	656	
TOTAL	144	13,974	3,383
Germany	141[c]	7,378[d]	2,445[e]

II. AIR FORCE

	Fighters	Bombers	Reconnaissance planes	Total aircraft
France	637	242	489	1,368[f]
Britain[b]	261	135	60	456
Belgium	90	12	120	250
Netherlands	62	9	50	175
Britain (home-based)	540	310		850
TOTAL	1,590	708	719	3,099
Germany (total)	1,736	2,224	700	5,446
Germany (operational 4 May 1940)	1,220	1,559	535	4,020

[a] North-eastern front alone, including reserves and one Polish division.
[b] Forces transferred to the Continent.
[c] See Table VI.II.1.
[d] Excluding Norway and east.
[e] Total available.
[f] Operational aircraft with front-line formations in metropolitan France.

Sources: Figures are balanced from Liss, *Westfront*, 145; Charles, *Forces armées belges*, 24; Hillgruber and Hümmelchen, *Chronik*, 9-10; Service Historique de l'Armée de Terre, *Les Grandes Unités françaises* (9 May 1940); Buffotot and Ogier, 'L'Armée de l'Air', 201. The computation of aircraft totals, in particular, is based on very unreliable data. About 30% of aeroplanes were probably not operational at some time or other. According to Uhle-Wettler, *Höhe - und Wendepunkte*, 256 ff., the Allies were in fact numerically superior to the Germans. He postulates, for example, 13 British and 10 Dutch divisions and puts the total of German aircraft available for the western campaign at 2,700-3,500. The continued divergence of numerical data on air strength emerges clearly from Bédarida's compilation, *Stratégie secrète*, 546-7; cf. also Gunsburg, *Divided and Conquered*, 108-9. Paillat, *Guerre éclair*, 631 ff., argues for a clear inferiority of the Allied forces.

and in some respects numerical advantage, greater combat experience after the campaigns fought so far, and the application of modern tactical principles in the use of resources—all these factors ensured German superiority for the time being and inspired greater confidence in victory on the part of the army command.

2. DETERMINATION OF THE DAY OF ATTACK

Hitler had hesitated for a long time in deciding whether to launch the attack on Denmark and Norway before or after the western campaign. However, Operation Weserübung (the attack on Norway and Denmark) could no longer be postponed; he gave orders at the end of March for this to be launched between 8 and 10 April, and for the offensive in the west to be started about the middle of the month. However, the not entirely smooth course of the surprise attack and the tying down of strong air forces in the north made a postponement of the western campaign necessary, although by then the army command was calling for a swift blow. Selection of a day during the first week of May was repeatedly revised because the weather conditions then forecast would render full air force employment difficult. A conspicuous intensification of Dutch defence measures, suggesting betrayal of German plans, as well as the fear that the enemy might advance into Belgium and Holland, eventually led to the choice of the one day for which good weather could be safely predicted. The attack was ordered for Friday, 10 May, at 05.35 hours. On the previous evening, in conditions of maximum secrecy and camouflage, Hitler and his staff moved to a newly established Führer headquarters at Münstereifel. He wished to be near the front to experience the western campaign, which he did not doubt would result in 'the greatest victory in world history'.

Germany policy and propaganda benefited from a number of British documents captured in Norway. From these it emerged that the enemy, regardless of the planning of Weserübung, had themselves been preparing for a landing in Norway. The Germans had merely been faster in their ruthless violation of neutrality.

In the case of Belgium and Holland Hitler nevertheless took the trouble to justify German aggression. Shortly before the launching of the attack the two ambassadors in Berlin were handed memorandums accusing their governments of a series of violations of neutrality:[4] one-sided troop deployment against the east, anti-German sentiments in the press and among the public, support for the British intelligence service, unopposed penetration of British aircraft into Dutch air-space, and military arrangements with the enemy for the purpose of an Allied thrust into the Ruhr. Nevertheless, the Reich government asserted, the German troops were not entering as enemies, and the sovereignty of the two countries would not be interfered with. A special envoy was envisaged for The Hague, to invite the queen to accept the country's occupation without opposition; the Dutch government, however, succeeded in preventing his arrival. It had again been warned: by Oster and by the German troop movements, which had not gone unnoticed. The Dutch and Belgian requests for Allied assistance were nevertheless made only on the morning of 10 May, when the German attack had become a terrible certainty for the two countries.

---

[4] German memorandums of 9 May 1940 to the Belgian and Dutch governments, in *Dokumente zur Vorgeschichte*, 215 ff.; *Weitere Dokumente*, 5 ff.

3. THE CAMPAIGN IN THE WEST[5]

The fact that for eight months France and Britain had more or less inactively watched the German war in Poland and the German deployment in the western territories of the Reich was to cost them dearly the moment Germany once more seized the initiative. The German attack came at a rather unexpected time for the Allies. All they could do was react to it, and that too slowly and unimaginatively. Within a short period the Allies were tactically and strategically outmanœuvred.

The success of the German plan of campaign depended on whether the enemy was taken by surprise and on whether the complicated system created for bringing up troops and supplies proved its worth. The special operations, on whose preparation Hitler had spent so much time, had only been partially successful.

In Maastricht the Dutch managed to blow up the bridges in good time, before the German commandos arrived.[6] The deception based on faked Dutch uniforms proved useless. The two operational squads of counter-intelligence came under fire and suffered considerable losses. Even so, only one bridge over the Albert Canal escaped the German *coup*, and at Gennep members of the Construction Training Battalion 800 succeeded in capturing a bridge over the Meuse. Elimination of Fort Eben-Emael by the air-landed Koch Assault Detachment was very largely successful. In consequence it was possible, despite a 24-hour hold-up in Maastricht, to burst through a defence system which could not have been overcome so quickly by traditional means. At the same time these spectacular special operations concealed the real main effort of the German operation.

The occupation of The Hague by paratroops and by units of 22nd Airborne Division was a failure.[7] Numerous transport aircraft were lost during the approach, and less than half the forces earmarked for the operation arrived at the selected airfields of Valkenburg, Ypenburg, and Ockenburg. Dutch opposition proved too strong. In the course of the day the Germans had to give up the airfields; the number of troops killed, wounded, or taken prisoner was considerable. More successful were the paratroops of the 7th Air Division and Infantry Regiment 16 (22nd Airborne Division) in the Dordrecht–Moerdijk–Rotterdam area, with the Waalhaven airfield as their base, who succeeded in seizing the principal bridges over the Meuse, the Waal, and the Lek.

Simultaneously, the German Army Groups A and B—Army Group C contented itself with minor attacks on the sector of First Army—had started moving according to plan. Across the frontier they initially encountered no major opposition. Very useful from the outset were the relatively numerous sapper units which followed the German spearheads and helped with the removal of obstacles and with the

---

[5] Blumentritt, 'Westfeldzug'; *Dokumente zum Westfeldzug*; Jacobsen, *Dünkirchen*; Benoist-Méchin, *Soixante jours*; Horne, *To Lose a Battle*; Ellis, *War in France*. On the crossing of the Meuse by 7th Armoured Division at Dinant cf. now the detailed account by Frieser, 'Rommels Durchbruch'.

[6] Melzer, *Albert-Kanal*, 56 ff.; Buchheit, 'Regiment Brandenburg', 130-1.

[7] 'Comment le Corps aéroporté', 9 ff. On the composition of the German forces cf. Edwards, *Airborne Troops*, 71 ff.

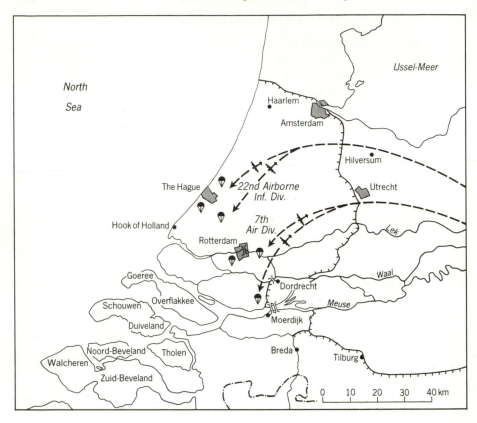

MAP VI.v.1. Airborne Operation Holland

crossing of rivers. The shortage of bridge-building equipment was not too important, considering that time and again undamaged bridges fell into German hands.

The Luftwaffe meanwhile, with the use of strong forces, was striving to eliminate the enemy's anti-aircraft defences over Holland and Belgium, as well as on the French Channel coast, and to neutralize his air forces concentrated in eastern France. The past few months' short-range and long-range reconnaissance provided a good basis for German activity. Support for ground operations consisted mainly of ceaseless bombing of railways, roads, command posts, and troop concentrations, designed to cover their exposed flanks. Skill in the establishment of rapidly effective communications and flexibility in bringing forward its ground organization—which shortened approach-flights and increased the number of daily missions to between five and nine—were the basis of a virtually 'classic' co-operation between army and air force. Indirect or direct support for the army, to the point of smashing enemy tank attacks, was increasingly becoming the main task of the German air force, which, after one week, achieved a clear superiority in the air and after a further week a degree of air supremacy that was but temporarily interrupted by enemy fighters.

The ceaseless, and costly, operations of the Luftwaffe played a decisive part in the success of the German campaign in the west.

On the enemy side an advance had been ordered on the morning of 10 May, in accordance with the Dyle Plan, for Army Group 1, for Seventh Army, and for the troops of Army Group 2 earmarked for Luxemburg. Gamelin at once made sure of the necessary contacts with the Belgian and Dutch high commands. The Belgian forces, like the BEF, were nominally subordinated to Army Group 1. However, it was not until the evening that all French formations were set in motion. Only hesitantly did formations of effective combat power cross the Meuse south of Namur, which rendered the rapid advance of the Germans easier. Among the French top command doubts concerning the effectiveness of the Dyle Plan were already beginning to be entertained in various quarters.

In Holland the German Eighteenth Army reached the IJsselmeer on the very first day. By the evening the Peel position had been overrun. The airborne landings had caused considerable confusion among the Dutch and had tied down several divisions. Although they scored no tactical success, they made a strategic one possible. The defenders managed to press the as yet isolated attackers very hard, but were unable, during the next few days, to liquidate them. Nor did the Dutch succeed in recapturing the vital bridge across the Waal, the access to 'Fortress Holland', from the paratroops dropped at Moerdijk. By the third day the advance guards of the German 9th Armoured Division arrived on the spot and on 13 May they thrust northwards behind the Grebbe Line still held by the Dutch. The French formations of Seventh Army at Breda, exposed to massive attacks by the Luftwaffe, still felt too weak to intervene at once. As there was little chance of establishing contact with the Dutch now withdrawing into their 'Fortress', Seventh Army after its useless engagement withdrew to the Antwerp area. The Germans had thus succeeded in isolating the Dutch army. On the evening of 13 May Eighteenth Army headquarters gave orders 'to break resistance in Rotterdam by all possible means'.[8] On the following day, just as, after some delay, negotiations were proceeding for the surrender of the city, the German Bomber Group 54, for whose first wing the countermanding order arrived too late, made a by then unnecessary attack on the city. Its effects were devastating. There were over 800 fatalities among the civilian population alone. In view of a hopeless military situation and in order to avoid similar disasters in other cities, the Dutch commander-in-chief, General Winkelman, decided to surrender. He signed the document on the morning of 15 May, jointly with the commander-in-chief of the German Eighteenth Army, in a little village between Dordrecht and Rotterdam. A few units in Zuidbeveland (Scheldt estuary) were exempted from laying down their arms, but these had to surrender a little later. Hitler ordered a demonstrative march through Amsterdam by parts of 9th Armoured Division and his SS-Leibstandarte.

---

[8] Eighteenth Army war diary, 13 May 1940, BA-MA N 126/19. Details of the air raid on the centre of Rotterdam in Uhle-Wettler, *Höhe- und Wendepunkte*, 277 ff. Deighton, *Blitzkrieg*, 225, gives the number of fatalities as 980.

Further to the south, meanwhile, the German Sixth Army had, after some delay, crossed the Meuse and the Albert Canal and surrounded the fortress of Liège. Most of its individual fortifications were overcome, before Belgium's capitulation, by the 223rd Infantry Division, placed directly under Army Group B. Dutch formations, as well as the Belgians and, after vigorous opposition near Gembloux, the most forward French formations withdrew by 14 May to Antwerp and to the Dyle line, where the bulk of the Allied forces in Belgium had gone into position.

Army Group A, to which the most important role was assigned by the German plan of operations, had likewise made rapid progress. The major roads were reserved for the mobile formations, while the infantry followed on lesser roads. By what was called a 'paternoster' procedure lagging formations and reserves were brought up according to a previously prepared march-table. Fourth Army had reached the Meuse

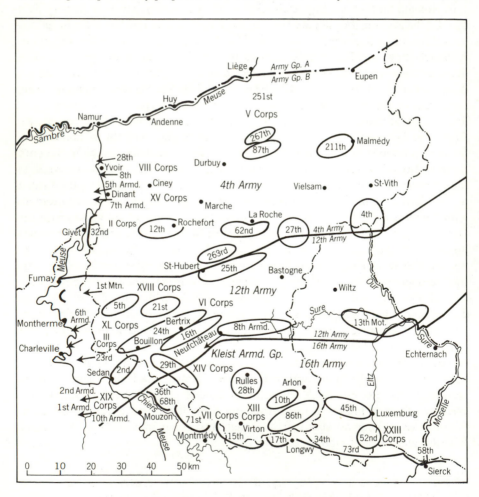

MAP VI.V.2. Meuse Crossings in the Area of Army Group A, 14 May 1940

at Dinant after three days and forced the Belgian troops to the north. On 13 May XV Army Corps, in which the two armoured divisions of the army had by then been concentrated, succeeded in forcing the difficult crossing of the river. The bridgeheads were held against fierce attacks by the French Ninth Army and soon extended.

At the same time Guderian's XIX Army Corps of Kleist's armoured group, the 'spearhead' of the German offensive wedge, had reached Sedan. Opposition by advanced French troops and by Belgian defending forces, as well as traffic congestion at the break-out from the Ardennes, only briefly delayed the corps. In the afternoon of 13 May, following massive Luftwaffe operations, the crossing of the Meuse was accomplished here too, albeit with heavy losses. By the evening of the following day the left bank of the river was firmly in German hands. Further to the north, at Monthermé, Reinhardt's XLI Army Corps had meanwhile gained the western side of the river. Thus, the breakthrough of the most difficult part of the Allied front had been accomplished. The hinterland was lying open for wide-scale operations.

While on the southern wing of Army Group A the Sixteenth Army was relieving Kleist's armoured group, which had been briefly held up, by providing flank cover towards the south—regarded as particularly important—Army High Command soon pulled I and XVI Corps out of the sector of Army Group B in order to exploit the success on the French sector of the front and to repulse any counter-attacks against the northern wing of Fourth Army, which by then had advanced far to the west. Following the subordination of Kleist's armoured group and the formation of a Hoth armoured group from XV and XVI Army Corps, nearly all the mobile troops were now gathered together. They were to push swiftly towards the west, starting on 18 May, between Arras and the Somme, and cut off and destroy the enemy now withdrawing further north in the face of Sixth Army. Infantry formations were always immediately brought up behind the motorized troops. Even more important than an early arrival at the Channel coast, in Hitler's eyes, was to ensure that the German advance did not suffer any local reverse anywhere, 'which might provide a fatal fillip not only to the military but mainly also to the political leaders of our enemies'.[9]

The Allies—such, at least, was the impression of the Germans—had still not clearly identified their enemies' deliberately camouflaged point of main effort. They were also wrong in their estimate of the time the Germans would need for crossing the Meuse. When on 13 May Gamelin visited the headquarters of the commander of the north-eastern front, General Georges, it seemed that he, as well as Army Group 1, still expected the main German attack on the north-eastern sector. Not until the evening of that day did the Allied command learn that further to the south the Germans were already west of the Meuse. General Huntziger (Second Army), however, did not succeed in mounting the immediately ordered counter-attack. By then the breakthrough, which was taking on an ever clearer outline, was no longer to be prevented either by the withdrawal of formations from the Maginot Line or

[9] Army Gp. A war diary West No. 2 (draft), 17 May 1940, BA-MA RH 19 I/37.

by a massive self-sacrificing employment of the Allied air force. Hurriedly Georges tried to insert a new Army headquarters under General Touchon (the subsequent Sixth Army) into the front and to establish a new line of defence north-east of Reims.

Holland's surrender had enabled the Germans to turn their Eighteenth Army against Antwerp, where it soon fought its way through the fortifications. By 18 May the city was in German hands; only the crossing of the Scheldt proved a protracted enterprise. The Allied Dyle position was similarly unable to hold up the German assault for long. The Germans had concentrated their efforts on the left wing of Sixth Army, and on 15 May had broken through to the west on the sector of the French First Army south of Brussels. Halder repeatedly intervened to prevent Fourth Army from getting too far to the north and bypassing the French frontier fortifications in the Valenciennes–Maubeuge area.

Not only Hitler but also Rundstedt and General Busch, the commander-in-chief of Sixteenth Army, continued to worry about a possible French attack against the southern flank. This was to lead to continuous tensions within the German command. The 'progressives' called for an immediate westward attack with armoured spearheads, while the safety-first concept of the 'old school' preferred to see all the divisions gathered on the western bank of the Meuse first and the infantry following up. Army High Command was in favour of not granting the enemy any respite and, at an early date, designated the lower Somme as the next objective for Army Group A. It still reserved for itself the decision on the further direction of the attack. First of all, bridgeheads were to be established across the Somme. Second Army was now inserted south of Fourth Army, while Twelfth Army took over the flank cover towards the south along a line Rethel–Laon–La Fère. Army Group A could count on further reinforcements, also from the sector of Army Group C.

In front of Army Group C the enemy fell back to the Maginot Line. Gamelin, while still not excluding the possibility of a German invasion of Switzerland, hurriedly transferred further formations to the north. But the massive attack on their southern flank, feared by the Germans, did not materialize. Only the French Second Army tried to break into the German front at Montmédy and Sedan.

On 15 May the Allied command performed a further regrouping. With freshly brought up forces it reinforced its Sixth Army to defend the Aisne, while on the Somme the pulled-back remnants of Seventh Army (General Frère) gradually took up position. Both armies were soon to be placed under the command of Army Group 3 (General Besson), which had until then been kept back on the Swiss frontier.

Ahead of this new line of defence, and also in Belgium, the situation had by now become very threatening to the Allies. Army Group 1 had been retreating to the Scheldt since 16 May. The French Ninth Army adjoining in the south—General Corap had been replaced by Giraud—was torn apart, with a 100-km. gap opening between its two sections, and the German armoured formations were now driving into it. Major reserves to close the gap were not available. The struggle for the Meuse was thus finally lost by the Allies.[10] Attempts by their air forces to attack the

---

[10] Gamelin, *Servir*, i. 342.

German river crossings merely brought them painful losses. A request by the French premier, Reynaud, for a stronger engagement of the Royal Air Force was turned down by the cabinet in London on 15 May. Only forces in excess of the 25 groups considered the minimum necessary for the defence of the British Isles could be transferred to France.[11] Churchill saw himself faced with the impossible task of, on the one hand, giving material and moral support to his ally and, on the other, having to strengthen the defence potential of his own country. In Paris the ministries started to burn their papers.

The Germans no longer needed to fear a counter-offensive. Yet the argument about strategy continued. Halder was already considering an early armoured thrust to the south-west across the Aisne, while Hitler, supported by Rundstedt, mistrusted his own luck and continued to worry about the southern flank. On 16 May, therefore, Rundstedt ordered a temporary halt for XLI and XIX Army Corps as soon as they had reached the Oise. Army High Command, less nervous, intervened by telephone: only the more exposed supply units were to wait for the arrival of the infantry formations; the tanks could roll on. At Saint-Quentin there was a quarrel between Kleist, who quoted Hitler as his authority, and Guderian, who wanted to press hard on the enemy's heels. Guderian was actually asking to be relieved of his command. Rundstedt approved List's compromise proposal that 'battle-worthy reconnaissance formations' might continue in the direction of the coast. Steadily, though not quite as quickly, the flank cover pushed forward to the Aisne.

In front of Army Group B the enemy had, in some areas, already withdrawn towards the lower Scheldt and begun to evacuate Belgium. The Belgian formations meanwhile formed the northern wing of Army Group 1 along a section of the Scheldt and along the Ghent–Terneuzen Canal. On 21 May they were ordered to withdraw to the Yser, where they were to cover Army Group 1 towards the east. This movement was executed by them only as far as the Lys, to avoid having to give up too much of their own territory. Ghent fell on 23 May.

Between Arras and Valenciennes, before the front of the German Fourth Army, British troops formed a barrier, from which an attack was to be mounted towards the south to cut off the German armoured spearheads from the infantry divisions which followed them. Simultaneously, French formations of Seventh Army were expected, in a northerly direction, to break through the not yet consolidated German flank cover. By means of a concentrated employment of the Luftwaffe the Germans prevented this threatening pincer attack. They succeeded in establishing isolated bridgeheads across the Somme and in generally forcing the enemy on to the defensive. The Allied thrust towards the south, limited though it was by a lack of forces, nevertheless had a considerable effect. On 21 May two British battalions succeeded south of Arras in penetrating the flank of Hoth's group, causing the Germans some anxiety. Fourth Army HQ and Army Group A HQ overrated the enemy's chances of exploiting this 'crisis of Arras', and on the evening of 23 May Rundstedt stopped the advance of Kleist's armoured group towards Boulogne and Calais. The French,

---

[11] Müller, *Entente Cordiale*, 5.

however, had been unable to get their formations ready in time, and the British were largely left to their own resources.[12]

Meanwhile, by an order of 18 May, effective from 20 May, a change took place in the Allied high command. General Weygand, whose name alone was expected to have an effect on morale, replaced Gamelin, who had resigned. Simultaneously the French ambassador to Spain, Marshal Pétain, was summoned to the government as vice-premier. The ministry of the interior was taken over by Mandel, known to champion a resolute conduct of the war. Daladier handed the defence ministry over to Premier Reynaud, with de Gaulle, promoted brigadier-general, supporting him in this additional function as under-secretary of state from 6 June.

As the danger of Army Group 1 being cut off had been taking on clearer outline Gamelin, as early as 19 May, had considered evacuation by sea.[13] The French admiralty considered such an operation to be virtually impossible, and instead recommended having the troops who were cut off supplied by the navy. The required shipping-space was quickly made available. The British, on the other hand, were beginning to make preparations for a rapid withdrawal across the Channel if the need should arise. This could not long be kept secret. It weakened morale and worsened relations between the French, Belgian, and British staffs.

On 20 May the German tanks, heedless of their rearward communications, were in Amiens and Abbeville. The sickle-cut movement was almost complete. Kleist's armoured formations now turned east against the ports of Bologne and Calais, threatening to cut off the Allied troops still holding out at Valenciennes from the coast, which was their only salvation. The planned breakthrough to the Somme—still recommended by Gamelin to the commander-in-chief of the north-eastern front on 19 May and more or less adopted by his successor (the 'Weygand Plan')—soon became illusory. The directives of the top political and military commanders struck the commanders in the field, whose operations by now were scarcely co-ordinated, as pure wishful thinking. Weygand had inherited a virtually hopeless situation and was soon to realize it. The withdrawal of further forces from the Maginot Line, which he ordered, was unable to save the situation. A break-out to the south-west was no longer possible for Army Group 1, weakened as it was by combat, forced into a desperate position, and cut off from its supply-lines—even less so after the British had abandoned Arras during the night of 23-4 May and after the line held by the Belgians had been penetrated. The British were the first to realize this. Lord Gort, having abandoned hope of a favourable issue of the battle in Flanders, regrouped his formations and decided in favour of a re-embarkation of the BEF which had been planned throughout the past week as a precautionary measure, and which for some of the rearward services had in fact begun.

The War Office for its part recommended the withdrawal on 26 May. That same evening it followed this up by a definite order. The situation of the BEF was seen

---

[12] Cf. Ellis, *War in France*, 87 ff.   [13] Müller, 'Dünkirchen', 135.

in London as so threatened that Lord Gort was even granted authority to surrender if necessary.[14]

The French high command was not immediately informed of the British intentions. New discussions between the Allies for a co-ordination of the withdrawal were conducted with opposite objectives. The British wanted to get to the coast in order to embark, while Weygand had ordered his own troops to form a bridgehead around Dunkirk and Calais and to hold it at all costs. Not until 28 May did the Allied commander-in-chief receive definite knowledge of the evacuation of the BEF. He was angered, even more than by the decision itself, by the furtiveness with which the British withdrawal had been prepared. Weygand felt he had been let down by a selfish ally, intent only on preserving his own interests. Following the Belgian surrender on the same day and the commencement of the embarkation by the British, all that was left to him was to order the evacuation of the bridgehead. However, the order was not issued until the morning of 29 May, so that in the event a disproportionately small number of French escaped from Dunkirk—which immediately triggered off a Franco-British controversy.

The deepening of the Franco-British conflict had first become obvious at the meeting of the Allied Supreme War Council on 25 May. Weygand described the hopeless military situation, and Pétain, referring to the slight degree of assistance, claimed the right to question the alliance as such. The agreement of 28 March 1940, which ruled out a separate peace by either partner, should, he believed, be revised. On 26 May, on a visit to London, Reynaud again stressed his difficult position *vis-à-vis* the champions of a conclusion of hostilities.

The precariousness of the enemy's position was certainly not fully appreciated by Hitler, who was not feeling very secure yet in his position as supreme war-lord. He was still worried about the southern flank. Army High Command's intention, in agreement with several commanders in the field, to turn sections of Army Group A around for a thrust to the west, in line with the old Schlieffen Plan,[15] to prevent the enemy from establishing a solid defensive front there, was not approved by Hitler. He was now—not for the first time in the western campaign—overrating the French army. To him it seemed advisable to concentrate all motorized formations in the area between Arras and Étaples and to wait for the infantry to close up behind them. He thereby created a pause which, contrary to Halder's intentions, divided the campaign in the west into two phases. He also prevented a swift operation towards the north-east by the mobile formations which had broken through: with parts of Army Group A as the 'hammer' and Army Group B as the 'anvil'.

Hitler's special concern was the state of the armoured forces, on which he had himself continually informed. His concern was shared by the commanders in the field, including Guderian. (For German tank losses during the campaign see

---

[14] Id., *Entente Cordiale*, 17.
[15] Fourth Army war diary, 21 May 1940, BA-MA W 6965a.

TABLE VI.v.2. *German Tank Losses, May–June 1940*

	10–20 May	21–31 May	1–10 June	11–30 June
Panzer I	41	101	28	12
Panzer II	45	150	32	14
Panzer III	26	84	16	9
Panzer IV	14	63	9	11
Panzer 35/38 (t)[a]	1	87		10
TOTAL[b]	127	485	85	56

[a] (t) = manufactured in Czechoslovakia.   [b] Grand total for the period = 753.

Source: OKW/WiRüAmt: Ten-day surveys 1939–41, BA-MA Wi/IF 5. 366.

Table VI.v.2.) On 23 May Kleist reported that more than half of his tanks were out of action: his formation had lost a lot of its fighting-power and would not be able to stand up to a major counter-attack.[16] Against Halder's wishes Army High Command issued an order in the evening, at the request of the commander-in-chief, that the defeat of the encircled enemy was to be effected by Army Group B. In line with its repeated requests, not only was Fourth Army placed under its command but so were all German forces north of a line Huy–Dinant–Philippeville–Le Cateau–Bapaume–Albert–Amiens. Army Group A had to hand over further formations, devote itself to covering the southern flank, and prepare for new tasks. Considerable anxiety was caused by the bridgeheads on the southern and western bank of the Somme. It was feared that it might not be possible to hold them against the enemy, who was now attacking in greater strength. The Germans did in fact have some difficulty in maintaining the Abbeville bridgehead against a massive attack by the French 4th Armoured Division under Brigadier-General de Gaulle.

The north-eastern front—this was a view shared also by Rundstedt—need no longer interest Army Group A. The fact that this sector of operations was regarded by the Germans, or at least by many of them, as finished was largely due to the apparently hopeless situation of the Allies. The commander-in-chief of Army Group 1, General Billotte, had lost his life in a road accident. His place was taken, four days later, by General Blanchard. Weygand was trying hurriedly to organize a new defensive front along the rivers Somme, Oise, and Aisne.

The Germans failed to exploit their favourable situation systematically. On 24 May Hitler visited Army Group A headquarters. He concurred with Rundstedt's view that it would be more useful to leave the further attack to the infantry and to halt and bring together the badly worn-out armoured forces. Besides, he wanted to save the latter for a further thrust to the west, and not have them incur losses fighting for localities or in unsuitable terrain. He wanted to leave the destruction of the cut-off enemy formations to the Luftwaffe, which—as Göring in his eagerness

[16] Fourth Army War Diary, 23 May 1940, BA-MA W 6965a.

for glory had suggested on 23 May, against the misgivings of several commanders—could tackle this task every bit as well. Hitler next saw to it that the 'unauthorized' reallocation of formations between the army groups was countermanded. The tanks were not allowed to cross the canal running via La Bassée–Béthune–Saint-Omer to Gravelines. Although Army High Command on 25 May[17] permitted the continuation of the attack, Rundstedt did not pass on this order because he regarded it as overtaken by events and because Hitler had given him a free hand. Besides, new consultations with the air force would have been necessary, and this would at least have cost time. Fourth Army was merely given permission to let Hoth's group attack in the direction of Lille. Hitler was convinced that the enemy would, even so, 'soon be softened up'.[18]

Not until 26 May, when the armoured formations had closed up, did the conviction gain ground among all concerned that only a further employment of the mobile forces could put an end to the 'patchwork' (Kluge) and bring the battle in north-eastern France to a sufficiently rapid conclusion. In the course of the day, when the enemy's withdrawal across the Channel became generally known, Hitler eventually authorized an advance by Kleist's armoured group, but only to the point where Dunkirk could be subjected to artillery fire.

From 27 May onwards a hail of shells and bombs came down on the port and town, without being able to prevent the embarkation of Allied, predominantly British, troops. The Luftwaffe, badly weakened by earlier operations, was unable to meet the demands made on it. It often took off from distant bases, sometimes situated in the Reich, found itself over Dunkirk without adequate fighter escort, and, frequently identified at an early stage by enemy radar, suffered considerable losses from squadrons of highly effective Spitfires, taking off from nearby southern England and employed in increasing numbers, as well as from concentrated AA artillery. Nevertheless, it inflicted major losses in personnel and especially in material on the Allied troops. Now and again, however, unfavourable weather conditions prevented any Luftwaffe intervention, quite apart from the fact that this had to be restricted to daylight hours anyway. At night embarkation could proceed virtually undisturbed. The Germans succeeded neither in totally destroying the harbour nor in interfering with troop withdrawals from the beach. In the sand of the dunes the effect of bombs on the less concentrated targets was slight. Moreover, the Luftwaffe called off its attacks on Dunkirk on 3 June and, for predominantly propagandist reasons, used all available forces to fly missions against the aircraft industry concentrated on the outskirts of Paris and against French ground services. Parts of the Luftwaffe had earlier been employed against Marseilles and against transport routes in the Rhône valley.

In these circumstances the Allied withdrawal, having been made an unexpected present of time for the improvement of defensive positions by the two-day halt of the German armour, was reduced to a transport problem, and this was mastered from

[17] Jacobsen, *Dünkirchen*, 100–1.
[18] Fourth Army war diary, 25 May 1940, BA-MA W 6965a.

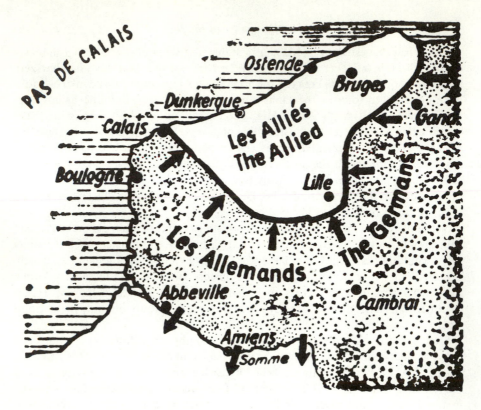

Camarades!

Telle est la situation!
En tout cas, la guerre est finie pour vous!
    Vos chefs vont s'enfuir par avion
A bas les armes!

British Soldiers!

Look at this map: it gives your true situation!
Your troops are entirely surrounded —
    stop fighting!
Put down your arms!

FIG. VI.v.i. German leaflet

the British Isles with astonishing organizational skill and improvisation, though at the cost of painful losses. The German air force, on the other hand, lost its 'aura of invincibility', even though it claimed Dunkirk as one of its successes.

For the number of Allied troops evacuated from the Dunkirk area see Table VI.V.3. Including the roughly 28,000 men evacuated before 27 May, a total of just under 370,000 Allied troops (139,000 of them French) succeeded in evading capture by the Germans.[19]

TABLE VI.V.3. *Evacuation of Allied Troops from the Dunkirk Area*

Date	From the beaches	From Dunkirk harbour	Total	Running total
27 May		7,669	7,669	7,669
28 May	5,930	11,874	17,804	25,473
29 May	13,752	33,558	47,310	72,783
30 May	29,512	24,311	53,823	126,606
31 May	22,942	45,072	68,014	194,620
1 June	17,348	47,081	64,429	259,049
2 June	6,695	19,561	26,256	285,305
3 June	1,870	24,876	26,746	312,051
4 June	622	25,553	26,175	338,266
TOTAL	98,671	239,555	338,226	338,266

Source: British Admiralty data; cf. Jacobsen, *Dünkirchen*, 182; Harris, *Dunkirk*, 151.

There has been much subsequent speculation about 'Hitler's halt order' outside Dunkirk. Did he, as Rundstedt claimed after the war in his own justification,[20] wish to spare the British and enable them to escape from the Continent painlessly? Did he wish to meet half-way those circles in Britain which, unlike Churchill, would have been ready to make peace with the Hitler regime? After all, Hitler had repeatedly stated—most recently on a visit to Army Group A headquarters—that he was seeking contact with Britain 'on the basis of a division of the world'.[21] Some currency was also given to an alleged remark by Hitler that he wanted to spare the British a 'humiliating defeat'.

[19] Liss, *Westfront*, 211.
[20] Rundstedt, 'Feldzug im Westen', 4; cf. also Blumentritt, 'Kritik', 28.
[21] Blumentritt, 'Westfeldzug', 63; Halder, *Diaries*, i. 413 ff. (21 May 1940).

TRANSLATION OF FIGURE VI.V.1.

Comrades!
This is the situation.
The war's over for you anyway.
    Your leaders will get away by air.
Lay down your arms!

It seems likely that a sharing of power with Britain appealed to Hitler no more than temporarily. The victory that was taking shape in the west, on a scale scarcely expected at the outset, soon provided fuel for new and even bolder ambitions. Perhaps Britain's heritage might be taken up in those parts of the world which seemed to Hitler suitable for an imperialist expansion of Germany or her partners. Britain at any rate would have been no more than a junior partner in any reallocation of spheres of influence.

That the victory over France was sufficient to make the British amenable to German ideas of a mutual 'adjustment of interests'[22] was a feeble hope and scarcely tallied with Hitler's assessment of the British national character. A long-term military weakening of the adversary, such as now seemed to offer itself, must, on the other hand, be welcome to Hitler with a view to forcing London to come to terms. At the same time he relied optimistically on the effectiveness of his air force, which had, in the course of the war to date, performed very impressively against ground targets. Neither it nor Army Group B had been ordered to spare the British.[23] Hitler was unlikely to want to lose the unique, indeed enormous, propaganda advantage that the annihilation of the BEF would have represented. However, the German armoured formations were to be saved as far as possible. They had new tasks awaiting them—in the next few weeks and perhaps again in the not too distant future.

At any rate, the events around Dunkirk revealed a Hitler who, supported by some commanders in the field, for the first time massively intervened in the conduct of operations through Army High Command, having previously been nervous at the pace of the German advance. Now he compelled Brauchitsch to rescind an order already given and ruined Halder's strategy—and in the end yet claimed credit for the overall success. The army command had to reconcile itself in the future to having a self-assured supreme commander of the armed forces, one who had no intention of exercising that office purely nominally. The propaganda, soon to be launched, about the inspired 'greatest general of all time', with the Wehrmacht contributing its share to Hitler's glorification,[24] was intended, despite errors in leadership, to make clear to the Germans the new allocation of roles.

On the morning of 27 May, therefore, the tanks too assembled for a by no means massive attack towards the east and north-east, and a few days later they were gradually pulled out again. No one, it seemed—such at least was Kluge's impression[25]—had any real further interest in Dunkirk. On 30 May Kleist's group was also permitted to attack the harbour town. But this made no difference to the 'patchwork'. The final battle in the pocket was poorly co-ordinated on the German side. Eighteenth Army was eventually ordered to liquidate the last resistance in Dunkirk. At Lille Sixth Army took approximately 35,000 prisoners from what was left

---

[22] Hitler in a conversation with Mussolini, 18 Mar. 1940, *Staatsmänner und Diplomaten*, i. 93, 102.

[23] Meier-Welcker, 'Entschluß', 286. Uhle-Wettler, *Höhe- und Wendepunkte*, 293, on the other hand, charges Hitler with lack of resolution, if not indifference.

[24] Cf. ObdH order of the day, 25 June 1940, in Messerschmidt, *Wehrmacht*, 251.

[25] Fourth Army war diary, 30 May 1940, BA-MA W 6965a.

of the French First Army. Around Dunkirk, eventually, more than 80,000 prisoners and a vast quantity of modern war material fell into German hands. According to initial French calculations, France had by that time lost at least 250,000 of her best troops (a total of 10 per cent), as well as 1,800 guns, 930 armoured vehicles, and, last but not least, the economically important northern French industrial region.[26] But the bulk of the British forces had escaped. Their losses amounted to roughly 68,000 men. They also lost more than 100 tanks, a large part of their artillery and vehicles, and considerable stores.[27]

On the evening of 27 May Sixth Army headquarters reported that the Belgians were requesting surrender negotiations. Further resistance on their part seemed pointless. Hitler decided that only unconditional surrender would be considered. On 28 May this was signed at Sixth Army headquarters.

Special attention had been paid throughout the campaign to an adequate supply organization. As the rail network of the territories to be occupied was expected to be wrecked, the armies had been assigned additional transport space. This made it possible to bridge the approximately 250 km. from the railheads to the front line. For these transports, as well as for the return of the empty trucks, certain roads had been designated 'supply arteries'. Sapper units and Todt Organization personnel immediately embarked on the repair of bridges, railway lines, and roads.

However, as the motorized troops were advancing faster than had been calculated, the Generalquartiermeister had to draw on all reserves and create points of main effort at the expense of Army Group B. But distances in excess of 350 km. could not be mastered in this manner. The situation in the area of Army Group B was greatly relieved by the fact that, along with the relatively low expenditure of ammunition, at least by the army, motor-fuel as well as foodstuffs and animal feed could in part be taken straight from the occupied country. German supply-bases were transferred to Holland and Belgium at an early date, trucks were requisitioned, repair workshops set up, and numerous skilled workers flown in from Germany.

By contrast, the spearheads of Army Group A had occasionally to be supplied by air. Rail-borne supplies initially got as far as Luxemburg. The next base was established at Mézières. But this was not sufficient for the rapid advance. Major bottlenecks were at first avoided only by skilful improvisation until the rich booty taken in northern France relieved the situation, and the supply organization in the rearward area, centred on Belgium, functioned properly. To replenish stores, civilian transport from the Reich territory had to be handed over to the Wehrmacht. Sea-borne supplies were still beyond the capabilities of the navy.

On 27 May Halder came to Charleville to discuss with the army group staffs the continuation of the campaign, 'Phase Red'. Army High Command meanwhile moved its quarters to Chimay. Regrouping of the formations, with two new army commands being inserted into the front, took some time. Mopping up of the Dunkirk pocket proved tedious. Only Fourth Army was able to halt at the line reached; it would

---

[26] Reynaud's address to the Senate Army Commission, 7 June 1940; German trans. of a captured French document, BA-MA RW 4/v. 310.   [27] Barker, *Dunkirk*, 224; Ellis, *War in France*, 327.

have preferred an earlier date of attack in order to extend the bridgeheads over the Somme.

The German plan of operations was based on the assumption that the enemy no longer possessed any major reserves and that the ratio of strength now stood at two to one in favour of the attacker. Brauchitsch reported to Hitler that the campaign was won already.[28] Therefore the improvised defensive front in the area of the Somme, the Oise, and the Aisne should be speedily overrun in order to prevent any kind of orderly retreat or the establishment of new defensive lines. To that end Army Group B, with Fourth Army, was to attack further towards the west, capture Le Havre and Rouen, cross the Seine, and wheel towards the south. With two of its armies, however, the main part of its effectives, it was to cross the Aisne in order to thrust towards the south in a second phase, and still bypassing Paris in the east. The plan to bypass Paris in the west with the bulk of the mobile forces, as intended by Army High Command, was first approved by Hitler and later rejected.[29] Adjoining in the east, Army Group A—as soon as its armour was operational again and French forces had (possibly) been pulled back because of the operations of Army Group B—was to break through to the south-east. In this way the enemy was to be encircled with the bulk of his forces still in eastern France, and the Maginot Line taken from the rear. At a later point Army Group C might then attack in the direction of Nancy and on the Upper Rhine. Eighteenth Army, meanwhile, being directly subordinated to Army High Command, had the task of securing Flanders and Artois. The Luftwaffe had orders to continue supporting the ground operations and to screen them against the west. On the strength of past experiences, however, flank cover need no longer be given so much attention. For the envisaged attack the number of operational tanks was increased (from 50 to 70 per cent), supplies were organized, and the communications network was improved.

Weygand, for his part, had used the short pause to reinforce his north-eastern front. At the cost of further weakening Army Group 2 in the Maginot Line, further armies were inserted into the battle front under Groups 3 and 4. At the same time, however, new defensive lines in the hinterland were already being considered in secret. Officially the Somme–Aisne position (the 'Weygand Line') was to be held at all costs, as was the eastern French fortification line, although some commanders had proposed that the latter should be given up. However, the French commander-in-chief had also informed his government that any further withdrawal would be tantamount to final defeat. All the army could then fight for was its honour, and it was up to the politicians to find a way out of the situation. In Weygand's view—and on this he was entirely at one with Pétain—France's entry into the war had been an irresponsible political decision.[30] But the army should be spared the ultimate sacrifice, as it was indispensable as a guarantor of internal order.

Reynaud, supported by Churchill, tried to counteract the pessimism among the generals. The British prime minister had gone to France again on 31 May; without

[28] Liss, *Westfront*, 212.   [29] Jodl, 'Tagebuch 1940', 431–2 (21 May 1940).
[30] Müller, *Entente Cordiale*, 19.

being able to convince his interlocutors, he declared his determination to continue the war even if the Germans succeeded in landing in England. Churchill's main objective, after the reverse in north-eastern France, was to gain time and to keep France on Britain's side at least with its colonial empire and with its fleet intact. He viewed the war on a global scale, he felt more strongly than the French military leaders the ideological conflict with Nazi Germany, and he relied on the economic strength of the British Empire and, ultimately also, the United States. Reynaud, sharing this point of view, was in favour of continuing the struggle, if necessary, from North Africa. The armistice terms to be expected from Germany would certainly not be acceptable. But there was no proof of that as yet, and no amount of Franco-British talks, nor the intensive exchange of notes, was able to prevent increasing French resentment, especially among military leaders, of their ally's behaviour and his inadequate military contribution. The majority thought in continental terms, and the lost battle in Flanders weighed more heavily with them than with those whom they regarded as the incurably selfish islanders. Pétain, already working for an armistice, denied the British any further right to be consulted in decisions concerning the future of France.

On the morning of 5 June Army Group B moved off as scheduled. Fourth Army immediately succeeded in extending the bridgeheads across the Somme. On the Aisne, however, there were difficulties. Weygand's recipe of defence in deep echelon seemed at first to work. It rendered effective Luftwaffe intervention against ground targets difficult. 'It looks as if we are stuck.'[31] Army Group B was already considering concentrating its armoured formations at a few crucial points. When the tanks eventually pushed forward, the infantry was prevented from following up by the numerous centres of resistance which had simply allowed the tanks to pass through. Nevertheless, plans were already being made by the Germans concerning how and when the operation might be turned towards the south-west and pushed forward into the heart of France.

Within a few days XV Corps had reached the lower Seine at Rouen, having split the French Tenth Army, some of whose parts, including British troops, had still been holding the Bresle and subsequently the Béthune Line. Towards the south, too, Army Group B had made important tactical penetrations into the French lines and thereby assumed the main burden in opening the second phase of the campaign; this made it possible for Army Groups A and C (with First Army) to be ordered to mount the attack. There was still no agreement on the general direction of the attack—Army High Command favoured the south-west, while Hitler and the High Command of the Armed Forces favoured the south-east. In any case, priority had first to be given to a tactical breakthrough along the entire front.

To this end—before Army Group C had completed its preparations—Army Group A attacked on 9 June. On the very first day it managed to cross the Aisne at several points, albeit with considerable losses. Following the tactical breakthrough there was soon the necessary space for major strategic movements in the direction of the

---

[31] Bock, 'Tagebuch-Notizen', iii. 47 (6 June 1940).

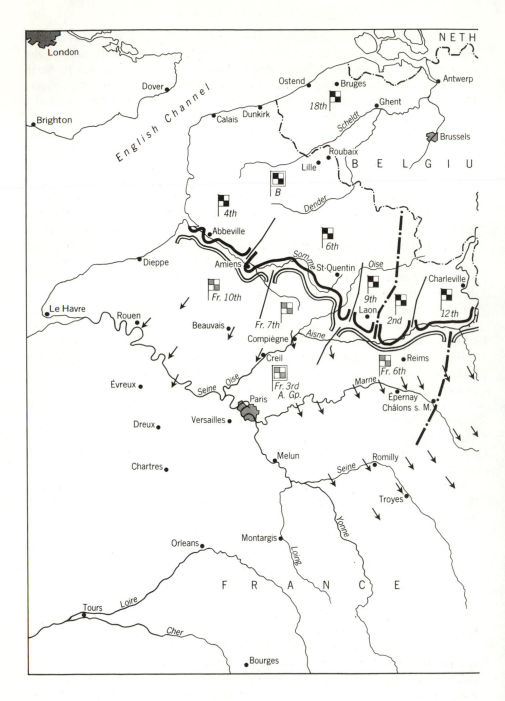

MAP VI.v.3. German-French Front Line for 'Operation Red': Situation on 5 June 1940, 05.00 hrs.

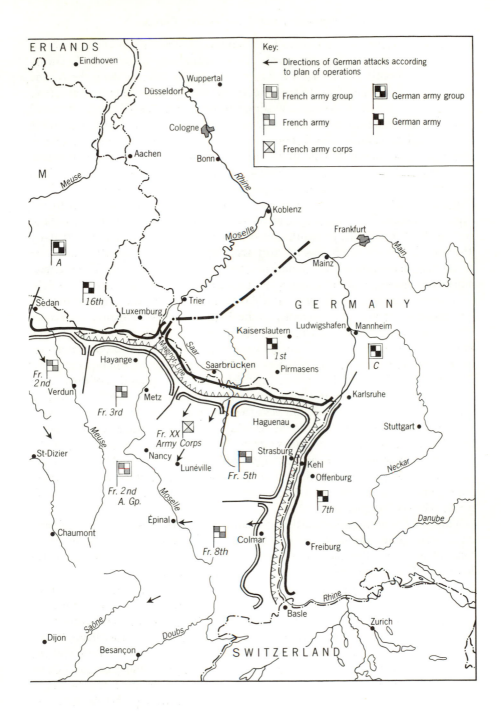

Key:

⟵ Directions of German attacks according to plan of operations

French army group

German army group

French army

German army

French army corps

Marne. Army High Command immediately reinforced this sector by creating a point of main effort with newly brought up reserves. It seemed doubtful whether the enemy was still in a position to maintain a continuous line of defence along the Marne from Alsace-Lorraine to Paris. In any case, it was the German operational objective to break through such a line and, by using mobile formations—Kleist's armoured group was retransferred from Army Group B to Army Group A and had orders to move via Dijon to the Swiss frontier—to bar the French forces in eastern France from moving westwards. Simultaneously, Eighteenth Army, again pulled forward, was committed against Paris. The French armies were still resisting fiercely. But the lines had been penetrated in many places and had begun to move. On 10 June Weygand found it necessary once more to point out to Premier Reynaud that it would not now take much to bring about the total disintegration of the army. Reynaud and the 'hard core' of the government soon considered a withdrawal into Brittany (the *réduit breton*), but this was by then scarcely feasible in military terms. The government and military headquarters had to withdraw to the Loire. The German ministry of foreign affairs was already 'perturbed by the idea that a situation might arise where France would be without a government in a position to negotiate'.[32]

Growing symptoms of distintegration in the French army led to increasing freedom of operation on the German side and vice versa. French combat strength diminished rapidly. The columns of French soldiers streaming away from the broken front and intermingling with millions of refugees and evacuees were continuous targets of the German air force, which, against a final self-sacrificing opposition of the French fighter force, was once more engaged in hard and costly combats. Clashes also occurred with Swiss air-defence forces in the frontier area. German air supremacy was at times lost. But superiority in the air was preserved and enabled the Luftwaffe, by missions against northern and western French ports, to interfere with the embarkation of troops. Attacks against targets on the roads, with bombs and machine-gun fire, caused panic and resulted in heavy losses also among the fleeing civilian population. Although this may not have been intended by the Luftwaffe command, it was accepted as a necessity.

While the Germans swiftly reached the Marne Line, the French high command on 11 June prepared, as far as possible, for an orderly disengagement of its formations towards the south-west in order to prevent the bulk of the forces still in eastern France from being encircled there. Attacks from the Argonne against Guderian's armoured group, which was first committed against Verdun and then against Langres, no more than temporarily slowed down the German main push towards the south and south-west. Weygand had Paris declared an 'open city'.

Churchill was still trying to stiffen French resistance. On the other hand, he did not wish to promise the intensified employment of the Royal Air Force that the French had always demanded. The French military leaders, Weygand and Pétain, believed that after the German breakthrough on the Somme line a request for an armistice was unavoidable. The French domestic controversy on this issue was

---

[32] Halder, *Diaries*, i. 457 (11 June 1940)

moving towards its climax. Churchill again intervened in the discussion when on 11 June he came to a conference at Briare near Orleans. Prior to that he had sent a telegram to Roosevelt—whom Reynaud had also repeatedly asked for assistance, and indeed urged to enter the war—requesting him to use his influence with the French. No decision was taken at that conference. Churchill insisted that, prior to a French cabinet decision, he should once more be consulted. What he was most concerned about was the fate of the French navy; if it fell into the hands of the Axis Britain's chances of survival could be greatly jeopardized.

Developments in France moved faster than Churchill expected. The position of Reynaud, who tried to postpone a final decision, was becoming weaker all the time. He once more asked the British prime minister to come to France for talks. However, the final meeting of the Supreme Allied War Council in Tours on 13 June still brought no decision. A rupture occurred within the French cabinet, where Pétain now, in the language of an ultimatum, insisted on the conclusion of an armistice. Roosevelt's reply to Reynaud's request for assistance was not exactly a rejection, but neither did it go far enough to heal the breach in the French government. Its value was further diminished by Roosevelt's refusal to have the text of his reply published. In Bordeaux, the last refuge of the French government, Reynaud made preparations for a withdrawal to North Africa and dispatched his under-secretary of state de Gaulle to London for appropriate negotiations. His attempt to get Weygand to agree to a military surrender in the metropolis that would leave the government a free hand in France's colonies failed in the face of the commander-in-chief's opposition. And within the cabinet the view was gaining ground that an enquiry should first be made as to the German terms and that any decision could be taken later. Reynaud succeeded in winning a short postponement of this *démarche* in order to seek British approval, while making clear to the British that a refusal on their part must result in his resignation. London's reply on 16 June was on the hoped-for lines—except that it contained the condition that the French navy be moved to British ports prior to an armistice with Germany. Shortly afterwards, influenced by de Gaulle, Churchill withdrew his approval and made a new proposal,[33] for a political union of the two countries. This would have served British interests even better, by securing the French navy and the continuation of the war effort from France's colonies.

The armistice party in the French cabinet was not impressed by the proposal for political union. It believed that Britain too was at the end of her strength. Reynaud resigned—in the hope, which was shared by Britain, that the humiliating German armistice terms would soon bring him back to power again.

Meanwhile the German advance continued. On 14 June Army Group C ordered First Army to attack on both sides of Saarbrücken (Operation 'Tiger'). The troops made good progress in the forefield of the Maginot Line. The French had for the most part retreated. Only rearguards were still slowing down the German advance.

---

[33] De Gaulle, *Call to Honour*, i. 80 ff.

While Fourth Army was already setting its sights on a thrust to the Loire, having encircled and taken prisoner major enemy forces west of Béthune, troops of Eighteenth Army entered Paris. In the late afternoon of 13 June Eighteenth Army headquarters in a signal to Paris police headquarters had announced the dispatch of a negotiator under a flag of truce. However, as he approached the French lines he found himself under fire and had to turn back. General von Küchler therefore demanded in an ultimatum the dispatch of a French negotiator, who in fact arrived the following morning and gave assurances that the city would be evacuated by French troops. At midday Bock and Küchler reviewed a march-past of German units at the Arc de Triomphe. It was less spectacular than Hitler would have wished from the point of view of foreign policy.[34]

On 15 June French resistance was finally broken. The crossing of the Upper Rhine by Seventh Army could probably have been dispensed with. However, the conquest—as distinct from a mere occupation—of Alsace, Lorraine, and 'the ancient German land of Burgundy'[35] was also of political importance, quite apart from the prestige associated with it. In eastern France Army Group C, which for this purpose had Sixteenth Army and tactically also Guderian's armoured group placed under its command, succeeded in encircling numerous enemy formations. Capture of individual fortifications of the Maginot Line became unnecessary. Hitler already ordered the reorganization of the German army, considering that the main burden in the elimination of Britain, should it become necessary, would be borne by the air force and the navy. The only task remaining for the land forces in France was to consolidate their success by a rapid pursuit of the enemy.

In military terms the Germans had no problems left in France. Guderian had reached the Swiss frontier. The isolated French troops, after bitter opposition, were taken prisoner or escaped to Switzerland for internment. Further west the Loire had been crossed in places by formations of Army Group B. After 17 June there were no longer any solid front lines of major extent left, and no orderly French resistance worth mentioning. The British withdrew their last troops from the Continent, taking with them nearly 30,000 Poles and Czechoslovaks. General Brooke as commander-in-chief of what remained of the BEF (over 140,000 men) had not been subject to any French command since 15 June.

Churchill, however, was not prepared simply to release Britain's erstwhile ally from her obligations under the alliance. French assurances did not satisfy him. Even within the French leadership there was still a dispute over whether a move to North Africa might not provide a greater latitude for action. But Pétain categorically rejected the idea.

The final German army thrusts were motivated by political considerations: taking possession of the 'ancient imperial territories' as far as the Verdun–Toul–Belfort line,[36] as well as the Channel and Atlantic coasts—apart from the city of Bordeaux,

---

[34] Halder, *Diaries*, i. 464 (13 June 1940).
[35] Order of the Day of OB H.Gr. C., 23 June 1940, BA-MA RH 19 III/7.
[36] Hitler's order to the Wehrmacht, 17 June 1940, BA-MA W 3654e.

to which the French government had withdrawn—and an advance to Lyons and into the Rhône valley in order to offer the Italians an easier military success in the Alps. To this end a 'Lyons group' was put together, which on 23 June, without taking any risks and at a more leisurely pace than Rome would have liked, advanced further to the south and the south-east. The coming into effect of the armistice two days later saved the Germans from what would undoubtedly have been difficult military operations in the mountains. The rest of the German troops had halted at the proposed demarcation-line between occupied and unoccupied France. Regrouping of formations began at once. Army Group A, now joined by Sixth Army, turned to face England, while Army Group B initially received the 'inglorious task of occupation';[37] presently, however, it was relieved by Army Group C and moved to the east. The British Channel Islands, finally, changed hands without any fighting at the end of June.

From the second half of June onward the Luftwaffe operated on an increased scale against the not yet occupied French ports, and increasingly also against the British Isles. It was allowed scarcely a breathing-space. The fact that it was soon, with weakened forces, to face the British air force, which had partly been held in reserve, was bound to have some effect on the outcome of the 'Battle of Britain'.

The agencies of military administration had followed the fighting forces to the west. Kommandanturen gradually assumed administration at provincial, *département*, and district level. They were soon placed under the command of newly appointed military commanders, though these remained in office for a short time only: Colonel-General Blaskowitz as military commander in France, responsible at first only for six eastern *départements*, and General von Vollard-Bockelberg as military commander in Paris.

The Germans had been prepared since the middle of the month for a French government request for an armistice, such as the new premier Pétain announced on 17 June. Following the receipt in Berlin, through the mediation of the Spanish government, of a French request for information on Germany's terms not for an armistice but for peace, the High Command of the Armed Forces on 20 June invited the Pétain government to send a delegation with powers to negotiate to the German lines at the bridge over the Loire at Tours. Its arrival was delayed. Not until the afternoon of 21 June did talks begin at Rethondes near Compiègne; Hitler chose this place of negotiation in order to make it clear to the vanquished that the results of the First World War were about to be reversed. The setting for this revenge was to be the saloon car in which Marshal Foch in 1918 had informed a German delegation of the Allies' terms for an armistice. A few weeks after the meeting of 1940 the railway carriage was taken to Germany as booty and the French memorial site, except for the monument to Foch, was destroyed.[38]

---

[37] Bock, 'Tagebuch-Notizen', iii. 69 (26 June 1940).
[38] Signal from AOK 16/A.Pi.F. to XXXII Army Corps, 14 July 1940, BA-MA 11301/2.

TABLE VI.V.4. *German Losses of Personnel 1939–1940*

	1st part of war in west 1 Sept. 1939–9 May 1940		2nd part of war in west 10 May–31 Aug. 1940		Total losses in 1st year of war (all theatres) 1 Sept. 1939–31 Aug. 1940	
	No.	Officers	No.	Officers	No.	Officers
Army						
Killed	1,139	49	26,972	1,253	36,752	1,709
Wounded	2,550	62	113,152	3,440	143,791	4,080
Missing	293	11	13,307	288	19,476	380
TOTAL	3,982	122	153,431	4,981	200,019	6,169
Navy						
Killed	1,612	90	453	15	2,856	152
Wounded	431	18	272	11	1,115	43
Missing	2,374	135[a]	326	17[b]	3,406	177
TOTAL	4,417	243	1,051	43	7,377	372
Air force						
Killed	847	176	2,668	386	4,016	650
Wounded	353	70	4,191	441	5,047	596
Missing	363	84	2,923	638	3,750	777
TOTAL	1,563	330	9,782	1,465	12,813	2,023
Wehrmacht total						
Killed	3,598	315	30,093	1,654	43,624	2,511
Wounded	3,334	150	117,615	3,892	149,953	4,719
Missing	3,030	230	16,556	943	26,632	1,334
TOTAL	9,962	695	16,264	6,489	220,209	8,564

[a] Of these 360 (36 officers) were taken POW; 1,097 (31 officers) interned; and 917 (68 officers) presumed drowned.

[b] Of these 69 (7 officers) were taken POW; 257 (10 officers) presumed drowned.

Source: OKW/WFSt/Abt I, No. 3340/40 g. (I M²), 9 Sept. 1940—German casualties during the first year of the war, 1 Sept. 1939 to 31 Aug. 1940, BA-MA RW 4/v. 170.

Table VI.V.4 gives the total German losses of personnel during the first year of the war.

4. ITALY'S ENTRY INTO THE WAR

In spite of a generally good personal rapport between the two dictators, German–Italian relations, even after the signing of the 'pact of steel' of 22 May 1939, had never been free from mental reservations on both sides.[39] The Italians were by no means happy that the Reich, without prior consultation, concluded a pact with the

[23] Schreiber, *Revisionismus*; cf. also vol. i of the present work, IV.VI.4.

Soviet Union. They regarded this and other unilateral steps by Germany as offending against the spirit of the alliance.[40] Italy, on the grounds of earlier German statements as well as Keitel's talks with the Italian chief of the general staff Pariani in April 1939, had counted on a longer period of peace and felt she had been bypassed by the German attack on Poland. Italy's attitude had disappointed Hitler. Her non-belligerent status, though highly advantageous to Germany and implying at least benevolent neutrality, fell short of Hitler's expectations. Moreover, the Allied governments had been informed about it at an early date. Italy's deliberately exorbitant requests to Germany for supplies of raw materials and armaments had not been fulfillable. Rome's contacts with Germany's adversaries, Ciano's unwelcome plans for the establishment of a Balkan bloc, information on German aggressive intentions leaked to Belgium from the Italian ministry of foreign affairs and discovered by Berlin—all these fuelled Hitler's mistrust. By the end of 1939 the German–Italian alliance had reached a low point. For a time Italy reinforced its frontier security in the north, where the still unsettled South Tyrol issue gave rise to German–Italian tensions.

The greatest interest in Italy's entry into the war had originally been shown by the German naval warfare command.[41] It expected Italy to tie down the enemy in the Mediterranean, thereby facilitating what Germany considered the decisive battle in the Atlantic. But this interest soon diminished. After months of vainly attempting to bring about camouflaged co-operation in the employment of German U-boats in the Mediterranean, Italy was regarded as an unreliable ally who would not, for the time being, support Germany.[42] Hitler did not yet share this negative estimate of his ally. At least he believed he could trust the Duce, though the latter seemed to vacillate between his preferred role of war-lord and the unheroic role, scarcely compatible with the nature of Fascism, of peace mediator. At times, under the influence of the anti-German, neutrality-minded minister of foreign affairs, Count Ciano, Mussolini's realization of his own military weakness and his irritation at the Germans seemed to gain the upper hand. But fundamentally Mussolini was determined to go to war. The only question was the choice of a favourable moment, when the greatest possible success might be achieved in return for a slight commitment of his own forces. Renewed German–Italian trade agreements, a conversation between General Roatta and the German military attaché, a visit by Ribbentrop to Rome and Hitler's talks with Mussolini on the Brenner on 18 March 1940 gave new buoyancy to the alliance. In May, at Germany's request, a new ambassador was appointed to Berlin to replace Attolico.

At the meeting on the Brenner—the last time the two dictators had met was towards the end of August 1938—Hitler assured Mussolini that he did not wish to influence his decision in any way.[43] He tried, however, to impress him with the warning that

[40] Siebert, *Italiens Weg*, 278; letter by Ambassador von Mackensen to State Secretary von Weizsäcker, 29 Aug. 1939, *DGFP* D vii, No. 438.

[41] Salewski, *Seekriegsleitung*, i. 128.

[42] Siebert, *Italiens Weg*, 302; Schreiber, *Revisionismus*, 271 ff.

[43] *Staatsmänner und Diplomaten*, i. 87-106.

mere neutrality would not help Italy overcome its status of a second-rate Mediterranean power. Germany needed a 'great partner'. When precisely Mussolini wished to participate in the conflict was entirely up to him. In view of Italy's inadequate military preparations Hitler suggested a deferred date, the moment when the outcome had already been decided and the Western powers would merely have to be dealt the final crushing blow. This Mussolini was prepared to agree to for the sake of Italy's 'honour' and interests, and also because he found himself under economic pressure from Britain's blockade and from unsatisfactory trade negotiations. The Allied attack in North Africa, which he had earlier feared, seemed hardly likely once Germany launched her attack in the west. Nevertheless, a period of three to four months for preparations seemed to him to be indispensable. Hitler, for his part, avoided being committed to a timetable. He proposed to his partner a participation, with some 20 divisions, in an attack across the Upper Rhine in the direction of the Burgundian Gate and the Rhône valley as soon as the German military success in northern France was a fact; an offensive on the Italo-French Alpine frontier would scarcely be profitable. The High Command of the Armed Forces, on the other hand, believed that an Italian attack towards the Suez Canal might be useful.[44]

Hitler's purpose was that German–Italian talks at the highest military level should now clarify all outstanding questions.[45] The High Command of the Armed Forces, however, charged with these negotiations, could afford to take them at a leisurely pace. It was not allowed to divulge Germany's offensive plans against northern and western Europe, nor was it to tackle the thorny problem of a joint high command. An Italian move towards the Balkans was undesirable from the German point of view. Italy's task was to tie down the maximum number of enemy forces in the Mediterranean area and to disrupt British and French sea communications. That was to apply even if Italy did not send any troops to the Upper Rhine front. Italy was also expected to operate vigorously on the Alpine front and to land in Corsica, although, according to German information, the Italians had no intention of doing so.[46] In point of fact, a secret memorandum of Mussolini's, dated 31 March 1940, envisaged an offensive on the Alpine front only in the event that France was already defeated by Germany. Otherwise the Italian forces were to adopt a defensive stance, both there and with regard to Corsica, as well as in the Aegean and North Africa. Any offensive operations in an Italian 'parallel war', apart from the war at sea, would be a possibility only in East Africa and, just possibly, in the Balkans.[47] The general staffs of the separate services were to prepare appropriate plans.

The joint project suggested by Hitler failed in the face of Mussolini's idea of an independent Italian 'parallel war'. A new German offer of 10 April remained unanswered;[48] in consequence the German command saw even less reason to

---

[44] OKW 494/40 g.Kdos. WFA/Abt. L—Ausl/Abw, 21 Mar. 1940: The military-political situation in the Middle East (copy), BA-MA RW 4/v. 35.

[45] The Führer and supreme commander of the Wehrmacht No. 22140/40 g.Kdos. Chefs., 4 Apr. 1940, BA-MA Case 1203.

[46] Halder, *Diaries*, i. 340 ff. (4 May 1940).

[47] Siebert, *Italiens Weg*, 426-7.   [48] Rintelen, *Zusammenarbeit*, 17.

inform its Italian ally of its own intentions. An attack across the Upper Rhine did not absolutely require Italian participation.[49]

Mussolini realized perfectly well that his country could not survive a prolonged war. The Italian army consisted of 73 divisions—51 of them in the mother country, 5 in Albania, 14 in Libya, 2 in east Africa, and 1 in the Aegean—each comprising 2 infantry regiments and 3 artillery groups. There was a shortage of well-trained officers and non-commissioned officers, and equipment was as inadequate as it was outdated. There was a lack of substantial stores and of armour-piercing weapons, anti-aircraft guns, and heavy tanks.[50] Motorization too was inadequate, and the artillery, in consequence, lacked mobility.

The following list shows the distribution of Italian army formations on the eve of Italy's entry into the war.

Western Alpine frontier	Army Group West: First and Fourth Armies with altogether 6 army corps, as well as a few divisions and further reserves
Italy's eastern frontier	Army Group East: Second Army, Po Army, Eighth Army (being raised) with altogether 7 army corps and some smaller formations
Central and southern Italy	Army Group South: Third Army and a few large formations, together of the strength of 3 army corps
Albania	1 army corps
Aegean	1 division
North Africa	Fifth Army (Tripolitania) and Tenth Army (Cyrenaica) with 5 army corps, 2 Libyan divisions, and lesser formations
East Africa	2 divisions, 29 colonial brigades, and a few native units

Of the 73 divisions, only 19 could be described as 'ready', 34 were regarded as 'operational though not ready' (possessing the scheduled equipment but only 75 per cent of their personnel), and 20 divisions had to be classified as 'scarcely operational'. These still had gaps in their armament, and had only half of the necessary vehicles and draught animals, and merely 60 per cent of their personnel. The numerically impressive Italian navy—with 6 battleships and over 100 submarines—was only partially operational. It lacked fuel, as did the air force with its approximately 1,800 planes, only a third of which, however, were operational. Supplies of further armaments and of urgently needed raw materials could now, at best, come from Germany—which, from the German point of view, meant an additional strain on rather than an alleviation of Germany's own military operations.[51]

---

[49] Halder, *Diaries*, i. 411 ff. (21 May 1940).
[50] Pieri, 'Stratégie italienne', 65; *Esercito italiano: Immagini*, pp. xxix–xxx.
[51] Hillgruber, *Strategie*, 129.

These generally known weaknesses were glossed over in the official statements of the Italian armed forces. It was, above all, Mussolini who wanted Italy to get into the war; he had enviously watched Germany and the Soviet Union extend their territories. He believed that he need not consider either the mood among the population nor the sceptical views of his military advisers, one of whom, Marshal Badoglio, chief of the armed forces general staff, as late as 18 May 1940 caused Gamelin, a friend of his, to be informed that France need not fear any Italian intervention.[52]

Impressed by the German successes in the west and afraid that he might be left out in the new share-out of Europe—he wished to be an equal partner at the negotiating table—Mussolini decided on 26 May to enter the conflict. Perhaps he also wanted to prevent the Germans from advancing as far as the French Mediterranean coast. His intervention, after all, was to help Italy break out from its confinement to the central part of the Mediterranean. He was no longer to be talked out of his intention by appeals either from the Pope or from the American president, or by generous offers of territorial compensation from Paris and London. France's military situation was hopeless, and likewise that of Britain seemed to Mussolini now so precarious that Italy would effortlessly inherit Britain's position in the Mediterranean. King Victor Emmanuel III shared this assessment of the situation. He did not renounce the nominal supreme command of his armed forces, and merely charged the Duce with the conduct of the war.

On 30 May Mussolini informed Hitler that Italy would probably enter the war on 5 June. The German dictator, however, was not by then interested in such a move; he was afraid he might have to let Mussolini have access to his own planning for 'Operation Red'.[53] He recommended a postponement, justifying his request by his intention of first dealing a devastating blow to the French air force: an Italian declaration of war might cause the latter's disposition to be changed. Mussolini therefore decided on entering the war on 11 June. Hitler for a while considered the employment of German mountain troops on the Alpine front.[54] He thought that Italy had operations planned against Malta, Corsica, and Tunisia, which could no longer be delayed. The Italian move evoked many a sarcastic comment among the Germans, not excluding Hitler. Italian non-belligerence would now have been preferable,[55] especially as it soon emerged that the Italian forces had made no preparations whatever for any offensive. Only the navy seemed capable of going into action straight away. The submarines were permitted to operate against French naval forces.

In order to be able to make a show of major military actions, Mussolini ordered an attack on the Alpine front. There, in accordance with orders, the Italian Army Group West, commanded by Crown Prince Umberto, with the Po Army now deploying behind it, had been prepared with its 22 divisions for defence. Facing it was the French Alpine Army under General Olry, weakened by the troops detached

---

[52] Azeau, *Guerre franco-italienne*, 35.
[53] Halder, *Diaries*, i. 435 (1 June 1940).   [54] Ibid. i. 439 (4 June 1940).
[55] Cf. Naval Warfare Command war diary No. 1, pt. A, 18 May 1940, BA-MA RM 7/12.

from it for the north-eastern front; its barely 200,000 men represented only two-thirds of the Italian strength.[56] On 16 and 17 June orders were received by Army Group West to the effect that, in addition to previously ordered local operations, it was to prepare within ten days—the date being subsequently advanced to 23 June—for an offensive operation with Marseilles as its final objective. The news of French efforts for an armistice with the Germans, however, induced the Italian command to order its western armies, without giving them time for regrouping, to move off, if possible, on the following morning. In these circumstances no systematic operation and none of the hoped-for territorial gains were possible.

Thus, while the Germans and French were already negotiating with each other, the Italian command had to confine itself to a few attacks which—in rainy weather and hence without appreciable air support, and moreover in the snow-covered mountains—did not yield much profit. The Germans, having occupied Lyons, had to be asked to execute the relief attack they had offered to make towards Grenoble. Neither were the Italian troops able to break into the French fortified line nor did an attempted flanking move at the Little St Bernard Pass get beyond its initial phase. The Italians' sole success was the capture of Menton, the township on the Riviera, which did not earn the Italian command much glory. Spectacular actions were confined to Italy's enemies: the French navy shelled Genoa and Savona, and the Royal Air Force made a raid on Turin. The sinking of a British cruiser and a few submarines by the Italian navy, and air raids on targets in southern France, Corsica, and North Africa, were not enough to offset that loss of prestige. In vain did Mussolini try to delay the conclusion of an armistice in order first to capture Nice.

At the Italo-French armistice talks in Rome on 24 June the Italian position was accordingly weak. Hitler had not agreed to joint negotiations by the Axis powers, and the French did not regard themselves as vanquished by the Italians.[57]

It was not German pressure but a realization of his own weakness and dependence that induced Mussolini[58] to conform to Hitler's calculations and not to jeopardize the latter's plans by an intransigent attitude. Hitler was anxious, by means of moderate armistice terms, to make it easy for France to get out of the war, lest Britain should be strengthened by her former ally's fleet and colonial empire and thus encouraged to continue fighting.[59] Mussolini therefore had no choice but to postpone his demands on France until what he thought was an imminent general peace settlement. His ambitions were in fact very extensive: annexation of Nice, Corsica, Tunisia, Malta, Corfu, British and French Somaliland, Aden, and the Sinai peninsula, not to mention parts of Algeria, Morocco, the Sudan, and French Equatorial Africa, and the inclusion of the Near East in Italy's sphere of influence.[60] He was, however, reasonable enough to forgo, for the time being, an occupation of the left bank of the Rhône and of a land-link with Spain, as well as Corsica and Jibuti, and

[56] *Battaglia delle Alpi*, 38-9.　　　　[57] Michel, 'Relations franco-italiennes', 487.

[58] Catalano, 'Économie de guerre', 118.

[59] Conversation between Hitler and Mussolini in a wider circle, 18 June 1940, in *Staatsmänner und Diplomaten*, i. 139 ff.

[60] Hillgruber, *Strategie*, 130-1.

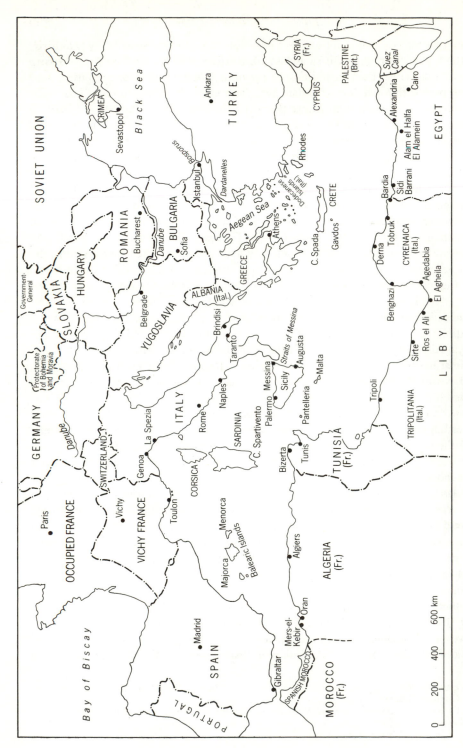

MAP VI.v.4. The Mediterranean Area, 1940

naval bases in Algeria, Morocco, and Tunisia. In Tunisia, as in Algeria and French West and Equatorial Africa, he contented himself with a demilitarization of the area adjoining Libya. He also abandoned his original claim for a total disarmament of all French fighting forces. Badoglio, as the Italian negotiator, did not even insist on the handing over of his *émigré* compatriots (an analogous demand had been successfully made by the Germans). On all other points the armistice agreements were similar, apart from the lesser extent of the occupied territory demanded by Italy and the provisional renunciation of occupation costs. By the time the High Command of the Armed Forces took up an earlier suggestion that the Italian zone of occupation be extended to the whole of Savoy as far as the German-occupied area, in order to separate truncated France from Switzerland, the agreement had already been signed.[61] German counter-intelligence was therefore ordered to mount a commando raid to disrupt rail communications between the two countries on a long-term basis. The operation, executed by Belgian agents, resulted only in the blowing up of one viaduct.

The Italian zone of occupation—832 km.^{2} in extent, with 28,500 inhabitants, Menton being the only town of any size—was confined to those areas, up to 15 km. deep, which lay east of the line reached by the Italian troops. To the west of it lay a strip of territory, equally deep in parts, whose lines of communications the Italian army was entitled to use for supplying its bases. A demilitarized zone of 50 km. depth protected the Italian zone of occupation, in which they soon introduced a number of measures which amounted to *de facto* annexation and immediately produced French protests.

For the implementation of the armistice treaty Italy, on the same lines as Germany, established a special commission with its seat in Turin. The French government sent a delegation there which, in view of the special importance of naval questions to Italo-French relations, was headed by an admiral.

Italian supervisory rights with regard to the French fighting forces extended to the area east of the Rhône and south of the Lyons–Geneva line, as well as to all French possessions in the Mediterranean region, including the big ports of southern France. The armaments industry was to be jointly supervised by Germans and Italians. To that end a special Italian controlling authority was set up in Grenoble. This supplemented the close network of twelve commissions which, under managements in Marseilles and Valence, as well as a president at Gap (later in Nice), ensured strict observance of the treaty stipulations.

Subsequently Mussolini turned to other regions to accomplish Italy's rise to world-power status. Egypt and especially the Balkans again seemed to him to be rewarding objectives. But he did not lose sight of France. He never gave up his plan to occupy Corsica. He was merely waiting for a suitable occasion. Moreover, he offered Hitler a participation by Italian forces in the invasion of Britain. Hitler accepted only submarines for the base at Bordeaux and one air corps for the Channel coast. He also tried to dissuade his partner from any move towards the Balkans, and instead

---

[61] Rintelen, *Zusammenarbeit*, 23.

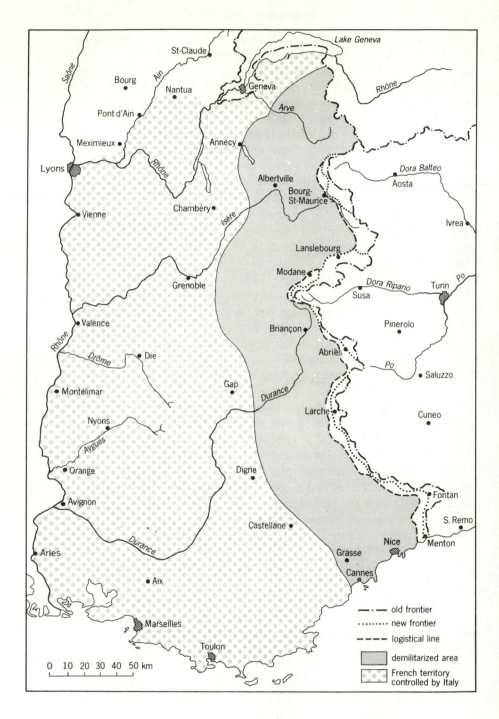

Map VI.v.5. South-eastern France after the Italo-French Armistice, 24 June 1940

urged him to conduct vigorous operations in Libya. But this required protracted preparations. The only success scored by Italy was in East Africa with the occupation of British Somaliland during the first half of August.

As for the realization of his territorial ambitions, Hitler persuaded his Axis partner to wait for the peace settlement. Mussolini's demands, extravagant measured against Italy's successes, threatened seriously to restrict Hitler's freedom of action in foreign policy. For a short time it even seemed that there might be some Italian-French collaboration: this was aimed at by Badoglio but at once rejected by Mussolini. On 7 July 1940 the Vichy government declared its agreement to the establishment of an Italian air force base at Oran, whereas a week later it emphatically refused a German application for airfields in Morocco. The Oran project did not materialize. But the Germans gained the impression that Italy was 'only very hesitantly' approaching the implementation of the armistice terms.[62]

The power-ratio in the Mediterranean had scarcely been changed by Italy's entry into the war.[63] Britain again consolidated her position in the Mediterranean and subsequently strengthened it further. The Italian armed forces had not succeeded in developing the area allowed them by their German ally into a basis for Italy's hoped-for hegemony. Hitler still inclined to dispense with any engagement in that region—out of consideration for Mussolini and so as not to provoke any secession of the French colonial empire from the unstable government in Vichy.

5. THE GERMAN–FRENCH ARMISTICE

Total victory over France with a costly occupation of the whole country was not in Hitler's interest. It might all too easily have resulted in the government's flight to its colonial possessions or to Britain and rendered even more illusory Hitler's hopes of concluding a general peace in western Europe. His main concern was over the French navy, whose scuttling he would not have greatly minded. If, he calculated, there was any chance of convincing Britain of the 'hopelessness' of continuing the war, Britain had to be prevented at all cost from effecting a lasting improvement to her military, strategic, and economic position by acquiring the navy and overseas possessions of an ally confronted with unacceptable armistice terms. That was why, even before the start of German-French negotiations, Hitler had a meeting with Mussolini in order to win him over for his tactical moves.[64] Hitler was interested in allowing France to keep a government with which German demands could be negotiated. These demands were designed to prevent France from resuming the struggle; they were, however, to be sufficiently lenient to suggest to the enemy an arrangement with Germany. At the same time, the victor wanted to keep all his options open—for political changes in western Europe and, if necessary, for the continuation of the war against Britain. In this respect Hitler's ideas were more moderate than those of the military staffs, some of whom came up with excessive demands.

---

[62] Deutsche Waffenstillstandskommission/Chefgruppe Ia No. 3/40 g.Kdos. Chefs., 12 Aug. 1940: Italian attitude to the implementation of the armistice treaty, BA-MA RW 4/v. 706.

[63] Hillgruber, *Strategie*, 126.   [64] *Staatsmänner und Diplomaten*, i. 139 ff.

The Germans were more or less aware of the arguments within the French cabinet. After the fall of Paris Hitler expected a request for a cessation of hostilities and on 15 June instructed the High Command of the Armed Forces to draft the text of a treaty.[65] The armistice of 1918 was to serve as a model.

This draft was submitted to Keitel the following day. It envisaged the occupation of the whole of France. The ideas of the Army High Command at this time were more modest. Although the army called for the occupation of the Rhône valley, it was ready to dispense with the Massif Central. Hitler, who joined in the planning on 17 June, was satisfied with even less. He probably regarded the Rhône valley as part of the Italian sphere of interest. In consultation with the ministry of foreign affairs, the draft was appropriately amended and then revised by Hitler himself. Individual agencies were given an opportunity on 19 June to introduce their special requirements into the draft of the treaty. Thus, counter-intelligence made sure its agents were released, while Himmler stipulated the handing over of German *émigrés*. In the evening of 20 June Hitler finalized the text, of which a French translation was then hastily made.

Before the armistice conditions were communicated to the French negotiating delegation, headed by General Huntziger, in the saloon car at Rethondes, Keitel read out a political declaration. This preamble was not intended as part of the treaty. It merely recalled the end of the previous war, in German eyes the 'greatest disgrace of all time', which now had to be wiped out. Hitler, Hess, Ribbentrop, and the commanders-in-chief of the three Wehrmacht branches followed the ceremony with emotion. Only then did the negotiations begin.

The Germans declared their text to be immutable and were merely prepared to give explanations. Keitel insisted on immediate signature, but Huntziger was not authorized to do that. Jodl, who at times relieved the chief of the High Command of the Armed Forces in conducting the talks, struck a more conciliatory note.[66] But neither his efforts nor the atmosphere of mutual respect in which the unequal negotiations took place were able to assuage the bitterness of the vanquished. Although Huntziger noted with some relief that the feared surrender of the navy was not a condition, he made it clear that, if the Italians were to make similarly tough conditions, his country would prefer to continue the struggle. Rome was informed of this attitude when the Italo-French negotiations followed, and could not avoid making allowance for it. In the evening Huntziger was given an opportunity to consult his government by telephone. The Germans listened in. On the following day, 22 June, the French delegation succeeded in wresting two concessions from the victors. Thus, the Germans waived the handing over of the French air force and contented themselves with its disarmament under German supervision. They also promised, in their economic measures in the occupied territory, to bear in mind the needs of the population in the southern zone. They did not, however, waive their demand for the handing over of German *émigrés* in unoccupied

---

[65] Böhme, *Entstehung und Grundlagen*, 16 ff.
[66] Jäckel, *Frankreich*, 40; Böhme, *Entstehung und Grundlagen*, 216.

France. Following an ultimatum by Keitel, Huntziger had to sign the treaty that evening.

The armistice clauses, deliberately vaguely formulated by the Germans,[67] envisaged the cessation of all hostilities in metropolitan France and in the colonies (article 1) and the occupation of three-fifths of the national territory by German troops (article 2). Occupied and unoccupied territory were divided by a demarcation-line whose approximate course from the Swiss to the Spanish frontier[68] had been notified to the German command authorities in advance and which had determined the further advance or halting of the formations. Delimitation of the zone of occupation was based not so much on French administrative boundaries as on the victors' political, military, and economic interests: isolation of France from undesirable British influence, a land-link between Germany and Spain, inclusion of the industrial region of Le Creusot, securing of the Channel and Atlantic coasts for future operations against Britain. Germany thereby—apart from the just under 2 million French prisoners-of-war (article 20)—had in her hands an important pledge, which she did not intend entirely to abandon even at the end of the German–British conflict (article 3). The French government, which was to be free to move into the German zone of occupation if it so desired, undertook to obey the orders of the German military administration and to ensure due co-operation by national authorities. It further promised to prevent any action favouring the enemy (article 10), to regard anyone who, like de Gaulle, might continue the struggle at the side of Britain as an irregular, and to maintain all military, telecommunication, transport, and vital installations in the occupied zone in good condition or to restore them to such condition (article 13). Article 18 envisaged the payment of occupation costs, and article 19 ensured for the Reich the handing over of German prisoners-of-war and *émigrés*, as well as civilian prisoners sentenced for pro-German actions. Article 21 regulated compensation for any damage that might be caused to the occupying power by French infringements of the treaty. Germany assumed the unspecified obligation to take account of the vital economic needs of the unoccupied part of France (article 17), and reserved the right to give notice of termination of the armistice treaty at any time if the opposite party failed to meet its obligations (article 24). But France in that case would scarcely have been in a position to continue the war. After all, the French armed forces had to be demobilized and disarmed, with the exception of an armistice force for the preservation of law and order (article 4). War material, in so far as it had not already been seized by the Germans as booty, was to be handed over or put in store (article 5). The navy was expressly exempted from this provision. The Reich government contented itself with the demobilization of naval units not required for the maintenance of the colonial empire, and 'solemnly' declared that, even in the peace settlement, it would lay no claim to the French fleet (article 8). In the unoccupied zone German and Italian controlling authorities would supervise the implementation of the stipulations (article 12). Supervision over French North Africa—the Germans

---

[67] Text in Böhme, *Entstehung und Grundlagen*, 364 ff.   [68] See Map VI.v.6.

renounced supervision of Morocco only temporarily—was to be exercised by Italy. Any questions arising from the treaty would be dealt with, on the German side, by an armistice commission to which the French government was to send a delegation (article 22). Hostilities were to cease 6 hours after the Reich government was informed of the conclusion of the Italo-French treaty. This was signed on 24 June at 19.15 hours, and 20 minutes later the German embassy in Rome was notified. This first phase of the war cost France some 92,000 men killed and 200,000 wounded. Just under 2 million went into captivity.

In the British view the armistice terms were incompatible with the existing Franco-British alliance. Disarmament of the navy in the ports of metropolitan France seemed to hold out no real assurance that the Germans or Italians might not, after all, gain control of the ships. The clearance of French mine-booms in the Channel and the stipulated use of French territory for Germany's further conduct of the war were bound to be seen in London as a threat to important British interests. The British ambassador, Sir R. Campbell, outraged at not having been consulted, announced his departure during the night of 22–3 June.

6. The 'New Order' in Western Europe

The National Socialist regime and Hitler in particular were incapable, after the elimination of France, of giving Europe a durable political order that was based 'on more than mere force'.[69] The German–French armistice treaty had limited itself to a stopgap regulation of the most urgent military problems. It was not a suitable basis for a permanent clarification of relations between the two countries. That could only be achieved by a peace treaty, preparatory work on which was beginning on the German side but the conclusion of which Hitler did not yet regard as opportune. He was hoping to make the advantages which had accrued to Germany from her successful campaign in the west the basis of his expected negotiations with Britain, when a redelimitation of spheres of power was to be effected. But this did not stop him from anticipating by unilateral measures some of the officially still postponed demands.

Hitler's temporary lack of interest in administrative matters had come to an end with Holland's elimination from the war. Even before General von Falkenhausen, appointed military commander in The Netherlands on 16 May, arrived at The Hague, Hitler had ruled that the country would shortly be given a German civil administration under Reich Minister Seyss-Inquart.[70] Hitler's decision gave rise to misgivings and disappointment in military circles, but it had to be accepted.[71] Although Army High Command understood from rumours that a civil administration

---

[69] Hillgruber, *Strategie*, 65.

[70] Comprehensive report on the activity of the military commander in The Netherlands during the term of Gen. von Falkenhausen from 20 May to noon on 29 May, BA-MA RW 36/1; Kwiet, *Reichskommissariat*, 48 f.

[71] Halder, *Diaries*, i. 406 (17 May 1940); Bock, 'Tagebuch-Notizen', iii. 15 (17 May 1940); Kwiet, 'Vorbereitung', 129.

was planned for Belgium as well, it assigned to Falkenhausen, in expectation of a prolonged period of transition, executive power for The Netherlands, the occupied parts of Belgium, and northern Luxemburg.

Seyss-Inquart, however, assumed office as early as 29 May. Although this move met the wishes of Mussert, the leader of the Dutch National Socialists,[72] it had to be seen as an indication of long-term annexation plans. However, in view of the Dutch colonial possessions with their wealth of raw materials, Hitler decided that the conquered country—like Belgium and likewise only for the time being—should 'be preserved as a political and economic entity' and serve as 'a bridge for opportunities offering themselves at the time of a peace treaty'.[73]

Eupen, Malmédy, and Moresnet had already been severed from Belgian state territory on 18 May and incorporated into the Reich.[74] Plans were canvassed in Germany immediately after the Belgian surrender. Belgium's future relations with Germany were to depend on the attitude of the king, who regarded himself as a prisoner-of-war and was interned at the palace of Laeken. Originally Hitler intended to talk to Leopold III himself, but later sent his state secretary Meissner to discover the monarch's views. Belgium was either to be preserved as a kingdom closely linked to the Reich or to be incorporated into Germany at some future time as the 'Flanders Gau' in much the same way as The Netherlands.[75] On 1 June Hitler visited the Belgian capital. He had given orders earlier for the chief towns of Flanders to be spared from destruction whenever possible.[76] The subordination of the French-Flanders *départements* Nord and Pas-de-Calais to the military commander in Brussels, and the preferential treatment the commander was instructed to give to the Flemish part of the population—Flemish prisoners-of-war could expect earlier release—represented an early hint of Hitler's greater-Germanic reorganization plans in north-western Europe.

Belgium was to remain under military administration for the time being. The appointment of Gauleiter Kaufmann as Reich commissioner, already under consideration, was abandoned. Attempts by the Belgian government, which had fled to France, to negotiate with the Germans concerning the repatriation of refugees and an armistice treaty met with rejection on Hitler's part. To him there was no longer any Belgian government.

In Luxemburg the grand-ducal family and most of the ministers had succeeded in escaping the commandos and advance units of Sixteenth Army. Their request for Allied assistance served the Reich government as a pretext for not keeping its assurance of 10 May that the territorial integrity and political independence of the small country would be respected. Army Group A had charged Oberfeldkommandantur 520, under Major-General Gullmann, and after 25 May Feldkommandantur 515, under

---

[72] Halder, *Diaries*, i. 428 (27 May 1940).

[73] Note on State Councillor Wohlthat's report on the situation in Holland on 12 June 1940, PA Bureau St.S.: Niederlande, fo. 84372.

[74] *RGBl.* (1940), i. 777, 804.   [75] Bock, 'Tagebuch-Notizen', iii. 39–40 (31 May 1940).

[76] Order from OKH/GenStdH/Op.Abt. (Ia) No. 5848/40 g.Kdos., 23 May 1940, to Army Gps. A and B, BA-MA RH 19 I/38.

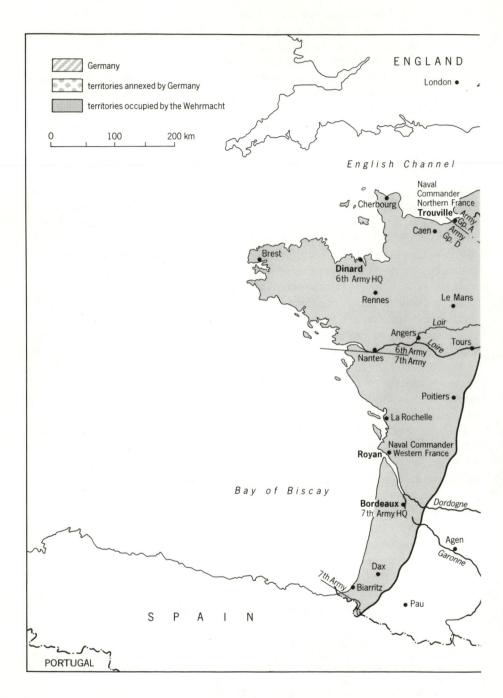

Map VI.v.6. Western Europe under German Hegemony, Autumn 1940

Commander-in-Chief Netherlands
Naval Commander in the Netherlands
The Hague

Utrecht Commander of Army Forces
in the Netherlands

• Münster

• Breda

Dover

16th Army

Ostend

Scheldt

• Antwerp

• Dortmund

• Kassel

Naval Commander
Channel Coast
Wimille

Boulogne
Air Fleet 2
HQ

Tourcoing
16th Army HQ

Brussels
Mil. Commander
in Belgium and
Northern France

Cologne

Aachen

Rhine

Eupen-
Malmedy

• Koblenz

Frankfurt

Main

• Würzburg

16th and 9th Army

Limésy
9th Army HQ

Amiens

p.

Laon

Luxemburg

Meuse

Metz

• Karlsruhe

Danube

Seine

Navy Group Command West
Air Fleet 3 HQ
Mil. Commander in France

St-Germain **PARIS**
Commander-in-
Chief West
(Army Gp. A HQ)

Army Gp. D HQ
Melun

St-Dizier

North-east line

Nancy
1st Army HQ

L o r r a i n e

Strasburg

Neckar

Ulm

A l s a c e

Rhine

Kolmar

Troyes

Chaumont

Langres

Saône

Belfort

Dijon

Doubs

Aare

• Innsbruck

Orleans

Bourges

demarcation-line

Chalon-s.-S.

Dole

Berne

S W I T Z E R L A N D

Châteauroux

Moulins

Saône

Mâcon

Rhone

Vichy

• Limoges

Clermont-Ferrand

Loire

Lyons

• Milan

Po

Tulle

Grenoble

• Turin

I T A L Y

Mende

Rhone

• Gap

Genoa

• Digne

Toulouse

Nîmes

Avignon

Nice

Marseilles

Perpignan

CORSICA

Colonel Schumacher, with the military administration of Luxemburg. The Germans found a native governmental commission under Secretary-General Wehrer, whose powers had to be confirmed by the Luxemburg parliament on 11 May.[77] Army High Command did not regard the grand duchy as an enemy country and intended, if only for the sake of German economic interests—the objective of the *coup*-like occupation of the country had been the swift seizure of its important industrial potential—to govern it, on the model of Denmark, 'on a loose rein'.[78] But this was no longer in line with the intentions of the political leaders. At the end of the first week of occupation Wehrer was informed that Luxemburg would henceforth be considered an enemy country and his commission no longer recognized as a government. He could, however, continue to stay in office as the representative of the local authorities. The provisional government was thereupon transformed, by the Luxemburg Chamber, into a commission for the administration of the country, but German Party officials increasingly narrowed its scope for orderly work.

Luxemburg was soon lifted out of the area of military administration and, along with Alsace-Lorraine, i.e. the French *départements* Moselle, Bas-Rhin, and Haut-Rhin, came under German civil administration. In mid-July the Verstärkte Grenzaufsichtsdienst (VGAD: Reinforced Frontier Surveillance Service) moved to the west, 'initially'[79] as far as the German frontier of 1918. At the beginning of August these territories were *de facto* incorporated into the Reich and allocated to the neighbouring Reich Gaue. Their Gauleiters had even earlier functioned as chiefs of civil administration under those army commanders-in-chief who practised executive power in their areas. They retained the designation of chiefs of civil administration, but were directly responsible to Hitler. Germanization of the territories began at once. Only refugees of 'German ethnic character' were allowed to return to Alsace-Lorraine.

Another indication of German annexation plans was the creation of a northern French closed zone. In connection with the repatriation of the population who had fled before the armies, the German military authorities set up several blocking-lines in the occupied territory. The one closest to the Reich, the so-called north-east line,[80] was kept in existence and returning refugees were denied access to their homes. Derelict farms were soon managed in trust by the German Ostland corporation. This closed zone comprised, along with the industrial region of Briey–Longwy, the economically important *départements* Nord and Pas-de-Calais, which originally, presumably for purely administrative and military reasons, had been assigned to the German military commander in Brussels. For political reasons these areas, whose detachment the Germans might possibly demand at the peace settlement,[81] continued even later to be outside the military administration in Paris, which was responsible for France.

---

[77] Minute by the Oberfeldkommandant, 21 May 1940, MA-BA E 138/8.
[78] Minute by Legation Counsellor von Nostitz, 14 May 1940, PA St.S.: Invasion of Belgium, Holland, and Luxemburg, fos. 114864-5.
[79] First Army command Oberquartiermeister's war diary, 9 July 1940, BA-MA W 6575/1.
[80] See Map VI.v.6.
[81] Study by the ministry of economic affairs, Oct. 1940, in *Anatomie der Aggression*, Doc. 21, pp. 108 ff.

The first steps had thus been taken towards a territorial and political new order in western Europe, for which the success of German arms had created such favourable prerequisites. Hitler still had no clear idea of the extent to which he could combine the consolidation of German hegemony in western Europe with a redrawing of the political frontiers. He wanted to await the clarification of German–British relations in order to see whether France or Britain would foot the bill for the new peace order. A return to conditions prior to the First World War, a mere revision of the treaty of Versailles, was out of the question for him. The 'new order' in Europe would presumably have aimed at the creation of an enlarged 'Greater German Reich' on an 'ethnic', i.e. Germanic, basis, around which a number of client states with limited sovereignty were grouped. Hitler instructed State Secretary Stuckart of the ministry of the interior to make proposals to him concerning a German western frontier.[82] This secret draft envisaged an outward shift of the frontier to a line running from Lake Geneva to the Somme estuary, which allowed for economic as well as transport considerations, and which roughly corresponded to the existing north-east line. Military quarters came up with their own preferences.

Inside Germany a lively concocting of plans had begun by competent as well as incompetent circles and individuals, frequently, in the general euphoria of the early summer of 1940, reverting to German wishful thinking of earlier times. A common feature of all these projects was the liberality with which the territory of alien states was disposed of regardless of the wishes of the affected population. Not all plans bore the character of non-committal extemporizations. Even when they merely took up some chance remark by Hitler they at once triggered off political or economic measures. Thus, the intention to shift the Reich frontier far to the west had transcended the realm of pure theory with the creation of the north-east line. The idea of an independent Brittany likewise did not remain without consequences,[83] until the project was dismissed as inopportune in the summer of 1940 and, like the revival of a Burgundian state, soon forgotten.

Politicians and groups in the occupied territories likewise believed at the time that they should adapt to an apparently permanent new situation. Authoritarian and Fascist forces came to the fore. Adoption of German models seemed a commandment of political wisdom and progressiveness. Even outside the German sphere of power, in the neutral countries, there was a temporary increase in readiness for a *rapprochement* with the Reich. Hopes of a German-aided 'reorganization of the world' ranged as far afield as Afghanistan.[84]

The new situation also offered an opportunity for a reshaping of economic relations and dependences. Governmental authorities and economic leaders believed that the time had come to assert a dominant economic position for the Reich in Europe, in line with its military and political hegemony. Some vague plans already existed, such as the reflections of prominent scholars like Haushofer and Schmitt, or those of a *de facto* official 'Association for European Economic Planning and Large-Area

---

[82] Jäckel, *Frankreich*, 46–7.
[84] Hillgruber, *Strategie*, 71.

[83] Umbreit, 'Bretonenbewegung'.

Economics', founded in September 1939.[85] The independence of neighbouring countries, of which there was still some talk at first, seemed overtaken by events. The ministry of foreign affairs saw good chances of a 'large-area economy' under German leadership, now that 'final victory has been won and that, therefore, England accepts all Germany's conditions';[86] it had earlier called an interdepartmental meeting to discuss these questions on 22 May. A month later Göring instructed the ministry of economic affairs to begin planning in conjunction with all interested state and Party authorities. An immediate start was made on incorporating the occupied territories into the Reich's war economy. German industry, with financial assistance from the state, was able to buy up foreign enterprises or at least acquire major shares. The ultimate objective—not to be stated publicly as yet but to be concealed by a nebulous European ideology—was, also for economic reasons, an extensive amalgamation of the conquered countries with the Reich, possibly with the exception of France.[87] In the view of the ministry of finance they should not only be made to pay war compensation but also make 'appropriate contributions' towards their future military protection, to be effected by the Wehrmacht.[88] There was to be no more independent economic policy even by neutral neighbouring countries. A revealing document was the proposal for a territorial division circulated by Hans Kehrl of the ministry of economic affairs on 12 August 1940 as a discussion paper.[89] It suggested that future planning should embrace the following spheres: (1) the 'Greater German economic sphere' (Sphere A), to comprise, in addition to Reich territory, the Polish Government-General, the Protectorate of Bohemia and Moravia, Slovakia, Alsace-Lorraine, Luxemburg, Holland, and Belgium, as well as the African colonies yet to be acquired; (2) the 'continental sphere' led by Germany (Sphere B), comprising, in addition to Sphere A, the Nordic and the Balkan countries (excluding Albania); and (3) a 'continental sphere in the broader sense' (Sphere C), which would include, in addition to Sphere B, France and Switzerland, but probably not permanently.

There existed, in consequence, a multitude of proposals from state and military authorities, as well as from interested industrial circles, for the extension and final structure of a 'large-scale economic sphere' oriented towards German requirements and advantages, as well as for a territorial 'new order' in general. Business circles scented undreamt-of opportunities for an expansion of their own activities and for an elimination of the foreign competition of the past. No decision in favour of any of these territorial or economic plans was ever to be made. Hitler saw no reason why he should reveal his intentions just then. But this did not rule out the implementation of some very far-reaching ideas, formulated for the most part regardless of legal considerations, at least to the extent permitted by Hitler's further

---

[85] Volkmann, 'Autarkie', 70.

[86] 'Most secret' minute by Minister Clodius, 30 May 1940, on 'aspects of the economic shaping of the peace', *DGFP* D ix, No. 354; minute by Ambassador Ritter, 1 June 1940, on large-area economics, ibid., No. 367.

[87] Minute by the ministry of economic affairs, 9 July 1940, BA R 43 II/311.

[88] Minute of a top-level conference at the ministry of economic affairs, 22 July 1940, in *Anatomie der Aggression*, Doc. 7, pp. 67 ff.   [89] Ibid., Doc. 12, p. 83 ff.

policies and military operations from time to time. This was true, up to a point, of a rather autarkical continental-European large-area economy from the Iberian peninsula to the Urals, pursued initially by peaceful and subsequently by warlike means. 'Decidedly premature', on the other hand, was a maximalist programme prepared by the naval war staff in early June 1940 for a spatial expansion and the establishment of bases not only on the Norwegian and northern and western French coasts, but throughout the world;[90] so was the broadly conceived redistribution of colonial possessions in Africa (mainly French) as a complement to the large-area European economy. Preparatory work, begun on a considerable scale (especially in terms of personnel), had soon to be stopped. A similar failure was a plan for transferring the Jewish population of Europe to Madagascar.

The ministry of foreign affairs tried stubbornly to keep future planning—for peace, as it was hoped for a while—in its own hands. However, it was unable to prevail in the long run against Göring and the economic departments under him.

On Ribbentrop's instruction a group of experts on France turned their minds to a new German western policy. This group was headed by Minister Abetz, the future diplomatic representative of the Reich in France. In May 1940 Abetz still favoured a cautious approach: co-operation with political groupings close to National Socialism, and support for regionalism and minorities, though without breaking up existing countries or offending their populations' sense of cultural identity.[91] Simultaneously he recommended skilful propaganda to make the vanquished aware of the weaknesses of their past governments, and emphasizing the advantages of Nazism, for instance in the social sphere.

The recommendations for Wehrmacht propaganda of July 1940 were along similar lines: emphasis on the failure of past governments and on the constructive action of the Germans; these were approved, *ex post facto*, by the minister of foreign affairs. However, they foreshadowed a harder line. Anti-democratic propaganda in territories earmarked for annexation or for direct German influence was to awaken sympathies for National Socialism among Belgians, Luxemburgers, Alsatians, and Lorrainers. The French, on the other hand, were to be reminded of the 'sins' of their former governments; by means of 'psychological terror' the Franco-British rift was to be widened, the French share of war-guilt emphasized, and the country prepared for harsh peace terms. Anything that might enhance 'national consolidation' had to be avoided.[92] Altogether, the future peace must put an end, once and for all, to France's hegemony in Europe. Germany's neighbour, Goebbels declared in a press directive of 9 July, would never be considered as an ally. As an 'enlarged Switzerland', France, following the detachment of her eastern and northern industrial regions, was to be only a 'tourist country' and, in total dependence on Germany, would

---

[90] Nuremberg document C-041, *IMT* xxxiv.

[91] Letter from Minister Abetz, western department of the Dienststelle Ribbentrop, to OKW/WFA/WPr, 24 May 1940, BA-MA RW 4/v. 187.

[92] Notes for a report by the Wehrmacht propaganda department in OKW/WFA, July 1940, BA-MA RW 4/v. 187; Sündermann, *Tagesparolen*, 110; *Secret Conferences of Dr Goebbels*, 66–7.

manufacture 'certain fashionable products'.[93] A resurgence of France, therefore, was not in the German interest.

On identical lines were the ideas of the ministry of economic affairs, as formulated in a memorandum of 29 October 1940: detachment of the eastern and northern French industrial regions, followed by a retro-development of the country into an agrarian state.[94] It was not yet, however, advisable to let the French know these intentions. A German–French separate peace, such as the Pétain government had hoped to achieve at Rethondes, was therefore out of the question. Belgium, which according to these plans would be situated within the westward-shifted Reich frontier, was to be divided into a Walloon and a Flemish area and absorbed into the 'Germanic living-space'.

There was no agreement on the question of which bodies were to be responsible for this policy, which was still undefined in details. No sooner was Paris in German hands than Ribbentrop decided to attach the Abetz group to the newly appointed military commander and charge it with cultural and propaganda tasks. This was opposed by the Wehrmacht propaganda department in the High Command of the Armed Forces and by the propaganda ministry, who were anxious to preserve their exclusive joint competence in this field.[95] They saw at once to the establishment of a propaganda machine aimed at the French population and nominally subordinated to the military administration, whose chief, General Streccius—replacing the meanwhile relieved military commanders in France and Paris, and working closely with the army command nearby—was to ensure the uniformity of the administration. He did not have much success in this, however. Abetz was received by Hitler at the beginning of August and appointed ambassador, thus becoming the sole authority for political matters in occupied France. He was merely to co-operate with the military administration and with the army general staff, both of whom viewed him with a good deal of mistrust. By establishing a 'German embassy in Paris', not accredited to the Vichy government, Ribbentrop emphasized in November 1940 the independent position of his representative Abetz.

In practice this imprecise delimitation of functions proved troublesome. Clashes of competence soon became an everyday feature among the ever more numerous official agencies in occupied France. Added to these was the armistice commission, provided for in the treaty and set up on the model of that of 1918-19. For reasons of prestige this had to have its seat in Reich territory, though not in Berlin—which seemed a rational arrangement—but demonstratively in Wiesbaden, in the erstwhile French-occupied Rhineland.[96] The commission, unlike the military administration, did not come under the Army High Command but under the High Command of the Armed Forces. A fairly close link between the two chains of command was provided, at least during the initial period, by the person of its chairman, the former Oberquartiermeister I in the Army General Staff, General Carl Heinrich von Stülpnagel. Major problems, on the other hand, were soon raised by the German armistice delegation for economic

[93] Jäckel, *Frankreich*, 57-8.   [94] *Anatomie des Krieges*, Doc. 139, pp. 300-1.
[95] Signal from OKW/WFA/WPr Ia No. 4431/40 g. to Chef WFA, 14 June 1940, BA-MA RW 4/v. 187.
[96] Jäckel, *Frankreich*, 72.

affairs, which was supposed to relieve the armistice commission of a large part of its non-military matters and which was headed by Minister Hemmen. Although this was an agency of the ministry of foreign affairs, it had to concede extensive influence also to the economic departments represented by Göring.

To the French this multiplicity of offices—with inadequate delimitation of their responsibilities—was more than confusing. At times, however, it provided them with an opportunity to play off the diverse German agencies against one another, to their own advantage. France meanwhile, without any kind of pressure from Germany—which indeed was hoping for an opposite domestic political development—had given itself an authoritarian state system. In the belief that the military catastrophe stemmed from a political system that was no longer suited to modern needs, the majority of the members of parliament assembled in Vichy voted for the abolition of the constitution then in force. Pétain, nominated head of state, was furnished with extensive powers and given the task of having a new constitution drawn up. Pierre Laval moved up to become deputy premier and Pétain's official successor. General Weygand was given the post of minister of war.

In view of the continuation of the war, until Britain either gave in or was defeated, the bulk of the German army had remained in occupied France. In early July the Army General Staff moved its headquarters to Fontainebleau, in order to be close to the army group headquarters which were preparing for a landing in England or were in charge of security in the occupied territory. The Army High Command at the same time wished to keep a say in the military administration in France.

Military organization in the occupied western territories did not assume clear forms until the autumn of 1940, when the operational plans against the British Isles were abandoned. Army Group B was transported to the east in October, in connection with the incipient deployment against the Soviet Union.

Next, Army Group C was moved back into the Reich, and in November the Army General Staff returned to Zossen. Before this move, Army High Command had ordered the raising of a fourth army group, Army Group D, which, under the former commander-in-chief of First Army, Field Marshal von Witzleben, was to be responsible, as of 26 October, for more 'local' tasks. Subordinated to it were First, Sixth, and Seventh Armies.

In operational matters the new army group came under the commander-in-chief of Army Group A (Ninth and Sixteenth Armies), Field Marshal von Rundstedt, who had just been appointed 'Commander-in-Chief West' (OB West). 'OB West', however, had powers of command only over the army formations. Naval Group Command West (General-Admiral Saalwächter) and the commands of Air Fleet 2 (Field Marshal Kesselring) and of Air Fleet 3 (Field Marshal Sperrle) were merely enjoined to co-operate with Rundstedt. A certain autonomy was enjoyed also by the newly appointed military commander in France (from 26 October 1940), General Otto von Stülpnagel, and the military commander in Belgium and northern France, General von Falkenhausen, in the execution of their territorial authority in line with Army High Command directives. Totally independent of 'OB West' was the Wehrmacht commander in The Netherlands, General Christiansen, who answered to the High Command of the Armed Forces. Command relations were not helped by the fact that Army High Command assigned to Christiansen a 'commander of army forces in The Netherlands' to whom 'OB West' was entitled to send directives. This scarcely efficient structure in the western territories already contained the seeds of the endless clashes of competence throughout the war years. This was not changed even by Witzleben's appointment as 'OB West' when Rundstedt left France with Army Group A in April 1941.

The establishment of German hegemony over extensive parts of northern and western Europe was the result of the risky conduct of the war that Hitler had forced on his generals. The fact that these successes were scored against greatly inferior or, as was not initially obvious, poorly prepared opponents in no way diminished the euphoria which seized virtually all strata of the German nation. Hitler's prestige as 'the greatest general of all time' reached its first climax and buttressed his self-assurance in a dangerous way. The army command, which had distinguished itself with wrong predictions, correspondingly lost much of its reputation.

The consequences which Hitler had expected from the campaign in the west did not, however, materialize as yet. The Germans, as de Gaulle was quick to assure his fellow countrymen from London, had won only a battle, not the war.

The German dictator was in fact soon facing a dilemma. True enough, Europe, at least the north and west of the continent, was now under German hegemony. But there had not so far been any acknowledgement of German dominance by Britain, the principal enemy, and that was what Hitler wanted most. His next objective, therefore, had to be to make London recognize what seemed so obvious to him—that only by an arrangement with the powerful German Reich could Britain retain its position as a great power, albeit outside Europe.

PART VII

The Operational Air War until the Battle of Britain

Klaus A. Maier

WITH the declaration of war by the Western powers on 3 September 1939, Hitler had to accept a military conflict with Britain earlier than he had originally calculated and, compared to his previous alliance plans, with reversed fronts; moreover, he was forced to include the United States in his current strategy even before achieving an autarkic, dominant position in Europe. The parallel policies[1] of Britain and the United States, which had been clearly expressed, for instance in Roosevelt's speech of 5 October 1937 and the Anglo-American trade treaty of November 1938,[2] meant that time was working against the realization of Hitler's strategic and war-economy programme. If he wanted to continue to pursue his aims, he could solve this problem only by repeated, risky military initiatives.

At first, however, Hitler found this situation quite acceptable, as the Western powers did not launch a major attack and the Wehrmacht was able to subdue Poland quickly. While the last military resistance in Poland, in Warsaw and Modlin, collapsed under the ruthless attacks of the Luftwaffe,[3] most of the German units which had taken part in the Polish campaign were already being transferred to the west. However, Hitler's military operations in the west were accompanied by peace-feelers even after 3 September,[4] all of which were intended to make it possible to revert to his original design based on a partnership with Britain, or at least on British toleration. Hitler's intention to 'force Britain to her knees' and not, as in the case of France, 'to smash' her[5] reflected this hope.

Apart from the need to maintain the fighting strength of the Luftwaffe for the decisive battle with the Western powers, Hitler's lingering hope of a 'reversal of alliances' led him to prosecute the air war against Britain with great restraint, though stepping it up by degrees.[6] The German air commands were ordered to 'leave clearly the responsibility for initiating air attacks to Britain and France'.[7] But because of the inferior strength of their air forces, the Western powers sought to gain time.[8] Moreover, in spite of reports about the use of the Luftwaffe against Polish towns,[9] they found it advisable to abide by their declaration of 2 September, according to which they intended to attack only 'strictly military objectives in the

---

[1] Confidential instructions to the press (June 1938), quoted in Schröder, 'Drittes Reich', 355.

[2] Hillgruber, 'Faktor Amerika'.   [3] Speidel, 'Luftwaffe im Polenfeldzug'.

[4] Cf. Martin, *Friedensinitiativen*; on Göring's role cf. III.1 above; Hildebrand, 'Hitler's "Programm"', 673 n. 64.

[5] Halder, *KTB* i. 86–90 (27 Sept. 1939). The trans. in *Diaries*, i. 91–2, is incomplete.

[6] Trevor-Roper, *Directives*, Nos. 1–4; cf. on this and the following passage the accounts of the air war in Murray, *Strategy*, and Overy, *Air War*.

[7] ObdL Füst. Ia No. 5293/39, g.Kdos. Chef-S., 23 Sept. 1939, BA-MA Lw 107/22.

[8] On the air strategy of the Western powers cf. Butler, *Strategy*, ii. 33 ff., 153 ff., 165 ff., 567 ff.

[9] Cf. Aide-Mémoire for Chiefs of Staff Committee on Polish Situation, Annex to C.O.S. (39) 8th meeting, 9 Sept. 1939, PRO Cab 79/1.

narrowest sense of the phrase'.[10] Because of the assumed fourfold German superiority in bombers, the French in particular feared serious losses if industrial areas should become targets in an air war.[11]

After the rejection of his proposal of 6 October 1939 for a separate peace with Britain, Hitler decided, against the opposition of the army leaders, to attack in the west at the earliest possible opportunity. On 9 October 1939 he explained his ideas to the commanders-in-chief and the head of the Wehrmacht High Command in a long memorandum.[12] Basing his arguments on the assertions that the military utilization of German national strength (*Volkskraft*) had reached a level 'which no efforts can improve significantly, in the short term at any rate', and that the increase in German military strength to be expected in the next few years could be matched, not indeed by France but probably by the growing British forces, Hitler pressed for quick exploitation of current German superiority, now that the successful campaign in Poland had given Germany the possibility, which for decades she had longed for in vain, of fighting a war on a single front. Time was very probably working for the Western powers. Among the resulting dangers for Germany Hitler described the disruption of production in the Ruhr by air attacks as the 'most serious and greatest danger'; a halt in production there could not be compensated for elsewhere, and 'sooner or later' would inevitably lead to the collapse of Germany's war economy and her defensive strength. The possibility of defence against night attacks was already limited; deterrence through retaliation seemed to Hitler to be the most reliable method at the moment. But it had to be expected that 'in the course of a long war' as soon as one warring state believed it had a clear superiority in certain armaments, it would make use of that superiority regardless of reprisals. But the longer the war lasted, the more difficult it would be to maintain German air superiority, especially offensive superiority. In this regard Hitler referred to the importance of Belgium and The Netherlands for the defensive as well as the offensive German conduct of the war. If the Western powers occupied Belgium and Holland, 'the air forces of our enemies, striking at the industrial heart of Germany, would have to fly hardly a sixth of the distance which a German bomber must fly to hit really important enemy targets. If we had Holland, Belgium, or even the Pas de Calais as offensive bases for the Luftwaffe, we could undoubtedly strike at the heart of Britain and accept even the harshest reprisals.' For this reason the operations plan for the German attack in the west,[13] which Hitler described in his memorandum, envisaged an attempt to 'penetrate the area of Luxemburg, Belgium, Holland as rapidly as possible'. In carrying out this operation Hitler demanded that the entire

---

[10] This declaration is printed in Butler, *Strategy*, ii. 568. It was preceded by an appeal from President Roosevelt on 1 Sept., which Hitler also answered affirmatively: *DGFP* D vii. 506-7.

[11] According to Villelume (*Journal*, 43), on 25 Sept. the French believed that Germany had 1,872 bombers, 507 dive-bombers, 1,278 fighters, and 312 heavy fighters; the British estimated a total of 2,130 bombers and 1,215 fighters: Butler, *Strategy*, ii. 33-4.

[12] 'Denkschrift und Richtlinien über die Führung des Krieges im Westen', 9 Oct. 1939, printed in *Dokumente zur Vorgeschichte*, 4 ff.; *IMT* xxxvii. 466 ff.; cf. also Hitler's speech to Gauleiters on 21 Oct. 1939 in Groscurth, *Tagebücher*, 385.

[13] Trevor-Roper, *Directives*, Nos. 6-8.

leadership 'always remember that the annihilation of the Anglo-French army is the great goal; achieving it will make possible later, successful operations of the Luftwaffe against other targets. The Luftwaffe can and will be used for ruthless attacks to destroy the basis of Britain's will to resist at the appropriate time.'

In contrast, the Luftwaffe Command Staff Ic (intelligence; previously department 5 of the Luftwaffe General Staff) argued on 22 November 1939 that actual attacks on Britain should be started 'as soon and as vigorously as possible, no later than this year', in order to prevent the enemy from utilizing previous experience in the war in order to improve his defences against German offensive weapons, and to keep him from completely encircling Germany economically with the help of the Anglo-French colonial empires and the neutrals, 'especially the United States'. Unlike Hitler, who sought to reach a decision about a general offensive in the west with the aim of improving Germany's geographical position in an operational air war against Britain 'at the proper time', the Luftwaffe Command Staff Ic wanted to achieve a decision by 'ruthlessly taking advantage of all possibilities' in a war to be started immediately against British overseas trade. In their opinion the following 'main target groups' could be attacked in a war against supplies for Britain: (1) British ports; (2) enemy ships at sea between latitude 61° N. and longitude 10° E., with a southern and western limitation of the operations area determined by the aims of the naval war staff but including the English Channel; and (3) the British navy. The Command Staff Ic expected the greatest successes in air attacks on merchant ships in ports as, in addition to numerous secondary effects, for example, on the morale of the population, it was highly probable that great losses of shipping capacity could be inflicted on the enemy. All the most important ports should be attacked at the same time at as many points as possible day and night, even with small and very small units. The fact that harbour and residential areas in some British port cities were not clearly separated should not be a reason for 'refraining from attacking these ports'. All attacks on other targets, such as industrial ones or air-bases in Britain, should be considered 'mistakes', as they ignored the final goal of paralysing British overseas trade as far as possible. From this direct strategy against Britain, which showed a general ignorance of Hitler's plans, the Luftwaffe Command Staff Ic expected a quick success and favourable political effects on enemies, neutrals, and allies. With regard to France, they argued: 'In so far as we refrain from any attacks on that country, the great mass of the French population will come to understand our argument that we are fighting against Britain alone, and our quick, visible successes will have a favourable influence on the government's attitude.' American intervention or restraint would largely depend on how effectively Germany waged the war.[14]

In contrast to this alternative plan for an offensive in the west, on 22 November 1939 the operations department of the Tenth Flying Corps concerned itself with the question of how an air war should be conducted against Britain 'as long as the

---

[14] Luftwaffenführungsstab Ic No. 7300/39 g. Kdos. (I) Beurteilung der Kriegführung gegen Großbritannien vom Standpunkt der Luftwaffe, 22 Nov. 1939, BA-MA RL 2/342.

idea of an offensive in the west is maintained'.[15] It was planned to tie British fighter aircraft down at home by air attacks on Britain in order to support a later offensive against France and, with the help of other diversionary measures, to guarantee that the offensive in the west would achieve surprise. Priority would be given to attacks on British warships and port facilities. The latter were considered especially important because of 'large shipments of supplies from overseas which have only just begun'. Moreover, the Tenth Flying Corps expected to be able to intensify the 'already existing unrest in the country' and to prevent orderly supplying of the population with essential goods by disrupting the unloading of imports. In choosing targets, however, it was not assumed that attacks on them meant from the very beginning the opening of an unrestricted operational air war by the Luftwaffe: 'If this were done, the consequence would be attacks by the British air force on open cities in Germany. Responding to such attacks would inevitably mean that a significant part of the Luftwaffe would not be available to support a later offensive in the west.'

Meanwhile the Western powers had been able to reach agreement on the use of their air forces in the event of a German attack on Belgium only with considerable effort. While initially the Royal Air Force was permitted to attack advancing German columns even if this endangered the civilian population, the French air force was under orders to obtain prior permission from the government in Paris. Moreover, the Royal Air Force could expect to receive permission from the War Cabinet to attack the Ruhr, whereas the French rejected the idea of bombing that area before the spring of 1940. At the meeting of the Supreme War Council on 17 November, Chamberlain and Daladier agreed that the Royal Air Force would be permitted to attack industrial targets in Germany without additional consultation with Paris only in the event of German air attacks on British or French industry, especially the aircraft industry. With this exception Allied conduct of the war was to be confined to strictly military targets even if Germany attacked Belgium.[16]

Göring played a double role in the debate concerning the offensive in the west. Available sources show that he vacillated between loyalty to Hitler and his own responsibility for the inadequately equipped Luftwaffe. Dahlerus, who, very probably with Hitler's knowledge, served as Göring's intermediary in extending peace-feelers to Britain, was clearly convinced of Göring's sincerity, but he qualified this by adding that Göring repeatedly left the 'final form of the decision' open and did not know himself how Hitler would decide. Sometimes he was not sufficiently circumspect and displayed a 'boundless admiration of the Führer's genius'.[17] On 4 November 1939 information was provided by Schulze-Boysen of the Luftwaffe Command Staff Ic that Göring and Reichenau had twice attempted independently of each other to

---

[15] Chef. 1. Abt. 'Luftkriegführung gegen England', 22 Nov. 1939, BA-MA RL 2 II/24.

[16] C.O.S. (39) 63rd Meeting, 30 Oct. 1939, PRO Cab 79/1. Cf. Butler, *Strategy*, ii. 168–9; Gamelin, *Servir*, iii. 144.

[17] Cf. record, dated 26 Oct. 1939, of a conversation between Göring and Dahlerus on 25 Oct., printed in Groscurth, *Tagebücher*, 387 ff., doc. 28; Leeb, *Tagebuchaufzeichnungen*, 193 ff.; Irving, *Rise and Fall*, 83; Brügel, 'Dahlerus'.

persuade Hitler to change his mind. As he was not successful, Göring had definitely abandoned all attempts to get Hitler to take a more moderate position and was now determined to 'obey like a soldier'.[18]

In his talk to the commanders-in-chief of the Wehrmacht services and line officers of the army on 23 November 1939[19] Hitler attempted to overcome the opposition of the army leaders to the offensive in the west by repeating the arguments in his memorandum of 9 October 1939 and describing the offensive as a question of 'the nation's very existence'. Again he stressed the strategic military aspects of the matter, especially the danger to the Ruhr (Germany's 'Achilles' heel'). This problem had to be solved even if it meant disregarding Belgian and Dutch neutrality. The occupation of Belgium and Holland was, however, the precondition for fighting a war against Britain: 'Our submarines, mines, and air force (also for minelaying operations) will be much more effective against Britain if we have a better starting-position. . . . Aircraft will be the main minelayers. We shall saturate the British coasts with mines that cannot be cleared. This mine-war using the Luftwaffe requires a new starting-position.'[20] Open threats against 'all gripers', combined with the reference to the military importance of the Low Countries, where both defensive and offensive interests of Germany were involved, seemed to Hitler especially well suited to win the support of the hesitant army leaders for the offensive in the west. In 'Führer Directive No. 9',[21] issued on 29 November 1939, he ordered that proper measures be taken in time to 'deal an annihilating blow to the English economy'. Once the army had succeeded in defeating the Anglo-French army in the field and in capturing and holding a part of the coast across the Channel from Britain, the navy and the Luftwaffe would have the following tasks, in order of importance: (1) to attack the main British unloading ports, using aircraft as minelayers; (2) to attack British merchant ships and the navy protecting them; (3) to destroy British reserves (of, among other things, oil and foodstuffs); (4) to disrupt British troop and supply transports to France; and (5) to destroy industrial plants vital to the British war effort, 'in particular key points of the aircraft industry and factories producing heavy artillery, anti-aircraft guns, munitions, and explosives'. The removal of previous restrictions on the conduct of the war in the air and at sea was to take place at the beginning of the offensive in the west.[22]

On 7 December 1939 Göring issued Directive No. 5 for the preparation of the Luftwaffe for the campaign in the west.[23] The purpose of the offensive was 'to defeat the French army and its allies as completely as possible in Belgium and France,

---

[18] Groscurth, *Tagebücher*, 403–4, doc. 33.

[19] Jacobsen, *Fall Gelb*, 59 ff.; *Lagevorträge*, 49–55; Groscurth, *Tagebücher*, 414 ff., doc. 40; *IMT* xxvi. 327 ff.   [20] *Lagevorträge*, 53–4.   [21] Trevor-Roper, *Directives*, No. 9.

[22] Directive No. 7 of 18 Oct. 1939 (Trevor-Roper, *Directives*, No. 7) authorized the Luftwaffe to attack British naval forces at their bases.

[23] ObdL Füst. Ia No. 5330/39 g.Kdos., 7 Dec. 1939. Cf. also Der Chef der Luftflotte 1 und Befehlshaber Nord, Führungsabteilung Ia No. 7300/39 g.Kdos., Chefsache, 11 Dec. 1939, 'Weisung Nr. 5 zur Abwehrschlacht'; Der Chef der Luftflotte 3 und Befehlshaber West, Führ. Abt. No. 324/39. g.Kdos. Chefs., 23 Dec. 1939, Weisung für die Kampfführung in der Abwehrschlacht; Speidel, 'Westfeldzug', annexes 4, 8, 13 to ch. II.

to occupy Holland, at first up to the Grebbe–Meuse line, and to seize as much territory as possible in Belgium, Holland, and northern France'. The task of the Luftwaffe was to continue the war against the British navy and its bases while using most of its aircraft to support the attacks of the army by concentrating on certain targets. The direct support of the army was entrusted to Air Fleets 2 and 3, while Lieutenant-General Geisler's Tenth Flying Corps (which had been directly subordinate to Göring since 25 October)[24] was to attack the British navy and merchant ships in the North Sea and the Channel. It was ordered to attack (1) ships and port facilities, (2) the ground-support units of the Royal Air Force in Britain in so far as they supported British air operations against targets on the Continent, and (3) troop transports to the Continent in the ports of embarkation and at sea. Among the German military leaders heavy attacks on the German war economy were expected only later, 'most probably only if such attacks can be plausibly represented as retaliatory blows'. For this reason cities with more than 5,000 inhabitants and containing military targets were not to be attacked without Göring's express permission.

The Luftwaffe Command Staff Ic now pressed for starting the operational air war against Britain as early as possible. In their 'assessment of the air armaments position of the Western powers as of 1 January 1940'[25] they presented the statistical argument that the situation of the Western powers would become all the weaker 'the earlier they suffer heavy losses, even if this also involves heavy German losses'. Assuming a total of 2,660 first-class British front-line aircraft[26] (220 long-range reconnaissance aeroplanes, 1,357 bombers, and 1,083 fighters), the staff argued that losses of 30 per cent beginning on 1 February 1940 would inevitably result in a decline of the effective strength of the bombers to 800 in the period from 1 June to 1 November, and of fighters to 600 or 700 between July and the end of October. On the basis of these figures the staff expected that Britain would then have only 400 bombers and about 300–50 fighters ready for action. This meant that it would be impossible to re-equip reserves (training units), whose second-class aircraft were of only limited use in combat. If, however, the losses of 30 per cent were assumed to apply only on and after 1 April 1940, the staff believed that this delay would ease the British armaments situation with regard to all types of aircraft, allowing a continuation of the re-equipping of the training units (at a somewhat reduced pace). In summary the Luftwaffe Command Staff Ic pointed out correctly that in terms of strength and equipment the combat-ready aircraft of the British and French air forces were clearly inferior to the Luftwaffe at the beginning of 1940. However, they also claimed that a decisive improvement of the air armaments of the Western powers compared with Germany in 1940 could not simply be assumed even if the United States placed most of its aircraft production at their disposal. The personnel problems of the enemy were thought to be 'considerably greater' than the purely material ones.

---

[24] ObdL Füst. Ia No. 5334/39 g.Kdos., Weisung für das X. Fliegerkorps, 25 Oct. 1939 (copy), BA-MA L 107/22. [25] 12 Jan. 1940, BA-MA RL 2/342.
[26] This was understood to mean 'usable front-line aircraft or aircraft of recent type in the process of being overhauled'.

As was made clear in the directive of the commander-in-chief of the Luftwaffe of 7 December 1939, the Command Staff Ic did not find the necessary support for their idea of starting an operational air war against Britain as soon as possible. In their directive of 17 January 1940 on 'more energetic measures for the war at sea and in the air'[27] for the duration of the offensive in the west, the Wehrmacht High Command placed the main emphasis in the air war on the support of army operations. Permission to attack British transports to the Continent, as well as their ports for loading and unloading, and the Royal Air Force in Britain, in so far as it carried out air attacks from there, was subject to the restriction that 'unleashing a full air war against Britain before we have acquired a favourable starting-position and have strong forces suitable for that purpose is incompatible with our overall strategy'. The staff had obviously underestimated the war-economy factor in Hitler's demand for an improvement of the German starting-position.[28] Against the background of strains and problems in the German war economy, it inevitably seemed more than doubtful that an air war conducted from within Germany itself against supplies for Britain could be successful. On 24 October Göring spoke of a 'total' war 'whose end no one can estimate even approximately'[29] and whose three fronts—the actual military front, the armaments industry, and the German nation at home—had to be 'kept in balance'. Göring was mainly concerned about the exemption of qualified skilled workers from military service. In this regard he spoke of 'serious problems' in the armaments industry caused by a lack of such workers. Every metal-worker was needed in ship and aircraft construction 'in order to carry out even the minimum programme'. The situation in agriculture was also very serious: 'If everything possible is not done there, the prospects could be bad.' To maintain healthy morale at home, all 'divinely gifted' artists were to be exempted from military service 'by order of the Führer'.

On 29 November General Thomas demanded in an even more radical fashion a war effort 'which in its size and the speed with which it is carried out will far exceed the Hindenburg programme,[30] in order to convert Germany into a single large, powerful arsenal that would be able to match Anglo-French armaments production and, in an emergency, even that of the United States'.[31] The Nazi leaders did not dare endanger their policy of keeping the population content with

---

[27] OKW/WFA/Abt. L (Ib), No. 22010/40 g.Kdos. Chefs. 17 Jan. 1940, PS NOKW 2267 (copy quoted in Speidel, 'Westfeldzug', annex 17 to ch. II).

[28] On the Low Countries cf. Volkmann, 'Autarkie'.

[29] Göring's speech to the defence replacement inspectors. The text was distributed down to battalion level on the orders of the C.-in-C. of the army: Annex to ObdH/AHA/Ag/E(Vb) No. 3412/39 geh. of 6 Nov. 1939, BA-MA RL 3/63, pp. 7301 ff. Göring also justified the measures to tighten the control of economic policy, which suffered from overlapping between the special representative for the Four-year Plan and the plenipotentiary for the economy, by pointing out the 'necessity to concentrate all our strength on a war of some duration': Ministerpräsident Generalfeldmarschall Göring, Vorsitzender des Ministerrates für Reichsverteidigung und Beauftragter für den Vierjahresplan, St. A. Bev. 11260, 7 Dec. 1939, BA-MA RL 3/63 lxv, fos. 7299–300.

[30] i.e. Hindenburg's proposal of 31 Aug. 1916 for increasing armaments production; or possibly an incorrect reference to the Auxiliary Service Law of 5 Dec. 1916.

[31] Quoted in Eichholtz, *Kriegswirtschaft*, 115.

an adequate supply of consumer goods; in their eyes, therefore, the annexation and exploitation of foreign industrial potential seemed a logical alternative.[32] This policy was reflected in the order forbidding bombing of towns and industrial plants without compelling military reason[33] during the attack on Belgium and Holland. Allied retaliation against the Ruhr was to be avoided, and the industry of the Low Countries was to be kept intact for German use.

Until a more favourable starting-position had been reached and was producing results, however, a maximum effort with all available resources was necessary in all areas, including air armaments. On 30 January 1940 Thomas accordingly presented plans to Göring,[34] who, at a conference on 'measures to support and accelerate rearmament' on 9 February,[35] ordered as a basic guide-line that 'regardless of previous tendencies, supplies of all raw materials etc. are to be stretched as far as possible in order to produce the greatest possible quantity of armaments as rapidly as possible with the material available'. Most important were those projects which 'will produce results in 1940 or at the latest 1941'.

In view of these difficulties in German armaments production, the question arises whether a determined Allied air offensive against the Ruhr could have prevented Germany from continuing the war. In contrast to France's obsolete bomber fleet, in the spring of 1940 Britain had 450 long-range bombers in front-line units. Apart from 100 Bristol Blenheims, which were not planned to take part in an attack on the Ruhr, and minus aircraft not ready for action and the losses suffered in the Norway campaign, Bomber Command still had 240 heavy bombers, of which only about half were available for an attack on the Ruhr at any given time. With these few aircraft the British air staff believed they could destroy German oil refineries, vital factories, and railway stations in the Ruhr by dropping 28 tons of bombs each night for eleven to eighteen days. In view of the later experience with major air offensives in the Second World War, these expectations were even more unrealistic than the successes the Luftwaffe considered possible in its attacks on Britain.

The German invasion of Denmark and Norway increased British fears that Hitler would attack Belgium and Holland next in order to use them as a base from which to conduct the possibly decisive air offensive against Britain. For this reason the British wanted to use the Royal Air Force to gain as much room as possible for the Allied land forces in Belgium. The medium-range bombers were to attack the German spearheads; a small number of the heavy bombers were assigned to attack the German deployment areas between the Rhine and the frontiers with Belgium

[32] Cf. Mason, 'Innere Krise und Angriffskrieg'.

[33] Trevor-Roper, Directives, No. 8.

[34] Eicholtz, Kriegswirtschaft, 113 ff.

[35] BA-MA RL 3/63, p. 7281 (participants: Funk, Keitel, Milch, Witzell). According to a report of GL 1 on the procurement situation in Dec. 1939 (12 Jan. 1940), the situation with regard to non-ferrous metals had to be described as 'extremely tight' as a result of constantly increasing requirements (BA-MA Lw. 103/65). On the air-armaments situation in general cf. Irving, Rise and Fall, 81 ff.

[36] The daylight attacks by the RAF against ships in the Heligoland Bight on 4 and 28 Sept. had resulted in heavy losses because of the Bristol Blenheim's poor defences against fighters. This made it advisable thereafter to carry out long-range attacks only at night.

and Holland. The mass of heavy bombers stood ready to attack industrial facilities, oil refineries, and communication lines in the Ruhr.

On 14 April the commander-in-chief of the British air units in France, Air Marshal Barratt, attempted to work out common guide-lines with General Gamelin for an air attack in the event of a German invasion of Belgium and Holland. Gamelin and the Comité de Guerre were still extremely cautious about air attacks to slow the German advance if the civilian population would also be affected. On 3 April the plan to disrupt German coal deliveries to Italy by bombing the railway between Freiburg and Basle had been dropped.[37] With regard to an attack on the Ruhr, the French leaders stressed again that it was not in their interest to start a war against German industrial areas and thus give Germany a justification for attacking French industry. At the meeting of the Supreme War Council on 23 April a compromise was achieved. If Germany attacked Belgium and Holland, British air units were authorized to attack railway stations and oil refineries in the Ruhr without further consultations with the Allied governments and high commands. This arrangement, however, did not permit air attacks on other industrial facilities.[38]

When the German attack in the west began on 10 May after numerous postponements, caused mostly by the weather, the Luftwaffe had about 1,180 bombers, 341 dive-bombers, 970 fighters, and 270 heavy fighters ready for action.[39] Although the Allies should have been warned by reports of the use of the Luftwaffe in Poland, the Luftwaffe succeeded in surprising their air units on the ground as well as their air command centres. As no persistent Allied attacks on the Ruhr took place, most of the fighter units assigned to defend that area were transferred to the operations area and used to achieve air supremacy there and to support the army.

As had been done against Warsaw, the Luftwaffe was used without regard to civilian casualties to break the last enemy resistance. When strong resistance in Rotterdam threatened to delay the quick occupation of Holland, Göring ordered a concentrated air attack on the city on 13 May to force an early capitulation.[40] According to the notes of the chief of the operations department of the Luftwaffe command staff, General von Waldau, this 'radical' method was the only possible one: 'The attack by two bomber and dive-bomber wings transformed the southern part of Rotterdam into a pile of rubble just like Warsaw. The complete surrender of Holland followed only two hours later. "Operation Holland" was thus finished.'[41]

---

[37] Villelume, *Journal*, 250, 259.

[38] Butler, *Strategy*, ii. 169 ff.; Woodward, *British Foreign Policy*, i. 145 ff.; PRO Cab 80/105: Air Policy, Draft Report, C.O.S. (40) 286 (S), 10 Apr. 1940; German invasion of the Low Countries, Memorandum of the Chiefs of Staff, C.O.S. (40) 292 (S), 18 Apr. 1940; Review of the strategic situation on the assumption that Germany has decided to seek a decision in 1940, Draft Report, C.O.S. (40), 29 Apr. 1940. Cf. also the discussion on the planned mining of the Rhine ('Royal Marine'), V.II above.

[39] According to the quartermaster-general, 6. Abt., 4 May 1940, BA-MA RL 2 III/707.

[40] Thus Schmid in a report written in 1945: 'Die 5. Abteilung des Generalstabes der Luftwaffe (Ic)', extracts in BA-MA Lw. 107/22, No. 57.

[41] Gen. von Waldau, 'Persönliches Tagebuch', 25 May 1940, copy of extracts, BA-MA Lw. 107/22, No. 79. Cf. Swint, 'Rotterdam'; Butler, *Strategy*, ii. 569-70.

According to Waldau, the attack 'planned in loving detail' against the airfields around Paris and parts of the engine and aircraft factories there on 3 June was likewise a 'desirable exercise of moral influence' on the capital.[42] However, the results of the action, carried out by 600 bombers and 500 fighters, were as scanty as those of the attacks on the harbour in Marseilles. It became clear that much stronger forces and frequent attacks would be necessary to achieve success.[43]

The British Bomber Command had similar experiences. The mining of the Rhine (Operation 'Royal Marine') had no influence on the course of the German offensive. The German attack on Rotterdam removed the War Cabinet's remaining moral reservations about an attack on the Ruhr, in which victims among the civilian population were to be expected. On 10 May the Western Allies threatened to carry out such attacks as retaliation for similar German actions against their civilian populations or those of countries they defended.[44]

As early as 12 May the Chief of Staff Committee was of the opinion that an attack on the Ruhr should be carried out as soon as possible, as it was perhaps the last chance to stop the German advance. An attack on oil refineries was, however, dependent on good visibility by moonlight and would be possible only on the nights of 16 and 17 May.[45] An attack on industrial plants in the Ruhr carried out with about 100 heavy bombers on 15 May achieved only slight results and had no effect on the battle in France, which, on the same day, the French premier Reynaud described to Churchill as lost.

The British decision on Reynaud's request the day before for ten additional fighter squadrons was determined by the impression of an imminent French defeat. On 15 May Sir Hugh Dowding, Chief of Fighter Command, was opposed to sending any more fighters to France as this would not change the situation there. He argued that if Fighter Command were not weakened by having to send more aircraft to France, he would be able to repel a German air offensive against the British Isles even if it were carried out from bases in Holland, Belgium, and France.[46]

Hitler's Directive No. 13 of 24 May 1940 authorized the Luftwaffe to start a 'full-scale' air offensive against Britain as soon as sufficient forces were available. It was to begin with a 'devastating retaliatory attack' for the British bombing of the Ruhr. The specific targets were to be determined by Göring on the basis of Directive No. 9 of 29 November and supplementary directives to be issued specifically for that purpose by the Wehrmacht High Command.[47]

In the 'Supplement to Directive No. 9' issued two days later the Wehrmacht High command came to the conclusion that no decisive result could be achieved by attacks

---

[42] Gen. von Waldau, 'Persönliches Tagebuch', 25 May 1940, extracts in BA-MA Lw 107/22, No. 79.

[43] Schmid, report on 'Die 5. Abteilung des Generalstabes der Luftwaffe (Ic)', extracts in BA-MA Lw 107/22, No. 57. On the effect in Paris cf. Villelume, *Journal*, 376.

[44] Woodward, *British Foreign Policy*, i. 176–7.

[45] PRO Cab 79/4, C.O.S. (40) 125th Meeting, 12 May 1940.

[46] PRO Cab 79/4, C.O.S. (40) 133rd meeting, 15 May 1940; Woodward, *British Foreign Policy*, i. 191 ff.; Butler, *Strategy*, ii. 179 ff.; Villelume, *Journal*, 336–7; Deighton, *Fighter*, 71 ff.

[47] Trevor-Roper, *Directives*, No. 13.

on British imports alone. On the other hand, 'at the crucial moment of the attack on the British economy, the disruption of the utility system (gas, water, electricity) could be of decisive importance'. Apart from the targets listed in Directive No. 9, the most urgent task of the Luftwaffe during the operations in the west was to destroy the British air armaments industry in order to deprive the British air force, the last weapon which could be used directly against Germany, of its industrial base.[48] That this would not be easy became clear when the Luftwaffe attacked the British expeditionary corps, which was able to escape annihilation primarily because of British air superiority over the Channel, although on 25 May Göring had promised Hitler he would destroy it.[49] Not the least important reason for this first success of Fighter Command was the fact that its fighter units had not been weakened by any significant new transfers to France and could be used within the framework of the British command and supply organization.

[48] Trevor-Roper, *Directives*, No. 9a.
[49] Meier-Welcker, 'Entschluß'; Irving, *Rise and Fall*, 90-1; notes of Luftwaffe Gen. Hans Seidemann (ret.) on the use of the Luftwaffe at Dunkirk, 4 Dec. 1954, PA-MA Lw 107/22.

PART VIII

The Second Phase of the War at Sea
(until the Spring of 1941)

BERND STEGEMANN

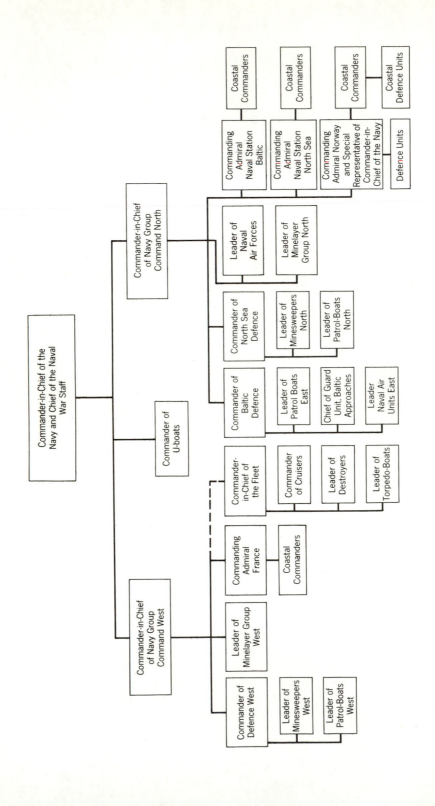

DIAGRAM VIII.I.I. Command organization of the navy at the end of 1940

I. The Submarine War

AT the end of 1940 the starting-position for the German U-boat fleet had greatly improved. After the occupation of Norway, the British were no longer able to block the exits from the North Sea with mine-barrages, something which had been a cause for concern because of their attempts to do so in the First World War. After the defeat of France, bases for U-boats could be built on the Atlantic coast, which reduced the distance from the operations area west of the British Isles by about 450 nautical miles. As early as July U-boats could be resupplied at Lorient. In August the shipyard there, which was more efficient than the German shipyards, was again in operation. Finally, the commander of U-boats transferred his command centre to neighbouring Kernevel.

This favourable development for the conduct of the submarine war was made even better by the weakness of British submarine defences. During the operations in and off Norway and in the evacuation of Dunkirk the Royal Navy had suffered heavy losses, especially of escort vessels. Moreover, until autumn strong destroyer units had to be kept ready to repel an invasion of the British Isles. For this reason until October the escorting of arriving and departing convoys could only be extended from longitude 12° W. to 19° W. In addition, the approaches for ships south of Ireland could not be used after 15 July because of the danger of air attacks. This made it necessary for all ships to use the North Channel and much easier for U-boats to find targets.

In spite of these favourable conditions, U-boat successes were limited because the number ready for action remained small. Between 1 June 1940 and 31 March 1941 72 were commissioned with only 13 losses; the total number of U-boats rose to 109. But the number of front-line U-boats available declined to 22 by February 1941 because many of them were required for training; a large number were undergoing sea trials and their crews were being trained. Raeder was still attempting to push U-boat construction, but with little success. At first Hitler told him to wait until after the campaign in France; then preparations for 'Operation Sea-Lion', the invasion of Britain, were given priority, and finally, armaments priorities were determined by the campaign against the Soviet Union planned for 1941.

After the defeat of France had considerably improved the raw-material situation, a continuation of the limited U-boat construction programme beyond 1 January 1942 and an increase to 25 submarines per month seemed possible. Raeder obtained Hitler's approval of this expanded programme on 31 July 1940, but at the same time he demanded that all measures for 'Sea-Lion' should be given greater priority. The introduction of priorities and special levels of urgency did not lead to any real improvements, as many more programmes were classified as extremely urgent than there were means and facilities available to carry them out. This situation became even worse when, in addition to U-boat construction, in a directive of 28 September

1940[1] for the equipping of 200 divisions special priority was given to most areas of aircraft production and the production of tanks and anti-tank weapons. On 27 December 1940 Raeder again complained to Hitler that the priority given to U-boat construction within the total armaments programme did not correspond at all to the importance of the submarine war. With the available work-force it would be possible to deliver only 12 or at most 18 U-boats per month. Hitler also wanted to accelerate U-boat construction as much as possible, but he pointed to political developments that made it necessary to strengthen the army in order to eliminate the Soviet Union.

Even after additional workers had actually been provided for the naval armaments programme in January 1941, the Navy High Command estimated that because of labour shortages and increased requirements they would still need 67,500 workers by 30 September. On 18 March 1941 Raeder informed Hitler that if these labourers were provided and material requirements met, it would be possible to increase monthly U-boat production in 1941 to 20 and in 1942 to 24; otherwise the number, which would be 18 in the second quarter of 1941, would decline to 15. As earlier, Hitler mentioned his intention to make the greatest efforts to expand the navy and the Luftwaffe after the conclusion of 'Barbarossa'.[2] Under these conditions, no decisive success could be expected, i.e. no level of sinkings that would reduce British shipping to the point where it would be impossible to replace losses. The U-boat fleet first had to be built up in 1940 and 1941. Only then would it be possible to see if the hopes were justified which Dönitz, especially, placed in the U-boats.

On 15 May, after the actions connected with 'Operation Weserübung', the first U-boat again put to sea for the war against British shipping in the Atlantic. As earlier, the magnetic detonators of the torpedoes often failed, and therefore the commander of U-boats had to forbid their use altogether.[3] On the whole, however, the operation was a success. In the following period the U-boats concentrated on shipping off the North Channel. It proved difficult to locate arriving and departing convoys in time to mass strong U-boat groups before they had passed the operations area. Finding a convoy was largely a matter of chance, as usually not even ten U-boats were in the operations area, and two of them were stationed far to the west as 'weather-boats'. Reconnaissance possibilities were obviously very limited. Signal intelligence provided important help here, as it repeatedly succeeded in deciphering British radio messages on course-changes and meeting-points in good time.[4]

Additional successes in the tonnage war were expected with the help of Italian U-boats in the Atlantic, which the Italian navy offered on 24 July. Bordeaux was

[1] Printed in Thomas, *Wehr- und Rüstungswirtschaft*, 432–6.
[2] 'Führer Conferences', 188. On this section cf. Rössler, *Ubootbau*, 202–3; Salewski, *Seekriegsleitung*, i. 261–5.
[3] Cf. IV.VII above.
[4] On this aspect of the war cf. esp. Rohwer, *Geleitzugschlachten*; id., 'Einfluß'; *Funkaufklärung*. On the individual phases of the Battle of the Atlantic cf. the chapter on the submarine war in Potter and Nimitz, *Sea Power* (German trans.), 521–50; Costello and Hughes, *Battle of the Atlantic*; Brennecke, *U-Boot-Krieg*; for a British account of the second phase of the submarine war cf. Roskill, *War at Sea*, i. 343–65.

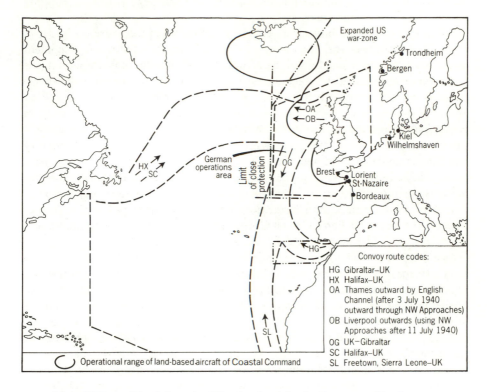

MAP VIII.I.I. The Submarine War in the Atlantic, June 1940–March 1941

placed at the disposal of the Italians as a base; an Italian leader of U-boats was placed under Dönitz. After operating near the Azores, 27 Italian U-boats arrived at their new Atlantic base. In October and November Dönitz sent them into action west and south-west of the German U-boats off the North Channel, but they did not succeed in directing German U-boats to convoys or in finding convoys themselves which had been reported and attacked by German U-boats. This was due partly to the fact that the Italian captains had been trained for isolated attacks by individual U-boats waiting for targets, and not for group operations against convoys; also, the Italian U-boats were poorly suited for a war in the Atlantic. For this reason Dönitz called off the attempt at co-operation on 5 December; the Italian U-boats were successfully deployed against individual ships in the southern and western part of the German operational area. Following these successes, Dönitz made a second attempt at co-operation beginning on 18 February 1941 and used the Italian U-boats to extend the area covered by German U-boats south of Iceland even further south. But by 5 May it had become clear that this effort was also a failure. Following the Italian defeats in the Mediterranean, the Italian U-boats returned home. Only 10 large ones remained in the Atlantic to continue the war against British shipping outside the German operations area.[5]

In October 1940 the U-boats achieved their best record of the entire war per day-at-sea. In the winter of 1940 the successes declined. One cause of this development was seasonal weather conditions in the North Atlantic, but far more important was the strengthening of British submarine defences. Through the 'destroyers for naval bases' deal of 5 September Britain received 50 American destroyers from the First World War in exchange for turning over to the United States a total of 8 bases in British possessions in the New World. Moreover, corvettes now entered the war—primitive, quickly constructed ships which would soon bear the main burden of anti-submarine defence. In and after November 1940 the first radar equipment, which still had a short range, was put into service on British destroyers in the area of the Western Approaches; and other escort vessels received radio telephones also. A usable radio direction-finder could not, however, be developed in this period. Units of the Royal Air Force Coastal Command were gradually strengthened, and after April 1941 Iceland was used as an air-base.

As a reaction to the declining sinkings in the North Atlantic, Dönitz decided in February 1941 to send more large U-boats of Type IX to the area off Freetown in Sierra Leone; individual U-boats had previously operated there on three occasions. Earlier he had rejected the idea of sending so many to that area because the number of sinkings per U-boat day-at-sea was inevitably lower than in the North Atlantic as a result of the great distance. This was incompatible with Dönitz's principle of the economical use of U-boats. But in March 5 U-boats were lost in the area south of Iceland, the first since November 1940. Among them were those of the most successful captains: Kretschmer, Schepke, and Prien, who had sunk the British battleship *Royal Oak* in Scapa Flow. These losses were not at first recognized as a coincidence, and the lack of reports on enemy convoys, however, caused Dönitz to shift the operations area of the U-boats 200 miles to the south-west, where the convoys could no longer be protected by land-based aircraft of Coastal Command.

Between June 1940 and March 1941 German U-boats sank a total of 446 ships of 2,430,386 gross registered tons, and Italian U-boats 37 ships with 157,699 gross registered tons.[6] Long-range aircraft sank an additional 52 ships of 207,889 gross registered tons.[7] Only in June and October were the U-boats able to sink more than 300,000 gross registered tons. They were still far from reaching the level of the First World War, but even the loss of almost 6 million gross registered tons of merchant shipping in 1917 had not meant defeat for Britain.[8]

---

[5] Cf. Dönitz, *Memoirs*, 140–5; Salewski, *Seekriegsleitung*, i. 299, 325–6.

[6] Figures according to statistics by Jürgen Rohwer, based on his *Submarine Successes*. Rohwer suggested including Apr. and May 1941 in this phase of the Battle of the Atlantic because thereafter the British breaking of the German ciphers created a completely new situation.

[7] Figures from Rohwer, 'U-Bootkrieg', 333.

[8] In 1917 the German navy command promised that a monthly total of 600,000 GRT sunk would force Britain to her knees within five months. This enabled them to push through their demand for unrestricted submarine warfare, which led to the entry of the US into the war.

II. Co-operation with the Luftwaffe[1]

OF special importance for the conduct of the submarine war in the Atlantic was the question whether it was possible to use aircraft to improve reconnaissance for U-boats to the point that the few available could at least be guided to convoys. In a protocol of 27 January 1939 Raeder and Göring had agreed that 'Aerial reconnaissance for naval purposes is a special task of the navy.'[2] The seaplanes and flying boats of the Küstenfliegergruppen, which were operationally under the command of the navy, could not, however, reach the operations area of the U-boats in the North Atlantic. Moreover, they were technically obsolete and no match for land-based aircraft in combat. The Luftwaffe did equip the Küstenfliegergruppen one after the other with land-based aircraft (the KFG 606 with the Do 17, the KFGs 806 and 106 with Ju 88s), but even these aircraft did not have sufficient range to fly reconnaissance for the U-boats. These wings were in fact withdrawn from the war at sea and used for attacks on Britain, which was in accordance with their own wishes as they, like the leader of Naval Air Forces West and Group Command West, were of the opinion that reconnaissance on the scale desired by the naval war staff was superfluous. The only aircraft in production that fulfilled the reconnaissance requirements somewhat better was the Fw 200.

The only Gruppe equipped with this aircraft, the I/KG 40, was under the Ninth Flying Division and had been operating since August 1940 from the airfield of Mérignac near Bordeaux against enemy shipping. The Luftwaffe, however, was more interested in increasing its own sinkings of enemy ships than in flying reconnaissance for the commander of U-boats.

The efforts of the naval war staff to recover their Küstenfliegergruppen, equip them with adequate aircraft, and persuade the Luftwaffe to carry out more intensive reconnaissance[3] were at first successful in one respect: Dönitz was permitted to present his views to the Wehrmacht operations staff on 18 and 30 December, and obtained a 'Führer order' that placed the I/KG 40 tactically under his command as of 7 January 1941. But the subsequent attempts to conduct joint operations showed that the Fw 200s did not have sufficient range to direct U-boats to convoys they had sighted. The navigation of the aircraft, however, was so imprecise that the U-boats were usually unable to use their position reports to find convoys. Finally a system was developed whereby an aircraft that had discovered a convoy transmitted a direction-finding signal which was zeroed in on by the U-boats. Using cross-bearings they were then able to mark the exact position. An extensive search for convoys was not possible as on average only two aircraft were available each day.

---

[1] Cf. IV.II above.

[2] Quoted in Hümmelchen, *Seeflieger*, 18; cf. also the first attempt to provide an account—Gaul, 'Marinefliegerverbände'; Dönitz, *Memoirs*, 128–37; Salewski, *Seekriegsleitung*, i. 254–7, 266–7, 427–36.

[3] Cf. also 'Führer Conferences', 156–7, 160–3 (3 and 27 Dec. 1940).

Göring, however, did not agree that the I/KG 40 should be placed under the commander of U-boats for tactical mission assignments. He was finally able to persuade Hitler to place the aircraft of KG 40, together with those of the Küstenfliegergruppen in the area, under a newly created 'air leader Atlantic' on 15 March 1941. Moreover, on 1 March the position of 'leader of reconnaissance Norway' had been created, subordinate to the Luftwaffe; the area for which the leader of the naval air forces was responsible was restricted to the North Sea itself and the Baltic approaches. This meant that Raeder had not been able in the end to push through his demands of 4 February, that the naval air forces in the west and the North Sea should each have one Gruppe for long-range reconnaissance and two for coastal-zone reconnaissance, escort duty, and anti-submarine operations.[4]

The Luftwaffe was also able to have its way in the dispute about the use of aerial torpedoes, which took place at the same time. At first such torpedoes had been used only by the naval air forces equipped with He 115 seaplanes. With these rather inadequate aircraft they had been able only to sink several merchant ships off the east coast of Scotland: at the start of the war the torpedoes still had a failure rate of 35.6 per cent. But after ten obsolete British torpedo-bombers had been able to put three Italian battleships out of action in the harbour of Taranto on the night of 11–12 November, Göring decided to create a torpedo-bomber Gruppe of his own with which to attack British battleships in Alexandria or Gibraltar. On 26 November he therefore ordered the naval air forces to stop using aerial torpedoes immediately. The naval war staff, on the other hand, considered the torpedo to be a weapon of the war at sea which only experienced naval officers could use effectively, and therefore demanded that the naval air forces should be equipped with the He 111 and the Do 217,[5] which the Luftwaffe planned to use as torpedo-bombers. The dispute, which was conducted with considerable bitterness on both sides, was provisionally settled by the decision that the navy should receive a third and the Luftwaffe two-thirds of aerial torpedo production. But this arrangement did not satisfy anyone, and on 23 April 1941 the Luftwaffe was able to persuade the Wehrmacht High Command to order the navy to turn over all its aerial torpedoes (a total of five) to the Tenth Flying Corps, which was stationed in the Mediterranean. This conflict between the Luftwaffe and the navy was less about technical or purely military questions than about principle: Göring wanted to prevent the development of an independent naval air arm; Raeder for his part wanted to ensure that the Küstenfliegergruppen, which on a tactical level were subordinate to the navy, were not further downgraded by being inadequately supplied with aircraft or by their tasks being taken over by the Luftwaffe.

---

[4] Cf. *Lagevorträge*, 4 Feb. 1941, annex 2.
[5] Details ibid., 3 Dec. 1940, annex 2; 27 Dec., annex b.

III. Armed Merchant Raiders
in the War against Shipping

DÖNITZ, at least, understood the submarine war as a tonnage war: i.e. the aim was to sink more tonnage than the enemy was able to build, buy, or charter, in the area where the U-boats could achieve the highest number of sinkings with the fewest losses. In this way Britain's transport-shipping capacity was to be reduced to the point where she would no longer be able to continue the war. On the other hand, the naval war staff, as regards the use of armed merchant raiders, were not primarily interested in sinking the maximum number of enemy merchant ships. In their view,

The main task is to inflict damage on the enemy and tie down his naval forces to take pressure off our home front:

(a) by forcing him to use convoys and strengthen protection for his shipping, even in remote areas of the ocean;
(b) by consequently placing a strain on his naval forces;
(c) by deterring neutral ships from transporting enemy cargoes; and
(d) by bringing about additional harmful trade and financial consequences.

For this task it is more important to tie down and distract the enemy for a long time than to achieve high sinking-rates, which would necessarily quickly wear out our armed merchant raiders.[1]

The use of armed merchant raiders was not envisaged in German mobilization plans, although the navy of imperial Germany had had considerable experience in this area during the First World War and the use of such ships had always played a role in German operational thinking between the wars. It had been realized that the use of large, fast passenger ships like those of the Allies would serve no real purpose because such ships were easy to recognize and their high fuel consumption limited their cruising range. More suitable were freighters with a great range, which could change their appearance more easily to resemble neutral or Allied ships in order to deceive their hunters as well as their victims.

Planning for the use of armed merchant raiders was begun after the start of the war, and by the end of September envisaged the equipping of a first group of six freighters. They were to be armed with 6 15-cm. guns, 4 2-cm. anti-aircraft guns, and 4 torpedo-tubes. Equipment for 400 mines and two seaplanes was also planned. The ships were to be able to remain at sea a year and cruise about 40,000 nautical miles with a crew of 284. According to the plans of the naval war staff, the first

---

[1] From the operations order for 'Ship 16', printed in Hümmelchen, *Handelsstörer*, 494–507, here 498–9. This is the definitive work on the German side. On the period treated here cf. Roskill, *War at Sea*, i. 277–92, 367–87; Potter and Nimitz, *Sea Power* (German trans.), 503–8.

armed merchant raider was to put to sea as early as November 1939, but this plan could not be realized. The first ship left port on 31 March 1940, the last only on 3 July. In November 1939 the naval war staff decided to send out a second wave of six armed merchant raiders in the summer of 1940, but this project proved even more difficult to realize with existing shipyard and armaments facilities.[2] Four ships of this second group were made ready for action, but only the first was able to put to sea in 1940, on 3 December. The fourth ship had to abandon the attempt to pass through the Channel in February 1943 after one armed merchant raider had already been lost there on 14 October 1942. Thereafter it was no longer possible for such ships to enter the Atlantic from Germany.

By the end of March 1941 the seven German armed merchant raiders in service had sunk or captured 80 ships of 494,291 gross registered tons. The naval war staff were quite satisfied with this result, which they evidently had not expected. They were apparently especially surprised that it had been possible to establish a smoothly functioning supply and support system in spite of British surveillance forces. On 14 October Raeder informed Hitler: 'Tanker Rekum has returned after successfully refuelling three auxiliary cruisers in the North and South Atlantic. The achievement of this vessel gives an indication of the possibilities of refuelling auxiliary cruisers and the prospects for our merchant shipping in the Atlantic.' A month later he reported that the 'Supplies from non-German sources have up to now been secured with only slight losses, in spite of a very sharp watch being kept by the enemy.'[3] On 20 April he again reported on this aspect of the war against enemy shipping: 'The numerous supply-ships engaged in replenishing the supplies of auxiliary cruisers and U-boats in the Indian and South Atlantic oceans have hitherto been remarkably successful. Only one prize tanker was lost.'[4]

The use of armed merchant raiders was especially important for the naval war staff because until the end of October 1940 no other surface ships were available which could operate in the North Atlantic, not to mention more distant oceans. The lack of a fleet was also reflected in Raeder's intention to use armed merchant raiders to take possession of colonies, whose return was expected after the conclusion of peace with Britain.[5] Thus, armed merchant raiders became a modest substitute for the more powerful ships actually envisaged by the Z plan.

The successes of the armed merchant raiders were made possible by several factors. Because of the collapse of France, the entry of Italy into the war on the side of Germany, and the need to keep forces ready in order to repel the threatened invasion, the Royal Navy was unable to assign the necessary ships to pursue them. The Royal Air Force was also fully occupied at home with preparations to repel a landing and by the Battle of Britain, and was therefore unable to devote enough aircraft to patrolling the North Atlantic or more distant oceans. Effective radar systems for

---

[2] Cf. Salewski, *Seekriegsleitung*, i. 383-4.
[3] 'Führer Conferences', 144, 151.
[4] Ibid. 190.   [5] Ibid. 113.

ships and aeroplanes were still lacking. The British had not yet succeeded in breaking the German codes and were thus still not able to intercept instructions regarding meeting-points of ships at sea, although the Admiralty was already concentrating all its efforts on that goal.[6]

---

[6] Cf. Rohwer, *Geleitzugschlachten*, 37-40, and the definitive work on the British side: Beesly, *Intelligence*.

IV. The Use of Large Surface Ships

AT the end of June 1940 the naval war staff still regarded the northern waters as by far the most important operations area, as 'Operation Juno' and the subsequent use of the heavy cruiser *Hipper* clearly showed.[1] Trondheim was to become the great naval base used by German battleships and heavy cruisers to attack British surveillance forces between The Faeroes and Greenland, and by torpedo-boats and destroyers, covered by heavy and light cruisers, to protect Norwegian coastal waters.[2] An expansion of operations into the North Atlantic and the use of bases in western France were not planned for the time being. By August this thinking had changed: the *Hipper* was recalled to break through into the Atlantic in conjunction with 'Operation Sea-Lion' (the invasion of Britain), and to call at Saint-Nazaire after doing so. When the order to start 'Operation Sea-Lion' failed to materialize, it was intended for the *Hipper* to carry out her operation nevertheless.

The reason was that, in the mean time, the naval war staff had begun to develop a plan for waging war in the Atlantic. The units of the fleet—battleships, heavy and light cruisers, and destroyers—were now to be used against enemy shipping there. Raeder described it as 'imperative' to concentrate all forces of the navy and the Luftwaffe on blocking the shipments of supplies to Britain.[3] This aim was to be reached partly by operational and partly by tactical co-operation. The time seemed to have come to use heavy surface ships once again in the war against such shipments. The U-boats and the armed merchant raiders had long been bearing the brunt of the fighting in the Atlantic alone; now the naval war staff wanted to start a new phase.[4]

On 14 September, however, the tanker *Uckermark*, which had been intended to refuel the *Hipper*, struck a mine south of Haugesund, and another tanker had to be provided. After this had been done, the *Hipper* put to sea again on 24 September but developed serious engine trouble off the Norwegian coast. Her captain was forced to break off the operation and return to Kiel on 30 September.[5] The forced cancellation of the operation was all the more vexatious to the naval war staff as destroyers had already been sent west and the second ship planned for the operation, the pocket battleship *Admiral Scheer* (Captain Krancke), also had engine problems and could not be made ready for action by 10 September as scheduled. She was able to put to sea only on 27 October, a week after her supply-ship, the tanker

[1] Cf. V.III above.
[2] Directive of 29 June 1940, printed in Salewski, *Seekriegsleitung*, i. 524-7; cf. ibid. 212.
[3] 'Führer Conferences', 150.
[4] Cf. for the following section also Salewski, *Seekriegsleitung*, i. 375-89.
[5] Cf. Bidlingmaier, *Einsatz*, 121; for the following section ibid. 123-34, 146-56, 184-98; and Hümmelchen, *Handelsstörer*, 188-90, 192-4, 278-91.

Nordmark. After a brief call at Stavanger, she passed through the Denmark Strait on 1 November, where she was able to avoid two British patrol vessels with the help of her radar (*DT-Gerät*).[6] Thereafter she began to search for convoys on the route between Halifax and Britain. During the morning of 5 November her seaplane discovered the convoy HX 84 protected only by the armed merchant cruiser *Jervis Bay*. Delayed by the sinking of a banana-carrier, the *Scheer* reached the convoy only late in the afternoon and opened fire at 4.40 p.m. on the armed merchant cruiser, which was finished off eight minutes later. By 9.30 p.m. the *Scheer* was able to sink five additional ships of the disintegrating convoy. This attack caused a twelve-day interruption of convoy traffic in the North Atlantic.

The *Scheer* was refuelled on 12 November by a tanker and from 16 to 20 November by the *Nordmark*. She then sailed for the area north of the Caribbean, where she also sank a ship. After an additional sinking off the Canary Islands, she set a course for the South Atlantic, resupplied again on 14–15 December by the *Nordmark*. On 18 December near the Equator she captured the refrigerator-ship *Duquesa*, which served the German ships in the South Atlantic as a food depot until her stocks were used up on 18 February. On 22 December the *Scheer* again met the *Nordmark* and was joined in the following days by Ship 10, a German tanker, and a captured Norwegian tanker. After her engines had been overhauled, the *Scheer* entered the waters west of central Africa on 8 January 1941, where she sank two ships and captured another tanker, which was equipped by the *Nordmark* and sent to western France with prisoners. Between 24 and 28 January the *Scheer* took on new supplies from the *Nordmark* and the *Duquesa*, transferred prize crews to whaling-ships captured by Ship 33, met Ship 10 again, and then entered the Indian Ocean, passing the Cape of Good Hope on 3 February. There she met her supply-ship, Ship 16, with two captured vessels on 14–17 February for mutual resupplying and to exchange information. Subsequently she captured a tanker and sank three ships north of Madagascar. After this last sinking the *Scheer* was discovered by a seaplane from the British light cruiser *Glasgow* but was able to shake off her pursuers by heading east. On 2 March she returned to the Atlantic. On 8 March she met the *Nordmark* and a freighter, which took off her prisoners; on 10 March she met a supply-ship, which brought ammunition and a new seaplane, and on 16 March she met Ship 41, with whose radar system she was able to repair her own. During the night of 28 March she succeeded in passing through the Denmark Strait after avoiding contact with two British light cruisers. On 30 March she reached the Norwegian coast and anchored in Kiel on 1 April. In 161 days the *Scheer* had sunk or captured 17 ships with a total of 113,233 gross registered tons.[7]

The *Admiral Hipper* (Captain Meisel) put to sea on 30 November and took on additional fuel in Norway on 1 December, but had to postpone passing through

---

[6] *Dezimetertelegrafie-Gerät.*

[7] This operation is regarded as the most successful carried out against enemy shipping by a regular warship during the Second World War (Hümmelchen, *Handelsstörer*, 291). The most successful U-boat captain, Lt.-Cmdr. Kretschmer, sank 37 ships totalling 241,523 GRT between July 1940 and his capture on 17 Mar. 1941.

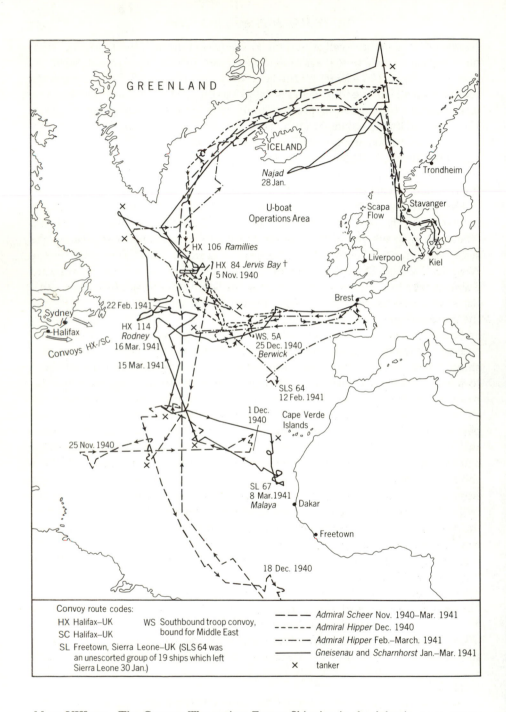

Convoy route codes:

HX Halifax–UK
SC Halifax–UK
SL Freetown, Sierra Leone–UK (SLS 64 was
      an unescorted group of 19 ships which left
      Sierra Leone 30 Jan.)

WS Southbound troop convoy,
      bound for Middle East

– – – *Admiral Scheer* Nov. 1940–Mar. 1941
- - - - *Admiral Hipper* Dec. 1940
–·–·– *Admiral Hipper* Feb.–March. 1941
——— *Gneisenau* and *Scharnhorst* Jan.–Mar. 1941
× tanker

MAP VIII.IV.I. The German War against Enemy Shipping in the Atlantic, 1940–1941

the Denmark Strait until a replacement ship was in position for one of her three refuelling tankers, which was not available because of engine damage. Continually refuelled by a tanker, the *Hipper* waited north of Iceland until 5 December and passed through the Denmark Strait two days later. When she reached her operations area, the convoy route between Halifax and Britain, she suffered serious engine problems, which were, however, repaired within two days. On 11-12 December she took on fuel from her second tanker. After two more fruitless attempts to locate convoys on the Halifax–Britain route, the *Hipper* returned to her tanker on 20 December, and her captain decided to change to the route Britain–Sierra Leone. There too he looked in vain for two convoys and had to take on fuel again on 23 December. On the evening of the following day, his radar located the troop convoy WS 5 A escorted by the aircraft-carrier *Furious*, the heavy cruiser *Berwick*, and the two light cruisers *Bonaventure* and *Dunedin*. After an unsuccessful torpedo attack during the night, the *Hipper* opened fire on the *Berwick*, the first target sighted, at 6.38 a.m. When the two light cruisers (at first taken for destroyers) came into view at 6.40 a.m., the *Hipper* turned away and was able to shake off her enemies at 7.20 a.m. She remained undamaged but had herself scored several hits on the *Berwick* and two troop-ships.

After this engagement Meisel decided to break off the operation and head for Brest because of the frequent problems with his engines. On the way to Brest the *Hipper* sank one more ship and on 27 December became the first heavy German ship to reach the base on the French west coast. In the mean time the British began patrolling the entrances to the North Atlantic with ships of the Home Fleet; only on 4 January did they discover the *Hipper* in Brest. Between that day and her departure from Brest on 1 February, aircraft of Bomber Command flew 175 missions over the city and dropped nearly 85 tons of bombs, but without hitting her. They did clearly demonstrate, however, that Brest was anything but a safe base.

In her next operation the *Hipper* took up a waiting-position north of the Azores, where she received fuel from her tanker. When she was sent into action again on 9 February, she sailed to intercept the convoy HG 53, with which the *U 37* was keeping in touch off Gibraltar. The *U 37* was able to sink 3 ships and direct aircraft of the I./KG 40 to the convoy; these sank an additional 5 freighters. The *Hipper* arrived on the scene on 11 February, but by then the convoy had been disbanded; she found only one ship. However, the convoy of 16 ships had lost a total of 9, totalling 15,218 gross registered tons.

In the following night, with the help of her radar, the *Hipper* discovered the unprotected convoy SLS 64, which consisted of 19 ships. She attacked on 12 February at 6.18 a.m. and by 7.40 a.m. had sunk 7 ships with a total of 32,806 gross registered tons. Two other ships totalling 9,899 tons were heavily damaged. Because his ammunition stocks were now low, Meisel broke off the operation and returned to Brest on 14 February. In view of the serious damage to his engines which was discovered there, the naval war staff decided to drop plans for another operation in the Atlantic and ordered the *Hipper* to return to Germany. As the British were still not able to score any bomb hits on the ship, she could sail for home on 15 March.

After taking on more fuel off the southern tip of Greenland, she passed through the Denmark Strait during the night of 23-4 March, avoiding two British cruisers. Two days later she took on more fuel in the Grimstad Fiord and reached Kiel on 28 March.

The climax of the war against shipping in the Atlantic using surface ships was 'Operation Berlin', the use of the two battleships *Scharnhorst* and *Gneisenau* under the commander-in-chief of the fleet, Admiral Lütjens. After the damage suffered in 'Operation Juno' had been repaired,[8] the two ships were able to leave the shipyard at the beginning of December 1940 and prepare for action during that month. On 28 December they put to sea, but the *Gneisenau* suffered such heavy damage in moderate seas off Norway that the naval war staff ordered the two ships to return home. On 22 January they were again able to put to sea; Lütjens intended to pass between The Faeroes and Iceland on the night of 28 January. But there he met British patrol-ships; his sailing had been reported to the commander-in-chief of the Home Fleet, Admiral Tovey, who had taken up a position to intercept him south of Iceland. The light cruiser *Naiad*, which had reported sighting the German ships at 8.15 a.m., lost contact with them as they turned away to the north-east at high speed. In the northern waters between 30 January and 2 February they took on more fuel from one of the seven tankers assigned to them, and then made an attempt to pass through the Denmark Strait. Using their radar, they succeeded in avoiding contact with a British patrol-ship on the morning of 4 February. As he had considered the report of the *Naiad* mistaken, Admiral Tovey had returned to Scapa Flow with the Home Fleet on 30 January.[9]

On 5-6 February the two German battleships received more fuel south of Greenland and operated against the Halifax-Britain convoy route. There they sighted the convoy HX 106 on the morning of 8 February. However, as it was escorted by the battleship *Ramillies*, Lütjens decided not to attack. After taking on additional fuel on 14 February, he was finally able to sink 5 individual ships on 22 February. As the British had now been alerted, however, he decided to shift his operations to the convoy route Sierra Leone-Britain. On 3 March, after being refuelled in mid-Atlantic, the two battleships had reached the area west of the Canary Islands. They continued on a southward course and sighted the convoy SL 67, which was also escorted by a battleship, the *Malaya*, on the morning of 7 March. After some difficulties caused by the fact that code-group radio transmissions were only possible via Germany, the *Gneisenau* and the *Scharnhorst* were able to direct the U-boats *U 124* and *U 105* to the convoy. In the early morning of 8 March the two U-boats sank 6 of its ships, but they could not eliminate the battleship. Lütjens decided to return to his tankers and then to the Halifax-Britain route. After sinking a lone ship, he met the tankers *Uckermark* and *Ermland*, which he retained as reconnaissance ships, on 11 March. With their help he achieved his greatest success

[8] Cf. V.III above.

[9] On 'Operation Berlin' cf. Bidlingmaier, *Einsatz*, 156-65, 169-84; Hümmelchen, *Handelsstörer*, 299-308. On the British side, as well as for the operations of the *Scheer* and the *Hipper*, cf. Roskill, *War at Sea*, i. 367-80.

on 15–16 March: on these two days he sank 13 ships of a dispersed convoy and sent 3 captured tankers to German bases on the western coast of France, where, however, only one was able to break through. In the evening the *Gneisenau* was challenged by the British battleship *Rodney*, but the German ships were able to shake her off and took a south-easterly course.

On 18–19 March Lütjens replenished his fuel again and decided to break off the operation. His two ships had to be ready to sail once more at the end of April, as the first cruise of the battleship *Bismarck* and the heavy cruiser *Prinz Eugen* in the Atlantic was planned for that date. While the British concentrated their surveillance on the northern entrances to the Atlantic, Lütjens set a course for Brest. An aeroplane of the British Force H from Gibraltar sighted the German ships on the evening of 21 March, but the exact information reached the British commander-in-chief too late. On the morning of 22 March the *Scharnhorst* and the *Gneisenau* arrived in Brest. They had sunk or captured 22 ships totalling 115,622 gross registered tons.

Sinkings and captures by the heavy German ships between July 1940 and March 1941 totalled 47 ships of 256,496 gross registered tons, a figure far below that achieved by the armed merchant raiders and which had almost been reached by the bombers. Nevertheless, the use of heavy cruisers, pocket battleships, and especially battleships endangered the British convoy system in the North Atlantic. Against such ships, armed merchant and old light cruisers could not provide adequate protection. But the British could not protect every convoy with battleships, and it had been a fortunate accident for them that the two convoys discovered by the *Scharnhorst* and the *Gneisenau* had been escorted by battleships. The cruise of the battleship *Bismarck*, planned by the naval war staff for April, would represent an even greater danger. Unlike the *Gneisenau* and the *Scharnhorst*, which were not really full battleships, the *Bismarck* did not need to fear an engagement with British battleships, which were mostly veterans of the First World War. On the other hand, it was felt on the German side also that the conditions of surface warfare in the North Atlantic would inevitably become worse for Germany and better for the enemy. The expansion of air surveillance, the increasing use of aircraft-carriers, and the equipping of British ships with radar were observed with growing concern. Greater involvement or even active intervention by the United States would make completely new decisions necessary.[10]

The use of the heavy surface ships showed once again how unreliable their engines were. After two months at sea the two battleships required overhauls in a shipyard lasting several weeks. It also became clear that the cruising range of the heavy cruiser *Hipper* was completely inadequate; she was dependent on frequent refuelling by tankers. Moreover, because of their construction the two battleships could hardly be used in wind and sea force greater than 6.[11] In addition to the problems with the engines, crews often changed when the ships had to spend a long time in a shipyard. When they were again ready for action, the new crews had to get used to their duties, which could require several additional weeks. For this reason the naval war staff

---

[10] Cf. Salewski, *Seekriegsleitung*, i. 390; Brennecke, *Bismarck*, 169–71.   [11] Cf. II.II above.

could never achieve their goal of a continuous use of the heavy surface ships. A good example of this was the seven-month repair and training period preceding the Atlantic operations of the two battleships after they had received only one torpedo hit each during 'Operation Juno'.[12] In view of these shortcomings the skill of the naval war staff in this phase of the war in directing and co-ordinating the operations of the battleships, cruisers, armed merchant raiders, and U-boats, and in designating meeting-points, using captured ships, and preparing them to be sent to Germany, is all the more remarkable. Especially noteworthy was the creation of a supply network at sea—the providing of fuel and other supplies from Germany, France, and even neutral countries to ships in the operations area. Without such a supply organization it would have been possible to conduct the war at sea only with U-boats in the North Atlantic and with armed merchant raiders. For the operation of the two battleships alone the naval war staff used seven tankers. How many would have been necessary if they had wanted to have four or even six heavy ships operating continuously in the Atlantic? Here the decisive weakness of the German Strategy becomes apparent again: without overseas bases the ability to conduct a naval war in the Atlantic, even with the Z-plan fleet, remained dependent on this extremely vulnerable supply system, a perfect target for the enemy.

[12] Cf. V.III above.

V. The Organization of the German Navy in the West

THE victorious conclusion of the campaign in the west meant for the German navy not only that it now had bases on the French west coast for surface and submarine warfare in the Atlantic, but also that it had to take over the task of defending the coast of Europe from Emden to the Spanish border. And this was only a month after the German north flank had been extended from Sylt to the North Cape. Although the British, who had just been forced to withdraw from the Continent, did not represent any immediate danger to the coasts occupied by German troops, the navy did not have the forces to provide ships and support for the invasion of Britain.[1] Even protecting coastal shipping, which had now been resumed, required an organization of numerous improvised units to defend harbours and for minesweeping, patrol and defence duty, and anti-submarine warfare. Providing and manning coastal artillery for defensive and offensive purposes also made heavy demands on material resources and personnel.[2]

The Group Commander West, Admiral Saalwächter, had suggested the creation of a new group command in the occupied areas to the naval war staff on 11 June 1940.[3] The staff reacted hesitantly, however, and only on 31 July did Raeder order the reorganization of the command system. Group Command West was transferred to Paris; its area of command was now to be the Channel and the Atlantic to latitude 53° N. Group Command East was renamed Group Command North and transferred from Kiel to Wilhelmshaven-Sengwarden. Its area of responsibility was expanded to include the North Sea and the Arctic Ocean. Already in June 1940 a navy commander in The Netherlands was placed under the naval station North Sea; this officer was in charge of a port-defence flotilla, the Rhine flotilla, a river minesweeping flotilla (from December 1940 onwards), three commanding officers of ports (responsible directly to the navy commander), and finally the two officers commanding the sea defence of northern and southern Holland. These latter were in charge of the remaining officers in command of the ports as well as the naval artillery and naval anti-aircraft units in their areas.

In the same month the commanding admiral for France was transferred to Paris. Operationally he was under Group Command West and was himself in charge of, among other commands, primarily the navy commanders of the Channel coast, northern France, Brittany, and western France. In the areas of the Channel coast and northern France the commanders were in direct charge of the commanding

---

[1] On 'Operation Sea-Lion' cf. IX.II below.
[2] Cf. Harnier, *Artillerie*, 33-5, 59-61.
[3] On this section cf. also Salewski, *Seekriegsleitung*, i. 208-9, 223-4; Lohmann and Hildebrand, *Kriegsmarine*.

officers of the ports and their port-defence flotillas (in so far as these had already been created), while the commanding officers of the sea defences (Seekommandanten) there were only in charge of the naval artillery units. On the Channel coast there was at first only one port-defence flotilla, which was also directly subordinate to the commander. In February 1941 the navy commander of the Channel coast took over, in addition, the area of northern France, and the commanding officers of the sea defences received the title of Marineartilleriekommandeure. At the same time new commanding officers of the sea defences were installed as intermediate officers between the commanders and other authorities and units. In December 1940 the navy commander in Brittany took over the area of western France and divided his area into three sea-defence commands, under which were the port-defence flotillas, the officers in command of the ports, the naval artillery, and the naval anti-aircraft units. With this reorganization (which is by no means described in full here and which was at this time still incomplete) the areas under the remaining three navy commanders in the west were also redelimited.

The Leader (Führer) of Minesweepers West was transferred to the Commander-in-Chief of the Fleet at Trouville in August 1940, who also performed the functions of Commander of Defence West until October. The Leader of Patrol Boats West had been stationed in Trouville since July. The Leader of Minesweepers West divided his area into three parts, whose commanding officers were given the title of Deputy Leader (II. Führer) of Minesweepers of western France, northern France, and The Netherlands and Belgium. The Deputy Leader of Minesweepers in Belgium and The Netherlands, as the officer in charge of Escort Service West, was also given the task in the period between August and October 1940 of protecting the movement of ships needed for the invasion of Britain to ports between Rotterdam and Cherbourg. This organization was changed in February so that the Leader of Minesweepers West also took over the tasks of the Commander of Defence West, while the offices of the Leader of Minesweepers West and the Leader of Patrol-Boats West were abolished. The minesweeping, auxiliary minesweeping, barrage-breaking, patrol-boat, and anti-submarine flotillas with a total of 433 boats and ships were divided among four defence divisions.[4]

---

[4] Ruge, *Küstenvorfeld*, 72–3. In his foreword Ruge calculates the strength of all German forces used for these tasks at 3,000 ships and boats and about 100,000 men.

PART IX

Direct Strategy against Britain

HANS UMBREIT

AND

KLAUS A. MAIER

I. Churchill's Determination to Continue the War

HANS UMBREIT

ON 4 June, the last day of the withdrawal of British troops from the Dunkirk pocket, Churchill declared in the House of Commons that his government would never give up the struggle. If necessary it would pursue it alone from overseas.[1] His uncompromising attitude prevailed against certain figures who, given acceptable conditions, would not have dismissed peace with Germany out of hand. Apart from Churchill's opposition to the Nazi regime, there was also his conviction that Hitler would not content himself with hegemony on the European continent.

As far back as 25 May the British chiefs of staff had proposed that, in the event of a French collapse, Germany's defeat should be brought about solely by a purposeful economic and air war, as well as—and this was now to be given priority—the creation of widespread revolt in Germany's conquered territories.[2] On 17 June, when the French government asked Germany to communicate its peace conditions, Churchill reiterated Britain's intention to pursue the struggle until victory was won. When, towards the end of the month, Pope Pius XII offered himself as a mediator, he met with no interest on the part of the British prime minister. Hitler's 'peace appeal' of 19 July fared no better. So long as her own navy was intact and her air-space was not yet dominated by the Germans, Britain need not fear an invasion. Calculations of a long-term weakening of the Germans were partly based on expectation of support from the United States and of a future German–Soviet conflict or indeed a war.

Churchill reinforced the weight of his declaration by demonstrative actions motivated both by military and by domestic and foreign-policy considerations. On 3 July he ordered his troops to occupy any French ships still in British ports. British naval units prevented the portions of the French fleet assembled in Alexandria and Mers-el-Kebir from putting to sea and confronted them with the choice of continuing the struggle on Britain's side, being transferred to neutral waters, scuttling themselves, or being sunk. In Alexandria the local commanders agreed to demobilization of the French ships. At Mers-el-Kebir, however, the British eventually opened fire. Over 1,200 French sailors were killed, as well as a further 154 in a second attack on 6 July.

---

[1] Klee, *Seelöwe*, 26. Yet at times even Churchill did not entirely rule out a negotiated peace with Germany: Reynolds, 'Churchill and the British "Decision"', 149 ff.

[2] Foot, *SOE* 18. Initially it was even thought possible that active resistance to the regime might be mobilized in Germany itself. See Keyserlingk, 'Deutsche Komponente'. On the build-up of the RAF, simultaneously promoted by Churchill at this time because he expected it to decide the war, cf. Reynolds, 'Churchill and the British "Decision"', 156–7.

In France the ruthless actions of her former ally caused considerable anger. The commander-in-chief of the French navy, Admiral Darlan, gave orders for counter-measures. Air force units carried out a demonstrative raid on Gibraltar. Diplomatic relations between Vichy and London were severed. On 8 July a British attack was mounted on Dakar. France now positively authorized her naval forces to engage British ships and—pointing to her determination to resist Britain,[3] which was registered with satisfaction by the Germans—obtained a number of alleviations in the implementation of the military armistice terms.

Simultaneously Churchill endeavoured to improve British–Soviet relations, without as yet being ready to recognize the changed status quo brought about, with Stalin's co-operation, in east central Europe. In the first half of June he sent Sir Stafford Cripps as ambassador to Moscow, thereby increasing Hitler's latent mistrust and his conviction that British stubbornness was based on the hope of a long-term change in Soviet policy and of American support.

A future alliance with the United States against Hitlerite Germany was in fact the basis of all British war plans. Ever since his assumption of government Churchill had worked for more extensive American assistance. He was anxious to dispel American mistrust arising from Britain's past policy of appeasement, and to convince both President Roosevelt and the American public that any agreement with Germany which might jeopardize American security interests was out of the question. By the summer of 1940 Churchill had such a close relationship with the president that he consulted Roosevelt on all major decisions.[4] British–American staff discussions were laying the groundwork for a future alliance.

At first the prospects for such an alliance were anything but favourable. American policy had been dominated by isolationist tendencies since the First World War. This had resulted in a neutrality legislation designed to prevent any new American involvement in European conflicts. Military expenditure was correspondingly low. It was just sufficient for the defence of the American sphere of interest, i.e. against Japan.

Roosevelt was by no means in tune with public opinion in his country or with the ideas of leading military figures when he supported Anglo-French resistance to German expansion. By relaxing embargo regulations in the autumn of 1939 he enabled the Allies to purchase war material that was still scarce in the United States. France's elimination and a possible collapse of Britain, assumed to be almost certain by the American military, upset what had been the foundations of American strategy. On 27 June Secretary of State Hull suggested a transfer of the British navy to American ports, to prevent it from falling into German hands in the event of an end to the war in Europe.[5] It was to Roosevelt's credit that calls for a return to total isolation did not succeed. His faith in Britain's ability to survive was restored and he regarded it as a moral obligation, as well as being in the United States' own

---

[3] Naval staff war diary No. 1, pt. A, 3 July 1940, BA-MA RM 7/14.

[4] Hillgruber, *Strategie*, 84; Butler, *Strategy*, ii. 243. On Churchill's dissatisfaction with US policy, however, see also Reynolds, 'Churchill and the British "Decision"', 161 ff.

[5] Martin, *Friedensinitiativen*, 282.

military and economic interest, to maintain Britain's defence capacity.[6] The president thus ensured a stepping up of armament production and, from the summer of 1940 onward, an increased allocation of war material to Britain. That was as far as Roosevelt was able to go in view of the opposition within his own administration and of the presidential election due in November. But he made no secret of his opposition to the Axis powers, and by the time the destroyers-for-bases agreement was concluded on 2 September 1940 it became obvious that the American government, by then with the approval of the majority of the population, would throw the country's growing industrial and military weight into the balance in favour of Britain.

After Roosevelt's re-election in November 1940 it must have been clear to Hitler that American entry into the war could scarcely be avoided in the long run. Appropriate plans had begun to be drawn up in the United States. The defeat of Germany seemed more urgent then than the elimination of the Japanese danger. Britain, along with Canada, was now able to count on half the American armament production.

[6] Hillgruber, *Strategie*, 96 ff.; Bedts, *American History*, i. 245-6; Lukacs, *European War*, 100.

II. Plans and Preparations for a Landing in England

HANS UMBREIT

HITLER had confidently expected that with his victory over France the war in the west would be at an end. For a period he believed that Britain would agree to a 'compromise peace',[1] which would result in recognition of German rule over Continental Europe and in the return and redistribution of colonies at France's expense. Such a peace, moreover, would safeguard the British Empire against Italian aspirations and hence cover Germany's rear when she proceeded to solve the 'eastern problem'.

The German press, in consequence, was instructed to take the line that the continuation of the war was necessary 'not so much in order to destroy the British Empire as to break British hegemony on the Continent'.[2] But this did not offer a way out of the German dilemma. Hitler had no ready answer to the situation which had now arisen—that Churchill was not acting 'according to plan', i.e. that he was not willing to give in or to accept Germany's forcibly restored position as a world power. Yet Hitler had been so confident that London would 'cry off'[3] that, even before the conclusion of the western campaign, he had given orders for a diminution of land forces and, to be on the safe side, a reallocation of armaments in favour of the other two—until then somewhat neglected—Wehrmacht services.

The German 'peace army' had originally been envisaged as consisting of 120, then of 146, divisions, with the current number of armoured divisions (10) being doubled.[4] On 9 July Hitler once more ruled that German war production was now to be focused predominantly on the requirements of the navy and the air force. Two days later he authorized the navy to have the construction of capital ships, suspended in September 1939, resumed after the end of the war. Meanwhile, the U-boat programme was to be pursued without restrictions.

Once again Hitler's demands upon the armament industry were self-contradictory. While the inevitable cut in ammunition, gunpowder, and explosive production was in itself questionable, the shift of emphasis to the navy and the air force meant that the equipment ordered for the new armoured divisions required a great deal of time for its production.[5] Other projects, such as the replacement of captured weapons by German weapons, the establishment of railway troops, an increase in the number

---

[1] Hillgruber, *Strategie*, 144.   [2] Sündermann, *Tagesparolen*, 47 (25 June 1940).
[3] OKW/WFA/Abt. L No. 33110/40 g.Kdos. Chefs., 24 June 1940: Minutes of WFA on conference Hitler–OBdH on 23 June 1940, BA-MA RW 4/v. 581.
[4] Mueller-Hillebrand, *Heer*, ii. 62 ff.
[5] OKW/WiRüAmt/Stab Ic: Minute of a conference with Lt.-Gen. Thomas on 20 June 1940 concerning redirection of armament production, BA-MA Wi/IF 5.378.

of artillery regiments, and the construction of an 'East Wall', would have to be abandoned or substantially modified. In mid-July the High Command of the Armed Forces defined three points of emphasis: the Ju 88 programme, U-boat construction, and the equipment of mobile troops.[6] A few weeks later even this makeshift solution was overtaken. Hitler's faith in Britain's readiness to come to an agreement had weakened, and he saw the pursuance of a 'solution in the east' as almost inevitable.[7] At the beginning of August he demanded an increase of the wartime army to 180 divisions by 1 May 1941. In spite of the increasing exploitation of the occupied territories and an intensification of foreign trade, the armament industry, in view of the ever more frequent changes of programme, was facing virtually insuperable tasks.

German strategy, in other words, had been planned only as far ahead as the expected victory in the west; this, it was thought, would decide everything. There were scarcely any strategic ideas looking beyond this. Not until shortly before the armistice with France did the possibility of an invasion of England come on the *tapis*. That such an operation might one day become necessary, however, had been pointed out even before the war in a Luftwaffe study.[8] The naval staff had gone as far as having certain contingency studies made, and the navy's commander-in-chief had used his conferences with Hitler to explain the prerequisites of air supremacy in greater detail. The subject had also been briefly discussed in the High Command of the Armed Forces and in the Army High Command. On 20 June Brauchitsch raised the question of transferring troops to England but met with scepticism from Hitler.[9] No precise plans then existed. Only the Luftwaffe had studied the possibility of an air landing in southern England in some detail and on 27 June submitted a plan, which Hitler, however, dismissed. The risks of a landing operation seemed to him too great, and moreover avoidable while he was still hoping for a political solution to the British problem. These expectations, incidentally, were shared by the leading groups in the Reich.

The Wehrmacht command nevertheless studied alternatives to the evidently elusive peaceful solution. The first to make this attempt was the chief of the Wehrmacht operations staff, Major-General Jodl. In a memorandum of 30 June[10] he outlined a number of alternatives which would arise in the event of Britain being unwilling to make peace. Only if Britain could not be made to see reason by political means—Jodl regarded her military situation as hopeless—did he recommend a defeat of the enemy by the navy and the air force: by the elimination of Britain's air force, the paralysing of her war economy, the cutting off of her imports, terror raids against the population, and, as a last resort and assuming air supremacy, by a landing. As an alternative or as a complement he suggested an indirect strategy on the periphery, with the assistance of all those countries which might expect advantages from a break-up of the British Empire. These plans included the seizure of Gibraltar in co-operation with Spain and the capture of the Suez Canal in conjunction with Italy.

---

[6] OKW/WiRüAmt/Rü IIb No. 1448/40 g.Kdos., 15 July 1940, concerning redirection of armament production, ibid.

[7] Halder, *Diaries*, i. 530 ff. (31 July 1940).   [8] Klee, *Seelöwe*, 43.

[9] *Heeresadjutant bei Hitler*, 83 (20 June 1940).   [10] *IMT* xxviii, PS-1776, pp. 301 ff.

Hitler rejected terror raids, at least at that phase of the war. He wanted the British population to be treated with consideration in order to 'drive a wedge between the people and their leaders'[11] and to bring about a change in political direction. German military means were insufficient for bringing the enemy to his knees solely by the cutting off of his supplies; they were equally insufficient for an intensified U-boat campaign as proposed by Admiral Dönitz. Hitler rejected the latter idea[12] because, on a sober estimate of the situation, he did not expect it to produce short-term results.

From the German point of view, therefore, it seemed that only a landing in England could bring about the desired speedy conclusion of the war. Hitler ordered plans to be prepared accordingly. To him, however, just as to the Wehrmacht, a landing was only the last resort. He continued to shrink from this risky enterprise which, even if successful, might have undesirable consequences: the break-up of the Empire or the flight of the British government to Canada in order to continue the war from there. Failure, on the other hand, would drastically weaken the German position, both political and military, for the impending confrontation with the Soviet Union. The High Command of the Armed Forces warned against incalculable consequences.[13] An operation based on inadequate foundations would be an 'act of desperation', which Germany had no cause to resort to, especially as Britain might still be 'brought . . . to her knees' by indirect measures.

Hitler put his hopes on a 'peace trend' among prominent British politicians, about which he had received some information through diplomatic channels. As exponents of this trend he saw, among others, the foreign secretary Lord Halifax, the ambassador in Madrid, Sir S. Hoare, as well as Lloyd George and also the Duke of Windsor. However, there was no reaction to soundings made via certain neutral countries. As he was convinced that 'the outcome of the war had already been decided' and that 'Britain, however, was still not aware of it', Hitler concluded that London was waiting for a 'turn-about in America' and for a 'change in Russia's attitude'.[14] He was already more or less aware of the falsity of his calculations when on 19 July he read out his postponed (and by now purely propagandist) 'peace appeal' in the Reichstag. Three days later Lord Halifax announced Britain's rejection. Churchill's intransigence had won the day in the British cabinet. Although Hitler did not finally abandon hope of an arrangement, he increasingly came to the conclusion that a military show of strength was needed to make the enemy come to terms. By then he had already given orders for plans for a possible landing in England, code-named 'Sea-Lion', to be prepared. Yet he disliked the idea of smashing the Empire, even though, given the ratio of military strength in the summer of 1940, he considered it entirely feasible. For his turn towards the east, which he had in mind in the long term, Hitler would have preferred an intact British Empire as a stabilizing factor in the world. Churchill's attitude was beyond Hitler's mental range. Hitler began

---

[11] Sündermann, *Tagesparolen*, 47 (5 July 1940).   [12] Hillgruber, *Strategie*, 159 ff.
[13] Chef WFSt, estimate of the situation on 13 Aug. 1940, BA-MA RW 4/v. 590.
[14] Conference of the commanders-in-chief of the three services with the Führer and supreme commander of the Wehrmacht, Naval War Staff war diary No. 1, pt. A, 21 July 1940, BA-MA RM 7/14.

to conceive the idea of defeating Britain, if necessary, through the Soviet Union. In this way his short-term strategic objective and his ancient political long-term objective[15]—'living-space' in the east—might be attained at a single stroke.

The uncertainty of the political and military situation in the east—where Army High Command was carrying out a command restructure—and in the Mediterranean induced the army commander-in-chief to complete the army reorganization only partially. On 13 July Brauchitsch obtained Hitler's permission to dissolve only 17 of the envisaged 35 divisions. The remaining 18 divisions were merely stripped of 60 per cent of their personnel.

On 2 July 1940[16] the Wehrmacht was officially informed of Hitler's decision that, given certain conditions (mainly the achievement of German air supremacy), a landing might be made in England. Two weeks later Hitler instructed the three services to intensify preparations so that the necessary measures were completed by mid-August.[17] However, he let it be understood that the operation represented only a last expedient, which perhaps would not be necessary and on which he was not particularly keen. His relative lack of interest could not fail to have its effect on the respective planning staffs. The army and navy, moreover, were hoping that success in the air war would make a landing unnecessary.

Thus, the preparations for the landing were predominantly an instrument of psychological warfare; at times Hitler did not rule out the operation—which the British government by then firmly expected—but soon he again lost interest in an enterprise for which the indispensable prerequisites seemed unattainable.

The most important precondition of numerous preparatory moves, and subsequently of the success of the landing, was German air superiority over the Channel and southern England. This had also been made a condition by the navy, which, weakened in Norway, was not fully operational. Moreover, it lacked the means for ferrying across the first contingent of the landing forces, expected to number approximately 100,000 men with equipment, tanks, motor vehicles, and horses. Without a solution to these problems any attempted landing was entirely out of the question from the point of view of the navy, which felt overtaxed by its new task. At an early stage it concluded that 'assuming the [militarily] correct reaction by the enemy, the execution of the operation' must be 'called in doubt'.[18] By the end of July the naval operations staff came to the conclusion that Operation Sea-Lion was inadvisable, at least in 1940.[19]

The Army General Staff at Fontainebleau was in close geographical contact with Army Groups A and B, which had established a front line against Britain from Holland down to Brittany. Supply-dumps were set up, map-exercises and embarking- and disembarking-exercises were carried out, occupation authorities were formed

---

[15] Jäckel, *Frankreich*, 56-7.

[16] OKW/WFA/L No. 33124/40 g.Kdos. Chefs., 2 July 1940, concerning conduct of war against Britain, in Klee, *Dokumente*, 301-2.

[17] Directive No. 16 of the Führer and supreme commander of the Wehrmacht/OKW/WFA/L No. 33160/40, g.Kdos. Chefs., 16 July 1940, ibid. 310 ff.

[18] Naval War Staff war diary No. 1, pt. A, 17 July 1940, BA-MA RM 7/14.

[19] Ibid., 30 July 1940.

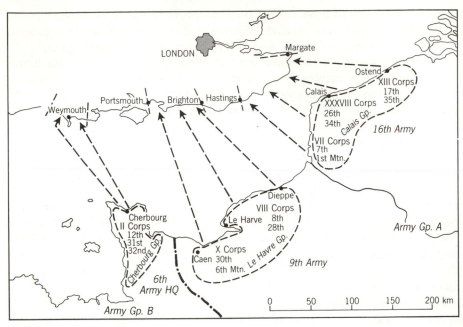

MAP IX.II.1. First Plan of the Army High Command for 'Operation Sea-Lion' (Ferrying of First Operational Troops)

for employment in England, and ferrying-craft, heavy artillery, and anti-aircraft artillery were assembled. All available sea and river craft in Germany and in the occupied territories were recorded. Diversionary manœuvres were to camouflage Germany's intentions as far as possible.

Operation Sea-Lion collapsed not only because air superiority could not be established over the Royal Air Force but also because a vast number of technical details of a maritime nature remained insoluble—which, with an enemy still in command of the seas, was of crucial importance. Moreover, the Germans were under pressure of time. Once the autumnal period of bad weather had set in, a landing would be even less practicable.

Exceptional difficulties were encountered in attempts to secure sufficient shipping-space and personnel in view of the effect this had on the civilian economy; the necessary rebuilding and the need for material detrimentally affected current production programmes; there were major difficulties with minesweeping in the Channel, the laying of German mine-barrages, and the protection of the ships and troops concentrated in the launching-ports against British air raids. The navy was unable to meet the army's demands for shipping-space and the air force's demands for transport for its anti-aircraft artillery. There was no agreement on the best time of day for disembarkation or for bringing up the second and third wave, nor even—the principal problem—on the extent of the landing-areas. Only with difficulty were partial compromise solutions reached between the widely dispersed headquarters of the different services. These compromises were preceded by protracted mediation by the High Command of the Armed Forces; on some occasions appeal had to be made to Hitler for a decision before the army would adapt to the limited facilities of the navy. Only the two armies of Army Group A were now to provide the divisions for the first landing-wave. The attack, finally, had to be made on such a narrow sector of the coast that the most the Army General Staff dared hope for was that it would 'give the *coup de grâce* to an enemy already prostrated by the air war'.[20]

Thus, the closing date for all preparations was delayed until mid-September,[21] and it soon seemed doubtful whether 'Sea-Lion' could still be mounted in the autumn of 1940 or, as the navy believed, not until May 1941. Hitler reserved his decision pending a 'further clarification of the overall situation', i.e. he wished to await the effects of the air offensive which, since the beginning of September, had been directed increasingly against Britain's economic potential. Göring was increasingly conducting a strategic war in the air, which only indirectly served the preparations for a landing operation. His generally shared expectation that Britain could in this way be forced into readiness for peace was not to be realized.

Hitler's decision on whether or not to execute the landing operation was still awaited. There was no doubt that the most important prerequisite, German superiority in the air, had not been achieved. Even less had it been possible, by the means employed to date, to compel Britain to change her attitude.[22]

Increasingly, Hitler had to turn his attention to east and south-east Europe, where German and Soviet imperialist interests were slowly moving towards a clash. Work was begun by Army High Command in early July, and actually ordered by Hitler towards the end of the month, on preparations for a campaign in the east, as well as on planning the employment of troops to support the Italians in North Africa, and on an operation for the seizure of Gibraltar. For a time Hitler saw a way out of his dilemma in a political unification of the Continent against Britain. Yet total abandonment of the landing in England seemed to him inopportune, despite the strain on German shipbuilding and transport. He regarded a continuing threat to Britain as useful if only for psychological reasons. Besides, he feared the political consequences of the loss of prestige he would suffer by calling off the enterprise. For internal purposes the decision was postponed 'until further notice' on 17 September, and on 12 October it was definitively deferred until the spring of 1941.[23] Withdrawal of troops and reduction of transport assembled in the Channel ports, where they had been exposed to British air attacks, had begun as early as September. Various technical preparations proceeded for some time, and the

[20] OKW war diary, i. 53 (30 Aug. 1940).
[21] OKW/WFSt/L No. 33229/40 g.Kdos. Chefs., 16 Aug. 1940, concerning 'Sea-Lion', in Klee, *Dokumente*, 356–7.
[22] Hillgruber, *Strategie*, 274.
[23] OKW/WFSt/Abt. L(I) No. 33318/40 g.Kdos. Chefs., 12 Oct. 1940, in Klee, *Dokumente*, 441–2.

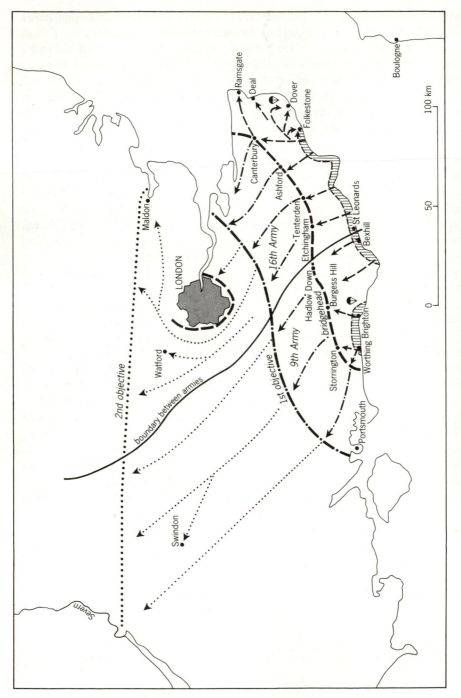

MAP IX.II.2. Landing Sectors According to the Final Plan for 'Operation Sea-Lion'

Luftwaffe continued, weather permitting, to employ its entire strength against the British Isles. But in fact 'Sea-Lion' now only served the deception of the enemy, to be kept up into 1942. In the German operation plans a landing in England eventually occupied the lowest place—to be resorted to when the situation on all other fronts had been settled in the desired way.[24]

[24] Klee, *Seelöwe*, 229.

III. The Battle of Britain

Klaus A. Maier

1. The Solution of a Strategic and Tactical Dilemma

In his memorandum of 30 June 1940[1] on continuing the war against Britain Jodl mentioned attacks on the British homeland and expanding the war to peripheral areas as measures which in his opinion should be used 'if political means do not produce the desired results'. In the war against the British homeland, which he preferred, he distinguished between three possibilities: (1) a 'siege': an air and naval war against imports and exports, the British air force, and all sources of strength of the British war economy: (2) the 'terror attack' against British population centres; and (3) a landing with the aim of occupying Britain.

Basing his arguments on the mistaken assessment that final victory over Britain was only a question of time, and Germany could therefore choose a form of military action which would 'spare her strength and avoid risks', Jodl recommended the elimination of the British air force as the first and most important aim: 'The war against the British air force must be the very first task in order to reduce and finally put a stop to the destruction of the foundations of our war economy.' For this purpose the British air force had to be defeated over parts of Britain within the combat-range of German heavy fighters (Me 110s) or at least forced to withdraw to bases in central Britain. This would make it possible to 'destroy the entire southern part of Britain with its armaments industry and greatly reduce the effectiveness of British bombers against the western parts of Germany'. Eliminating the aircraft industry concentrated around London and Birmingham would make it impossible for the British air force to replace its losses. This would mean 'the end of Britain's ability to carry out military actions against Germany'. The destruction of the British aircraft industry should be complemented by a simultaneous campaign against supply-depots and exports and imports, at sea and in ports: 'Combined with propaganda and occasional terror attacks—to be represented as retaliation—this accelerating decline in the food supply of the country will paralyse and finally break the will of the people to resist and thus force their government to capitulate.' In Jodl's opinion a landing should only be carried out 'to deal a death-blow to Britain when her war economy has been paralysed and her air force destroyed, if it should still be necessary'. For Jodl, too, German air supremacy was therefore an essential condition of a landing.

This condition was also laid down by the Wehrmacht High Command in its directive of 2 July,[2] in which the high commands of the three services were

---

[1] Klee, *Dokumente*, 298-9; *IMT* xxviii. 30 ff.; cf. Ansel, *Hitler*, 114 ff.; Klee, *Seelöwe*, 61-2.
[2] Klee, *Dokumente*, 301-2.

instructed to initiate preparations for carrying out a landing 'at the earliest possible date'. The directive stated: 'Under certain conditions, the most important of which is air supremacy, a landing in Britain can be envisaged.' It then emphasized that all preparations must take into consideration that 'The plan for a landing in Britain has by no means assumed concrete form, and only preparations for a possible operation are involved.' On 13 July the question of greatest concern to Hitler was 'why Britain is still unwilling to make peace'. Halder noted in his diary: 'He believes, as we do, that the answer to this question is that Britain is still placing her hopes in Russia. He therefore expects that it will be necessary to force Britain to make peace.'[3]

Three days later, on 16 July, Hitler issued Directive No. 16 'on preparations for a landing operation against England',[4] in which he announced his decision to prepare and, if necessary, to carry out such an operation. As the first prerequisite he mentioned that the British air force must be crushed to the point that it would not have the strength necessary to mount a significant attack on a German attempt to cross the Channel. In conferences with the commanders-in-chief of the Wehrmacht services on 21 July[5] Hitler repeated his doubts about a landing operation: 'If it is not certain that preparations can be completed by the beginning of September, other plans must be considered.'[6] Among these plans was an attack on the Soviet Union.[7]

Above all the navy voiced serious doubts about the feasibility of a landing. The importance of air supremacy was increasingly emphasized, not only for the crossing but also for the orderly deployment of the transport fleet and the necessary minesweeping operations. On 11 July Raeder explained to Hitler that a landing could only be a 'last resort'. He demanded 'strong air attacks', for example on Liverpool, 'so that the whole nation will feel the effect'.[8] On 23 July the naval war staff warned against any further delay in achieving air supremacy, as this would be decisive in determining when the navy could consider its own preparations complete.[9] In a memorandum of 29 July[10] the staff even concluded that they could not accept responsibility for an attempt to carry out a landing in 1940 and that it seemed 'extremely doubtful' that a landing could be carried out at all.

After Raeder had informed him on 31 July that the navy's preparations for a landing could not be concluded before 15 September, Hitler decided that all preparations should take that date as a deadline, but his final decision would depend on victory in the air war. Eight or, at most, fourteen days after the start of the 'great air campaign against Britain', which could begin at any time from about 5 August, he intended to decide whether or not Operation Sea-Lion should take place in 1940, depending on the outcome of the air battle.[11]

---

[3] Halder, *Diaries*, i. 506 (13 July 1940), on a talk by Hitler at the Berghof (trans. amended).
[4] Trevor-Roper, *Directives*, No. 16; Klee, *Dokumente*, 305 ff.
[5] Halder, *Diaries*, i. 515 ff. (22 July 1940); 'Führer Conferences', 119-20.
[6] Quoted in 'Führer Conferences', 119-20.
[7] Halder, *Diaries*, i. 515-17; Hillgruber, *Strategie*, 207 ff.
[8] 'Führer Conferences', 114. [9] BA-MA PG 32431, Case GE 385.
[10] Klee, *Dokumente*, 315 ff. [11] Ibid. 335.

Drohend liegen die Schatten des Wirkungsbereichs der deutschen Luftwaffe über
England. — Frankreich, Belgien, Holland und Norwegen, die bestimmt waren, den
Krieg von Englands Küsten fernzuhalten, umschließen heute als Startplätze der
überlegenen deutschen Luftwaffe die britische Insel.

L'Angleterre sous l'ombre sinistre des ailes de l'Arme Aérienne du Reich. La France, la Belgique, la Hollande, la Norvège
sont aujourd'hul les points de départ des avions allemands.

The mighty German Air Force throws its
greedy shadow over England – no longer safe
behind France, Belgium, Holland and Norway.

FIG. IX.III.I. German leaflet

In Führer Directive No. 17 issued on 1 August for 'the conduct of air and sea warfare against England',[12] Hitler announced his intention to intensify the air and sea battle so as 'to establish the necessary conditions for the final conquest of England'. The Luftwaffe was to overpower the Royal Air Force as soon as possible by attacks 'primarily against flying units, their ground installations, and their supply organizations, but also on the aircraft industry, including the manufacturing of anti-aircraft equipment'. After the Luftwaffe had achieved temporary or local air superiority, the air war should be directed against the harbours and stocks of foodstuffs there and in the interior of the country. However, attacks on ports of the south coast were to be kept to a minimum 'in view of our forthcoming operations'. Generally the Luftwaffe was to be maintained at full fighting strength and ready for Operation Sea-Lion: according to the directive it would be possible to begin the intensified air war on or after 5 August. Hitler left the choice of the exact date to the Luftwaffe—which, however, was not ready. On 1 August Jodl was informed that, while the Luftwaffe had long been ready for the intensified air war in accordance with Führer Directive No. 17 in terms of supplies and the ability to perform the tasks involved, it had not yet been possible for the commanders of the air fleets to reach agreement on the tactics to be used against Britain, as Göring himself had not made any decision in this regard.[13]

After the campaign in the west the Luftwaffe was in a very favourable geographical position for operations against Britain, but it did not have any overall tactical plan in spite of the ideas developed by Air Fleet 2 in 1938, which of course assumed a much less favourable geographical situation. A plan had seemed unnecessary because of the general expectation that Britain would come to terms after the victory over France. For the first time the Luftwaffe was forced to carry out an attack on an enemy air force across the sea without the advantage of surprise and without an accompanying army offensive. Hitler's general dilemma with regard to the necessary new (direct) strategy against Britain made it difficult for the Luftwaffe to find an immediate way out of its own tactical dilemma. In spite of Hitler's orders to prepare an invasion of Britain, his hesitation about carrying it out greatly

[12] Trevor-Roper, *Directives*, No. 17.
[13] *KTB OKW* i, 1 Aug. 1940.

TRANSLATION OF FIGURE IX.III.1

There are no islands any more!

[The curved lines give the flying-time (*Flugzeit*) to locations in the British Isles from German-occupied territory.]

The operational range of the German air force casts threatening shadows over Britain. France, Belgium, Holland and Norway, which were intended to keep the war away from Britain's shores, are now taking-off grounds from which the German air force with its superior strength can attack Britain from all sides.

[The French text is an abbreviated version.]

complicated the problem of setting consistent priorities and goals in an air war against that country. However, there was general agreement that domination of the air, or at least regional air supremacy, was essential for a landing as well as for an independent operational air war against Britain.

The Luftwaffe command staff had as yet made no preparations for a landing. General von Waldau (Luftwaffe Command Staff Ia (operations)) declared that, as the chief of the Luftwaffe General Staff was of the opinion that the Führer was not seriously considering a cross-Channel invasion, he refused to take a position with regard to the ideas developed in 'The Role of the Luftwaffe in a Landing in Britain', a draft memorandum submitted by Jodl's Wehrmacht command office for comment on 25 June.[14] A landing in Britain was also not mentioned in the 'General Directive for the War of the Luftwaffe against Britain' issued by the commander-in-chief of the Luftwaffe on 30 June. During the deployment the Luftwaffe units were to concentrate on disruptive attacks with light forces on industrial and air force targets and on reconnaissance and orientation flights. In doing so they should 'try to avoid causing serious losses among the civilian population for the time being'. Jodl's memorandum assigned the Luftwaffe the following tasks when it was completely combat-ready:

1. to create conditions for an effective campaign against imports, supplies, and the British war economy, and thus for the protection of Germany herself, by attacks on the enemy air force, its ground-support organization, and the British armaments industry;
2. to destroy the British supply system by attacks on ports of entry, their installations, transport ships, and warships.

Both tasks were to be carried out simultaneously. The directive concluded: 'As long as the enemy air force has not been smashed, the basic principle for conducting the air war will be to attack enemy air units at every opportunity, night and day, in the air and on the ground, regardless of other targets.'[15]

Only on 21 July,[16] in a conference of the heads of the air fleets and corps commanders, did Göring forbid attacks on installations 'which will be needed to carry on the war later'. Among such installations were primarily loading and unloading facilities in harbours between the south-eastern corner of Britain and the Isle of Wight. The Ninth Flying Division, which had been given the task of laying the necessary mines around Britain, was also instructed to leave the south coast free.

Until the start of the intensified air war, which would be possible on or after 28 July, the Luftwaffe was to try to avoid losses. Göring mentioned British convoys and naval forces as the main targets. Attacks on land targets were to be carried out

---

[14] Klee, *Dokumente*, 296–7.

[15] Quoted in Klee, 'Luftschlacht', 68–9. On 11 July a new 'Directive for Intensified Air War Against Britain' (not found) was issued: Genst. Lw. 8. (Kriegswissenschaftliche) Abt., Luftkrieg gegen England, Gefechtskalender, Weisungen und Befehle (only in the form of a reference), Aug. 1940, BA-MA RL 2/v. 3021; cf. Klee, *Seelöwe*, 167; Wheatley, *Sea Lion*, 52 ff.

[16] Besprechung Reichsmarschall (21 July 1940), BA-MA RL 2 II/30; cf. Milch, 'Merkbuch', 21 July 1940; cf. Irving, *Rise and Fall*, 95 ff.

at every opportunity, but only by individual aircraft. Specialists were to be trained for night attacks on the air armaments industry, munitions factories, and oil-storage depots.

The first aim of the intensified air war would be to achieve air supremacy over southern Britain against strong fighter forces and anti-aircraft units, as well as a smoothly functioning reconnaissance and early warning network. It would be necessary to defeat the British fighters before the German bombers could be used; the latter would then be able to attack the ground support installations of the Royal Air Force more easily. Göring called for suggestions from the air fleets and flying corps for the tactical execution of this plan, especially for the employment of fighters. He proposed to issue a new order with the exact date for the attacks on the British armaments industry, with concentration on engine-production facilities. For the 'final battle', in which fighter aircraft carrying bombs were to be used for the first time, Göring called for 'heavy attacks to wear down (*zermürben*) the whole country'.[17]

On 30 July the Wehrmacht High Command and the Wehrmacht command office informed Göring of Hitler's order that preparations for the 'great battle of the Luftwaffe against Britain' were to be made as fast as possible and in such a way that the battle could begin twelve hours after the necessary 'Führer order' had been issued.[18]

On 1 August the air fleet commands submitted their revised suggestions for the conduct of the intensified air war, together with suggestions of the flying corps, to Göring, who provided his own comments the same day.[19] In the suggestions on conducting an air war against Britain presented by the First Flying Corps, the following aims were mentioned: (1) achieving air supremacy, i.e. the destruction of the enemy air force and its sources of supply, especially the engine industry; (2) protection of the army crossing the Channel and of airborne operations by (*a*) attacks on the enemy fleet, (*b*) intercepting attacking enemy aircraft, and (*c*) direct support of the army; (3) 'strangling' Britain by paralysing her harbours, destroying her stocks, and preventing the arrival of new supplies; (4) 'apart from these tasks, ruthless, unrestrained terror attacks on large cities can be considered as means of reprisal'. In the view of the First Flying Corps, the battle for air supremacy was thus primarily a prerequisite for a later landing operation. The Second Flying Corps proposed attacking London so as to draw British fighters from airfields beyond the range of German fighters and engage them in battles over the capital. Large-scale bomber attacks were envisaged after British defences had been weakened. As Hitler had

---

[17] Cf. Irving, *Rise and Fall*, 97.

[18] Klee, *Dokumente*, 324.

[19] According to Genst. Lw. 8. Abt., Luftkrieg gegen England, Gefechtskalender, Weisungen und Befehle (BA MA RL 2/v. 30321), the air fleets had presented their first suggestions on 24-5 and 27 July; Göring commented on them on 29 July. On Göring's conference with the air fleet commanders on 1 Aug. cf. the memorandum of 2 Aug.: BA-MA RL 2 II/30. The views of the First and the Eighth Flying Corps have also been preserved, MGFA Sammlung v. Rohden, Film No. 2; Klee ('Luftschlacht', 72) cites the proposals of the chief of staff of the Second Flying Corps, Deichmann, which were recorded after the war.

reserved the right to order terror attacks in his Directive No. 17 of 1 August, this tactic was not to be used for the time being.[20]

On 2 August Göring issued the order for the attack 'Adler' (Eagle) with the same aims as those discussed on 21 July: destruction of the British air force, achieving air supremacy over southern Britain, and attacks on the British fleet.[21] In telephone instructions to the air fleets on 3 August, Göring ordered them to use special units to attack the British early-warning system with the first attack-wave.[22] After the tactics had been tested in a map-manœuvre on 4 August, in a conference with the air fleet commanders on 6 August[23] Göring referred to the possibility of breaking off the attack early and presenting it in the press as an isolated instance of retaliation. This was presumably intended to anticipate any unfavourable effects caused by a failure, but it is also possible that Göring took into consideration the continuing peace-feelers being extended via Albert Plesman, the director of the Dutch airline KLM.[24]

In an assessment of the situation by the Luftwaffe Command Staff Ic of 16 July[25] the Luftwaffe was described as 'clearly superior' to the Royal Air Force in terms of training, strength, equipment, and command. It was also in an advantageous geographical position and, 'in view of the inadequate air-defence system of the island, able to go over to decisive daylight attacks'. A 'decisive effect' in 1940 was possible if the Luftwaffe took advantage of the relatively favourable weather between July and the beginning of October. The Staff Ic estimated that the Royal Air Force had a total of 900 fighter aircraft, of which about 675 (40 per cent Spitfires and 60 per cent Hurricanes) were ready for action. While this estimate was indeed close to the actual number of British fighters (700), the production of the British aircraft industry was far greater than the 180–200 fighters the staff assumed: it was on average 470 fighters a month, twice as many as the German aircraft industry (see Tables IX.III.1, 2). A comparison produced on 10 August by the director-general of air armaments (Udet) in co-operation with staff Ic also described the Luftwaffe as superior in almost all respects. For example, the last chapter dealt with 'the special weaknesses of British research and development institutions with regard to the timely, correct recognition of important new weapons and new methods of attack, in contrast to comparable German institutions, which especially in this respect have a very positive attitude and are responsive to new ideas'. After a comparison of repair possibilities in relation

---

[20] In the conference notes of 21 July (BA-MA RL 2 II/30) the following was subsequently put into brackets: 'Question of combining forces of Air Fleet 2 + Flying Corps VIII + fighter forces of Air Fleet 3 for battle against RAF over London'; cf. n. 22 below.

[21] Original not found; cf. Klee, 'Luftschlacht', 74; Irving, Rise and Fall, 99.

[22] Note for files on telephone instructions to Air Fleets 2 and 3 of 8 Aug., BA-MA RL 2 II/30. According to this source, an increase in fighter strength in air districts VI and XI (of Air Fleet Command 2) was requested on and after the third day of the attack, probably in connection with the note: 'The attack of Air Fleet 3 planned for 3rd day will be directed only against L[ondon].' In fact the first attack on the London area took place on 24 Aug.: Mason, Battle over Britain, 297–8; Klee, 'Luftschlacht', 79.

[23] Note for oral report: 'Flottenchef-Besprechung 6.8. [6 Aug.] in Karinhall', BA-MA RL 2 II/30; cf. Irving, Rise and Fall, 99.

[24] Cf. Martin, Friedensinitiativen, 323 ff.; Das 'Andere Deutschland', 177.

[25] Luftwaffenführungsstab Ic, Beurteilung der Schlagkraft der britischen Luftwaffe im Vergleich zur deutschen Luftwaffe (Entwurf), 16 July 1940, BA-MA (without signature).

TABLE IX.III.1. *British Aircraft Production (1940), as Estimated by Luftwaffe Command Staff Ic*

	Fighters	Bombers[a]	Other aircraft[b]	Total
Jan.	200	200	400	800
Feb.	200	200	400	800
Mar.	220	230	450	900
Apr.	220	230	450	900
May	225	310	465	1,000
June	225	310	465	1,000
July	380	310	410	1,100
Aug.	280	240	280	800
Sept.	280	290	230	800
Oct.	250	250	200	700
Nov.	180	200	220	600
Dec.	130	165	205	500
TOTAL	2,790	2,935	4,175	9,900

[a] Including Blenheim, Beaufort, Botha.

[b] Fleet Air Arm, transports, short-range reconnaissance, all school and training aircraft.

Source: Luftwaffenführungsstab Ic/III, A, Ausbringung der britischen Flugrüstungsindustrie im Jahre 1940, 17 Feb. 1941, BA-MA RL 2/744.

to estimated losses, the director-general emphasized the 'supreme importance' of destroying the British air armaments industry, the repair industry, and ports in the west of England, where deliveries from American aircraft producers were to be expected. This would be true above all if Britain succeeded in 'staving off her final defeat until the winter of 1940–1'.[26]

The Wehrmacht High Command also believed that the Luftwaffe would be successful. In a situation assessment of 13 August[27] Jodl warned that the political consequences of a failure of the landing operation would extend far beyond its mere military aspects. He believed that the Luftwaffe would create the conditions necessary for successfully carrying out 'Sea-Lion', i.e. the prevention of counter-attacks by the British air force and navy on the southern coast: 'We shall know definitely in the next eight days.' If, however, the German navy should not be able to secure a landing front for ten divisions from Folkestone to Brighton in four days, the landing would be an act of desperation which there was no reason to undertake at that time. Instead, there were other ways to force Britain to her knees. Among the alternatives Jodl mentioned was the 'continuation of the air war until the war economy in southern Britain has been completely destroyed'. This would also require the use of all available Italian air units. Jodl argued that Germany should not concentrate on purely military objectives, but on victory: 'Britain's will to resist must be broken by spring.'

[26] Der Generalluftzeugmeister Gl No. 740/40 g.Kdos., 10 Aug. 1940, BA-MA RL 2/356.

[27] Klee, *Dokumente*, 353 ff. Keitel, the head of the Wehrmacht High Command, agreed with Jodl's assessment and presented it 'in general terms' to Hitler.

TABLE IX.III.2. *Actual Monthly British Aircraft Production, 1940–1941*[a]

	Heavy Bombers	Medium Bombers	Light Bombers	Fighters	General Recon- naissance	Naval	Trainers and Mis- cellaneous	Total
1940								
Jan.	—	96	86	157	24	19	420	802
Feb.	—	66	65	143	29	20	296	719
Mar.	—	91	75	177	31	25	461	860
Apr.	—	130	91	256	37	32	535	1,081
May	1	183	124	325	52	33	561	1,279
June	1	239	167	446	64	43	631	1,591
July	4	242	173	496	34	47	669	1,665
Aug.	1	214	177	476	41	56	636	1,601
Sept.	3	163	112	467	22	43	531	1,341
Oct.	4	167	154	469	18	54	553	1,419
Nov.	14	169	163	458	18	60	579	1,461
Dec.	13	165	134	413	17	44	443	1,230
TOTAL	41	1,926	1,521	4,283	387	476	6,415	15,049
1941								
Jan.	17	150	117	313	15	69	517	1,198
Feb.	21	220	196	535	16	74	525	1,587
Mar.	37	231	163	609	19	81	590	1,730
Apr.	27	212	163	534	13	88	492	1,529
May	38	232	147	580	23	109	579	1,708
June	39	231	136	556	17	114	,535	1,628
July	38	232	130	572	12	110	574	1,668
Aug.	50	237	99	645	3	121	638	1,793
Sept.	60	253	85	747	14	122	634	1,915
Oct.	57	275	70	676	13	122	634	1,847
Nov.	59	268	48	653	27	116	635	1,806
Dec.	55	236	39	644	24	106	581	1,685
TOTAL	498	2,777	1,393	7,064	196	1,232	6,934	20,094

[a] There was no production of transports and air-sea rescue aircraft.

Source: Postan, *British War Production*, 484–5. Several small mistakes in addition have been retained as it was not possible to determine their source.

When the battle for air supremacy over Britain began on 13 August 1940,[28] seven weeks had passed since the end of the campaign in the west, during which time Britain had been able further to improve her air defences. But Germany still had no clear strategy with regard to Britain. Not only did the argument about the necessity of Operation Sea-Lion continue,[29] but preparations were also being made for the

[28] The original attack set for 8 Aug. had to be postponed because of the weather.
[29] Cf. Hitler's statements on 14 Aug. on the occasion of the presentation of marshals' batons: Leeb, *Tagebuchaufzeichnungen*, 251–2; Bock, 'Tagebuch-Notizen', i, 14 Aug. 1940. On 17 Aug. Goebbels

attack on the Soviet Union, 'Britain's last hope on the Continent'.[30] Thus, the Battle of Britain took the form of a strategically and tactically improvised air offensive against an air defence which the British had been building up systematically for four years.[31]

2. THE BATTLE FOR AIR SUPREMACY

In August 1940 the British air-defence system (see Map IX.III.1) consisted of a chain of 52 radar stations along the coast from Pembrokeshire to the Shetland Islands which provided exact information about the distance and direction of attacking aircraft at a range of about 120 km., as well as approximate data on their altitude and number. After crossing the coast, the aircraft were tracked by the Royal Observer Corps.[32] The information provided by the radar stations and the Royal Observer Corps was fed to the four group command posts of Fighter Command. These group areas were in turn divided into several sections whose commanderrs directed the deployment of their fighters according to instructions they received from the group command posts. In the Fighter Command headquarters at Stanmore a constantly updated picture of the total situation was produced. The ability to react quickly of the British air-defence system, which also disposed of 1,300 heavy and 700 light anti-aircraft guns and 1,500 barrage-balloons, made possible an extremely economical use of available fighters. Extensive fighter patrols were unnecessary.

The weak point of the British air-defence system was the shortage of personnel in Fighter Command, which had lost 300 pilots in France, about a third of its total. In spite of replacements from the Empire and from countries occupied by Germany, Fighter Command still lacked 154 pilots in August 1940. However, because the air war took place over British territory, many British pilots who had been shot down were able to return to duty immediately if they had not been injured.

An invaluable contribution to British air defence and to the conduct of the war in general was made by information gained from deciphered German radio messages, as the British had been able to read messages encoded by German Enigma machines since April 1940.[33] Subject to a precise evaluation of recently declassified files

---

issued the propaganda directive that neither at home nor abroad should the statement be repeated that Hitler intended to subdue Britain with the Luftwaffe alone and abandon the plan for an invasion: *Wollt Ihr den totalen Krieg?*, 118 (trans.: *Secret Conferences*, 79).

[30] 'Betrachtungen über Rußland', BA-MA, Sammlung Raeder, xxiii; *KTB OKW* i, 1 Aug. 1940, 'Tarnbefehl für den Aufbau Ost', *Weizsäcker-Papiere*, 216. In the Luftwaffe files that have been preserved 'Russia' appears for the first time as a point for discussion in a note for an oral report dated 3 Aug. 1940: MGFA, Sammlung v. Rohden, Film No. 2. Cf. Hillgruber, *Strategie*, 222 ff.; Ansel, *Hitler*, 177 ff.

[31] On the Battle of Britain see Köhler, *Bibliographie*, 168 ff.; Butler, *Strategy*, ii. 286 ff.; B. Collier, *Defence*, 147 ff.; Mason, *Battle over Britain*; Taylor, *Breaking Wave*; Dowling, 'Battle of Britain'; Deighton, *Fighter*; id., *Battle of Britain*; Gropman, 'Battle of Britain'; Irving, *Rise and Fall*, 94 ff.; R. Collier, *Eagle Day*; Ishoven, *Luftwaffe*. The two studies of the 8th (military sciences) department of the Luftwaffe General Staff are also informative: BA-MA RL 2/v. 3015 (Bechtle) and 3019 (Hesler).

[32] Cf. Wood, *Attack Warning Red*; Volkmann, *Britische Luftverteidigung*.

[33] Kahn, *Codebreakers*; Winterbotham, *Ultra Secret*; Jones, *Most Secret War*; Lewin, *Ultra goes to War*; Stafford, 'Ultra'; Hinsley, *British Intelligence*, vol. i.

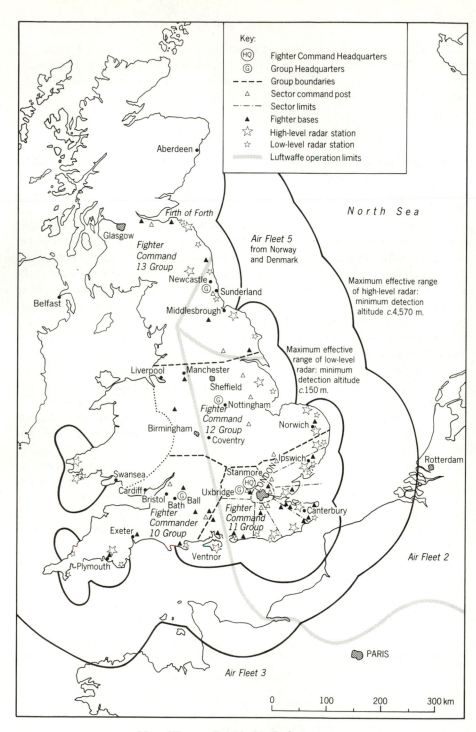

Key:
- ⓗ Fighter Command Headquarters
- Ⓖ Group Headquarters
- – – – Group boundaries
- △ Sector command post
- –·–·– Sector limits
- ▲ Fighter bases
- ☆ High-level radar station
- ✩ Low-level radar station
- ▨▨▨ Luftwaffe operation limits

North Sea

Aberdeen

Firth of Forth

Glasgow

Fighter Command 13 Group

Newcastle

Belfast

△ Sunderland

Ⓖ

Middlesbrough

Air Fleet 5 from Norway and Denmark

Maximum effective range of high-level radar: minimum detection altitude *c.*4,570 m.

Maximum effective range of low-level radar: minimum detection altitude *c.*150 m.

Liverpool   Manchester

Sheffield

Fighter Command 12 Group

Ⓖ Nottingham

Norwich

Birmingham

Coventry

Rotterdam

Swansea

Ipswich

Stanmore

LONDON

Cardiff

Bristol   Uxbridge Ⓖ

Bath   Ball

Fighter Commander 10 Group

Canterbury

Fighter Command 11 Group

Exeter

Ventnor

Plymouth

Air Fleet 2

▨ PARIS

Air Fleet 3

0   100   200   300 km

MAP IX.III.1. British Air Defences, 1940

of the Secret Intelligence Service (SIS), it can already be assumed that the British leaders were fully informed of numerous German plans, including the planning of air attacks and the command of air units during the Battle of Britain.

Even the first large-scale attacks revealed the shortcomings in armaments and training of the Luftwaffe. Of the 520 bombers and 1,270 fighters and heavy fighters sent against Britain on 15 August, 57 were lost.[34] As a rule British fighters attacked the lightly armed bombers and avoided dogfights with German fighters. German fighter pilots, however, were less experienced in escorting bombers in formation than in 'free fights'. Moreover, the available German fighter forces were simply not sufficient to provide adequate protection. In the opinion of Air Fleet 2, 36 bombers were such an extended formation that even a complete heavy fighter group (a maximum of 106 aircraft) could not provide enough protection. And the heavy fighter (the Me 110) did not come up to expectations. So many Me 110s were lost that replacements of personnel and aircraft could not keep pace. Finally, mixed fighter and heavy fighter groups were demanded.[35] The daylight use of bomber formations was thus limited in range and strength of attack because of the inadequate fighter protection.

As most of the British air armaments industry was beyond the range of German fighters, on 19 August Göring ordered missions against it 'as long as enemy defences are still strong' to be flown only by individual aircraft and in weather conditions permitting surprise attacks: 'We *must* succeed in largely destroying the material-support base of the enemy air force by attacking its aircraft-engine industry and aluminium production.'[36] These targets were therefore of special significance, but 'in the present phase of the air war, in which it is important to wear down the enemy by attacking him day and night', this did not mean that if they could not be found other important targets should simply be ignored: 'At the present time we cannot afford to be shy in choosing our targets. I have only reserved to myself the right to order attacks on London and Liverpool.'[37] Summing up, Göring explained:

We have entered the decisive period of the air war against Britain. Everything depends on using all possible means to defeat the enemy's air force. To achieve this our first aim is to destroy his fighters. If they avoid combat in the air, we shall attack them on the ground or force them to accept a fight by using bombers to attack targets within the range of our fighters. Moreover, we must constantly intensify the battle against enemy bomber units by attacking

---

[34] 8. Abt. Genst. Lw., Studie Hesler, BA-MA RL 2/v. 3019.

[35] Jafü 1, Gedanken zum Einsatz von Zerstörern, 15 Sept. 1940; Stellungnahme des Jafü 2, 24 Sept. 1940; Stellungnahme des Befehlshabers Lfl. 2, 4 Oct. 1940: MGFA, Sammlung v. Rohden, Film No. 9.

[36] 'Bemerkung des Herrn Reichsmarschalls über die Kampfführung in der Besprechung vom 19.8.1940', BA-MA RL 2 II/27; MGFA, Sammlung v. Rohden, Film No. 9. The corresponding directive of the C.-in-C. of the Luftwaffe Command Staff Ia 'for the continuation of the war against the British air force' was issued on 20 Aug. 1940: 'Schwächung der feindl. Jagdfliegerkräfte, Bekämpfung d. feindl. Bodenorganisation, der Flugrüstungsindustrie, der Aluminium- und Walzwerke', Genst. Lw. 8. Abt., Luftkrieg gegen England, Gefechtskalender, Weisungen und Befehle, Aug. 1940, BA-MA RL 2/v. 3021; extracts quoted in Bechtle, Der Einsatz der Luftwaffe gegen England, 6, BA-MA RL 2/v. 3015.

[37] Milch noted in his 'Merkbuch' on 19 Sept.: 'General disruptive attacks on industry or cities, only London not yet.'

their ground support. When the enemy air force has been defeated, the Luftwaffe will continue its attacks on vital targets to be specified then.

Air Fleets 2 and 3 were ordered to prepare a night attack on Liverpool or Glasgow using the strongest possible bomber formations.[38]

In the mean time the deadline Hitler had given the Luftwaffe to achieve the air supremacy necessary for Operation Sea-Lion had passed. When the Luftwaffe with its record of victories was not able to achieve a fast and decisive success, pessimism began to spread. On 23 August Goebbels found it necessary to 'prepare the nation gradually for the possibility that the war may continue through the winter'. The stubbornness of the British decision to continue the war was to be placed in the foreground. Only in exceptional cases would reports be presented on the triviality (*Lächerlichkeit*) of British everyday life.[39]

Under these circumstances it was not surprising that in its attempt to force the British fighters to accept a battle the Luftwaffe soon succumbed to the temptation to attack London, although the lack of sources makes it impossible to reconstruct exactly how this decision was taken.

3. The Extension of the Air Attacks to London

Although a directive of the Wehrmacht High Command issued on 24 August still made attacks on London dependent on Hitler's decision,[40] the next day at about 10 p.m. a Luftwaffe formation of about 100 bombers attacked the British capital. The British fire brigades reported a total of 76 'incidents' in the City and the adjacent areas of Bethnal Green, East Ham, Stepney, and Finsbury.[41] In retaliation the Royal Air Force bombed Berlin on 25-6 August,[42] which resulted in few victims and little damage but caused Hitler to demand retaliation.[43] On 31 August the Luftwaffe command staff issued an order for the second and third air fleets to prepare

[38] Milch, 'Merkbuch': 'Tenth Flying Corps Glasgow/Clyde—Shipyards, city too, no restraints [*keine Rücksicht*], free.'

[39] *Wollt Ihr den totalen Krieg?*, 121 (not in English trans.). This change in propaganda aimed at Britain had been recommended on 19 Aug. by Warlimont, head of the home defence department in the Wehrmacht Command Staff: Steinert, *Hitlers Krieg*, 145; cf. Martin, *Friedensinitiativen*, 333.

[40] Klee, *Seelöwe*, 171 n. 469.

[41] Mason, *Battle over Britain*, 297-8. According to Klee ('Luftschlacht', 79), Göring had already given permission to attack the British ground-support installations in the London area in his directive of 2 Aug. (cf. nn. 20-1 above). The Second Flying Corps took the initiative on 24 Aug. and was followed in the next few days by the remaining units.

[42] Cf. Jones, *Most Secret War*, 127. Between 25 Aug. and 21 Dec. 1940 Berlin was bombed by a total of 493 aircraft; the next occasion was on 12-13 Mar. 1941, with 48 aircraft. The total quantity dropped was 33,837 tons of high-explosive bombs and 5,800 tons of incendiary bombs: Headquarters, Bomber Command, Photographic Interpretation Section, Interpretation Report No. 653, 20 Mar. 1941, PRO Air 29/432; Tress, 'First Berlin Raids'.

[43] Cf. Hitler's speech of 4 Sept. in Berlin on the occasion of the inauguration of the Kriegswinter-hilfswerk (war winter relief) 1940-1: 'If they say they will attack our cities on a large scale, we shall obliterate their cities! We shall put a stop to the game of these night pirates, so help us God. The time will come when one side breaks, and that will not be National Socialist Germany!': Domarus, ii. 1575 ff.

TABLE IX.III.3. *British Civilian Casualties, July–December 1940*

	Men		Women		Children under 16		Total	
	Killed	Injured	Killed	Injured	Killed	Injured	Killed	Injured
July	178	227	57	77	23	17	258	321
Aug.	627	711	335	448	113	102	1,075	1,262
Sept.	2,844	4,405	2,943	3,807	1,167	2,403	6,954	10,615
Oct.	2,791	4,228	2,900	3,750	643	717	6,334	8,695
Nov.	2,289	3,493	1,806	2,251	493	458	4,588	6,202
Dec.	1,838	2,962	1,434	1,775	521	307	3,793	5,044
TOTAL	10,567	16,026	9,475	12,108	2,960	4,004	23,002	32,138

Source: Mason, *Battle over Britain*, 615.

a 'retaliatory attack on London'. Two days later the air fleets submitted their suggestions and orders. After Hitler had chosen the afternoon of 9 September for the attack, the Luftwaffe Command Staff Ia issued the necessary order on the same day.[44]

The retaliatory attack on London was mainly aimed at the docks and was carried out with such strong forces that the British government declared the highest invasion alert. By the standards of the time the losses were high: in the city 306 dead, 1,337 seriously injured; 142 dead in the suburbs.[45] (For British civilian casualties in the whole period July–December 1940 see Table IX.III.3.)

In spite of Hitler's 'directive for disruptive attacks on the population and air defences of major British cities, including London, by day and night' of 5 September 1940,[46] the attacks on London did not mark the adoption of a purely 'terrorist' policy in the conduct of the air war against Britain. The terror effect on the population was at first merely a secondary goal or regarded as a desirable secondary effect. Most important for the Luftwaffe itself was the fact that London was now a permitted target area. The main aim of the air war was still to destroy the British air force and air-armaments industry. On 1 September the Luftwaffe command staff had chosen thirty factories of this industry as targets. On 9 September they made a distinction between the 'big attack on London' and disruptive attacks on armaments and port facilities. It was planned to have Air Fleet 2 carry out daylight attacks escorted by very strong fighter and heavy fighter formations; Air Fleet 3 would fly night attacks 'until the docks and all supply- and power-sources of the city have been annihilated'.[47]

---

[44] Genst. Lw. 8. Abt., Luftkrieg gegen England, Gefechtskalender, Weisungen und Befehle, Sept. 1940, BA-MA Rl 2/v. 3021; Einsatzbefehle des I. Fliegerkorps, MGFA, Materialsammlung v. Rohden, Film No. 2. On Göring's and Jeschonnek's views regarding an air war with terror attacks cf. Irving, *Rise and Fall*, 12.

[45] Mason, *Battle over Britain*, 358 ff.

[46] Genst. Lw. 8. Abt., Luftkrieg gegen England, Gefechtskalender, Weisungen und Befehle, Sept. 1940, BA-MA RL 2/v. 3021.   [47] Quoted in Klee, 'Luftschlacht', 81.

TABLE IX.III.4. *Aircraft Losses of Fighter Command, August–September 1940*

August		September	
Day	Losses	Day	Losses
1	1	1	15
2	—	2	31
3	—	3	16
4	—	4	17
5	1	5	20
6	1	6	23
7	—	7	28
8	20	8	2
9	4	9	19
10	—	10	1
11	32	11	29
12	22	12	—
13	13	13	1
14	8	14	14
15	34	15	26
16	21	16	1
17	—	17	5
18	27	18	12
19		19	
20		20	
21	} 11	21	
22		22	} 22
23		23	
24	22	24	
25	16	25	4
26	31	26	9
27	1	27	—
28	20	28	49
29	9	29	—
30	26	30	20
31	39		
	TOTAL 359		TOTAL 364

Source: Collier, *Defence*, 450 ff.

The shift of focus of German air attacks from the air-bases in southern England to London represented an important change in the Battle of Britain from the British point of view. Between 31 August and 6 September Fighter Command had lost 185 aircraft (see Table IX.III.4); in the same period losses of fighter pilots reached 10 per cent of total strength.[48] Damage to the infrastructure of the Royal Air Force

---

[48] Dowling, 'Battle of Britain', 122.

in southern England had been so serious that the Luftwaffe was close to achieving air supremacy over Sussex and Kent. The extension of German attacks to London took the pressure off the air defences in south-east England and increased the distance German bombers had to fly to their targets. This in turn gave British interceptors more time to attack them and reduced the time German fighters could remain over the target area.

Although on 5 September an order was issued by the commander-in-chief of the Luftwaffe concerning its tasks in Operation Sea-Lion, Göring seems to have concerned himself little with this operation. A situation report of the Wehrmacht High Command and the Wehrmacht command office of 5 September complained that Göring was not interested in the preparations for 'Sea-Lion' as he did not believe it would be carried out.[49]

Since on 29 August the Fighter Commander 2 had the impression that 'a clear fighter superiority' had already been achieved,[50] it is not surprising that Raeder became more optimistic with regard to 'Sea-Lion'. On 6 September he informed Hitler that the new deadline (20 September) could be met[51] if 'domination of the air is consolidated'. However, on 29 August he had also submitted a memorandum by Wagner (Chief 1 of the naval war staff) to Hitler on the 'conduct of a war against Britain in the event that "Sea-Lion" is cancelled'.[52] Wagner assumed that it was still possible to force Britain to conclude peace by massive air attacks in the foreseeable future, or at least to create a situation in which 'Sea-Lion' could be carried out successfully in the autumn of 1940. But he also believed that because the air war and the landing operation were dependent on the weather, the prospects for ending the war in autumn were uncertain: 'We must realize that Britain will defend herself to the last man, especially as she hopes that the entry of the United States into the war, and possibly other political developments in the spring, will create more favourable conditions for continuing the fight if she can only hold out until winter.' It would not be until spring that more favourable conditions prevailed for direct attacks on Britain by the Luftwaffe alone or in conjunction with Operation Sea-Lion, and in the mean time Britain would be able to increase her strength considerably as a result of American help. Hence, other possibilities for attacking her Empire had to be considered, such as establishing Axis dominance in the Mediterranean.

The Luftwaffe, too, attempted to take stock after its experiences of the preceding weeks. According to an 'Assessment of the Situation of Great Britain' of 10 September by the Luftwaffe command staff,[53] all signs indicated that the British

---

[49] Klee, *Dokumente*, 106. Milch noted after a conference with Göring on 15 Aug.: 'South coast in part less important' ('Merkbuch', 15 Aug. 1940).

[50] Führungsstab Ia, Besprechungsnotizen, 29 Aug. 1940, MGFA, Materialsammlung v. Rohden, Film No. 2.

[51] On 30 Aug. the naval war staff reported to the Wehrmacht High Command and the Wehrmacht Command Staff that the original date (15 Sept.) could not be met because of 'deployment difficulties of the transport fleet' owing to 'particular effects of the air war'. The naval war staff asked for 20 Sept. as the earliest date for the transport fleet to put to sea. On 3 Sept. the Wehrmacht High Command agreed to these suggestions: BA-MA PG 32430/31, Case 385.

[52] *Lagevorträge*, 138 ff.

[53] Intelligence, Ic/III, A1, Maj. von Dewitz, BA-MA RL 2/671, 185 ff.

government believed that by accepting great losses and difficulties they would be able to hold out until either the Luftwaffe was destroyed or the United States intervened with shipments of military equipment or even as an ally. For this reason the British were trying to spare their bomber units. Only 'business circles' took a more sober view of the situation and feared the economic losses a long war would cause. Therefore an increasing readiness to end the war could be expected from these groups. And British military leaders, with the exception of the navy, were also likely to be realistic in their views: 'The army, after its experiences in Flanders, and the air force, after the losses of recent weeks, must be gravely concerned, to say the least, about the near future.' The British people had relatively little interest in the war, but, given their inherent toughness, their will to resist would become stronger if they were directly affected. 'A collapse of this will can be expected only after long direct and indirect exposure to the effects of war.' In conclusion the intelligence staff pointed out that a readiness to make peace could not be expected from the Churchill government. No government could be formed by revolutionary methods, as the British people were simply not revolutionary; and, even if they were driven to extremes, no revolutionary leaders were at hand. (For examples of German attempts to influence the British population by propaganda see Figs. IX.III.2–3.)

A legal change of government would require that 'circles ready to make terms with Germany influence the king and parliament so strongly that Churchill's fall would be inevitable'. In the opinion of the intelligence department, the groups which were 'able to initiate the formation of a new government' were 'the leading business circles' and the army and air force leaders. Both could be influenced by attacking the British armaments industry. Terror attacks would at present affect the population only in so far as productivity would be reduced or eliminated, and this would lead indirectly to a paralysis of enterprises engaged in the war economy. On the basis of this assumption Dewitz suggested the London docks area and the city utilities as targets for attacks. An attack on the docks would reduce the efficiency of the population in the entire industrial area of London, force great changes and shifts in the economy, and destroy enormous economic assets. An extension of the attacks to other parts of London would, in the department's view, be useful only if industrial areas and workers' residential districts were hit. Decisive results could not be expected from attacks on the City and residential areas of the wealthier classes. Attacks on the London area alone could not inflict a devastating blow on the British armaments industry. To achieve that, the intelligence department believed, the target area around Coventry and the steel-producing area of Sheffield presented a 'unique opportunity'. The destruction of Sheffield as the 'vulnerable point' of British warship construction and naval armaments production would be an especially telling blow against the navy.

On 14 September 1940 Hitler informed the commanders-in-chief that the navy had completed preparations for 'Sea-Lion', but in spite of the 'enormous' successes of the Luftwaffe, the preconditions for the operation did not yet exist.[54] For the

---

[54] Quotations in this paragraph from Halder, *Diaries*, i. 583 ff. (trans. slightly amended). Cf. also *Lagevorträge*, 142; *KTB OKW* i, 14 Sept. 1940; Milch, 'Merkbuch', 14 Sept. 1940; Hillgruber, *Strategie*, 176–7.

air attacks to achieve 'total victory' four or five days of good weather were necessary. The enemy was seriously weakened, but his fighter units had not yet been completely eliminated. German reports of successes did not suffice to provide an accurate picture. Although domination of the air, which was necessary for a successful landing, had not been achieved, Hitler did not want to cancel 'Sea-Lion' as yet because that would destroy the effect of the air attacks on the enemy's morale.

Attacks to date have had enormous effects, though perhaps chiefly upon nerves. Part of that psychological effect is the fear of invasion. That anticipation of its imminence must not be removed. Even though victory in the air should not be achieved before another ten or twelve days have passed, outbreaks of mass hysteria may yet occur in Britain. If within the coming ten or twelve days we achieve mastery of the air over a certain area, we could, by a landing operation, compel the enemy to come out with his destroyers against our landing fleet. We could then inflict such losses that he would no longer be able to protect his convoys.

Whereas earlier the purpose of the air war had been to create the preconditions for a landing, Hitler now evidently viewed the landing preparations as a psychological instrument to support the air war, which had been indecisive but might still lead to victory. The now declared aim of a possible landing had little in common with the earlier expectations that it would decide the war. Raeder suggested 8 October as the next date for a landing, as the situation in the air would not change before the next favourable invasion dates, 24–7 September. His remark that a Channel crossing would not be necessary if the Luftwaffe had been completely successful by then, and his demand for air attacks 'without regard to "Sea-Lion" ', suggest that by this time he had ruled out a landing in 1940. Hitler, however, ordered preparations to be made for 27 September and named 17 September as the date for confirmation or otherwise. Only after that should 8 October be considered. The main thing was, however, that the air attacks should be continued without interruption. Hitler's emphasis on the effect of the attacks on enemy morale apparently encouraged Jeschonnek, the chief of the Luftwaffe General Staff, to demand that attacks on residential areas be permitted. Halder noted down his arguments: 'Physical destruction exceeds our expectations. But there has as yet been no mass panic, because residential districts have not been attacked and destroyed so far. Wants free hand in attacking residential areas.' However, Hitler, fearing retaliatory attacks on German cities, refused to change his view that air attacks on the British population must remain the last 'terrible threat': 'As long as there is still a strategic target left, we must concentrate on it.' In this regard he mentioned railway stations, targets in suburban areas, water and gas installations.

These ideas were repeated in a directive of the Wehrmacht High Command the same day:

Air attacks on London, even with expanded target areas, should continue to concentrate primarily on targets vital to the war effort and the functioning of the city (including railway stations) as long as they can still be found. Terror attacks on residential areas are to be kept as a last possible means of applying pressure and are therefore not to be used now.[55]

[55] Klee, *Dokumente*, 406.

WHOSE FAULT?

The German Airforce knows what you think about it. It unterstands your horror and dismay.

Germany has not deliberately chosen this method of warfare. It has been forced upon her by the irresponsability of the British government.

Up to this moment

— according to the instructions of the German High Command — the German Airforce has not attacked one single non-military object. This is a well known and established fact.

The Führer himself gave the order to distinguish clearly between civil population and fighting troops. In contrast to this attitude however

the R.A.F. has bombed again and again undefended German cities.

The British Government has shown its incapability to beat the German forces. Therefore they have attempted to terrorise the civil population in Germany.

Under brutal violation of the laws of international warfare the German women and German children have been wantonly murdered, by the R. A. F. German hospitals have been ruthlessly bombed, though they have been clearly marked by the International Red Cross.

And everyone of these abominable deeds has been praised in Britain as

a victory for the R.A.F.

FIG. IX.III.2. German leaflet

You have been warned

again and again by the German Broadcasting and by German Official Statement that such crimes would not be left unpunished by Germany.

So the German Airforce is now willing to take up the challenge — thought it will still refrain from imitating the unfair methods forced upon the R. A. F. by Mr. Churchill.

The German Airforce will hit back

from now on by powerful attacks on Great Britain in order to retaliate for the unlawful British attacks against civilians in Germany.

The first answer to the attacks of the R. A. F. will have been given by the German Airforce when you read this leaflet.

If in consequence of this intensification of air-warfare the civilian population of Great Britain should suffer, we do regret it.

Remember that

any casualty or any suffering is solely due to one man, Mr. WINSTON CHURCHILL,

who brought this upon you.

Reverse side

WANTED

FOR INCITEMENT TO
MURDER

FIG. IX.III.3. German leaflet

This gangster, who you see in his element in the picture, incites you by his example to participate in a form of warfare in which women, children and ordinary civilians shall take leading parts.

This absolutely criminal form of warfare which is forbidden by the

HAGUE CONVENTION

will be punished

according to military law

Save at least your families from the horrors of war!

Reverse side

Göring also maintained this view in a conference with the air fleet chiefs on 16 September,[56] at which, referring to the weather, he also ordered a change in tactics. Until then the Luftwaffe had tried to force the enemy to accept combat in the air. But because of the weather he had had time to reorganize. All available fighters had been concentrated in the area of London. The pressure on the enemy must be kept up 'as, if his heavy losses continue, he will be finished in four or five days as far as fighters are concerned'. Subsequent German attacks 'spread all over Britain' would then encounter no British fighters at all in some areas. To achieve this it would of course be necessary to prevent replacement, i.e. to eliminate factories. Göring seemed optimistic: 'attacks on London make it absolutely necessary for the enemy to accept combat. If, contrary to expectations, he should not do so, all the better, since we can use increasingly powerful forces to destroy his capital.' Göring distinguished between disruptive attacks, which were to be carried out against London day and night with the strongest possible forces, and destructive attacks flown by individual, specially trained crews as part of a plan to destroy the British air-armaments industry. He assigned the individual air fleets the following tasks:

Air Fleet 2: good-weather attacks on London with small formations and strongest possible fighter and heavy fighter protection to wear down and decimate enemy fighters; Air Fleets 2 and 3: bad-weather disruptive attacks on London as strong as possible; Air Fleets 2 and 3 continue disruptive attacks on Liverpool; Air Fleet 3: by day further attacks on Southampton and Bristol; Ninth Flying Division: dropping mines on London and mining the Thames; Air Fleets 2 and 3: with special crews destructive attacks on thirty targets of the British aircraft industry. Alternative targets will be assigned soon by Command Staff Ic.

For night attacks on large industrial cities Göring wanted to provide the air fleets with about 100 converted Ju 52 transport aircraft. His remark that ' "Sea-Lion" must not disturb or burden the operations of the Luftwaffe' and his reference to 'subsequent attacks spread all over Britain' show that Göring, like Raeder, no longer expected the landing operation to be carried out. In view of the first dispersal order of the Wehrmacht High Command of 19 September, for the 'Sea-Lion' transport fleet to avoid further losses as a result of British air attacks, and the instructions to halt further deployment of the transport ships where this had not already been completed, serious preparations by the Luftwaffe had become superfluous.[57]

Although the attacks on London had not achieved the expected air supremacy and therefore the bomber formations had to be used primarily at night, the Luftwaffe still seemed optimistic. On 16 September Göring believed that the last British fighter forces were now being drawn together and estimated that they had only 177 aircraft.[58] The Luftwaffe crews were supposedly still 'full of optimism about a successful conclusion of the air war': British units were thought to have about 300 fighters

---

[56] MGFA, Materialsamlung v. Rohden, Film No. 2; Milch, 'Merkbuch', 16 Sept. 1940.

[57] Klee, *Dokumente*, 436. Already on 17 Sept. Dept. L of the Wehrmacht High Command and the Wehrmacht Command Staff had informed the C.-in-C. of the navy of the postponement of the original landing 'until further notice': BA-MA PG 32431, Case GE 358, p. 127. On the losses of the transport fleet cf. BA-MA PG 32441, Case GE 403, p. 117.

[58] Milch, 'Merkbuch', 16 Sept. 1940.

left, with reserves of at most 50 and monthly deliveries of 250. Opinions differed about the strength of the British bomber fleet, which had been kept in reserve in expectation of a German landing. In general it was assumed to have about 800 aircraft.[59]

Although the attacks on the British air-armaments industry (fighter replacements) continued, strikes were now increasingly extended to other targets. Among the Luftwaffe leaders and in the Luftwaffe Command Staff Ic differences of opinion about the value of purely terror attacks continued.[60] In a note of 20 September for an oral report by the head of Ic on the 'selection of primary targets in the near future',[61] attacks on British ports and in particular the London docks area were suggested because of the effect already achieved and in the light of the experience gained in Air Fleet 2 before the war. With the start of attacks on London it had seemed advisable 'to try to achieve the maximum effect on the unique concentration of 8 million people in the city, in addition to the strong attacks on the dock facilities'.

This basic aim was also considered a guide-line for the coming weeks. The intelligence department expected a lasting effect on the ability of the London docks to function if electricity production could be destroyed as far as possible. If the gas and sewage pump-works could also be put out of operation at the same time, that would do more than seriously impair the ability of the docks to function; it would also affect British industry, including the armaments industry, as well as the cost of living and the 'health of the nation'. In accordance with these priorities the department divided London into four target areas and added a fifth on the lower Thames, outside the actual city, including the Tilbury Docks. An expansion of the suggested target areas to include residential districts could not, it was held, be expected to produce any devastating effect: 'The direct effect on the population of bomb explosions in residential areas will be achieved even if attacks are clearly restricted to limited target areas, as a result of scattering and emergency drops.'

With regard to attacks on the air-armaments industry, the intelligence department pointed out that the selection of thirty targets was based on the assumption that by destroying key production centres of general importance within the industry and annihilating the fighter factories, fighter production would be paralysed as quickly as possible. Targets of general importance had been given priority over fighter-airframe factories. Fighter production had now been disrupted to a certain degree by the attacks. Asserting again the view that the most important aim was still a further destruction of enemy fighter production, the intelligence department made several suggestions for achieving a general paralysis of the British aircraft industry on the broad scale necessary in the event of a long war, and emphasized especially the significance of the large industrial regions of Coventry, Birmingham, and Sheffield.

[59] Cf. statements of the chief of staff of Air Fleet 2, Lieut.-Gen. Speidel, in Warlimont's report of 23 Sept. 1940, *KTB OKW* i, 23 Sept. 1940. On the question of aircraft strength cf. the figures of Ic/III A 1, BA-MA RL 2/671, pp. 182–3.

[60] On 20 Sept. Hitler ordered a retaliatory attack on Cambridge for the night of 21–2 Sept. Göring's corresponding order is dated 23 Sept.: Genst. Lw. 8. Abt., Luftkrieg gegen England, Gefechtskalender, Weisungen und Befehle, Sept. 1940, BA-MA RL 2/v. 3021.

[61] BA-MA RL 2/671, pp. 147 ff.

Attacks on Coventry would have a double effect: they would 'destroy industrial installations and directly affect workers there, who live near their factories. Because the factories and residential structures are built close together in a small area, an especially powerful effect is to be expected from the use of incendiary bombs.'

The most radical position with regard to the use of attacks on the civilian population was advocated by the 'England Committee' of the foreign ministry.[62] On 20 September they argued that 'there are no longer any reasons to refrain from attacks on the civilian population because of fear of enemy propaganda', as not only the British but also the American press already presented German attacks as directed exclusively against civilians, especially workers. The committee attached particular importance to air attacks on working-class districts in London, as they would destroy the illusion that the Germans were giving up attacks on civilian areas. Moreover, such raids would cause the workers to flee to the wealthier sections in the west of London, 'which will accentuate the breach between the classes'. Soon there would be complete dislocation in the food supply and serious unrest in London: 'If the poorer classes are actually exposed to real want, this will put increasing pressure on the Labour Party to force the government to end the war.' In the committee's opinion raids on working-class areas should be supplemented by attacks on radio stations and on Fleet Street: 'Without newspapers political life in Britain will come to a stop.'

Against these ideas, which were reminiscent of the German 'stab-in-the-back' myth, it was pointed out in Command Staff Ic that 'if at some point it should be intended to terrorize the whole London area', this could best be done by paralysing the utilities. The main aim must be to strike at those people who could produce a 'legal' change of government: 'Since for the most important people (among the civilians) in the final analysis everything is at stake, the fate of several hundred thousand of their countrymen is a matter of indifference to them, but not the prospect of their own ruin.' The 'absolutely logical' conclusion was therefore that British heavy industry and the armaments industry had to be hit as quickly and directly as possible. Any deviation from this aim meant a waste of energy and prolonged the war. With regard to London this meant 'not losing sight for a moment of the goal clearly recognized in the England Study of destroying the vital utilities'.[63] Dewitz was still of the opinion that the British air-armaments industry could be weakened in an extremely short time by planned attacks on the chosen targets and by extending these attacks to include supplier industries, with a decisive effect on the outcome of the war. On 28 September he demanded renewed attacks on the target areas Coventry and Sheffield.[64] The head of the operations department, General von Waldau, was less confident. On 7 October Halder summarized the latter's statement: 'Air Force Command has underestimated British fighter strength by about 100 per cent. . . . At the beginning of the air battle over Britain we had about 950 fighters and now

---

[62] BA-MA RL 2/671, pp. 124 ff.

[63] Dewitz to Lindeiner (Robinson Ic), 23 Sept. 1940, BA-MA RL 2/671, pp. 141 ff.; cf. Ic/III, note for an oral report of 25 Sept. 1940, ibid., pp. 129-30.

[64] Ic/III, note for an oral report of 28 Sept. 1940, BA-MA RL 2/671, pp. 116-17.

we have 600; about 1,100 bombers, and now we have 800.' As targets until mid-October, Waldau named vital installations in London, industry (individual attacks), convoys, and the British navy. On the general strategic situation he noted:

American production will not get into its stride before spring 1941. We shall have to keep a bomber fleet and strong fighter forces in readiness against that time. Russian air force is large, but of poor quality. Our air strength by next spring will at best have regained the level held at the beginning of the air war against Britain. We would need four times that strength to force Britain into surrender. Two-front war [i.e. against Britain and the Soviet Union] cannot be sustained.[65]

(For total German personnel and aircraft losses in this period see Table IX.III.5.)

On 10 October the group from the Luftwaffe Command Staff Ic in Göring's command train 'Robinson' came to the conclusion that a 50 per cent reduction of British aircraft engine and airframe production could be expected. Total British losses of 1,770 fighters were calculated for the period 1 July to 9 October. 'In agreement with reports from the intereception service' the number of remaining British fighters ready for action was given as 300–400. Other successes were the London docks, which were 'largely' destroyed, and British losses of at least 10,000 dead and 20,000 injured. Even more serious than these losses was the poor health of the population: 'The constant air-raid warnings, spending part of every night for at least five weeks in an air-raid shelter, difficulties in food distribution, and damage to important sanitation and other facilities will surely lead to a great increase in illnesses, which could easily become epidemics.' Although the concentration of previous attacks on utilities had not yet achieved any lasting effect, a continuation of such attacks was necessary.

Even within the intelligence department this evaluation of the successes of the German air attacks was viewed with scepticism. Commenting on the alleged effect of bombing on the thirty-three targets of the air-armaments industry, the intelligence department in Berlin (Major von Dewitz) recommended to the group in 'Robinson': 'In view of the tendency of some people to see things too optimistically, I would personally take good care to protect myself by pointing to the lack of photographs.' In his assessment of the 'current situation' of 17 October, Dewitz came to the conclusion that the position in London was approaching a kind of stalemate. Despite every effort it had still not been possible to destroy the utilities, as in night attacks the targets could not be recognized, and during the day low-level attacks were not possible because of the enemy defences. Therefore Dewitz suggested the following three stages: (1) shifting the focal point of the attacks to the outer areas of London (industrial and residential sections); (2) the use of stronger attacking forces against the industrial Midlands (Coventry, Birmingham, Sheffield) to paralyse the air-armaments industry and disperse the air defences massed around London; and (3) then suddenly shifting the weight of the attacks back to central London. The intelligence department believed that a surprise resumption of bombing in central

[65] Halder, *Diaries*, i. 614 (7 Oct. 1940).

TABLE IX.III.5 *Total Personnel and Aircraft Losses of the Luftwaffe, 1 August 1940–31 March 1941*

PERSONNEL LOSSES

	Dead		Captured/Missing		Wounded	
	Total	Officers	Total	Officers	Total	Officers
Front losses						
Flying personnel in units	1,741	367	2,537	601	891	158
Ground personnel	117	3	12	1	133	2
Flak	116	3	8	—	263	8
Air signal troops	21	4	34	1	11	—
Paratroops	—	—	—	—	15	1
TOTAL	1,995	377	2,591	603	1,313	169
Home losses						
Flying personnel in units	588	101	27	3	246	43
Other flying personnel and schools	780	63	23	2	558	54
TOTAL	1,368	164	50	5	804	97
TOTAL LOSSES OF THE LUFTWAFFE	3,363	541	2,641	608	2,117	266

AIRCRAFT LOSSES

	Complete losses	All losses[a]	Replacements on and after 1 Aug. 1940	Replacements available on 31 Mar. 1941
Bombers	1,142	1,817	1,919	—
Fighters	802	1,166	1,191	—
Heavy fighters	330	468	776	—
Dive-bombers	128	208	447	33
Long-range reconnaissance	136	204	526	—
Units of the C.-in-C. of the navy	102	136	88	39
Others	69	133	195	47
Army reconnaissance	33	80	156	18
Special bomber units	37	61	209	—
Battle	26	48	—	
Courier squadrons	11	18	—	—
Weather squadrons	12	18	—	—
Corps transport squadrons	8	16	—	—
Local transport flights	4	10	—	—
TOTAL LOSSES	2,840	4,383	5,507	137
LOSSES FROM ENEMY ACTION	2,265	3,132		

[a] Figure includes complete losses and all damage amounting to more than 10% of the aircraft.

Source: Compiled according to ObdL, Genst., Gen. Qu. G. Abt. No. 1437/41 g.Kdos. (IA), 2 Apr. 1941; from Klee, 'Luftschlacht', 85.

London would make it possible to destroy the principal utility installations in low-level attacks and thus 'strike a devastating blow against the capital'. The resulting disruption of 'life in the City, which has undergone a strong revival' and of clearing operations would have a particularly lasting material and moral effect.[66]

The suggestion to extend the air attacks to the industrial Midlands received the support of the political department of the Luftwaffe Command Staff Ic (Ic/Pol.), who argued that, unlike the case of industry in London, which was dominated by British finance capital, most British investment capital, especially that of those circles who formed the main support of the government, was in the industry of the Midlands. Serious damage to that industry would therefore not only reduce Britain's armaments potential considerably 'but would also affect that class of well-to-do British capitalists who cannot simply transfer their capital to somewhere in the Empire or abroad'. Central England, moreover, unlike the cosmopolitan port city of London, was the home of 'the really conservative, stubborn British, who constitute the psychological and spiritual basis of Britain's will to resist and to continue the fight'. This group must be made to feel the effects of the air war so that they would no longer stiffen the gradually weakening will of the population of London.[67]

The Luftwaffe command accepted the idea of extending the air war to the industrial Midlands,[68] but without stopping the attacks on London. The order of 19 October[69] in fact listed so many targets that it was impossible to speak of a concentrated attack. Moreover, authority to give the orders was divided between the commander-in-chief of the Luftwaffe and subordinate commands. For example, the bomber wing commanders were given considerable freedom for attacks aimed at the air-armaments industry. These attacks were to be continued with vigour. Attacks on the London utilities were also to be continued day and night 'with the minimum interruption'. British fighter forces would suffer heavy losses from frequent changes in German fighter tactics and from surprise attacks, by fighters carrying bombs, on British aircraft on the ground. Even if no fighter cover was available, disruptive attacks by bomber formations should be carried out if at all possible: 'The purpose of these attacks is to disrupt seriously the lives of the people. They are therefore to be extended to the whole area of London.' Until further notice about 50 bombers of Air Fleet 2 and about 150 of Air Fleet 3 were to be kept ready for night attacks on London. The target areas for these attacks were to be changed frequently 'to achieve the desired effect on the population and constantly confront the British defences with new problems'. The Ninth Flying Corps was ordered

---

[66] Letter from Lindeiner (Robinson Ic) to Dewitz (Füst. Ic/III) of 11 Oct. 1940 with two annexes of 10 Oct. 1940: 'Angriffswirkung gegen die 33 wichtigsten Ziele der britischen Jagdflugindustrie' and 'Beurteilung der britischen Jägerlage', BA-MA RL 2/671, pp. 88 ff. Remark of Ic/III of 13 Oct. 1940, BA-MA RL 2/671, pp. 84-5. Assessment of Ic/III A 1 of 17 Oct. 1940, BA-MA RL 2/671, pp. 64 ff.

[67] Note for an oral report of 21 Oct. 1940, seen by Chef Ic "Robinson", BA-MA RL 2/671, pp. 67-8.

[68] On 4 Nov. Maj. von Dewitz (Ic/III) said that he realized that his remarks encroached on the area for which Ia (operations department) was responsible, 'but, after all, at present the war against Britain is being run more by Ic than Ia': BA-MA RL 2/671.

[69] In *KTB OKW* i. 977 ff. Cf. Genst. Lw. 8. Abt., Luftkrieg gegen England, Gefechtskalender, Weisungen und Befehle, Oct. 1940, BA-MA RL 2/v. 3021.

to mine British seaports, especially the Thames estuary, the Bristol Channel, and Liverpool. Air Fleet 2, in addition to night attacks on targets in London, was also to fly such attacks against the industrial areas of Liverpool and Birmingham–Coventry with its remaining 100 bombers. If other aircraft were available, it would also carry out disruptive attacks on east-coast ports. Göring reserved for himself the authority to order attacks on Bomber Command bases in the event of good weather. Air Fleet 3 was ordered to continue the war against British fighters in south-western Britain and to use bomb-carrying heavy fighters to attack Southampton. In addition, it was to use dive-bombers to prevent a revival of coastal shipping along the British south coast, and long-range bombers to carry out disruptive attacks on the northern entrance to the Irish Sea (the North Channel) and Glasgow, in so far as such bombers (Fw 200 Condor) were available for that purpose. Bombers of Air Fleet 3 equipped with Plendl devices[70] were to be put on stand-by for use against London as well as Birmingham and Coventry. Moreover, Air Fleet 3 had to be prepared to attack either Liverpool or Birmingham with all its strength at short notice, on Göring's orders. In that event the Second Flying Corps (Air Fleet 2) was to mount disruptive attacks on London as a diversion.

4. THE 'WAR OF ATTRITION'

Although the battle to achieve air supremacy by attacking British fighters and the air-armaments industry was not abandoned, the air war henceforth assumed more and more the character of a war of terror and exhaustion. With winter approaching, the Luftwaffe would have to reduce its activities because of the weather (cf. the high losses through accidents as early as October, Table IX.III.6), while increased British aircraft production and American supply shipments were to be expected. German hopes could only be centred on a collapse of the British will to resist. This hope in fact dominated the thoughts of the Luftwaffe command staff on 25 October when they called upon the fighter-bomber units once more to impress upon all their crews the importance of the 'war of attrition'. A decline in the intensity of the attacks at the wrong time could destroy the chances of achieving a rapid victory in the war and thus make all earlier sacrifices useless.[71]

The hope that the British will to resist would collapse suddenly was to be found not only in the Luftwaffe. As late as 3 November the state secretary of the foreign ministry, von Weizsäcker, noted that the possibility should not be excluded that 'things will one day become too tedious [*sic*] in the East End of London and negotiations with Germany, perhaps even a new cabinet, will be demanded'.[72]

Although the night attacks on Midland industrial cities registered successes, as the organization of British night-fighter units was still in the initial stages, hopes for a collapse of the British will to resist rapidly disappeared. Attacks such as that

---

[70] These were radio navigation aids (*Funkleitvorrichtungen*), the so-called *X-Geräte* for the bombing system developed by Dr Hans Plendl in 1933 according to the Lorenz blind-landing procedure: Price, *Instruments*, 21 ff.; Niehaus, *Radarschlacht*, 35 ff.; Irving, *Rise and Fall*, 61; Jones, *Most Secret War*, 135 ff.
[71] Fernschreiben Füst. Ia, 25 Oct. 1940, MGFA, Materialsammlung v. Rohden, Film No. 9.
[72] *Weizsäcker-Papiere*, 222–3.

TABLE IX.III.6. Losses of German Front-line Air Units, 1–31 October 1940

	Enemy action		Special circumstances		Total destroyed	Total damaged	Total damaged and destroyed	Losses as % of effective strength			Monthly effective strength	
	Destroyed	Damaged	Destroyed	Damaged				Total	Damaged	Total %	Oct.	Sept.
Army reconnaissance	1	—	6	6	7	6	13	2.2	1.6	3.8	320	320
Long-range reconnaissance	9	—	9	6	18	6	24	6.3	2.1	8.4	285	300
Fighters	123	15	40	51	163	66	229	14.8	6.0	20.8	1,100	950
Heavy fighters	12	3	17	6	29	9	38	8.1	2.5	10.6	360	310
Bombers	71	16	112	91	183	107	200	12.3	7.2	19.5	1,485	1,420
Dive-bombers	—	—	7	4	7	4	11	1.6	0.9	2.5	430	460
Transport aircraft	—	—	4	3	4	3	7	0.8	0.6	1.4	470	470
Courier aircraft	—	—	—	2	—	2	2	—	1.7	1.7	115	200
Units of the C.-in-C. of the navy	4	—	9	—	13	—	13	4.2	—	4.2	215	240
TOTAL	220	34	204	169	424	203	527[a]	8.9	4.3	13.2	4,780	4,670

[a] In original document mistakenly given as 627.

Source: Luftwaffenführungsstab Ic/III, 16 Nov. 1940, BA-MA RL 2/671

on Coventry on the night of 14–15 November, in which twelve armaments factories and the fourteenth-century cathedral were destroyed and 380 persons were killed,[73] actually strengthened British determination, as did the large-scale attacks on London. In the following months German air attacks still concentrated on British cities, but they were increasingly directed at targets whose destruction would have no decisive effect on the war but would at most relieve the western front in the approaching two-front war against the Soviet Union and Britain. Increased attacks were carried out on the night-bases of British bombers and on port facilities and merchant ships, coupled with the mining of estuaries and coastal waters.[74] For overall statistics on the Battle of Britain see Table IX.III.7.

The Luftwaffe Command Staff Ic also ceased to evaluate the air war over Britain in terms of a possible decisive event, and instead considered primarily its effects on the course of the war as a whole. It was easier to present the conduct of the air war against Britain as a success within the framework of such long-term developments than to justify it in terms of the original German aims and expectations. Weizsäcker noted: 'Incidently, in spite of Coventry etc. the view now prevails that starvation caused by a blockade is the most important weapon against Britain, and not smoking the British out.'[75] On 21 December Major von Dewitz regarded the large-scale Luftwaffe attacks on Britain as having led to a decline in production, above all in the aircraft-engine industry, which had to be described as 'for the first time of decisive importance to the conduct of the war'. Dewitz predicted a 'catastrophic situation' with regard to the supply of aircraft engines in January and February 1941.[76] Observing that the direct effects of attacks on airframe and engine factories on the edge of industrial cities had to be considered small, compared with the indirect effects on supplier industries in the cities, the intelligence department on 14 January 1941 called urgently for attacks by strong forces on 'large areas' in which targets in the air-armaments industry were located: 'Even if factories are not directly hit, production will be indirectly reduced by the effects of the attack on the workers.' 'Area target maps' were submitted to 'Robinson' accordingly.[77]

The assumed successes of the German attacks were reflected in the completely inaccurate estimates of British aircraft production in 1940 (see Tables IX.III.1, 2), on the basis of which extremely rash predictions were made for 1941. In the belief that 'production in January 1941 will be about the same as in November 1940, and production for the entire year 1941 will remain on average at about the same level', the intelligence department predicted that total British aircraft production for 1941 would be 7,200: 2,160 fighters, 2,400 bombers and long-range reconnaissance

---

[73] Göring's directive (*inter alia*) to prepare the attacks on Coventry ('Mondscheinsonate'), Birmingham ('Regenschirm'), and Wolverhampton ('Einheitspreis'), 7 Nov. 1940: Vorbefehl und Weisung ObdL Füst. Ia an Lfl. 2 u. 3 für Angriff auf Coventry in der Nacht v. 14-15 Nov. 1940 ('Mondscheinsonate'), 14 Nov. 1940, BA-MA RL 2/v 3021 (Gefechtskalender); Mason, *Battle over Britain*, 473-4; Longmate, *Air Raid*; Evans, 'Air Intelligence'; Jones, *Most Secret War*, 146 ff.

[74] Genst. Lw. 8. Abt., Luftkrieg gegen England, Gefechtskalender, Weisungen und Befehle, Dec. 1940–Mar. 1941, BA-MA 2/v. 3021.

[75] *Weizsäcker-Papiere*, 225 (17 Nov. 1940).

[76] LwFü. Stab Ic/III, Britische Flugzeugindustrie, 21 Dec. 1940, BA-MA RL 2/744.

[77] Ic/III, Flugzeugindustrie G.B., 14 Jan. 1941, BA-MA RL 2/447.

aircraft, and 2,640 other aircraft.[78] In spite of the proviso that Britain's aircraft production could only be kept down to the level of November 1940 if her aircraft industry and imports of materials from the United States 'are seriously disrupted', the intelligence department's figures were in fact only an attempt to gloss over their own ignorance. In reality Britain produced more than 20,000 aircraft in 1941 (Table IX.III.2).

The German failure to achieve air supremacy and the unfavourable time of year reduced British fears of a landing. In fact war-economy considerations forced a disbanding of the deployment for Operation Sea-Lion, which since 14 September 1940 at the latest had been a mere psychological support-measure for the air war. Because of the losses caused by British air attacks, on 2 October Hitler ordered that all measures taken in conjunction with 'Sea-Lion' were to be 'largely dismantled'. If this meant that the previous preparation time of nine to ten days for 'Sea-Lion' could not be maintained, this was to be accepted.[79] In his Directive No. 18 of 21 November[80] Hitler again stated that 'changes in the general situation may make it possible, or necessary, to revert to "Sea-Lion" in the spring of 1941'; but he evidently expressed himself more plainly on 5 December, when Halder noted: '"Sea-Lion" can be left out of our consideration.'[81] At the same conference at which Hitler made this remark the situation in the air was discussed. It was believed that the British air force 'had not been greatly weakened'. 'Perhaps the stopping of our daylight air attacks saved the British fighters from total defeat. But our attacks on British industry cannot destroy it.' However, Britain could not replace her losses herself, and deliveries from the United States should not be overestimated: 'Until next summer no significant increase in American aid is to be expected (new factories will be ready only in 1941).' Whereas the British would not have a stronger air force in the spring of 1941 than in December 1940 and would therefore not be in a position to carry out any real offensive against Germany, the Luftwaffe would be 'significantly stronger' then than it had been in the spring of 1940. In May and June 1941 the first series of new-model aircraft would be produced and sent to the western front. The older models would be used against the Soviet Union. In conclusion it was remarked: 'For the situation in the air to remain acceptable it is essential that rapid progress be made in land operations.'

On 18 December 1940 Hitler issued Directive No. 21 ('Case Barbarossa'), in which he ordered the Wehrmacht to be prepared to 'crush Soviet Russia in a rapid campaign' even before the end of the war with Britain.[82] In this way Hitler attempted to correct the priority of the two fronts, deriving from his basic aim of

---

[78] Ic/III, A (Ausbringung der brit. Flugrüstungsindustrie im Jahre 1940 und erwartete Ausbringung der brit. Flugrüstungsindustrie im Jahre 1941), according to a handwritten note: 'Vortragsnotiz f. Chef zur Vorlage Chef Genst.', 17 Feb. 1941, BA-MA RL 2/447.

[79] OKW WFst/Abt L (I) No. 00811/40 g.Kdos., 2 Oct. 1940, betr.: Luftangriffe im Kanalgebiet, BA-MA PG 32430, Case GE 385, p. 37a. Cf. also Klee, *Dokumente*, 441-2.

[80] Trevor-Roper, *Directives*, No. 18, p. 43.

[81] Halder, *Diaries*, i. 722-3 (5 Dec. 1940); cf. Klee, *Seelöwe*, 215 ff.

[82] Trevor-Roper, *Directives*, No. 21.

TABLE IX.III.7. *German Aircraft Used*[a] *and Tons of Bombs Dropped in the Battle of Britain, 1940–1941*

AIRCRAFT

	Concentrated large-scale attacks	Disruptive attacks and attacks on alternative targets	Against ships	For mine-laying	Total no.
1940					
Aug.	404	3,898	239	246	4,779
Sept.	4,755	2,136	90	279	7,260
Oct.	3,826	5,415	60	610	9,911
Nov.	3,142	3,008	23	605	6,778
Dec.	2,082	1,562	8	192	3,844
1941					
Jan.	1,730	655	22	58	2,465
Feb.	329	762	103	207	1,401
Mar.	3,309	952	139	234	4,364
Apr.	3,681	1,292	263	212	5,448
May	2,311	1,538	211	222	4,282
June	312	410	312	371	1,405

BOMBS (t.)

	Large-scale attacks		Disruptive attacks and attacks on alternative targets		Attacks on ships	Total tons		Total no. of air-dropped mines
	Explosive	Incendiary	Explosive	Incendiary		Explosive	Incendiary	
1940								
Aug.	387,800	25,776	3,946,850	164,332	113,150	4,447,800	189,108	328
Sept.	4,687,250	345,908	1,884,500	81,906	43,750	6,614,500	427,886	669
Oct.	4,642,950	143,328	4,011,782	179,964	135,800	8,790,632	323,292	562
Nov.	3,736,800	230,795	2,449,250	74,172	18,850	6,204,900	305,507	1,215
Dec.	1,998,395	365,492	1,808,008	144,691	6,250	3,812,653	510,183	557
1941								
Jan.	1,469,940	309,954	425,250	61,630	23,500	1,952,690	471,584	144
Feb.	288,950	68,746	661,300	36,060	71,000	1,021,250	105,806	376
Mar.	2,959,150	593,745	806,748	96,162	122,850	3,888,748	689,907	410
Apr.	4,684,330	394,821	1,553,110	181,476	285,650	6,523,090	576,297	433
May	2,973,690	352,018	1,666,850	132,703	181,800	4,822,340	494,721	363
June	471,200	24,666	492,493	30,593	103,250	1,066,943	55,259	647

[a] Excluding fighters and reconnaissance aircraft.

Note: Several small mistakes in addition in the original document have been retained, as their individual sources could not be determined.

In addition, in Sept. 1940 62 containers (ABB 500) with 140 incendiary bombs each were dropped. In Nov. 1940 105 mine-bombs (1,800 kg.) were dropped in destructive attacks. In Dec. 1940 50 mine-bombs were dropped in large-scale attacks and 40 in destructive attacks (1,800 kg.). In Jan. and Feb. 1941 2 large bombs were dropped each month in destructive attacks. In Mar. 4 were dropped in large-scale attacks (2,500 kg.). In Apr. 1941 21 mines were dropped in destructive attacks.

Source: Compiled on the basis of: Oberkommando der Luftwaffe, Chef Genst. 8. Abt., Luftkrieg gegen England, Gefechtskalender 1 Aug. 1940–30 June 1941; from Klee, 'Luftschlacht', 84.

conquering 'living-space' in the east. Contrary to his original intentions, he was unable to begin his campaign against the Soviet Union with the necessary cover in the west, and certainly not with British toleration or support. His hope of being able to force the British to capitulate by achieving a quick victory in the east meant that his 'living-space' war against the Soviet Union also had a strategic function in the west, on a front where the Wehrmacht had lost its first decisive battle and consequently also the strategic initiative. This fact not only caused countries as yet unaffected by Nazi aggression to reorientate their policies; the nascent resistance movements in areas occupied by German troops also drew hope from the German failure.

IV. The Return to an Indirect Strategy against Britain

HANS UMBREIT

HITLER had been realistic enough to want to risk a direct attack on Britain only under quite definite favourable conditions. The invasion across the Channel was merely to administer the *coup de grâce* to an already weakened enemy. Essentially Britain's will to resist had to be broken first. If, therefore, the conflict could not be ended by political means, then the preconditions of a military solution would have to be created by a 'siege' of Britain, using the navy and the air force to this end. As a further possibility, towards the end of June 1940 Jodl suggested an extension of the war on the periphery: by military operations against the overseas Empire, in conjunction with those states which stood to gain from a British defeat.[1] He had in mind support for Italy in Libya with a view to occupying the Suez Canal and joint action with Spain for the seizure of Gibraltar. Counter-intelligence was to discover what other British possessions offered a chance of successful operations under an indirect strategy.[2] Jodl also believed that support for Arab independence moves might be useful.

The naval operations staff developed similar ideas.[3] Ever since August 1940 it had entertained serious doubts about the feasibility of 'Sea-Lion', as well as about Germany's ability to force Britain to come to terms solely by the war at sea and in the air. The staff therefore recommended, in the event that the landing plans had to be abandoned or postponed, the capture of that area of the Mediterranean which was as important to the Axis powers as to the enemy. The seizure of Gibraltar, jointly with Spain, and the closure of the Suez Canal by a German–Italian thrust into Egypt would be sufficient, in the opinion of the German navy, to bring the Mediterranean into the Axis sphere of power. This would ensure undisturbed naval transport throughout the Mediterranean, safeguard the Balkans against British intervention, and make the Middle East available to the Axis powers as a source of raw materials and a base for future moves towards India. Italian forces would be freed for military operations. The conquest of Gibraltar and Spain's previous entry into the war would prevent the secession of further French colonies and widen the basis for the naval war in the Atlantic. Moreover, German bases on Spain's and Portugal's Atlantic islands—in line with Hitler's intentions, as was a naval base in Dakar—seemed within the realm of the possible and might influence the attitude

---

[1] Cf. IX.II above.　　　　　　　　　　　　　　　[2] OKW war diary, i. 15 (8 Aug. 1940).
[3] Memorandum by Capt. Wagner of 29 Aug. 1940 on 'Conduct of the war against Britain in the event of the non-materialization of Operation "Sea-Lion"' and the navy C.-in-C.'s report to Hitler on 6 Sept. 1940, in *Lagevorträge*, 134 ff.

of the United States. Control of the Mediterranean, in the view of the naval operations staff, was 'of decisive importance for the further conduct of the war'. It did not rule out the possibility that in such an event Britain would at last cease resistance.

In parallel to their 'Sea-Lion' preparations, the High Command of the Armed Forces and the Army High Command also gave detailed consideration to various alternatives in order to be able to submit proposals to Hitler for action in the event that the direct strategy against Britain did not produce the expected results. At the end of July—the Germans having previously failed to establish themselves in Morocco—a proposal was made for an expeditionary corps to support an Italian offensive against Egypt.[4] The army commander-in-chief was ordered to have the technical prerequisites examined.[5] The home defence department of the High Command of the Armed Forces thought that the period until the spring of 1941, when all armoured formations might again be needed, would probably be sufficient to 'destroy . . . the British position in the Mediterranean'.[6] And Jodl believed that the time had now come for arrangements with Rome, so that Germany and Italy could wage the 'final struggle' against Britain—not separately, but together.[7] Mussolini, however, thought he could still do without the German help offered him at the beginning of September. He calculated that he had a good chance against Egypt once the German landing in England had begun. When this was abandoned, the Italian push into Egypt, started on 13 September, lost its prerequisite for success.

Hitler had another reason in September 1940 for close co-operation with Mussolini. To the extent that the chances of 'Sea-Lion' were dwindling he became more amenable to the navy's ambitious suggestions for operations in the Mediterranean and in the Atlantic. The Azores, the Canary Islands, and the Cape Verde Islands increasingly seemed to him attainable objectives of a German-Italian-Spanish conduct of the war.[8] In this area he wanted to forestall Britain and, in the long term, the United States. From the Azores, which according to Hitler's ideas would come to Germany under the peace treaty, future long-range bombers would be able to threaten North America.[9] Gaining a foothold in Ireland was also considered for a time. However, the logistical problems proved insuperable.

As for joint operations with Italy, Hitler had meanwhile reduced any possible German assistance to one mixed armoured brigade with modern equipment, and demanded further details from Army High Command before approaching the Italians again. The Italians, however, now expressed greater interest in support by Luftwaffe formations.[10] As the German Army High Command also viewed the employment of armoured formation in North Africa with some scepticism, a German-Italian war plan did not come about by the winter of 1940-1.

---

[4] OKW war diary, i. 11 (7 Aug. 1940).

[5] OKW/WFSt/Abt. L(I) No. 33217/40 g.Kdos. Chefs., 12 Aug. 1940, BA-MA RW 4/v. 590.

[6] OKW war diary, i. 17 (9 Aug. 1940).

[7] Chef WFSt, estimate of the situation on 13 Aug. 1940, BA-MA RW 4/v. 590; OKW diary, i. 32 (14 Aug. 1940).

[8] OKW war diary, i. 63-4 (5 Sept. 1940).   [9] Ibid. 177 (15 Nov. 1940).

[10] Ibid. 119 (10 Oct. 1940)

For reasons of prestige, however, Mussolini felt under pressure to act. Even though his first attempt to make the Mediterranean the Italians' mare clausum had not succeeded, he still thought there was a chance of a 'lesser solution'—extension of the Italian zone of influence in south-east Europe. Hitler, however—as soundings in July 1940 elicited—was opposed to an Italian attack on Yugoslavia. He did not wish for a military conflict in the Balkans and prohibited the Wehrmacht from having staff discussions on this issue and also from passing on any information concerning the Yugoslav fortifications.[11] Britain was to be given no opportunity for establishing herself in the Balkans, lest the Romanian oil-fields should come within the range of her air force. The German military attaché in Rome reported that Marshal Badoglio, at any rate, was very pleased by the German veto. It was supposed that Italy had dropped all plans of expansion against Yugoslavia and Greece.[12] This, however, was only half true. In Italian eyes Hitler seemed to be less inimical to the idea of an attack on Greece. The Italian commander-in-chief in Albania was therefore instructed in mid-August to resume offensive planning. Preparations for Italy's 'separate war'[13] were to be completed by October.

Italy's attack on Greece made Hitler temporarily lose 'all inclination for close military co-operation'.[14] His exasperation with an ally who would not (as yet) subordinate himself to German strategy was tempered, however, by the realization that any loss of prestige by the Axis must be avoided to prevent American intervention in the war.

The creation of such new fronts did not suit Hitler's book at the time. However, he did not himself feel bound by the kind of self-restraint he demanded of his ally. He was, in his own mind, moving ever closer to the ancient object of his ambitions, the destruction of the Soviet Union, and Stalin's expansionist policy was, in Hitler's eyes, making a solution of this problem unavoidable. When precisely Hitler decided in favour of a military operation which he had first given orders to prepare for in the summer of 1940 cannot be stated with certainty. It would seem that the final decision in favour of this operation—the gravity of which was universally misjudged by the German leaders—was not taken until near the end of the year. This turn to the east was based not only on the alleged need for 'living-space'—the war to date had brought Germany a greater territorial accretion than the nation could cope with in the foreseeable future—but his *idée fixe* that solely the elimination of the last continental great power could make Britain comprehend the hopelessness of her situation.

There was not much time left to bring this about. Hitler realized that Britain was relying on support from the United States, and he knew of the American president's increasing dislike of National Socialist Germany. A conflict with the United States, which seemed to be getting ready to enter the war and was making its resources increasingly available to the British war-machine, would not be avoidable in the long run, unless the development of Japan's world-power status resulted in

---

[11] OKW war diary, i. 36 (15 Aug. 1940).
[12] Situation report OKW/WFSt/L, 2 Sept. 1940, in Klee, *Dokumente*, 103.
[13] Hillgruber, *Strategie*, 134.   [14] OKW war diary, i. 144 (1 Nov. 1940)

the neutralization of America. (This purpose was intended to be served by the German-Italian-Japanese pact of 27 September 1940, but it proved to have no practical effect.) It was important, therefore, to bring the European war to a conclusion, or at least to make Germany's position more or less unassailable.

This objective was initially to be achieved also by another project, one suggested by Ribbentrop and for a time strongly supported by Hitler—the establishment of a 'continental coalition' against Britain. Such an alliance, under German leadership, was, as far as possible, to unite Spain, France, Italy, the Soviet Union, and also Japan against Britain and prevent the enemy from ever again gaining a foothold on the European continent. It also promised to influence the attitude of the United States and to open new opportunities for the elimination of threatening British positions along the fringes of the German power-sphere. The continental bloc—a favourable basis for the conquest of Gibraltar and the extension of Germany's base of operations to North Africa—to this extent fitted into Hitler's peripheral strategy against Britain.

Assuming, however, that Hitler unswervingly regarded the expansion of German 'living-space' at the expense of the Soviet Union as his life's purpose, then this coalition represented no more than an expedient in a tight situation,[15] a provisional alternative to a merely postponed war in the east, or possibly a safeguard in the west for the realization of his real war aim. In the situation of October 1940, however, the continental alliance might also have offered itself to Hitler as a basis for long-term clarification of German-Soviet relations, provided that Soviet imperialism could be deflected to those regions—Persia, India—which were not of direct interest to Germany.

An important part in Hitler's plan was played by Spain. After initial neutrality, Franco on 12 June 1940 chose the status of 'non-belligerent' for his country, and a week later, after the defeat of France, allowed it to be understood that he would be ready to join in the war—but by then there was no immediate German interest in his doing so. As a prior condition he stipulated German assistance with armaments, and as his reward he expected Gibraltar and the extension of Spanish colonial possessions in North and West Africa, mainly at the expense of France. In mid-June he had already occupied the international zone of Tangier.

With Spain's entry into the war—and this made Franco's offer attractive to Hitler after all, following his failure to come to terms with Britain—the corner-stone of the British Empire in the western Mediterranean could be liquidated and increasing pressure brought to bear on French North Africa. Plans for a conquest of Gibraltar began at the end of July. Department 'L' of the Wehrmacht operations staff submitted a paper[16] based on counter-intelligence findings. It met with Hitler's approval, and he thereupon ordered the High Command of the Armed Forces to prepare a detailed operations study (code-named 'Felix'), which was to serve him as a basis for negotiations with the Spanish head of state.[17] Department 'L' demanded for

---

[15] Hillgruber, *Strategie*, 178, 274 ff.   [16] OKW war diary, i. 17 (9 Aug. 1940).
[17] Ibid.

foreign-policy propaganda reasons that, prior to the start of the enterprise, Spain should openly place herself on the side of the Axis.[18] Franco seemed prepared to do this, but stepped up his requests for economic and military aid.[19] Hitler for his part did not see any problem in these demands: their fulfilment would be accomplished 'by victory in the field'.[20]

His optimism proved unrealistic. The Caudillo came to the conclusion that Britain had by no means lost the war yet, and that Germany's colonial ambitions and demands for bases were scarcely compatible with his own interests. Hitler, moreover, soon realized that, in view of the diverging interests of the Mediterranean littoral states, his continental bloc could only be accomplished by a 'gigantic fraud'. This did not make him shrink from the attempt. However, his meeting with Franco at Hendaye on 23 October yielded no results. Germany's deliberately soft treatment of the Vichy government aroused Spanish suspicions. Hitler did not want Vichy to learn the full extent of its future territorial losses—however generously compensated from British bankruptcy assets—in order not to provoke the defection of further French colonial possessions to de Gaulle.

The Spanish foreign minister Suñer gained the impression 'that Germany's attitude towards France had changed' and 'that this would render void Spain's maximum demands'.[21] Thus, Franco did not consider it advisable to adhere to the German treaty system and join the war against Britain in return for what were only vague promises of territorial gain. He avoided committing himself. Placed under economic pressure by the United States, Franco on 7 December refused to take part in the German plans, by then limited to Gibraltar. He stated plainly to the German counter-intelligence chief Canaris, who had been sent to Spain, that his country must adhere to 'non-belligerence'. Thus, the prerequisites of 'Operation Felix' were lost for the time being.

Meanwhile Hitler was not sure what to make of France's attitude. Suspiciously he watched developments in occupied France, where the German authorities were attentively registering any sign of a resurgence of French nationalism. Hitler was convinced that in the 'État Français' influence was still wielded by circles from the army, the churches, and big business, who, like the anti-German 'bourgeoisie', 'Jewry', and the 'Communists', would not reconcile themselves to France's defeat. But so long as his hoped-for arrangement with Britain remained unaccomplished he had to take account of the Vichy government, which still held two weighty trump cards with the navy and the colonial empire. The Germans had also been impressed by the fact that after the armistice the colonies had not gone over to the French National Committee proclaimed by General de Gaulle in London and that the naval units attacked by the British had shown remarkable loyalty to Vichy. Any openly voiced claims to French colonial possessions, however, might lend unwelcome support to defection. Thus, the Vichy government retained some political weight

---

[18] OKW war diary, i. 40 (20 Aug. 1940).   [19] Ibid. 48 (24 Aug. 1940).
[20] Ibid. 56 (2 Sept. 1940).
[21] Minute of a conversation between the German minister of foreign affairs and Serrano Suñer at Hendaye railway station, 23 Oct. 1940, *DGFP* D xi, No. 221.

for further negotiations with the occupying powers who, mainly in exchange for economic advantages, were prepared to make military concessions. The Germans did not insist on the air-bases in Morocco they had asked for in mid-July 1940, nor did they enforce the dispatch of control authorities to that French possession. When de Gaulle in August 1940 succeeded in persuading the administrations in French Equatorial Africa, the Chad, and Cameroon to defect from the 'illegitimate' Vichy government, this merely emphasized the need to enable France to defend her colonies—and that was what mattered to the Axis powers in the circumstances. That such a readiness for defence existed was proved by the repulse of a British-Gaullist operation against Dakar from 23 to 25 September. However, as a result, France's situation became even more complicated than the Germans, primarily those quarters which championed a military alliance with France, were prepared to admit. Vichy, having made two retaliatory bombing raids on Gibraltar between July and September 1940, was risking war with its former ally, on whose side, moreover, some Frenchmen were fighting.

After Dakar France continued for only a short period to play a major part in Hitler's political and strategic thinking.[22] None the less Hitler began to doubt whether his fundamental mistrust of the French was justified. He hesitated over whether in his plans he should not, if necessary, give France precedence over Spain. The High Command of the Armed Forces and the Navy High Command repeatedly pointed out the advantages which might accrue to the German conduct of the war from some kind of German–French alliance. The Army High Command also inclined towards a main effort in the Mediterranean region and favoured negotiations with Vichy. All three high commands, however, misjudged the extent of the necessary German concessions, which Hitler, who was predominantly interested in utilizing France's economic power for the German war effort, was not really prepared to make. He was also aware that major concessions to France would hardly be compatible with Italian or Spanish ambitions. He nevertheless tried to get France—if it could be accomplished—'harnessed to the German cart', and was considering a meeting with François-Poncet, the former ambassador in Berlin, or with Pétain.[23] On 4 October Hitler had a meeting with Mussolini and obtained his approval of his plans. The two dictators assured each other that their territorial demands in the peace negotiations would be moderate. The Spanish too were to be advised to restrain themselves.

The talks with the French leaders at Montoire on 22 and 24 October, however, were not very specific. A maximum programme drafted in the German ministry of foreign affairs,[24] calling for unilateral actions by France all the way to a declaration of war against Britain, was not even discussed. Pétain himself made a good impression on Hitler; Laval he regarded rather more sceptically.[25] Although the French head of state declared himself ready for 'collaboration', he was in no great hurry to translate this formula into practical politics. Soon the possibility could

---

[22] Hillgruber, *Strategie*, 136.
[24] Jäckel, *Frankreich*, 113.

[23] OKW war diary, i. 93 (26 Sept. 1940).
[25] OKW war diary, i. 137 (29 Oct. 1940).

no longer be ruled out that Britain might after all survive the war better than had originally been assumed. In that case there was even less hope for France to escape more or less lightly in the peace terms. Passiveness and awaiting further developments seemed to Pétain to be his best course. In this attitude he was confirmed by warnings from King George VI and the American president. Pétain had secretly assured the London government that he had no intention of changing the status quo by, for instance, ceding African bases to the Germans. Weygand, shunted to North Africa as delegate-general on 6 September, even hoped that France might re-enter the war against Germany at a later date.

The Pétain government was obliged to coexist with the occupation powers, which in practice meant ever new concessions. Advocates of an alliance with Germany, such as Laval, who was convinced of Germany's superior strength, did not have an appreciable following. The failure of a peace treaty to materialize, the Germans' disinclination to make binding and satisfactory statements regarding France's future destiny, and the increasing hardships of life under foreign occupation—all these made it obvious that co-operation with the Axis was scarcely worth while.

None the less, Laval, appointed foreign minister on 27 October, and the commanders of the French armed forces were able to invoke the Montoire conversations when they embarked on detailed negotiations with the Germans in the late autumn of 1940. The promised protection and, where necessary, reconquest of the colonies provided the generals with the longed-for opportunity to demand a fundamental strengthening of the French armed forces and armament industry. Laval saw a chance to secure his demands, which would have strengthened his position in the country: German concessions in the matter of the French prisoners-of-war, of the demarcation and north-east lines, and the onerous occupation costs. He also regarded a guarantee of the colonial empire, with the exception of Cameroon, as indispensable if France, as Laval at least was ready to do, were to risk war with Britain.[26]

In spite of considerable economic contributions by France, Laval was unable to point to any success of his policies. He had placed his hopes in Abetz, Ribbentrop's representative in Paris, but had overrated his influence. Although Germany still believed that France would adopt the stance of a 'benevolent neutral' and tolerate or support German military operations from French sovereign territory, especially in Africa,[27] Hitler's interest in co-operation with France proved short-lived. The massive deportation, approved by Hitler, of Lorrainers and German Jews into unoccupied France was bound to be felt as an affront by Pétain. Hitler, moreover, was by then again more interested in Spain, as well as having to show reluctant consideration for Italy, which, after her failure in North Africa and her unsuccessful attack on Greece, was in need of support—possibly by a rapid seizure of Gibraltar or by the occupation of the Atlantic island possessions of Spain and Portugal. The

[26] OKW/WFSt/Abt. L(I) No. 001131/40 g.Kdos., 13 Dec. 1940: Minute of Paris conference on 10 Dec. 1940, in OKW war diary, i. 984 ff.
[27] Ibid. 145 (1 Nov. 1940); memorandum OKW/WFSt/Chef L No. 33351/40 g.Kdos. Chefs., 2 Nov. 1940, BA-MA RW 4/v. 574.

Wehrmacht operations staff translated this indecisive estimate of the situation into 'Führer directive No. 18' of 12 November, which more than anything else was a testimony of the crisis into which Hitler's overall strategic concept had slipped.[28]

In Vichy, Pétain got rid of his deputy premier Laval, whom he no longer found acceptable, on 13 December. Hitler, when Japan had shown no interest in his plans and Molotov's visit to Berlin had led to no satisfactory result, again dropped his idea of a continental coalition. This gave him a pretext for putting an end to his half-hearted wooing of France. His mistrust revived again. A few days before Laval's dismissal, when the Gibraltar plan had fallen through owing to Franco's refusal and when Vichy might once more have played a greater part on Germany's side, he instructed the Wehrmacht[29] to react to a possible defection of French North Africa under General Weygand with a swift occupation of the remainder of France ('Operation Attila'). Strict secrecy covering the preparations, even *vis-à-vis* Italy, was to prevent the escape of those parts of the French fleet and air force that were in metropolitan territory.

Hitler, who on 13 December signed the directive for the Balkan campaign and who five days later, it seems, finally made up his mind to go to war against the Soviet Union, was by then interested only in maintaining the status quo in the west. There was just a hope left that Spain might change her attitude.

[28] Trevor-Roper, *Directives*, 39 ff.; Hillgruber, *Strategie*, 325.
[29] Supreme commander of the Wehrmacht/OKW/WFSt/Abt. L No. 33400/40 g.Kdos. Chefs., 10 Dec. 1940: Directive No. 19 for 'Operation Attila', in Trevor-Roper, *Directives*, 44 ff.

Conclusion

GERMANY'S SITUATION IN THE LATE AUTUMN OF 1940

BY the early summer of 1940 Hitler and the Wehrmacht could boast of 'a military promenade unique in history'[1]—the conquest of Poland, Denmark, Norway, Holland, Belgium, Luxemburg, and France, which had brought the greater part of Europe under German rule. Immediate steps were taken to establish the 'new order' in the countries thus placed under German hegemony. The precise form of the new structure in German-dominated Europe was not yet specified. German measures were confined to single initiatives pending a decision by Hitler that the moment had come to adopt a definite programme.

Hitler had only partly achieved the aims for which he had gone to war—a war that was his deliberate intention, though not in the form it actually took. He had failed in his attempt to localize the 'settling of accounts' with Poland. True, the entry of Britain and France into the conflict did not at once lead to the 'war on two fronts' that was Germany's perennial nightmare. Thanks to the Allies' strategy of holding back and trusting to their own stronger economic position, which, they believed, was bound to ensure victory in the long run, Hitler was able to make full use of the military superiority that Germany still enjoyed, and to knock France out of the war.

The Wehrmacht itself was still in the process of development in September 1939, and had evinced considerable weaknesses in respect of organization, personnel, and equipment. But its adversaries during the first year of war were far less well prepared for the conflict. Moreover, the Germans had not only developed a new method of mobile warfare but had to a large extent transformed it into practice. For this purpose they had the Luftwaffe co-operating closely with the army and efficiently organized armoured formations. Consequently, in the western campaign they were able to out-manœuvre an enemy whose ideas of warfare were still largely rooted in the past. The high-pressure development of the Wehrmacht and the systematic preparation for a war of aggression bore fruit, even though for a long time the military leaders were not in agreement as to the most effective methods of warfare, and there were in this initial stage violent controversies, particularly over the use of the latest weapons. In the western campaign in particular there were errors of command due to lack of consistency in exploiting opportunities: these were symptomatic of the uncertainty of judgement that still characterized Hitler as a supreme commander. These errors and the Führer's occasional loss of nerve—most evident during Operation Weserübung—were thrust into oblivion by the successful outcome. On the whole, Hitler showed a clearer intuition in his judgement of the adversary than did his generals. The resulting boost to his self-confidence was zealously encouraged

[1] Jacobsen, in *KTB OKW* i. 66E.

by his entourage and by Goebbels's obedient propaganda-machine, and persisted even when Germany's military successes failed to produce the desired political results. Hitler no longer had the necessary patience for solutions and compromises requiring shrewd judgement; he relied more and more on violence to secure his ends.[2] Increasingly, it was he who drew false conclusions based on ideological obsession. He had indeed succeeded in virtually driving Britain out of Europe; the Anglo-French entente, which had been an agreement of substance despite considerable conflicts of interest, had broken up in discord. But he had not managed to end the war by overthrowing Britain, which he had from the beginning regarded as his chief adversary. The British were not even so far impressed by German power as to be willing to conclude a 'compromise peace' with the Nazi regime. Hitler's insistence that the British, though they did not know it, were already beaten sounded increasingly like a mere exhortation. He had not foreseen the situation that existed in the summer of 1940. This was the penalty for not having devised an overall war plan in the autumn of 1939, even after it was clear that the attempt to isolate Poland was a partial failure.[3]

After the German victory in the west a stalemate arose, since even the united forces of the Commonwealth would probably not have sufficed to destroy German military power. The British, however, were not prepared to abandon the Continent to Hitler. The war, to them, was no longer a question of territory, bases, or spheres of influence, but of victory or defeat. The war had become an all-or-nothing struggle—a fact that Hitler took time to understand—and the British would have been prepared to negotiate only if he had completely desisted from his aims. Peace initiatives no longer had any chance of success. Britain fought on in the hope of American support and of a change in German–Soviet relations.

In Germany the three successful campaigns made the regime probably more popular than ever before. Earlier misgivings over Hitler's war policy seemed refuted by its brilliant success; opposition no longer had a leg to stand on. Scarcely anyone felt scruples at a time when services were being rewarded and rich spoils awaited distribution. Peace was expected on all sides; and, even when it failed to materialize, there was no appreciable dissent from official expectations of victory.

Within the German leadership, however, a state of perplexity set in for the first time. New initiatives promised an escape from the dilemma, but soon proved ineffectual. Hitler's last peace offer to Britain in July 1940 was already designed chiefly for its propaganda effect on the German people. Certainly the successes gained had considerably strengthened Germany's position for carrying on the war. But her power was insufficient for a direct attack on Britain; the latter's sea power and overseas resources were, given the geographical conditions, proof against attack by the land power of Germany. No decisive action could be expected from the German navy, which was no match for Britain's at the outset and had been further weakened by the hostilities of 1939-40. The Luftwaffe, imposing as it was, was not equal to the task of breaking the British defences and destroying the war industry of southern

---

[2] Cf. Bogatsch, 'Probleme', 17.   [3] Ibid. 29.

England. In the economic field there was no provision for a long war against an opponent possessed of far greater resources. True, Germany could look forward to an increase in arms production, as her own potential was not yet fully engaged and she now had the benefit of that in the occupied countries also. But the resources available to the Axis powers were limited, and, as in the case of Romanian oil, whether they could be fully used depended on the unforeseeable fortunes of war. By the late autumn of 1940 Germany's arms production was already behind that of Britain.

Hitler for his part was unable to create the political conditions for an indirect strategy—the 'gigantic fraud' met with justified scepticism on the part of those whom he had earmarked as fresh associates—and in addition he began to find that time was working against him. Anglo-American co-operation was developing more and more into an alliance against the Axis, and its military-economic potential must before long impair Germany's strategic and operational freedom of movement.[4] If Hitler wished to continue 'calling the shots' after the makeshift political solution of a Continental bloc had foundered on the conflict of interests between Germany and the Soviet Union, he had no alternative but to resort to precipitate military action. This brought with it fresh risks and a greater strain on the available forces, including the Luftwaffe, which had already suffered considerably in the Battle of Britain. The Mediterranean had been left to Mussolini; the German admirals pressed for a campaign there, and the generals would have preferred it to fighting in the east, but Hitler did not regard this as a sound alternative. He refused to envisage doing more than come to the rescue of Mussolini, whose 'parallel war' had proved a disaster, because, while a determined push in the Mediterranean area seemed to promise success for a time,[5] it could not be decisive for the outcome of the war. Hitler continued to postpone the solution of the 'problem of Britain'. As he saw it, another 'blitz campaign' in the east would bring back the war to the direction originally intended; moreover, by removing Germany's last potential adversary on the Continent it would destroy British hopes and thus put an end to the conflict. 'It followed, however, that if Hitler failed in this, he would have lost not merely a campaign, but the war itself.'[6]

---

[4] Hillgruber, *Strategie*, 389.   [5] Bogatsch, 'Probleme', 145.   [6] Hillgruber, *Strategie*, 392.

Bibliography

FOR the English edition works published between 1979 and 1987 have been added, as far as they were available to the authors. Edited works which have no single author are listed under titles.

ACKERMANN, JOSEF, 'Der begehrte Mann am Bosporus: Europäische Interessenkollisionen in der Türkei (1938-41)', in *Hitler, Deutschland und die Mächte* (q.v.), 489-507.

Akten zur deutschen auswärtigen Politik 1918-45, Series B: *1925-33* (Göttingen, 1966-78); Series C: *1933-7* (Göttingen, 1971-5); Series D: *1937-45* (Baden-Baden, 1950-). [For trans. of Series C and D see *Documents on German Foreign Policy.*]

ALLARD, SVEN, *Stalin und Hitler: Die sowjetrussische Außenpolitik 1930-41* (Berne and Munich, 1974).

Anatomie der Aggression: Neue Dokumente zu den Kriegszielen des faschistischen deutschen Imperialismus im zweiten Weltkrieg, ed. with intro. by Gerhart Hass and Wolfgang Schumann (East Berlin, 1972).

'Andere Deutschland' im Zweiten Weltkrieg, Das: Emigration und Widerstand in internationaler Perspektive, ed. Lothar Kettenacker (Veröffentlichungen des Deutschen Historischen Instituts in London, 2; Stuttgart, 1977).

ANSEL, WALTER, *Hitler Confronts England* (Durham, NC, 1960).

AZEAU, HENRI, *La Guerre franco-italienne, juin 1940* (Paris, 1967).

BACHMANN, HANS R., 'Die polnische U-Boot-Division im September 1939', *MR* 67 (1970), 17-35.

—— 'Der Kampf um Hela (1. September-1. October 1939)', *WWR* 20 (1970), 275-96.

—— 'Die deutsche Seekriegführung in der Ostsee nach Ausschalten der polnischen Marine im Herbst 1939', *MR* 68 (1971), 197-224, 273-82, 352-62, 407-13.

BARKER, ARTHUR J., *Dunkirk: The Great Escape* (London, Toronto, and Melbourne, 1977).

Battaglia delle Alpi Occidentali, La: Giugno 1940. Narrazione, documenti (Opere dell'Ufficio Storico SME sul Secondo Conflitto Mondiale, 3. 1; Rome, 1947).

BAUERMEISTER, HERMANN, 'Die Entwicklung der Magnetminen bis zum Beginn des Zweiten Weltkrieges', *MR* 55 (1958), 25-31.

BAUMGART, WINFRIED, 'Zur Ansprache Hitlers vor den Führern der Wehrmacht am 22. August 1939', *VfZG* 16 (1968), 120-49.

BAYER, JAMES A., and ØRVIK, NILS, *The Scandinavian Flank as History, 1939-1940* (National Security Series, No. 1/84; Kingston, Ont., 1984).

BÉDARIDA, FRANÇOIS, 'France, Britain and the Nordic Countries', *Scandinavian Journal of History*, 2 (1977), 7-27.

—— *La Stratégie secrète de la drôle de guerre: Le Conseil Suprême Interallié, septembre 1939-avril 1940* (Paris, 1979).

BEDTS, RALPH F. DE, *Recent American History*, i. *1933 through World War II* (Homewood, Ill., 1973).

BEESLY, PATRICK, *Very Special Intelligence: The Story of the Admiralty's Operational Intelligence Centre, 1939-1945* (London, 1977; rev. edn. 1978).

BEKKER, CAJUS, *Angriffshöhe 4000: Ein Kriegstagebuch der deutschen Luftwaffe* (Oldenburg and Hamburg, 1964).

BENOIST-MÉCHIN, JACQUES, *Soixante jours qui ébranlèrent l'Occident: 10 mai–10 juillet 1940,* 3 vols. (Paris, 1956). [Trans. Peter Wiles, *Sixty Days that Shook the West: The Fall of France* (London, 1963).]

—— *Wollte Adolf Hitler den Krieg 1939? Generalprobe der Gewalt* (Preußisch-Oldendorf, 1971).

BERBERICH, FLORIAN, 'Die deutschen militärischen Planungen gegenüber Polen vor dem Hintergrund der deutsch-polnischen Beziehungen von Januar 1933 bis zum September 1939' (unpubl. diss. Freiburg, 1982).

BERGH, HENDRIK VAN, *Die Wahrheit über Katyn: Der Massenmord an polnischen Offizieren* (Berg am See, 1986).

BERTRAND, GUSTAVE, *Enigma ou la plus grande énigme de la guerre 1939–1945* (Paris, 1973).

BEST, GEOFFREY, *Humanity in Warfare: The Modern History of International Law of Armed Conflicts* (London, 1983).

BIALER, URI, 'The Danger of Bombardment from the Air and the Making of British Air Disarmament Policy 1932–4', in *War and Society: A Yearbook of Military History,* i (London, 1975), 202–15.

—— ' "Humanization" of Air Warfare in British Foreign Policy on the Eve of the Second World War', *Journal of Contemporary History,* 13 (1978), 79–96.

BIDLINGMAIER, GERHARD, *Einsatz der schweren Kriegsmarineeinheiten im ozeanischen Zufuhrkrieg* (Die Wehrmacht im Kampf, 35; Neckargemünd, 1963).

—— 'Die Grundlagen für die Zusammenarbeit Luftwaffe/Kriegsmarine und ihre Erprobung in den ersten Kriegsmonaten', in *Die Entwicklung des Flottenkommandos* (Beiträge zur Wehrforschung, 4; Darmstadt, 1964), 73–112.

BIRKENFELD, WOLFGANG, *Der synthetische Treibstoff 1933–1945: Ein Beitrag zur national-sozialistischen Wirtschafts- und Rüstungspolitik* (Studien und Dokumente zur Geschichte des Zweiten Weltkrieges, 8; Göttingen, Berlin, and Frankfurt am Main, 1964).

—— 'Stalin als Wirtschaftspartner Hitlers (1939–1941)', *Vierteljahrsschrift für Sozial- und Wirtschaftsgeschichte,* 53 (1966), 477–510.

BIRNBAUM, FRIEDRICH KARL, 'Der Untergang der "Blücher" am 9. April 1940', *MR* 62 (1965), 76–84.

BLUMENTRITT, GÜNTHER, 'Der deutsche Westfeldzug: Kritik' (unpubl. Study P-208, vol. ii, sect. E, MGFA).

—— 'Der Westfeldzug, ii. Darstellung der Operationen' (unpubl. Study P-208, vol. ii, MGFA).

BOCK, FEDOR VON, 'Tagebuch-Notizen', pt. 1: 'Polenfeldzug'; pt. 2: 'Westen, Vorbereitungs-zeit'; pt. 3: 'Westen, Offensive und Besatzungszeit' (unpubl. Study P-210, MGFA).

BOEHM, HERMANN, 'Seekriegsleitung, Gruppen- und Flottenkommando im Zweiten Weltkrieg', *Atlantische Welt,* 7/11 (1967), 24–6.

—— 'Eine Richtigstellung', *MR* 67 (1970), 289–93.

—— 'Zur deutschen Seekriegführung 1939–40, Stellungnahme von Generaladmiral a.D. Hermann Boehm, Flottenchef bis 20.10.1939', *MR* 69 (1972), 42–55.

—— and BAUMGART, WINFRIED, 'Zur Ansprache Hitlers vor den Führern der Wehrmacht am 22. August 1939: Miszelle', *VfZg* 19 (1971), 294–304.

BOGATSCH, RUDOLF, 'Politische und militärische Probleme nach dem Frankreichfeldzug', in *Vollmacht des Gewissens,* ii (Frankfurt am Main and Bonn, 1965), 11–145.

BÖHME, HERMANN, *Der deutsch-französische Waffenstillstand im Zweiten Weltkrieg,* i. *Entstehung und Grundlagen des Waffenstillstandes von 1940* (Quellen und Darstellungen zur Zeitgeschichte, 12; Stuttgart, 1966).

BOLLMUS, REINHARD, *Das Amt Rosenberg und seine Gegner: Studien zum Machtkampf im nationalsozialistischen Herrschaftssystem* (Studien zur Zeitgeschichte; Stuttgart, 1970).

BOOG, HORST, *Die deutsche Luftwaffenführung 1935–1945: Führungsprobleme — Spitzengliederung — Generalstabsausbildung* (Beiträge zur Militär- und Kriegsgeschichte, 21; Stuttgart, 1981).

BRAUSCH, GERD, 'Sedan 1940: Deuxième bureau und strategische Überraschung', *MGM* 2 (1967), 15–92.

—— 'Der Tod des Generalobersten Werner Freiherr von Fritsch', *MGM* 7 (1970), 95–112.

BRENNECKE, JOCHEN, *Schlachtschiff Bismarck: Höhepunkt und Ende einer Epoche* (Jugenheim an der Bergstraße, 1960).

—— *Die Wende im U-Boot-Krieg: Ursachen und Folgen 1939–1943* (Herford, 1984).

BROCKDORFF, WERNER, *Geheimkommandos des Zweiten Weltkrieges: Geschichte und Einsätze der Brandenburger, der englischen Commands und SAS-Einheiten, der amerikanischen Rangers und sowjetischer Geheimdienste* (Munich, 1967).

BROSZAT, MARTIN, *Zweihundert Jahre deutsche Polenpolitik* (Munich, 1963).

—— *Nationalsozialistische Polenpolitik 1939–1945*[2] (Schriftenreihe der Vierteljahrshefte für Zeitgeschichte, 2; Frankfurt am Main and Hamburg, 1965).

BRÜGEL, JOHANN WOLFGANG, 'Dahlerus als Zwischenträger nach Kriegsausbruch', *HZ* 228 (1979), 70–97.

BUCHBENDER, ORTWIN, and HAUSCHILD, REINHARD, *Geheimsender gegen Frankreich: Die Täuschungsoperation 'Radio Humanité' 1940* (Herford, 1984).

BUCHHEIT, GERT, *Der deutsche Geheimdienst: Geschichte der militärischen Abwehr* (Munich, 1966).

—— 'Die Anfänge des Regiments Brandenburg', *Feldgrau*, 18 (1970), 125–32.

BUFFOTOT, P., and OGIER, J., 'L'Armée de l'Air pendant la bataille de France (du 10 mai à l'armistice): Essai de bilan numérique d'une bataille aérienne', in *Service historique de l'armée de l'air: Recueil d'articles et études (1974–1975)* (Vincennes, 1977), 197–226.

BURCKHARDT, CARL J., *Meine Danziger Mission 1937–1939* (Munich, 1960).

BUTLER, Sir JAMES RAMSAY MONTAGU, *Grand Strategy*, ii. *September 1939–June 1941* (History of the Second World War, United Kingdom Military Series; London, 1957).

CARL, HELMUT, *Kleine Geschichte Polens* (Frankfurt am Main, 1961).

CATALANO, M. F., 'L'economia di guerra italienne', in *La Guerre en Méditerranée* (q.v.), 101–38.

CHARLES, JEAN-LÉON, *Les Forces armées belges au cours de la Deuxième Guerre Mondiale 1940–1945* (Brussels, 1970).

CHASSIN, L.-M., 'Un Plan grandiose: L'attaque des pétroles du Caucase en 1940', *Forces aériennes françaises*, 176 (1961), 821–49.

CHEW, ALLEN F., *The White Death: The Epic of the Soviet-Finnish Winter War* (Detroit, 1971).

CHRISTIENNE, CHARLES, 'L'armée de l'air française de mars 1936 à septembre 1939', in *Deutschland und Frankreich 1936–1939*: 15. Deutsch-französisches Historikerkolloquium des Deutschen Historischen Instituts Paris (Bonn, 26.-29. Sept. 1979) (Beihefte der Francia, 10; Munich, 1981), 215–48.

CHURCHILL, WINSTON S., *The Second World War*, i. *The Gathering Storm*: bk. 1, *From War to War*; bk. 2, *The Twilight War*; ii. *Their Finest Hour*: bk. 1, *The Fall of France*; bk. 2, *Alone* (London and Boston, Mass., 1948–9).

COLLIER, BASIL, *The Defence of the United Kingdom* (History of the Second World War, United Kingdom Military Series; London, 1957).

COLLIER, RICHARD, *Eagle Day: The Battle of Britain, Aug. 6-Sept. 15, 1940* (London, 1980).

'Comment le Corps aéroporté allemand attaqua les Pays-Bas en mai 1940', Service Historique de l'Armée Néerlandaise, *L'Armée — la Nation*, 9/4 (1954), 3–19.

COSTELLO, JOHN, and HUGHES, TERRY, *The Battle of the Atlantic* (London, 1977).

COWIE, JOHN STEWART, *Mines, Minelayers and Minelaying*[3] (London, 1951).

CYNK, JERZY B., *History of the Polish Air Force 1918-1968* (Reading, 1972).

DEIGHTON, LEN, *Fighter: The True Story of the Battle of Britain* (London, 1977).

—— *Blitzkrieg: From the Rise of Hitler to the Fall of Dunkirk* (London, 1979).

—— *Battle of Britain* (London, 1980).

DELMAS, J., 'Les exercices du Conseil supérieur de la Guerre 1936-1937 et 1937-1938', *Revue historique des armées*, 4 (1979), 28-56.

DENNE, LUDWIG, *Das Danzig-Problem in der deutschen Außenpolitik 1934-39* (Bonn, 1959).

DERRY, T. K., *The Campaign in Norway* (History of the Second World War, United Kingdom Military Series; London, 1953).

Deutsche Reich und der Zweite Weltkrieg, Das, 6 vols. so far published by MGFA:

    i. *Ursachen und Voraussetzungen der deutschen Kriegspolitik*, by Wilhelm Deist, Manfred Messerschmidt, Hans-Erich Volkmann, and Wolfram Wette (Stuttgart, 1979). [Trans. P. S. Falla, E. Osers, and Dean S. McMurry, *Germany and the Second World War*, i. *The Build-up of German Aggression* (Oxford, 1990).]

    ii. *Die Errichtung der Hegemonie auf dem europäischen Kontinent*, by Klaus A. Maier, Horst Rohde, Bernd Stegemann, and Hans Umbreit (Stuttgart, 1979). [Original of the present vol.]

    iii. *Der Mittelmeerraum und Südosteuropa: Von der 'non belligeranza' Italiens bis zum Kriegseintritt der Vereinigten Staaten*, by Gerhard Schreiber, Bernd Stegemann, and Detlev Vogel (Stuttgart, 1984).

    iv. *Der Angriff auf die Sowjetunion*, by Horst Boog, Jürgen Förster, Joachim Hoffmann, Ernst Klink, Rolf-Dieter Müller, and Gerd R. Ueberschär (Stuttgart, 1983).

    v. *Organisation und Mobilisierung des deutschen Machtbereichs*, pt. 1: *Kriegsverwaltung, Wirtschaft und personelle Ressourcen 1939-1941*, by Bernhard R. Kroener, Rolf-Dieter Müller, and Hans Umbreit (Stuttgart, 1988).

    vi. *Derglobale Krieg. Die Ausweitung zum Weltkrieg und der Wechsel der Initiative 1941-1943*, by Horst Boog, Werner Rahn, Reinhard Stumpf, and Bernd Wegner (Stuttgart, 1990).

Deutschland im zweiten Weltkrieg, i. *Vorbereitung, Entfesselung und Verlauf des Krieges bis zum 22 Juni 1941*, by a group of authors under the direction of Gerhart Hass (Cologne, 1974).

DGFP: see *Documents on German Foreign Policy*.

Diensttagebuch des deutschen Generalgouverneurs (Hans Frank) in Polen 1939-1945, Das, ed. Werner Präg and Wolfgang Jacobmeyer (Quellen und Darstellungen zur Zeitgeschichte, 20; Stuttgart, 1975).

DILKS, DAVID, 'Great Britain and Scandinavia in the "Phoney War"', *Scandinavian Journal of History*, 2 (1977), 29-51.

DINKLAGE, LUDWIG, and WITTHÖFT, HANS-JÜRGEN, *Die deutsche Handelsflotte 1939-1945* (2 vols.; Göttingen, 1971).

Diplomacy and Intelligence during the Second World War: Essays in Honour of F. H. Hinsley, ed. Richard Langhorne (Cambridge, 1985).

Documents on German Foreign Policy, Series C and D (London, 1957-83; 1949-64).

Dokumente zum Westfeldzug 1940, ed. Hans-Adolf Jacobsen (Studien und Dokumente zur Geschichte des Zweiten Weltkrieges, 2b; Göttingen, 1960).

Dokumente zur Vorgeschichte des Westfeldzuges 1939-1940, ed. Hans-Adolf Jacobsen (Studien und Dokumente zur Geschichte des Zweiten Weltkrieges, 2a; Göttingen, 1956).

DOMARUS, MAX, *Hitler: Reden und Proklamationen 1932-1945. Kommentiert von einem deutschen Zeitgenossen*, i. *Triumph (1932-1938)* (Würzburg, 1962); ii. *Untergang (1939-1945)* (Würzburg, 1963).

DÖNITZ, KARL, *Zehn Jahre und zwanzig Tage*[6] (Munich, 1977). [Trans. R. H. Stevens and David Woodward, *Memoirs: Ten Years and Twenty Days* (London, 1959).]

DOUHET, GIULIO, *Il dominio dell'aria* (Verona, 1932). [Trans. Dino Ferrari, *The Command of the Air* (London, 1942); German trans. *Luftherrschaft* (Berlin, 1935).]

DOWLING, CHRISTOPHER, 'Battle of Britain', in *Decisive Battles of the Twentieth Century, Land-Sea-Air*, ed. Noble Frankland and Christopher Dowling (London, 1976), 114-26.

DRECHSLER, KARL, 'Die Zersetzungsarbeit der Geheimsender des Goebbels-Ministeriums in Frankreich Mai/Juni 1940', *ZfG* 9 (1961), 1597-607.

DÜLFFER, JOST, *Weimar, Hitler und die Marine: Reichspolitik und Flottenbau 1920-1930*, with appendix by Jürgen Rohwer (Düsseldorf, 1973).

DUTAILLY, HENRY, 'Faiblesses et potentialités de l'armée de terre (1939-1940)', in *Les Armées françaises pendant la seconde guerre mondiale 1939-1945: Colloque International, École Nationale Supérieure de Techniques Avancées, Paris, du 7 au 10 mai 1985* (Paris, 1986), 23-32.

EDWARDS, ROGER, *German Airborne Troops, 1936-45* (London, 1974).

EICHHOLTZ, DIETRICH, *Geschichte der deutschen Kriegswirtschaft 1939-1945*, i. *1939-1941* (East Berlin, 1969).

EISENBLÄTTER, GERHARD, *Grundlinien der Politik des Reichs gegenüber dem Generalgouvernement: 1939-1945* (diss. Frankfurt am Main, 1969).

ELBLE, ROLF, 'Mobilmachung als politisches Problem, gezeigt am Beispiel der Mobilmachung des deutschen Heeres im Sommer 1939', *Wehrkunde*, 20 (1971), 365-73.

—— *Die Schlacht an der Bzura im September 1939 aus deutscher und polnischer Sicht* (Einzelschriften zur militärischen Geschichte des Zweiten Weltkrieges, 15; Freiburg, 1975).

ELLIOT, PETER, *Allied Minesweeping in World War 2* (Cambridge, 1979).

ELLIS, L. F., *The War in France and Flanders 1939-1940* (History of the Second World War, United Kingdom Military Series; London, 1953).

Entscheidungsschlachten des Zweiten Weltkrieges, ed. Hans-Adolf Jacobsen and Jürgen Rohwer (Frankfurt am Main, 1960).

Esercito italiano nella 2ª guerra mondiale, L'; Immagini (Stato Maggiore dell'Esercito, Ufficio Storico; Rome, 1976).

EVANS, N. E., 'Air Intelligence and the Coventry Raid', *RUSI Journal*, 121 (Sept. 1976), 66-74.

Événements survenus en France de 1933 à 1945, Les: Témoignages et documents recueillis par la Commission d'Enquête Parlementaire (10 vols.; Paris, 1947-54).

FABRY, PHILIPP WALTER, *Der Hitler-Stalin-Pakt 1939-1941: ein Beitrag zur Methode sowjetischer Außenpolitik* (Darmstadt, 1962).

—— *Die Sowjetunion und das Dritte Reich: Eine dokumentierte Geschichte der deutsch-sowjetischen Beziehungen von 1933 bis 1941* (Stuttgart, 1971).

FECHTER, HELMUT, and SCHOMAEKERS, GÜNTHER, *Der Seekrieg 1939/45 in Karten*, i. *Nordsee-Atlantik* (Preetz, 1967).

FEUCHTER, GEORG W., *Der Luftkrieg: Vom Fesselballon zum Raumfahrzeug*[2] (Frankfurt am Main and Bonn, 1962).

FOOT, MICHAEL RICHARD DANIEL, *SOE in France: An Account of the Work of the British Special Operations Executive in France 1940-1944* (History of the Second World War, Secret Service, 1; London, 1966).

FÖRSTER, GERHARD, *Totaler Krieg und Blitzkrieg: Die Theorie des totalen Krieges und des Blitzkrieges in der Militärdoktrin des faschistischen Deutschlands am Vorabend des zweiten Weltkrieges* (Militärhistorische Studien, NS 10; East Berlin, 1967).

FRIEDENSBURG, FERDINAND, 'Die sowjetischen Kriegslieferungen an das Hitlerreich', *Vierteljahrshefte zur Wirtschaftsforschung* (1962), 331-8.

FRIESER, KARL-HEINZ, 'Rommels Durchbruch bei Dinant: Der Maas-Übergang der 7. Panzerdivision vom 12. bis 14. Mai 1940', *Militärgeschichtliches Beiheft zur Europäischen Wehrkunde/Wehrwissenschaftlichen Rundschau*, 2/1 (1987), 1-16.

FRITZ, MARTIN, *German Steel and Swedish Iron Ore: 1939-1945* (Publications of the Institute of Economic History of Gothenburg University, 29; Gothenburg, 1974).

'Führer Conferences': see *Lagevorträge*.

Funkaufklärung und ihre Rolle im Zweiten Weltkrieg, Die, ed. Jürgen Rohwer and Eberhard Jäckel (Stuttgart, 1979).

GAMELIN, Général, *Servir*, i. *Les Armées françaises de 1940* (Paris, 1946); ii. *Le Prologue du drame (1930-août 1939)* (Paris, 1946); iii. *La Guerre (septembre 1939-19 mai 1940)* (Paris, 1947).

GARLIŃSKI, JÓZEF, *Poland in the Second World War* (London, 1985).

GAUL, WALTER, 'Marinefliegerverbände und operative Luftwaffe im Einsatz über See 1939-1945', *MR* 50 (1953), 24-739-43, 65-7, 106-14.

GAULLE, CHARLES DE, *Mémoires de guerre*, i. *L'Appel: 1940-1942* (Paris, 1954). [Trans. Jonathan Griffin, *The Call to Honour: 1940-1942* (London, 1955).]

GEHRISCH, WOLFGANG, *Die Entwicklung der Luftfahrtindustrie im imperialistischen Deutschland bis 1945* (diss. East Berlin, 1974).

GEHRTS, ERWIN, 'Gedanken zum operativen Luftkrieg: Eine Studie', *Die Luftwaffe*, 2/2 (1937), 16-39.

GEMZELL, CARL-AXEL, *Raeder, Hitler und Skandinavien: Der Kampf für einen maritimen Operationsplan* (Bibliotheca Historica Lundensis, 16; Lund, 1965).

Geschichte des Panzerkorps Großdeutschland, Die, ed. Helmuth Spaeter (3 vols.; Duisburg, 1958).

GEYR VON SCHWEPPENBURG, Freiherr LEO, *Erinnerungen eines Militärattachés, London 1933-1937* (Stuttgart, 1949). [Trans. *The Critical Years* (London, 1952).]

GIBBS, NORMAN HENRY, *Grand Strategy*, i. *Rearmament Policy* (History of the Second World War, United Kingdom Military Series; London, 1976).

GIESSLER, HELMUTH, 'Die Revolutionierung des Seekrieges durch Funkmeß', *MR* 65 (1968), 181-91.

—— *Der Marine-Nachrichten- und -Ortungsdienst* (Wehrwissenschaftliche Berichte, 10; Munich, 1971).

GLADISCH, WALTER, *Der Krieg in der Nordsee*, vii. *Von Sommer 1917 bis zum Kriegsende 1918* (*Der Krieg zur See 1914-1918*, I/vii; Frankfurt am Main, 1965).

GOLCZEWSKI, FRANZ, *Das Deutschlandbild der Polen 1918-1939: Eine Untersuchung der Historiographie und der Publizistik* (Geschichtliche Studien zu Politik und Gesellschaft, 7; Düsseldorf, 1974).

'Great Powers and the Nordic Countries 1939-1940, The' (collected lectures), *Scandinavian Journal of History*, 2 (1977).

GROHMANN, JUSTUS ANDREAS, *Die deutsch-schwedische Auseinandersetzung um die Fahrstraßen des Öresunds im Ersten Weltkrieg* (Wehrwissenschaftliche Forschungen, Abteilung Militärgeschichtliche Studien, 19; Boppard am Rhein, 1974).

GRÖNER, ERICH, *Die Schiffe der deutschen Kriegsmarine und Luftwaffe 1939-45 und ihr Verbleib*[8] (Munich, 1976).

GROPMAN, ALAN L., 'The Battle of Britain and the Principles of War', *Aerospace Historian*, 18/3 (1971), 138-44.

GROSCURTH, HELMUTH, *Tagebücher eines Abwehroffiziers 1938-1940*, ed. H. Krausnick and H. C. Deutsch with the assistance of H. von Kotze (Quellen und Darstellungen zur Zeitgeschichte, 19; Stuttgart, 1970).

Guerre en Méditerranée 1939-1945, La: Actes du Colloque international tenu à Paris du 8 au 11 avril 1969 (Comité d'Histoire de la Deuxième Guerre mondiale; Paris, 1971).

GUNDELACH, KARL, 'Gedanken über die Führung eines Luftkrieges gegen England bei der Luftflotte 2 in den Jahren 1938/39', *WWR* 10/2 (1960), 33-46.

GUNSBURG, JEFFREY A., *Divided and Conquered: The French High Command and the Defence of the West, 1940* (Contributions in Military History, 18; Westport, Conn., and London, 1979).

HADELER, WILHELM, *Der Flugzeugträger* (Wehrwissenschaftliche Berichte, 5; Munich, 1968).

HAGEN, W., 'Stellungnahme zu dem Aufsatz von Hermann Bauermeister', *MR* 55 (1958), 25-31, 272-6.

HÄIKIÖ, MARTTI, 'The Race for Northern Europe, September 1939-June 1940', in *Scandinavia During the Second World War*, ed. Henrik S. Nissen (Oslo and Minneapolis, 1983), 53-97.

HALDER, FRANZ, *Generaloberst Halder, Kriegstagebuch: Tägliche Aufzeichnungen des Chefs des Generalstabes des Heeres 1939-1942* (pub. by Arbeitskreis für Wehrforschung Stuttgart, ed. Hans-Adolf Jacobsen and A. Philippi), i. *Vom Polenfeldzug bis zum Ende der Westoffensive (14. 8. 1939-30. 6. 1940)* (Stuttgart, 1962); ii. *Von der geplanten Landung in England bis zum Beginn des Ostfeldzuges (1. 7. 1940-21. 6. 1941)* (Stuttgart, 1963). [Trans. and ed. Trevor N. Dupuy, *The Halder Diaries, 1939-1942* (2 vols.; Boulder, Colo., 1975); German edn. cited as Halder, *KTB*.]

HARNIER, WILHELM VON, *Artillerie im Küstenkampf* (Wehrwissenschaftliche Berichte, 7; Munich, 1969).

HARRIS, JOHN, *Dunkirk: 'The Storms of War'* (Newton Abbot, 1980).

Heeresadjutant bei Hitler 1938-1943: Aufzeichnungen des Majors Engel, ed. Hildegard von Kotze (Schriftenreihe der Vierteljahrshefte für Zeitgeschichte, 29; Stuttgart, 1974).

Heil Beil! Flugblattpropaganda im Zweiten Weltkrieg: Dokumentation und Analyse, ed. Ortwin Buchbender and Horst Schuh (Schriftenreihe der Studiengesellschaft für Zeitprobleme, 1, Militärpolitik, 10; Stuttgart, 1974).

HEIMANN, BERNHARD, and SCHUNKE, JOACHIM, 'Eine geheime Denkschrift zur Luftkriegs-konzeption Hitler-Deutschlands vom Mai 1933', *ZMG* 3 (1964), 72-86.

HENKE, JOSEF, *England in Hitlers politischem Kalkül 1935-1939* (Schriften des Bundesarchivs, 20; Boppard, 1973).

HERHUDT VON ROHDEN, HANS-DETLEV, 'Betrachtungen über den Luftkrieg', *Militärwissen-schaftliche Rundschau*, 2 (1937), 198-214, 347-61, 504-17, 623-32.

HERZOG, BODO, *60 Jahre deutsche Uboote 1906-1966* (Munich, 1968).

HEUSINGER, ADOLF, *Befehl im Widerstreit: Schicksalsstunden der deutschen Armee 1923-1945* (Tübingen and Stuttgart, 1950).

HILDEBRAND, KLAUS, *Vom Reich zum Weltreich: Hitler, NSDAP und koloniale Frage 1919-1945* (Veröffentlichungen des Historischen Instituts der Universität Hamburg, 1; Munich, 1969).

—— *Deutsche Außenpolitik 1933-1945: Kalkül oder Dogma?* (Stuttgart, 1971). [Trans. Anthony Fothergill, *The Foreign Policy of the Third Reich* (London, 1973).]

—— 'Hitlers "Programm" und seine Realisierung 1939-1942', in *Hitler, Deutschland und die Mächte* (q.v.), 63-93.

HILLGRUBER, ANDREAS, 'Quellen und Quellenkritik zur Vorgeschichte des Zweiten Weltkrieges', *WWR* 14 (1964), 110-26.

—— *Hitlers Strategie. Politik und Kriegführung 1940-41* (Frankfurt am Main, 1965).

—— *Deutschlands Rolle in der Vorgeschichte der beiden Weltkriege* (Die deutsche Frage in der Welt, 7; Göttingen, 1967). [Trans. William C. Kirby, *Germany and the Two World Wars* (Cambridge, Mass., 1981).]

—— 'Militarismus am Ende der Weimarer Republik und im "Dritten Reich" ', in id., *Deutsche Großmachtpolitik und Militarismus im 20. Jahrhundert: 3 Beiträge zum Kontinuitätsproblem* (Düsseldorf, 1974), 37-51.

—— 'Der Faktor Amerika in Hitlers Strategie 1938-1941', in *Nationalsozialistische Außenpolitik* (q.v.), 493-525.

—— *Zur Entstehung des Zweiten Weltkrieges: Forschungsstand und Literatur. Mit einer Chronik der Ereignisse September–Dezember 1939* (Düsseldorf, 1980).

—— 'Noch einmal: Hitlers Wendung gegen die Sowjetunion 1940. Nicht (Militär-)"Strategie oder Ideologie", sondern "Programm" und "Weltkriegsstrategie" ', *Geschichte in Wissenschaft und Unterricht*, 33 (1982), 214-26.

—— *Der Zweite Weltkrieg: Kriegsziele und Strategie der großen Mächte*[4] (Stuttgart, 1985).

—— and HILDEBRAND, KLAUS, *Kalkül zwischen Macht und Ideologie: Der Hitler-Stalin-Pakt, Parallelen bis heute?* (Texte und Thesen, 125, Sachgebiet Politik; Zurich and Osnabrück, 1980).

—— and HÜMMELCHEN, GERHARD, *Chronik des Zweiten Weltkrieges* (Arbeitskreis für Wehrforschung; Frankfurt am Main, 1966).

HIMMLER, HEINRICH, *Geheimreden 1933 bis 1945 und andere Ansprachen*, ed. Bradley F. Smith and Agnes F. Peterson, with intro. by Joachim C. Fest (Frankfurt am Main, Berlin, and Vienna, 1974).

HINSLEY, FRANCIS HARRY, *British Intelligence in the Second World War: Its Influence on Strategy and Operations*, i (London, 1979).

Hitler, Deutschland und die Mächte: Materialien zur Außenpolitik des Dritten Reiches, ed. Manfred Funke (Bonner Schriften zur Politik und Zeitgeschichte, 12; Düsseldorf, 1976).

Hitlers Weisungen für die Kriegführung 1939-1945: Dokumente des Oberkommandos der Wehrmacht, ed. Walther Hubatsch (Frankfurt am Main, 1962). [Trans. with comment by H. R. Trevor-Roper, *Hitler's War Directives 1939-1945* (London, 1964).]

HODGSON, JOHN, *Communism in Finland: History and Interpretation* (Princeton, NJ, 1967).

HOFER, WALTHER, *Die Entfesselung des Zweiten Weltkrieges: Eine Studie über die internationalen Beziehungen im Sommer 1939*[3], enlarged edn. (Frankfurt am Main, 1964). [Trans. Stanley Goodman, *War Premeditated, 1939* (London, 1955).]

HOMZE, EDWARD L., *Arming the Luftwaffe: The Reich Air Ministry and the German Aircraft Industry, 1919-39* (Lincoln, Nebr., 1976).

—— 'The Luftwaffe's Failure to Develop a Heavy Bomber before World War II', *Aerospace Historian*, 24/1 (1977), 1-24.

HOOP, JEAN-MARIE DE, 'Les projets d'intervention des Alliés en Méditerranée Orientale (septembre 1939-mai 1940)', in *La Guerre en Méditerranée* (q.v.), 237-56.

HORNE, ALISTAIR, *To Lose a Battle: France 1940* (London, 1969).

HUBATSCH, WALTHER, *'Weserübung': Die deutsche Besetzung von Dänemark und Norwegen 1940*[2] (Studien und Dokumente zur Geschichte des Zweiten Weltkrieges, 7; Göttingen etc., 1960).

HÜMMELCHEN, GERHARD, 'Der Untergang der Zerstörer "Z 1" und "Z 3" ', *MR* 52 (1955), 62-5.

—— 'Der Einsatz deutscher Luftstreitkräfte über der Nordsee vom 3. 9. 1939-9. 5. 1940', *MR* 55 (1958), 301-11.

—— 'Die Handelskriegsoperationen der deutschen Panzerschiffe 1939', *MR* 56 (1959), 333-45.

—— *Handelsstörer: Handelskrieg deutscher Überwasser-Streitkräfte im Zweiten Weltkrieg* (Munich, 1960).

'Minenerfolge deutscher Zerstörer an der englischen Ostküste (Oktober 1939-März 1940)', *MR* 57 (1960), 45-7, 105.

—— *Die deutschen Seeflieger 1935-1945* (Wehrwissenschaftliche Berichte, 9; Munich, 1976).

HYDE, H. MONTGOMERY, *British Air Policy between the Wars 1918-1939*, with foreword by Sir John Slessor (London, 1976).

IMT (International Military Tribunal): see *Trial*.

IRVING, DAVID, *The Rise and Fall of the Luftwaffe: The Life of Luftwaffe Marshal Erhard Milch* (London, 1973). [Previously published as *Die Tragödie der deutschen Luftwaffe: Aus den Akten und Erinnerungen von Feldmarschall Milch* (Frankfurt am Main, Berlin, and Vienna, 1970).]

—— *Hitler's War* (London, 1977). [Previously published as *Hitler und seine Feldherren* (Frankfurt am Main, Berlin, and Vienna, 1975).]

ISHOVEN, ARMAND VAN, *The Luftwaffe and the Battle of Britain* (London, 1980).

JÄCKEL, EBERHARD, *Frankreich in Hitlers Europa: Die deutsche Frankreichpolitik im Zweiten Weltkrieg* (Quellen und Darstellungen zur Zeitgeschichte, 14; Stuttgart, 1966).

JACOBMEYER, WOLFGANG, *Heimat und Exil: Die Anfänge der polnischen Untergrundbewegung im Zweiten Weltkrieg September 1939 bis Mitte 1941* (Hamburg, [1973]).

—— 'Die polnische Widerstandsbewegung im Generalgouvernement und ihre Beurteilung durch deutsche Dienststellen', *VfZG* 25 (1977), 658-81.

JACOBSEN, HANS-ADOLF, *Fall Gelb: Der Kampf um den deutschen Operationsplan zur Westoffensive 1940* (Veröffentlichungen des Instituts für europäische Geschichte Mainz, 16, Abt. Universalgeschichte; Wiesbaden, 1957).

—— *Dünkirchen: Ein Beitrag zur Geschichte des Westfeldzuges 1940* (Die Wehrmacht im Kampf, 19; Neckargemünd, 1958).

—— *Die nationalsozialistische Außenpolitik 1933-1938* (Frankfurt am Main and Berlin, 1968).

—— *Der Weg zur Teilung der Welt: Politik und Strategie 1939-1945* (Koblenz and Bonn, 1977).

—— and ROHWER, JÜRGEN, 'Planungen und Operationen der deutschen Kriegsmarine im Zusammenhang mit dem Fall "Gelb" ', *MR* 57 (1960), 65-78.

JÄGER, JÖRG-JOHANNES, 'Sweden's Iron Ore Exports to Germany, 1939-1944: A Reply to Rolf Karlbom's Article on the Same Subject', *The Scandinavian Economic History Review*, 15/1-2 (1967), 139-47.

JAKOBSON, MAX, *Diplomatie im finnischen Winterkrieg 1939/40* (Düsseldorf and Vienna, 1970).

JODL, ALFRED, 'Dienstliches Tagebuch [Service Diary], 1. 4. 1937-25. 8. 1939; Dok. 1780-PS', in *IMT* xxviii. 345-90.

—— *Dienstliches Tagebuch* (13 Oct.-20 Nov. 1939), ed. Walter Hubatsch, in *Die Welt als Geschichte*, 12 (1952), 274-87; (22 Nov. 1939-30 Jan. 1940), ibid. 13 (1953), 58-71.

—— 'Dienstliches Tagebuch, 1. 2.-26. 5. 1940', in *IMT* xxviii. 397-435.

JONES, REGINALD VICTOR, *Most Secret War* (London, 1978).

JONG, LOUIS DE, *Die deutsche Fünfte Kolonne im Zweiten Weltkrieg* (Quellen und Darstellungen zur Zeitgeschichte, 4; Stuttgart, 1959).

—— *Het Koninkrijk der Nederlanden in de tweede Wereldoorlog (1939)*, ii. *Neutraal* (The Hague, 1969).

KAHLE, GÜNTER, *Das Kaukasusprojekt der Alliierten vom Jahre 1940* (Rheinisch-Westfälische Akademie der Wissenschaften, Geisteswissenschaftliche Vorträge, G 186; Opladen, 1973).

KAHN, DAVID, *The Codebreakers: The Story of Secret Writing* (New York, 1968).

KARLBOM, ROLF, 'Sweden's Iron Ore Exports to Germany 1933-1944', *Scandinavian Economic History Review*, 13/1-2 (1965), 65-93.

Keesing's Contemporary Archives (London, 1931-).

KENNEDY, ROBERT M., *The German Campaign in Poland 1939* (Department of the Army Pamphlet, No. 20-255; Washington, 1956).

KENS, KARLHEINZ, and NOWARRA, HEINZ JOACHIM, *Die deutschen Flugzeuge 1933-1945*[5] (Munich, 1977).

KEYSERLINGK, ROBERT H., 'Die deutsche Komponente in Churchills Strategie der nationalen Erhebungen 1940-1942: Der Fall Otto Straßer', *VfZG* 31 (1983), 614-45.

KIMCHE, JOHN, *The Unfought Battle* (London, 1968).

KLEE, KARL, *Das Unternehmen 'Seelöwe': Die geplante deutsche Landung in England 1940* (Studien und Dokumente zur Geschichte des Zweiten Weltkrieges, 4a; Göttingen, 1958).

—— *Dokumente zum Unternehmen 'Seelöwe': Die geplante deutsche Landung in England 1940* (Studien und Dokumente zur Geschichte des Zweiten Weltkrieges, 4b; Göttingen, 1959).

—— 'Die Luftschlacht um England 1940', in *Entscheidungsschlachten des Zweiten Weltkrieges* (q.v.), 61-89.

KLESSMANN, CHRISTOPH, *Die Selbstbehauptung einer Nation: Nationalsozialistische Kulturpolitik und polnische Widerstandsbewegung im Generalgouvernement 1939-1945* (Studien zur modernen Geschichte, 5; Düsseldorf, 1971).

KOCH-KENT, HENRI, *10 mai 1940 en Luxembourg: Témoignages et documents* (Luxemburg, 1971).

KOELTZ, L., *Comment s'est joué notre destin: Hitler et l'offensive du 10 mai 1940* (Paris, 1957).

KÖHLER, KARL, 'Douhet und Douhetismus', *WWR* 14 (1964), 88-91.

—— *Bibliographie zur Luftkriegsgeschichte* (Schriften der Bibliothek für Zeitgeschichte, 5; Frankfurt am Main, 1966).

—— 'Operativer Luftkrieg: Eine Wortbildung zur Bezeichnung unterschiedlicher Vorstellungen', *Wehrkunde*, 16 (1967), 265-9.

KREBS, GERHARD, *Japans Deutschlandpolitik 1935-1941: Eine Studie zur Vorgeschichte des Pazifischen Krieges* (2 vols.; Mitteilungen der Gesellschaft für Natur- und Völkerkunde, 91; Hamburg, 1984).

Kriegsbeginn 1939: Entfesselung oder Ausbruch des Zweiten Weltkrieges?, ed. Gottfried Niedhart (Wege der Forschung, 374; Darmstadt, 1976).

Kriegstagebuch des Oberkommandos der Wehrmacht (Wehrmachtführungsstab) 1940-1945 [War diary of the OKW (Wehrmacht operational staff)], compiled by H. Greiner and P. E. Schramm; ed. by P. E. Schramm for the Arbeitskreis für Wehrforschung, i. *1. August 1940-31. Dezember 1941*, with comments by H.-A. Jacobsen (Frankfurt am Main, 1965).

KUBY, ERICH, *Als Polen deutsch war: 1939-1945* (Ismaning near Munich, 1986).

KUHN, WALTER, 'Das Deutschtum in Polen und sein Schicksal in Kriegs- und Nachkriegszeit', in *Osteuropa-Handbuch: Polen* (q.v.), 138-64.

KUTZLEBEN, KARL VON, SCHRÖDER, WILHELM, and BRENNECKE, JOCHEN, *Minenschiffe 1939-1945* (Herford, 1974).

KUUSINEN, AINO, *Der Gott stürzt seine Engel* (Vienna, 1972). [Trans. P. S. Falla (as Paul Stevenson), *Before and After Stalin: A Personal Account of Soviet Russia from the 1920s to the 1960s* (London and New York, 1974); US title *The Rings of Destiny*.]

KWIET, KONRAD, *Reichskommissariat Niederlande: Versuch und Scheitern nationalsoziali-stischer Neuordnung* (Schriftenreihe der Vierteljahrshefte für Zeitgeschichte, 17; Stuttgart, 1968).

—— 'Vorbereitung und Auflösung der deutschen Militärverwaltung in den Niederlanden', *MGM* 5 (1969), 121–53.

Lagevorträge des Oberbefehlshabers der Kriegsmarine vor Hitler 1939–1945, ed. Gerhard Wagner (Munich, 1972); trans. (with some omissions) as 'Führer Conferences on Naval Affairs, 1939–1945', in *Brassey's Naval Annual* (Portsmouth, 1948), 25–496.

LEE, BRADFORD A., 'Strategy, Arms and the Collapse of France 1930–40', in *Diplomacy and Intelligence* (q.v.), 43–67.

LEEB, Generalfeldmarschall WILHELM RITTER VON, *Tagebuchaufzeichnungen und Lage-beurteilungen aus zwei Weltkriegen,* ed. from posthumous papers with biographical notes by Georg Meyer (Beiträge zur Militär- und Kriegsgeschichte, 16; Stuttgart, 1976).

LE GOYET, PIERRE, *Le Mystère Gamelin* (Paris, 1975).

LEWIN, RONALD, *Ultra Goes to War: The Secret Story* (London, 1978).

LIPSKI, JOZEF, *Diplomat in Berlin 1933–1939: Papers and Memoirs of Jozef Lipski, Ambassador of Poland,* ed. Wacław Jędrzejewicz (New York, 1968).

LISS, ULRICH, *Westfront 1939/40: Erinnerungen des Feindbearbeiters im O.K.H.* (Neckargemünd, 1959).

LOEBER, DIETRICH, A., *Diktierte Option: Die Umsiedlung der Deutsch-Balten aus Estland und Lettland 1939–1941. Dokumentation*[2] (Neumünster, 1974).

LOHMANN, WALTER, and HILDEBRAND, HANS H., *Die deutsche Kriegsmarine 1939–1945: Gliederung — Einsatz — Stellenbesetzung* (3 vols.; Bad Nauheim, 1956–64).

LONGMATE, NORMAN, *Air Raid: The Bombing of Coventry, 1940* (London, 1976).

LOOCK, HANS-DIETRICH, *Quisling, Rosenberg und Terboven: Zur Vorgeschichte und Geschichte der nationalsozialistischen Revolution in Norwegen* (Quellen und Darstellungen zur Zeit-geschichte, 18; Stuttgart, 1970).

—— 'Nordeuropa zwischen Außenpolitik und "großgermanischer" Innenpolitik', in *Hitler, Deutschland und die Mächte* (q.v.), 684–706.

—— 'Weserübung: A Step towards the Greater Germanic Reich', *Scandinavian Journal of History,* 2 (1977), 67–88.

LORBEER, HANS-JOACHIM, *Westmächte gegen die Sowjetunion* (Einzelschriften zur militärischen Geschichte des Zweiten Weltkrieges, 18; Freiburg i.Br., 1975).

LUDLOW, PETER W., 'Scandinavia between the Great Powers: Attempts at Mediation in the First Year of the Second World War', *Historisk tidsskrift* (Stockholm, 1974).

Luftwaffen-Druckvorschrift 16, *Luftkriegführung* [regulation concerning aerial warfare] (Berlin, 1936).

LUKACS, JOHN, *The Last European War: September 1939–December 1941* (London, 1977).

LUTZHÖFT, HANS-JÜRGEN, 'Deutschland und Schweden während des Norwegenfeldzuges (5. April–10. Juni 1940)', *VfZG* 22 (1974), 382–416.

—— *Deutsche Militärpolitik und schwedische Neutralität 1939–1942* (Skandinavistische Studien, 15; Neumünster, 1981).

MACHT, Major, 'Die wehrwirtschaftlichen Grundlagen Deutschlands und ihr Einfluß auf die Luftwaffe', pt.3, *Die Luftwaffe,* 2/1 (1937), 150–74.

MACKIEWICZ, JÓZEF, *The Crime of Katyń: Facts and Documents* (London, 1965).

MAIER, KLAUS A., *Guernica, 26. 4. 1937: Die deutsche Intervention in Spanien und der 'Fall Guernica'* (Einzelschriften zur militärischen Geschichte des Zweiten Weltkrieges, 17; Freiburg i.Br., 1975; Spanish edn. 1976).

MAIER, KLAUS A., 'Total War and German Air Doctrine before the Second World War', in *The German Military in the Age of Total War*, ed. Wilhelm Deist (Leamington Spa, 1985), 210-19.

MÄKELÄ, JUKKA L., *Im Rücken des Feindes: Der finnische Nachrichtendienst im Krieg* (Frauenfeld and Stuttgart, 1967).

MANN, GOLO, *Deutsche Geschichte 1919-1945* (Frankfurt am Main, 1973).

MARDER, ARTHUR J., *From the Dardanelles to Oran: Studies of the Royal Navy in War and Peace 1915-1940* (London, 1974).

MARSCHALL, WILHELM, 'Vorstoß gegen Färöer-Island-Passage', *Atlantische Welt*, 6/11 (1966), 22-4.

—— 'Unternehmen "Juno" ', *Atlantische Welt*, 7/6 (1967), 4-7; ibid. 7/7: 5-7.

—— 'Zur deutschen Seekriegführung 1939-1940: Stellungnahme von Generaladmiral a. D. Wilhelm Marschall, Flottenchef bis 8. 7. 1940', *MR* 69 (1972), 55-79.

MARTIN, BERND, *Friedensinitiativen und Machtpolitik im Zweiten Weltkrieg 1939-1942* (Geschichtliche Studien zur Politik und Gesellschaft, 6; Düsseldorf, 1974.

MASON, FRANCIS K., *Battle over Britain: A History of the German Air Assaults on Great Britain 1917-18 and July-November 1940, and of the Development of Britain's Air Defences between the World Wars* (London, 1969).

MASON, TIMOTHY W., 'Innere Krise und Angriffskrieg 1938/1939', in *Wirtschaft und Rüstung am Vorabend des Zweiten Weltkrieges*, ed. Friedrich Forstmeier and Hans-Erich Volkmann (Düsseldorf, 1975), 158-88.

MAZOUR, ANATOLE G., *Finland between East and West* (Princeton, NJ, 1956).

MEIER-DÖRNBERG, WILHELM, *Die Ölversorgung der Kriegsmarine 1935-1945* (Einzelschriften zur militärischen Geschichte des Zweiten Weltkrieges, 11; Freiburg i.Br., 1973).

MEIER-WELCKER, HANS, 'Der Entschluß zum Anhalten der deutschen Panzertruppen in Flandern 1940', *VfZG* 2 (1954), 274-90.

MELZER, WALTHER, *Albert-Kanal und Eben-Emael* (Die Wehrmacht in Kampf, 13; Heidelberg, 1957).

MESSERSCHMIDT, MANFRED, *Die Wehrmacht im NS-Staat: Zeit der Indoktrination* (Hamburg, 1969).

—— 'Kriegstechnologie und humanitäres Völkerrecht in der Zeit der Weltkriege', *MGM* 41 (1987), 63-110.

MICHALKA, WOLFGANG, *Ribbentrop und die deutsche Weltpolitik 1933-1940* (Veröffentlichungen des Historischen Instituts der Universität Mannheim, 5; Munich, 1980).

MICHEL, HENRI, *La Drôle de guerre* (Paris, 1971).

—— 'Les relations franco-italiennes (de l'armistice de juin 1940 à l'armistice de septembre 1943)', in *La Guerre en Méditerranée* (q.v.), 485-511.

MIKOLA, K. J., *Finland's War during World War II (1939-1945)* (Mikkeli, 1973).

MILCH, ERHARD, 'Merkbuch' (Xerox copy in MGFA; original in the possession of David Irving).

MILWARD, ALAN S., *The German Economy at War* (London, 1965).

—— 'Could Sweden have Stopped the Second World War?', *The Scandinavian Economic History Review*, 15/1-2 (1967), 127-38.

MOLOTOV, V. M., *Soviet Peace Policy: Four Speeches* (London, 1941).

MUELLER-HILLEBRAND, BURKHART, *Das Heer 1933-1945: Entwicklung des organisatorischen Aufbaues*, i. *Das Heer bis zum Kriegsbeginn* (Darmstadt, 1954); ii. *Die Blitzfeldzüge 1938-1941* (Frankfurt am Main, 1956).

MÜLLER, KLAUS-JÜRGEN, *Das Ende der Entente Cordiale: Eine Studie zur Entwicklung der englisch-französischen Beziehungen während des Westfeldzuges 1940* (Beihefte der Wehrwissenschaftlichen Rundschau, 3; Frankfurt am Main, 1956).

—— 'Dünkirchen 1940: Ein Beitrag zur Vorgeschichte der britischen und französischen Evakuierung', *MR* 57/3 (1960), 133-68.

—— *Das Heer und Hitler: Armee und nationalsozialistisches Regime 1933-1940* (Beiträge zur Militär- und Kriegsgeschichte, 10; Stuttgart, 1969).

MUNTHE-KAAS, OTTO ULRIK, 'The Campaign in Norway in 1940 and the Norwegian and British War Direction Machineries', *Revue internationale d'histoire militaire*, 47 (1980), 36-59.

MURRAY, WILLIAMSON, 'German Air Power and the Munich Crisis', in *War and Society: A Yearbook of Military History*, ii (New York, 1977), 107-18.

—— 'British and German Air Doctrine between the Wars', *Air University Review*, 31/3 (1980), 39-58.

—— 'The German Response to Victory in Poland', *Armed Forces and Society*, 7/2 (1981), 285-98.

—— 'The Luftwaffe before the Second World War: A Mission, a Strategy?', *Journal of Strategic Studies*, 4/4 (1981), 261-70.

—— *Strategy for Defeat: The Luftwaffe 1933-1945* (Washington, 1983). [British title *Luftwaffe* (London, 1985).]

MYLLYNIEMI, SEPPO, *Die baltische Krise 1938-1941* (Schriftenreihe der Vierteljahrshefte für Zeitgeschichte, 38; Stuttgart, 1979).

Nationalsozialistische Außenpolitik, ed. Wolfgang Michalka (Wege der Forschung, 297; Darmstadt, 1978).

Nauticus: Handbuch der Seemacht und Seegeltung, 20 (1936); 22 (1939).

Nazi-Soviet Relations 1939-1941: Documents from Archives of the German Foreign Office, ed. Raymond J. Sontag and James Stuart Beddie (Department of State; Washington, 1948).

NEVAKIVI, JUKKA, *The Appeal that was Never Made: The Allies, Scandinavia and the Finnish Winter War 1939-1940* (London, 1976).

NIEHAUS, WERNER, *Die Radarschlacht, 1939-1945: Die Geschichte des Hochfrequenzkrieges* (Stuttgart, 1977).

NYMAN, KRISTINA, *Finland's War Years 1939-1945: A List of Books and Articles concerning the Winter War and the Continuation War, Excluding Literature in Finnish and Russian* (Publications of the Society of Military History, 4; Mikkeli, 1973).

OBERDÖRFER, LUTZ, 'Militärische Pläne und Aktivitäten der europäischen Westmächte und Deutschlands gegenüber Nordeuropa während des "seltsamen Krieges" ', *Militärgeschichte*, 21 (1982), 430-42.

Osteuropa-Handbuch, ii. *Polen*, ed. Werner Markert with the collaboration of many specialists (Cologne and Graz, 1959).

OVERY, RICHARD JAMES, 'The German Pre-war Aircraft Production Plans: November 1936-April 1939', *English Historical Review*, 90 (1975), 778-97.

—— 'From "Uralbomber" to "Amerikabomber": The Luftwaffe and Strategic Bombing', *Journal of Strategic Studies*, 1/2 (1979), 154-75.

—— *The Air War 1939-45* (London, 1980).

—— 'Hitler and Air Strategy', *Journal of Contemporary History*, 15/3 (1980), 405-21.

OWENS, FRANK E., 'Anatomy of Defeat: France 1940', *Army*, 22/12 (1972), 32-8.

PAILLAT, CLAUDE, *Dossiers secrets de la France contemporaine*, iv. *Le Désastre de 1940*, 1: *La Répétition générale* (Paris, 1983); 2: *La Guerre immobile, avril 1939-10 mai 1940* (Paris, 1984); v. *Le Désastre de 1940*, 3: *La Guerre éclair, 10 mai-24 juin 1940*, with the collaboration of Francis Boulnois (Paris, 1985).

PIEKALKIEWCZ, JANUSZ, *Polenfeldzug: Hitler und Stalin zerschlagen die polnische Republik* (Bergisch-Gladbach, 1982).

PIEKALKIEWCZ, JANUSZ, *Der Zweite Weltkrieg* (Düsseldorf, 1985).

PIERI, PIERO, 'La stratégie italienne sur l'échiquier méditerranéen', in *La Guerre en Méditerranée* (q.v.), 61–78.

Polskie Siły Zbrojne w Drugiej Wojnie Światowej (The Polish Armed Forces in the Second World War), ed. General Sikorski Historical Institute (London, 1950–75).

POSTAN, M. M., *British War Production* (History of the Second World War, United Kingdom Civil Series; London, 1957).

POTTER, ELMER B., and NIMITZ, CHESTER W., *Sea Power: A Naval History* (London, 1960; 2nd, rev. edn. Annapolis, 1981). [German trans., *Seemacht: Eine Seekriegsgeschichte von der Antike bis zur Gegenwart*, ed. Jürgen Rohwer under the direction of the Arbeitskreis für Wehrforschung (Munich, 1974).]

POWERS, BARRY D., *Strategy without Slide Rule: British Air Strategy 1914–1939* (London, 1976).

PRICE, ALFRED, *Instruments of Darkness* (London, 1967).

PSZ: see *Polskie Siły Zbrojne.*

RAUCH, GEORG VON, 'Der deutsch-sowjetische Nichtangriffspakt vom August 1939 und die sowjetische Geschichtsforschung', in *Kriegsbeginn 1939* (q.v.), 349–66.

RAUSCHNING, HERMANN, *Die Revolution des Nihilismus* (Zurich and New York, 1938; new edn. by Golo Mann, Zurich, 1964). [Trans. E. W. Dickes, *Germany's Revolution of Destruction* (London, 1939).]

RAUTENBERG, HANS-JÜRGEN, *Deutsche Rüstungspolitik vom Beginn der Genfer Abrüstungskonferenz bis zur Wiedereinführung der allgemeinen Wehrpflicht 1932–1935* (diss. Bonn, 1973).

RÉAU, ÉLISABETH DU, 'Haut commandement et pouvoir politique', in *Les Armées françaises pendant la seconde guerre mondiale 1939–1945: Colloque International, École Nationale Supérieure de techniques avancées, Paris, du 7 au 10 mai 1985* (Paris, 1986), 67–86.

REINHARDT, HANS, 'Die 4. Panzer-Division vor Warschau und an der Bzura vom 9.–20. 9. 1939', *Wehrkunde*, 7 (1958), 237–47.

Relations militaires franco-belges, de mars 1936 au 10 mai 1940, Les: Travaux d'un colloque d'historiens belges et français (Paris, 1968).

REYNOLDS, DAVID, 'Churchill and the British "Decision" to fight on in 1940: Right Policy, Wrong Reasons', in *Diplomacy and Intelligence* (q.v.), 147–67.

RHODE, GOTTHOLD, 'Die politische Entwicklung Polens im Zweiten Weltkrieg', in *Osteuropa-Handbuch: Polen* (q.v.), 194–220.

RINTELEN, ENNO VON, 'Die deutsch-italienische Zusammenarbeit im II. Weltkrieg' (unpubl. Study B-495, MGFA).

ROHDE, HORST, *Das deutsche Wehrmachttransportwesen im Zweiten Weltkrieg: Entstehung, Organisation, Aufgaben* (Beiträge zur Militär- und Kriegsgeschichte, 12; Stuttgart, 1971).

ROHWER, JÜRGEN, 'Der U-Bootkrieg und sein Zusammenbruch 1943', in *Entscheidungsschlachten* (q.v.), 317–94.

—— 'U-Bootoperationen vor der englischen Südostküste und im Ost-Kanal 1939/40', *MR* 57 (1960), 104–5.

—— *Geleitzugschlachten im März 1943: Führungsprobleme im Höhepunkt der Schlacht im Atlantik*, ed. Arbeitskreis für Wehrforschung (Stuttgart, 1975).

—— 'Der Einfluß der alliierten Funkaufklärung auf den Verlauf des Zweiten Weltkrieges', *VfZG* 27 (1979), 325–69.

—— *Axis Submarine Successes 1939–1945* (Annapolis, 1983).

—— and HÜMMELCHEN, GERHARD, *Chronik des Seekrieges 1939–1945* (Oldenburg and Hamburg, 1968).

ROOS, HANS, 'Die militärpolitische Lage und Planung Polens gegenüber Deutschland 1939', *WWR* 7 (1957), 181–202.

—— 'Polen in der Besatzungszeit', in *Osteuropa-Handbuch: Polen* (q.v.), 167–93.

—— 'Der Feldzug in Polen vom September 1939', *WWR* 9 (1959), 491–512.

—— *Geschichte der polnischen Nation 1916–1960: Von der Staatsgründung im ersten Weltkrieg bis zur Gegenwart*[2] (Stuttgart, 1964). [Trans. J. R. Foster, *A History of Modern Poland* (London, 1966).]

ROSKILL, STEPHEN W., *The War at Sea 1939–1945* (3 vols.; History of the Second World War, United Kingdom Military Series; London, 1954–61).

RÖSSLER, EBERHARD, *Geschichte des deutschen Ubootbaues* (Munich, 1975).

RUGE, FRIEDRICH, *Im Küstenvorfeld* (Wehrwissenschaftliche Berichte, 15; Munich, 1974).

RUNDSTEDT, GERD VON, 'Bemerkungen zum "Feldzug im Westen" ' (unpubl. Study C-053, MGFA).

RUNZHEIMER, JÜRGEN, 'Der Überfall auf den Sender Gleiwitz im Jahre 1939', *VfZG* 10 (1962), 408–26.

SALEWSKI, MICHAEL, 'Erwiderung zu der Stellungnahme von Generaladmiral a. D. Boehm', *MR* 69 (1972), 737–41.

—— *Die deutsche Seekriegsleitung 1939–1945*, i. *1935–1941* (Frankfurt am Main, 1970); iii. *Denkschriften und Lagebetrachtungen 1938–1944* (Frankfurt am Main, 1973).

—— 'Basis Nord', *Schiff und Zeit*, 3 (1976), 11–17.

—— 'Das maritime Dritte Reich: Ideologie und Wirklichkeit 1933-1945', in *Die deutsche Flotte im Spannungsfeld der Politik 1848–1985*, ed. Deutsches Marine Institut and MGFA (Schriftenreihe des Deutschen Marine Instituts, 9; Herford, 1985), 113–29.

SALMON, PATRICK, 'Crimes against Peace: The Case of the Invasion of Norway at the Nuremberg Trials', in *Diplomacy and Intelligence* (q.v.), 245–69.

SCHALL-RIAUCOUR, Countess HEIDEMARIE, *Aufstand und Gehorsam: Offizierstum und Generalstab im Umbruch. Leben und Wirken von Generaloberst Franz Halder, Generalstabschef 1938–1942* (Wiesbaden, 1972).

SCHIEDER, WOLFGANG, 'Spanischer Bürgerkrieg und Vierjahresplan: Zur Struktur national-sozialistischer Außenpolitik', in *Der Spanische Bürgerkrieg in der internationalen Politik (1936–1939)*, ed Wolfgang Schieder and Christof Dipper (Munich, 1976), 162–90.

SCHINDLER, HERBERT, *Mosty und Dirschau 1939: Zwei Handstreiche der Wehrmacht vor Beginn des Polenfeldzuges*[2], enlarged edn. (Einzelschriften zur militärischen Geschichte des Zweiten Weltkrieges, 7; Freiburg i.Br., 1979).

SCHMITZ, ERNST, and STAUFFENBERG, Count BERTHOLD SCHENK VON, 'Erlaubte Angriffsziele im Luftkrieg', *Wissen und Wehr*, 20 (1939), 521–8.

SCHREIBER, GERHARD, *Revisionismus und Weltmachtstreben: Marineführung und deutsch-italienische Beziehungen 1919–1944* (Beiträge zur Militär- und Kriegsgeschichte, 20; Stuttgart, 1978).

—— 'Zur Kontinuität des Groß- und Weltmachtstrebens der deutschen Marineführung', *MGM* 26 (1979), 101–71.

SCHRÖDER, HANS-JÜRGEN, 'Das Dritte Reich, die USA und Lateinamerika 1933-1941', in *Hitler, Deutschland und die Mächte* (q.v.), 339–64.

SCHUUR, HEINRICH, 'Auftragserteilung und Auftragsdurchführung beim Unternehmen "Juno" vom 4. bis 10. Juni 1940', in Wolfgang Köhler, Rolf Martens, and Heinrich Schuur, *Führungsprobleme der Marine im Zweiten Weltkrieg* (Einzelschriften zur militärischen Geschichte des Zweiten Weltkrieges, 13; Freiburg i.Br., 1973), 9–53.

Secret Conferences of Dr Goebbels: see *Wollt Ihr den totalen Krieg?*

SENGHAAS, DIETER, *Rüstung und Militarismus* (Frankfurt am Main, 1972).

Service Historique de l'Armée de Terre, *Les Grandes Unités françaises: Campagne 1939-1940. Atlas des situations quotidiennes des armées alliées* (Paris, 1964).

SIEBERT, FERDINAND, *Italiens Weg in den Zweiten Weltkrieg* (Frankfurt am Main, 1962).

SKODVIN, MAGNE, 'Norwegian Neutrality and the Question of Credibility', *Scandinavian Journal of History*, 2 (1977), 123-45.

SMITH, MALCOLM, 'The Royal Air Force: Air Power and British Foreign Policy 1932-1937', *Journal of Contemporary History*, 12/1 (1977), 162-74.

SMITH, PETER CHARLES, *Hold the Narrow Sea: Naval Warfare in the English Channel 1939-1945* (Ashbourne, Derby., and Annapolis, 1984).

SOHLER, HERBERT, *U-Bootkrieg und Völkerrecht* (*Marine-Rundschau*, suppl. 1; Frankfurt am Main, 1956).

SOMMER, THEO, *Deutschland und Japan zwischen den Mächten 1935-1940: Vom Antikomintern-pakt zum Dreimächtepakt* (Tübinger Studien zur Geschichte und Politik, 15; Tübingen, 1962).

SOUTHWORTH, HERBERT RUTLEDGE, *Guernica! A Study of Journalism, Diplomacy, Propaganda and History* (Berkeley, Los Angeles, and London, 1977).

SPEER, ALBERT, *Erinnerungen* (Frankfurt am Main, 1969). [Trans. Richard and Clara Winston, *Inside the Third Reich* (London, 1970).]

SPEIDEL, WILHELM, 'Die Luftwaffe im Polenfeldzug' (unpubl. Study Lw 2/1-6, MGFA).

—— 'Der Einsatz der operativen Luftwaffe im Westfeldzug 1939/40' (unpubl. Study Lw 3/1-4, MGFA).

Staatsmänner und Diplomaten bei Hitler: Vertrauliche Aufzeichnungen über Unterredungen mit Vertretern des Auslandes 1939-1941, ed. with comments by Andreas Hillgruber (Frankfurt am Main, 1967).

STAFFORD, DAVID A. T., ' "Ultra" and the British Official Histories: A Documentary Note', *Military Affairs*, 42 (1978), 29-31.

STEGEMANN, BERND, 'Hitlers Ziele im ersten Kriegsjahr 1939/40: ein Beitrag zur Quellen-kritik', *MGM* 27 (1980), 93-105.

—— 'Der Entschluß zum Unternehmen "Barbarossa": Strategie oder Ideologie?', *Geschichte in Wissenschaft und Unterricht*, 33 (1982), 205-13.

—— 'Geschichte und Politik: Zur Diskussion über den deutschen Angriff auf die Sowjetunion 1941', *Beiträge zur Konfliktforschung*, 17/1 (1987), 73-97.

STEINERT, MARLIS G., *Hitlers Krieg und die Deutschen: Stimmung und Haltung der deutschen Bevölkerung im Zweiten Weltkrieg* (Düsseldorf and Vienna, 1970).

STJERNFELT, BERTIL, and BÖHME, KLAUS-RICHARD, *Vägen till Westerplatte* (*Militärhistoriska Studier*, 2; Kristianstad, 1978). [German trans. *Westerplatte 1939* (Einzelschriften zur militärischen Geschichte des Zweiten Weltkrieges, 23; Freiburg i.Br., 1979).]

SÜNDERMANN, HELMUT, *Tagesparolen: Deutsche Presseweisungen 1939-1945. Hitlers Propaganda und Kriegsführung*, ed. from posthumous papers by Gert Sudholt (Deutsche Argumente, 1; Leoni am Starnberger See, 1973).

SWINT, WILLIAM A., 'May 14, 1940 Revisited: The German Air Attack on Rotterdam', *Aerospace Historian*, 21/4 (1974), 14-22.

SYWOTTEK, JUTTA, *Mobilmachung für den totalen Krieg: Die propagandistische Vorbereitung der deutschen Bevölkerung auf den Zweiten Weltkrieg* (Studien zur modernen Geschichte, 18; Opladen, 1976).

TALÓN, VICENTE, *Arde Guernica* (Madrid, 1970).

Talvisodan historia [History of the Winter War]: *Toimittanut Sotatieteen Laitoksen*

Sotahistorian toimisto (4 vols.; Sotatieteen laitoksen julkaisuja, 16; Porvoo, Helsinki, and Juva, 1977-9).

TAYLOR, TELFORD, *The Breaking Wave: The German Defeat in the Summer of 1940* (London, 1967).

TESSIN, GEORG, *Verbände und Truppen der deutschen Wehrmacht und Waffen SS im Zweiten Weltkrieg 1939-1945*, vols. ii-v (Frankfurt am Main, n.d.); vols. i, vi-xiii (Osnabrück, 1972-6).

THOMAS, GEORG, *Geschichte der deutschen Wehr- und Rüstungswirtschaft (1918-1943/5)*, ed. Wolfgang Birkenfeld (Schriften des Bundesarchivs, 14; Boppard am Rhein, 1966).

THOMSEN, ERICH, *Deutsche Besatzungspolitik in Dänemark 1940-1945* (Studien zur modernen Geschichte, 4; Düsseldorf, 1971).

TIPPELSKIRCH, KURT VON, 'Operativer Überblick über den Feldzug in Polen 1939', *WWR* 4 (1954), 252-67.

—— 'Der Westfeldzug 1940', vol. i. 'Die Vorgeschichte', pt. 1. 'Der Westkriegsschauplatz während des Feldzuges in Polen' (unpubl. Study P-208; vol. i, MGFA).

TOPITSCH, ERNST, *Stalins Krieg: Die sowjetische Langzeitstrategie gegen den Westen als rationale Machtpolitik* (Munich, 1985).

TRESS, HARVEY B., 'Churchill, the First Berlin Raids, and the Blitz: A New Interpretation', *MGM* 32 (1982), 65-78.

TREUE, WILHELM, 'Hitlers Denkschrift zum Vierjahresplan 1936', *VfZG* 3 (1955), 184-210. [Trans. in Jeremy Noakes and Geoffrey Pridham (eds.), *Documents on Nazism 1919-1945* (London, 1974), 401-8).]

TREVOR-ROPER, *Directives*: see *Hitlers Weisungen*.

Trial of Major War Criminals by the International Military Tribunal Sitting at Nuremberg, Germany (42 vols.; Nuremberg, 1947-9). [Vols. i-xxii are cited according to the English version; the remaining vols. according to the German text, which was not translated.]

UEBERSCHÄR, GERD R., 'Generaloberst Halder im militärischen Widerstand 1938-1940', *Wehrforschung*, 2 (1973), 20-31.

—— *Hitler und Finnland 1939-1941: Die deutsch-finnischen Beziehungen während des Hitler-Stalin-Paktes* (Frankfurter Historische Abhandlungen, 16; Wiesbaden, 1978).

UHLE-WETTLER, FRANZ, *Höhe- und Wendepunkte deutscher Militärgeschichte* (Mainz, 1984).

UMBREIT, HANS, *Der Militärbefehlshaber in Frankreich 1940-1944* (Wehrwissenschaftliche Forschungen, Abteilung Militärgeschichtliche Studien, 7; Boppard, 1968).

—— 'Zur Behandlung der Bretonenbewegung durch die deutsche Besatzungsmacht im Sommer 1940 (Dokumentation)', *MGM* 3 (1968), 145-65.

—— *Deutsche Militärverwaltungen 1938/39: Die militärische Besetzung der Tschechoslowakei und Polens* (Beiträge zur Militär- und Kriegsgeschichte, 18; Stuttgart, 1977).

VAUTHIER, P., *La Doctrine de guerre du Général Douhet* (Paris, 1935).

VILLELUME, PAUL Marquis DE, *Journal d'une défaite (23 août 1939-juin 1940)* (Paris, 1976).

VÖLKER, KARL-HEINZ, 'Die Entwicklung der militärischen Luftfahrt in Deutschland 1920-1933: Planung und Maßnahmen zur Schaffung einer Fliegertruppe in der Reichswehr' (Beiträge zur Militär- und Kriegsgeschichte, 3; Stuttgart, 1962), 121-292.

—— *Die deutsche Luftwaffe 1933-1939: Aufbau, Führung und Rüstung der Luftwaffe sowie die Entwicklung der deutschen Luftkriegstheorie* (Beiträge zur Militär- und Kriegsgeschichte, 8; Stuttgart, 1967).

—— *Dokumente und Dokumentarfotos zur Geschichte der deutschen Luftwaffe: Aus den Geheimakten des Reichswehrministeriums 1919-1933 und des Reichluftfahrtministeriums 1933-1939* (Beiträge zur Militär- und Kriegsgeschichte, 9; Stuttgart, 1968).

VOLKMANN, HANS-ERICH, 'Autarkie, Großraumwirtschaft und Aggression: Zur ökonomischen Motivation der Besetzung Luxemburgs, Belgiens und der Niederlande 1940', *MGM* 19 (1976), 51-76.

VOLKMANN, UDO, *Die britische Luftverteidigung und die Abwehr der deutschen Luftangriffe während der Luftschlacht um England bis Juni 1941* (Studien zur Militärgeschichte, Militärwissenschaft und Konfliktforschung, 30; Osnabrück, 1982).

VORMANN, NIKOLAUS VON, *Der Feldzug 1939 in Polen: Die Operation des Heeres* (Weisenburg, 1958).

WAGNER, GERHARD, *Lagevorträge*: see *Lagevorträge*.

WAGNER, WILFRIED, *Belgien in der deutschen Politik während des Zweiten Weltkrieges* (Wehrwissenschaftliche Forschungen, Abteilung Militärgeschichtliche Studien, 18; Boppard, 1974).

WARLIMONT, WALTER, *Im Hauptquartier der deutschen Wehrmacht 1939-1945: Grundlagen, Formen, Gestalten* (Frankfurt am Main and Bonn, 1962); trans. R. H. Barry, *Inside Hitler's Headquarters 1939-45* (London, 1964).

WATT, DONALD CAMERON, 'Restraints on War in the Air before 1945', in *Restraints on War: Studies in the Limitation of Armed Conflict*, ed. Michael Howard (Oxford, 1979), 57-77.

WEBER, PAUL, *Geschichte Luxemburgs im Zweiten Weltkrieg*[2] (Luxemburg, 1948).

WEGENER, WOLFGANG, *Die Seestrategie des Weltkrieges*[2] (Berlin, 1941).

WEHLER, HANS-ULRICH, 'Der Verfall der deutschen Kriegstheorie: Vom "Absoluten" zum "Totalen" Krieg oder von Clausewitz zu Ludendorff', in *Geschichte und Militärgeschichte: Wege der Forschung*, ed. Ursula von Gersdorff (Frankfurt am Main, 1974), 273-311.

Weißbuch des Auswärtigen Amtes 1939-1941, vi. *Die Geheimakten des französischen Generalstabes* (Berlin, 1941).

Weitere Dokumente zur Kriegsausweitungspolitik der Westmächte: Die Generalstabsbesprechungen Englands und Frankreichs mit Belgien und den Niederlanden, ed. Auswärtiges Amt (Weißbuch des Auswärtigen Amts, 5; Berlin, 1940).

Weizsäcker-Papiere 1933-1950, Die, ed. Leonidas E. Hill (Frankfurt am Main, Berlin, and Vienna, 1974).

WESCHE, HANS-HENRIK, 'Die dänische Marine während des Zweiten Weltkrieges', *MR* 62 (1965), 141-52.

WESTPHAL, SIEGFRIED, *Heer in Fesseln* (Bonn, 1950).

[WEVER, WALTER], 'Vortrag des Generalmajors Wever bei der Eröffnung der Luftkriegs-akademie und Lufttechnischen Akademie in Berlin-Gatow am 1. November 1935', *Die Luftwaffe*, 1/1 (1936), 5-9.

Weyers Taschenbuch der Kriegsflotten, ed. Alexander Bredt, xxxiii (Munich, 1939).

WHEATLEY, RONALD, *Operation Sea Lion: German Plans for the Invasion of England, 1939-1942* (Oxford, 1958).

WINTERBOTHAM, FREDERICK WILLIAM, *The Ultra Secret* (London, 1974).

WITTMANN, KLAUS, *Schweden in der Außenwirtschaftspolitik des Dritten Reiches 1933-1945* (diss. Hamburg, 1976).

WOLLSTEIN, GÜNTER, 'Die Politik des nationalsozialistischen Deutschland gegenüber Polen 1933-1939/45' in *Hitler, Deutschland und die Mächte* (q.v.), 795-810.

Wollt Ihr den totalen Krieg? Die Geheimen Goebbels-Konferenzen, 1939-1943, ed. with comments by Willi A. Boelcke (Stuttgart, 1967). [Trans. Ewald Osers, *The Secret Conferences of Dr Goebbels* (London, 1970).]

WOOD, DEREK, *Attack Warning Red: The Royal Observer Corps and the Defence of Britain 1925 to 1975* (London, 1976).

WOODWARD, Sir LLEWELLYN, *British Foreign Policy in the Second World War*, i (History of the Second World War, United Kingdom Civil Series; London, 1970).

YAKUSHEVSKY, A. S., 'Vymysly i pravda o sovetsko-germanskom dogovore o nenapadenii 1939 goda', *Voennoistorichesky zhurnal*, 28/1 (1986), 59-65.

ZAWODNY, JANUSZ K., *Death in the Forest: The Story of the Katyn Forest Massacre* (Notre Dame, Ind., 1962).

ZENTNER, CHRISTIAN, *Der Kriegsausbruch, 1. September 1939: Daten, Bilder, Dokumente* (Frankfurt am Main, Berlin, and Vienna, 1979).

ZETZSCHE, HANS-JÜRGEN, *Logistik und Operationen: Die Mineralölversorgung der Kriegsmarine im Zweiten Weltkrieg* (diss. Kiel, 1986).

ZIEMKE, EARL F., *The German Northern Theater of Operations, 1940-1945* (Department of the Army Pamphlet No. 20-271; Washington, 1959).

ZIESE-BERINGER, HERMANN, 'Der Begriff des moralischen Gefährdungsraumes als strategisches Element', *Die Luftwaffe*, 2/2 (1937), 40-91.

ZIPFEL, FRIEDRICH, 'Hitlers Konzept einer "Neuordnung" Europas: Ein Beitrag zum politischen Denken des deutschen Diktators', in *Aus Theorie und Praxis der Geschichtswissenschaft: Festschrift für Hans Herzfeld zum 80. Geburtstag*, ed. Dietrich Kurze (Berlin, 1972), 154-74.

Index of Persons